John's Wisdom

Also by Ben Witherington, III
from Westminster John Knox Press

Paul's Narrative Thought World:
The Tapestry of Tragedy and Triumph

John's Wisdom

A Commentary on the Fourth Gospel

Ben Witherington, III

 Westminster John Knox Press
Louisville, Kentucky

Except where noted, the scripture quotations contained herein are from the New Revised Standard Version of the Bible, copyright © 1989 by the Division of Christian Education of the National Council of the Churches of Christ in the U.S.A., and are used by permission. All rights reserved.

Grateful acknowledgment is made to Harcourt Brace & Company, for excerpts from "As the Ruin Falls," in *Poems,* by C. S. Lewis, copyright © 1964 by the Executors of the Estate of C. S. Lewis and renewed 1992 by C. S. Lewis Pte. Ltd.

Book design by Drew Stevens
Cover design by Kim Wohlenhaus
Cover illustration: The Last Supper *by Frans Pourbus the Younger. Louvre, Paris/E.T. Archives, London. Courtesy of Superstock.*

First edition

Published by Westminster John Knox Press
Louisville, Kentucky

This book is printed on acid-free paper that meets the American National Standards Institute Z39.48 standard. ∞

PRINTED IN THE UNITED STATES OF AMERICA

95 96 97 98 99 00 01 02 03 04 — 10 9 8 7 6 5 4 3 2 1

Library of Congress Cataloging-in-Publication Data

Witherington, Ben, 1951–
    John's wisdom : a commentary on the fourth Gospel / Ben Witherington, III.
      p.   cm.
    ISBN 0-664-25621-X (alk. paper)
    1. Bible. N.T. John—Commentaries.   I. Title.
    BS2615.3.W57   1995
    226.5'077—dc20   95-30831

Contents

Part V. The Passion Narrative: Phase Two
John 18:1–19:42

Part VI. The Resurrection Narratives: Including the Epilogue
John 20:1–21:25

Excursus List

Preface

The Fourth Gospel is certainly one of the most beloved and belabored of all New Testament documents, and yet there are dimensions and depths in this rich work that still have not been adequately explored. In particular, the great debt to the wisdom tradition that this Gospel reflects has been under-appreciated. This commentary does not intend to try to be all things to all people. Instead, its aim is to read this Gospel in the light of Jewish and early Christian wisdom material, ranging from Proverbs to the Wisdom of Solomon to the early Christian christological hymns, and then to help the reader see how some of this material can be applied in church settings today.

I have deliberately written this book at a level that is intended to make the material accessible for pastors, teachers, and seminary students wishing to study the Gospel in some detail without being overwhelmed by scholarly jargon and debate. I hope there is enough interaction with the wealth and breadth of scholarly discussion of this Gospel to stir up the scholarly pot some as well, perhaps adding a few new ingredients to the Johannine stew.

There are, basically, two sections in each unit of text: (1) a discussion of the historical and theological context and content of the material; (2) an attempt to build a bridge from the original context of this material to our modern world. The latter section is accordingly called Bridging the Horizons. Because the audience for this commentary is a broad one, the reader will find in the second section some general and introductory suggestions about the application of this material. These remarks are intended to serve as catalysts for the hermeneutical exercise, not definitive or exhaustive examples of that enterprise.

Finally, it is important that I recognize those in the modern Johannine community to whom I am most indebted in this commentary: J. Ashton; C. K. Barrett; R. E. Brown; A. Culpepper; J. Painter; and D. M. Smith. May their tribe increase!

This commentary is dedicated to my many foot washing friends, especially Fred, Mary Ellen, Jerry, and Charles. It is also dedicated to my Durham mentors and colleagues who have labored long and profitably in the Johannine vineyard—Kingsley Barrett, John McHugh, John Painter, Bill Domeris, and Judy Lieu. I couldn't have done this without their help. A blessing on all their houses.

B.W., III

Abbreviations

1QH	The Thanksgiving Hymns (Qumran)
1QS	The Community Rule (Qumran)
3Q15	The Copper Scroll (Qumran)
4QTest	Testimonia (Qumran)
11QPs	Apocryphal Psalms (Qumran)
Adv. haer.	*Adversus haereses* (Irenaeus)
Ant.	*Antiquities of the Jews* (Josephus)
Apol.	*Apologeticum* (Tertullian)
b.	Babylonian Talmud
CD	Cairo Document (Damascus Rule; Qumran)
Dial.	*Dialogue with Trypho* (Justin Martyr)
Digest	*Digest* (of laws; Justinian)
Ep.	*Epistulae* (Letters)
Ephes.	*To the Ephesians* (Ignatius of Antioch)
H.E.	*Historia Ecclesiae* (Eusebius)
Histor.	*Historia* (Tacitus)
Jub.	*Jubilees*
Leg. all.	*Legum allegoriae* (Philo)
m.	Mishnah
Magn.	*To the Magnesians* (Ignatius of Antioch)
NIV	New International Version
Orac. Sib.	*Sibylline Oracles*
P. Flor.	*Papyri Fiorentini* (G. Vitelli)
P. Oxy.	*Oxyrhynchus Papyri* (B. P. Grenfell et al.)
par.	parallel(s)
Ps. Sol.	*Psalms of Solomon*
Sir.	Sirach
Syll.	*Sylloge Inscriptionum Graecarum* (W. Dittenberger)
t.	Tosephta
Test. Naph.	*Testament of Naphtali*
Trall.	*To the Trallians* (Ignatius of Antioch)
Vit. cont.	*De vita contemplativa* (Philo)
War	*Jewish War* (Josephus)
y.	Jerusalem Talmud

Introduction

The Background and Foreground
of the Fourth Gospel

G. R. Beasley-Murray begins his recent commentary on the Gospel of John by remarking, "The last of the four Gospels appears among the rest in a manner reminiscent of Melchizedek to Abraham: 'without father, without mother, without genealogy' (Heb. 7.3)."[1] This judgment is not without foundation. The presentation of Jesus' words and deeds and person is in so many ways so strikingly different from the Synoptic portraits of Jesus that the Fourth Gospel seems both at first glance and after careful study an independent testimony to the Christ. Here we have a Jesus who speaks no parables but rather offers long discourses; a Jesus who, far from silencing messianic acclamations, personally offers various "I am" utterances; a Jesus who is said to have preexisted, to be the Logos in human form, and yet is also depicted as radically dependent on and subordinate to the Father and his will. This Jesus speaks rarely of kingdom and often of eternal life. He does not so much call disciples as exercise some kind of mysterious spiritual gravity, attracting them from among the world's many truth seekers. It is no wonder that E. Käsemann once suggested that the Johannine Jesus bestrides the stage of history like some sort of colossus or deity,[2] and various other scholars have noted that this Gospel's waters are shallow enough for a baby to wade in, yet also deep enough for an elephant to drown in. Before one can study particular passages of this Gospel it is necessary to get one's bearings, or else suffer an inevitable case of theological vertigo, especially when one tries to coordinate one's findings with the Jesus one reads about in the Synoptic Gospels.

What follows here is an attempt to help the reader be able to place the Fourth Gospel in its proper literary, historical, social, and theological contexts and, having done so, to help prepare the reader to study this Gospel in a manner that comports with the way the Fourth Evangelist intended to have it read, heard, and understood. Whatever contemporary use we may wish to make of this Gospel must be grounded in a proper understanding of its historical character.

By way of anticipation, the reader should be alerted at the outset that this Gospel focuses on Christology, and only secondarily and in a few places (e.g., John 13—17; John 21) on matters of discipleship and community life. It intends to inculcate faith in Jesus Christ as the Son of God and the Christ. We should not, then, expect it to give us a great deal of teaching material for those who are already Christians, unlike, for example, Matthew, which gives us the Sermon on the Mount. We will look in vain for extended discussions

1

in this Gospel about marriage and divorce, singleness for the sake of the kingdom, or other relevant Christian ethical topics. This is not to say that Christians cannot and have not gained a great deal spiritually by reading or hearing this Gospel, but only to note that the material in this Gospel is largely geared for use in evangelistic and missionary work. It can profitably be used with Christians to strengthen faith in Christ and his work, but some adjustments will need to be made from time to time, depending on the level of Christian maturity of the audience. One will have to ask, How clearly does my audience understand the character, work, and career of Christ?

The Genre of the Fourth Gospel

In some ways the most crucial issue for proper study of the Fourth Gospel is determining its genre or literary kind. Different genres of literature convey different sorts of information in differing ways and must be evaluated in terms of their differing literary kinds and purposes. For example, poetry sets up a different set of expectations in the audience than prose does, and even within the realm of prose, different kinds of prose compositions must be evaluated differently. A historical novel must be evaluated differently from a serious piece of history writing, even though they both may share a prose narrative format and may be talking about historical subjects and events. Making a mistake about the category the Fourth Gospel belongs to can lead to all sorts of errors in evaluating the document, as well as frustration because one is not deriving from this Gospel what one hoped to get out of it. For example, looking in the Fourth Gospel for a detailed treatment of proper church polity or structure would be rather like looking in a telephone directory to find the definition of a word.

Once the genre of a document is recognized, it sets up a sort of compact between author and audience, in which the former attempts to meet certain kinds of expectations associated with that genre of literature, and the audience will be looking or listening for the author to do so. Accordingly, we must spend some time dealing with the issue of the Fourth Gospel's genre.

Because of the influence of R. Bultmann, and more recently Johannine scholars such as J. Painter, many New Testament scholars still hold the view that the Gospels are unique, their genre being determined by and developed out of the distinctive primitive Christian preaching.[3] While I would grant that the Gospels contain the unique Christian message about Jesus and that their form is somewhat conditioned by their contents, it is not the case that the form is without analogy in certain types of biographical and historical writings in antiquity.[4] In fact, the recent work of R. Burridge, which provides a detailed comparison between the Gospels and other ancient biographies, has now provided us with compelling reasons for seeing John's Gospel, along with the Synoptics, as a subspecies of the ancient biography.[5] Though the Gospels are not biographies in the modern sense of the word (i.e., they do not reflect much interest in personal appearance, the sociological and psychological factors of character development, or consistently precise chronology),[6] it does not follow that they were not intended or understood as biographies by the standards of antiquity, for these were not elements characteristic of such ancient literature.

Burridge has shown that the ancient biographical genre was somewhat flexible and there was room for variations of features within it, but that there were nonetheless certain common features that provide a family resemblance in all such ancient documents. These common features included:

1. A prologue or introduction.
2. Focus on a particular individual (unlike ancient histories, which were generally much broader in scope). This individual is introduced by name directly after the prologue if not in the prologue itself.
3. The use of chronological, geographical, and topical categories to arrange the material. "This structure of a chronological framework with a topical material inserted . . . is typical of the structure found in many *Bioi*."[7] There was normally an interest in saying something about the origins and outcome of the subject's life; thus the normal "life" began with the character's origins and concluded with statements about his or her death and ongoing impact.
4. Records of deeds and words used to build up a portrait or characterization of the subject of the biography with a focus on incidents that were especially revealing of that person's character. Normally incidents were selected to present the character in a particular light (favorable or unfavorable), and the mode of presentation was some form of continuous narrative, with some interruptions and digressions.
5. A length that tended to be medium-sized—more than a record of a speech, but less than that of a work of general history writing. For example, biographical works such as Philo's *Life of Moses* or Nepos's *Atticus*, or Xenephon's *Agesilaus* range from 3,500 words (the *Atticus*) to 32,000 in the case of Philo's work, but the latter is a two-volume work. In general, they tended to be no more than could be fitted on one papyrus roll (21,000–24,000 words), or for that matter what could be read aloud in one long sitting to an audience. The Fourth Gospel is 15,416 words, which places it about halfway between the length of Mark and the other two Synoptics and well within the requisite length to fit on one papyrus roll.[8]
6. A tone in most of these biographies, especially those which intended to present their subject in a positive light, that tended to be serious in character, inculcating an atmosphere of respect or even reverence in the audience for the subject.

A few more points are critical in order to grasp the impact of suggesting that the Fourth Gospel is deliberately written as a form of ancient biography. "If genre is the key to a work's interpretation, and the genre of the gospels is *Bios*, then the key to their interpretation must be the person of their subject, Jesus of Nazareth."[9] The subject matter of the Fourth Gospel is *not* the contemporary experience of Johannine Christians, or even the history of the Johannine community, though we can learn something indirectly from the Fourth Gospel about such matters, but rather the story of Jesus Christ as sifted, ruminated on, and interpreted by the Beloved Disciple. While this Gospel, like the Synoptics, deals by implication with a variety of matters, "to place such subjects as their primary concern above the person of Jesus is to miss the fact that they are *Bioi*. . . . Christology . . . affects every area."[10] To put it another way, "The simple fact that the evangelist has chosen to express himself through the means of the gospel indicates that there is a real historical human life at the root of the central character of his witness. If flesh is irrelevant to the evangelist or if the revealer in no sense really took upon himself fleshly existence why did the evangelist write a *gospel?*"[11]

A biographer could come at his subject with a variety of interests and aims—the desire to persuade, which entailed the art of rhetoric, the desire to convey a certain amount of historical information about the subject, the desire to dramatize certain facts about a historical person, the desire to teach or instruct by presenting a subject's discourse, the desire to praise a dead hero.[12] The Fourth Gospel means to persuade people to believe certain things about Jesus (see below). This leads us to our next point.

If we are to ask more specifically about the Fourth Gospel, it will appear that it is in some respects most like ancient philosophical biographies, because of its lengthy discourse material, and in some respects like ancient political biographies in some of its handling of the polemics between Jesus and the Jewish leaders and the events that lead up to Jesus' death. As Burridge says, the ancient biographical form was well known throughout the Roman Empire, and was used to address not only highly literate audiences, but also more popular ones. Even a general audience would have been familiar with the conventions of ancient biographies, and one need not have had more than a secondary level of education to produce such a document.[13] As will be made clearer a bit later in this introduction, I believe that this Gospel should be seen as a dramatic biography written for Christians to use for evangelistic purposes. (It is not simply a missionary tract to be handed out, but rather a document for Christians to use for evangelistic and missionary purposes.)

The Mode of the Fourth Gospel

It has been noticed that the Fourth Gospel in particular has certain affinities with ancient drama, in particular ancient tragedy.[14] As Burridge says, this is not a matter of genre, but of the *mode* of presentation in this particular biography.[15] There are too many features of ancient drama (as, for example, the choral interludes) that are missing from the Fourth Gospel for us to see this work simply as a play. It is, however, precisely in this area of mode that we can detect and explain some of the major differences between the Fourth Gospel and the Synoptics.

I would suggest that what the Beloved Disciple, or the final editor of this Gospel, has done is to choose to present the story of Jesus in a dramatic mode, drawing on certain familiar elements and techniques from the theater such as (1) the initial hymn of homage found in John 1[16]; (2) the use of irony throughout—the technique of using two levels of discourse at once, saying one thing, apparently mundane in character, while referring to something on a higher plane; (3) the stress on the stupendousness of Jesus' miracles and other actions in the story—gallons of wine are produced, a man born blind is healed, a man four days dead is raised, Jesus is buried in a veritable mountain of spices, Roman cohorts fall down when Jesus approaches;[17] all of this is meant to stress the importance and magnitude of the main character of the story; (4) the playing up of dualisms—light and dark, good and bad, friend and foe, offense and commendation; (5) the use of the crescendo effect—the crescendo of the miraculous, the crescendo of confessions, the crescendo of opposition to Jesus climaxing at the end of the drama in the resurrection stories; (5) the almost self-contained nature of certain scenes, like scenes in a play (e.g., the incident with the Samaritan woman, the drama with the blind man); (6) the use of rhetoric at key junctures for the sake of persuasion; (7) the usual following of the rule in Greco-Roman drama of having no more than three figures speak in any one scene (see John 3, 4, 9); (8) the emphasis on surprising revelations that come to Jesus and dictate the action—he can't go up to the feast, or go to Lazarus unless the Father gives the orders; this is meant to show the central figure's dependence on God, and thus his heroic and positive character, as is also the case in Greco-Roman drama when the main character receives visions or dreams from the gods for guidance.

In these and other ways the Fourth Evangelist has drawn on the conventions of Greco-Roman drama to reveal the character of someone who he believed truly is the divine Son of God, as opposed to the Emperor Domitian, who in this same time period was publicly making claims to be "Deus et Dominus Noster" ("Our God and Lord") and was honored as such in Asia Minor.[18] In short, there is much that can be learned from evaluating the Fourth Gospel in light of its literary, as well as its social and political, context.

The Sources of the Fourth Gospel

The Relation of John to the Synoptics

After the time of B. H. Streeter, when most scholars held that the Fourth Evangelist used Mark, probably Luke, and possibly Matthew, a new consensus arose, chiefly in the wake of the works of P. Gardner-Smith and C. H. Dodd, favoring the independence of John from the Synoptics. It is fair to say that at the present time the pendulum has begun to swing back in the other direction.[19] "We have now reached a point at which neither assumption is safe, that is neither can be taken for granted. Any exegete must argue the case afresh on its merits."[20] I intend to provide such an argument in a moment, but in view of our earlier discussion of the genre of the Fourth Gospel two important points must first be noted.

First, since it is very likely that the Fourth Gospel is a type of ancient biography, it is not necessary to argue that the Fourth Evangelist must have known other Gospels such as Mark if we are to explain why he chose to write a document that takes the form of the Fourth Gospel. The evangelist need not be seen as the second inventor of some unique genre called Gospel. Rather he, like Mark and others, will simply have been adapting and adopting the widely known form of the ancient biography, which begins with the main subject's origins, concludes with his death and legacy, and in between provides a mixture of chronological narrative and topically arranged material, or discourses, or dialogues, in part depending on whether the biography is about a philosopher or teacher on the one hand, or a great political figure on the other. Ancient biography chiefly differs from a historical monograph in that it has a deliberate and relentless focus on one particular individual.

Second, it is not necessary to argue that the writing of a Gospel *must have* required a long gestation period, presupposing a long traditioning process, developing the Gospel form *out of* earlier traditions and collections of material. Gospels need not have been the end result of a long evolutionary process from smaller- to larger-sized units of materials about Jesus. As it happens, I think in the case of the Fourth Gospel we *are* talking about a document that reflects the fact that the Beloved Disciple did meditate on, and preach and teach, the Jesus traditions for a long period of time, at some point casting the material into his own style and idiom, likely before writing it down. This conclusion does not, however, require us to think that there was a comparable length of time between when the Beloved Disciple wrote down his version of the Jesus traditions and the time when the Fourth Evangelist gathered them up and cast them into the biographical document we call the Fourth Gospel. In other words, I do not think that the form of this Gospel in any way requires us to think of its material as having been passed down for many years in the hands of the Johannine *community* and reflecting *its* various stages and crises. When it came time to put the Beloved Disciple's material in the form in which we now have it, the ancient biography format was ready to hand, and the Gospel may have been compiled with some dispatch, caused by the death of the Beloved Disciple.

While I think there *are* a few hints in the Gospel's text that tell us something about the Johannine community, I am basically skeptical of the ability of scholarship to successfully excavate the mound known as the Fourth Gospel and make nice distinctions between earlier and later layers of Johannine tradition, *and then correlate them with stages in the development in the Johannine community.*[21]

My skepticism has several bases. First, all of this Gospel manifests a uniform style, even including the asides. Second, *all* of the material included in this Gospel in its present form has been included for a reason, and has a meaning at the Gospel level, whatever previous meanings the material may have had. I doubt there are any *pure* artifacts of earlier meanings to be found (e.g., earlier Christologies), though there may be some few traces left.[22] Third, reflexive reading of the text, taking what is said about Jesus, the first disciples, and their interlocutors and then *assuming* it is really talking about the Johannine community and its dialogue partners is fraught with perils and lacks external controls to provide limits to speculation. It would be better to speak of how the author uses Jesus material, cast in the Johannine idiom, and *applies* it to later settings. The hermeneutical drive has *not* created these source materials—they are the testimonies of the Beloved Disciple— but it has affected how they have been edited, and why they have been put together in biographical form. Fourth, what we *do* know about the Johannine community from the only external and partially objective sources we have, the epistles and perhaps the seven letters in the book of Revelation, does not suggest this community was *ever* part of some diaspora synagogue, but at least Revelation suggests it had controversies with the synagogue. Using synagogue controversy and in particular expulsion from the synagogue as *the clue* to the development of this community (and thus to the meaning of some layers of the text) is overemphasizing one clue in the Gospel at best.[23] In this commentary we will concentrate on the meaning of the final form of the text, and make what few literary critical comments that can judiciously be made about the source material.

In another context, I have argued at length for the literary independence of John from the Synoptic Gospels, though the author clearly enough knows about various of the events that are recorded in the Synoptics.[24] The case for dependence on Matthew is generally recognized to be weak; the case for dependence on Luke depends on certain names and details shared in common, which can as easily be attributed to the use of common sources. The case for dependence on Mark is more substantial, however, and may lead to the conclusion that the evangelist at least had heard this Gospel at some point. In regard to *literary* dependence of the Fourth Gospel on Mark, the case is not compelling.

C. K. Barrett places particular emphasis on the argument from order.[25] His list includes: (a) the work and witness of the Baptist (Mark 1:4–8/John 1:19–36); (b) departure to Galilee (Mark 1:14f./John 4:3); (c) feeding the multitude (Mark 6:34–44/John 6:1–13); (d) walking on the lake (Mark 6:45–52/John 6:16–21); (e) Peter's confession (Mark 8:29/John 6:68f.); (f) departure to Jerusalem (Mark 9:30f.; 10:1, 32, 46/John 7:10–14); (g) the entry and the anointing (Mark 11:1–19; 14:3–9; transposed in John 12:12–15; 12:1–8); (h) the Last Supper, with predictions of betrayal and denial (Mark 14:17–26/John 13:1–17:26); (i) the arrest (Mark 14:43–52/John 18:1–11; and (j) the Passion and resurrection (Mark 14:53–16:8/John 18:12–20:29).

At first blush, this list appears very formidable evidence for dependence, but first impressions can be deceiving. There seems to be no likelihood that pericopes f–g, and h–j could be in any other place than their present one in either Gospel. Jesus must depart for Jerusalem before he enters it; the Last Supper must precede the arrest; the arrest must precede the Passion and resurrection. There is, however, room for rearranging the order of the entry and the anointing and, significantly, Mark and John differ at this point, as they do even more dramatically on the placement of the temple cleansing as well. Furthermore, unlike the case in John, there is a considerable amount of material that separates Mark's entry and anointing stories.

The first half of Barrett's list is more problematic. Nonetheless, the pericope he lists as a logically precedes b, c, d, and e, since it is the Baptist who prepares the way by appearing before Jesus and announcing his coming. This is true even in the Fourth Gospel (see 1:15 and 1:27), though it is also true that John continues to play a role in both Gospels even after the coming of Jesus on the public scene (see Mark 6 and John 3:22ff.). Pericope b must precede pericope c, for all four evangelists locate the feeding of the multitude in Galilee and Jesus must depart for Galilee before the feeding can be recorded. Similarly, Jesus must finish his Galilean ministry before he makes his final trip up to Jerusalem; thus pericope f must follow a–e.

The parallels in the sequence c, d, e are more impressive, but even here there is room for doubt. In John's framework, e must precede f. Peter's confession in John occasions a reference to Jesus' betrayal (6:70–71) and his not going up until his time has come (7:1, 6), both of which set the stage for Jesus' trip to Jerusalem. The order e–f can be explained in terms of the internal framework of the Fourth Gospel. Finally, the order c–d, d–e may be explained without the dependence theory if one accepts C. H. Dodd's argument that Mark had a general narrative framework that helped him order some of the pericopes about Jesus' Galilean ministry, which the Fourth Evangelist may also have access to,[26] or one may choose to accept Dodd's suggestion that "there is good reason to believe that in broad outlines the Markan order does represent a genuine succession of events,"[27] in which case Mark may have known the outline and the Beloved Disciple may have known the actual sequence of events, which the Fourth Evangelist did not choose to rearrange at this point. In conclusion, the arguments from order are not sufficient to make probable, much less force, the conclusion that John knew Mark's order.

The case for verbal dependence is also less than compelling. Of the twelve examples Barrett cites,[28] which represent the best of the possible list of parallels, the longest is no more than three and a half lines in the Greek text— one average-length sentence and one shorter sentence (Mark 14:7–8; see John 12:7–8). We have word-for-word agreement in none of these twelve examples, not even in the shortest ones (Mark 6:50; John 6:20; cf. Mark 8:29; John 6:69). D. M. Smith stresses "precisely in those passages which have obvious synoptic parallels the extent of divergence is considerable, and difficult to account for on the basis of clear Johannine interests."[29] These points about verbal dependence are of somewhat limited value since Barrett, and others of his persuasion, do not tend to argue that John simply copied Mark; some weight must be given to them, however, because they show that the verbal similarities come not so much from unusual words, graphic details, or peculiar turns of phrase, but primarily in *ordinary* words and phrases. This is surely significant, since it is reasonable to expect that the unique or striking words or phrases would be what the Fourth Evangelist or the Beloved Disciple would primarily remember and reproduce from Mark.

Finally, since the case for literary dependence of John on Mark is often thought to be secured because of detailed parallels between the two versions of the feeding of the five thousand story, a few closing remarks on that narrative are in order. This is the only ministry miracle story recorded in all four Gospels, which suggests that it was deemed crucial by *all* the evangelists, and it is not likely that their judgment differed much from that of many other early Christians. In other words, this miracle story must have had very widespread and early circulation due to its importance and popularity. In such a circumstance it is hardly necessary to argue for John's dependence on Mark to explain the similarities. We thus must conclude that the case for dependence of the Fourth Gospel on any of the Synoptics is not compelling or even necessarily the most plausible explanation of all the relevant data.

John and the Signs Source

Since R. Bultmann first made the theory of a signs source popular,[30] this particular source theory has eclipsed all others in gaining acceptance among Johannine scholars, though on occasions the arguments for the dependence of John on the Synoptics has temporarily gained great popularity. In the wake of R. Fortna's second book on the subject, the theory of the signs source has gained new adherents and strengthened old ones.[31] Fortna, in distinction from Bultmann, argues that the composer of the signs source combined a signs source and a Passion source, in effect creating a minigospel which ended at John 20:30–31. He then maintains that the Fourth Evangelist created his Gospel out of this source, adding discourse material and critiquing the view of signs and Christology he found in the source material.

There are some serious problems with this theory, not the least of which is explaining why the evangelist was careful enough to record so much of this source, and yet not careful enough to edit out the christological and sign material with which he disagreed. In view of the pervasive evidence that the Fourth Evangelist made all of his source material his own, as is reflected by the distinctive Johannine style and themes that are found throughout the Gospel, it is hard to accept the view that this evangelist was a careless editor—for instance, leaving in the numbering of the first two signs while excluding the original third sign and removing the numbering on the rest. As Painter suggests, it is much easier to believe that the Fourth Evangelist numbered the two Cana signs, and so intentionally set them apart from the other ones, highlighting them.[32] Another complaint that may be made about Fortna's treatment is that it does not do justice to the intricate relationship of signs and discourses at various key points, and this in turn leads to an unsatisfactory treatment of the signs themselves in the completed Gospel.[33] If the Christology inherent in the sign narratives is at odds with that of the evangelist, how is it that the same Christology can be found in the discourses connected to various of the signs (e.g., in John 6)? I am much more inclined to agree with Painter that the Fourth Evangelist began not with a signs Gospel, but with a loose collection of traditional stories and discourses which he has edited and used.[34]

My own source theory involves several deductions. First, the Beloved Disciple is, as John 21 suggests, the source of the material in this Gospel, and it owes most of its distinctive traits to him and his casting of the material into his own idiom (see below). It is his eyewitness testimony that is largely incorporated into this Gospel, but the way he has handled his material, namely, by presenting it in a sapiential or wisdom format, sets it apart from most Synoptic traditions.

Second, I would suggest that there were primarily two sorts of traditions the Fourth Evangelist derived from the Beloved Disciple—traditions used in preaching to and teaching of nonbelievers (the signs material, the Passion material), and traditions mainly used to encourage those who were already Christians and needed to learn how to remain in Christ and carry on in the faith and with the mission of the church (e.g., the farewell discourses and John 21). The Fourth Evangelist has edited both of these sorts of traditions to serve his overall evangelistic purposes in his Gospel (see below).

Third, it seems clear enough from John 20:30, from the character of the appendix in John 21, and from the free-floating Johannine tradition of the woman caught in adultery (which in all likelihood was not originally part of this Gospel),[35] that there were many other Johannine traditions available to the Fourth Evangelist that he did not use, and that at least some if not all of the traditions he did use were independent stories like the story of the blind man (e.g., John 9), or brief collections that could and did stand on their own (e.g., the Cana traditions). In other words, the Fourth Evangelist, not his source, is likely to have taken a disparate collection of written (and perhaps even a few oral) traditions and formed them into this Gospel. We are not told that his source wrote down these stories in some kind of order or in Gospel form; we are simply told the Beloved Disciple testified and had these things written down (21:24).

Fourth, the intention of the Fourth Evangelist was to present a life or biography of Jesus in the Johannine key, and he selected and arranged his source material to that end. I suspect that this Gospel as a publication never existed without the prologue, since that was standard fare in ancient biographies and since the Logos hymn is in many ways the key to understanding the portrayal of Jesus throughout the Gospel. It is possible that John 21 was added later in a second edition, but I doubt it, since it provides us with data that explains why the Gospel was in fact published at all—namely, the death of the Beloved Disciple. The Fourth Evangelist thus likely used the traditions found in John 21 as an epilogue when the Gospel was first put together, in part because they did not neatly fit within the narrative framework of the events recorded in John 20; in part because they suited well his purpose of strengthening one more time the essential message of the Gospel about inculcating faith through an active mission; in part because they gave him an occasion to correct the false impression that the Beloved Disciple would live until Christ returned.[36]

Fifth, it was the intention of the Fourth Evangelist to provide a Johannine biography of Jesus, with all credit being given to the source of the eyewitness traditions, not to himself, and thus, rightly, he remains an anonymous member of the Johannine community, likely a close friend and disciple of the Beloved Disciple. The Fourth Evangelist should be seen not as a pneumatic prophet generating words of the exalted Jesus and placing them on the historical Jesus' lips, but as a redactor or editor, skillfully editing his sources into a biographical format.

Sixth, the purpose of this document is not to be a missionary tract that would simply be handed out, but rather to be a tool for Johannine Christians to use to inculcate faith in nonbelievers, and perhaps as a secondary purpose to encourage those who already believed.[37] Little signals like John 11:2 let us know that the evangelist expects that Christians with a Christian memory of these stories will be using them—the Gospel is not meant simply to be passed out to the nonbeliever without interpretation or explanation by a Christian witness. John 11:2 is *not* a reminder from the narrator to the reader or first-time hearer of the Gospel, for the anointing story is not presented until John 12! Nonetheless, the dominant evangelistic purpose and focus of the document must not be missed, and this probably sets it apart from the Synoptics. It is the unbelieving world more than anyone else that is meant to hear this biography given a dramatic reading, or explained or proclaimed (see below).

Unlike the Johannine epistles, the Gospel is not in the main directed toward internal problems or conditions in the community. The Gospel is meant to provide biographical ammunition for Johannine Christians to use in the witness to the world; and even a good deal of the material in the farewell discourses is used to stress the importance of the disciples remaining faithful to Jesus and his mission, taking up this task, though these discourses were originally addressed to those who already believed.

The Authorship and Editorship
of the Fourth Gospel

As scholars liberal, conservative, and moderate recognize, the *text* of the Fourth Gospel as we have it, which begins at John 1:1 and ends at John 21:25, does not reveal the name of the author, any more than any of the Synoptics do. What then of the superscription, "The Gospel according to John"? This superscription is in fact found in P[66], which perhaps comes from the late second century, and in P[72], which is a little later, but appears to have been first added to the Gospel when it was brought together with the other three canonical Gospels and they were circulated as a collection, perhaps as early as A.D. 125.[38] If this title had been attached to the Gospel before the fourfold collection, we would have expected it to read "The Gospel *of* John," not "The Gospel *according* [*kata*] to John," because the latter expression surely implies that there were tellings of the Gospel according to others, and so this form of a title would be used to *distinguish* this Gospel from the others with which it was placed together.[39] In any case, this attestation must be taken as part of the *external*, not internal, evidence for the authorship of this document, however early it was attached to the document. It is an error to begin the discussion of authorship by looking first at the external and secondary data and then turning to the Gospel itself, as has recently been the case with D. Carson's and M. Hengel's discussions of the matter.[40] What then do we learn from the Gospel itself about the originator of the traditions found in this Gospel?[41]

First, we learn that he is a person with a Jewish background who is interested in things like the Jewish discussion about Messiah, the Jewish festivals, the law, and distinguishable groups found on the fringes of early Judaism such as John the Baptist and his followers and the Samaritans. Second, in view of the interesting parallels between the Fourth Gospel and the Qumran material, which are now widely recognized (including such dualisms as light and dark, truth and falsehood, flesh and spirit, life and death, and the discussion of knowledge),[42] it would seem that at some point the originator of this Gospel material had some sort of connection with what could be called sectarian Judaism. I would suggest the connection is a mediated rather than an immediate one, namely, that the Beloved Disciple was probably at one time a disciple of John the Baptist and the latter had, at some point, some kind of contact and relationship with the Qumran sect.[43] One important feature of this Gospel is the polemics directed against certain Jewish officials, in particular those in Jerusalem, who are regularly called "the Jews" in this Gospel. Such polemics are not surprising from a disciple of either John or Jesus, and were a regular feature of the critique by Qumran of institutional Judaism.

It is not likely that it was just a product of the later Jewish-Christian squabbles in the Diaspora after A.D. 70. The originator of the traditions found in this Gospel was a Jewish Christian who had become convinced not only that the existing institutions of mainstream Judaism were corrupt and needed replacement, but that Jesus had in fact replaced them by means of his life, death, and resurrection. What early Jews were looking for in terms of life, light, power, healing, forgiveness, cleansing, knowledge, and the like was to be found in Jesus the Christ, not in Jewish purification rituals, or in Temple-centered worship, or in attending Jewish festivals, or even by and large in the law, though the Beloved Disciple believed the Torah most certainly pointed forward to the fulfillment of all Jewish hopes and dreams in the coming messianic One. In other words, the originator of the Johannine tradition was a Jew engaged in a radical critique of early Judaism, but he would have been horrified to have been labeled anti-Semitic, not least because he earnestly believed salvation came forth to the world from the Jews in the person of Jesus (John 4:22).

We learn, third, that like many other early Jews, the originator of this Gospel's substance knew enough Greek to communicate well in that language, though no one would accuse the Beloved Disciple or the Fourth Evangelist of writing anything more than readable, simple Greek. He likely acquired these skills well before he moved to the Diaspora (if he did so), since the Holy Land, including Galilee and Judea, had long before his time felt the pervasive influence of hellenization, and Greek was the lingua franca for business and general communication of the empire, especially east of Rome.

The fourth major thing one can learn about the originator of the Johannine traditions from the text itself is that he had at some point gathered a community of disciples around him as the "we" in John 21:24 makes abundantly clear. While I am skeptical about the ability to trace a history of this community from the Gospel itself, when one combines what is implied in the Gospel with what one learns from the Johannine epistles a somewhat clearer picture emerges of a community that during the lifetime of its leader had some serious internal problems, created by differences over christological and ethical matters, among other things, as well as having, apparently, *some* external problems, to judge from the stress on being cast out of the synagogue in John 9:22 and 12:42.[44] It is by no means clear, however, that the Johannine community as a whole had ever been a part of a synagogue. More likely the Beloved Disciple had formed a separate community from the outset when he arrived in Asia, but there were repeated attempts to evangelize in and through the local synagogue(s), and there were Christian sympathizers who sought to remain in the synagogue, which in due course led to the expulsion of both the visitors and the sympathizers from that venue.

In other words, the missionary nature of the Johannine community must not be underestimated, as that was characteristic of early Christianity in general. The Johannine community was not a merely sectarian community, but rather one that sought to maintain a careful balance between clear and faithful allegiance to its own identity, as the Johannine epistles reflect, while still being part of a missionary movement. In principle, this is not different from what we find in the Pauline communities, which also had to establish boundaries for its communities, while at the same time putting doors in those boundaries so outsiders could be brought in and, if necessary, troublemaking insiders could leave or even be expelled (compare 1 Cor. 5 to 2 and 3 John).

The fifth major thing one can learn about the originator of these traditions is that he had a clear and accurate knowledge of conditions in Judea and Jerusalem *prior* to A.D. 70 (see, e.g., especially John 5:2). In fact, the extensive Judean traditions in this Gospel, including the material about Mary, Martha, and Lazarus, about the festivals, knowledge of the high priest (John 18:15) and other matters strongly suggest that we are dealing with a disciple of Jesus who came from or at least was located in Judea for some time prior to becoming a follower of Jesus, if in fact he traveled with Jesus.[45] A case can be made that this Judean disciple, who does not *clearly* appear in the narrative before John 13:23, did not travel with Jesus, but was only present whenever Jesus was in Jerusalem, and especially during the last week of Jesus' life. This might account for why in John 13:23 the Beloved Disciple was reclining next to Jesus, namely, because it was in his house that this supper transpired, and following normal Greco-Roman custom the host and guest of honor sat closely together at or near the head of the table. Indeed, a case could be and has been made that the Beloved Disciple was Lazarus of Bethany, not only because of the meal celebrated in his home in John 12, which immediately precedes the story in John 13, but also because he is the only male disciple other than the Beloved Disciple who is specifically labeled "he whom you love" (John 11:3; cf. 13:23) in this Gospel. This theory might also explain how it is that some of the Beloved Disciple's own disciples later came to believe he would live until Christ returned (see John 21:23)—they had heard the story that he had been raised from the dead by Jesus, and assumed that it meant he would not die again! As tempting as this theory is, it would be difficult then to explain how this Gospel ever came to be associated with anyone named John.

What we can say with more certainty is that it is likely the Johannine traditions originated with a Judean follower of Jesus, who was an eyewitness of at least the closing stages of Jesus' life, and probably to all his visits to Jerusalem. Since there is some evidence that the Beloved Disciple may have been influenced in his thinking by and have been a disciple of John the Baptist first before joining Jesus, perhaps he was with Jesus even from the time Jesus parted company from John the Baptist.[46]

We must consider one further bit of information from John 21 sometimes thought to force the conclusion that John, son of Zebedee, was the Beloved Disciple. In John 21:2 a list of disciples is mentioned, including the two sons of Zebedee and two anonymous disciples. The Beloved Disciple is said to recognize Jesus first, and here in John 21:7 he is closely associated with Peter, as he is in John 13 and 20 and in 21:20ff. While it is possible to conclude that the Beloved Disciple is John the son of Zebedee in John 21, especially if one comes to this text predisposed to favor such a view, this is by no means a necessary conclusion. The Beloved Disciple could well be one of the two anonymous disciples mentioned in 21:2, whose anonymity is not violated by the reference to the Zebedees, but rather carried on at 21:20ff., where again he is referred to as the Beloved Disciple, not as a son of Zebedee. All that the Beloved Disciple traditions in John 13—21 suggest on their own is that this disciple was very close to Jesus' heart, as was Peter, and thus was closely associated with Peter as well.

What the internal evidence of this Gospel read critically does *not* suggest is that the Beloved Disciple was John son of Zebedee, for not only does this Gospel not focus on the Galilean ministry of Jesus, it omits the crucial events that happened in Galilee about which John the son of Zebedee could have provided eyewitness testimony. For example, the Fourth Gospel totally omits the narrative of the calling of the sons of Zebedee from their nets at the Sea of Galilee; the "in house" story of Jesus' healing of Peter's mother-

in-law at which John was present; a second "in house" story, about the raising of Jairus's daughter where the three main disciples were present; the
transfiguration narrative; the request by the Zebedees to sit on Jesus' right
and left in the kingdom; and the Gethesemane prayer session at which John
was present (see Mark 14:33).[47] While it might be possible to account for the
omission of one or two of these stories, it is extremely improbable that all of
them would be absent from this Gospel if it is in essence the eyewitness testimony of John the son of Zebedee. It is for this reason that even moderate
to conservative scholars like R. Schnackenburg, G. R. Beasley-Murray, R. E.
Brown, and J. W. Pryor have come to abandon the theory that this Gospel
is attributable to John the son of Zebedee, and instead are content to affirm
that it goes back to the Beloved Disciple who was another, and likely Judean,
disciple and an eyewitness of at least some of the ministry.[48] The internal evidence of the Gospel supports such a conclusion.

What of the external evidence, and how much weight should it be given?
There is, of course, the evidence of the superscription, but all it tells us is that
this Gospel is according to someone named John—it does not specify which
John, a very common name in the New Testament (cf., e.g., John the Baptist, John son of Zebedee, John Mark). The first unambiguous quotation of
this Gospel that ascribes it to John son of Zebedee is that of Theophilus of
Antioch (A.D. 181), some ninety years after this Gospel was likely published.
But the two crucial witnesses come from even later, in the testimony of Irenaeus at the end of the second century A.D. and the testimony of Eusebius
from the early fourth century A.D.

It must be remembered when evaluating these testimonies that by the
end of the second century A.D. two trends were already in evidence: (1) the
desire and felt need to associate all the sacred traditions of Christianity with
apostolic witness; (2) the Gnostic controversies of the second century,
which made it especially crucial to associate the Fourth Gospel with apostolic testimony, since this was the Gospel that was the favorite of various
Gnostics, and the representatives of more orthodox Christianity wanted to
reclaim it for their own communities.

In a letter to someone called Florinus (see Eusebius, *H.E.* 5.20.5–6), Irenaeus recalls what he heard from Polycarp, who in turn claimed to have spoken to one named John and other eyewitnesses of Jesus' ministry: "The
blessed Polycarp . . . reported his converse with John and with the others
who had seen the Lord, how he remembered their words, and what were the
things concerning the Lord which he had heard from them, including his
miracles and his teaching." Irenaeus (in his *Against Heresies* 3.1.2) also says,
"John, the disciple of the Lord who leaned back on his breast, published the
Gospel while he was resident at Ephesus in Asia." Several points about this
testimony are notable: (1) Irenaeus is passing along secondhand information; he himself had not spoken to any of the eyewitnesses; (2) Polycarp's
testimony does not *say* that the John he was speaking about was John son of
Zebedee, only a John who had been an eyewitness of the ministry of Jesus
and was the Beloved Disciple; (3) in his own deductions in *Against Heresies*

Irenaeus assumes that this John is the Beloved Disciple mentioned in John 13:23, but even there he does not clearly equate this John the Beloved Disciple with John the son of Zebedee.

In Eusebius we are dealing with a tendentious fourth-century writer quoting a second-century source, namely Papias, who likely wrote somewhere between A.D. 125 and 135. Eusebius quotes Papias (in *H.E.* 3.39.3–4) as saying: "And if anyone chanced to come who had actually been a follower of the elders, I would inquire as to the discourses of the elders, what Andrew or what Peter said, or what Philip, or what Thomas or James, or what John or Matthew or any other of the Lord's disciples [said]; and the things which Aristion and John the elder, the disciples of the Lord, say." This tradition has been endlessly debated: was Papias referring to one John or two? The one thing that is clear about this testimony is, there is a striking affinity between the disciples named in it and those listed in John 1:35–51 (Andrew, Peter, and Philip in this same order) and those mentioned in John 21:2, a fact which strongly suggests Papias knew the Fourth Gospel.[49] In this testimony of Papias, even if the two Johns are in fact taken as one and the same, this does not prove that he is referring to John the son of Zebedee, one of the Twelve, any more than the reference to Aristion proves he was one of the Twelve or one of the original apostles. All it proves is that Papias takes all these persons to be eyewitnesses of the ministry of Jesus. Furthermore, the opening of this quotation does not suggest that Papias himself spoke with this John or with any of these eyewitnesses, but rather with "those who had been followers of the elders," through whom he got his information.

A reasonable case can be made for distinguishing the John listed with members of the Twelve, and the John the elder mentioned with Aristion, who was still living when Papias gave this testimony.[50] This latter John was perhaps called the elder because he lived to a ripe old age, or perhaps he had gained such a title because he called himself *ho presbyteros*, "the old man," in his letters to his disciples (cf. 2 John 1, and 3 John 1). I for one do not think we should cavalierly dismiss the external testimony of Irenaeus and Papias, but their testimonies do not force the conclusion that their sources were referring to John the son of Zebedee when they spoke of John, the Beloved Disciple, who was responsible for the testimony in the Fourth Gospel.

To sum up, the internal evidence suggests that the testimony enshrined in the Fourth Gospel is that of the Beloved Disciple, a Judean disciple who was an eyewitness of at least some of the ministry of Jesus, including at least the occasions when Jesus was in or near Jerusalem, especially during the closing weeks of Jesus' life. It is also very possible, but not certain, that this same disciple was originally a follower of John the Baptist and joined Jesus' entourage at some point, perhaps even early in his ministry. Notice that the ministry of John is characterized in John 3:22–23 as transpiring in Judea, not in Galilee, which may support the connection of the Beloved Disciple with the followers of the Baptist.

The external evidence, so far as it goes, does not necessarily contradict this conclusion, and does not require the conclusion that there was an early insistence in the church that John the son of Zebedee was the author or source of the Fourth Gospel. What it does suggest is that someone named John was the Beloved Disciple, and that he may have been called, or called himself, John the elder, or perhaps John the old man.

We have not suggested to this point that we should equate the Beloved Disciple and the Fourth Evangelist. In part this equation reflects a particular view of the *degree* to which the testimony of the Beloved Disciple was edited and put into final form by another hand. My own personal view is that it is this other hand which gathered the various Johannine traditions, some written and perhaps some oral, and put them into the form of an ancient biography which we call a Gospel. Clearly, John 19:35 and John 21:24 require some such theory. The former text distinguishes between the Beloved Disciple who has testified and the voice of the evangelist who speaks about him in the third person. The latter text distinguishes between the Beloved Disciple, again spoken of in the third person and so distinguished from the writer, and "we"—the Johannine community, of which the final editor of this document must have been a part.

Some, of course, have taken a minimalist view of the final editor's role, even suggesting that John 21:24 refers only to the material in the appendix in John 21, but it appears to me that this view is not sound, and not just because of John 19:35. It is very difficult to believe that any disciple of Jesus would go around regularly styling himself "the one whom Jesus loved" (*heis . . . hon egapa ho Iesous,* John 13:23; cf. 20:2; 21:7), but quite believable that members of the Johannine community who admired him might do so, highlighting his closeness to Jesus. These texts do not, however, merely claim that Jesus loved this person, but insist on using a phrase that characterizes this disciple in this way, to some degree setting him *apart* from others. On the one hand, those who wish to insist the Beloved Disciple produced the final form of this Gospel argue that the author was too modest to mention his own personal name, but on the other hand he was not modest enough to refrain from calling himself the Beloved Disciple! This strains credulity to the breaking point.[51] It is much easier to believe that the phrase in question reflects the hand of the final editor, whom I am referring to as the Fourth Evangelist.

As is widely known, there are also various gaps (*aporia*) or unexplained shifts or references in the Fourth Gospel; for example, in John 14:31 Jesus says, "Rise, let us be on our way," but in fact goes on discoursing until 18:1, at which point we find the proper sequel: "After Jesus had spoken these words, he went out with his disciples across the Kidron valley." Or again, one may point to the numbering of the first two signs in Cana without numbering any others, or the reference to the third day in John 2:1. All of this is more easily explained if a cautious editor who was not an eyewitness of these events was attempting to put together in some sort of coherent order a collection of written (and oral?) Johannine traditions after the time when the Beloved Disciple could be consulted, namely, shortly after the death of the

Beloved Disciple—an editor conservative enough to leave in some of these small things without attempting to smooth out all the rough or unexplained spots in the source material.

Some of the editorial remarks are more easily explained if they were inserted after the Beloved Disciple's death, when the materials were being put into the biographical format to be used as an evangelistic tool with a predominantly Gentile audience (see John 4:9b; 5:2; 6:4). Indeed, the use of the phrase "of the Jews" may even point to the final editor's hand. Would the Beloved Disciple in his teaching really have felt it necessary to say to a Christian audience, at least some of whom were probably Jewish converts, "Now the Passover, *the festival of the Jews,* was near" (6:4, emphasis added)?

Furthermore, the arrangement of seven signs, seven "I am" sayings, seven discourses, a crescendo of the miraculous signs climaxing not merely in the raising of Lazarus, but in the ultimate sign, the death and resurrection of Jesus, and a crescendo of confessions climaxing in John 20:28 before the original ending of the book reflects an editor with some rhetorical purposes to arrange his material in as persuasive a form as possible without drastically altering the individual units he is compiling and putting together, so that the testimony can still be said to be the Beloved Disciple's.

For these and other reasons which will be discussed in the commentary itself I am led to the conclusion that we should call the final editor the Fourth Evangelist, for he has made a significant contribution in compiling, selecting, arranging, inserting the odd parenthetical remark, and editing the whole into the form of an ancient biography, a life of Jesus, to be used in the mission work of the Johannine churches. He deserves to be called more than just a redactor or editor, but on the other hand, in view of the Johannine epistles, which were written by John the Beloved Disciple himself as an old man, and which share the same style, vocabulary, and ethos as the Gospel, the Fourth Evangelist was not the creator of the special Johannine vocabulary or thought world. It is a difficult and delicate matter to get the balance right between attributing too little or alternatively too much to the role the Fourth Evangelist played in the production of this Gospel.

The Johannine Voice and Style

Scholars have long wondered about the source of the distinctive style and idiom of the Fourth Gospel. Style is not to be confused with a mode of presenting a narrative (see above), but is rather the combination of grammar, syntax, and vocabulary and the use made of language that goes into making this Gospel distinctive in its form. I have argued elsewhere that the Fourth Gospel should be seen as an attempt to read and present the story of Jesus in a sapiential manner (i.e., a manner that reflects ways of speaking found in Jewish wisdom literature), and has arisen out of what may be called a school setting that centered on the teaching and thought of a particular sage—the Beloved Disciple.[52] I would include as members of this school the

Beloved Disciple, John the seer who wrote the Revelation, and the Fourth Evangelist. This Gospel has been written for Christian teachers or evangelists to use, teachers and evangelists who have been trained in a school setting where sapiential thinking and wisdom literature like that found in Proverbs, Job, and especially the Wisdom of Solomon and Sirach were important formative influences.

Wisdom literature was, from all available evidence, tremendously popular in early Judaism. This was in part because it gave advice about everyday life, helping God's people to learn how to live well and wisely. It was also popular because it provided answers to difficult questions about how one could believe in the God of the Bible when the world seemed such a dark and dangerous place and God's people often suffered. Where could wisdom be found in such a fallen world? This question was in fact a more universal question, and was raised outside as well as inside Jewish contexts. Because of the more universal character of this sort of discourse and the fact that it provided answers about where light could be found in a dark world, this form of discourse was ideally suited for a Jewish Christian to use when addressing a diverse audience of religious seekers in the Diaspora. The Fourth Evangelist wished to present Jesus as a universal savior who is God's Wisdom come in the flesh to reveal God's character and to gather a community of the faithful from both Jews and Greeks.

The discussion of the wisdom influences on the Fourth Gospel normally begins and all too often ends with the discussion of the Logos hymn in John 1. This is a mistake, especially since the Logos hymn strongly shapes the way the story of Jesus is told thereafter.[53] C. H. Dodd affirms the main point to be made here about John 1:

> The evangelist does not, like some Gnostics, set out to communicate an account of the origin of the universe, as a way to that knowledge of God which is eternal life, and then fit Christ into the scheme. He says, in effect, "let us assume that the cosmos exhibits a divine meaning which constitutes its reality. I will tell you what that meaning is: it was embedded in the life of Jesus, which I will now describe." . . . the Prologue is an account of the life of Jesus under the form of a description of the eternal Logos in its relations with the world and with man, and the rest of the gospel an account of the Logos under the form of the record of the life of Jesus; and the proposition *ho logos sarx egeneto* [the Word took on flesh] binds the two together.[54]

The prologue and the wisdom trajectory it evokes of one who came down and must go back up into heaven again shapes the whole Gospel considerably, as will now be shown by some telling examples.[55]

Once one recognizes that the Logos hymn sets the interpretative agenda for the Gospel, it is important for the author to show Jesus revealing directly or indirectly at various points that he is the preexistent Logos. A. Culpepper aptly sums up this postcreation but preincarnational work of the Logos as follows:

During the historical past, the history of Israel, he came into the world and enlightened those who had eyes to see him (1.9). Moses and the prophets wrote about him (1.45; 5.46), and Abraham saw his "day" (8.56). Isaiah, presumably in the heavenly vision (Isaiah 6) saw "his glory" (12.41). No one actually saw him, just as no one was able to see God (1.18; 6.46), but there is little doubt that for John the *logos* was the inspiration of the prophets and Jesus was the fulfillment to which they pointed.[56]

What is most intriguing about all this is that in Wisdom of Solomon 10—19 similar sorts of roles are predicated of Wisdom.[57] She was present in the wilderness and provided water from the rock (11:4); she sustained Israel with manna (16:26); she rescued various righteous men including Lot and Joseph (10:6ff.), and helped Abraham (10:5); she entered Moses, allowing him to perform wonders and signs (10:16) and gave him the gift of prophecy (11:1; cf. 7:27). The Johannine Jesus understands himself to be the Word or Wisdom who had aided God's people throughout all previous generations.[58]

The V pattern of the trajectory of Jesus' career, which is distinctive to this Gospel[59] and affects the plot of the Gospel itself in numerous ways is indebted to the plot of the course of Wisdom and her career with God, descending to God's people, and returning to heaven.[60] Knowing Jesus' origins and his destiny leads to both knowing who Jesus is and knowing God as Father. In other words, recognizing that Jesus is being portrayed as God's Wisdom, indeed Wisdom incarnate, in this Gospel is *the key* to understanding the presentation of the central character of the story. This is made very plain in the opening Logos hymn, which presents the story of the pre-existent Word/Wisdom of God who comes to earth, and is an adaptation of the various wisdom hymns found in Prov. 8; Sir. 24; and elsewhere. The rest of the story is meant to be read in light of this prologue, and those who do so have the key to understanding who Jesus is throughout the drama. (I do not say that Wisdom is the key to every aspect of this complex work, but I would insist that it is the key to understanding the central issue of this biography, which is Christ and his character.) From the outset, the Gospel is set up to encourage the reader to expect a sapiential presentation of Jesus, and in the plot of the Gospel, as well as in the "I am" sayings, in the sign narratives, in the discourses, in short, in all the material that sets this Gospel apart from the Synoptics, this sapiential portrayal is played out in detail. Jesus in his career is portrayed as Wisdom bringing God's word and redemption and then returning to heaven, having been rejected by many.

The language of what precedes and follows grows out of thinking sapientially about Jesus and his story, and then about the story of his converts who must be born from above even if they have not, like Jesus, come from above (see John 3). The initial plan of the plot was announced in John 1:11–14—he came to earth, took on flesh, was rejected by his own but accepted by a few followers. These latter he empowered to become children of God.[61] The story ends, appropriately enough, with the Risen One (incarnate and now glorified Word/Wisdom) speaking a wisdom saying, a beatitude:

"Blessed are those who have not seen, and yet come to believe." Hearing, believing, understanding are what disciples are to do. Seeing is not required for full faith. This is only what one would expect when the object of faith is the *Word* or *Wisdom*. In effect, the evangelist says to his audience, "Let the one who has ears to hear about and believe in Wisdom and Wisdom's pilgrimage do so."

Similarly sapiential is the language about before and after, such as we find on the lips of the Baptist in John 1:30. Scholars have been puzzled about the combination of Son of man language with the language of ascending and descending (cf. John 6:62), but once one sees the Wisdom trajectory of Jesus' career, or reads such wisdom texts as *1 Enoch* 70–72, where Enoch ascends and is identified with the Son of man, the language becomes understandable.[62] This is the paradigmatic sage, or, in some texts, Wisdom in person.

Note the elliptical reference to angels "ascending and descending" on the Son of man (John 1:51). Jesus *is* the juncture between earth and heaven, the one through whom the two realms are linked. In John 3:2, Nicodemus admits that Jesus is a teacher who comes from God, but of course the remark is ironic, for he has said more than he realizes. He is not merely a teacher, but that which must be taught—the Word that comes from God. The birth that comes through Jesus is a birth from above (*anothen*, vv. 3, 7); Jesus is the only one who has both descended from heaven and ascended into it as Son of man (v. 13).[63]

One also finds in 3:14 the first presentation of the theme that the Son must be lifted up (on the cross) in order that salvation may come. In John's theology the cross is the first step on Jesus' way back to heaven and therefore the moment at which he begins to be glorified, the moment at which his decisive hour has come. What this passage and the rest of John 3 shows, we see then as follows: (1) The Fourth Evangelist's theology of the Son of man is conditioned by the Wisdom trajectory, perhaps in light especially of *1 Enoch* 70:2; 71:1, where Enoch ascends and is identified with the Son of man, and *1 Enoch* 42, where Wisdom descends to earth and then returns to heaven rejected. This is important because it has been indicated in various places throughout the Similitudes of Enoch that their subject matter is in fact Wisdom (see 46:3; 48:1–2, 7; 49:1–3; 51:3).[64] (2) John's theology of the cross is affected by how he views the trajectory—dying on the cross is the first stage of being lifted up (see also John 8:28). (3) Even the larger theology of Jesus as God's beloved Son and God the Son (see the NRSV on John 1:18) who is begotten, not made, is affected, for it is as the Son that the Logos was sent into the world, as John 3:16–17 make clear.

It is not just that Jesus has come from God in heaven, for that could be said of angels as well, but that he has been sent on the mission of redemption, with both a special character and a special relationship with the Father—he is the only one who has actually *seen* the Father (6:46). As such this especially equips him to speak for the Father, and indeed to give the teaching which is from God (7:16–17).

If understanding in this Gospel amounts to knowing where Jesus came from and where he is going, then misunderstanding normally manifests itself in having a false conception of where Jesus has come from (and is going). For example: (1) In John 7:25 the people of Jerusalem say they know where Jesus is from, but they do not know his ultimate origins. (2) In John 8:41 it is implied that Jesus came from a woman who bore him out of wedlock, while his opponents are true and legitimate sons of Abraham. To this Jesus counters that he precedes Abraham, indeed, he simply exists ("Before Abraham was, I am," 8:58). (3) In John 8:48 it is asked if he is not from Samaria. (4) In John 18:5ff. the opponents stress they are looking for Jesus from Nazareth. The errors about who Jesus is come from not knowing his ultimate origins, which is to say, not knowing he is the Logos, the Son sent from God, the Son of man who descends and ascends.

In John 7:35 the puzzlement over who Jesus is comes from not knowing where he is going. The Pharisees show their lack of understanding by conjecturing that he intends to go to the Diaspora among the Greeks and teach the Greeks, when he says he is going somewhere they cannot follow. A variety of further examples could be cited, including the fact that Mary Magdalene in John 20 misunderstands the divine nature of Jesus (calling him only *Rabbouni*), precisely because she is trying to renew earthly relationships with Jesus and has not understood that Jesus must ascend so he can have a new form of relationship with all his disciples. Notice Jesus chooses to reveal who he truly is to the disciples through Mary by having her say that he is ascending to his and their Father, his and their God (20:16–17). It is only when she understands his pilgrimage that she is able to proclaim "I have seen the [risen] Lord."[65]

The above is only a very cursory sketch of the use of the language about coming from and going to heaven, but enough has been said to warrant the conclusion that the Fourth Evangelist makes understanding that Jesus is the one who has come from and returns to heaven a key, if not *the* key, to understanding his identity in this Gospel.[66] In short, proper christological understanding requires a knowledge of the trajectory traced by Wisdom, now seen in the person of Jesus, the incarnation of God's Word/Wisdom.

In the seven key "I am" sayings, Jesus is characterized variously as living bread, light of the world, the door, life, and the authentic vine (cf. 6:35, 51; 8:12; 10:7, 9; 10:11, 14; 11:25; 14:6; 15:1, 5). *All* of these things are said at one point or another to come from or characterize personified Wisdom. Thus, for instance, in Prov. 8:35 Wisdom says, "Whoever finds me finds life and obtains favor from the LORD." In Wisd. Sol. 7:26 she is said to be a reflection of eternal light. The characterization of Jesus as vine should be compared to the characterization of Wisdom in Sir. 24:17–19, 21, where it says, "Like the vine I bud forth delights, and my blossoms become glorious and abundant fruit. Come to me, you who desire me, and eat your fill of my fruits. . . . Those who eat of me will hunger for more, and those who drink of me will thirst for more." This passage from Sirach also seems to inform John 4:13–14: "Everyone who drinks of this water will be thirsty again, but those who drink of the water that I will give them will never be thirsty. The water that I will give them will become in them a spring of water gushing up to eternal life."[67] Perhaps also one may compare "I am the bread of life. Whoever comes to me will never be hungry, and whoever believes in me will never be thirsty" (John 6:35). The latter text is also close to Prov. 9:5, where Wisdom beckons "Come, eat of my bread and drink of the wine I have mixed. Lay aside immaturity, and live, and walk in the way of insight." Wisdom is said to be a tree of life in Prov. 3:18, and in the immediately preceding verse there is a discussion of her ways and paths. The disciple is meant to see following her as a way to life and peace. Whether or not the absolute *"ego eimi"* in John 8:58 owes anything to wisdom material, the "I am" sayings with predicates likely do.

Many have said that what sets the Fourth Gospel off from the Synoptics more than any other one thing is the discourses, and that it is here especially that the Johannine style becomes evident and dominant. I would suggest that this judgment is basically correct, and the reason for the distinctiveness is that Jesus' teaching takes the form of wisdom discourses not unlike the material we find in Prov. 8, or Sir. 24 or Wisd. Sol. 1—11. Not only do the "I am" sayings become comprehensible in light of this sort of sapiential material, but the discourses do as well, as we shall show in the commentary itself. The discourses expand and expound on the basic saying. The use of food and drink metaphors to refer to deeper spiritual sustenance is characteristic of both these sources. The point in the wisdom corpus is that all one truly longs for and needs can be found in Wisdom, and the Fourth Evangelist is trying to make the same point about Jesus.[68]

The "I am" discourses are also linked with the sign narratives, which are clustered in the first half of the Fourth Gospel. These sign narratives are in a variety of ways different from the tales of "mighty works" in the Synoptics, and scholars have offered many explanations for the difference. Perhaps the most convincing explanation of at least the Johannine approach was offered by G. Ziener some years ago in two much-neglected articles.[69] The author of the Wisdom of Solomon treats the serpents in the desert as a sign or symbol of something else. In fact, he sees all the wonders performed by God as the Israelites left Egypt and wandered in the wilderness as symbols of salvation (*symbolon soterias*) for God's people (Wisd. Sol. 16:6). Like John, he thinks of a miracle as a *semeion* (Wisd. Sol. 10:16). Ziener shows how in his conception of Jesus' signs the Fourth Evangelist is drawing on the presentation of God's miracles for Israel, not simply in Exodus but in the retelling of those stories found in the historical review section of Wisd. Sol. 11—18.[70] What the author of the Wisdom of Solomon says about God's Word could just as easily have been said by John of Jesus, with little alteration: "For the one who turned toward it was saved, not by the thing that was beheld, but by you, the Savior of all. . . . For neither herb nor poultice cured them, but it was your word, O Lord, that heals all people. For you have power over life and death; you lead mortals down to the gates of Hades and back again" (16:7, 12–13).

We can also see in several further examples that what the author of the Wisdom of Solomon attributes to Wisdom or God's personified Word (e.g., water from the rock in the desert, 11:1–4) is in John attributed to Jesus. For instance, in Wisd. Sol. 16:20–26 the author discusses how "without their toil you supplied them from heaven with bread ready to eat." This in itself appears on the surface to be just another discussion of the exodus wonders, until one arrives at the punch line in v. 26 and hears, "So that your children, whom you loved, O Lord, might learn that it is not the production of crops that feeds humankind but that your word sustains those who trust in you."[71] This is the same sort of point the Fourth Evangelist is driving at in the discourse in John 6—"Do not work for the food that perishes, but for the food that endures for eternal life, which the Son of Man will give you" (6:27). In both cases the wonder is seen to point to a larger verity outside itself which is much more important. In Wisd. Sol. 18 the author discusses the miracle of light even at night that God provided the Israelites as they left Egypt, but again his interest lies in the fact that "their enemies deserved to be deprived of light and imprisoned in darkness, those who had kept your children imprisoned, through whom the imperishable light of the law was to be given to the world." This should be compared to the symbolic treatment of Jesus as the light of the world in John 9, but which is presaged in the saying "Whoever follows me will never walk in darkness but will have the light of life" (8:12). The two-level discussion about physical and spiritual sight and insight and physical and spiritual blindness is meant to make much the same point as is made in Wisd. Sol. 18, especially as Jesus says not merely that his followers are being given light but that his opponents are being deprived of light (John 9:39—"I came into this world for judgment so that those who do not see may see, and those who do see may be deprived of light").

Another clue to the sapiential character of this Gospel's style is the high incidence of Father and Father-Son language used, which is not characteristic of the Old Testament naming of God in general but is characteristic of especially late sapiential literature.[72] In the Fourth Gospel God is called Father no fewer than 115 times, compared to only five in Mark and fifteen in Luke. In the Fourth Gospel it is affirmed that one can only truly come to know God as Father through Jesus, his unique Son. The resonances here especially with the presentation of Solomon and his relationship to the Father in Wisd. Sol. 1—11 are notable.

The two-level discussion of wonders in both John and the Wisdom of Solomon is made possible because both authors have a theology of eternal life and its negative counterpart. This theology, in the *way* it is expressed, reflects the use of sapiential language to cope with an idea that likely does not appear in the wisdom corpus before the Wisdom of Solomon, the idea of a positive afterlife.[73] Thus, for the author of the Wisdom of Solomon, as for the Fourth Evangelist, physical death is not the end of the story. In Wisd. Sol. 3:1–4 the author stresses "But the souls of the righteous are in the hand of God, and no torment will ever touch them. In the eyes of the foolish they seem to have died . . . but they are at peace. . . . Their hope is full of immortality." This statement about only appearing to have died is similar to the discussion in John 11 when Jesus insists that Lazarus is sleeping. This is because death in the hands of the God of Life is not necessarily the end. The author of the Wisdom of Solomon in fact is willing to say that God did not make death (1:13); it entered the world through the devil's envy (2:24) and only the devil's followers truly experience it.[74] It was God's intention that human beings were created for "incorruption," being made in the "image of his eternity" (2:23). By contrast with the wicked, "the righteous live forever" (5:15).[75]

The need for a birth from above, which is discussed in John 3, seems to owe something to the discussion in Wisd. Sol. 7:14ff., where Wisdom is said to be the one who, coming down from above, passes into human souls, renewing all things, and makes them friends of God and even prophets. A bit later, in John 3:14, the puzzling remark about Moses lifting up the serpent in the wilderness is made, and it is likened to the act of salvation provided on the cross by the Son. What is the connection? Dodd rightly points to Wisd. Sol. 16:6, where "readers of the LXX however would remember that the serpent was, in the words of the Book of Wisdom, *symbolon soterian* [a symbol of salvation] (Wisd. 16.6); it signified the means by which men [*sic*] passed from death to life."[76] The Gospel of John makes a great deal more sense when read in light of the sapiential literature, and in view of the numerous similarities it has with it, it is hard to doubt the evangelist intended it to be read that way.

The Fourth Gospel speaks of salvation in a way (usually as life or eternal life) and to a degree that is not characteristic of the Synoptics, but it is certainly reminiscent of the Wisdom of Solomon, where not only is immortality the reward for seeking and finding or receiving wisdom, but there it is also said, "Who has learned your counsel unless you have given wisdom and sent your holy spirit from on high? And thus the paths of those on earth were set right, and people were taught what pleases you, and were saved by wisdom" (Wisd. Sol. 9:17–18). It is striking too that John's theology of the penetration of believers by Christ, so that he will dwell in them (John 14:23) seems to echo the idea found in Wisd. Sol. 7:24, 27 that salvation amounts to Wisdom's penetrating and indwelling human beings.

Not only in what he says about death and eternal life, but also in the role he allots to the devil in such matters, the Fourth Evangelist seems very close to the author of the Wisdom of Solomon. For example, John 8:44, where the devil is said to be the father of the wicked and to be "a murderer from the beginning [who] does not stand in the truth," could just as easily have been said by the earlier sage. In the minds of both authors it was not the intention of God to condemn the world, even the fallen world, but rather to save it (compare Wisd. Sol. 2—3 to John 3:16–21).

As Moeller says, with Jesus in John as with Wisdom in the wisdom corpus, but especially in the Wisdom of Solomon, one's destiny, whether life or death, hangs on whether one accepts or rejects Jesus or Wisdom.[77] The coming of Wisdom causes a division among human beings—some seek and find (see Prov. 8:17; Sir. 6:27; Wisd. Sol. 6:12), others to their cost do not seek and regret it too late (Prov. 1:28). "The same language in John describes the effect of Jesus upon men [*sic*] (7.34; 8.21; 13.33)."[78]

Because the author of the Wisdom of Solomon equated Wisdom with God's Spirit and the Fourth Evangelist seems to be drawing on his work, or perhaps sharing common late wisdom material,[79] it is not surprising that our author sometimes uses this material to characterize not just Jesus but also the other Paraclete whom he will send (compare esp. John 14:16–17, 26–27 to Wisd. Sol. 1:6ff.; 6:17ff.; 7:7–14, 22–29; 9:17–18). The Fourth Evangelist's ideas about the Spirit as well as his Christology owe something to the sapiential corpus.

There are also points in Jesus' teaching where he seems to speak as Wisdom. For example, when he says to his disciples "If you love me you will keep my commandments" (John 14:15), one cannot help but hear an echo of Wisd. Sol. 6:18, where one hears, "And love of Wisdom is the keeping of her laws, and giving heed to her laws is assurance of immortality." To this one should add the fact that John in chaps. 13—17 seems to characterize Jesus as a sage or as Wisdom conveying his legacy of wisdom to his "learners" in private, which is in many ways reminiscent of what one finds in Ben Sira and what he conveys in his house of instruction to his charges (cf. Sir. 51:23ff.).

Again, when Jesus gives his private teaching to his disciples and closes it in John 14—17, it appears he is speaking as Wisdom, for the echoes of Sir. 4:11–13 are hard to miss. Compare the following:

Wisdom teaches [Heb.]/exalts [Gr.] her children and	(cf. John 14—16)
gives help to those who seek her.	(cf. John 14:16ff.)
Whoever loves her loves life, and	(cf.John 14:15)
those who seek her from early morning are	
filled with joy.	(cf. John 15:11)
Whoever holds her fast inherits glory,	(cf. John 17:22)
and the Lord blesses the place she enters. . . .	
the Lord loves those who love her.	(cf. John 17:26)

It is also telling that in John disciples are called Jesus' little children (John 13:33), just as they are said to be Wisdom's children in Sir. 4:11; 6:18, and earlier in Prov. 8:32–33.[80]

There is a great deal more that could be said when one begins to compare John's Gospel to the wisdom corpus, especially the late wisdom material, but the above must suffice for now. It has been pointed out that: (1) in the Logos hymn; (2) in the V-shaped plot of the Gospel; (3) in the "I am" sayings and discourses; (4) in the conception and character of the signs; (5) in the use of Father language and teacher-learner language; (6) in various aspects of Christology, soteriology, and pneumatology this Gospel reflects a notable similarity to late wisdom material, especially the Wisdom of Solomon. What the author of the Wisdom of Solomon says about Wisdom/

Word, John says about either Jesus or, in one place, the Paraclete he will send. This Advocate is so closely connected to Jesus that it is called "another" Paraclete, just as Wisdom, Word, and Spirit are very closely intertwined in the Wisdom of Solomon.

The Fourth Evangelist has been deeply affected by the wisdom corpus and draws on it in his presentation of Jesus. The elements listed above encompass most of the primary things that distinguish the Fourth Gospel from the Synoptics, and so it is perhaps not too much to say that a primary cause of the major differences between the Fourth Gospel and the Synoptics is the *way* he draws on wisdom material to shape the source material that he *does not* share with the Synoptics, and even some of the common material.[81]

The Date and Provenance of the Fourth Gospel

It has been pointed out with some regularity that one must evaluate the entire Johannine corpus together when considerations of date and provenance are at issue. Thus I must first state my view of the interrelationship of the Johannine documents, before discussing in some more detail the date and provenance of the Fourth Gospel itself.

There are very good reasons for arguing that the book of Revelation must surely be by someone other than the author (or source) of the Gospel or epistles. The author writes in very different style from the author of the Gospel and epistles. No one who has taken a basic course in Greek will deny that the Gospel and epistles are written in very simple and readable Greek. This is hardly the case in the Apocalypse. Furthermore, the author of the Revelation uses some words to mean quite the opposite of what the same words mean in the Gospel or epistles. Thus in the Revelation *ethne* and *ethnos* and Jerusalem are associated with the Gentile nations, but in the Gospel these terms are associated with the Jews. In addition, the Revelation is dominated by futurist eschatology, something that is at most only occasionally mentioned in the Gospel. Finally, the author of Revelation is identified as a seer, and should be seen as a prophet of Jewish Christian extraction in all probability. He *seems* to speak of the apostles in 18:20; 21:14 as people other than himself. I take it, then, as most unlikely that the same author wrote all five Johannine documents. Nevertheless, there is more than enough of an affinity between the Revelation and the rest of the Johannine corpus to strongly suggest that the author of the former had at some point been a member and perhaps even one of the founders of the Johannine community (yet another John! cf. Rev. 1:1),[82] for he addresses the churches in Ephesus and elsewhere as an authority over them. I would suggest that this Apocalypse was written after the Beloved Disciple had died and when the Johannine communities lacked, and desperately needed, some guidance during the reign of Domitian. The author was deeply influenced by, having been a member of, the Johannine school of sapiential and eschatological interpretation of the Jesus tradition.

When we turn to the question of possible common authorship of the Gospel and the epistles, we are on different ground altogether. There are few if any scholars who would deem it impossible that these four documents come from the same pen. Only by examining the evidence can the issue be decided. There is, first of all, no real case that will stand close scrutiny for arguing that 2 and 3 John were written by two different authors. They both identify themselves as having been written by *Ho Presbyteros*, they both have the same style, length, nature, form—in short, they are surely by the same person.

What, then, of 1 John and its relationship to 2 and 3 John? Here there is considerable debate, and various scholars such as Barrett have argued that 1 John and 2 and 3 John are by different authors.[83] Against this is the very strong evidence that all three letters share the same style, vocabulary, and concepts. Second John 4ff. especially has numerous parallels with 1 John. Furthermore, all three letters share the same sort of polemic against heretical *gnosis* (knowledge). The differences are small in comparison to these notable similarities, and I suspect many of the differences can be explained by the view that 1 John was originally a homily, not a letter, while 2 and 3 John were always letters.[84] This is an important conclusion, especially because the material in 1 John 1 is most naturally taken as the testimony of an eyewitness of the ministry of Jesus.

The relationship between, especially, 1 John and the Fourth Gospel in vocabulary, style, and content is quite close. Even authors who maintain the three epistles weren't all written by the same person allow that 1 John and the Gospel seem to have a common source. Yet there are differences, notably a time difference, for in the first epistle we hear of abiding in the now solidified old teaching. Also the opponents now are not the Jews, or the world, but the false teachers, labeled antichrists. This could be explained as due to a change in situation at the time of writing 1 John from that at the time when the Fourth Gospel traditions were written down, rather than a change of author; but equally plausible is the suggestion that the epistles are addressed to the internal situation within the Johannine Christian community, whereas the Gospel is directed outwardly toward the world—hence the discussion about the synagogue, the Greeks, and others.

I tentatively conclude that the Johannine epistles were written by the Beloved Disciple toward the close of his life. Many if not most of the Gospel traditions, including John 1, may have already been written down and were in any case familiar to the communities John was writing to, but they were not yet collected and put into Gospel form, something that was likely accomplished after the Beloved Disciple died. Perhaps even a bit later than this the Revelation was written and sent to the Johannine communities in western Asia, perhaps toward the end of the reign of Domitian in A.D. 96. I am thus suggesting the epistles were likely written in the late 80s or early 90s, and the Gospel written in the early to mid-90s.

We are able to establish a rather firm upper limit for the writing of the Gospel because papyrus 52 (P52), dating from about A.D. 130 and coming from Egypt, contains a portion of John 18. One must allow time for the

Gospel to have been written, to have traveled to Egypt, and to have been copied before A.D. 130. In regard to the lower limits of when this Gospel may have been written, several points are in order. If indeed Papias, who was bishop of Hierapolis in Phrygia in the first half of the second century A.D. had contact with the Johannine community and even with the Beloved Disciple, this must mean that the Beloved Disciple/John the elder lived well into the first century A.D., probably into its last decade. Eusebius quotes Irenaeus as saying that this John lived until the time of Trajan (*H.E.* 3.23.3–4), and while that may be pushing things a bit, it seems likely he made it into the last decade of the first century A.D.

The question of the *birkat ha minim,* or ban on heretics, and the expulsion of Christians from the synagogue must be broached at this point. Most scholars think this ban did have to do with Christians, among others, and that it dates from the 80s A.D.[85] Nevertheless, the practice in the Diaspora and practice in Israel at Jamnia may have and probably did differ. As Hengel points out, there is considerable evidence from the Pauline corpus and Acts that expulsions from synagogues were happening much earlier than this in any case,[86] and it is difficult to know what the practice was in synagogues in Asia in the 80s and 90s, and whether there was ever a general ban enforced throughout the empire by Jews in the first century. It is possible that Justin Martyr (*Dial.* 16.4; 47.4; 93.4; etc.) alludes to the practice in the early second century,[87] but even this may be debated. What happened to Johannine Christians could have predated or postdated the ban. It is thus precarious to use the ban as a means of dating the Gospel's publication, and even more precarious to use it as a means of discerning how, why, and when the Johannine community developed as it did. I am only willing to say that some Johannine texts *may* reflect a time when the ban was already enforced in Asia.

We have been regularly mentioning Asia and Ephesus in our discussion, and now we must sum up the reasons why it seems likely that this is the locale of the Johannine community: (1) First, there is the evidence that the Revelation was addressed to Christians in the western part of Asia, including Ephesus, and the author of the document was surely influenced by Johannine thought and forms of expression; (2) there is considerable testimony to the Beloved Disciple's being in Ephesus in Asia until the end of his life, in Irenaeus, Eusebius, and elsewhere (cf. Eusebius, *H.E.* 3.23.3ff., and Irenaeus, *Adv. haer.* 2.22.5; 3.34); (3) the ethos of the Fourth Gospel suggests a place that is predominantly Gentile in character, but which nonetheless has a strong Jewish presence. No locale as well suits the internal hints of this Gospel as Ephesus.

The Purpose(s) of the Fourth Gospel

Quite naturally, the discussion of purpose in regard to the Fourth Gospel always begins with, and frequently gets no farther than, the discussion of John 20:31. Before we discuss the probably insoluble dilemma in regard to the original verb form and its meaning, it is crucial to note that, regardless of how we read the key verb, the "evangelist's expressed purpose in writing the gospel provides a clear biographical intent with the whole focus upon the person of Jesus: it is an account of 'signs' which *he* did, that people may believe who *he* is, and have life in *him*."[88] Overconcentration on the verb has led to too little focus on the fact that the evangelist is trying to inculcate or encourage a certain kind or content of belief in and about Jesus. This sort of didactic or evangelistic aim was quite common in ancient biographies, especially those originating in philosophical schools, and those which had certain rhetorical aims involving the art of persuasion.[89] A good deal of the content of this Gospel is framed so as to be suitable for use in debate with opponents or possible converts.

Let us consider now the vexed question about the verb "believe" in John 20:31 and the two purpose clauses. G. D. Fee has pointed out that the textual evidence for the reading *pisteuete* (present subjunctive) is in fact superior to the evidence for *pisteusete* (aorist subjunctive), and that since the aorist would have been the more common Greek idiom, scribes would be more likely to change a present subjunctive to an aorist, rather than the reverse.[90] As Fee admits, however, an aorist could be used to simply refer to the act of believing, without making a point of when, and, on the other hand, the present subjunctive does not in itself demonstrate that the Gospel was intended for the believing community.[91] The string of present subjunctives in John 13—17 is probably best explained as meaning that the disciples should keep on doing, knowing, believing as they had already begun to do. The real question, however, is whether the Fourth Evangelist is consistent in observing the proper state or kind (and so time) of action of a given verb, and here I think the answer must be no.

Consider John 6:29–30. Here we have Jesus saying, "This is the work of God, that you believe [*pisteuete*—present subjunctive] in him whom he has sent." The inquisitors who have prompted this response are not the disciples but the crowd (vv. 22, 25), who are not regarded by the evangelist as already *properly* believing in who Jesus really is at this point; hence his attempt to escape from them (see 6:14–15). The proof that they are not yet proper believers is shown by the sequel in 6:30, where they respond to Jesus' pronouncement with the question "What sign are you going to give us then, so that we may see it and believe you?" The fact that this question comes *after* Jesus has already performed the miracle of loaves and fish must not be overlooked, because it shows the spiritual obtuseness of the audience. To be sure, Jesus wishes for them to engage in a life of faith, but this discussion is about the beginning of faith, the initial act, and the crowd is asking for *more* signs, more reason to begin believing in Jesus.[92] The present subjunctive here should not be read as a present continual tense.

Even less convincing is Fee's treatment of John 17:21, where again we have a present subjunctive form of *pisteuo*, and the world is the one that is to do the believing. Jesus has just said that he and his disciples do not belong to the world, which is seen in this Gospel as a place of darkness, and when the word refers to humankind it is viewed as lacking spiritual comprehension, being unsaved (see John 1:10–11). It is the world that God loved and sent Jesus to save (John 3:16). It is not convincing to argue that *kosmos* here is seen as unredeemable, whereas in John 3:16 it is the object of missionary outreach. John 17:20 refers to those who "are believing" (timeless present-tense participle, though it could be translated "will believe"; see NRSV), through the missionary work of the disciples, and the goal here is that "the world may believe that you have sent me." Again in this text the present subjunctive likely is used to refer to the act of coming to saving faith, something neither the crowds nor the world had yet done when this Gospel was written.

From the evangelist's point of view the only fully adequate or saving faith is the faith that matches up with the statement in John 20:31,[93] the faith that matches up with the proclamation of the prologue and the confession of the climactic scene in John 20:28. Any confession short of that may well be good and accurate (cf., e.g., John 4:29), but it is not fully adequate, and this is surely how we are meant to see almost all the confessions from John 1:35 through John 19, leading up to the ones in John 20. What we have leading up to Easter is a series of people on the way to becoming full-fledged Christians, whether we think of Jesus' mother, the Samaritan woman, Nicodemus, Peter, or others. The process of coming to adequate faith is described, and is seen by the end of the Gospel to involve more than just a belief in Jesus' signs. It must also entail a belief in Jesus as divine Son of God, having come from and returned to God, and having been glorified in his death, resurrection, and exaltation. This Gospel wishes to make abundantly clear the extent of what one must believe about the person and works of Christ.

It has been frequently argued that the Fourth Evangelist has taken various of his source narratives and cast them into quest stories.[94] While agreeing that we have a goodly number of quest and re-quest stories in this Gospel, I am not at all certain that the Fourth Evangelist has significantly redirected these stories. I suspect the Beloved Disciple himself used these stories in his evangelistic preaching as examples of all the different sorts of people who could come to fully adequate faith in Jesus "the Savior of the world" (John 4:42)—Greeks, Samaritans, a variety of different kinds of Jews, Jesus' family members, and of course Jesus' own disciples. Whether in the source material or the result of redaction, the quest form of so many of these stories tells us something significant about the purpose of this Gospel. Burridge puts it aptly:

> The writer must provide information about Jesus in order for the reader to come to believe, and he chooses to do this by narrating the Signs. In fact through the *chronological narrative,* all the necessary information about Jesus' cosmic origins, earthly ministry, Passion and Resurrection is provided for the reader to realize the true identity of Jesus, while through the *discourse material* the reader comes to appreciate the teaching of Jesus and the Christian faith.[95]

It is no accident that so much stress is placed in this Gospel on witnesses, witnessing, and adequate testimony. Such is the lifeblood of missionary work.

What then is to be made of John 13—17? I suspect that here we are dealing with material that the Beloved Disciple originally used to encourage and nurture the Johannine community, showing them what fully adequate faith looks like, and what the responsibilities are of those who truly believe—among other things, sharing their faith. It appears likely that the Fourth Evangelist has somewhat rearranged and recast this material, so that it better suited the evangelistic purposes of the document as a whole. For example, I would suggest that the evangelist has placed the high-priestly prayer where it now is so that he could end these "in house" discussions on the missionary note that we have already discussed is to be found in 17:20–21. As Carson says, even in a largely evangelistic document like this one it is necessary to speak not only about how to become, but also how to remain or be, a Christian, and this latter is especially addressed in John 13—17, but the missionary note is not entirely absent even in these chapters.[96] One of the essential stresses of the prayer in John 17 is to make clear to the disciples their mission and obligation to carry on Jesus' work and witness in the world. Thus, we conclude: This Gospel is written as a tool to be used by Christians who already know a good deal of the gospel tradition (cf. 11:2) in their evangelistic and missionary work. They are to share the testimony of the Beloved Disciple with the world.[97] The Johannine Christians do not need to be told or convinced that "He who saw this has testified so that you also may believe. His testimony is true . . ." (John 19:35), but their audience, with whom they would share these stories, did need such assurances.

The Audience of the Fourth Gospel

A detailed study of the parenthetical remarks, asides, or explanations in the Fourth Gospel leads to some very interesting conclusions.[98] We have already stressed that the primary audience to whom the material in the Fourth Gospel is directed by the evangelist is *not* the Johannine community, but rather nonbelievers, but with a careful scrutiny of certain remarks in the Gospel I think we can be more specific and develop a running profile of the audience.

There are seven cases of translation or explanation of Hebrew or Aramaic terms, some of which, like "rabbi" or "messiah," must surely have been familiar to even diaspora Jews (cf. 1:38, 41d, 42e; 9:7; 19:13d, 17; 20:16). If these sorts of explanations were in the source the Fourth Evangelist drew on and he did not think the audience would need such explanations, it is hard to explain why he would have left them in the text. I think we must assume they tell us something about the audience the Fourth Evangelist was addressing.

The second sort of remarks of interest are explanations of national and religious customs, of which there are a variety of examples. For instance, in John 2:6 the jars are explained to be for the purpose of holding Jewish purification water. John 4:9 refers to the lack of table fellowship, or sharing of

food and water, between Jews and Samaritans. John 5:16, 18 explains that
Jesus' death was being sought because he was breaking Sabbath regulations,
and even making himself equal with the Father (see 9:14, 16). In 19:31 the
Day of Preparation (see v. 42) and the great solemnity of the Passover Sabbath is referred to, to explain why the Jews did not wish Jesus' body to be
left on the cross during that time. In 19:39–40 the burial customs of Jews are
described. These remarks are surely best explained as directed at a largely
Gentile audience, and one not generally familiar with early Jewish practices
or religious terms.

There are up to fifty possible examples of indications of localities, times,
or events. For example, at John 1:28 we are told that Bethany is across the
Jordan. At 2:1 we are told that Cana is in Galilee. At 3:23 we are reminded
that John was baptizing at Aenon near Salim because water was abundant
there. At 4:3–4 it is explained that in order to go the most direct route from
Judea to Galilee one must go through Samaria, and this in turn is followed
by an explanation that Jacob's well is near Sychar. At 5:2–3 it is explained
that in Jerusalem by the Sheep Gate there is a pool called in "Hebrew"
Bethzatha, which has five porticoes. At 6:1 it is explained that the Sea of
Tiberias (see 21:1) is also called the Sea of Galilee. At John 11:18 it is said
that Bethany is to be found outside of Jerusalem about two miles. These
sorts of examples could be multiplied, but they are sufficient to show that:
(1) the audience of the Gospel is surely not in Palestine; (2) the evangelist
does not think they know the geography or locations in the Holy Land, including Galilee, Judea, and Samaria, very well if at all; (3) the repeated reference to the name Sea of Tiberias (cf. John 6:1; 21:1), which is also called
the Sea of Galilee, surely presupposes an audience that, if it knows anything
about the geography of the Holy Land, will know the Roman designations,
not the Jewish ones.

There are a few comments such as John 11:2, or John 3:24, or John 4:46
which I would call reminders from the evangelist to the Christian users of
this Gospel about key persons or events, reminders presupposing they had
heard of certain of these events or persons before. There are also some comments that are most naturally taken as the the Beloved Disciple's remembering something incidental about the things that happened during Jesus'
ministry or the places where they transpired (cf., e.g., 6:10—in that place
there was a great deal of grass; or more importantly 9:14—it was a Sabbath
day when Jesus made the mud to put on the blind man's eyes), or even
something important that the audience would not know (e.g., 7:5—even
Jesus' brothers didn't believe in him). These kinds of remarks show us that
this Gospel is meant to be used by Christians, but do not indicate how it is
to be used.

There is a good deal of material about disciples' not understanding during Jesus' ministry but remembering and understanding later (cf. 10:16—
failure to understand metaphorical language; 2:12—remembered what
Jesus said and understood after the resurrection; 20:9—did not yet understand the scripture that he must rise). This surely amounts to an apologetic

for the disciples' lack of understanding before Easter, and is part of the larger agenda of this Gospel, to show how even the disciples were in the process of coming to fully formed faith during the ministry—a process not brought to satisfactory fruition prior to the resurrection appearances and the sending of the Paraclete that aided them to remember, understand, and properly interpret the past. This sort of apologetic could be useful in explaining things either to believers or nonbelievers, with questions that a telling of the basic gospel story would raise.

There are some asides about scripture fulfillment that could be said to suggest that there were at least some of Jewish extraction in the audience. John 12:14–15 comes to mind, or especially 12:37–41. Another good example would be 19:24, about not tearing Jesus' robe, or 19:28, explaining why Jesus said, "I am thirsty" (cf. 19:36–37). Now it will be seen that all these examples come from the Passion narrative, which shows that it was felt there was more that needed the defense or support of scripture in this section of the Gospel.[99] This would more naturally be taken as an attempt to convince Jews, or possibly Gentile synagogue adherents, of the Christian interpretation of crucial last days of Jesus' life. The same may be said about the evangelist's explanation of the "prophecy" of the high priest in 11:50–51. If the Passion narrative was put together in substantially its present form at an early date by the Beloved Disciple, this could explain these references' origins, but that the Fourth Evangelist leaves them in suggests he thinks Jews or synagogue adherents are still potentially part of the audience for this Gospel.

There are even places where it appears that parenthetical remarks are added to clarify, if not correct, false impressions of some of the characters in the text. This is apparently done where the evangelist seems to assume that the remark, if left unqualified, might mislead an audience that was not familiar with the basic gospel story. A good example of this would be John 4:1–2, where the Pharisees remark that Jesus is baptizing and making more disciples than John, but the evangelist corrects this immediately, saying that it was not Jesus but his disciples who were doing the baptizing. This is not so much a correcting of the source as a clarifying of it to prevent false impressions.

What all these sorts of comments show is that the Fourth Evangelist is more intrusive with his text than any of the Synoptic writers, which suggests he believes he is dealing with an audience that needs a lot of explanation of the text.[100] G. Van Belle believes most, if not almost all, of these intrusions into the text may be traced back to the Beloved Disciple himself, in part because their style is the same as the rest of the text, and he may well be right. If this is the case, then it seems that already before the Gospel was composed the Beloved Disciple was preaching and teaching to a mainly Gentile audience, though apparently one that also included some Jews or at least some Gentile synagogue adherents for whom a scripture apologetic might be effective. If the Fourth Evangelist found most if not all of these comments in his source, the fact that he has *retained* them is important. It means that he perceives the audience for this biography of Jesus still to be mainly Gentile, though presumably including some Jews or synagogue adherents. I see no clear evidence to suggest a total shift in audience from the time when the Beloved Disciple promulgated these traditions to the time when the Fourth Evangelist redacted them into the form of this Gospel. There are some hints, however, that the Fourth Evangelist may be responsible for some of these asides, directing the Gospel more toward Gentiles and seeking to prevent misunderstandings of the original telling of the story.

Finally, another important thing that can be deduced from a study of these intrusions into the text is that the evangelist has a firm grasp on historical distinctions, particularly on the difference between disciples' faith or knowledge before and after Easter. His historical consciousness is also reflected in the stress on gospel events fulfilling earlier prophecies, showing that all that transpired in the story happened according to God's plan.[101] This is only what one would expect from a person who was serious about writing a biography for missionary purposes. The biography is, of course, tendentious and intended to persuade, but it has as one of its main concerns conveying a certain amount of historical information about, as well as theological interpretation of, Jesus.

History and the Fourth Gospel

The problem of the relationship of the Fourth Gospel to history is an acute one, precisely because John is so different from the Synoptics. The problem becomes somewhat less complicated if, as we have argued, the Fourth Evangelist did not use the Synoptic Gospels.[102] As even so conservative a commentator as L. Morris has remarked, it helps us to recognize that like the Synoptists:

> John is not attempting to set forth an objective unbiased account of certain historical events. He is a convinced believer and he wants his readers to see the saving significance of what he narrates. He is not recording facts for facts' sake. We completely miss his purpose if we assess his work on narrowly historical lines. There is no question then as to whether John is giving us interpretation. . . . The question is whether his interpretation is a good one and soundly based, or whether he allows his presuppositions to dominate the facts in the interests of buttressing up a dogmatic position.[103]

But the fact remains that though the Fourth Evangelist shares a Christian perspective and motivation with the Synoptists, his Gospel has turned out very differently from the Synoptics.

The explanation for these differences is not to be found in the suggestion that John is a "theological" or "spiritual" Gospel while the Synoptics are historical, since redaction critics have demonstrated how thoroughly theological are the Synoptics, and Dodd and others have shown that a considerable amount of historical material can be derived from the Fourth Gospel.[104] This is why, despite disclaimers about John's interest in precise chronology or "scientific" history, Barrett still affirms: "Yet at every point history underlies what John wrote."[105]

But does the Fourth Gospel have only a substratum of history, overlaid by a thick, and one might add distorting, veneer of interpretation? As we have already stressed, the Fourth Evangelist wrote as an ancient, tendentious biographer with historical interests but also missionary purposes. He wrote that his audience might believe something about Jesus, and he presented an interpretative character sketch by revealing some of Jesus' words and deeds. I suspect that the crisis manifest in the Johannine epistles had by no means disappeared by the time the Gospel materials were collected and put together, and therefore surely one, though not the only, purpose, as is shown not just by the prologue but by a host of other texts, was to refute various docetic and perhaps even some proto-Gnostic arguments about Jesus' nature and life. He seems also to make his case both on the level of facts *and* on the level of their interpretation. While he is primarily concerned to bring out the important meaning of this or that saying or event in Jesus' life (notice how the words of Jesus to Nicodemus blend right into the theological commentary of the evangelist in John 3), he does not neglect to narrate the factual foundation of that meaning, lest he himself be accused of Docetism or some sort of mysticism for which historical contingencies are of little or no importance.

If we allow that conveying some historical information is at least *part* of the Fourth Evangelist's purpose, the question of why John is so unlike the Synoptics becomes even more acute. My explanation for these differences is severalfold.

First, the primary missionary purpose of this Gospel distinguishes it from the Synoptics. In this Gospel we have a veritable parade of non-Christians, representing a variety of different sorts of people (the Baptist, Nicodemus, the Samaritan woman, various Jewish officials, the Greeks in John 12:20) who come to speak to or question Jesus, and the evangelist goes out of his way to demonstrate that Jesus has the answers for all these varied sorts of people. Being the universal Savior, he is "the way" for them all into eternal life. Then, too, the main point of including discussions about being born again, about the source of living water, about the nature of true worship, about Jesus' testimony being greater than John's, about Jesus as the bread of life, the true vine, the way, the truth, and the life seems to be to give Christians material to use to lead those in the position of the above mentioned inquisitors to Christ. The stress on Jesus' right to various titles, his oneness with the Father, and his power to perform stupendous miracles all comports with the basic evangelistic and missionary purposes of this document and so helps explain its differences from the Synoptics.[106]

Second, the evangelist has chosen to offer a *dramatic* mode of presentation of the life of Jesus, and has accordingly taken certain artistic liberties the Synoptics did not take. For example, he places the cleansing of the

Temple at the outset of the ministry, as it is part of his theological concern to show in clear and dramatic fashion at the beginning how Jesus replaces certain of the institutions of Judaism (e.g., purification water replaced by wine, Temple replaced by Jesus' body, Temple-centered religion replaced by a focus on Jesus and worship in spirit and truth).

Third, the Fourth Gospel writer drew on traditions not available to the Synoptic writers, in particular, discourse material, and all of this material is presented in a sapiential manner. While it has often been assumed and argued that there is likely little historical kernel and a great deal of theological expansion in these discourses, I would suggest that H. Schürmann's arguments for a pre-Easter "situation in life" for at least some of the Jesus logia material must be taken seriously.[107] Furthermore, H. Riesenfeld's suggestion commends itself, that the original situation in which some of this Johannine discourse material took shape was "in the discussions and 'meditations' of Jesus in the circle of his disciples such as certainly took place side by side with the instructions of the disciples proper, with its more rigid forms."[108] The Gospel itself presents us with a lengthy example of discourse material conveyed just to the disciples in an "in house" setting (John 13—17), and even goes so far as to suggest that while Jesus used figurative and metaphorical speech in such a context, he also "spoke plainly" and elucidated the meaning of such symbolic language as well (cf. John 16:25–29). This bears a striking similarity to the independent testimony of Mark that Jesus explained the mysteries of the kingdom and of his metaphorical wisdom speech to his disciples in-house (cf. Mark 4:34 and 4:10–13). By the criteria of multiple attestation we must take this suggestion of in-house explanation of Jesus' public teaching seriously. I would thus suggest that the discourse material in the Fourth Gospel has as its ultimate source this sort of setting, when Jesus explained himself to his disciples in private, and that the evangelist has portrayed this kind of discussion in John 13—17. In addition, he has taken some of these private explanations and appended them to the sign narratives and public logia of Jesus in John 2—12 in order to explain the signs by means of discourse material. This is not to deny that the Fourth Evangelist has himself added his own commentary here and there, as in John 3, but only to argue that his own commentary is appended to and developed out of material the Beloved Disciple passed on and had formulated in his own particular style, some of which probably ultimately goes back to Jesus himself.

The Social Setting of the Fourth Gospel

The social scientific study of the Fourth Gospel is only in its infancy, but there is already a good deal that can be said. In terms of methodology I would insist that direct evidence about the Johannine community must take precedence over indirect evidence, and this means starting with what we can know about the Johannine community from the epistles, especially since in my view they are the earliest Johannine documents, then turning to the Gospel itself, and finally looking for corroborating evidence from the book of Revelation. In the course of the commentary I will discuss among other things the social implications of the presentation of the Roman authorities, in particular Pilate. Here a few comments on some major studies are in order.

I am well aware of the weight that J. L Martyn and others have placed on how critical the expulsion of Johannine Christians from the synagogue was for the Johannine community and the formation of the Gospel material.[109] While I would not dismiss this as a possible formative influence on the Johannine community, including both the Beloved Disciple and the Fourth Evangelist, the fact remains that the epistles do not really reflect this sort of crisis. Indeed Moody Smith is willing to say, "Nor is it clear that the Gospel or Epistles in their present form are addressed entirely (or even primarily) to the Jewish-Christian controversy which underlies them. There are motifs in the Johannine literature that go beyond the controversy with Judaism and reflect a later stage in the development of the Johannine church."[110] While I would not dispute for a minute the likelihood that the Johannine community had controversies with the synagogue, I would suggest that from the very beginning of the Johannine community in Asia it was an essentially *separate* entity from the synagogue, but because it was made up of some Jewish Christians it was also one that at least in its early stages felt compelled to witness to and in the synagogue.

This is not any different from the general picture we get of Pauline Christianity from the Pauline corpus, or for that matter of Jerusalem Christianity in Acts, which from the outset had separate meetings with their own social organization, while they continued to also meet in the Temple precincts and probably went to synagogue as well (cf. Gal. 1:18–2:2; Acts 4:32–37). It seems likely to me that this ultimately goes back to the separate meetings that Jesus had with his disciples quite apart from what they did in the synagogue, meetings that were simply continued after Easter (cf. Acts 1:12–14).

It also seems probable that the history of controversy between mainstream Judaism and the Jewish followers of Jesus must be traced back to the controversies Jesus himself and his first disciples had with the synagogue, and especially with the Pharisees.[111] There are significant Synoptic traditions, some of which at least are likely to go back to Jesus, that warned that when the disciples went to a town to bear witness they might be rejected (cf. Mark 6:8–10 and par.).[112]

I suspect that skirmishing between followers of Jesus and other Jews, especially in the synagogue, continued until there was finally a full separation between the followers of Jesus and early Judaism centered on the synagogue. That this happened at different times in different places in the Diaspora is perhaps likely, but the point I wish to stress is that by the time the Johannine epistles were written in the 80s it appears that the full separation had already transpired, and by the time the Gospel was put into its final form in the 90s there was a clear and conscious distinction made between Jews and

Christians. The Fourth Gospel was not written to address a current social crisis between the synagogue and the Johannine community. Indeed, I would suggest that while the Johannine community may at one point have had basically friendly relationships with the Jewish community, which later went sour, it is likely that the Johannine community was never simply a part or subset of the synagogue. When the Beloved Disciple came to Asia Minor it is more than likely that he continued the practice of Christians' meeting in homes for their own distinctive forms of worship (see 3 John 9–10), though the Jewish members of the community likely also attended the synagogue and bore witness there.

If indeed we have enshrined in the Fourth Gospel essentially the individualistic testimony of the Beloved Disciple, an eyewitness of at least part of the life of Jesus, then it appears he wished to stress that Jesus foresaw expulsion from the synagogue coming for his followers.[113] Even if the Beloved Disciple was present only from the time of the climactic Judean events recorded in John 13 to the close of the Gospel, he could have heard personally Jesus' warning about this very matter (cf. John 16:2). The Fourth Gospel traces such expulsions back to the hostility that already existed during Jesus' ministry and to Jesus' own predictions.

Thus I would conclude that expulsion from the synagogue likely happened to Johannine Christians when they went to witness in such venues, much as was the case with Paul and his coworkers.[114] The Johannine community in Ephesus and its satellites in western Asia did not simply grow out of the synagogue, nor was that community born due to expulsion from the synagogue. By the time the Gospel is written we are dealing with a stage when polemical shots are being fired at each other from two already distinguishable and essentially distinct groups. The stress on witness, testimony, acceptance by some and rejection by other Jews in the Fourth Gospel must be evaluated in the light of this social context.

To this may be added that Rev. 2:1–7 comports remarkably well with and may illuminate further the internal struggles discussed in the Johannine epistles, while the material about Smyrna and Philadelphia in 2:8–11 and 3:7–13 may illuminate the hostility expressed toward the synagogue as an entity separate from the Johannine community in the Fourth Gospel, and 3:1–6 may be compared to the urgings to abide in Christ found in John 13—17.

Something should be said at this juncture about two recent studies by J. Neyrey and D. Rensberger on the Fourth Gospel, which have implications for evaluating the social outlook presented in this Gospel. Rensberger is right to point out that this Gospel, like the epistles, exudes the ethos of a minority group, and one that views the larger non-Christian world in apocalyptic terms as a spiritually dark and dangerous place. Jesus' coming into this sort of world and being rejected is no surprise, and his followers are forewarned to prepare for the same.[115] Yet it seems to me a significant mistake to simply read this Gospel as a manifestation of dualistic sectarianism bent on nurturing an "us versus them" mentality.[116] As even Rensberger admits, such an analysis does not do justice to the missionary thrust of a good deal of this Gospel.[117] That the disciples are prepared for rejection and persecution comes out of an ethos that calls for an aggressive witness to both Jews and Greeks but is preparing itself for the worst, since the world is indeed a dark place. This is a rather different matter than a community that, like the Qumran sect, has withdrawn from the center of the Jewish world (Jerusalem) and is basically satisfied to anathematize it from a distance as hopelessly corrupt. Rensberger is also right that this Gospel is urging a social program—many of the central institutions and authority figures of early Judaism are seen as not merely corrupt but obsolescent, having been fulfilled or replaced or both by a religion that centers on a person, not a place; on an unrepeatable event (Christ's death), not a ritual of sacrifice that must be repeated over and over; on grace, truth, and Spirit rather than on the law that came through Moses. This in turn has created a new sort of people of God made up of both Jew and Gentile—born "not of blood, or of the will of the flesh, or of the will of man, but of God." The creation of this sort of inclusive community requires a universe of discourse that speaks in terms of life, light, water and bread, spirit and truth, which are universal symbols.

The Fourth Evangelist, however, does not focus on sinful civilization in general as the matrix out of which people must be rescued, but focuses on what are in his view inadequate and in some cases corrupt religious communities. The world for this writer is civilization insofar as it is organized against Jesus, and that civilization is not the whole world, but specific kinds of religious and spiritual opposition. The Fourth Gospel does not offer us a polemic against the Roman Empire writ large, but focuses rather on the Jewish leadership as providing the decisive actions and impetus that led to Jesus' death. As such, this Gospel is not readily serviceable in the cause of some forms of liberation theology that focus on the (inherently?) corrupt social and power structures of society as a whole.

The study of J. Neyrey is in some ways more helpful.[118] He is quite right that this Gospel comes out of a group that is in significant tension with its neighbors, whose mood is "more one of revolt against discredited systems than sectarian defense from enemies. The strategy is not that of drawing the wagons into a circle so much as that of relentless criticism and attack, which is expressed in the extensive forensic processes in which the high Christology is expounded."[119] His basic conclusion is that the community that creates this sort of document manifests a lack of cohesiveness and a low degree of stratification. There is also something to the suggestion that one impetus for the stress on the power and deity of Jesus is that the Christian community is at least partly alienated from the power structures of the world and needing reassurance that "greater is he who is in us, than he who is in the world."

The problem with the analysis that Neyrey presents is that it tends to assume that spirit is necessarily set over against flesh in this Gospel, in almost Gnostic fashion, which in turn leads to an otherworldly, docetic Jesus and a community that rejects matter for spirit, and in fact rejects the very concept of society. It is not an accident that Neyrey does not deal in any depth with the prologue, which conditions how this whole Gospel ought to be read, nor does he really come to grips with the strong authority figures that are endorsed in this book (the Beloved Disciple, Peter) or the stress on mission in this Gospel. He fails to see that the revolt in this Gospel is not against any and all worlds, but a particular religious world and ethos, and is certainly not against any and all forms of society, but society as it is opposed to and organized against Jesus and his message. Neyrey argues that in this Gospel "all value was found in individualism rather than flesh, and in heaven, not earth. That the flesh is of no avail means that all things earthly are denied value, whether the flesh of the earthly Jesus, his signs, his death on the cross, or the apostolic tradition of eyewitness leadership and sacramental rituals."[120] This conclusion significantly skews the Johannine data.

In terms of Christology this Gospel stresses the importance of the divine Son of God coming in the flesh and dying as a human being on the cross. It affirms that God loves the world and that human beings as creatures are redeemable. Furthermore, it affirms, especially in John 13—17 that human and earthly community is not only possible but necessary "in Christ." The scope of rejection is limited, just as the scope of redemption is, and since the redeemed must come from human society, mission is necessary. A more balanced analysis of the tension between world and community of faith, between flesh and spirit, between strong community boundaries and openness to persons newly born of God is required. There are indeed social implications to be derived from the cosmology, Christology, and ecclesiology of this Gospel, but Neyrey is wrong in what he affirms, while being only partly right in what he denies (i.e., that this Gospel manifests a defensive strong sectarian position).

The Structure of the Fourth Gospel

As we conclude our initial discussions of the background and foreground of the Fourth Gospel, it is in order to say something about the structure of the Fourth Gospel. We have already pointed out that its macrostructure indicates it was intended to be read as a sort of ancient biography, with discussion of origins at the outset, death and impact at the end, and both chronological and topical material variously arranged in between.

If we consider the matter in some more detail, it seems clear enough that there are several major subsections to the material that stands between the prologue in John 1 and the epilogue in John 21. There are narratives, discourse, and dialogues between 1:19 and 12:50, meant to reveal something about Jesus' ministry. It is difficult not to see 12:37–50 as a theological summary and conclusion of the public ministry. On the other hand, since in 12:1ff. we actually begin to have the presentation of the events leading up to the passion of Christ, including the proleptic anointing of Jesus (for burial), it is perhaps best to see chapter 12 as a bridge passage linking the ministry and the Passion narrative and presenting some of both. What this means is that we have a longer Passion narrative in this Gospel than in any other Gospel, and that the so-called "farewell discourses" in John 13—17 are meant to be seen as part of the Passion narrative, or at least with chaps. 12—17 we have the events and discourses that prepare for the Passion events. In this view, 18:1–20:31 narrate the actual Passion events foreshadowed and prepared for in John 12—17.

Of the various suggestions about the structure of this Gospel, some are more revealing than others. For example, R. E. Brown's suggestion that chaps. 5—10 focus on the principal feasts of the Jews has its weaknesses, as very little is said about the Feast of Dedication in 10:22–39, as even Brown admits.[121] Much more revealing is Morris's breakdown of the signs and public discourses in 2:1–12:50:

a. First sign (2:1–11)—water into wine
b. First discourse (3:1–36)—the new birth
c. Second discourse (4:1–42)—the water of life
d. Second sign (4:46–54)—healing of the nobleman's son
e. Third sign (5:1–18)—healing of the lame man
f. Third discourse (5:19–47)—the divine son
g. Fourth sign (6:1–15)—feeding the multitude
h. Fifth sign (6:16–21)—walking on water
i. Fourth discourse (6:22–66)—bread of life
j. Fifth discourse (7:1–52)—life-giving Spirit
k. Sixth discourse (8:12–59)—light of the world
l. Sixth sign (9:1–42)—healing of the man born blind
m. Seventh discourse (10:1–42)—the Good Shepherd
n. Seventh sign (11:1–57)—raising of Lazarus[122]

While we may quibble with the naming of some of these sections and perhaps may question why the cleansing of the Temple is not a sign,[123] nevertheless this shows us a deliberate schematizing of this first major section of the Gospel, which has the "perfect" number of signs and discourses. The evangelist admits there are many more he could have added (20:30) and that he does not add more indicates that this sevenfold structure is intentional, showing that Jesus' actions and teachings amount to the perfect revelation of God's character and plan. Notice, however, that the section is not so schematized that signs and discourses always follow each other in the same order, and sometimes it is difficult to see the connection, if any, between some of the signs and some of the discourses. What this structure also shows is that the signs have been arranged to present a crescendo of the miraculous, climaxing with giving sight to the blind (a miracle not predicated of anyone in the Old Testament but God) and the raising of Lazarus, which foreshadows what will happen to Jesus. This arrangement did not happen by accident and may lead to some clues about how the Lazarus story plays such a crucial role in this Gospel, helping to precipitate and foreshadow the Passion events, while it plays no role at all in the Synoptics. The placement of the Lazarus story is likely theological rather than chronological.

The most recent detailed monograph on the structure of the Gospel has been penned by G. Mlakuzhyil and has a very helpful analysis of all the major proposals about this Gospel's structure.[124] Whether or not one accepts his arguments about various chiastic structures and bridge passages,[125] or his argument for dividing the Gospel into only two major parts, namely, 2:1–12:50 (the book of signs); and 13:1–20:29 (the book of Jesus' hour),[126] he is surely right that the evangelist has constructed a theological drama which "manifests the salvific mission and human-divine person of Jesus and the human response of faith or unbelief provoked by his revelation . . . for a specific purpose, namely so that the readers may believe that Jesus is the Messiah and the divine Son of God, and that through their personal existential faith in him they may have eternal, divine life."[127]

It becomes clear that for the Fourth Evangelist, like other ancient biographers, what is most crucial is an accurate presentation of Jesus' character and accomplishments through a presentation of his words and deeds, and that chronological considerations and in particular chronological precision take a back seat to these larger concerns. The Fourth Evangelist is deeply concerned with Jesus' hour, the significant and crucial time when salvation is made possible through the death and resurrection of Jesus, and less interested in some of the details about his hours. This is the sign of a writer who not only interprets time in the light of eternity, but knows that good historical biographies must focus on the historically (and in this case theologically) significant, not merely the historically interesting. The following is a brief structural analysis.

A Biography of Jesus:
The Testimony of the Beloved Disciple
as Told by the Fourth Evangelist

Part One. Prologue: John 1—The word takes on flesh

Part Two. Signs, seekers, and salvation—John 1:19–12:50

Part Three. Preparations, promises, provisions—John 13:1–17:26

Part Four. From gall to glory—John 18:1–20:31

Part Five. Epilogue: Reunion, reassurances, recommissioning—John 21

A slightly different breakdown of this outline can be found on the Contents pages.

Part I. Beginnings:
Including the Prologue (John 1:1–2:12)

1. The Prologue to the Fourth Gospel: Wisdom's Way into the World (John 1:1–14)

1:1   In the beginning was the Word, and the Word was with God, and the Word was God. [2]He was in the beginning with God. [3]All things came into being through him, and without him not one thing came into being. What has come into being[4] in him was life, and the life was the light of all people. [5]The light shines in the darkness, and the darkness did not overcome it.

6   There was a man sent from God, whose name was John. [7]He came as a witness to testify to the light, so that all might believe through him. [8]He himself was not the light, but he came to testify to the light. [9]The true light, which enlightens everyone, was coming into the world.

10   He was in the world, and the world came into being through him; yet the world did not know him. [11]He came to what was his own, and his own people did not accept him. [12]But to all who received him, who believed in his name, he gave power to become children of God, [13]who were born, not of blood or of the will of the flesh or of the will of man, but of God.

14   And the Word became flesh and lived among us, and we have seen his glory, the glory as of a father's only son, full of grace and truth.

I. The Historical Horizon

As we have noted in the Introduction to this commentary, it was not uncommon in Roman drama to sing a hymn to the emperor (sometimes as divine) prior to the presentation of the drama itself,[1] and I suspect the Fourth Evangelist may be adopting this custom here. The function of this material here, however, is to provide a key for the hearer or reader to understand what follows in the dramatic presentation of Christ's life in this Gospel. Throughout the Gospel, knowing where the Son of God came from and where he is going is the key to understanding who he is, and thus is also a key to understanding why so many misunderstand and reject him.[2] The hymnic structure of this material is more easily seen in the following arrangement of the material.

> *First Strophe*
> In the beginning was the Word;
> and the Word was with God,
> and the Word was God.
> He was with God in the beginning.

Second Strophe
Through him all things were made.
Without him nothing came to be.
In him was life,
and this life was the light of humanity.
The light shines in the darkness,
and the darkness has not overcome/understood it.

(Verses 6–9 are an insert by the evangelist introducing the Baptist and his relationship to the Word.)

Third Strophe
He was in the world,
and though the world was made by him,
it did not recognize/respond to him.
To his own he came,
yet his own did not receive him.
But all those who did accept him,
he empowered to become children of God.

(Verses 12b–13 are an explanatory insertion by the author about how one becomes such a child.)

Fourth Strophe
And the Word became flesh,
and dwelt among us.
And we beheld his glory.
The glory of the only begotten Son of the Father,
full of grace and truth.[3]

There is some question as to whether vv. 16–18 should be seen as a fifth strophe, but probably they should not be included. Roughly speaking, the hymn can be broken down into several major themes: (1) the preexistent Word (*logos*); (2) the Word and creation; (3) the response of those created—rejection; (4) the incarnation and revelation; (5) the response of the faithful community (i.e., "we have seen his glory"). Without question, John 1:1–14 has had more impact on Christian thinking about the Son of God as preexistent and a divine being than any other New Testament passage. Here is where the early church derived its *logos* (i.e., the Son of God as the "Word") Christology and its basic understanding of the incarnation. In its pattern it is not unlike the two hymns in Phil. 2:6–11 and Col. 1:15–20 (cf. also Heb. 1:2–4). Like the hymn in Heb. 1, this material serves both to establish the identity and reveal the scope of the deeds and career of the main character of the book. While in Heb. 1 the hymn is part of the prologue, in John 1 it has basically become the prologue, along with the parenthetical remarks about the Baptist and the birth from above.

In John 1 there is only really an account of the first two of the normal three stages in the V pattern of Wisdom hymns of preexistence, earthly existence, and existence in heaven after death, perhaps because the author wishes to develop the glorification theme later in the Gospel. He is trying to make clear that Jesus' ministry and person can only be understood if one recognizes where Jesus came from and where he is going. In short, the Son of God is only explicable if one understands that here is a divine being who came from and returns to heaven. Yet it is striking also in this Gospel that, in order to make clear that the Son of God does not exhaust the Godhead, we are constantly being told in John that Jesus is dependent on the Father—he cannot speak or act except as the Father grants him to do so.

There is some evidence that this is an independent hymn that has been incorporated into this Gospel, for there are various key terms in this hymn that one finds nowhere else in the Gospel, including the word *logos,* the word for grace (*charis*), and the word for fullness (*pleros*).[4] Furthermore, the idea found in v. 14 of the Word coming and tabernacling or setting up his tent in our midst is found only in this passage of the Gospel. On the other hand, the Beloved Disciple or the Fourth Evangelist may have composed this based on precedents in wisdom literature, and thus the special vocabulary would reflect the source of influence, not its authorship. This description of the Logos echoes the story of the coming of the law to Israel, especially in its retelling in Sir. 24, where the Torah is identified with Wisdom. Here, however, the author is making a very different hermeneutical move—instead of identifying Wisdom or Word with Torah, Wisdom is identified with Christ, who is seen as eclipsing the law of Moses in v. 17. Already, then, in this first section of the Gospel the evangelist wishes to make clear how the coming of Jesus both fulfills and so makes obsolescent the earlier institutions of Judaism.[5]

The best way to describe this hymn is to call it poetry, with some lapses into prose at the end, or poetic prose.[6] In the Greek it has a certain rhythmic cadence, which can even be picked up in a good English translation. The cadence is established by the repetition of certain key words (v. 1 Word, Word, God, God; vv. 4–5 life, life, light, light, darkness, darkness; vv. 10–12 the world, the world, the world, his own, his own, receive/accept, receive). Note also that the phrase "his own" apparently has a different meaning in the hymn than elsewhere in John. The only real difficulty is in deciding what originally belonged to the hymn. The simplest solution is to see the material on the Baptist in vv. 6–8 as an addition by the evangelist. There is certainly a stylistic difference between vv. 6–8 and the rest of the hymn up to v. 11.[7] One must always bear in mind that the Christian authors who used these hymns or hymn fragments also edited them to some extent to suit their own purposes.

EXCURSUS: EARLY CHRISTIAN HYMNS ABOUT CHRIST[8]

Though it is perhaps an exaggeration to say that early Christology was born in song, one may certainly say that early Christology grew out of the worship of Christ and was accordingly expressed in various liturgical forms—hymns, prayers, creedal statements, *testimonia,* and doxologies. Some of these forms no doubt came initially from a spontaneous response in worship to what was felt to be the leading of the Holy Spirit, but some also seem to reflect a careful and calculated composition prepared in advance for use in worship. Various sources suggest that psalms, hymns, and spiritual songs were perhaps the most crucial forms not only in the earliest period (ca. A.D. 35–55) but at least well into the second century. It is not just Pliny the Younger (*Ep.* 10.96.7) who bears witness to the fact that that which distinguished early Christians was "the singing of hymns to Christ as to a god."[9] Indeed, there is telltale evidence of such practices well before the time of Pliny in the New Testament (cf. 1 Cor. 14:26; Col. 3:16; Eph. 5:19).[10]

Also important for our purposes are the words of Philo (*Vit. cont.* 28–29, 68–80) about the Jewish Therapeutae in the first century A.D. who were "yearning for Wisdom" (68), and so they studied scripture.

> Then the President rises and sings a hymn composed as an address to God, either a new one of his own composition or an old one by poets of an earlier day who have left behind them hymns in many measures and melodies. . . . They all lift up their voices, men and women alike (80) . . . [in] two choirs one of men and one of women (83). . . . After choric dancing they form a single choir and sing until dawn (89).[11]

Especially telling is the fact that Eusebius interprets this discussion in Philo as referring to early Christian worship (cf. *H.E.* 2.17, 21ff.).

If one considers the possible analogies with Qumran, one will not be surprised that Christians were in the business of composing hymns. Certainly this was a regular practice in the Qumran community (see especially the 1QH material), and there is evidence that the psalms and perhaps also such hymns were the result of being filled with God's wisdom and Spirit, which resulted in a prophetic utterance. This is, in fact, what is claimed for David in 11QPs.,[12] which reads in part, "And Yahweh gave him a wise and enlightened spirit. . . . The sum [of his songs] was 4050. These he uttered through prophecy [*bnbw'h*] which had been given him by the most high." This should be compared with the previous discussion about Solomon and his songs[13] but also with what is said about Solomon in Wisd. Sol. 7:7— "Therefore I prayed, and understanding was given me; I called on God and the spirit of wisdom came to me." This is followed by the wisdom hymn in 7:22ff., which near its conclusion says, "In every generation she passes into holy souls and makes them friends of God and prophets; for God loves nothing so much as the person who lives with Wisdom." The point of the previous discussion is to show that there is a precedent for the earliest Christians' composing hymns and, in particular, hymns influenced by sapiential material.

In large measure the earliest Christian worship practices seem to have reflected and grown out of early Jewish worship, and so the quote from Philo is important, especially in view of the Pauline texts mentioned above. The connection between wisdom and the singing of hymns in the Philo quote, and also in the quote from the Qumran material, should not be missed, for there is also such a connection in the christological hymn fragments in the New Testament, as shall be shown shortly.[14] It was the focus on Christ, not the composition of hymns, even sapiential ones, that made early Christian worship and hymns stand out.[15] It is not historically improbable that the theological thinking that eventually led to the christological hymns originated very early and on Palestinian soil. In our case, it was a Judean disciple, the Beloved Disciple, or the one most influenced by him, the Fourth Evangelist, who created the hymn we find in John 1.

There seem to have been three primary sources that are drawn on to compose the christological hymns: (1) earlier Jewish discussions about personified or even hypostasized Wisdom; (2) the earliest Christian preaching about the life of Jesus, in particular about his death and vindication beyond death; and (3) the christological use of the psalms, especially Ps. 110 but also Ps. 8 among others.[16] Though this study intends to focus on the degree of indebtedness to the first source, the importance of the other two is not being minimized. It appears that in general the protological and incarnational language draws on the sapiential material; the language about Jesus' death or sacrifice draws on the Passion material and the early preaching; and the references to Jesus' exaltation and vindication draw on material from the psalms. The V narrative *pattern* of these hymns, discussing in turn the pretemporal, temporal, and posttemporal nature, life, and activity of the Son, favors the suggestion that the dominant influence on these hymns is the earlier Jewish reflection on the career of personified Wisdom, who is said in Prov. 8 to be involved in the work of creation, who is said in Sir. 24 to have come and dwelt in in the midst of God's people, and who is said in *1 Enoch* 42 to have been rejected by those people and so returned to dwell in heaven with God. Wisdom thinking to the extent that it is theology is a form of creation theology, and thus one should not be surprised that a considerable amount of space could be devoted to what was true of the Son before and during the event of creation in a Christian wisdom hymn. Indeed, in some of the christological hymns at least as much time (and in some instances more time) is spent on protological matters as on anything else (cf., e.g., Col. 1 and John 1). Christ's career is envisioned as having both heavenly and earthly scope, and the attempt to adequately express the theological significance of this career led early Jewish Christians to draw on the most exalted language they could find—Jewish wisdom speculation, coupled to some degree with messianic interpretation of the psalms and soteriological reflections on Christ's death. Since wisdom thought is a form of creation theology, it is also not surprising that it is in these sorts of Christian hymns (rather than, for instance, in hymns that were simply a form of messianic exegesis of a psalm), that we find the first reflections about what it might mean to say that the preexistent Redeemer took on human flesh or became a human being. One must keep steadily in mind that the V pattern *and* the theme of rejection are already found in the earlier Jewish material about personified Wisdom.[17]

The point of these remarks is just this: these hymns do not appear to be hymnic adaptations of the early Christian kerygma or basic teaching about Jesus' death and resurrection. One should look for their provenance elsewhere. Even where soteriology is suggested in these hymn fragments, one must not forget that in the Wisdom of Solomon, written probably only a few decades before the christological hymns, not only does one find various hymns praising Wisdom but also the words, "Who has learned your counsel, unless you have given Wisdom and sent your Holy Spirit from on high? And thus the paths of those on earth were set right, and people were taught what pleases you, and were saved by Wisdom" (9:17–18). E. Schüssler Fiorenza is right to stress how astonishing the exalted language of the christological hymns is, for "they do not belong to a later stage of christological development but are among the earliest christological statements found in the New Testament."[18]

There is in this hymn an obvious drawing on material from Gen. 1. Both documents begin with the words "In the beginning." Then too the Genesis story is about how God made a universe by means of his spoken words. Here too creation happens by *the* Word. But whatever debt the author of this hymn has to Genesis, Gen. 1 is not about a personified attribute, much less a person assisting God in creation. It is the use of the Genesis material in the hymnic material about Wisdom, both in the Old Testament and in later Jewish sapiential writings, that provides the font of ideas and forms used in creating this hymn. Not only Prov. 3 but also Prov. 8:1–9:6 should be considered.[19] There one learns that personified Wisdom was present at creation, but also that she called God's people back to the right paths and offered them life and favor from God (cf. 8:35).[20] These are the very things being said of the Word as well in this hymn. This sort of Wisdom speculation had gone a step farther by the time of Ben Sira, to include speculation about God's written word, the Torah. Torah and Wisdom were seen as interrelated, the former being the consummate expression of the latter (cf. Sir. 24). At the end of the hymn in John 1 it is said that the Son eclipses this Torah, for Torah which came from Moses gave the law, but through the Logos one gets grace and truth.

The Wisdom character and background of the Logos hymn has long been recognized. One can point out the remarkable parallel in 1QS 11:11: "All things come to pass by his knowledge. He establishes all things by His design, and without Him nothing is done [or made]."[21] On the idea of Wisdom providing life and light, one thinks again of Wisd. Sol. 7:27, where Wisdom is said to be the effulgence of eternal light, and she is said to be the very life breath of God in Wisd. Sol. 7:25a.

This hymn, then, emphasizes the goodness of creation—both God and the Word are involved with it, and both are involved with its redemption as well. Thus, however dark and fallen the creation may have become, it must be remembered that our author is not supporting the views held in the second century by Gnostics that matter and the material world were inherently evil and spirit was inherently good. The Fourth Evangelist does not believe in a permanent, irreconcilable dualism in the universe of good vs. evil, spirit vs. matter.

Perhaps this hymn was composed in part to combat heretical ideas that plagued the church even in the first century. For instance, the idea of docetism (that Jesus only appeared to be human and have a human body) and/or the ideas of proto-Gnosticism (that there were many intermediaries between God and human beings; that matter is evil, spirit good) may be in mind here.[22] The evangelist makes clear that the Logos really took on human flesh, and that he is the only intermediary between human beings and God.

In regard to the old problem of why *logos* and not *sophia* is used here, it seems doubtful that the reason is because Jesus was a male. Certainly that did not stop the other evangelists from using Sophia of Jesus (see Matt. 1:19; Luke 11:49).[23] It has also been pointed out that in Wisd. Sol. 9:1–2 Word (*en logo*) and Wisdom are used in synonymous parallelism, an idea that Philo takes much farther.[24] Furthermore, the Logos is personified already in Wisd. Sol. 18:15, where it is said that God's "all-powerful Word leaped from heaven, from the royal throne into the midst of the land." Since it had already been said in 9:10 that Wisdom was present and sent forth from the throne, one can see how interchangeable the terms were in the Wisdom of Solomon. This is also the case in the earlier writing of Ben Sira, for at Sir. 24:3 it is Wisdom that is said to come forth from the mouth of God. It may be that the evangelist simply used the term Logos to better prepare for the replacement motif—Jesus superseding Torah as God's Logos.[25] Perhaps it was thought that the *logos* concept better united creation and salvation history.[26] Finally, there is also the matter of the tabernacling of the Logos with God's people.[27] This idea was already manifested in Sir. 24:8, where it speaks about the Creator choosing a place for Wisdom to tent, namely, in the earthly tabernacle in Zion (v. 10), and in particular in the book of the covenant in that tabernacle (v. 23). In the Logos hymn one finds the idea of Wisdom in the person of the divine Logos tabernacling in the midst of God's people. As J.D.G. Dunn argues, it is the idea of the Word's taking on human flesh (not historical form of just any sort) that makes the Logos hymn stand out from its sapiential background.[28] I would add that the explicitly incarnational expression in John 1:14 is just a further clarification of the already incarnational thought present in the earlier christological hymns.

There are many important theological ideas that this hymn causes one to reflect on, but this study can mention only a few of the more important ones by looking at several verses in more depth. This Logos, or Word, was present with God before the space-time continuum, or universe, was created. Not only so, this Word is said to be God. The key phrase *kai theos en ho logos* does not mean "the Word was a god," but rather "the Word was God." Notice it does not say "the Word was *the* God" for this then would mean the Word was all there was to the Godhead, and the evangelist does not want to convey that idea. It is also pertinent to note that there is mention of the *pleros*, or full grace and truth, in the Logos, as in Col. 1:19 we are told that the *pleroma* (the fullness of God, cf. 2:9) dwells in him. The various parallels and similarities between the hymns should not be overlooked as they suggest they all came out of the same sort of situation in life, prone to thinking in certain sapiential ways about Christ.[29] The recent study by M. J. Harris rightly stresses the importance for the Fourth Evangelist of the idea that the Son was divine as well as human.[30]

M. D. Hooker has argued that the whole Gospel must be read in light of this prologue, and this is surely correct.[31] She maintains that the "messianic secret," if one should call it that, in the Fourth Gospel is that Jesus is the Logos, the one who has come from above and returns to the Father. But this is hidden to all but the reader who starts with John 1, just as in Mark 1 the story is incomprehensible without knowing the content of the very first verse. Thus the christological hymn is used as a christological basis for the argument in the rest of the Fourth Gospel. This argument is supported by the point that P. S. Minear makes that understanding Jesus in the Fourth Gospel depends on knowing where he has come from and where he is going.[32] The whole of the Fourth Gospel is dependent on the Wisdom hymn in the first chapter to set the stage for the story about the One who comes from and returns to the Father. This is why, on the one hand, the Johannine Jesus can say, "Before Abraham was, I am," and on the other hand he can convey the idea that he is not glorified until he is lifted up on the cross first and then returns into heaven. It should also be stressed that this is the only christological hymn that begins a *Gospel,* and it is likely because of this fact that the normal second half of the V pattern is basically missing here.[33] Had it been fully included here it would have preempted the conclusion of the Gospel story. The hymn is meant to introduce the Gospel, *not* provide a synopsis of the *whole* plot. Neverthless, it makes the listener begin to think about the Son as Wisdom, and thus one is not surprised to find that roughly the first half of this Gospel, composed of the Book of Signs found in John 2—12, is about the descent and engagement of God's Wisdom/Son into and with the world, while the second half, composed of the farewell discourses and the Passion narrative, is about Wisdom's rejection and consequent death, departure, and exaltation.

I would go farther than Hooker and suggest that the whole of this Gospel must be read in light of this very first verse, for it means that the deeds and words of Jesus are the deeds and words of a divine being, and not a created supernatural being, either, for he existed prior to all of creation. Later, in v. 18, one hears that this Son of God is the *monogenes* Son, but this may mean the unique (only one of its kind) Son or it may mean the "only begotten Son" as distinct from a created Son. This latter understanding would suggest that in eternity the Son proceeded from the Father as like produces like kind, but he was not created by the Father as something that was inherently distinct from the Father's being.[34] Jesus is, then, the natural Son of God, while mere mortals may be the adopted sons and daughters of God through the new birth. Thus the Son is set apart from other human beings in his divine nature.

This Word was involved in the whole act of creation. Nothing was made without him. Also he is involved in the whole work of redemption. Nothing is saved without him. The words "light" and "life" are major theological

terms in this Gospel, and they begin to be used here in this hymn. It is helpful to remember that light is a metaphor for revelation or enlightenment
that comes from God, and life or eternal life is the Fourth Gospel language
for salvation, or at least the benefit of salvation. The light and life offered
through the Son are not temporal or temporary, like the life and light referred to in Gen. 1, which are part of material creation. This hymn is saying
that in the Logos lie the gifts of eternal life and eternal light. The darkness
the author talks about is not just physical darkness like that referred to in
Gen. 1 but a spiritual darkness that involves not only ignorance of the truth
but also moral darkness and fallenness, which lead one to reject the light and
life even when they are offered. Thus our author wishes to stress the ultimate irony of this all. The creatures reject their own creator when they
reject the Son of God. At v. 5b we probably have a double entendre—the
darkness has not understood the light, but in addition the verb *katelaben*
may also mean the darkness has not overcome that light, it has not snuffed
it out.[35] This rejection motif is a part of what had already been said about
Wisdom, in particular in *1 Enoch* 42, but it is not irrelevant to point out that
this same theme of the rejection of Wisdom can be found in the Q material
(e.g., Matt. 23:37–39/Luke 13:34–35).

At v. 14 the *logos* finally reaches the human stage. The strophes before this
were not in any direct way talking about the incarnation, but here the subject is directly treated. Here one finds "*ho logos sarx egeneto.*" This means
"the Word became flesh." It certainly does not mean that the Word turned
into flesh with no remainder, because he remains the Word who is beheld
by the community at the end of the hymn. Thus it might be better to say that
what is meant is either the Word took on flesh, or the Word came on the
human scene.[36] The Word became more than he was before, not less. To his
divine nature he added a human one.[37] The word translated "tabernacled"
or "set up tent" seems to allude more remotely to the tabernacles period of
Jewish history, when God's presence was to be found in the tent of meeting.
Just as the Israelites saw the Shekinah glory, so the believers now have seen
an even greater glory, *the* glory, the bright and shining presence of the only-
begotten Son. As has already been said, however, its more proximate parallel is found in Sir. 24, which speaks of Wisdom in the tabernacle, and Wisdom as the book of the covenant, God's holy Word.

Glory is a familiar concept from the Old Testament which refers to the
splendor or majesty or overwhelming weightiness of the divine presence
here. It is in order to note that *doxa,* or radiance, is regularly associated with
Wisdom as well (see Wisd. Sol. 6:12; 7:10; 7:26; 9:10). From the tabernacling
of the Word temporarily here on earth, there was the benefit not just that
some believers saw his glory (possibly an allusion to Jesus' resurrection appearances)[38] but also that all believers receive grace (God's unmerited favor)
and truth (something the Spirit conveys to people who have been born anew
by the Spirit). Truth in this Gospel refers to saving truth, not just any sort
of accurate information. This grace and truth has led to one blessing after
another. Thus while Moses/Torah provided a certain knowledge of God's

will, Jesus gave the ability through dispensing grace to know the truth *and* to perform it. The great theme of this hymn is that God, in the person of the Word, did what was necessary not only to inform humankind about the gift of salvation but also to reach out and transform some with that gift so that they might be, like the Logos who is the Son, children of God.

In this hymn there are two ways that the Logos is given historical location and presence: through the mention of the incarnation in v. 14, and by associating the coming of this Logos with a historical person, John the Baptist. The story of Wisdom is thereby given further historical concreteness and specificity.

It is probably wrong to suggest that the Logos hymn marks a significant new step or radical departure in early Christology. Closer to the mark, though underestimating things a bit, is the judgment of E. D. Freed that "It may not be going too far to say that the writer of the *logos* verses in John has scarcely done more than add the technical term *logos* to a Christology which had already been formulated by Paul and others."[39]

At this point some comments on the parenthetical but crucial remarks found in vv. 12–13 are necessary. Here we have a crucial clue to the purpose for which this Gospel was written, and to how the material that follows in this Gospel is meant to be read. The evangelist has inserted this material into the hymn to prepare the reader or hearer for what follows. The aim of this Gospel is that people might receive the Christ and become children of God, and this requires of them that they be born of God. Particular ethnic origins, or merely human desires or designs, or human decisions about marriage ("the will of man") will not be sufficient to make one a disciple of Christ. This birth is possible only because of the will and power of God operating in a human life.[40] "Here is no known, natural sonship, the result of mixing of bloods, of natural desire, and of an exercise of human will. Here is the ultimate and primal sonship that has as its origin the creative gift of the will and power of God."[41]

Verses 12–13 will be further commented on in John 3 in Jesus' famous discussion with Nicodemus, but they are inserted here for a very important reason. Birth from God is here linked with the understanding that the one known as Jesus had a prehistory as the Word of God in heaven and was involved in the work of creation as well as redemption. In other words, Jesus must be seen as the divine Son of God who has come in the flesh. A confession of Jesus that does not equal the one found in this christological hymn is seen by the evangelist as inadequate, and something less than a full Christian confession. This in turn means the confession of Jesus as the divine Son and Word of God is seen as primary evidence that one is born of God. This conclusion is borne out by a careful reading of 1 John, and leads us to think that the situation addressed there is likely very similar to the one addressed in this Gospel, though there is obviously more concern in the Gospel with outsiders and their reaction to the Christ. First John is primarily addressed to Christians with problems, while the Gospel is primarily a retelling of the story of Jesus in a sapiential fashion for outsiders. Both, however, are about what amounts to adequate faith in and confession of Jesus.

This Gospel was written in order that the audience might believe in Jesus as the divine Son of God and the Christ, and so have life (John 20:31). In fact, we will see in this Gospel a parade of witnesses who confess Jesus in various terms, beginning in this very first chapter. While many, indeed nearly all, of these acclamations are indeed true confessions, the point is that they are not fully adequate confessions. What we find in this Gospel is a plethora of people on the way to becoming full-fledged disciples, including Jesus' mother, his disciples, John the Baptist, the blind man, and a host of others, but they have not yet fully arrived.[42] This Gospel is meant to lead such seekers to the full and adequate faith in Christ so they may have life. It is no accident that the climax of this Gospel comes *after* Jesus' death and resurrection, when doubting Thomas finally offers a confession that matches the lofty tones of the prologue, acclaiming Jesus as "my Lord and my God." It was not until after Easter that such a confession was possible. Only then was fuller understanding possible, and only then was the Paraclete sent that could lead one into all truth and empower believers to be children of God. It is only after the resurrection, after Jesus' glory had been seen and the Spirit received, that people like the Beloved Disciple could reflect back on the story of Jesus and understand its real significance and deeper meaning.

The evangelist reminds us at various points that this was the case, and that it was a matter of remembering and rereading the story of Jesus in light of its conclusion (see John 2:22; 20:9) and the post-Easter confessions.[43] This is what we find in this Gospel, and it is no doubt this sort of reflective meditation on the story in light of the Easter events and the confessions they prompted that in due course led to a reading of the story of Jesus in light of the story of Wisdom. If Jesus could indeed be confessed as "my God," then something in scripture, God's very Word, must have hinted at such things in advance of the appearance of Jesus on the human scene. In the minds of the Beloved Disciple and the Fourth Evangelist that something was the story of Wisdom, who came forth from the side of God to dwell in the midst of God's people, but was rejected and returned to dwell on high. The course of the life of Jesus was not fortuitous; it was part of God's plan from all eternity to save the world, and was foreshadowed if not also foretold, according to this Gospel's creators, in the story of Wisdom.

It is important to see the order in which this process proceeded: (1) the actual course of Jesus' life, and particularly its outcome, caused various people to reflect again on the scriptures in comparison with the life and teachings of Jesus, since early Jews were not looking for a crucified and risen manual worker from Galilee to be the messiah; (2) when such reflection was undertaken after Easter it was seen how Jesus was foreshadowed in the figure of personified Wisdom, and his life, even in various of its more troubling aspects, was a fulfillment of the Hebrew scriptures (see John 19:24); hence (3) though Jesus' course of life may have seemed surprising on initial scrutiny, seen with the eyes of faith it was actually part of God's divine plan from before the foundation of the world.

II. Bridging the Horizons

In order for this text to be used with a modern audience, pastors and teachers will necessarily have to familiarize themselves and their audience with Jewish wisdom literature, including Proverbs, Ecclesiastes, Job, Sirach, and Wisdom of Solomon. It is equally crucial to be clear about what wisdom really amounted to in the Jewish world. Briefly wisdom can be defined as skill in living well, making the right decisions, which prolong and promote life, health, and happiness, even in a dark world. This wisdom was thought to be gained by studying the parables, aphorisms, riddles, and other forms of metaphorical speech offered by Jewish sages. I would suggest that the Beloved Disciple was seen as such a sage, and this is one reason why his homilies and memoirs about Christ were preserved and finally put in biographical form. By the time Wisdom of Solomon was written, around the turn of the era, wisdom had come to be associated with concepts like eternal life, resurrection, and salvation, as some of the quotes in this section from this book show. This is also the ethos out of which the Johannine literature is produced, the major difference being that now Jesus is seen as Wisdom in the flesh, and knowing him is the key to obtaining eternal life and light. Unless the audience the pastor or teacher is addressing has some familiarity with biblical wisdom literature and its development, much of the Fourth Gospel will remain mysterious and impenetrable.

The second thing to be said about using this text today is that some serious reflection must be undertaken about one's view of heaven and the material world, as well as the use of metaphor in this hymn. The Son of God was not literally God's speech or Word, though he may be said to be the exegesis, the explanation and revelation, of God's true character. Furthermore, if indeed by heaven one means God's eternal dwelling place, then by definition heaven is not part of the material universe. The Son did not arrive here by descending through the Milky Way galaxy and turning left at Earth's moon. In short, the language of down and up in this Gospel must not be overpressed. The point is that the Son came from God's side to be with humankind on earth and returned to the place from which he had come after his death and resurrection. Heaven must be seen as a parallel and presumably nonmaterial dimension of reality, not part of the material universe.

Third, before one preaches on or teaches this text, it must be balanced against the rest of the Gospel, where the Son is seen to be clearly subordinate to the Father and dependent on his will and guidance. Jesus is depicted, as we shall see, as God's agent on earth, just as the Spirit is later seen as Christ's agent once he departs from earth. If one is going to stress the divinity of the Word or Son, one must also be prepared to stress the humanity and subordination of the Son to God. Sometimes, especially in conservative circles, the divinity is preached in such a way that the humanity of Christ is denied or sublimated or consumed. The consequence of this is, of course, that when the Johannine Jesus says things like "You will do even greater works than these" such sayings become inexplicable if the Son is nothing more than God bestriding the earth, disguised as a human being. The humanity and self-limitation of Christ is an important aspect of this Gospel, which must not be neglected, especially since the death of Christ is crucial in this Gospel to the fulfillment of God's plan for Jesus as well as for his followers.

Fourth, the incarnation, so often preached and taught about at Christmas, cannot be reduced to simple explanations; it involves a considerable element of mystery. As John Donne once put it, "Twas much, that man was made like God before, But that God should be made like man, much more."[44] This means that one must resist the urge to overexplain, which so often leads to the trivializing of the subject matter. The Logos hymn here does not tell us *how* the Word took on flesh or came on the human scene, it only insists that he did so. It must be kept steadily in view that this is a hymnic or poetic passage, and some of its imagery should not be overpressed (such as the use of the term "word," or "tabernacled").

If one is stumped at how to use this or any other narrative text in this Gospel, I would suggest that three fundamental questions can be asked of such texts: (1) What does it tell us about God? (2) What does it tell us about humankind? (3) What does it tell us about God's relationship to humankind?

2. A Cloud of Witnesses (John 1:6–9, 15–51)

I. The Historical Horizon

A. *The Witness from the Wilderness (John 1:6–9, 15–34)*

1:6 There was a man sent from God, whose name was John. ⁷He came as a witness to testify to the light, so that all might believe through him. ⁸He himself was not the light, but he came to testify to the light. ⁹The true light, which enlightens everyone, was coming into the world. . . .

15 (John testified to him and cried out, "This was he of whom I said, 'He who comes after me ranks ahead of me because he was before me.'") ¹⁶From the fullness we have all received, grace upon grace. ¹⁷The law indeed was given through Moses; grace and truth came through Jesus Christ. ¹⁸No one has ever seen God. It is God the only Son, who is close to the Father's heart, who has made him known.

19 This is the testimony given by John when the Jews sent priests and Levites from Jerusalem to ask him, "Who are you?" ²⁰He confessed and did not deny it, but confessed, "I am not the Messiah." ²¹And they asked him, "What then? Are you Elijah?" He said, "I am not." "Are you the prophet?" He answered, "No." ²²Then they said to him, "Who are you? Let us have an answer for those who sent us. What do you say about yourself?" ²³He said,

"I am the voice of one crying out in the wilderness,
'Make straight the way of the Lord.'"
as the prophet Isaiah said.

24 Now they had been sent from the Pharisees. ²⁵They asked him, "Why then are you baptizing if you are neither the Messiah, nor Elijah, nor the prophet?" ²⁶John answered them, "I baptize with water. Among you stands one whom you do not know, ²⁷the one who is coming after me; I am not worthy to untie the thong of his sandal." ²⁸This took place in Bethany across the Jordan where John was baptizing.

29 The next day he saw Jesus coming toward him and declared, "Here is the Lamb of God who takes away the sin of the world! ³⁰This is he of whom I said, 'After me comes a man who ranks ahead of me because he was before me.' ³¹I myself did not know him; but I came baptizing with water for this reason, that he might be revealed to Israel." ³²And John testified, "I saw the Spirit descending from heaven like a dove, and it remained on him. ³³I myself did not know him, but the one who sent me to baptize with

water said to me, 'He on whom you see the Spirit descend and remain is the one who baptizes with the Holy Spirit.' 34And I myself have seen and have testified that this is the Son of God."

Various commentators have rightly pointed out that there is a major focus in this Gospel on witnesses, and on Jesus being on trial, even long before the Passion narrative. A. E. Harvey has put the matter as follows: "The underlying pattern [of the Fourth Gospel] is of two parties in dispute, Jesus and 'the Jews'; and the dispute has to be presented in such a way that the reader is persuaded of the justice of Jesus' case."[1] This is not surprising in a missionary document that necessarily must have an apologetic thrust, in view of the way Jesus' life ended. Harvey has even suggested that the structure of the Gospel is often conditioned by the attempt to produce a case on behalf of Jesus, beginning with the witnesses and following with an account of the events that led up to Jesus' trial, verdict, execution, and vindication by God. I am largely convinced by this argument. Harvey's argument strongly suggests that the author expects resistance and even opposition in the audience to persuasion about Jesus' true character. This in turn requires that we see the primary audience of this Gospel as not disciples, but those as yet unconverted. But, one may ask, why was it necessary to defend or provide an apologia for the story of Jesus?

As M. Hengel has made very clear, there was no positive evaluation of crucifixion in the ancient world; it was seen as a disgraceful way to die, the proper punishment for the dregs of society—rebellious slaves, bandits, and revolutionaries.[2] Crucifixion was not seen as an honorable or noble or heroic way to die. In such a context, it became crucial for Christians to provide an adequate explanation for the outcome of Jesus' life in its witness to the world.

The strategy of the Fourth Evangelist is to make clear even in the testimony of the first witnesses to Jesus that Jesus' death was planned by God, and that in fact Jesus was in control of his life and his death. Crucifixion did not happen to him by accident, nor was it evidence of Jesus' powerlessness and weakness. Rather, even in the case of Pilate, Jesus can say, "You would have no power over me unless it had been given you from above" (John 19:11).

Commentators have also rightly remarked on the fact that John has so transformed the telling of Christ's passion that, unlike the stark and gutwrenching portrait found in Mark, complete with the cry of dereliction "My God, my God, why have you forsaken me?" we have a Jesus in the Fourth Gospel who is already on his way back to heaven when he is "lifted up" on the cross, the cross having become the first of several stages in his exaltation and glorification. Rather than being the hour of the great triumph of the powers of darkness, Christ's death is his own hour, which he has long prepared for and during which he even makes a last will and testament involving his physical family and the family of faith (see commentary below on John 19). In fact, Jesus does not die in this portrayal until he announces, "It is finished"—he must "give up the ghost" (i.e., his human spirit); no one can take it from him. The point is, it is not just Jesus' death, but now the entire story, even beginning with that first witness John the Baptist, that has been transfigured by looking at it in the light of the resurrection and the events that followed Easter morning. John, like all the others in this Gospel, has been summoned upon the stage as part of a positive portrayal of and witness to Jesus and his enduring significance.

Since I have elsewhere discussed the relationship of Jesus and John the Baptist in some detail, I will simply summarize my conclusions here about what we can know about the actual historical relationship of Jesus to John, and the character and mission of John the Baptist.[3] This is of paramount importance, especially in view of the likely historical evidence in John 1 and 3 that Jesus not only drew some of his early disciples from the followers of the Baptist, but was himself involved in John's ministry and was acting as a support for it, or at the very least had a parallel ministry involving baptizing prior to the imprisonment of John and the beginning of Jesus' own ministry.

The Synoptic portrayal of the relationship of Jesus and John, particularly the Lukan portrayal that intimates they were related (see Luke 1—2), suggests a closeness between the two men both in origins and in lifework. The Q saying in Matt. 11:7–11/Luke 7:24–28 shows that Jesus is by no means stinting in his praise of John, calling him the greatest man ever born of woman and more than a prophet. It must steadily be kept in mind that Jesus even submitted to John's baptism, which to the casual onlooker would have suggested John's precedence and authority over Jesus. Who then was John and what was he about?

On the one hand, John appears like an Old Testament prophet in both his oracles of doom and his ascetical behavior. On the other hand, his practice of baptizing has no precedent in the Old Testament prophetic literature and is like the practices of Qumran and other baptist-type sects. . . . John cannot be seen as simply a reformer of society like the Pharisees because he calls even the ritually pure and righteous to repentance and baptism and he threatens that one's descent from Abraham was neither a protection from the coming judgment nor a guarantee of one's place in God's final dominion, and because he did not write off the nation as the sons of darkness—he calls them to repentance. Yet John, unlike Jesus, apparently performed no miraculous deeds or signs. John's water rite, however, seems to have a different focus than the practices of Qumran, coming closer to what we know of Jewish proselyte baptism.[4] . . . Although John may have been a part of the Qumran community, he is no longer a member when we encounter him in the Gospel literature because 1) he calls the nation to repentance, 2) he allows both the unclean and clean, the sinners and the righteous, to come into contact with him and 3) his water rite is not merely a repeatable ritual ablution. . . . Jesus recognized John as a prophetic figure, and there is no reason to dispute this identification. There is also no reason to see John as the founder of a messianic movement because neither in the Gospels nor in Josephus (*Ant.* 18.5.2) is there any evidence that John viewed himself in such a light. Nevertheless, he seems to have felt that the final and decisive judgment of God was about to fall on Israel. Finally John should not be seen as a reformer in the same manner that the Pharisees or Zealots were reformers. He urges neither a levitical nor a revolutionary program to cure the nation's ills. He was in many ways a unique figure that caused a stir among the religious and in the halls of power in the region because he was perceived to be a threat to various authority figures, a threat to the religious and political status quo.[5]

I would argue that John likely was at some point part of the Qumran community, and that he conveyed some of their emphases and their universe of discourse to his own disciples, among whom may well have been the Beloved Disciple.[6] "If this is true, and if . . . the Evangelist was his disciple, we can explain very well the Qumran impact on the Fourth Gospel."[7] I would suggest also, however, that some of the strong contrasts in this Gospel between dark and light, truth and falsehood, can at least in part be explained by the impact of the wisdom tradition on the Beloved Disciple and the Fourth Evangelist (see, e.g., Prov. 1—2; Sir. 37:16–26).

Why is there so much emphasis on John in the beginning of this Gospel, when he had been dead for perhaps seventy years when it was published? I would suggest that the answer is that there continued to be followers of John even into the second century A.D., and therefore the Fourth Evangelist has shaped especially some of the material in chaps. 1 and 3 as a witness to such folk. I doubt that it is accidental that in the only passage outside the Gospels that refers to those baptized by John, Acts 19, we are told that Paul encountered these disciples in Ephesus, also the traditional locale from which this Gospel was written. I would suggest that one group of dialogue partners of the members of the Johannine community were those who continued to be followers of John. This would explain why there is so much stress here both on John's denial of being Elijah or a messianic figure, and his strong affirming witness to Jesus. With this background we must consider the text itself.

The first mention of John in v. 6 affirms that John was one sent from God, a description also applied to Jesus (cf. 3:17). There is no attempt here to cast John in a bad light, only to cast him in the shadow of Jesus and stress his witness to and about Jesus. We are told that the specific reason that John came was to be a witness to the light, "so that all might believe through him." We are thus informed from the outset that the function of this witness (and others as well) is that all the audience might come to true faith in the one who is the Light of the World.

As Harvey stresses, John's words have the character not of prophecy or proclamation but of a legal witness. Thus it is said of John that "he gives evidence [*martyrei*] about him" (1:15), and then at v. 19 we hear explicitly, "This is the evidence of John." Furthermore, "the striking phrase with which John answers the deputation from Jerusalem also has the ring of the law court: 'He affirmed [*homologesen*], and did not deny, but affirmed'"

(1:20).[8] The testimony character of these scenes must be borne in mind as one works through the chapter.

Verse 8 makes explicit from the outset that John himself was not the light and would repudiate any such suggestions (see vv. 15ff.). Verse 9 speaks of the "true light." Here, as in various other places in this Gospel (cf. 15:1) the Greek word translated true (*alethinos*) means genuine as opposed to inauthentic, not true as opposed to false. We may already here be in the provenance of the language of the law court. There is considerable question as to whether the phrase "coming into the world" modifies the noun "light" or "every human being"—probably the former.[9] The term *kosmos* is an important one in this Gospel. It refers to the human world, probably without a pejorative sense here, but in due course the term comes to mean in this Gospel humanity organized against God and needing redemption (cf. 3:16–17).

Verse 15 provides us with the next reference to the Baptist, and, as various translations suggest, this is likely a parenthetical remark of the evangelist. This is an important point, for the evangelist has summed up the gist of John's testimony in his own style and language—Jesus ranks ahead of John, even though he appeared on the public scene after him, because he was *before* John. Here already, especially in light of John 1:1–14, is a hint of the preexistence of the Son. The Synoptic testimony of John does not include such a statement, but comes closer to what we find in v. 27.[10]

The real testimony of John begins with v. 19 and culminates with v. 34. It is cast in the form of a quest story, as Painter has shown, and prepares the reader for questions to be raised by inquirers about Jesus.[11] In the Fourth Gospel seekers track down John and Jesus to ask questions, sometimes offer professions, and sometimes become followers.[12] This is the opposite of what we find by and large in the Synoptics, where Jesus goes around the Sea of Galilee selecting people to become fishers of human beings.[13] The differences in the two sorts of narratives can be accounted for, I think, in part by the missionary focus of this Gospel, aimed as it is at religious seekers, so that they might believe in Jesus. The Fourth Evangelist is also interested in portraying Jesus as a sage and Wisdom, and by definition potential disciples of Jewish sages were expected to seek the sage and seek out Wisdom (see Sir. 51:23). In other words, the details of the story are shaped to serve the larger purposes, both historical and theological, of the evangelist.[14] Here in chap. 1 we have a sort of synopsis of true confessions about Jesus, revealing to the listener in advance insights into who Jesus was, insights that only truly and fully dawned on the disciples later, and for the most part after Easter.

In v. 19 we come across the first reference to one of the most crucial phrases in the whole Gospel—*hoi Ioudaioi*, variously translated "the Jews" or sometimes "the Judeans." This is a term found some seventy times in the Fourth Gospel and only five or six times in each of the Synoptics. This shows that "the Jews" are a major concern of the evangelist. Properly speaking, the term derives from the old tribal distinctions, in this case from the tribe of Judah (cf. Josephus, *Ant.* 11.173), but it is unlikely that it has such a reference in the Fourth Gospel. It is conceivable that it could mean Judean Jews as opposed to those in the Diaspora, but nothing in the Fourth Gospel actually favors such a suggestion. More clearly, the term cannot mean any and all Jews, as later anti-Semitic readings of this Gospel unfortunately claimed, since all the earliest people who responded positively to Jesus, whether as disciples or sympathetic listeners like Nicodemus, were Jews, and the evangelist singles out a variety of early Jews to bear witness to Jesus in this very chapter, including the Baptist.

Much the most probable solution is the suggestion that when the term "the Jews" has a pejorative sense, and this is by no means always the case in this Gospel (cf. John 4:22), it refers first and foremost to those Jewish leaders who opposed Jesus and the Jesus movement, and perhaps by implication those Diaspora Jewish leaders who opposed the Johannine community and its witness to Jews and others. As J. Ashton says, "In the Gospel itself, the only clear synonym for 'Jews' is 'the chief priests and Pharisees' (not the Pharisees alone)."[15] It is this group that sends priests and Levites from Jerusalem to inquire of John, according to John 1:19. A careful scrutiny of the meaning of this phrase in this Gospel, then, will show that the focus is on the Jerusalem leadership that opposes Jesus at various points throughout the Gospel, not primarily on later synagogue leadership.[16] Finally, it is in order to add that not even all Jewish leaders are said to oppose Jesus, Nicodemus and Joseph of Arimathea being examples of a differing viewpoint. The use of this phrase does, however, tell us one crucial thing about the Fourth Evangelist and the Johannine community—he is part of a community that distinguishes itself from "the Jews" and perhaps also from the Jewish community.

The testimony of John found in vv. 19–22 involves three negations: (1) He is not the messiah; (2) he is not Elijah (come back from the dead, and sometimes associated in Jewish tradition with the messiah's forerunner—see Mal. 4:5); (3) he is not the prophet. This latter does not amount to a claim not to be a prophet, but likely refers to the specific Mosaic prophet promised in Deut. 18:15–18. At Qumran there is reference to "the coming of the prophet and the messiahs of Aaron and Israel" (1QS 9:11). When John is then asked who he thinks he is, especially since he is going around baptizing people, he refers to the text of Isa. 40:3, which not coincidentally is the very text that the Synoptics use to describe John's mission (see Matt. 3:3; Mark 1:3; Luke 3:4). It is also important to point out that this same text crops up at Qumran in 1QS 8:13–16, but is interpreted as a command, not a prediction.[17] Possibly the Baptist came across the usage of this text at Qumran and adapted it for his own purposes when he left the community.

John's answer in v. 26 to his inquisitors is that his baptism is with water, but that there is one present in their midst that they do not know. Here already we see the major theme of spiritual ignorance and obtuseness introduced and associated with these Jewish leaders and their emissaries. John says of this unknown one that he is unworthy to loose his sandal thongs, which suggests he is unworthy even to be his servant. There may be something in the suggestion that since students of sages were expected to do any task for a teacher, except the slave's task of taking off the master's shoes, John is here ranking himself lower even than a disciple of Jesus.[18] In any case, the seekers should be busy looking for someone much more important than John, someone who is already in their midst.

Verse 28 adds an interesting note about the locale where this encounter occurred, namely, Bethany across the Jordan. Unfortunately, we do not know where this village may have been. Some have suggested the reference is to a region, not a city, known as Batanea (called Bashan in the Old Testament), but why then did the Fourth Evangelist write Bethany? D. A. Carson suggests the location may have been Batanea, but that the evangelist uses an alternate spelling in order to emphasize that Jesus' public ministry began and ended at a Bethany, one across the Jordan mentioned here and one at 10:39–40, which in both cases is associated with Jesus' connection to John the Baptist.[19] The other Bethany is of course the one only a few miles outside Jerusalem, where Jesus concluded his sign ministry by raising Lazarus, according to John 11.

The heart of John's positive witness comes in the much-debated v. 29. Perhaps as part of his intent to cast John in Jesus' shadow, the Fourth Evangelist nowhere narrates Jesus' baptism by John. Instead, John confesses Jesus to be "the Lamb of God who takes away the sin of the world." As Carson says, "Modern Christians are so familiar with the entire clause that it takes an effort of imagination to recognize that, before the coming and death of Jesus, it was not an obvious messianic designation."[20] There is some reason to think that if this acclamation was ever made by John (who, according to the Synoptics, had doubts about Jesus, apparently because he was not prepared for a suffering messiah; see Matt. 11:2–19), that it did not have the later Christian connotations it is assumed now to have.

There is evidence in some early Jewish material influenced by wisdom, prophetic, and apocalyptic material that an image of a warrior lamb was well known, an image we find later in the Johannine corpus in Rev. 7:27 and 17:14. For instance, in *Testament of Joseph* 19:8 we read, "And I saw that a virgin was born from Judah, wearing a linen stole; and from her was born a spotless lamb. At his left there was something like a lion, and all the wild animals rushed against him, but the lamb conquered them."[21] This may suggest that John's phrase originally referred to a conquering lamb who comes for judgment on all things dark and dangerous.[22]

A second possibility would be an allusion to the scapegoat of Lev. 16, which was sent out to the desert bearing away someone's sins. The problem, of course, with this suggestion is that it involves a goat, not a lamb. Furthermore, in the Old Testament the Passover lamb was not seen as a sin offering, but rather as a sacrifice that averted God's wrath.

Perhaps the identification of Jesus as the one who takes away the sin of the world, followed quickly by the reference to John's baptizing with water, is meant to stress that while John's baptism was to be "a baptism of repentance for the forgiveness of sins" (Mark 1:4), in fact it was in Jesus', not in John's, baptism that sin would actually be dealt with. John goes on to say that he himself did not know Jesus (or at least know who he truly was), but that his mission in baptizing with water was so that Jesus might be revealed to Israel.[23] This suggests that the Fourth Evangelist views John's mission as the setting for the initial unveiling of the unknown messiah. John further explains that he did not know who Jesus truly was until two things happened: (1) John saw the Spirit descend on and remain on Jesus; and (2) God spoke to him and told him that this one who was permanently Spirit-endowed was the one who would be the Spirit bestower. Several things about this testimony are striking: John is depicted as a prophet, who from time to time at moments of divine inspiration has divine insight into persons and things and hears God's word explaining such things. Jesus, by contrast, is seen here not as one who merely has intermittent inspiration from God, but rather as one who is permanently endowed with the presence and power of God. This is consistent with the overall effort here to cast John in Jesus' shadow.

Finally, Hoskyns suggests a not-implausible reading of this crucial verse. In the Jewish way of thinking about things, "salvation presupposes sacrifice. Salvation from sin depends upon that sacrifice of which lambs, consecrated morning and evening in the Temple to be the possession of God, provide the proper analogy. As the consecrated property of God, Jesus possesses the power of God unto forgiveness."[24] This is a plausible reading of the phrase if one is not meant to think of the Passover lamb.

This segment of the chapter comes to a close with John under inspiration declaring Jesus to be the Son of God. In view of the earlier statement of the Baptist about Jesus coming before him, it is possible that the evangelist intends for the reader to see the content of this confession as implying some sort of divine status, but if so, it is at most implied, not made clear.[25]

The term Son of God in itself, while having rather clear royal associations, did not convey overtones of divinity in early Judaism. Even at Qumran where we have the now-famous 4Q246, rulership but not divinity is predicated of the looked-for king: "[He] shall be great upon the earth . . . and all shall serve [him] . . . and by his name shall he be named. He shall be hailed [as] the Son of God, and they shall call him the Son of the most High."[26] If the acclamation here has some historical foundation, it likely was John's way of calling Jesus Messiah.[27] Since salvation came into the world in the form of a Word from God, it is only fitting that the first witness to this Word be a voice—the voice of one crying in the wilderness. Thus close days one and two; thus ends the first act of this drama of witnesses.

B. The Witness of the Disciples:
What's in a Name? (John 1:35–51)

1:35   The next day John again was standing with two of his disciples, [36]and as he watched Jesus walk by, he exclaimed, "Look, here is the Lamb of God!" [37]The two disciples heard him say this, and they followed Jesus. [38]When Jesus turned and saw them following, he said to them, "What are you looking for?" They said to him, "Rabbi" (which translated means Teacher), "where are you staying?" [39]He said to them, "Come and see." They came and saw where he was staying, and they remained with him that day. It was about four o'clock in the afternoon. [40]One of the two who heard John speak and followed him was Andrew, Simon Peter's brother. [41]He first found his brother Simon and said to him, "We have found the Messiah" (which is translated Anointed). [42]He brought Simon to Jesus, who looked at him and said, "You are Simon son of John. You are to be called Cephas" (which is translated Peter).

43 The next day Jesus decided to go to Galilee. He found Philip and said to him, "Follow me." [44]Now Philip was from Bethsaida, the city of Andrew and Peter. [45]Philip found Nathanael and said to him, "We have found him about whom Moses in the law and also the prophets wrote, Jesus son of Joseph from Nazareth." [46]Nathanael said to him, "Can anything good come out of Nazareth?" Philip said to him, "Come and see." [47]When Jesus saw Nathanael coming toward him, he said of him, "Here is truly an Israelite in whom there is no deceit!" [48]Nathanael asked him, "Where did you get to know me?" Jesus answered, "I saw you under the fig tree before Philip called you." [49]Nathanael replied, "Rabbi, you are the Son of God! You are the King of Israel!" [50]Jesus answered, "Do you believe because I told you that I saw you under the fig tree? You will see greater things than these." [51]And he said to him, "Very truly, I tell you, you will see heaven opened and the angels of God ascending and descending upon the Son of Man."

The second act of this drama focuses on Jesus gaining disciples and their initial reactions to him. Scholars have often puzzled over the time references found in 1:29, 35, 43, and 2:1, since the last refers to "the third day," or possibly "the day after tomorrow." This chronology makes very good sense, however, if we are meant to group together the three stories about the initial experiences of the disciples prior to the public ministry of Jesus. In this case the first "day" of the disciples would be recorded in 1:35–42, the second in 1:43–51, and the third in 2:1–11, with v. 11 bringing to a close the entire sequence with the pronouncement "and his disciples believed in him."[28] Thus this subsection of the Gospel discusses what the disciples initially heard, said, and saw of Jesus.

As Painter has pointed out, we have here quest stories, not call narratives. I have suggested that this reshaping of the original stories that *can* be said to be call narratives (cf. Mark 1:16ff.) has been undertaken because this Gospel is intended as a missionary document, reaching out to a variety of sorts of people. Also since these quest stories involve pronouncements, they should likely be seen as a subspecies of the pronouncement story. "Pronouncement stories are an expression of the rhetoric of persuasion related to the literary milieu of Greco-Roman biography."[29] What is interesting in this case is that the pronouncements about who Jesus is are being made by someone other than Jesus, until the climactic saying in 1:51 which climaxes day two of the first three days of the disciples, though Jesus makes pronouncements about Peter and Nathanael in vv. 42 and 47 respectively.

These narratives have been put together in a careful and subtle manner, but in spite of all the labels placed on Jesus in 1:35–51 it is clear enough that the disciples understand only in part. Jesus promises they will see and learn much greater things than these (v. 51), things, for example, involving Jesus' being the Son of man, through whom the avenue to heaven is opened and made "visible," for he *is* the way.

Accordingly, on the one hand when we are told that the disciples believed (cf. 1:50, 2:11), it is appropriate to note that we are not told precisely what the content of this faith was, and to stress that the evangelist, while certainly not intimating the disciples were guilty of a false faith, nonetheless is not suggesting that they already manifested a full Christian faith in Jesus as the one who died and rose again for the sins of the world. They believed, but were only on the way to becoming full-fledged disciples of Jesus. This entire Gospel is in many ways about the pilgrimage that leads to a fully adequate faith in Jesus, and repeatedly the evangelist, showing some concern for historical accuracy and distance, intimates that fully adequate understanding and faith come only after Easter. This means that the characters in this drama, including not only the disciples but Jesus' mother, Nicodemus, the Samaritan woman, the blind man, and others, are *not* being portrayed as full-fledged Christians,[30] but rather as examples of how to come to an adequate faith in Jesus. The faith of these characters in Jesus is seen as salutary, but only the first step along the way to a belief in Jesus as the Word of God, the divine Son of God, or, as Thomas finally puts it, "My Lord and my God." Rhetorical investigations of this Gospel merely confirm these conclusions: "From this movement the critic might infer that the disciples' following will be based not so much upon a full knowledge of who Jesus is and what his 'work' will be, as upon incomplete and undigested knowledge. The disciples' rash confessions which follow, clearly point to this possibility, for they are confessions based upon minimal knowledge of Jesus . . . as Jesus' surprised question confirms (v. 50)."[31] This must be kept steadily in view throughout the reading of this Gospel.

The story begins with Jesus passing by and John telling his own disciples that Jesus should be seen as the Lamb of God, which in turn leads two of John's disciples to follow him. In many dramas the first words of the main character are critical, and this is certainly the case here. Jesus asks, "What are you looking for?" It is the question that this Gospel asks of all questers, all seekers who hear these narratives. Jesus is initially addressed as "Rabbi," which is explained to mean teacher.[32] This explanation suggests, as do other similar explanations, an audience that does not know Hebrew or Aramaic, or at least an audience of which a significant portion is assumed to be Gentile.[33] I suspect the Gospel was intended to address a mixed audience of Jews and Gentiles, but that there were a significant enough number of the latter, many of whom may not have had prior contact with the synagogue, that explanations of this sort were felt to be needed.

In the typical fashion of potential disciples seeking out a famous sage or teacher, the question is raised about where Jesus' teaching house is, where he is staying (v. 38). I suspect it is hardly accidental that Jesus' response is

"Come and see," for here Jesus is being depicted not merely as a sage but as Wisdom, who elsewhere in early Jewish literature appeals to her audience: "Draw near to me, you who are uneducated, and lodge in the house of instruction. . . . Acquire wisdom for yourselves without money. Put your neck under her yoke, and let your souls receive instruction; it is to be found close by. See with your own eyes" (Sir. 51:23, 25–27; cf. Prov. 8). The most telling parallel is with the portrayal of Wisdom in Wisd. Sol. 6 where we hear: "Wisdom is radiant and unfading, and *she is easily discerned by those who love her, and is found by those who seek her.* . . . One who rises early to seek her will have no difficulty, for she will be found sitting at the gate [like a sage]. . . . She goes about seeking those worthy of her, and she graciously appears to them in their paths, *and meets them in every thought*" (emphases added). Jesus, then, is depicted here as at once sage and the Wisdom which the sages sought.[34] Thus the initial "following" of Jesus ends in a teaching session where Jesus was staying (v. 39b), which in turn leads to one of the first two disciples (Andrew) going and finding his brother (Simon). The other of the two disciples of the Baptist who first followed Jesus is not mentioned, perhaps because it was the Judean disciple we call the Beloved Disciple, who would become the focus in the concluding stages of the drama. In favor of this suggestion is the fact that the Fourth Evangelist portrays Jesus as turning and noticing the Beloved Disciple following him in John 21:20, which is very similar to the language used here in v. 38.[35]

Andrew tells Simon that Messiah (explained to mean Anointed) has been found. He brings Simon to Jesus, and then follows the nicknaming of Peter as Cephas ("which is translated Peter," from the Greek word for rock, *petra*), from the Aramaic word for rock, *kepha*. Nothing is made of this wordplay at this juncture. It is important to bear in mind that according to the Synoptic Gospels this incident of the nicknaming of Simon does not occur until much later in the ministry, at Caesarea Philippi (cf. Mark 8 and par.). The Fourth Evangelist has moved this tradition to this point because it is his purpose to say something up front about who Jesus truly was, and at the same time who the first disciples were, before recording the stories about the ministry. The cast of central characters needs to be introduced to the audience at the outset so that the deeds later recorded will make sense. This is a dramatically effective move, especially if the audience of this narrative was *not* primarily Christians, who already knew who the prime movers of the faith were and needed no such explanations.[36]

The second day of the disciples is said to take place in Galilee, unlike the first day, which was involved with disciples of John in or near Judea coming to follow Jesus. Here most scholars think we actually have a more Synoptic-like calling of Philip by Jesus, using the words "Follow me." Intriguingly we are told that this transpires in Bethsaida,[37] the city of Andrew and Peter. Are we meant to think that these latter two suggested to Jesus to go there to find disciples? Carson suggests that since the "he" in question in v. 43 is not clear in the Greek, it may refer to Andrew, who went to Galilee and retrieved Philip, a conjecture supported by the fact that everyone else who comes to

Jesus in this narrative does so not because Jesus sought them out but because of someone else's witness.[38] I am inclined to accept this view.

At v. 45 we are told that Philip, fulfilling his responsibility as a disciple by reaching out to others, finds Nathanael, whose name means "given by God." Hoskyns remarks that the gathering of the disciples is less an act of Jesus here "than the record of the gift to him of the disciples by the Father, as the name Nathanael—given by God—suggests."[39] This sort of subtle connection would have been missed by Gentile listeners. However, if this Gospel is not a missionary tract to be handed out without comment, but is rather a missionary tool for disciples to use with potential converts, then the disciples could have had occasion to explain such hints in the text. Nathanael is the first to voice serious skepticism about the suggestion of Philip that Jesus was what the disciples were acclaiming him to be. Notice that Philip says Jesus is not only the one foretold by Moses and the prophets but also "son of Joseph from Nazareth." It is possible that the Beloved Disciple and/or the Fourth Evangelist did not know the stories about the virginal conception of Jesus. But in view of John 6:42, a text laden with irony, it may be that the evangelist has deliberately included this remark here to show that while there was some initial insight on the part of the disciples into who Jesus was, there also was some considerable misunderstanding of Jesus' origins—the Son came from God, not born of the seed or will of a husband. "It is in accord with his ironical use of traditional material that he should allow Jesus to be ignorantly described as 'son of Joseph' while himself believing that Jesus had no human father."[40]

Nathanael's reply is the now-famous remark, "Can anything good come out of Nazareth?" to which Philip simply replies, "Come and see." It is hard to miss the hint here that Nathanael is meant to be seen as a type of the skeptical but honest Jewish person who will require some evidence and convincing before believing in Jesus. This should make his witness all the more compelling to listeners who may also have had considerable doubts. As we shall see, Nathanael gains credibility as a witness not only because he is not easily taken in, but also because we are told he is one without guile, an essential trait of a good witness.[41] If the reference to Nathanael's being under a fig tree is an allusion to the traditional place where a teacher would study the Torah, he may be being portrayed as an expert in the scriptures, who knows that Nazareth would not be the hometown of the Messiah.[42]

In any case, Jesus acclaims him "an Israelite in whom there is no deceit," which serves as an implicit warning to the audience that it is possible to make good professions of faith without actually believing or at least fully believing what one says. Better to be like a Nathanael with open doubts than a Judas who betrays Jesus even while kissing him and acclaiming him Master. It should be seen that Jesus' words about Nathanael, following as they do v. 46, suggest that open doubts or questions are not bad things, but reflect a spirit of honest inquiry that requires evidence for faith, which Israel at its best affirms and encourages. This attitude is not condemned, unlike the close-mindedness of the Jewish officials in John 9 who are deliberately spiritually obtuse, and so blind. Initial resistance to or questioning of the good news is not to be taken as a final rejection—a salutary warning to the Johannine community engaged in mission. Jesus' prophetic insight into Nathanael and Nathanael's character as reflected in his question, leads to Nathanael's calling Jesus rabbi, Son of God and King of Israel—the true Israelite recognizes his king. Yet it is impossible to escape the impression that, as true as these remarks are, Jesus' response in vv. 50–51 is meant to be seen as indicating that there is much more to Jesus and his works than these acclamations suggest. They are true and reflect traditional Jewish expectations but, precisely for this reason, do not plumb the depths of Jesus' character or works. Jesus is not merely the one about whom Moses and the prophets spoke; he is the Word through whom all creation and prophetic discourse was brought about in the first place.

A great deal could be said about the use of the phrase "Son of Man," which appears thirteen times in the Fourth Gospel and is most often found in contexts discussing revelation (6:27, 53), Jesus' death (3:14; 8:28), and the eschatological position and authority of Jesus (cf. 5:27; 9:39). This phrase was, historically speaking, probably the one phrase or title Jesus felt most comfortable using of himself.[43] I am in agreement with Ashton that Dan. 7 lies in the background of the use of the phrase in this Gospel, and that it seems to stress "the theme of Jesus' heavenly origin and destiny. . . . It therefore adds to Messiahship and Sonship . . . the notion of pre-existence. What it does *not* convey, paradoxically, is either humanity (which mostly rests upon messianic titles) or any suggestion of [special or royal] sonship. . . . Nor is the Son of Man ever said to be *sent*."[44]

Turning now to the first use of the phrase "Son of Man" in this Gospel at 1:51, it is right to point out that the text alludes to Jacob's dream at Bethel "that there was a ladder set up on earth, and the top of it reached to heaven; and behold the angels of God were ascending and descending on it" (Gen. 28:12). Here, though, the angels are said to be ascending and descending upon Jesus. The language that this verse is couched in is thoroughly apocalyptic, for it speaks of the opening of heaven so that Nathanael may see this sight (cf., e.g., Rev. 4:1). These words, then, are about having a vision that unveils the truth about Jesus—something that can only be known by revelation. The language of vision here is quite similar to what is said about the Baptist's seeing the Spirit descending upon Jesus in v. 32. What then is the meaning of this text? Ashton plausibly suggests that the saying means that there is no other *route* between heaven and earth than the Son of man.[45] I would suggest, however, that the meaning is that Jesus is the *place* where heaven and earth, God and humankind, meet. The angels ascend from and descend to the Son of man because he is now the touchstone on earth where the heavenly and earthly realms come together. Jesus is the Christian's Bethel.[46] This not only comports with the earlier incarnational themes in this chapter, but it also prepares for the discussion about Jesus' being the temple of God in chap. 2. In Jesus, not in the Temple, one finds the presence of God perfectly joined together with a human being. In such a context, worship need no longer be place-centered or dependent on locale, but rather person-centered, a worshiping in Spirit and truth wherever one may be, not necessarily on this or that holy mountain (John 4:20ff.).[47]

Jacob concluded, "How awesome is this place! This is none other than the house of God, and this is the gate of heaven" (Gen. 28:17), and the Johannine response to that is "How awesome is this person, who is the locus not only of God's revelation but also of God's presence on earth." The focus in this chapter is not on the function of Jesus for believers, but on the person, character, and true nature of the Christ who is also Son of man. Thus the second act of this initial part of the drama, which forms a bridge for the hearer between the prologue and the account of Jesus' public ministry (which begins in John 2:13ff.), ends with a dramatic proclamation about the character of Jesus. The prologue had ended by telling us that the Word became flesh. The testimony of John had ended by informing us that "this is the Son of God," and now the second act of the cloud of witnesses drama ends with the pronouncement about the Son of man.

II. Bridging the Horizons

In so many ways, the Fourth Gospel is an exercise in hermeneutics, the science of the interpretation and application of a foundational narrative, the taking of the story of Jesus and putting it into a language and form of narrative that will convey the significance and meaning of the Christ event for a new and different audience. It is not just a presentation of the facts about the life of Jesus, but a meditation on the meaning and application of those facts. It is easy for a person who studies all the Gospels to get confused and even lost in the maze of details, especially when there are obvious differences in the accounts. This often leads more conservative Christians to various sorts of false harmonizations that do justice to neither the differing texts of the Gospels nor their authors' intents and purposes. Each Gospel, and all the details in it, must be evaluated in light of the overall purpose and genre of each document as a whole. If the author's purpose is *simply* to convey some historical data, his data may be evaluated at that level. But, in fact, all the evangelists come at their historical data and sacred traditions with more than just historical agendas in mind. No document that says it is written "in order that you might believe that Jesus is the Christ" has *purely* historical aims, and the document should not be assessed as if it did. John's Gospel especially is as much proclamation, presenting a certain slant on the facts, as it is information. We do this Gospel no justice, then, if we read it as if it were of the exact same ilk as the six-o'clock news.

If we are to bridge the two horizons, we must realize that we live with a post-Enlightenment worldview of history and the cosmos dominating our thinking, which is very different from the worldview reflected in these Gospels. The modern worldview has little if any room for the supernatural, for miracles, or for the intrusion of angels, much less of God in person, into the flow of historical events. Too often we come to the text with certain modern urgencies and expectations, and accordingly interpret the text in a way that distorts the text's meaning and purpose.

A good example of this tendency is to note how those who have not studied the Gospels in light of ancient literary conventions, and especially the techniques of ancient biographies, handle the presentation of the way Jesus gained his first disciples in the Fourth Gospel as it differs from that in the Synoptics. The tendency is to ignore that the Synoptics present stories that are call narratives in form, while John offers quest stories, or to deny that there are really any significant differences in the telling of the stories. Perhaps the favorite harmonization is to argue that the disciples first sought out Jesus, then returned to Galilee, where Jesus called them to discipleship when he toured the Sea of Galilee at a later date.[48] The important thing to say about this reconstruction is that it is something that not a single Gospel suggests. The original hearers of Mark would never have guessed this to be true, nor would the readers or hearers of John. It is only when the Gospels began to be read together or by the same audience that such questions and suggestions would have arisen.

Yet surely the Fourth Evangelist has edited his material in such a way that it furthers his missionary purposes. In his view, this would not amount to a distorting of the historical data but would be rather a using of it in an appropriate rhetorical way to elicit a positive response from his target audience, by conveying certain theological, ethical, and social implications of the historical data. The almost telegraphic or bare-bones form of these narratives about the coming of the first disciples to Jesus shows that the author is much more interested in the significance of Jesus' having followers and their confessing him to be various things, than in the details of who joined Jesus' movement when, where, and under what circumstances. This is not to say that he has *no* interest in the historical data, but rather to make clear that for him they only serve as a starting point for reflecting on the larger significance of these events for himself and his audience.

The Fourth Gospel must be evaluated on the basis of its own terms of reference, not on ours, and this means learning about the worldviews of ancient Christians and imaginatively entering into their way of handling texts, reflecting on scripture, presenting history or theology or both. If we do not do this, instead of bridging the two horizons we will simply fuse and then confuse them, assuming that the ancient worldview and the way first-century Christians handled historical data are exactly the same as our own in the twentieth century. This will result in distortion, not illumination, of the meaning of the Fourth Gospel, which on any showing is a literary masterpiece.

What this means is that in order to properly use the Fourth Gospel, one must be prepared to do one's homework, studying ancient history, ancient literature, archaeology, and the like, or failing that, to rely on good scholarly commentaries that are conversant with the conventions, languages, and all the rest that goes into making a worldview.

I was once told by a young preacher that such detailed study of the background and foreground of the biblical text was unnecessary, since "All I need to do is step up into the pulpit and the Spirit will give me utterance." To this I somewhat abruptly replied, "It's a shame you didn't give the Spirit more to work with." One would think that especially a person who has studied the Fourth Gospel would realize that the role of the Paraclete is to illuminate those who are already pondering and meditating on the truth already given in the Jesus tradition, not to provide a substitute for careful and prayerful study of the scriptures. Christianity is a living religion, grounded in history. If we are to understand that historical foundation, historical study of the text is necessary, not optional. Another word of caution is in order: a person may be the most powerful preacher or witness in the world, testifying to all the wonderful things Jesus was and is, and yet if this person's audience is not prepared to listen, and if the Spirit is not moving, little if anything is likely to happen. Good technique, even with good material to proclaim, will not necessarily result in new creatures in Christ. This sobering fact should be sufficient to keep any witness for Christ humble, lest we think we are somehow indispensable. Furthermore, lest we get too excited about initial positive response to the Gospel, Jesus in this very chapter says to Nathanael, You haven't seen anything yet. Chapter 1 of the Fourth Gospel is but a preview of coming attractions. It should be treated as such.

3. The New Wine of the Gospel (John 2:1–12)

The presentation of the story of Jesus between the time of his appearance on earth and his public ministry, a time in which he meets and manifests himself to his disciples, is brought to a climax in John 2:1–12. Jesus attends a private affair, a wedding in Cana of Galilee at which his mother is present. Jesus' mother is never called Mary in this Gospel. The evangelist calls her "the mother of Jesus," indicating that her main significance in the story has to do with her unique relationship to Jesus (cf. John 2:1; 19:25–26), and Jesus always calls her "woman" (*gynai*; John 2:4; 19:26), *not* mother. We will shortly offer one possible explanation of why this is, but for now we will note that Mary plays no active role in the story of the ministry itself in this Gospel; her appearances frame the ministry, and this is not likely accidental. Jesus' ministry is not a family matter; indeed it is a matter in which Jesus must disengage himself from his physical family and any parental authority Mary may have over him, in order to establish the family of faith. The only parent to whom Jesus is subordinate in this Gospel is his Father in heaven, whose will he must and does follow in detail.

This passage also continues the trend of presenting Jesus as Wisdom in the flesh. As M. Scott has noted, it is Wisdom who offers a banquet imploring "Come, eat my food and drink the wine I have mixed" (Prov. 9:5).[1] Yet Jesus even surpasses this appeal by offering wine unmixed with water, wine *instead of* water. Another text of some relevance is Sir. 24:21, where Wisdom (as Torah) says, "Whoever drinks from me will thirst for more." As we shall see in John 4, Jesus as Wisdom surpasses the claim of the wisdom tradition about Torah, for he says, "Those who drink of the water that I will give will never thirst again" (John 4:14). The point of this portrayal of Jesus as Wisdom is then at least in part to suggest that what one might look for in Judaism, including in Torah/wisdom, one can find in Jesus, and in the finding discover that he surpasses claims about other sources or sorts of wisdom.[2]

2:1   On the third day there was a wedding in Cana of Galilee, and the mother of Jesus was there. [2]Jesus and his disciples had also been invited to the wedding. [3]When the wine gave out, the mother of Jesus said to him, "They have no wine." [4]And Jesus said to her, "Woman, what concern is that to you and to me? My hour has not yet come." [5]His mother said to the servants, "Do whatever he tells you." [6]Now standing there were six stone water jars for the Jewish rites of purification, each holding twenty or thirty gallons. [7]Jesus said to them, "Fill the jars with water." And they filled them up to the brim. [8]He said to them, "Now draw some out, and take it to the chief steward." So they took it. [9]When the steward tasted the water that had become wine, and did not know where it came from (though the servants who had drawn the water knew), the steward called the bridegroom [10]and said to him, "Everyone serves the good wine first, and then the inferior wine after the guests have become drunk. But you have kept the good wine until now." [11]Jesus did this, the first of his signs, in Cana of Galilee, and revealed his glory; and his disciples believed in him.

12 After this he went down to Capernaum with his mother, his brothers, and his disciples; and they remained there a few days.

I. The Historical Horizon

Besides the reference to the third day in 2:1, one thing that closely links this story to what immediately precedes it is the twofold reference to the disciples in 2:2 and 2:11. Jesus had promised Nathanael as a fledgling disciple that he would see greater things, and this promise is immediately fulfilled in part in 2:1–12.[3] Interestingly, the appendix in John 21:2 tells us that Nathanael was from Cana in Galilee; thus there may be a closer connection between the second and third acts of this first part of the drama than is usually thought. Perhaps we are meant to think of this wedding as being an event in Nathanael's family. This is possible but unprovable; it may in any case explain why we have two stories about Jesus visiting Cana in the Fourth Gospel (cf. John 4:46–54) and none in the Synoptics, just as we have no reference to Nathanael in the Synoptics.[4] Perhaps Nathanael was the ultimate source of these rather unique Cana traditions, which he passed along to the Beloved Disciple (if the latter was not present on that occasion).

Though Painter has seen this story as a quest story, it might be better called a request story, for Mary is not after Jesus, but after obtaining something from Jesus.[5] Yet in another sense this story is at least a prelude to a quest, for Mary's story is taken up again in 19:25–27, and there she is finally seen as a disciple ushered into the family of faith.

The historicity of this story has been long debated by scholars, not least because this miracle seems gratuitous, but I have elsewhere shown reasons why it is likely an authentic Jesus story, especially because of the potentially negative light in which it may cast Mary.[6] Nevertheless, the Fourth Evangelist has written up this first miracle narrative, the first of Jesus' "signs," in such a way that its similarity to Hellenistic miracle material is rather clear. Here Jesus appears as one greater than any Bacchus, due to the quantity of wine he produces.[7] I would suggest that there are two reasons for this way of framing the story of the miracle: (1) the evangelist is producing a document for missionary use in Asia Minor and (2) a goodly portion of his potential audience for this story is Gentiles. With this story we begin to see the subtlety of the art of the Fourth Evangelist, for the story works on two levels. There is the historical one, certainly, but the story has been told because it aptly displays the theological and social significance of Jesus—he is the one who brings the new wine of the Gospel, which eclipses and makes obsolete previous sources of life and health such as Jewish purification water. The miracle itself *would* be gratuitous, if it did not have this larger emblematic quality, for the Fourth Evangelist is clearly very selective in the miracles of Jesus he chooses to present (cf. John 20:30). It is also part of the evangelist's agenda to present the faith that is centered on Jesus as a more powerful, life-giving, and universally accessible faith than Judaism, but also, in this story, as more powerful and life-giving than any pagan religion such as the Dionysian rites.

Something should perhaps be said at this juncture about Jewish weddings in Jesus' day. What we need to know for our purposes is simply the following: (1) Such wedding parties could go on for days, and thus running out of wine must surely have been a rather frequent occurrence; (2) there were already in Jesus' day caterers who could have provided more wine should the wine run out, and thus Jesus' act was presumably not absolutely necessary to prevent the wedding party from fizzling;[8] (3) the beverage in question here is wine, which was the normal table beverage in the Greco-Roman world and was alcoholic, though it was customary in many contexts to dilute it with water in order to be able to consume more of it;[9] (4) it was customary to serve the best wine first, before the guests were too inebriated to appreciate the vintage.

The saying in v. 10b, however, is meant to work on two levels—just as the best wine has been served last at this banquet, so God's most powerful and life-giving force has only been unveiled at the end of the age; after all, the Old Testament prophets had already come on the stage. The wedding, including a meal with wine, was a normal image of eschatological fellowship in early Judaism (cf. Matt. 25:1–13; Mark 14:25; Luke 14:15–24, and par.), and it is intimated in John 2 that the eschatological age has already arrived with the appearance of Jesus on the human scene.[10] God has saved the best revelation, the most life-giving One, for last. It is for this reason that the evangelist concludes the discussion by saying that Jesus "revealed his glory" (v. 11). The very presence of God has now appeared on the human stage, which signals the climax or end of the human drama of redemption, the coming of the messianic age of miracles and blessing for God's people.[11]

We must focus at this point on the heart of this story, which is the dialogue between Jesus and Mary, which is not coincidentally the heart of the only other scene in this Gospel with these two characters, in John 19. In both episodes, Jesus addresses Mary as *gynai* and does something of benefit to or for her.

Verse 4 in both its parts is difficult on any showing. Should we take 4b as a statement ("My hour has not yet come") or a question ("Has my hour not come?")? How are we to translate v. 4a: (1) "What is that to me and you?"[12] (2) "What do you have to do with me?" (3) or more loosely, "Why do you involve me in this affair?"? It would appear that neither Mary nor Jesus had any obligation in this matter, since it is the bridegroom who is commended when the new wine is sampled (2:9–10).[13] It is possible to read 4a as a

Semitism, meaning something like "That is your business; do not involve me," but then that makes nearly inexplicable what follows, since Jesus seems to act on the basis of Mary's request. The most probable explanation, especially in view of 4b, is that translation 2 above is close to the mark. Jesus is disengaging, not from the need Mary is referring to but from Mary's authority over him. Implicit in her statement was an imperative—"Do something." Jesus responds in a way that distances him from Mary's authority, but does not reject the need. "Jesus' heavenly Father, not his earthly mother, must determine when his hour is to come and what he is to do until then."[14] Throughout this Gospel, Jesus acts only when the Father gives him the go-ahead.

In view of what has just been said, it may be best to take 4b as a question: "Has not my hour already come?"[15] In this case, then, "hour" would mean Jesus' time to go out into the world and begin his ministry and be independent of his mother's authority.[16] There is a focus in this Gospel on Jesus' time—the time for decisive action that manifests Christ's glory and fulfills God's will.

Verse 4a, then, is to be seen as a gentle rebuke, not an irretrievable rejection. Jesus shows respect by using the term *gynai,* but this also distances him from his mother and her authority. This is the way he respectfully addresses other women in this and other Gospels (cf. John 4:21; 20:13; Matt. 15:18; Luke 13:12). There are, however, *no known examples* of a son's using such a term to address his mother, and so this vocative must have more significance than it would when, for instance, Jesus used it to address Mary Magdalene.

If on the other hand one takes v. 4b as a statement, as in the translation above, then the point would seem to be that Jesus cannot act on behalf of his mother until his hour has come, until his death on the cross. In any case, 2:5 surely implies that Mary already had some knowledge of and confidence in Jesus' remarkable powers, and yet Jesus' response makes clear that she does not yet fully understand about Jesus' mission and "hour." She too is depicted as a person on the road to full comprehension and full discipleship. As "woman," Mary must work out the tensions between the physical family, from which Jesus is disentangling himself (cf. John 7:1–5), and the family of faith. Mary will later enter the family of faith at the cross, as an archetypal female disciple, as "woman," but not on the basis of being Jesus' mother.[17]

In terms of the christological significance of this story, the focus is on the deed of Jesus, which manifests his divine power and presence. The center of the story in terms of action is obviously the turning of water into wine, which serves as an invitation to faith for the audience.[18] The disciples are depicted as responding with faith in Jesus of some degree or sort (v. 11). As a sign narrative it requires a symbolic interpretation, for the function of a sign is to point away from itself to some larger reality of which it is but a symbol or representation. This sign is said to reveal Jesus' glory, that is, that God's life-giving and joyful presence can be found in him.

There are, in fact, several hints in the story that the story is supposed to be symbolic: (1) the wedding setting; (2) the huge volume of water; (3) the explicit reference to the Jewish purification water jars. The mention of the latter makes clear that the author wishes to intimate that Jesus replaces the rituals and institutions of early Judaism with something more life-giving and enduring. This will prove to be a major theme throughout this Gospel.

"This miracle, so different from those that were to come, resembles them in the most important point, for it too suggests by its very nature, the *kind* of faith it is designed to inspire: a faith of fulfilment and of transformation, of joy and celebration. Linked deliberately to the accounts of the testimony and the Discovery ('on the third day'), it completes the triptych with a symbolic affirmation that 'the old order changeth, yielding place to the new.'"[19]

The final verse of this subsection, v. 12, is in fact a transitional verse indicating we are still in the transitional period when Jesus is still with his physical family, yet already has disciples. What is intriguing about this verse is the reference to going to Capernaum, which in the Synoptics is said to be Jesus' home base during the Galilean ministry (cf. Mark 2:1). If we put this reference together with the reference to Jesus' operating with the Baptist, it appears that we are meant to think the evangelist is telling us that the transitional period for Jesus involved his operating in the presence of family, as in John 2, or friends such as the Baptist, as in John 1 and 3, before striking out on his own. This is historically very likely, and reminds us that Jesus and his ministry grew and developed over the course of time.

II. Bridging the Horizons

The following words of caution must be offered in the use of this text today. First, Jesus is not still on the earth performing signs, and there is no inspired Fourth Evangelist roaming around to give us the absolutely accurate interpretation of whatever miracles happen today. This means that miracles can at most bear some witness today, but they cannot be made to bear the whole weight of a proper witness. If this Gospel is any guide, even in the Fourth Evangelist's day signs *and* discourses, actions and words, were both needed to witness adequately to Jesus.

Second, this text, when combined with others, makes abundantly clear that Jesus was no teetotaler, or advocate of such a position. Indeed, there was a reason that he got the reputation of sharing wine with and being a friend of "sinners" (Luke 7:34 and par.)—the reason was because it was true.[20] Jesus was no killjoy, nor was he antisocial. When he was asked why his disciples didn't fast, his response was in essence that his presence should be cause for celebration, not ascetical practices (Mark 2:18–20).[21]

While there are many virtues in abstaining from alcohol, and in some cases total abstinence is not merely salutary but necessary, since one can become addicted to alcohol as one can to any other drug, the Bible cannot be made to say that the only possible Christian position on this issue is total abstinence. In North America, total abstinence is a position that arose out of all the problems created by excessive drinking in the nineteenth century, which led to the rise of various temperance movements. In the ancient world wine was drunk instead of water at most every meal, including ritual meals like Passover, and Jesus participated in such meals (see, e.g., the Last Supper). I bring this up for only one reason—not to be an advocate for imbibing wine, but because if one is going to be committed to the truth of God's Word, one must be honest about what God's Word does and does not say.[22]

A third caution in the use of this text is that one must beware of reading it in isolation, not only from the later texts that indicate that the disciples did not yet have full Christian faith during the ministry of Jesus, but also from John 19, which indicates that only later did Mary become a full-fledged follower of her son. It is a mistake to read all these stories as Christian allegories. They have more historical integrity than that, for they are meant to present to seekers the stories of those who were on the way to becoming full-fledged followers of Jesus during his ministry. They are models of initial seeking and partial finding, not models of full Easter faith prior to John 19—20.

In a modern world, where miracles, to the eye of the ordinary person, seem few and far between, there is a great temptation for a minister or teacher to play up the magnitude of this miracle. This approach seems to be based on the assumption that a person can be astounded or impressed into the kingdom. The stupendous quantity of water turned into wine in this story could be said to encourage such an approach—revealing Jesus' stupendous power. It is worth noting, however, that while the Fourth Evangelist again and again stresses the magnitude of Jesus' signs, he shows little or no interest in dwelling on *how* the miracle took place or was accomplished. We are simply told of the outcome, not about the means. The evangelist is not really interested in the miracle for its own sake, or as a historical curiosity, but because of what it reveals about the character of Jesus. In other words, the main value of these miracles is not intrinsic, but lies in what and to whom they point. A belief in miracles, after all, does not necessarily entail a belief in Jesus. Orthodox Muslims and Jews also believe in miracles, but this has not led them to faith in Jesus as the Son of God. Thus, a Christian must be careful how and in what way he or she uses the appeal to miracles to lead someone to Christ. The appeal may prove ineffective, or at least prove less than what the one doing the evangelizing may desire.

The argument for the divinity of Christ has often gone rather like this: (1) Jesus did stupendous miracles; (2) only someone with God's own power can do such things; (3) Jesus must be God. This argument has a significant flaw in it, as any careful reader of the scriptures will know. Elijah and others before Jesus also performed stupendous miracles, including raising the dead, and Peter and others did so after Jesus. While these miracles certainly bear testimony to the working of God's power through these human agents, they do not provide clear demonstration of divinity—otherwise Elijah, Peter, and others must be counted as divine.

This Gospel, while not belittling the power of mighty works to point to the real character of Jesus, also makes clear that the appeal to miracles is insufficient as proof of who Jesus is, and can even at times be misleading. It may encourage the audience to assume that unless they see such things they are not required to believe. Remember that this Gospel near its close has the benediction "Blessed are those who have not seen [Jesus or his signs or other deeds], and yet have come to believe" (John 20:28). It would be accurate to say that the Fourth Gospel's message is that believing leads to (spiritual) sight and insight, but physical sight does not necessarily lead to faith. A person without faith will normally interpret even a miracle within his or her own preexisting frame of reference. The defensive remark "I would believe in Jesus if you could only show me a miracle" most often reveals an attitude of a person not yet willing to step out on faith. Thus, the miracle at Cana should be appropriated now, as it was appropriated then, in the process of witnessing—as a sign and symbol of something and someone greater than itself, not as an end in itself. The goal is not to lead someone to a faith in the power and possibility of miracles, but to lead them to faith in Christ.

Fred Craddock has put it aptly: "This Gospel is full of accounts of those who believe he worked the signs but who did not believe in him as the revealing Son of God.... As significant as signs are in this Gospel, they are not simply presented as miracle stories to be investigated. Perhaps this is why details are so lacking. As signs these acts of Jesus are to function as windows rather than ornaments. Seekers after miracles usually need *one more* to be fully persuaded, all the while missing the signs along the way."[23]

The miracle found in this story has been called a nature miracle, and as such is not unlike the multiplication of the loaves and fish (cf. below on John 6). It demonstrates that the "all-creating Word cannot be held ransom by the constraints of his own creation. 'The modest water saw its God and blushed.'"[24]

Part II. The Public Ministry of Jesus: Phase One (John 2:13–4:54)

4. Cleaning House (John 2:13–25)

In chap. 2 the literary skill of the evangelist is quite evident, especially when one considers how the two stories told in this chapter are similarly shaped. "Both the wedding story and the temple cleansing are revelation events (manifest the glory of the Son); both are third day stories (resurrection symbolism); both focus upon a sign; both carry a polemic against religion centering upon ceremonies (water of purification in one, temple rites in the other); in neither does being present suffice to generate faith in Jesus; both conclude with references to disciples believing. But the differences between the two [are crucial]—In Galilee is the wedding; in Judea is the funeral ('Destroy this temple')."[1]

It is possible to see this as a quest story—Jesus is attempting to discover if true worship and worshipers can still be found at the heart of Judaism during one of its high and holy feasts.[2] It is also important to note the self-contained nature of this story despite its connections with what precedes: like a scene in a play, it has a beginning, middle, and end, though the conclusion, like that in the first Cana, is in fact open-ended, pointing forward to the conclusion of the drama in the death and resurrection of Jesus.

It is also worth noting the two-part internal structure of the cleansing story: (a) the action of Jesus, vv. 14–15; (a) the (re)action of the Jews, v. 18; (b) the words of Jesus, v. 16; (b) the enigmatic words of Jesus, v. 19; (c) the remembering of the disciples, v. 17; (c) misunderstanding by the Jews, v. 20, followed by disciples' remembering, vv. 21–22.[3] The typical intrusiveness of the evangelist can be clearly seen near the end of this passage (vv. 21–22), and once again it suggests an audience that needs the explanations of a theologically interpretative author to understand the larger significance of the story.

In regard to the basic historicity of this story, few scholars would dispute that Jesus performed some such action in the Temple at some point during his ministry, and equally few would suggest he did it twice.[4] Strongly favoring the basic historical character of this story is that: (1) the early church in Jerusalem was still involved in Temple worship prior to A.D. 70 (cf. Acts 2:46) and would have been unlikely to invent a story about Jesus taking action against the Temple; and (2) temples of all sorts were protected by the Romans, especially because sacrifices on behalf of the emperor were offered in them, even in the Jerusalem Temple, and Christians who wished to appeal to a Gentile audience or make clear that Christianity was no threat to the empire would hardly have concocted a story like this.

It is important to note that *no* Gospel suggests more than one cleansing of the Temple, and there are very plausible reasons for arguing that the placement of this episode in John is due to theological, not chronological considerations. First, the fact that this story follows a narrative that alludes to Jewish purification procedures is not likely accidental, especially in view of the other parallels already noted above between these two narratives.

Second, the story preserves the only record of a saying of Jesus (v. 19) that seems to have led to the charges made against Jesus at his Jewish trial (Mark 14:58 and par.), charges that are made in the context of the cleansing of the Temple during the last Passover Jesus spent in Jerusalem. Third, the action taken and the reporting of it in the Synoptics and John are far too similar, even down to some details, for it to be likely that the Johannine account is a record of a separate occurrence. Fourth, if in fact Jesus had taken such an action at the beginning of his ministry, it is hard to doubt that there would have been some sort of legal investigation of the matter, and Jesus would hardly have been welcome in the Temple precincts or even in Jerusalem thereafter.[5] I thus conclude that this story is placed here because it shows Jesus revealing himself at the very heart of Judaism, in the Temple, and revealing that Judaism's institutions needed a major reformation. This story also furthers the theme, already noted in this Gospel, of Jesus fulfilling, and thus in essence making obsolescent, the ritual institutions of early Judaism.[6]

2:13   The Passover of the Jews was near, and Jesus went up to Jerusalem. [14]In the temple he found people selling cattle, sheep, and doves, and the money changers seated at their tables. [15]Making a whip of cords, he drove all of them out of the temple, both the sheep and the cattle. He also poured out the coins of the money changers and overturned their tables. [16]He told those who were selling the doves, "Take these things out of here! Stop making my Father's house a marketplace!" [17]His disciples remembered that it was written, "Zeal for your house will consume me." [18]The Jews then said to him, "What sign can you show us for doing this?" [19]Jesus answered them, "Destroy this temple, and in three days I will raise it up." [20]The Jews then said, "This temple has been under construction for forty-six years, and will you raise it up in three days?" [21]But he was speaking of the temple of his body. [22]After he was raised from the dead, his disciples remembered that he had said this; and they believed the scripture and the word that Jesus had spoken.

23   When he was in Jerusalem during the Passover festival, many believed in his name because they saw the signs that he was doing. [24]But Jesus on his part would not entrust himself to them, because he knew all people [25]and needed no one to testify about anyone; for he himself knew what was in everyone.

I. The Historical Horizon

The passage begins with a reference to "the Passover of the Jews," a phrase that also occurs in 6:4 and 11:55 and strongly suggests: (1) a certain distance between the author and Judaism, and perhaps also (2) that the audience, being at least partly Gentile, might require some such explanation or reminder that this was a Jewish festival.[7] It may also suggest that the group the Fourth Evangelist is a part of no longer celebrates such a festival.[8]

We are not told when Jesus went to this festival, for the time connection between this event and the previous one in chap. 2 is conspicuously absent, another small piece of evidence that this story has likely been placed here for other than chronological concerns. If we do *not* count this story as a record of a Passover separate from the last one Jesus attended in Jerusalem, there is still a reference to Jesus' ministry's continuing through at least two Passover seasons (cf. 6:4; 11:55; 12:1), a fact that strongly supports the suggestion that Jesus' public ministry lasted longer than a year. Another factor that may support such a view is the reference in 2:20 to the Herodian Temple taking forty-six years to build, which, if one begins with the usual chronology of the eighteenth year of Herod the Great's reign,[9] means that the Temple construction began about 20–19 B.C., and forty-six years would bring us to A.D. 27–28.[10] If however we are meant to think of a Passover early in Jesus' ministry, this might suggest a three-year ministry period, but if this is an allusion to the time when Jesus had his final confrontation with the Jewish authorities in Jerusalem, this would put Jesus' death at a somewhat earlier date than the Synoptic chronology suggests (ca. A.D. 30). In any case, this Gospel, because of its mention of multiple Passovers attended by Jesus, bears strong witness to Jesus' ministry lasting longer than a year's time.

Two features that distinguish the Johannine account from the Synoptic ones are the reference to sheep and oxen and the reference to Jesus making a whip out of cords, in other words using a *flagellum*.[11] This last feature is not insignificant, since the gender of the word "all" (*pantas,* masculine) likely suggests Jesus was driving people as well as animals out of the Court of the Gentiles with this whip. Whatever else this story may say to us, it suggests that Jesus was not above using some force on occasion, apparently even against human beings, when the cause was just.

It will be noted, however, that Jesus takes action only against the sellers, not the buyers.[12] Jesus' anger is kindled against the various economic operations in the Temple precincts, including both the selling of sacrificial animals and the exchanging of money to pay the Temple tax.[13] Jesus did not believe in turning his Father's house into a marketplace, and there is evidence that at least the selling and buying of sacrificial animals in the precincts was not a practice of long standing. In any case, sacrificial animals could be bought on the Mount of Olives outside the Temple walls.[14]

The question then becomes, what sort of action are we to think was taken by Jesus in the Temple? In view of the fact that the outer court of the Temple was some 300 meters wide by 450 in length, and served as the marketplace for Jerusalem in various respects, it is unlikely that Jesus drove *everyone* out of the Temple court.[15] Much more likely is the suggestion that this was a limited action, meant in the main to be symbolic in character, demonstrating the need for the cleansing of the Temple. Notice that in 2:16 Jesus is not said to drive out the sellers of doves, but rather orders them to voluntarily take their wares away.

In 2:17 we have the first reference to the disciples "remembering," in this case remembering the words of scripture: "Zeal for your house will consume me." The quotation is taken from the Greek translation of the Old Testament (the LXX), from Ps. 69:9, *except* that the tense of the verb has been changed from past tense ("has consumed") to the future ("will consume"). Perhaps this is because there is an allusion here to Jesus' death. This death seems in part to have been precipitated by Jesus' zeal for and action in his Father's house, as the synoptics make clear. This conjecture becomes all the more likely when we notice that in 2:19ff. there is a clear reference to Jesus' death. This act of "remembering" likely transpired after Easter,[16] and reflects the Christian belief that all Jesus' actions, including the more controversial ones, were a fulfillment of scripture. For our purposes what is crucial is that Jesus' action and this reference to his zeal suggest not only that Jesus was attempting a radical reformation of Judaism, even at the heart of her faith, but also that his actions, including perhaps particularly the action in the Temple, were perceived as a serious threat to the status quo; this is what in the main led to the trial and execution of Jesus.

If this evaluation is correct and is how the Fourth Evangelist understood the matter, then we now see another reason why the cleansing story is found at the beginning of the ministry. The evangelist wants the audience to read the whole story of the ministry in light of the event that most led to Jesus' death, the cleansing of the Temple. With this story set out at the beginning as the revelation of Jesus' essential ministry aims and of his character as the locus of the presence of God on earth, the evangelist can then be justified in presenting the story of the ministry, especially from chap. 5 onward, as the story of an investigation, leading to a legal procedure, a trial, and execution, as Harvey has rightly argued.[17] Seen in this light, various of Jesus' actions from John 3 on are taken as further provocations precipitating confrontations between "the Jews" (the Jewish authorities) and Jesus. One of the driving passions of this evangelist is to present the course of events that led to Jesus' death in such a light that they will be seen from a human point of view to exonerate Jesus and his followers of any wrongdoing, and to convict their adversaries. The apologetic purposes of this Gospel, defending Jesus, must not be overlooked, as they would naturally have to be part of any public witness in the Greco-Roman world, in view of the fact that Jesus died by crucifixion.[18]

Jesus' action prompts an immediate response from "the Jews" in v. 18, surely a reference here to the Temple authorities. They ask, "What sign can you show us for doing this?" Here the word sign (*semeion*) has the sense of a validating action or miracle, providing evidence of one's divine authority and power to act the way Jesus had acted.[19] This request grows out of the teachings in Deut. 13:1–5 and 18:20–22 about testing prophets. But instead of performing a miraculous validating "sign" on the spot, Jesus offers a *mashal*, or figurative saying, in this case in the form of a riddle: "[You] destroy this temple, and in three days I will raise it up." Here, as so often in this Gospel, we have irony, the saying of one thing and meaning another; or to put it in a different way, we have a two-level conversation—Jesus is speaking on one plane, but it is being understood only at a much more mundane level (cf. 4:32–33). This reveals not only the depth of Jesus' sapiential speech, but the shallowness of the interlocutors in the text.

The form of Jesus' reply reveals Jesus to be a sage, offering riddles instead of clear speech in response to a confrontational audience. The use of wisdom speech in public, especially with outsiders, is also said to be typical of Jesus' modus operandi in Mark 4:11, and we may be reasonably certain that this did indeed characterize Jesus' public speaking. He often spoke in a metaphorical way, and probably did so for a variety of reasons. For one, he spoke in this way in order to force the audience into active contemplation and reevaluation of their presuppositions about God, the kingdom, messiah, and a host of other subjects. This can be seen in the Fourth Gospel even though it does not record a collection of parables like the Synoptics. Another possible reason for such speech patterns is that this method revealed to the audience their own lack of understanding. Finally, this sort of way of speaking, which was not novel but rather characteristic of Jewish sages,[20] prevented those who were hostile to Jesus from truly understanding him and thus having clear grounds for taking action against him prior to the time when Jesus decided to force the issue.

The evangelist clarifies Jesus' meaning in 2:21—Jesus was referring to his own body. The point then becomes that Jesus, not the Herodian Temple, is the locale of God's presence among God's people, and consequently an attack on Jesus will be an attack on God's presence on earth. Another reference to the disciples' remembering occurs at 2:22–23, but this time it explicitly tells us the remembering took place after Easter, and involved not only scripture, but the remembering of the words of Jesus. Here we have a telltale sign that Jesus' words were treasured along with scripture as something sacred—to be remembered, passed down, and meditated on. Remembering here is said to lead to believing, not only in the scriptures, but in the words Jesus spoke. As we shall see, this evangelist conceives of the community of Jesus' followers as a community grounded in historical memory, for it is remembering the story and sayings that prompts and nourishes faith.[21] In the 90s already, the Christian community had become a community of the Word, and so hearing rather than seeing was already primary then, as it is now (cf. John 20:29). Faith does not require seeing, but it does require hearing and understanding.

There are, however, different degrees and sorts of faith, and 2:23–25 speaks of those who *trusted* in Jesus' name because they *saw* the signs he was doing. Still, Jesus did not *entrust* himself into their hands because he knew what was in their hearts.[22] They were by no means manifesting an adequate or full faith in Jesus. The stress on a belief based on the seeing of miracles or signs would perhaps in particular be a criticism of the attitude of non-Christian Jews, who as Paul says demanded signs (1 Cor. 1:22).

Such a faith is not completely rejected (cf. 10:32–38); it is simply inadequate and can lead to misunderstanding of Jesus' purposes and character.

In any event, it is clear that the public response to Jesus in Jerusalem, whether of the Jewish authorities or of the people, is not viewed as positive. Only the disciples are depicted as models here, and even in their case it is made clear that they did not understand at first, but only after Jesus' resurrection.

II. Bridging the Horizons

This passage bristles with problems and possibilities for the person who wishes to teach or preach this material. A certain amount of understanding of the Temple procedures and practices of Jesus' day is necessary for a contemporary audience to make sense of this material. For instance, it cannot be stressed enough that the heart of ancient religion was animal sacrifice, which in turn meant the availability of animals for such practices in reasonable proximity to the Temple. Thus one must raise the question here whether Jesus is attacking the sacrificial system of worship per se, or merely the matter of where the economic transactions were taking place. It appears to be the latter, in which case this text does not provide a warrant for long harangues about God's desiring mercy *rather* than sacrifice, now that Jesus has arrived on the scene.[23] Indeed, since the evangelist will go on to portray Jesus as the ultimate and definitive Passover sacrifice that was necessary for redemption, it can hardly be argued that he or Jesus had an antisacrificial agenda. It is just that Jesus' sacrifice is seen as eclipsing all previous sacrifices and rendering unnecessary all future ones. Sacrificial death was as much at the heart of early Christianity as it was at the heart of early Judaism, however squeamish that may make a modern audience.

It might be useful, then, to spend some time depicting what actually went on in the Temple precincts and was considered an act of worship—from the slaughtering of the animal, to the pouring out of the blood and its sprinkling in the appropriate places, to the burning of the carcass, to the eating of sacrificial meat in some types of sacrifices that didn't involve whole burnt offerings. Whatever else one may say, this sort of worship could scarcely ever have suffered from being dull. The noises and smells alone would have kept most anyone awake. If this sort of worship seems alien to us, it reminds us of what a great distance there is between our culture and that of Bible times, and thus of the need for building bridges if modern people are to relate to this story.

One possible way of building bridges would be to talk about religious zeal then and now, and the sorts of actions it prompts. Most people living in the West today have both a fear and a loathing of what are commonly called "religious fanatics." They prefer their religion in measured, small doses that do not cause people to take leave of their "common sense." They prefer being innoculated with a slight case of Christianity, or some other faith, which in effect prevents them from catching the real thing. One may wish to ask, Is this the sort of religion Jesus had in mind when he began his religious movement? I personally doubt it. Jesus' own faith, and that which he sought to inculcate, involved a burning passion for what was right and true and honored God.

It is for this reason that I would caution against the all-too-common modern attempt to domesticate this text and try to contain its meaning merely to "spiritual" rather than also to "social" matters. Whether we like it or not, Jesus was attempting both a spiritual and a social reform of early Judaism, a reform that affected not just hearts but also religious rites, and in this case the basic economics of Temple religion. This being the case, this text provides an opportunity to talk about the economics of modern religion and the use and abuse of property and money in the church.

5. Nicodemus and Nativities (John 3:1–21)

The Nicodemus narrative is prepared for by the transitional material in 2:23–25. Nicodemus is seen as an example of those who believed in Jesus because of his signs, and thus believed inadequately.[1] The structure of this episode in the drama is paralleled by a similar structure in the Baptist narrative that concludes the chapter, as can be seen from the following:

(1) Report* 2:23–25	(1) Report 3:22–24
(2) Dialogue 3:1–12	(2) Dialogue 3:25–30
(3) Monologue/	(3) Monologue/
Commentary 3:13–21	Commentary 3:31–36[2]

(* providing the key to the following dialogue)

This source material, then, has been very carefully crafted by the evangelist, and it will serve us well to examine the material carefully. The Nicodemus story provides us with another excellent example of a quest narrative, meant to relate to those who were religious seekers. It is in various regards like the story of the quest of the rich young ruler in the Synoptics (Mark 10:17–22 and par.),[3] except that the quest of Nicodemus is left open-ended, and he will appear again in the narrative at various junctures (7:45–52; 12:42–43; 19:38–42). One suspects Nicodemus gets the play he does in the story because he strongly resembles and thus represents a certain type of person in the Jewish community to whom Johannine Christians are being called on to bear witness. The usefulness of this material for missionary or evangelistic purposes does not need to be belabored. That it is intended for such purposes becomes evident at 3:7, where Jesus says, "You [plural] must be born anew," making clear that Nicodemus is being addressed as an example of a particular type of potential convert. The audience of the Gospel are meant to see themselves as addressed by this imperative.[4]

What is striking about the characterization of Nicodemus is that though he actually appears in only seventeen verses in this Gospel, and speaks only sixty-three words, we feel we know him rather well, and apparently the audience is meant to develop a certain sense of kinship or identity with him. As A. Culpepper says,

> He is both individual and representative, a foil and a character with conflicting inclinations with which the reader can identify. . . . His confession . . . is perceptive and entirely proper so far as it goes: "You are a teacher

come from God." . . . The alert reader, however, will not expect too much of him: Jesus refused to trust himself to those who believed the signs in Jerusalem (2.24), Nicodemus came to Jesus in darkness (3.2) . . . Nicodemus quickly confirms his lack of understanding by . . . assuming Jesus was speaking of birth in the most physical and literal sense. As with all of the Johannine misunderstandings, Nicodemus serves as a foil, which enables Jesus to explain his meaning . . . . Nicodemus says Jesus is "from God," but he has not grasped the full implications of the origin.[5]

What all this means is that Nicodemus should be seen as a type of the sympathetic Jewish seeker, yet one who is still "in the dark,"[6] not as someone who is already a "secret" Christian but remains in the synagogue.[7] Nicodemus is the first full-fledged example in this Gospel of the types of seekers and people in need Jesus meets, and his story is meant to be seen as an example of one who is in pilgrimage toward a full and proper faith in Jesus but has not yet arrived, as the misunderstanding shows. Nicodemus must yet be born anew to become a Christian. It is a failure to see this that has led some commentators to wrongly suppose that this and other similar quest narratives are really about secret Christians within the synagogue, who simply need to grow in Christ and perhaps be prepared to leave or be cast out of the synagogue. It is not that Nicodemus is guilty of a false faith, only that a miracle-working faith is an inadequate one. As R. Bultmann stressed, "Such faith is only the first step towards Jesus: it has not yet seen him in his true significance, and it is therefore not yet fully established."[8] The chief cause of the inadequacy is that one cannot understand or confess who Jesus truly is unless one really understands where he has come from and where he is going, as John 1 made quite clear.

I. The Historical Horizon

A. *The First Dialogue (John 3:1–12)*

3:1 Now there was a Pharisee named Nicodemus, a leader of the Jews. [2]He came to Jesus by night and said to him, "Rabbi, we know that you are a teacher who has come from God; for no one can do these signs that you do apart from the presence of God." [3]Jesus answered him, "Very truly, I tell you, no one can see the kingdom of God without being born from above." [4]Nicodemus said to him, "How can anyone be born after having grown old? Can one enter a second time into the mother's womb and be born?" [5]Jesus answered, "Very truly, I tell you, no one can enter the kingdom of God without being born of water and Spirit. [6]What is born of the flesh is flesh, and what is born of the Spirit is spirit. [7]Do not be astonished that I said to you, 'You must be born from above.' [8]The wind blows where it chooses, and you hear the sound of it, but you do not know where it comes from or where it goes. So it is with everyone who is born of the Spirit." [9]Nicodemus said to him, "How can these things be?" [10]Jesus answered him, "Are you a teacher of Israel, and yet you do not understand these things?

11 "Very truly, I tell you, we speak of what we know and testify to what we have seen; yet you do not receive our testimony. [12]If I have told you about earthly things and you do not believe, how can you believe if I tell you about heavenly things?"

The name Nicodemus is Greek, adopted by Jews in the form Naqdemon.[9] It is possible that Nicodemus, besides himself being a member of the Sanhedrin, was part of an illustrious family, for later a certain Gorion, son of a Nicodemus, negotiated with the Romans for the conclusion of the Jewish war of A.D. 66–70. We are in any case told three important things about him: (1) he is a ruler of the Jews (i.e., probably a member of the Sanhedrin); (2) he is a Pharisee (who certainly believed in new life from God, but associated it with the final resurrection in the eschatological age); (3) he is a teacher. In the Greek v. 10 calls him "*the* teacher of Israel" (emphasis added), which may be meant to lead us to think he is Israel's leading sage.[10] He sees Jesus as in at least one key respect like himself, for he calls Jesus both "Rabbi" (respected one) and "teacher." But, we may ask, what sort of teacher or sage is Jesus portrayed as here? I would suggest he is portrayed as Wisdom here. For example, in Wisd. Sol. 10:9–10 it is Wisdom who rescues someone from troubles and "she guided him on straight paths; she showed him the kingdom of God, and gave him knowledge of holy things." Earlier in the same discourse on Wisdom it is not only said that people are "saved by Wisdom" (9:18), but even more strikingly we hear, "We can hardly guess at what is on earth, . . . but who has traced out what is in the heavens? Who has learned your counsel, unless you have given wisdom and sent your holy spirit from on high?" (9:16–17). Nicodemus did not know how much he was admitting to when he said that Jesus had come from God, for Jesus here and elsewhere is being portrayed as Wisdom "who formed humankind" (9:2), who "sits by your throne" (9:4), and whom God can send "forth from the holy heavens . . . for she knows and understands all things" (9:10–11). This is a dialogue between Nicodemus and God's Wisdom in the flesh. The narrative begins by telling us that Nicodemus came to visit Jesus at night. We are presumably meant to think that this occurred during Jesus' visit at Passover to Jerusalem. It is true that Jewish teachers were noted for their nocturnal study and dialogue sessions (cf. 1QS 6:7), but here, in view of the tone set in John 1, we are probably meant to think of Nicodemus coming to Jesus out of a world of spiritual and theological darkness (cf. John 9:4; 11:10; 13:30) into the presence of the true Light. About Wisdom it is said that she is "a pure emanation of the glory of the Almighty; . . . for she is a reflection of eternal light . . . and while remaining in herself, she renews all things." It is not necessary to look farther than the hellenized Jewish Wisdom material to find the primary source of the unique Johannine language and the explanation for its differences from the Synoptics.

The words "from God" in v. 2 are in an emphatic position, indicating that Nicodemus thinks highly of Jesus, perhaps seeing him as a prophet.[11]

While he understands that God is with Jesus, as is shown by the signs Jesus performs, he does not understand that Jesus is the human form that the divine Son of God sent from heaven has taken.

The discussion about birth and new birth is begun at v. 3, and much has been made of the fact that *anothen* can mean above, as well as again or anew. It does not follow from this that it means all these things in one sentence. I would suggest that we are not dealing with a double entendre or a pun here (Nicodemus thinking Jesus means born again, while Jesus means born from above),[12] but rather the characteristic Johannine problem of two levels of understanding. Both Jesus and Nicodemus are referring to being born anew or again; the problem lies not in the meaning of the word, but in what it refers to. Nicodemus assumes Jesus is referring to another physical birth by the phrase "born anew," whereas in fact Jesus is referring to a birth of a different sort, caused by the work of the Holy Spirit in someone's life. If there is a double entendre in these first twelve verses, it involves the word *pneuma*, not the word *anothen*. *Pneuma* can mean wind or spirit, just as in Hebrew *ruach* has both of these possible meanings (cf. below).

It will be worthwhile to say a few things about spiritual begetting at this point. The Jewish idea of a proselyte being like a newborn child is probably not entirely relevant, since this refers to a legal status, not a spiritual transformation.[13] The idea of spiritual rebirth, however, was very familiar in the Greco-Roman world,[14] and one may suspect that the Fourth Evangelist has couched this discussion in terms that a mixed Jewish and Gentile audience in the Diaspora could resonate with.

Reference to the dominion (or kingdom) of God is rare in this Gospel; in fact, it is found only in this passage at 3:3, 5 (but cf. 18:36), which is striking since it can be found on almost every page of the Synoptic Gospels as a phrase that characterized Jesus' speech. I have argued elsewhere that Jesus did in fact use this phrase to speak of the inbreaking saving activity of God during and through his ministry (cf. Luke 11:20/ Matt. 12:28), as well as to refer to the future eschatological realm that one could enter at the end of history.[15] Here the phrase could have either meaning, but appears to refer to a realm that can be seen as well as entered (cf. v. 5), although the parallel with Wisd. Sol. 10:10 cited above might suggest otherwise. The point here is that being born anew is the prerequisite for seeing the dominion of God.

In v. 4 Nicodemus characterizes himself as old, and intimates that Jesus is suggesting something humanly impossible—one cannot return into one's mother's womb. The mention of the womb prompts a response in vv. 5–6 by Jesus about birth out of water and out of Spirit, which has led to endless debate.

EXCURSUS: THE GOSPEL OF JOHN, SIGNS, AND SACRAMENTS

Over the course of this century a tremendous amount of ink has been spilt on the issue of whether we should read the Fourth Gospel in a sacramental or antisacramental fashion. This question usually arises when texts such as the Nicodemus story are under scrutiny. I am convinced that neither of these views nor the interpretations they have spawned does justice to this Gospel.

In the first place, the signs in this Gospel are not ritual procedures involving baptism or the Lord's Supper, but rather miracles, divine actions undertaken by Jesus that reveal something of his character and glory. The term *semeion* is not applied to ritual activities of any sort in this Gospel.

In the second place, there is a studied effort on the part of this evangelist to *avoid* talking about the possible sacramental occasions that might be seen as a basis for a sacramental theology. We have already noted[16] how the Fourth Evangelist avoids altogether mentioning or discussing Jesus' baptism by John in John 1. True enough, he is happy to mention John's baptism in general, but only as a precursor and foil for the baptism with the Spirit that will come from Jesus (see John 1:30–32). That latter Spirit baptism is linked not to any ritual activity of any sort but rather to an event, the return of Christ to heaven (cf. John 16:7).

Furthermore, when the Fourth Evangelist seems to be discussing the occasion on which the Lord's Supper took place he avoids saying anything substantive at all about the meal aspect of the supper, including omitting any comment about the significance or symbolic interpretation of the wine or bread (cf. John 13:1–12). Instead he discusses the act of foot washing as a symbol of Christ's cleansing of the disciples. It is not even clear in regard to this latter action that it is meant to be seen as an activity to be repeated, and potentially a ritual.

Then too, the "I am the bread of life" discourse of John 6 that follows the loaves and fish miracle provides no real encouragement for developing a Johannine theology of the sacraments. The sign miracle that prompted the discourse was about bread and fish, not bread and wine, as is also true of the story in the appendix in John 21:4–14. What this Gospel is interested in from first to last is the one person that all the Gospel signs and sayings point to— Jesus Christ. It does not pause more than briefly to reflect on a sign's qualities, characteristics, or elements as if it were an object that is intrinsically interesting, but focuses like a laser on the thing to which the sign points. This is shown clearly by the fact that in none of the seven sign miracles is there any real interest in describing *how* a miracle happened, only *that* it did happen and so intimated the power and glory of the one performing these signs. It is not accidental that neither Christian baptism nor the Lord's Supper is the subject of a discourse in this Gospel, even under the guise of discussing ritual washings, John's baptism, or the Passover meal.

This conclusion comports well with the general focus of this Gospel, which is christological, not ecclesiological, concentrating on Christ, not the Christian community. This is not surprising since this is a missionary document meant to focus on the substance of what one must believe in order to have life and have it abundantly. If anything can be read between the lines from an examination of the Fourth Gospel coupled with the Johannine epistles, it is this: that the Johannine community was neither a particularly sacramental nor an antisacramental group, unless one is referring to Jewish rituals, in which case those early Christians seem to have believed that they were fulfilled and so made superfluous by the coming of Christ. Rather, the Johannine community was interested in focusing on christological, not ecclesiological or sacramental matters, as is equally clear in the epistles and in the Gospel. This must be borne in mind when reading texts like John 3:1–12 or 1 John 5:6–8.

John 3:5 speaks of a birth "out of" or "from" water. As I have shown elsewhere, water was a regular metaphor for various facets of procreation—insemination, the child in the womb, childbearing, and childbirth (cf. Prov. 5:15–18; S. of Sol. 4:12–15; *m. Abot* 3:1; *3 Enoch* 6:3; 1QH 3:9–10).[17] Here birth out of water is coupled with a reference to birth out of or from Spirit. Water and Spirit are seen as the mediums or agencies through which birth comes about. The argument that because we have but one preposition (*ek*) before "water and Spirit," neither of which has the definite article, these two things must refer to one and the same birth is a possible but not compelling conclusion. In fact, in the parallel text in 1 John 5:6–8 we have articleless references to water and blood preceded by one preposition (*dia*, through), and it is very clear there that water and blood are metaphors for two *different* events. I submit that the context of John 3:5 does not favor the view that water and Spirit refer to one and the same event. Verse 6 says that flesh is born from (*ek*) flesh, and spirit (i.e., spiritual birth) is born from Spirit. This is a clear reference to two "births"—physical and spiritual birth. In other words, v. 5's mention of water and Spirit is explained in v. 6 as referring to physical and spiritual birth.[18] This being the case, John 3:5–6 tells us nothing about a view of water baptism—either John's or the Johannine community's. The issue here is physical and spiritual generation and the need for both in order to enter the kingdom of God. While there may be an antidocetic edge to this teaching, the main focus is on the need for all human beings, even Jews, indeed, even Jewish leaders and teachers, to be born again or anew. *Anothen* probably does not have the meaning "above" here, but rather "again" or "anew," for Jesus is talking about a second or new birth that is necessary, and by no means a duplicate of the first physical birth. The latter, while necessary, is no substitute for the other sort of birth. John 3:5–6 should be seen as a further development of themes already introduced in John 1:13, where physical human birth and the human decisions and activities that lead to it are *contrasted* with birth from God, just as being born of water and of Spirit are distinguished here.

Verse 7 indicates that Nicodemus is astonished by Jesus' initial response that he must be born anew. Such a birth is necessary if one is to understand where Jesus has come from and where he is going, or for that matter where the Spirit has come from and where it is leading. Verse 8 draws an analogy between the wind, which is invisible and so cannot be seen either coming or going though it can be heard, and the work of the Spirit. The analogy is apt not just because one can only detect the presence of the wind or Spirit by its respective effects, but also because in this Gospel *hearing*, not seeing, the

Word, is the prerequisite to new birth and entering the dominion of God. There is much that could be said at this point about the new birth coming from God through the Spirit and not being in any sense a human achievement. One cannot decide to be or work one's way into being born again any more than one decided to be physically born or achieved physical birth (cf. below). Everyone who is born of the Spirit has certainly heard about these things, but even then is not fully able to tell from whence the Spirit came in order to enter his or her life.

Nicodemus's only rejoinder at this point (v. 9) is, "How can these things be?" To which Jesus responds with the ironic remark, "How could you be a teacher of Israel and not understand these things?" The point here is that Nicodemus is overlooking or is ignorant of one of the most basic and fundamental truths of faith—that all life, including new spiritual life, comes from God, and that what is humanly impossible is nonetheless quite possible and even commonplace with God.

Verse 11 begins with the double Amen, often translated "Truly truly" or "Very truly." It seems to have been characteristic of Jesus to introduce important sayings of his with Amen. This also seems to have been a distinctive feature of his way of teaching, for the normal procedure was for someone else to vouch for the truth of what one had said by *responding* with an amen.[19] In typical Johannine fashion, what is always one introductory Amen in the Synoptics becomes two in the Fourth Gospel (compare Mark 14:30 to John 3:11).[20] Thereby the Fourth Evangelist makes this self-testimony to the truth of one's words very emphatic; this is characteristic of evangelistic speech patterns.

It becomes very apparent at v. 11, though it was already hinted at in v. 7, that what begins as a story about a private dialogue is used as the taking-off point for a public discussion of these fundamental matters. Thus v. 11 speaks of "our" speech and testimony, and we are meant to think not just of what Jesus once said, but of what the Johannine community continued to say to the inquiring minds of their age. Here also is the first real hint of the rejection of the testimony by Jewish rulers and authorities, and perhaps also by their counterparts in Asia Minor to whom the Johannine community had witnessed.

Verse 12 is intriguing and raises the question of what the earthly things and what the heavenly things are in this discussion. As R. E. Brown says, the simplest explanation is that the earthly things are what has already been referred to, and the heavenly things are the things about to be discussed in the following monologue and commentary.[21] Up to this juncture in the discussion Jesus has been talking about very basic spiritual things, which are in various ways analogous to earthly things—human birth, or the wind. How is one going to understand more esoteric and heavenly things, such as the Son of man's being lifted up, that have no such *simple* analogies in the material realm, if one misunderstands the basics?[22] There is an interesting rabbinic saying that is similar to what we have here. *b. Sanh.* 39a has Rabbi

Gamaliel say to the emperor: "You do not know that which is on earth. Should you know what is in heaven?"

It is of course difficult to know exactly where Jesus stops and the comment of the evangelist and his community begins, but I suspect that vv. 12–15 should be seen as transitional. More clearly, by vv. 16ff. we are hearing the voice of the evangelist commenting on the significance of Jesus' words.

B. The Monologue/Commentary (John 3:13–21)

3:13 "No one has ascended into heaven except the one who descended from heaven, the Son of Man. [14]And just as Moses lifted up the serpent in the wilderness, so must the Son of Man be lifted up, [15]that whoever believes in him may have eternal life.

16 "For God so loved the world that he gave his only Son, so that everyone who believes in him may not perish but may have eternal life.

17 "Indeed, God did not send the Son into the world to condemn the world, but in order that the world might be saved through him. [18]Those who believe in him are not condemned; but those who do not believe are condemned already, because they have not believed in the name of the only Son of God. [19]And this is the judgment, that the light has come into the world, and people loved darkness rather than light because their deeds were evil. [20]For all who do evil hate the light and do not come to the light, so that their deeds may not be exposed. [21]But those who do what is true come to the light, so that it may be clearly seen that their deeds have been done in God."

Verse 13 has been the subject of much controversy, especially when it is taken to be coming from the lips of Jesus. Why is there mention of ascending before the mention of descending, coupled with an analogy in the next verse to Moses' lifting up of the serpent in the wilderness? Perhaps the first clue to unraveling the mystery here is that while Nicodemus may have been thinking of Jesus as the expected Mosaic prophet (Deut. 18:15), Jesus does not accept such an identification. With a truly ironic twist he affirms that he is more like the snake lifted up by Moses, since he is the Son of man who must be lifted up, than he is like Moses. The bronze serpent referred to in Num. 21:8–9 was made to protect God's people from dying when they were bitten by a poisonous snake. The key ideas here are: (1) the bronze snake was lifted up on a pole so it could be easily seen; (2) those who looked on it lived. The crucial point in the analogy, then, is that for one to "live," in this case to have new life, one must "look at" the one who is lifted up—the Son of man. Jesus is one greater than Moses because of his descent and ascent; his ascent includes his death on the cross on the way back to heaven. In short, the Son of man is a divine figure who can convey life to those who "look at" him after he has been lifted up. As v. 15 puts it, he is lifted up *in order that* all those believing in him might have eternal life.

This key verse, v. 13, may in fact have a polemic edge, because it seems to be claiming that only Jesus has truly ascended into heaven, something claimed by early Jews for Moses, not only because he went up on Mount Sinai and received revelation from God, but in view of the conclusion of his life. The evangelist has just told us that Jesus is capable of revealing "heavenly things," but that Nicodemus is apparently not yet spiritually perceptive enough to receive and understand them. Verse 13 implies that the descent preceded the ascent, but the question becomes whether the ascent in view here is that of a seer or sage who, like Paul in 2 Cor. 12:1–7, is caught up into heaven and hears and sees heavenly things, or is the reference to the ascent on the cross.[23]

In view of what *precedes* in v. 12 it possible that the subject is the mystical ascent to hear things in heaven as a basis for offering revelation on earth, but in view of the echo of Wisd. Sol. 16 and the fact that the discussion moves on quickly in v. 14 to the equally or more crucial future ascent onto the cross, the ascent into heaven is likely meant.

> The son of man, the visible historical Jesus, must be lifted up on a cross and die in public for all to see as a dangerous disturber of the public peace. But for all those who have eyes to see, for those who believe, the place of death is the place of revelation. For this reason, the road to death, the death of the son of man, is the determined direction of the mission of the Son of God, determined not by fate nor by mischance nor by the will of his enemies, but by the love of God for [humankind]. The death of the son of man is not, properly understood, a mere spectacle on the plane of history; it is the place of faith, the place where [people] are enabled to apprehend the eternal realm of the kingdom of the Spirit of God, and where they are therefore enabled to enter into eternal life. They look—and live. This is the fulfilment of the mission of Jesus the only-begotten Son of God.[24]

This brings us to what has become in the twentieth century the most commonly quoted verse in the New Testament, John 3:16, most often correctly used in evangelistic contexts. Here Jesus is spoken of in the terms we have heard of in John 1 as the unique or only-begotten Son (cf. John 1:18), and surely the third-person discourse signals that here, if not before, we are meant to think that we are listening to the voice of the evangelist speaking *about* the significance of Jesus, as the Nicodemus story reveals it. Before discussing this verse further we must digress briefly to say something about the evangelist's method of operating here and elsewhere in the Gospel's discourse material.

EXCURSUS: THE AUTHORITY, INSPIRATION, AND CREATIVITY OF THE FOURTH EVANGELIST

John 3:13–21 says something to us about how the evangelist views the testimony of either the Beloved Disciple or himself or both.[25] It intimates that he believes that his own words, being inspired, have the same authority as Jesus' words, so that the two can be joined together in one discourse *without the need* of stopping to stress what is source and what is the evangelist's commentary.[26] There is a felt continuity of intent and content between what Jesus said and what the evangelist is saying.

This is *not*, I think, because the evangelist believed he could speak as if he *were* Jesus addressing a later life situation, or as if the risen exalted Lord were speaking through him and he was nothing more than a mouthpiece.[27] No, this document reflects a period of profound meditation on the Jesus tradition and a casting of it into one's own idiom, not a collection of spontaneous prophetic utterances. Nor is it a matter of this evangelist's trying to deceive the listener about who is saying what. In various respects he is just following normal operating procedures of writing an ancient biography, in which, since there were no footnotes, all commentary was put in the text along with the source material.

Nevertheless, there are factors that separate the Gospel of John from other ancient biographies. It because the evangelist believed he could speak authoritatively *about* Jesus, and in a sense *for* him as his agent in the new situation, that he joins together the Jesus tradition and his own commentary here and elsewhere in this Gospel, and also feels free to recast the Jesus tradition into his own style. In view of what the evangelist later conveys to his audience about the role of the Holy Spirit helping the believer "remember" the Jesus tradition and then leading him or her into all truth (i.e., learning its significance), in the commentary sections of this Gospel where the Jesus tradition is not being quoted it appears we are dealing with an inspired spinning out of the meaning of the Jesus tradition for the new situation with the aid and guidance of the Spirit, not an offering of words from the exalted Jesus. We may perhaps call this a homiletical use of and expounding on the Jesus tradition, and in particular, homiletics done in the service of evangelism.

It will be noted that John 3:16 speaks about God loving the *kosmos*, the world, not merely the elect, even though it is a world that neither understands, nor in most cases accepts, God and divine revelation. This use of *kosmos* here is not at odds with its use in the farewell discourses (cf. 15:18ff.), for John 3:16 is not meant to portray the world in a positive light, but rather to show the extreme graciousness of God's dealings with the world. "If the depth of love is measured by the value of its gift, then God's love could not be greater, for his love-gift is his most precious possession—his only, eternally beloved Son."[28]

The *houtos* which begins this verse can be translated "In this way" or "In the same manner" or "So." I suspect one of the former two renderings best does justice to the text. The evangelist means for us to link the allusion to Jesus' death in v. 15 to what is said in v. 16—"In this way [i.e., by means of Jesus' being lifted up on the cross] God loved the world, that he gave the unique (or only) Son, in order that all the ones believing in him should not perish but have everlasting life." Thus vv. 14b–15 and v. 16 are two different ways of saying the same thing.[29] Verses 14–15 speak of the Son of man's being lifted up as a necessity, if eternal life was to become available, though a full-blown theology of the atonement is not explicated here. Verse 16 tells us, however, that if God had not given the Son, the world would have perished and would not have had eternal life. Nevertheless, it is only all those who believe who obtain the gift of eternal life.

Verse 17 makes even more explicit that it was not God's desire to condemn the world. God did not send the Son into the world for such a purpose, but rather to save the world through him. Whatever one's own theology of the sovereignty of God, if it is to come to grips with the Johannine discussion of the matter, it must recognize the key fact that faith in Christ is what makes the difference between those who perish and those who obtain eternal life—not God's love or an elective intent on the part of God. God's love is directed toward the entire human world and does not wish the condemnation of any in the world. Having said this, no one in the world would have faith if God had not drawn them to Christ and graciously illuminated them. Furthermore, being born anew is not a human self-help program, but a work of God (cf. below). This Gospel stresses that before a human being has made a decision about Christ, God has already begun to work in that human being, illuminating and making possible a person's positive response to Christ. Indeed, this Gospel is about the pilgrimage from initial illumination and inadequate (though not necessarily inaccurate) faith responses to a full faith in Christ as Lord and God. Then, too, Jesus is portrayed in this Gospel as having true insight into human character and knowing who will and who won't respond in faith to the call of the Gospel (cf. John 2:23–25).

Thus, the mystery of God's sovereignty and the necessity of the human faith response to God are not resolved in this Gospel into the neat formulas of later theological controversies. The Gospel clearly affirms both things, and makes evident that it was God's intent from all eternity to send the Son to redeem the world, and Christ is viewed as God's elect one, who must come, must die, and must rise again in order for eternal life to be available at all. It is his life and work that is punctuated with the emphatic elective word *dei*, "It is necessary." The reasons why some respond positively in faith to the Son and some do not are not fully explicated in the Fourth Gospel, *except* that John 3:16–17 makes clear that the fault for some rejecting Christ cannot ultimately be laid at the door of God's elective intent, for God loves and does not wish to condemn the world. It may, perhaps, be explained in part by the fact that some love darkness more than they love light, because their deeds are evil (v. 19).

Verse 18 reveals that the evangelist believes not only that eternal life begins during one's earthly existence, but also that condemnation begins already in this life. Those who do not believe are *already* (*ēdē*) condemned, and have put themselves in this position by their failure to respond in faith.[30] It does not follow from this that one whose initial response is misunderstanding or rejection of, or having strong doubts about, the Gospel is eternally condemned—simply that there are negative consequences here and now to rejecting the Gospel. Thomas's initial lack of faith did not lead to his eternal undoing, as we shall see in John 20, but it did mean he missed out on the first appearance of Jesus to the inner circle of male disciples and the prophetic sign promise of the Holy Spirit!

Verses 19–21 offer an explanation of why some love darkness rather than light. The focus here is on human deeds. Evil deeds require the cover of darkness. Even more pointedly, we are told that people who do such things hate the light, for they hate to be exposed; they do not want to know or be revealed to be what they are—children of darkness. This is not just a matter of human beings' having an infinite capacity for self-justification, though that is also true, but the evangelist is suggesting that deep down those who do evil things know their deeds are evil, and so try their best to hide this fact from the light of day and, indeed, even from themselves apparently.[31] They are heavily into denial. They do not wish to give up certain kinds of behavior and actions, and accordingly they avoid coming into the light, for deep down they know it will entail their condemnation, including self-condemnation. This is a portrait of humanity, with a guilty conscience and yet not prepared to give up its sin.

II. Bridging the Horizons

Perhaps the first clue to a proper and cautious handling of this text is to recognize that the story of Nicodemus is not brought to a closure here, but is rather open-ended. He clearly does not understand, but his story is not yet complete. A key in many of these stories is that to evaluate characters, one must recognize what stage she or he is at, in their spiritual pilgrimage.

A second key is to recognize the homiletical use of the Jesus tradition here. In such evangelistic material, the stress on dualities (darkness and light, evil and good, condemnation and eternal life) and on clarity is customary. Life, including Christian life, is more complex than this passage, if read in isolation, might suggest. This is one good reason why the "sound bite" approach to the rich and complex theology of the Fourth Gospel should be avoided. It would be better to teach and preach one's way through a variety of passages to expose the variety and range of the evangelist's teaching and thought.

A third key to a proper handling of this text is to recognize that this is not an "us versus them" text, especially since we are told that God loves the world of fallen humankind. Nicodemus is not portrayed as a reprobate, just one who understands inadequately and has (to paraphrase Robert Frost) "miles to go before he sleeps." Jesus' message speaks of radical change in a person's life, but notice he does not say to Nicodemus, "You must change yourself" but rather, "You must be born anew," referring to God's work in the individual. This means that this text gives little if any warrant for the "Make a decision for Christ and you will receive the new birth" approach.

Faith is a response to what God has already begun to do in a person's life, or else one would not respond at all.

This text, like most in this Gospel, reveals that the key to all things salvific is a proper and full belief in Christ—who he is, where he has come from, what he has done to provide salvation. The Fourth Evangelist would surely urge on us that the one thing we must make abundantly clear to an un- or nonbelieving audience is the truth about Christ. He must be lifted up so all may see and have life. This in turn also means, however, that one must not treat those who have already come to Christ as though they need repeated doses of the same evangelistic message. The technique of this evangelist is repetition and some development of a few key themes throughout the Gospel,[32] and this is indeed a proper homiletical technique in an evangelistic situation. One must be crystal-clear about the things necessary for salvation. "Jesus is . . . the *plan* of God, his grand project for humanity (the world) made flesh and his glory made manifest."[33] There is also a time and a place for getting beyond John 3:16 in preaching, especially to Christians.

In a provocative and evocative discussion of the Nicodemus story F. Craddock suggests that the key to an adequate modern proclamation of a text like this is realizing that this Gospel speaks about levels and qualities of faith. He goes on to add that in "Jerusalem there was a kind of faith generated by Jesus' signs, but the fact that Jesus did not trust such believers testifies to the inadequacy or incompleteness of such faith. . . . We have already noticed that faith in Jesus' special power (Jesus' mother at Cana) and faith in his supernatural knowledge (Nathanael) are qualitatively different from the faith in him as the epiphany of divine glory."[34] This is all true as far as it goes, but in none of the cases just mentioned should we speak of those who are already disciples of Jesus at the juncture at which we encounter them in the text in John 1—3, so it is not just a matter of their being strengthened in their discipleship. What John 3:1–16 is telling us, however it may scandalize some moderns, is that there is a threshold that must be crossed in one's understanding of, relationship to, and belief in Jesus if one is to have eternal life. Of course it is true that "one does not decide for or against Jesus once and only once," and that "the life of faith [is] alive, capable of growth and regression,"[35] but that is not the issue here. The issue is not deepening levels of commitment by those who are already Christians, or an upward evolutionary process by which one naturally moves from less to more adequate faith,[36] but how one becomes a child of God in the first place, and what amounts to adequate or saving faith in Christ. What is being discussed in this text is an *event* of God's divine grace, called here by analogy a birth, which may be preceded or followed by a lengthy process but which in and of itself is not a mere human development, but rather a work of God. The new birth is seen as a matter of transformation, not just more information; new being, not merely new seeing.[37]

If we go back and reflect for a moment on John 1:12–13, we can see this point clearly. John 1:12 tells us that "to all who received him, who believed in his name, he gave power to become children of God." Now this tells us that the new birth has prior human conditions. It is to those who received and believed that the power was given from on high to be children of God. Nevertheless, the most important point is that God, not mere human choice or decision, is the change agent here. Conversion is a work of God, not of human beings, either evangelists or converts. Furthermore, one cannot be a little bit born of God any more than a woman can be a little bit pregnant. What the Fourth Evangelist is speaking of is an event that either has or hasn't happened in someone's life.[38]

It does *not* follow from a close reading of John 1:12–13 and of John 3:1–21, however, that a particular kind of conversion *experience* is being advocated in the text. The tendency in some conservative Protestant circles is to make the mistake of assuming that one has not been converted unless one has had a Damascus road experience like Paul's. This is a big mistake, as even a cursory reading of the other conversion stories in Acts will show. C. S. Lewis in his spiritual autobiography, *Surprised by Joy*, remarks that he was the most reluctant convert in all of Christendom, and that for him it was more a matter of giving in to the relentless pursuit of the Hound of Heaven than a joyful seeking after and finding Christ. The truth is that no two conversion *experiences* are exactly alike—God calls each one individually and by name. What the text of John 3:1–21 is about is the *fact* of the new birth, not the human experiences that accompany it.

If we wish to push the birth analogy a bit, we might say that one's labor before the birth may be long and painful or short and relatively uneventful. It may be attended by many or witnessed by none other than oneself. The new birth may involve a dramatic turning from darkness to light, or a quiet assurance after long searching that one truly is a child of God. The time of crossing the river may be noted on the occasion, or only realized long after one is on the other shore. One may know when one's spiritual birthday is, or, on the other hand, the records and remembrance of it may be lost.

If sociological studies of conversions tell us anything, they tend to suggest that the children of believers who have not significantly strayed from the faith tend to have quieter crossings from the womb of faith into the real world of new life in Christ, whereas those who come to Christian faith without any Christian background, or after having followed the path of the prodigal son only to return home, tend to have more dramatic conversion experiences.

What is critical is not the process, *how* one got there, but the result—*that* one has been born of God and has an adequate faith in Christ. Adequate faith in Christ is possible only if the power of God has worked in a human life, enabling such a response. Anything short of that and one is in the state we find Nicodemus in—believing and believing accurately something about Jesus, and yet still in the dark about the most fundamental christological and soteriological issues.[39]

We have listened here to a tale about both universalism (God loves all the world) and particularism (there is only one Son, through whom eternal life is available). There is one Savior sent for all, but whether the "all" will be for the "One" depends on a faith response. "The discourse cannot therefore come to rest, it cannot end with the assertions that love and not justice is the final truth of God and life and not death is the final destiny of [humankind]. The word *all* is qualified by the word 'faith'—*all who believe*—and the thought of the love of God is still crossed by the thought of his judgement. The discourse ends in a tension: it does not and cannot come to rest, for it is a human thing vibrating in the midst of a world that does not believe."[40] It is a discourse directed to a darkened world.

6. John, Jesus, and the Waterworks (John 3:22–36)

The structure of this passage, as we have already noted (cf. above) is basically the same as the Nicodemus story in the earlier part of the chapter, and this favors the suggestion made by some scholars that the words found in vv. 31–36 are words of Jesus, not of John.[1] We will take a different view (cf. below). In any event, it is worth asking why we seem to have a further story about John and Jesus, which adds only a few new things to what was said in John 1. I suggest it is because it was important to point out that John was a witness to the beginnings of the public ministry of Jesus.

It may be, as Brown has conjectured, that in terms of the actual chronological sequence of events this story may record the first encounter of John and Jesus, prior to the Lamb testimony of John to Jesus.[2] The placement of this material might have been originally between John 1:34 and 35. This might explain the hostile reaction of John's disciples to the Baptist's losing followers to Jesus—they did not yet know what John truly thought of Jesus. Whatever one thinks of this theory of the original historical setting of this material, it is clearly about a period *before* any of the Synoptic stories about the ministry of Jesus in Galilee. This material may have been of especial importance if there was an ongoing witness to John's followers in the area where this Gospel was published.[3] The evangelist's technique here as elsewhere in the Gospel is to address his audience by means of "the elucidation of themes by progressive repetition."[4] This is not surprising in a document meant for evangelistic use which has a homiletical character.

I. The Historical Horizon

A. The Report (John 3:22–24)

3:22 After this Jesus and his disciples went into the Judean countryside, and he spent some time there with them and baptized. [23]John also was baptizing at Aenon near Salim because water was abundant there; and people kept coming and were baptized [24]—John, of course, had not yet been thrown into prison.

The narrative begins by hinting that Jesus left Jerusalem and went out into the Judean countryside.[5] Judean here may reflect the Roman designation for the region (especially if this document was written outside Palestine), in which case it would include the relevant parts of Samaria. Probably Aenon near Salim is referring to the Salim near Shechem in Samaria, which makes good sense in light of what is said about Jesus' itinerary in 4:1–3, on his way back to Galilee. We are told at 3:22 that Jesus and his disciples were baptizing there, though this remark is either corrected or clarified at 4:2 to indicate that the disciples of Jesus were doing the baptizing. This in any case would have transpired only if Jesus had approved, and it suggests that early in his public ministry Jesus, like John, was engaged in calling God's people, even the righteous, to account in light of the new inbreaking work of God.

John was also baptizing in this area where there was plenty of water, and the evangelist adds that this all obviously happened prior to John's being put in prison (v. 24). This reminder might be necessary for those who had heard of the Baptist and his death but did not know the relationship of John's death to the rise of Jesus' ministry—in other words, diaspora Jews who did not know the Jesus tradition but knew of John. The Fourth Evangelist is interested in John only as a historical figure, insofar as he has some bearing on the story of Jesus, as is shown by the fact that he does not relate what happened to John after his imprisonment. His interests in John are primarily theological, as an important witness to the significance of Jesus.

B. The Dialogue (John 3:25–30)

3:25 Now a discussion about purification arose between John's disciples and a Jew. [26]They came to John and said to him, "Rabbi, the one who was with you across the Jordan, to whom you testified, here he is baptizing, and all are going to him." [27]John answered, "No one can receive anything except what has been given from heaven. [28]You yourselves are my witnesses that I said, 'I am not the Messiah, but I have been sent ahead of him.' [29]He who has the bride is the bridegroom. The friend of the bridegroom, who stands and hears him, rejoices greatly at the bridegroom's voice. For this reason my joy has been fulfilled. [30]He must increase, but I must decrease."

Verse 25 tells us that a dispute arose between John's disciples and a Jew over purification (*katharismos*). This provides a clue to the proper context in which the evangelist wants the hearer to reflect on John's baptism, but also on the practice of Jesus' disciples. The issue here is not Christian baptism, even when we are discussing what Jesus' followers were doing, but rather various forms of Jewish purification rituals and their respective merits.[6] This becomes especially clear in v. 26, where reference is made by these Jews to the baptizing by Jesus.[7] It seems plausible that some of the disciples of John who had become followers of Jesus may have continued John's baptizing practices, and perhaps Jesus endorsed or even encouraged this.[8] It is clear enough from a saying like Mark 11:27–33 (and par.) that Jesus believed that John's ministry and baptizing was of God. I have argued elsewhere that "it is quite plausible that Jesus, out of respect for John, ceased his own parallel ministry so as not to compromise John's work. Perhaps he saw his own efforts as an attempt to supplement, not supplant John's efforts. Perhaps when it became apparent that John would not minister anymore due to imprisonment, Jesus had to carefully evaluate the call of God on his life to see if God was urging him to go a step further than the Baptist. . . . Jesus would preach, heal, and fellowship directly with the people rather than wait for them to come to him."[9]

John's response in v. 27 to the indirect question of what John might think about his competition is couched in typical Johannine language—"No one can receive anything except what has been given from heaven" (cf. John 19:11). John does not see Jesus as competition, but as the One for whom he has had the honor of preparing the way. Once again, in v. 28, John disclaims that he is the messiah, saying he is only the forerunner of Messiah and claiming that his audience are the witnesses that he has made such a disclaimer.

This saying is followed in turn by a *mashal,* a parable about the bride and the bridegroom on their wedding day. This is interesting for it may suggest that Jesus chose to follow John's example of telling parables. For the Baptist this seems to have been only an occasional mode of speech, compared to prophetic oracles, but for Jesus it became his main manner of public discourse, leading to the impression that he was, and wished to present himself as, a Jewish sage. Probably John actually told such a parable about Jesus, which may explain why Jesus in turn referred to himself on a later occasion as the bridegroom, while distinguishing his lifestyle from that of the Baptist (cf. Mark 2:19–20).[10]

Although there is no evidence that it was traditional for early Jews to refer to the messiah as the bridegroom, the image is not unnatural, since there were traditions referring to Israel as the bride of God (cf. Isa. 49:14–26; 54:4–8; Jer. 2:2; Ezek. 16:8–14; Hos. 2:16–23). This parable is important because it suggests that what Jesus was trying to achieve was a more perfect union and harmony between Israel and her God. The mission of Jesus was not to reject but to reform Israel.[11]

A certain amount of knowledge of Jewish wedding customs aids in understanding this parable. John is portraying himself as assuming the role of the "friend of the bridegroom," whom we would call the best man. He was traditionally the groom's best friend, whose job was to take care of all the wedding arrangements.[12] Verse 29b may refer to the custom of the best man's standing guard outside the house while the groom goes in to share the wedding bed with the bride. The "voice of the bridegroom," then, refers to the shout of joy when the groom has successfully had marital relations with his bride on the wedding day. The other possibility is that this verse alludes to hearing the voice of the groom coming to fetch the bride for the wedding procession to his house.[13] In any case, the point is that the best man knows his place and role and is happy to fulfill it—it is not his place to marry the bride, but rather to rejoice over another who is doing so.

The last words of the Baptist in this Gospel are both appropriate and prophetic. "He must increase, but I must decrease" is the way the story goes henceforth, for John disappears from the drama, to be referred to only in the third person at John 10:40–42, as a figure in the past whose witness about Jesus had proved to be true. John is the first great witness to Jesus, and his testimony becomes crucial as Jesus' adversaries begin to gather evidence and the story takes on an increasingly judicial character, leading to the climactic trial and execution. The legal tone, however, is already fully in evidence in the monologue/commentary that follows.

C. Monologue/Commentary (John 3:31–36)

3:31   The one who comes from above is above all; the one who is of the earth belongs to the earth and speaks about earthly things. The one who comes from heaven is above all. ³²He testifies to what he has seen and heard, yet no one accepts his testimony. ³³Whoever has accepted his testimony has certified this, that God is true. ³⁴He whom God has sent speaks the words of God, for he gives the Spirit without measure. ³⁵The Father loves the Son and has placed all things in his hands. ³⁶Whoever believes in the Son has eternal life; whoever disobeys the Son will not see life, but must endure God's wrath.

As with the conclusion of the Nicodemus story we end this section with a monologue/commentary and it is once again difficult to tell who is speaking here. Is it John, or perhaps Jesus? I would suggest, in view of the character of the last commentary after the Nicodemus dialogue, that the NRSV has taken the right course and simply seen these words as the commentary of the evangelist, speaking of both John and Jesus in the third person and using typical Johannine diction. We have stressed that the Beloved Disciple was probably a disciple both of John and then of Jesus, and so it is right to note there are no derogatory things said about John. Indeed the veracity of his testimony to Jesus is seen as crucial. It is simply that his role is seen as preparatory and pales in comparison to that of Jesus. There is no polemic against the Baptist here; to the contrary he is coopted and given a very positive role in the Jesus story.[14]

    The contrast, then, between heaven and earth in vv. 31–36 is not meant to be seen as a contrast between good and bad, positive and negative, as is shown by the earlier discussion in which Jesus tells Nicodemus earthly things, which while basic are nonetheless of eternal significance (cf. vv. 1–12). The point, however, is that the one who has come from above is above all things and everyone else, and his testimony is the most crucial. Jesus, the stranger who came from heaven, testified and continued through his disciples to testify to the things he saw and heard, but his testimony was frequently rejected. We are not surprised by this conclusion, for we have already been told in John 1:11 that even some of Jesus' own had rejected him, and that in general such a reaction is to be expected when people love darkness more than light. When the Fourth Evangelist wrote this at the end of the first century, he wrote at a time when the rejection by Jews of the Christian message had only increased. For the evangelist this was a painful fact, and some of the polemics in the telling of Jesus' story reflect that ongoing rejection, no doubt. It is important to bear in mind, however, that the reason this was still an open wound for the evangelist is probably not because he was just "looking back in anger," but because the witness of the Johannine community to Jews continued despite repeated rejection. They continued to be cast out of the synagogue for such testimony (cf. below on John 9).

Yet there were those who did accept the testimony of and about Jesus, and they have "set a seal to" (NRSV: "certified") the fact that God is truthful. The metaphors here are all legal ones, and in this case the reference is to a seal indicating approval on a legal document.[15] The evangelist is already arguing his case here with his audience, and he knows that the case for the defense must be powerful if it is to be accepted, when so many have rejected such a testimony before. Yet argue he must, because in his mind it is not just the veracity of John or Jesus on the line, but that of God, for it is God who has sent the Son, God who speaks in and through Jesus, and God who has given Jesus the Spirit without measure (cf. 1:33). God has placed all things in the hands of the Son whom he loves,[16] the whole of the working out of the plan of redemption for humankind, and especially for God's people. Therefore, everything of consequence, everything of eternal significance is on the line here—"Whoever believes in the Son has eternal life; whoever disobeys the Son will not see life, but must endure God's wrath."

To reject the Son is to reject the Father, and so the writer believes that the stakes for his audience are very high. He writes with urgency, because he longs for the audience to believe in Jesus for who he is, and so have eternal life, and he is angry and grieved when the message is ignored, misunderstood, or flatly rejected. He writes as one who has known rejection, even though he believes he is offering something the audience cannot do without.

It is worth noting the strong contrast at the end of this monologue between believing and disobeying, which comports with the strong linking of obeying and believing in 3:18–21. For the evangelist faith and actions were not two alternatives to be set at odds with each other. Rather, having faith in Jesus both was an action itself and at the same time entailed living in a certain manner, and so encompassed various actions.

Just as the evangelist believed in eternal life as something that already begins for the follower of Jesus in this life, so he also believed in realized wrath; he believed that God's wrath is already on those who reject and disobey God, even prior to the last judgment. In short, the evangelist believed wholeheartedly that there were always moral consequences to one's actions, both sooner and later. This is only to be expected from the Gospel writer and/or from the Beloved Disciple who is so deeply steeped in the Jewish wisdom tradition. Even a cursory glance at the book of Proverbs shows over and over again the belief that actions always have moral consequences: "Whoever walks in integrity walks securely, but whoever follows perverse ways will be found out" (Prov. 10:9). The evangelist and/or the Beloved Disciple believed in the strong form of this equation—not merely pie in the sky by and by, or judgment at judgment day, but eternal life and wrath already partially realized in the here and now.[17] These conditions were not seen as written in stone, however, for those currently in darkness might yet come to the light, and on the other hand those currently in the light might finally be blinded and offended by it as it intensified in its brightness and power the closer one got to it.

II. Bridging the Horizons

Whatever else one may say, this passage provides no fodder for a discussion about Christian baptism, because that is not what is at issue here—rather, Jewish purification rituals are. The issue is, of course, ultimately Jesus and John's testimony to him, not the sacraments. Some very interesting sermons or lessons could be derived from this passage, however, about the real relationship of Jesus and John the Baptist.

It would be worthwhile to undertake some study of Jewish wedding customs, as this can illuminate not only John 3 but also John 2, as well as various other parts of the Jesus tradition, like the parable of the wise and foolish virgins in Matt. 25. One could then compare and contrast modern wedding customs with those in the text, and so give one's audience a sense of the similarities and differences. The fact of arranged marriages in antiquity, and the fact that in both Jewish and Greco-Roman settings the bride was often no older than twelve or thirteen, set these stories apart from modern Western customs. Such a study in turn sheds light on the teaching by Jesus and others in the New Testament about marriage, divorce, and singleness, and helps one to sift what principles are transferrable from then to now and which things are dependent on local customs and culture.

Another subject of importance this text addressed is Jesus' early "Judean" ministry, prior to the Galilean one, which is where the Synoptics begin and almost all they discuss. We are being told that Jesus' early ministry was similar to John's, apparently calling Jews to repentance in light of what was to come. It is hinted at that the turning point for Jesus was the imprisonment of John, something the Synoptics also suggest (Mark 1:14).

What we are being told, then, is that Jesus had a normal, progressive consciousness, and that awareness of what God wanted him to do did not come all at once at birth, or even at his baptism, but over the course of time and as a result of certain things that happened to his closest contemporary— John the Baptist. God gradually guided and instructed Jesus in the course in which he must go, and there were also times of supernatural insight into what was going to transpire. This is the way the story of Jesus is portrayed, not only in the Synoptics, but also in John. This is of great importance, for it means that Jesus was not only a divine being bestriding the stage of human history, but also a human being who learned things as time went on (cf. Luke 2:52), who suffered hunger, thirst, and the general weariness of the flesh (cf. John 4:6), who had on occasion to ask questions (cf. Mark 5:30), and admitted there were things God had not revealed to him (Mark 13:32). In other words, all the Gospels, and even John, which most clearly depicts Jesus as a divine figure, make clear that in the process of taking on flesh Jesus had also taken on certain human limitations of time, space, knowledge, and endurance. This is a great paradox, and even in John's Gospel the paradox is not resolved; the divine glory is just somewhat more in evidence than in the Synoptics. This must be borne in mind when one is presenting the story of Jesus and John.

Contemporary Christians have been so used to associating eternal life with going to heaven that it requires some careful instruction to enlarge their perspectives to see that "the future is now."[18] Eternal life has as much to do with a quality and direction of life as it has to do with the length of one's existence, for after all most early Christians believed that even the eternally condemned go on to exist beyond the grave, albeit in an unpleasant state.

There are many paradoxes about this term eternal life. In the first place, it means something more like everlasting life—a life that begins in this lifetime when one believes in Christ, and then continues on forever. It is a derivative life form, and not the same as God's eternal life, for God always has been and will be. Second, this gift of eternal life does not prevent one from physically dying, which in turn suggests that this life form is not dependent on physical existence nor terminated when physical life ends. Third, however, early Christians also believed in the resurrection from the dead. They were not looking forward to an eternal existence without a body in heaven, which as 2 Cor. 5:1–10 shows was seen as a state of nakedness (to be "away from the body and at home with the Lord"), but were looking forward to finally being made like the risen Christ—having a body immune to disease, decay, death, sin, and sorrow. This for them was the final and ultimately satisfactory form of eternal life, not pie in the sky by and by.

This in turn means that Christians who are convinced that they too should believe such things must not be purely otherworldly in their outlook on life. If indeed there will be a new heaven *and a new earth,* if indeed God's kingdom will one day fully manifest itself on earth, as we have been praying for for centuries in the Lord's Prayer, if indeed there will be a future resurrection of believers as 1 Cor. 15 says, then Christians must indeed be concerned not only about heavenly things, but also about earthly things—for both creatures and creation shall one day be redeemed (cf. Rom. 8:19–20). No one should be more concerned about caring for the earth and matters of worldly import than Christians, since that is evidently God's great concern. God not only made all of creation, God loves all of creation, and is already in the process of redeeming it. It is a truncated vision of the Gospel that cares for the souls of the unsaved but not their bodies or minds, that cares for heaven but not the conditions on earth, that cares for spiritual things but not also material things. God's present wrath, like God's ongoing love, shows precisely how much God cares about conditions and behavior on earth. Were God indifferent to material things, we could expect silence from heaven. "The wrath of God is a difficult notion to hold together with the love of God. . . . The place from which to view these divine perfections in their mutual relationship is the cross, to which John will bring us before long."[19] Strange as it may seem, the road to life passes through death, the road to heaven for Jesus through Golgotha, and the road to understanding heavenly things comes through greater insights into earthly things, like the Word made flesh and the cross he bore.

7. A Savior in Samaria (John 4:1–42)

One of the longest continuous narratives in the Fourth Gospel deals with Jesus' activities neither in Judea nor in Galilee, but in the region in between the two called Samaria. The narrative is surprising on at least three counts: (1) Jesus is dealing with Samaritans; (2) Jesus is dealing with a strange woman in public; (3) Jesus is dealing with an immoral woman. Yet the evangelist does not assume that his audience will understand that the first of the above-mentioned factors is strange; rather, he feels it necessary to explain: "Jews do not share things in common with Samaritans" (4:9). We will explain why this remark is made in the Historical section below, but for now it is sufficient to remark that this statement would certainly not have to be made to Palestinian Jews, and it probably would not have to be made to diaspora Jews who had any contact with the Holy Land and/or knew the history of the antipathy between Jews and Samaritans since at least the return from exile in the sixth century B.C. This strongly suggests that the original audience for this Gospel must have included a considerable number of Gentiles who were not aware of many Jewish customs and rivalries.

As we have already noticed in John 2 and 3, it is the practice of the evangelist to provide certain transitional material between major narratives in the Gospel. This transition is made in John 4:1–4. John 4:1–3 suggests that Jesus did not wish to detract from John's ministry, and thus, due to the complaint of the Pharisees, left the region where John was and began to travel back to Galilee. Considering where he was and where he wanted to go, this required that he go through Samaria if he was to go the most direct route. Josephus confirms that for rapid passage to and from the festivals the Galileans had to go through Samaria (cf. *Ant.* 20.118; *War* 2.232; *Life* 269), yet perhaps the necessity of traveling this way for Jesus was divine—God wanted him to have this encounter with the Samaritan woman.

4:1   Now when Jesus learned that the Pharisees had heard, "Jesus is making and baptizing more disciples than John" ²—although it was not Jesus himself but his disciples who baptized— ³he left Judea and started back to Galilee. ⁴But he had to go through Samaria. ⁵So he came to a Samaritan city called Sychar, near the plot of ground that Jacob had given to his son Joseph. ⁶Jacob's well was there, and Jesus, tired out by his journey, was sitting by the well. It was about noon.

7 A Samaritan woman came to draw water, and Jesus said to her, "Give me a drink." ⁸(His disciples had gone to the city to buy food.) ⁹The Samari-

tan woman said to him, "How is it that you, a Jew, ask a drink of me, a woman of Samaria?" (Jews do not share things in common with Samaritans.) [10]Jesus answered her, "If you knew the gift of God, and who it is that is saying to you, 'Give me a drink,' you would have asked him, and he would have given you living water." [11]The woman said to him, "Sir, you have no bucket, and the well is deep. Where do you get that living water? [12]Are you greater than our ancestor Jacob, who gave us the well, and with his sons and his flocks drank from it?" [13]Jesus said to her, "Everyone who drinks of this water will be thirsty again, [14]but those who drink of the water that I will give them will never be thirsty. The water that I will give will become in them a spring of water gushing up to eternal life." [15]The woman said to him, "Sir, give me this water, so that I may never be thirsty or have to keep coming here to draw water."

16 Jesus said to her, "Go, call your husband, and come back." [17]The woman answered him, "I have no husband." Jesus said to her, "You are right in saying, 'I have no husband'; [18]for you have had five husbands, and the one you have now is not your husband. What you have said is true!" [19]The woman said to him, "Sir, I see that you are a prophet. [20]Our ancestors worshiped on this mountain, but you say that the place where people must worship is in Jerusalem." [21]Jesus said to her, "Woman, believe me, the hour is coming when you will worship the Father neither on this mountain nor in Jerusalem. [22]You worship what you do not know; we worship what we know, for salvation is from the Jews. [23]But the hour is coming, and is now here, when the true worshipers will worship the Father in spirit and truth, for the Father seeks such as these to worship him. [24]God is spirit, and those who worship him must worship in spirit and truth." [25]The woman said to him, "I know that Messiah is coming" (who is called Christ). "When he comes, he will proclaim all things to us." [26]Jesus said to her, "I am he, the one who is speaking to you."

27 Just then his disciples came. They were astonished that he was speaking with a woman, but no one said, "What do you want?" or, "Why are you speaking with her?" [28]Then the woman left her water jar and went back to the city. She said to the people, [29]"Come and see a man who told me everything I have ever done! He cannot be the Messiah, can he?" [30]They left the city and were on their way to him.

31 Meanwhile the disciples were urging him, "Rabbi, eat something." [32]But he said to them, "I have food to eat that you do not know about." [33]So the disciples said to one another, "Surely no one has brought him something to eat?" [34]Jesus said to them, "My food is to do the will of him who sent me and to complete his work. [35]Do you not say, 'Four months more, then comes the harvest'? But I tell you, look around you, and see how the fields are ripe for harvesting. [36]The reaper is already receiving wages and is gathering fruit for eternal life, so that sower and reaper may rejoice together. [37]For here the saying holds true, 'One sows and another reaps.' [38]I sent you to reap that for which you did not labor. Others have labored, and you have entered into their labor."

39 Many Samaritans from that city believed in him because of the woman's testimony, "He told me everything I have ever done." [40]So when the Samaritans came to him, they asked him to stay with them; and he stayed there two days. [41]And many more believed because of his word. [42]They said to the woman, "It is no longer because of what you said that we believe, for we have heard for ourselves, and we know that this is truly the Savior of the world."

I. The Historical Horizon

The antipathies between Jews and Samaritans have a long history, and even continue today, for there is still a small group of a few hundred Samaritans offering sacrifice on Mount Gerizim at present. Samaria was the capital city (1 Kings 16:24) of the Northern Kingdom when Judah and Israel split, and at some point the term also came to be used of the region in general. After the invading Assyrians had captured Samaria in about 721 B.C., they deported most if not all of the ruling class of Jews to Assyria and settled the land partially with foreigners, partially with their own people. 2 Kings 17—18 says that some of these foreigners intermarried with some Israelites who were not deported.[1] Whether these Israelites are the ancestors of the group later called the Samaritans is not clear. In any case, once the exile was over, Judean Jews who returned home tended to view the Samaritans as half-breeds, whose religion had become tainted by non-Jews' ideas and practices (cf. Neh. 13; Josephus *Ant.* 11:297–347). So far as we can tell, there was not a lot of substance to the charge that Assyrian or other pagan elements were amalgamated with Samaritan religion, but there is no doubt that the Samaritan version of Judaism differed considerably from the Judean version after the exile. The Samaritans, for example, recognized only the Pentateuch as Holy Writ, and when they thought of a redeemer figure, naturally enough they conceived of him as being like Moses, or even being Moses come back from the dead (cf. Deut. 18:18–22). They called this redeemer prophet the Taheb ("the Restorer"). That the expectation of such a figure appearing was considerable around Jesus' time can be shown from the account in Josephus (*Ant.* 18.85–87), which records that only some six years after Jesus' death a Samaritan fanatic assembled a large group on Mount Gerizim, promising to reveal to them the sacred vessels thought to have been hidden there by Moses.

A particularly important event in the religous history of Samaria is that somewhere around 400 B.C. the Samaritans had built their own temple on Mount Gerizim and saw it as the proper place to hold and observe the true worship of God. The fact that John Hyrcanus, a ruler in Judea, came and destroyed this temple before the time of Jesus only fueled the animosities between Jews and Samaritans. It appears that by Jesus' day, Samaria as a land was regarded by many of the religiously observant Judean and Galilean Jews as unclean, and contact with these people, especially their women, or sharing a meal or common cup with them was widely held to render a Jew unclean. *m. Nid.* 4:1 records a saying that appears to go back at least to the middle of the first century A.D. which reads "The daughters of the Samaritans are menstruants from the cradle," in other words they are unclean from birth. It is in light of this background that one should read the story of the surprising encounter between Jesus and the Samaritan woman.[2]

Yet it is not just knowledge of the proximate background of the history of the Samaritans that illuminates this text, but also knowledge of the stories and ideas from the Hebrew scriptures that provide patterns and ideas for the way the evangelist tells this story. First of all, it has long been noted that this text should be read in light of the Old Testament stories about women's encounters at wells, especially the stories of the betrothal scenes involving Isaac (Gen. 24:10–61), Jacob (Gen. 29:1–20), and Moses (Ex. 2:15b–21).[3] The evangelist evokes such scenes by opening the telling of the story with remarks like "Sychar was near the field which Jacob gave to Joseph his son," referring to Jacob's well, and indicating that the woman asks "You're not greater than our father Jacob, are you?"[4] One must also bear in mind that in the previous chapter Jesus has just been called the bridegroom, raising the question, who is the bride? Who will be the one(s) to be Jesus' people, the true bride of Christ?

The basic pattern of these well stories is as follows:

1. The future bridegroom or his substitute travels to a foreign land (compare the Jacob story to John 4:3–5, where Jesus goes through Samaria)
2. He encounters a girl or girls at the well (compare the Jacob story to John 4:6–7a)
3. Someone draws water from the well
4. The girl or girls rush home to bring news of the stranger encountered there (compare Gen. 24:28ff. to John 4:28–30)
5. A betrothal is concluded between the stranger and the girl, generally only after he has been invited to a meal (compare Gen. 29:14 to John 4:31–34, 40–42).[5]

Notice how the Johannine story ends with Jesus speaking of what his true food is, and indicates his sharing a meal with the Samaritans, the implication being he is seeking union and fellowship with them, as their Savior. Of course the Johannine well story works at the spiritual, not the material, level. Jesus' accomplishment comes not in establishing a physical family by betrothal but by establishing a spiritual community, based on worshiping in Spirit and truth (cf. 10:7–30). The water he gives and the food he eats is spiritual food. "Therefore the relationship with the woman, and hence all believers, will not be based upon any physical relationship . . . , or physical betrothal . . . , or physical kingdom . . . but upon spiritual birth . . . and covenantal commitment."[6] The bride of the bridegroom turns out to have a surprising past and present, but a promising future.

Jesus is depicted in this narrative as the spring of living water and thus of life, which is striking because these were previously said to be attributes of Wisdom. For example, in Prov. 13:14; 18:4 Wisdom is said to be the spring of life. An even closer parallel is between Sir. 24:11 and John 4:14, but as we have already noted the point is that what Ben Sira predicates of Torah, the Fourth Evangelist applies to Jesus, and in fact goes beyond—Torah will make you thirst for more; Jesus as Wisdom quenches all thirsts.[7] Jesus as Wisdom is both the source and the substance of true life, light, and true worship; Torah ultimately points away from itself to God as the source of these things. Perhaps most interesting, as has been pointed out by Scott,[8] is that in this story it is *not* Jesus' disciples (who misunderstand) but the Samaritan woman by whom witness is borne. She is portrayed as assuming the role of Wisdom's maidservant who goes forth and calls others to come to Wisdom: "She has sent out her servant girls, she calls from the highest places in the town.... Come, eat of my bread and drink of the wine I have mixed. Lay aside immaturity, and live, and walk in the way of insight" (Prov. 9:3, 5–6). Here is a narrative loaded with artistic skill and irony, which Jewish listeners especially were likely to appreciate because of its echoes of early stories and ideas from the Hebrew scriptures.

The key to understanding this narrative is the recognition that the Samaritan woman and her fellow villagers are depicted as examples of those moving from no faith to some faith in Jesus, making progress toward an adequate faith in him. It is, then, a story not about Samaritans as examples of Christian faith, or Samaritans who have joined the Johannine community, but about the call of the Gospel to yet another sort of potential convert. John 4:35–38 makes clear its evangelistic focus and intent, and as such serves as an appeal both to the Christians who are passing on this Gospel to continue to do the work of sowing and reaping and to those in the audience to listen to the voice of Jesus calling them and to follow the example of the Samaritans in the text.

There is a certain continuity of themes in John 2—4, all of them having to do with water and its various possible metaphorical meanings. In John 2 it is purification water, in John 3 the waters of birth and baptismal water, in John 4 it is drinking water. In the narrative we are now examining Jesus persuades a woman that she needs to exchange drinking water for living water. Perhaps there is a contrast here between the Samaritan woman who gains some insight into Jesus' true character and Nicodemus, a teacher and representative of normative Judaism, who fails to understand Jesus.

It should be noticed that in the case of the Samaritan woman she is responding to Jesus' word, not to any previous signs he has performed, unlike the stories in John 2—3. "This story deals precisely with the process of coming to faith, but in it faith is a response to Jesus's word not to any sign."[9] There is also a continuation of the theme of Temple worship and true worship first introduced in John 2:13–22 and now more fully explored in 4:1–26.

Though the Samaritan woman may be portrayed as a particular type of potential convert, it is clear enough that she can't be seen as a type of the

Gentile world, for she is obviously a monotheist. From the way this story begins it is equally obvious that her situation in life is not an ordinary one. She comes to the well in the heat of the day, at noon. This suggests that she was attempting to avoid the company of other women, who would have come early in the morning. This in turn accents her moral situation—she was living with a man not her husband, and she had already had five husbands.

This narrative tells us a great deal about Jesus' attitude toward women, even women he knows would be considered immoral and unclean by most Jews. This is shown in his request of the woman for a drink, which surprises her on two counts: (1) he is a male, not supposed to be conversing with strange women in public, according to Jewish customs;[10] (2) he is a Jew, and Jews "don't have dealings with Samaritans"; it is possible, in fact, that what the aside of the evangelist means is that Jews do not share a common cup with Samaritans,[11] and in most regards this seems the more probable reading of v. 9b.

The Samaritan woman is in a somewhat similar position to that of Martha in Luke 10:38–42; she assumes she is the hostess, and Jesus needs something from her, even though it is actually Jesus who has real water to bestow—living water. Notice too that Jesus is never said to drink the water the woman could have given him. The request for water simply serves as the occasion for the dialogue on religion in which Jesus will offer the woman something far more valuable than ordinary water.

Here, as so often in this Gospel, we have two levels of speech and understanding. She is thinking on an earthly plane, and believes Jesus' reference to "living water" refers to running water, for the former was often a metaphorical way of speaking of a stream or river. Thus she assumes that what Jesus is offering is water that runs near her home, so she wouldn't have to come repeatedly to the well and carry water home.

The woman's pride in her Samaritan heritage comes to the fore when she asks if Jesus is saying he can give better water than father Jacob, whose well is the locus where they are having this conversation. The reader of the Fourth Gospel is reminded of the reference in John 1:51 (cf. above), where we learned that Jesus is one greater than Jacob, for he is the locus of God's presence on earth, through whom all divine communication comes and goes.

The Samaritan woman wins some admiration from the listener because her reaction to Jesus is one of inquiry, not rejection, and as such she can to a certain extent be seen as a model of the proper way to begin to respond to Jesus. Yet this is not totally so. When Jesus tells the woman to go and call her man, her response is deliberately evasive—"I do not have a man (husband)." She does not wish to reveal her true moral condition; apparently it was a sore point for her, as her presence at the well at noon likely implies—she wished to avoid inquiring eyes and lips. In early Judaism it was not the custom to have more than three marriages in a lifetime, and so her situation was morally very suspect. If this woman was living with a man who was not her husband, she was ritually unclean; yet here and elsewhere Jesus shows no interest in upholding the Jewish distinctions between clean and unclean, which, had he obeyed them, would have prevented him from reaching out to "sinners" of various sorts. Jesus not only speaks to the woman, but carries on a lengthy and theologically profound discussion with her, violating Jewish custom.[12]

Yet noticeably it is the woman who turns the discussion to the proper place of worship, changing the subject from her own personal life. Clearly, if Jesus had said Jerusalem was the proper place for true worship, she would have rejected him as a false prophet. But Jesus rejects the either/or she offers (either Gerizim or Jerusalem) and indicates that what really matters is the mode and manner of worship, not the place. The Samaritans may worship the true God, but they do not understand whom they are worshiping, and Jesus goes on to stress that salvation is "from the Jews." Still, as the narrative concludes, it becomes clear that this salvation is for everyone, not just the Jews. Whoever will worship in spirit and truth, even including the Samaritan woman, may get the benefit of this salvation, this living water. Jesus is suggesting a form of worship, unlike Temple worship, that would not separate men and women, that would not have special gender or ritual (clean/unclean) restrictions.

After the woman expressed her faith in the Coming One (likely the Samaritan Taheb; cf. above), Jesus responds, "*Ego eimi*, the one who is speaking to you." Scholars debate whether or not *ego eimi* should be seen as a theophanic formula here, a means of Jesus' revealing that he is and can speak as God did to Moses, using the "I am" formula. But the woman has spoken only of the one called the Christ/Messiah, and it is most natural to read Jesus' response to be, "I am (he); the one who is speaking to you is that person."[13] In either case, this amounts to at least a partial revelation of who Jesus truly is, and prompts the woman to return to town with the big news. The evangelist brings the first dialogue to a close dramatically, with the woman leaving for town just as the disciples arrive from town with food.

Apparently we are to think that the disciples not only saw Jesus talking to the woman, but perhaps also overheard the last few remarks. They are amazed that Jesus would speak to this woman, but they are reticent to ask Jesus about it. At this point the irony of the story begins to build—the disciples have left Jesus to find mere material sustenance, while this woman leaves her source of material sustenance behind (her water jug) to go to town and witness about Jesus. It is noticeable that the disciples do not play a major or even very positive role in the early stages of this Gospel, not only because they misunderstand, but also because others like the Samaritan woman assume the tasks, such as spreading the word, that Jesus wishes them to undertake.

It is crucial to note, however, that the woman's testimony is not a full-fledged Christian one. The evangelist summarizes it in v. 29—"Come and see a man who told me everything I have ever done![14] He cannot be the Messiah [Taheb], can he?" Craddock helpfully puts it this way: "Her repeated affirmation, beyond which she seems unable to move, was that here was a man 'who told me all that I ever did' (vv. 29, 39). One has the clear sense in this Gospel, however, that had she confessed Jesus to be the Christ, this would not have been adequate. . . . Jesus is not fully confessed when called the fulfillment of Jewish [or Samaritan] messianic hopes; he more than fulfills human expectation. Jesus is not simply God's Messiah; he is God's presence among them. In fact any single title by which one confesses faith in Jesus is insufficient and reductionistic."[15]

Notice, regardless, that the woman is open about her notorious past, a rather clear sign that she is making spiritual progress, though she has not yet fully arrived, for she, like Nathanael, seems mainly impressed with Jesus' supernatural knowledge of her past rather than Jesus' claims about himself. Her witness, despite its limitations, induces the townspeople to go out and meet Jesus for themselves, which is the aim of all good witnessing—to lead people to their own personal encounters with Jesus. While they are traveling to meet Jesus, the evangelist presents Jesus' second dialogue scene, this time with the disciples, and it is notable how they are spiritually less perceptive than the woman.

The disciples offer food to Jesus, but he remarks that he has a source of food unknown to them, namely, setting this woman on the pilgrimage toward an adequate faith in himself. The disciples, like the woman, misunderstand Jesus' remark about food, for they are thinking on a merely material level. Jesus then speaks metaphorically about teaching and witnessing as a matter of sowing seeds and reaping a crop of grain. Jesus tells them that the fields around them are already ripe for harvest, and here the meaning surely is that he is referring to the Samaritans now coming out of town to meet Jesus. The disciples should look up and see them coming, and seize the moment for harvesting.

In v. 37 Jesus clearly distinguishes between the sower and the reaper. The disciples have been urged to be the reapers, reaping where they have not sown. Who then are the others (plural) in v. 38 that have sown the word? The most natural answer is, of course, Jesus and the Samaritan woman, for they are the ones who have borne witness in this story. Jesus has sown the word in the woman, and she in turn has sown the word in her fellow Samaritans. Thus the disciples are not to be suspicious of Jesus' conversation with this woman—it has borne gospel fruit. The sowers and reapers are, rather, to rejoice together.[16]

While the Samaritans believed the word of the witnessing woman, this served only as a catalyst for them to go and find out things for themselves and to believe on the basis of hearing Jesus' own testimony, his word—a testimony we are apparently meant to think Jesus gave to them during the next two days when he stayed with them. The story is brought to a dramatic climax by the confession that Jesus is truly the Savior of the world, not just of Jews but of Samaritans as well, and we are told that "many" more believed because of his testimony in addition to the woman's testimony. The disciples have only brought Jesus physical food and have been exhorted to get on with the task of reaping a spiritual harvest. The woman of ill repute, ironically, brings Jesus his true food, by being the spark that brought the Samaritans into his presence. Here we see both reversal of expectations and also reversal of male-female roles, the woman taking the lead in sharing the good news.

As I have noted elsewhere, the evangelist intends to convey by this literary unit several things. "Jesus and the woman had discussed a more universal source of life and the basis of worship. The witness of Jesus and this sinful Samaritan woman bore fruit in Samaria and led to the confession and acknowledgement of the presence of the universal Saviour. 'The hour is coming and now is' when even women, even Samaritan women, even sinful Samaritan women, may be both members and messengers of this King and his Kingdom."[17]

II. Bridging the Horizons

One way of getting from the original setting of this text to our own setting is to analyze the text in terms of witnessing technique and results. If one examines Jesus' way of dealing with the Samaritan woman closely, one notices the degree to which Jesus converses with her in a way she can understand. Not only does he know (supernaturally) about her shady past, but he is well conversant with Samaritan ways of thinking about things. He couches his conversation in terms the woman can relate to. This suggests that knowing the views and belief system of the persons to whom one is witnessing is vital if real communication is going to happen.

Second, we notice about Jesus that he refuses to be sidetracked into focusing on interesting but subsidiary issues. Jesus deals directly with the woman's situation, what she needs in her life, and how he can help. His compassion and persistence until she is actually helped are clear throughout the passage. Jesus is not just interested in being right, or adding numbers to the grand total of his followers—he genuinely cares about this woman and her temporal and eternal future.[18]

Another key to moving from the text to our context is to focus on the realism of the text. The Samaritan woman is not depicted as having a full-fledged faith in Christ, but rather of being on the right road to such a faith. Likewise, she does not lead the Samaritans *to* Christ; more correctly, her witness leads them *toward* Christ, and then when they personally encounter Jesus and his word, at that point they more adequately confess Jesus to be the Savior of the world. In regard to the woman herself, the text is left open-ended. Her last words are "This can't be the Messiah, can it?" She is depicted as being a quester, now searching for the religious truth. Jesus is said to spend two more days with these Samaritans, presumably to solidify the gains of the dialogue he had begun with them. We are warned in such stories that witnessing often takes time, and that hearers' coming to an adequate faith in Christ seldom happens in an instant or overnight.

Another way of bridging the horizons using this text would be to see it as an example of how to witness to persons in groups that are unorthodox off-shoots of Christianity, such as Jehovah's Witnesses or Mormons or Christian Scientists. The example of Jesus suggests that such witnessing will require not only a Bible or training in evangelism but also a good knowledge of what one's audience believes and holds dear. If one does not do this, witnessing becomes a monologue, not a dialogue. Good witnessing begins where people in the audience are, not where one would like them to be, in their beliefs and practices.

One of the more disturbing trends in recent literature on evangelism is the emphasis on one's "target audience." The suggestion is that one should target certain *kinds* of people to recruit for one's church, because they can be more easily assimilated into the preexisting mix in one's congregation, for the very good reason that they are so much like the congregation in race, ethnic origins, socioeconomic status, education, and the like. This literature not only talks about things like "blue-collar" churches as opposed to "white-collar" churches, Irish Catholic churches as opposed to French Catholic churches, Dutch Reformed churches as opposed to Swiss or German Reformed churches, but it often seems to assume that such designations are both natural and normal and raise no questions about the character or unity of the church. It is one thing to talk about the American church as it is, it is another thing to baptize the status quo by a certain selective kind of evangelism strategy and assume that's the way it ought to be. Yet we would deem it very peculiar if not clearly prejudicial if people started talking about a gas station meant for blue-collar people rather than white-collar people, or a restaurant where only Polish Americans were welcome, or a United Way agency on which only men could serve. The point is that the Christian church in America, instead of trying to reach across barriers to share Christ, is often too comfortable sharing Christ within certain familiar categories and social lines. The Sunday morning worship hour in most churches is still one of the most segregated hours spent by any large number of people during the week. There is a fine line between ethnic pride and racial prejudice, and all too often we do not seem to be able to tell the difference.

The story of Jesus and the Samaritan woman is extremely potent to use as a tool both for sharing the Gospel across socioeconomic, ethnic, and racial barriers and for exhorting Christians to get on with doing so. Jesus in this story not only rejects the notion that he shouldn't associate with Samaritans, he also rejects the notion that he shouldn't talk with a "strange" woman in public, and furthermore rejects the idea that one shouldn't associate with notoriously immoral people. Besides that, Jesus' act involves witnessing to a person that many of his fellow Jews would have written off as both unclean and theologically out of bounds, a hopeless case. But this is not all.

In this story a woman is depicted as more spiritually perceptive than the male disciples, who are portrayed as misunderstanding Jesus and stuck in their thinking on the material level of things. It is precisely thinking stuck on the material level of things that too often leads to certain kinds of target-audience strategies. Furthermore, this woman is depicted as evangelizing for Jesus, even though she herself is not yet an example of full-fledged faith in Jesus. This may say something to us about the advisability of limiting our witness teams to mature Christian persons.

Finally, at the climax of the story Jesus is portrayed as the savior of the world, which means the savior of all races, ethnics groups, sexes, and ages, regardless of one's socio-economic status, health, or previous theological orientation. While it is true that no local church can be all things to all people, and that there is nothing wrong with sharing the faith with those sorts of people with whom one has various things in common, there *is* something wrong with an evangelism strategy that deliberately tries to *avoid* crossing lines, and ignores the mandate to reach out across social barriers as Jesus does in this story. We too easily forget that the community of Jesus is not intended to be a museum for a particular kind of saints, but rather is to be a hospital for sick sinners in a broken and divided world full of hate, prejudice, and discrimination. If one is going to preach or teach this text adequately, it will be necessary to stress the intentionality of Jesus and of God in reaching across lines, and to stress the way Jesus enables even despised and disfranchised people like Samaritans and women to become disciples and able witnesses for the Savior of the world. The question becomes, is the food that satisfies Jesus also the food that satisfies us, or are we settling for the more material fare that the disciples brought back from town? The fields are ripe for harvest, but the laborers are few.

8. The Second Sign at Cana (John 4:43–54)

As is his custom, the Fourth Evangelist provides a transitional passage between the story of the Samaritan narrative and that of the healing of the official's son. This particular transitional passage includes three things: (1) mention of Jesus' return to Galilee after his two days with the Samaritans (v. 43); (2) a familiar saying about prophets' being without honor in their home territory (v. 44); (3) an affirmation that Galileans welcomed Jesus home because they had seen all he did in Jerusalem during the festival.

Even a moment's reflection will show that the juxtaposition of v. 44 with v. 45 seems odd. On the one hand we have the saying that a prophet is not without honor save in his own country (cf. Mark 6:4 and par.),[1] and on the other hand we are told that Jesus was received warmly in Galilee. This has led so careful a commentator as Barrett to suggest that the evangelist is intimating that Judea is being called Jesus' country here, the place where he was not accepted and ultimately died, and this in spite of the fact that the Gospel writer clearly knows that Jesus is from Galilee (cf. John 1:46; 7:41, 52).[2] My own suggestion is that both in Judea (cf. 2:23) and Galilee people respond to Jesus' signs, but this does not lead Jesus to entrust himself to them, because he knows this does not amount to a full and adequate faith in him. The saying is included here because Jesus is moving from a place where he was surprisingly well received and proclaimed as savior of the world to a place he should have been fully received, but where the response was inadequate and superficial. Thus the saying refers to the general reaction of "his own" in both Judea and Galilee—initial acceptance of Jesus' signs and a belief in them, followed in due course by rejection when Jesus' real claims surface. Thus the response in v. 45 is to be seen as superficial and ultimately ironic—a faith based on signs or works will not only prove insufficient but in due course will turn into rejection.

4:43 When the two days were over, he went from that place to Galilee ⁴⁴(for Jesus himself had testified that a prophet has no honor in the prophet's own country). ⁴⁵When he came to Galilee, the Galileans welcomed him, since they had seen all that he had done in Jerusalem at the festival; for they too had gone to the festival.

46 Then he came again to Cana in Galilee where he had changed the water into wine. Now there was a royal official whose son lay ill in Capernaum. ⁴⁷When he heard that Jesus had come from Judea to Galilee, he went and begged him to come down and heal his son, for he was at the point of death.

[48]Then Jesus said to him, "Unless you see signs and wonders you will not believe." [49]The official said to him, "Sir, come down before my little boy dies." [50]Jesus said to him, "Go; your son will live." The man believed the word that Jesus spoke to him and started on his way. [51]As he was going down, his slaves met him and told him that his child was alive. [52]So he asked them the hour when he began to recover, and they said to him, "Yesterday at one in the afternoon the fever left him." [53]The father realized that this was the hour when Jesus had said to him, "Your son will live." So he himself believed, along with his whole household. [54]Now this was the second sign that Jesus did after coming from Judea to Galilee.

I. The Historical Horizon

This narrative of Jesus' second miraculous sign brings to a close the presentation by the Fourth Evangelist of the first major phase of Jesus' public ministry, which one scholar has summed up as "from Cana to Cana."[3] There are notable parallels between the first and second Cana signs. In both stories: (1) a need is expressed; (2) Jesus seems to offer resistance; (3) faith in his power persists; (4) Jesus deals with the matter in a manner different from what is requested and/or expected; (5) servants participate in the action; (6) some sort of faith results, and the mention of it concludes the narrative, but in each case the faith exhibited seems to be in Jesus' power, not a full-blown faith in who he is.[4] I would call these stories request rather than quest stories, for they involve people seeking something from Jesus, not seeking Jesus per se. I would agree, however, with Painter's summary about these stories and their function: "The evangelist's strategy was to narrate and interpret a selection of signs with a view to leading the readers to authentic faith in Jesus, a true understanding of his Messiahship (20:30–31)."[5] Once again we have a narrative in which the disciples play no role. In part this is because of the evangelist's focus and intent to concentrate on Jesus as the object on which the audience should focus their attention and devotion.

Our story reflects the considerable skill of the evangelist, who is able to round off a section of his Gospel so that it echoes the way the section began.[6] At 2:1 and 4:46 we have references to Cana; the miracle of water changed to wine is referred to at 2:1–11 and 4:46; there are references to Capernaum at 2:12 and 4:46; to inadequate faith based on miracles at 2:23–25 and 4:45, 48. These two signs are clearly numbered as first and second, drawing attention to their similarity.[7]

Many, perhaps most, scholars[8] have concluded that the story found in John 4:43–54 is a variant of the story of the healing of the centurion's son recounted in Matt. 8:5–13/Luke 7:1–10. I have argued elsewhere against this conclusion.[9] The proper explanation, in my view, lies in the fact that certain kinds of miracle stories tended to be told in similar fashion—in this case stories about healing at a distance. A good illustration of this point can be found in a Jewish tale from the end of the first century A.D. or beginning of the second about Gamaliel II and the famous Jewish healer and sage Hanina ben Dosa, which is clearly independent of both the above-mentioned Gospel stories and yet is told in a similar fashion. The story[10] can be briefly summarized: Once a son of R. Gamaliel II was ill, and so Gamaliel sent two of his disciples to ask Hanina ben Dosa that he might pray for mercy on Gamaliel's son. When ben Dosa saw them coming he went up into his upper room and pleaded for mercy. When he came down he said to the disciples, "Go, for the fever has left him." They responded: "Are you a prophet then?" He replied, "I am no prophet, nor am I a prophet's son; but I have received tradition—When my prayer flows freely in my mouth I know that the person concerned has been accepted; but if it doesn't I know he will be carried off." The disciples returned and noted in writing the hour ben Dosa said this. When they came back to Gamaliel he said to them, "By the Temple service! You have said neither too little nor too much; it happened exactly so in that hour—the fever left him and he asked for water." Stories of the same genre or type tended to be told in similar fashion.

Our story in the Fourth Gospel is about a royal official, likely someone who worked for Herod Antipas. The Greek word *basilikos* means a royal official or a person of royal blood, surely the former here. Josephus uses this term to refer to troops in service of the Herods (*Life* 400ff.), and so we may think of this person as an officer in the service of the king.[11] Evidence has now been presented to show that Roman soldiers served the Herods,[12] and so it may be that we are to think of this person as a Gentile, but if so the evangelist makes little or nothing of the fact.

The official's son lay ill in Capernaum, and we are told that the official went to Jesus when he heard he had returned from Judea and, not standing on his dignity, begged Jesus to come and heal his son, who was on the verge of dying.

Jesus' response in v. 48 seems and is brusque: "Unless you see signs and wonders you will not believe." Apparently we are meant to think that Jesus takes this man as representative of the attitude of the Galileans who "believed" in and and welcomed Jesus because of his notable deeds and miracles. This sort of faith, while not totally rejected by Jesus (cf. John 10:38; 14:11), is clearly not seen as adequate. We are meant to see the progress of a soul in this story, for while the official comes on the basis of Jesus' reputation as a miracle worker, he leaves on the basis of a trust in Jesus' word *without* seeing a miracle or validating sign that his son would be all right.

The official is not put off by Jesus' response, but simply pleads again, "Sir, come down before my little boy dies." The word properly translated "sir" here is *kyrie*, a vocative form of *kyrios* (lord), and does not suggest the official saw Jesus as Lord. He was simply using the common respectful form of address.[13] Jesus replied, "Go; your son will live." The official took Jesus at his word and started on his way.

In due course (since a journey back to Capernaum would likely have taken more than a day), he met his servants coming to tell him his son was alive, and he discovered that the fever had left his son at the precise hour

Jesus spoke the words "Your son will live." This in turn produced yet greater faith in the official and in his household, apparently including his servants. The use of the verb *pisteuo* without a direct object suggests a more substantial form of faith than mere miracle-working faith, yet the evangelist does not tell us this man had become a Christian. Among other things, he had heard nothing from Jesus about who he truly was, or what his mission in life was. The point of this story then, like various of the ones we have examined in this Gospel, is to reveal progress toward a more adequate faith on the part of a non-Christian. As such it would be appropriate to use with certain kinds of more notable (Roman?) potential converts.

Notice that there is no attempt by the evangelist to describe the miracle itself, but its supernatural character, which in turn reflects back on Jesus' supernatural character, is shown by the immediacy of the cure, as soon as Jesus spoke. Only God can act that quickly and across a considerable distance in space and time. Notice too that unlike the Hanina ben Dosa story Jesus does not have to pray to accomplish this miracle; he needs only to say the word.[14] For one who has followed the Fourth Evangelist's story this far, this is hardly surprising—the Word who created the world has no trouble making the return of good health to one individual into a reality by speaking.

II. Bridging the Horizons

Unless one has come from a church where faith healing is a regular practice, it may be easier to relate to the story of Hanina ben Dosa than to the healing of the official's son, for this is not a story about prayer working wonders, but about Jesus directly doing so. One point of contact between ourselves and the text, however, is clearly the desperate need expressed by the man. Most of us have experienced tragedy or close calls at some point in our lives when we did not know where to turn to get help. Yet this text is not encouraging a faith that is born out of mere desperation, but rather one that is tested and found true under such conditions.

I once worked for a man who had been badly injured in a car accident on the way to a church service. To my knowledge, he has never been back since, and he once told me why: "If there really is a God, God would never let something like that happen to a person on the way to worship." The truth is, however, that God allows all kinds of things to happen, and many apparently happen as intended trials of faith. The question this story raises is whether when we have trials in life we will put our faith on trial, or put God on trial instead. The royal official was not interested in laying blame for his son's illness, unlike my friend; he was interested only in getting help, and he would not let Jesus go until he had obtained a blessing from him.

Here as elsewhere we see an undercurrent in the Gospel tradition that shows that Jesus by and large did not set out to perform miracles—he did so in response to needs and requests. In other words he did not see miracles as his primary ministry task, and seems to have grown impatient with those who came to him and related to him only because of the miracles he had performed and could perform again. Notice how in Mark 1:38 Jesus leaves a region to avoid the clamoring after miracles and says, "Let us go on to the neighboring towns, so that I may proclaim the message there also; for that is what I came out to do." Jesus came to be the Word, not the Work, and he grew weary of those who were after him only for what he could do for them, not for who he was. The strong critique of the inadequacy of a miracle-working faith must not be missed in this Gospel, though it is also true that Jesus saw such faith as better than none. If one would be true to the evangelist's intent here, one should preach or teach this story not by playing up the miracle, but by stressing what it says about Jesus and his powerful word, for Jesus is the focus of this and all tales in this Gospel.

It is often argued by wistful Christians that if they could only get back to the first century and walk with Jesus where he walked, and talk with him and see his mighty works, then they would have truly authentic and muscular faith. This, I am convinced, is a mistaken impression. Not only does familiarity breed contempt, or at least breed a taking-things-for-granted attitude, but we must heed the warnings of this Gospel that those who walked and talked with Jesus were as prone to misunderstand him and have inadequate faith as we are, *if not more so.* Sometimes, as Kahlil Gibran, the Lebanese poet, once said, the mountain to the climber is clear from the plain, and very clearly it was only after Jesus' death and resurrection and many years of profound meditation that the Beloved Disciple came to the profound understanding of Jesus enshrined in this Gospel. Craddock is right that this story is telling us that the power of Jesus' word is not confined to the bodily presence of Jesus. What was spoken in Cana had effect in Capernaum.[15] Indeed, Christ can heal as easily from heaven as from someplace on earth, and we still have his word in our midst doing all kinds of marvelous things. The final benediction of this Gospel is on those who have not seen and yet have believed, like the royal official and like ourselves. There is a sense in which those who believe on the basis of the word have a stronger faith than those who will believe only on the basis of an observed work. The Gospel is for those who have ears, first and foremost, for hearing alone requires a full faith response, while seeing may prompt a trusting in only what one sees with one's own eyes. This text then challenges all generations to an adequate faith that goes beyond the signs to see the Sign, that goes beyond the healing words to hear the Word.[16]

Part III. The Public Ministry of Jesus: Phase Two (John 5:1–12:11)

9. Sabbatical Work (John 5:1–47)

In the first portion of the Fourth Gospel we have heard the clear testimony that Jesus was in fact Wisdom come in the flesh, and so divine; we have heard a cornucopia of testimonies to Jesus, including especially the testimony of John the Baptist; and we have seen various quest and request stories that reveal a series of people on the road to a more adequate faith in Jesus. The first two signs recorded in this Gospel both took place in Cana, and were more or less private affairs, but in this section of the Gospels Jesus goes much more public with his works and words, and as there is a crescendo of the miraculous and of the claims made by and about Jesus, so there is also a rising tide of opposition to him by a certain segment of Jewish society.[1] The reason for this opposition is made clear in the very first miracle story of this second phase of the public ministry—Jesus is making himself equal with God. In other words, Jesus is revealing by word and deed that the accolades to the Word/God's Wisdom in John 1 are true, and thus that the appropriate confession of Jesus involves a recognition that "I and the Father are one," that "Before Abraham was, I am," and the like. It is ultimately these sorts of claims, by word and by deed, that scandalize the "Jews" and lead to the trial, conviction, and execution of Jesus. The engine that drives this story forward is the view that Jesus was rejected for who he truly was as well as what he did, for if his claims and works were true, all that came before him had been eclipsed—when the author comes on the stage, the play is over, and following the script previously given is no longer appropriate.

That we are dealing with a new section of the story is shown by the general way the narrative is introduced ("After this," 5:1; cf. 6:1; 7:1; 13:7 [NRSV: "later"]; 19:38; 21:1).[2] It is also apropos to notice the self-contained nature of this scene, and the lack of smooth transition from it to the next narrative in John 6. At one moment we are hearing the dramatic climax of a discourse given in Jerusalem (5:47), at the very next we are in a boat headed across the Sea of Galilee (6:1), with no more connection between the two stories than "After this" (6:1). The evangelist seems to flash back and forth between Jesus in Jerusalem and Jesus in Galilee to show the mounting tide of opposition to Jesus in both places (cf. John 5—7). The judicial process has been set in motion, and Jesus is now a marked man. Now witnesses must testify on his behalf to exonerate him, not merely to bear witness to his merits. It seems clear at least to this author that such an extensive and intensive defense, or *apologia*, of Jesus and his words and deeds would not have been necessary if this Gospel was addressed primarily to Christians who already accepted and believed in the church's testimony about him. Rather, this is a Gospel born out of the fires of ongoing controversy between Christians attempting to witness, and Jews and others who doubted, rejected, or even attacked their witness. This text according to Beasley-Murray "owes its shape to its use in the defense and proclamation of Johannine preachers to Jews, who assailed the Christians for their understanding of the sabbath and still more for their belief about Jesus." It is "a prime example of the missionary apologetic of Christians to Jews."[3] But the evangelist is telling his audience that this controversy had already happened in the life of Jesus, which provided some guidelines for how Christians should handle later similar controversies.[4]

I. The Historical Horizon

It appears that this text falls into a pattern we have already recognized: (1) an event (vv. 1–9b) is followed by (2) a dialogue (9c–18), which in turn is followed by (3) a discourse/commentary, the latter of which can be divided into two parts (vv. 19–30 and 31–47).[5] The narrative of the healing follows the basic structure of such stories (cf. Mark 2:1–12 and par.), with the illness mentioned first, followed by an encounter with Jesus, which issues in healing. The healing then is demonstrated by an action the healed one undertakes, and this in turn is followed by the reaction(s) of one or more onlookers. From the evangelist's point of view, what is really crucial about this miracle is not so much what happened or who was involved—for in this narrative the healed man manifests no faith in Jesus either before or after the healing—but *when* the event took place, on the Sabbath, and the fallout that resulted from a healing on the Sabbath. Notice the artistic skill of the author in holding back until the end of the tale (v. 9) the information that this transpired on the Sabbath, giving it the rhetorically effective placement (end stress) for the fact to be especially noted.

In our last section of the commentary we noted that it was not Jesus' usual procedure to seek out people to heal; rather, they came to him. There is one exception to this rule—when healing was undertaken on the Sabbath. Both the Synoptics and the Fourth Gospel stress that Jesus *deliberately* sought out opportunities to heal on the Sabbath (cf. Mark 3:1–6; Luke 13:10–17; 14:1–6), which raises the question whether he did so as a provocation.[6] It is hard to underestimate how important Sabbath observance was to Jews. Along with circumcision and keeping kosher, it was seen as one of the most crucial marks of being Jewish. And yet Jesus felt free to act in ways that he knew would be seen as deliberate violations of the Sabbath. In this case, the violation is of the prohibition of work on the Sabbath unless life was endangered. This man had had his problem for some thirty-eight years. Clearly his healing could have waited one more day, and yet Jesus chose to act. The consequences of Sabbath violation could be as severe as death by stoning, and both Mark's Gospel and this one seem to agree that it was these sorts of actions on the Sabbath that caused some Jews to begin to make preparations to take action against Jesus. The Mishnah was also quite clear that carrying any burden on the Sabbath was explicitly prohibited (*m. Shabb.* 10:1–5); thus Jesus would be seen to be encouraging others to violate the Sabbath as well.

It is also worth noting that both in our story and in Mark 2, a very similar story where Jesus heals a paralytic using virtually the same words, "take up your mat and walk,"[7] the issue of blasphemy arises in connection with what Jesus says and does. There are several possible explanations for Jesus' behavior: (1) he believed he was bringing in the eschatological age, when the final sabbatical rest would ensue, and Sabbath regulations would no longer be in force; (2) Jesus believed he was divine, and so was not subject to such regulations; this explanation is clearly too neat, because Jesus was also human and a Jew, and one who surely revered the Hebrew scriptures; (3) Jesus believed that he with his ministry was bringing out the true intent and meaning of the sabbatical rest, namely, relieving people from their burdens both mental and physical; and thus healing on the Sabbath was carrying out part of the original intent of the Sabbath laws.[8] From the Johannine perspective, a fourth option arises, namely, that Jesus *is* the world's source of rest, and thus he fulfills and so makes obsolescent Jewish Sabbath regulations. This would be another example of the Johannine theme of Jesus' replacing the institutions of Judaism with something he has to offer that is superior and more lasting. This last explanation probably best describes how the Fourth Evangelist saw the matter.

Excursus: Laying Down the Law: Jewish Judicial Procedures

In order to understand this text and various texts that follow it in this Gospel, it is necessary to understand some things about Jewish judicial processes. As Harvey points out, Jewish courts were not really in a position to investigate the *facts* of a given case. They did not have detectives who went around evaluating clues and putting pieces of evidence together to form a case. Rather the whole Jewish judicial process revolved around deciding the competence of witnesses and the admissibility of their testimonies.[9] The person with the most impressive and honorable array of witnesses normally won in Jewish court, for the chief issue was whose testimony one trusted and believed. "If the witnesses were found to be admissible and competent, and if their evidence was clear and unambiguous, conviction would follow automatically; and in many cases it was the same witnesses who would have responsibility for carrying out the sentence. Evidence, sentence, and judgment were thus much less clearly separated than would be conceivable in a western court."[10] Now it must be remembered that, unlike in most Western and modern courts, there were very severe punishments for giving false testimony; at times the false witness even received the punishment that would have been given the accused, in a sort of boomerang effect. Thus the tendency was to follow careful procedures before making a serious charge.

The normal way of going about things was to give a formal and public warning to a person one believed was violating the law, in case he or she was doing so unintentionally. If the person persisted, next there was usually an attempt to discover if there were some extreme or at least mitigating circumstances or reasons why the person was acting this way. If there were no such factors, it was the duty of the witnesses—any law-abiding and, in this case, Sabbath-keeping Jew—to make sure the law's sanctions were enacted.

There were dangers at every step for such witnesses. Had they understood the law in all its intricacies properly? Had they overlooked or ignored any facts in the case that were relevant? Finally, failure to properly execute the sentence might put the witnesses in danger themselves. If the matter did come to a more formal conclusion by way of trial before the elders or Sanhedrin, the Old Testament requirement of two independent witnesses who were in substantive agreement also came into play (cf. Deut. 19:15; 2 Cor. 13:1).

Another factor that needs to be noticed about Jewish legal proceedings: In a given case, what started out with one party being the defendant and another the prosecutor (in both cases witnesses, not legal representatives, such as lawyers), could turn into a complete reversal of the original, with the accuser ending up being successfully accused and punished. Judges tended to have only confirming roles in Jewish courts; it was the witnesses who were taking action against others. Jewish legal proceedings also did not have the Western rule of trying only one person or group of persons at a time, so the person who started as a defendant could end up being a successful prosecutor during the same proceedings. Perhaps most crucially, a formal court was not necessary for proceedings to go forward in many cases, and thus Harvey is surely right that the Fourth Gospel portrays Jesus as on trial on various occasions long before he gets to the hearings before the Sanhedrin.[11] John 5 relates one such informal trial in which Jesus turns the tables on his accusers, and ends up making clear that it is they who are and will be judged.

A. The Miracle (John 5:1–9)

5:1   After this there was a festival of the Jews, and Jesus went up to Jerusalem.

2 Now in Jerusalem by the Sheep Gate there is a pool, called in Hebrew Bethzatha, which has five porticoes. [3]In these lay many invalids—blind, lame, and paralyzed. [5]One man was there who had been ill for thirty-eight years. [6]When Jesus saw him lying there and knew that he had been there a long time, he said to him, "Do you want to be made well?" [7]The sick man answered him, "Sir, I have no one to put me into the pool when the water is stirred up; and while I am making my way, someone else steps down ahead of me." [8]Jesus said to him, "Stand up, take your mat and walk." [9]At once the man was made well, and he took up his mat and began to walk.

Now that day was a sabbath.

The setting of this miracle is said to be during a feast, though which feast is not specified.[12] Apparently the evangelist mentions it only to explain why

Jesus was in Jerusalem at this time. The event itself is said to take place at the pool called in Aramaic[13] Bethzatha, or more likely Bethesda,[14] which had five *stoas*, or porticoes.[15] There is a reasonable degree of certainty that this location has been pinpointed as being in the northeast quadrant of Jerusalem near the church of St. Anne and the beginning of the Via Dolorosa, near Nehemiah's Sheep Gate.[16] It was a location where many of the sick and lame came, in hopes of a magical cure from the waters in the pool. Verses 3b–4 (NRSV margin: "waiting for the stirring of the water; for an angel of the Lord went down at certain seasons into the pool, and stirred up the water; whoever stepped in first after the stirring of the water was made well from whatever disease that person had") are not in our earliest and best manuscripts, but v. 7 makes clear enough that it was believed that healing happened when the water was stirred up, if one got into the water quickly enough. The problem was that the persons who most needed the cure would be least able to get into the water first, whereas those wanting healing of relatively minor ailments that did not immobilize them would have the advantage.[17] This story reveals the quiet desperation of people with ongoing illnesses in an age when medicine was either nonexistent or usually ineffective. This would be especially the case for someone who had had a malady for thirty-eight years.

We are told that Jesus saw the paralyzed man, knew (presumably by means of supernatural insight) he had been there a long time, and confronted him directly with a question, singling him out of the crowd: "Do you want to be made well?" It is an age-old question, with serious ramifications. Some prefer the sympathy, attention, and help a lingering but non-life-threatening illness brings to a cure that leaves them without such attention. The man's response is to complain, or make an excuse, that his problem is that he has no one to help him get into the water first. The man is not making a request for a cure from Jesus; he is not even thinking in those terms. He assumes that if there is to be a cure, it will come from the magical waters when they are moved. There is no evidence at all that the man knew who Jesus was or what he could do, or had any faith in Jesus.

Jesus abruptly responds: "Stand up, take your mat and walk." We are told that the man is healed at once, immediately after and because Jesus spoke, and he obeys the command, demonstrating he is well. It is only at this juncture in the story, at v. 9b, that we are told that this happened on the Sabbath, and since it is this fact which prompts all the following discussion, it is aptly placed here.

B. The Dialogue (John 5:10–18)

5:10 So the Jews said to the man who had been cured, "It is the sabbath; it is not lawful for you to carry your mat." [11]But he answered them, "The man who made me well said to me, 'Take up your mat and walk.'" [12]They asked him, "Who is the man who said to you, 'Take it up and walk'?" [13]Now the man who had been healed did not know who it was, for Jesus had disappeared in the crowd that was there. [14]Later Jesus found him in the temple and said to him, "See, you have been made well! Do not sin any more, so that nothing worse happens to you." [15]The man went away and told the Jews that it was Jesus who had made him well. [16]Therefore the Jews started persecuting Jesus, because he was doing such things on the sabbath. [17]But Jesus answered them, "My Father is still working, and I also am working." [18]For this reason the Jews were seeking all the more to kill him, because he was not only breaking the sabbath, but was also calling God his own Father, thereby making himself equal to God.

In v. 10 "the Jews" appear on the scene and criticize the man for carrying his mat on the Sabbath. The phrase here again seems to mean some Jewish authorities, or if it has a somewhat wider reference it refers to Torah-observant Jews who were zealous for the precise observance of the law.[18] The major issue here is what constitutes work which is forbidden on the Sabbath. For instance, some early Jewish teachers would have said that if the man in question was a furniture remover, then his carrying the mat constituted work, but if this was not the case, it did not. By the time the Mishnah was codified after the New Testament era, the rabbis had said that there were thirty-nine classes of activities prohibited under the Sabbath laws (cf. *m. Shabb.* 7:2). The problem was not just what constituted work, but also what constituted rest, especially in the case of God. What did it mean to say that God had rested on the seventh day? Who was running the universe while God rested? Philo, a famous Alexandrian Jewish scholar from the New Testament period, in fact denied that God ever ceased his work of creation, not least because *he* is the source of all activity in others (cf. *Leg. all.* 1.5, 18). The debate in part centers around whether the Hebrew verb *shabbat* means to cease or to rest. Thus, there was considerable debate on these issues, and it appears there was an ever-growing list of things that constituted the prohibited activities called work.

In v. 11 the cured man shows that he is adept at the fine art of passing the buck, by telling the Jews that it was the man who cured him (he doesn't even know his name) who told him to carry his mat. Jesus had managed to disappear into the crowd, and so the man is unable to single him out at that point. The story continues by saying that sometime later Jesus found the man in the Temple (notice it was not the other way around), and said to him: "See, you have been made well. Stop sinning, so that nothing worse happens to you." Here we have, juxtaposed side by side, a reference to sickness and a reference to sin. The question is, is Jesus making a connection? Is he suggesting that the man had been paralyzed because he sinned or was a sinner? Let us start with what is relatively more clear. The saying here does connect sinning with *future* consequences. The man must stop sinning lest something worse (than his previous lameness) happen to him. Carson thinks that the "unavoidable implication is that the bad thing that had already happened was occasioned by the sin which the person must not repeat."[19] This is not so obvious to me, especially in light of what is said in

John 9 about the man born blind (cf. below, on 9:1–4). Furthermore, Jesus could be referring to the man's willingness to pass the blame on to Jesus when confronted by the authorities. What can be said on the basis of this Gospel and other pertinent texts such as Luke 13:1–5, which has a very similar logic to John 5:14, is that there is no one-to-one correspondence between sickness and sin. While some illnesses certainly can be said to be caused by sin, the point is that not all illnesses can be explained in this fashion, as John 9:1–4 makes evident. Nevertheless, in Jesus' day there were many who presumed that various people's illnesses could be attributed to prior sin. Jesus *may* be saying this was the case with the man he just healed, but the text is not clear on this point. What it is clear is that sin ultimately has moral consequences, indeed, it seems to be implied here, eternal ones.

At this juncture (vv. 15–16), the man informs the authorities that it was Jesus who healed him, and we are told that the Jews *ediokon* (started persecuting) Jesus. This Greek word often is translated "persecute" in the translations of this verse, but as Harvey rightly points out it has a perfectly good forensic sense—namely, prosecute, bring to trial. Here these Jews believed they had discovered Jesus had violated the law, and so they set the process of inquisition in motion, seeing it as their religious duty. This is a crucial juncture in the telling of Jesus' story in the Gospel, after which there is no turning back from the judicial process of inquiry—what may be called pretrial hearings, prosecution, informal trial, and then finally formal trial and execution. From now on, the atmosphere during the rest of the narration of the ministry is dark and foreboding because of this ongoing judicial process. Jesus' initial response to the inquiry only serves to pour more fuel on the flames—"My Father is still working, and I also am working." The evangelist tells us that this response caused these Jews all the more to seek to kill Jesus, not only because he was breaking the Sabbath,[20] but also because: (1) he was calling God his own Father (i.e., claiming a special relationship with the Father); and (2) thereby he was making himself equal with God (i.e., his work was equivalent to or an expression of God's work, which implied something about him). Verse 18 must be read carefully, because it is a statement by the evangelist explaining why the Jews were seeking to kill Jesus. It boils down to Jesus' claiming a special relationship to the Father, and the implications of that claim.

The text does not say that the Jews were already charging him with claiming to be a god or equal to God—that comes later, after further confrontations (cf. 10.33; 19:7). The evangelist has made and will make clear that it was not so much a matter of Jesus' *making himself* equal to God, for in light of the prologue he has been in this condition from the outset.[21] The question becomes, in what sense was Jesus equal to the Father, especially in light of his evident subordination to the Father? This raises some important issues, which we must address under the heading of agency language.

EXCURSUS: AGENCY LANGUAGE IN THE FOURTH GOSPEL

In my judgment, one of the most important advances in understanding Johannine language about the Christ has come by exploring how the evangelist uses agency language to describe the relationship between the Son and the Father.[22] This is by no means the only way the author speaks about Jesus—the Son of man language and the Wisdom language add other ways the evangelist attempts to adequately express the character and significance of Jesus. Nevertheless, agency language is a crucial part of his christological vocabulary.

The Jewish concept of agency, which involved a legal relationship as much as anything else, can be summed up in the key phrase: "A person's agent is as himself." An agent is a person authorized to perform some specific set of tasks and empowered to speak and act for the one sending the person. The agent was acting for the sender on occasions when the sender could not or chose not to be personally present. This agent was to be treated as the one sending him or her would have been treated had that one come in person. An affront to the agent was an affront to the sender; a positive response or treatment of the agent was seen as a positive response or treatment of the sender. In many ways this was also how ambassadors or envoys were viewed in the ancient world—they were just other kinds of agents.

How, then, does this affect the way we read the Fourth Gospel? First, this Gospel stresses that Jesus is the Father's unique and special Son. This claim is reiterated over and over again in various ways in this Gospel. Now, in family affairs the agent of first choice for any family business dealing would be the eldest son, who was the chief heir, and if he was the only son, he would be the sole heir of all the father's property. He could be authorized to undertake a mission for the head of the family, and would be empowered to say or do whatever was necessary to accomplish the task; and the son would know that for all legal purposes he was not only acting and speaking *for* the father, but as the father would act. The son could do nothing beyond the scope of the power and commissioned authority given to him. If the Fourth Evangelist is using the Jewish concept of agency to describe Jesus' relationship with the Father, this will explain why it is said that the Son can do only what the Father authorizes him to do, or again, the Son can go only when the Father authorizes him to go somewhere. Jesus, the only Son, is his Father's sole agent on earth, commissioned and sent so that "whoever believes in him might have life." In short, he has been commissioned and sent to convey God's life and light to humankind. The negative side of this task is that if and when the light or life is rejected, then the Sender has been rejected as well, and so some type of judgment must follow. Basically, the Son is authorized to undertake a soteriological task and to do whatever is necessary while on earth to accomplish this task. To be sure he is acting appropriately, he consults with the Sender regularly (through prayer). The agency model explains how Jesus can be both equal in power and authority to the Father while he undertakes his mission and ministry, and yet clearly subordinate to the Father. It also partially explains why it was necessary for Jesus to return to the Father. All good agents must report directly to the sender about the outcome of their (joint) venture.

At this juncture, one may object: where in the Fourth Gospel is Jesus called, or does Jesus call himself, God's agent? The answer is that Jesus reveals this truth at the crucial last meal with his disciples, where he tells them before leaving the world, "The slave is not greater than his master, nor is the *apostolos* greater than the one who sent him" (John 13:16, alt.). Here the term *apostolos* must have its basic nonreligious sense of a "sent" one, an agent. Here, Jesus is at the point of authorizing the disciples to be his agents, his *apostoloi*, a word we transliterate as apostles. But he has also just said in 13:15, "I set you an example, that you should do as I have done."[23] This whole discourse comes to a preliminary climax at 13:20 where Jesus pronounces one of the most fundamental truths about a person and his agent: "Whoever receives one whom I send receives me; and whoever receives me receives him who sent me." Jesus is God's "apostle" or agent, and the disciples (apostles) are Jesus' agents, authorized and empowered to act for him in his absence.[24]

Now of course this model does not tell the whole story about the Fourth Evangelist's view of Christ. For one thing, the agent's "equality" with his sender was a legal fiction—he was to be treated *as if* he were the principal who sent him.[25] The Fourth Evangelist wants to say more than "as if" about Jesus' equality with the Father. Nevertheless, this concept unlocks many puzzling doors in the world of Johannine Christology. In closing, it is not only the Fourth Evangelist (and the Christ who speaks in his Gospel) who expresses this theme. The famous parable of the vineyard in Mark 12:1–12 (and par.), which is likely authentic,[26] tells an agency story of an only son sent by a father to deal with recalcitrant tenants in the owner's vineyard, a son who is recognized as the heir and thus the ultimate agent of the father and who gets himself killed in the bargain. Thus it appears that both the Synoptics and John are telling us that Jesus presented himself as God's unique agent, the only Son of the Father.[27]

C. The Discourse(s)
(John 5:19–30, 31–47)

5:19 Jesus said to them, "Very truly, I tell you, the Son can do nothing on his own, but only what he sees the Father doing; for whatever the Father does, the Son does likewise. [20]The Father loves the Son and shows him all that he himself is doing; and he will show him greater works than these, so that you will be astonished. [21]Indeed, just as the Father raises the dead and gives them life, so also the Son gives life to whomever he wishes. [22]The Father judges no one but has given all judgment to the Son, [23]so that all may honor the Son just as they honor the Father. Anyone who does not honor the Son does not honor the Father who sent him. [24]Very truly, I tell you, anyone who hears my word and believes him who sent me has eternal life, and does not come under judgment, but has passed from death to life.

25 Very truly, I tell you, the hour is coming, and is now here, when the dead will hear the voice of the Son of God, and those who hear will live. [26]For just as the Father has life in himself, so he has granted the Son also to have life in himself; [27]and he has given him authority to execute judgment,

because he is the Son of Man. [28]Do not be astonished at this; for the hour is coming when all who are in their graves will hear his voice [29]and will come out—those who have done good, to the resurrection of life, and those who have done evil, to the resurrection of condemnation.

30 "I can do nothing on my own. As I hear, I judge; and my judgment is just, because I seek to do not my own will but the will of him who sent me.

31 "If I testify about myself, my testimony is not true. [32]There is another who testifies on my behalf, and I know that his testimony to me is true. [33]You sent messengers to John, and he testified to the truth. [34]Not that I accept such human testimony, but I say these things so that you may be saved. [35]He was a burning and shining lamp, and you were willing to rejoice for a while in his light. [36]But I have a testimony greater than John's. The works that the Father has given me to complete, the very works that I am doing, testify on my behalf that the Father has sent me. [37]And the Father who sent me has himself testified on my behalf. You have never heard his voice or seen his form, [38]and you do not have his word abiding in you, because you do not believe him whom he has sent.

39 "You search the scriptures because you think that in them you have eternal life; and it is they that testify on my behalf. [40]Yet you refuse to come to me to have life. [41]I do not accept glory from human beings. [42]But I know that you do not have the love of God in you. [43]I have come in my Father's name, and you do not accept me; if another comes in his own name, you will accept him. [44]How can you believe when you accept glory from one another and do not seek the glory that comes from the one who alone is God? [45]Do not think that I will accuse you before the Father; your accuser is Moses, on whom you have set your hope. [46]If you believed Moses, you would believe me, for he wrote about me. [47]But if you do not believe what he wrote, how will you believe what I say?"

In light of the discussion above about agency, much of what follows is easier to understand. For instance, the very first strong assertion (with double *Amen;* cf. above), "The Son can do nothing on his own, but only what he sees the Father doing," is more than an ancient version of the aphorism "like Father, like Son." It is a statement saying that the Son's writ is only to do what he is authorized by the Father to do and in fact what the Father has shown him to do. Verse 20 indicates that this is an intimate partnership, for the Father loves the Son and shows him all that he is doing.

Part of what the Father has authorized and empowered the Son to do is to give life, to be able to raise the dead—a power early Jews believed was solely in the hands of God. But even further than this, v. 22 also says that the Son has been given the power to pass ultimate or final judgment—again a role that is exclusively in God's provenance. As is always true with an agent, anyone who doesn't honor the agent doesn't honor the sender. Verse 23 says precisely this, but using the terms Son and Father. The Son's words are in fact the words of "him who sent me" (v. 24), so that to hear and believe the

Son's words is to hear and believe the Father's words. The upshot is that one not only has eternal life, having passed from death to life already before physical death, but also one avoids present (and future?) judgment. Verse 25 speaks of the dead hearing the Son's voice and coming to life, and here the reference appears to be to the spiritually dead.

Notice that vv. 26–27 say the Father has *granted* the Son the privilege of having life in himself and has *given him authority* to execute judgment, "because he is the Son of Man." What this suggests is that while the term Son here amounts to agency language, the term "Son of Man" is in fact a higher term, implying that this person could suitably be given such powers because of his divine character.[28] One is reminded of the outcome of the discussion in *1 Enoch*, where Enoch is taken on a tour of heaven and told about the figure called the Son of man, and then informed he *is* the Son of man. The point is that in both contexts a human being is said to be one and the same as the divine Son of man.[29] Notice, too, the difference between v. 25a, which speaks of the hour coming and being *now here*, and v. 28, which speaks simply of the hour coming, which means that v. 28 is surely speaking of a future event—the resurrection of the dead, responding to the voice of the Son. This means that the writ of authority of the Son extends into the future, at least until the final resurrection and judgment. Verse 29 speaks of a resurrection of life for those who have done good, and of death for those who have done evil. This discourse is very similar to the one in Wisd. Sol. 16, where the roles of God and of Wisdom seem to be identical or blended together, and yet the two can be distinguished. After having spoken of the incident of the lifted-up snake in the desert (Num. 21), "For the one who turned toward it was saved, not by the thing that was beheld, but by you, the Savior of all,"[30] it is then said of God and/or of God's Wisdom, "For you have power over life and death; you lead mortals down to the gates of Hades and back again."[31] Jesus, then, assumes the role earlier predicated of Wisdom and God in the earlier Jewish sapiential literature. John 5:29 implies that judgment is rendered on the basis of deeds, and this is not seen as contradictory to grace, in part because the chief work or deed said to be necessary in this Gospel is belief in the Son. But it is also because this Gospel writer does believe that Jesus affirmed that one's eternal destiny will be affected by one's behavior, perhaps especially behavior subsequent to the new birth, for "From everyone to whom much has been given, much will be required." Verse 30 concludes this discussion of agency, making plain that the Son can only act and judge on the basis of the will of the Father. He does not seek to act independently, but rather to do the Father's will.[32]

The first discourse represents Jesus' response to what will become the two major charges against him: (1) violation of the Sabbath, and (2) blasphemy. The response to the first charge amounted to saying that Jesus was simply doing what the Father was doing on the Sabbath, which of course implied he was authorized to act this way and thus was intimate with, and in some sense equal to, God. In the second discourse, Jesus begins to line up his witnesses for his defense against the charges that are being brought against him, and the chief of these witnesses are John the Baptist, the works Jesus does, the Father, and the scriptures, *including Moses'* testimony.[33]

The witness of the Baptist is appealed to, because the audience knew of him and had in fact sent messengers to him to hear his testimony (cf. above on 1:19–28).[34] Jesus disclaims accepting human testimony, but he knows his audience does so, and so he hopes they will believe John's testimony, since they rejoiced in it for a while. He hopes they will believe it "so that you may be saved," which of course implies they are lost. Notice that John is said to be a burning and shining lamp (*lychnos*), not the light. "John is distinguished from the true self-kindled light, just as his witness is secondary to and derived from (1:33) that of the Father."[35] It appears likely that Ps. 132:17 stands in the background here: "Here [at Zion] I will make a horn grow for David, and set up a lamp for my anointed one."

Jesus sees the testimony of the works the Father sent him to complete as a higher testimony than that of John's, but it is also the case that the Father testifies on Jesus' behalf. Yet Jesus says they have never seen him *nor heard his voice*. Since there is no voice from heaven in this Gospel (the baptism and the transfiguration not being discussed), those scholars who think the Father's testimony to Jesus comes in the scriptures are likely right. The problem is that the hearers don't have God's word abiding in them, because they do not believe in the agent God sent.

Verse 39's main verb could be taken as either an indicative ("You search the scriptures"), or an imperative ("Search the scriptures"), but the context surely favors the former. Jesus says the Jews search the scriptures because they assume "in them you have eternal life," but this is a case of mistaking the means for the ends. It is God who bestows such life, in this case through the Son. The audience is said to be caught up in the cycle of trusting in human testimonies and accepting glory from one another, rather than accepting the testimony God sent in Christ and the glory that comes from God alone. Once again we are in a two-level discussion—Jesus is speaking and acting on one level, but the audience is operating and thinking on a more mundane level. The equality Jesus has with the Father is not that of an independent or competing deity, but as one who is subordinate to and works in harmony with the Father. He affirms strongly in v. 44 that there is only one true God; nothing he has said should be taken in any other sense. This can only mean that Jesus must be seen as one manifestation or represention of the one true God on earth, God in human form, not a second deity.

In a surprising turn at v. 45, Jesus says that Moses, far from testifying against him [Jesus] for what he did on the Sabbath, will testify against his accusers! The worm has now turned, and now it is "the Jews," not Jesus, who are or will be on trial. If they had believed Moses, they would believe Jesus, "for he [Moses] wrote about me." The discourse then comes to an abrupt halt, or, better said, is left open-ended, for this is only the first salvo in an ongoing series of confrontations and controversies. It is meant to be seen as a type of the kind of Sabbath controversies Jesus had with the authorities, as is shown by the fact that in v. 18 it is said Jesus *was breaking* (imperfect tense verb indicating habitual, ongoing action) the Sabbath. The evangelist leaves no doubt that the issue under debate is not just what Jesus did, but who he was.

II. Bridging the Horizons

This chapter is a gold mine of material, which if handled properly can lead to numerous pertinent applications and implications. I would suggest that one way to avoid misuse of this text is to familiarize oneself with the Jewish trial procedures and agency concepts as outlined above. This will prevent a lot of false starts or overdrawn conclusions.

A second key pointer is that it is usually wise to follow the flow of the text and emphasize what it emphasizes. As the amount of material devoted to the issue shows, for the evangelist the matter of real importance is not the miracle per se, but what it tells us about Jesus' character and mission.

Another possible line of approach would be to focus on the fact that Jesus is liberating the paralyzed man not just from his illness, but presumably also from a worldview that looked for healing in water or magic rituals rather than in God.[36] One could also dwell on the issue of wellness, and of people who would rather not be well for a variety of reasons.

The end of this chapter offers a warning that it is a mistake to search the scriptures as if in them one finds life. Again, this is to mistake the means for the ends. A good sermon could be preached on the problems of bibliolatry, a worship or overly high reverence of the Bible itself, rather than the God of the Bible.

God's Word is meant to lead one to God, and the study of God's Word is not meant to be an end in itself, however fascinating, but a means to a relationship or deeper relationship with God. "It is not the Scriptures as such, or mastery of them at the literary level, which will give eternal life. The Son alone gives life."[37]

One final word of caution should be issued about this text. This text does indeed suggest that according to Mosaic law, Jesus intentionally violated the Sabbath. Yet one cannot violate a law that is no longer in force! I would suggest that in order to make sense of this text we follow the leading of the Fourth Evangelist and see this as yet another example of Jesus' not merely correctly interpreting the law, but replacing the institutions of Judaism with himself, including replacing the Sabbath laws. Jesus gives the rest and restoration the law promised. The law came through Moses, but grace and truth through Jesus. In Jesus the new age has come, and new occasions teach new duties. Moses' law is viewed as no longer binding on Jesus or his followers, having fulfilled its purpose and having become obsolescent *except* insofar as it points to and testifies about Jesus. It is, then, a glorious and insightful anachronism from the Fourth Evangelist's viewpoint, but an anachronism nonetheless. This view is little different from what we find in Paul's letters, in Gal. 3—4 and 2 Cor. 3, and it reveals how Christians began to distinguish themselves from early Judaism. The radical implications of the Johannine approach to this matter must not be dodged. The Old Testament is seen to have a rather exclusively christological function in the new age, except where its dictates are reaffirmed as part of the new covenant. This text then must be taught or preached with caution, especially with an audience that has not been sufficiently instructed about the relationship between the testaments. At the very least, it is a PG-13 kind of text.

Were I to preach on this text on more than one occasion I would focus on very different aspects of the text. For one thing, it is crucial to focus on the characterization of Jesus here as God's Son and agent. Furthermore, the claims that Jesus makes, especially in regard to having a unique relationship with the Father, go well beyond the claims of a teacher or prophet. There is thus a place for a real evangelistic sermon based on this material, along the lines that C. S. Lewis long ago suggested:

> In the mouth of any speaker who is not God, these words would imply what I can only regard as a silliness and conceit unrivalled by any character in history. . . . You must make your choice. Either this man was, and is, the Son of God; or else a madman or something worse. You can shut him up for a fool, you can spit at him and kill him as a demon; or you can fall at his feet and call him Lord and God.[38]

The option one is not left with is the patronizing approach that sees Jesus as merely a good teacher or prophet, or a great man. As this Gospel makes clear, these are true but woefully inadequate confessions. It was the belief of the Fourth Evangelist that one was always in danger of saying too little about who Jesus really was, not saying too much.

On an entirely different front, a good sociological sermon could be preached based on this text. Sociologists tell us that either in a pluralistic society or in a society with strongly competing forms of monotheism (e.g., in Israel today), people who make exclusive claims are inevitably going to cause controversy and conflict. It is simply not possible to affirm *and bear witness to* the scandal of particularity that lies at the heart of the Gospel and at the same time expect to be everyone's friend and the toast of the town. The Johannine community was a minority community, which established its identity and distinctiveness by affirming a very high Christology—a Christology that set it at odds with many in the synagogue (especially its most zealous leaders), and many in the larger Greco-Roman world as well. The Johannine Christian was not content to have Jesus sit on Mount Olympus as one among many gods and lords. This Gospel tells us that *if* one is part of a witnessing community in a pluralistic or competitive monotheistic environment, *the higher one's Christology, the more separation and alienation from the larger culture is not only likely but almost inevitable.* One must ask oneself whether one's church is willing to pay the price of hostility, resistance, controversy, and rejection for a bold witness making exclusive claims about Jesus. The Johannine community did this, as I would suggest Jesus did, and the result was they were not welcomed with open arms by most. I am not proposing that one should ever be obnoxious for the sake of Jesus, merely that texts like John 5 ask us to count the cost before becoming a disciple. There is in most people a great desire and need to be loved, appreciated, affirmed.

For the Christian, these needs and desires must take a decided back seat if one is to live out the implications of the Gospel in one's day-to-day life in a pluralistic culture where Christians are a minority. One must decide whether integration with the dominant values of one's society or integrity as a Christian is more critical. We live in an environment not unlike the Johannine Christians' where one starts as a Christian witness with considerable disadvantages.[39]

10. Food for Thought,
Bread on the Waters (John 6:1–71)

If the healing of the paralytic on the Sabbath precipitated a crisis in the Judean ministry, the feeding of the five thousand has the same effect in Galilee.[1] The alert reader will note that John 6 is the only chapter where the evangelist treats the Galilean phase of Jesus' public ministry in any sort of detail, and it is not an accident that he has chosen the one incident that, if not bringing the Galilean ministry to a climax, at the very least brought it to a crisis stage, causing the withdrawal of Jesus, the falling away of some of the more peripheral disciples, and finally the confession of the faithful few.

That the feeding of the five thousand was a crucial event in Jesus' Galilean ministry is shown by the fact that it is the only ministry miracle that appears in all four Gospels. Whatever may be the reasons for its inclusion in the other Gospels, it is included here because it reveals something crucial about the character of Jesus himself and of his ministry. We have here yet another quest story, with the crowd pursuing Jesus around the Sea of Galilee, but they are after Jesus to be their political leader and/or to provide physical sustenance for them, and in both cases they miss the meaning of both the miracle and the miracle worker.

John 6 is a self-contained unit, and its internal structure is somewhat complex.[2] We have two miracle narratives (6:1–15, 16–21), the latter of which is exceedingly brief and serves mainly as an interlude between the feeding miracle and the dialogue about it. Yet there is a brief narrative introducing the dialogue at 6:22–25, and the dialogue continues to the end of the chapter, but with an ever-decreasing group of dialogue partners. At first the discussion is with the crowd (vv. 25–40), then with "the Jews," again clearly a smaller group of objectors within the audience (vv. 41–59),[3] and finally with the disciples, some of whom themselves "turn back" from Jesus, leaving Jesus with the inner circle of the Twelve, which here for the first time in this Gospel comes to the fore. Even then, while one makes a good confession, it is immediately stated that even one of them would prove to be an adversary.[4] Verse 59 marks off the public from the private discussion of the matter, indicating that what has preceded took place in the synagogue in Capernaum. The flow of the text suggests that Jesus' miracle of feeding was seen to be appealing by the crowd and raised many questions, but the farther the dialogue proceeded the more offensive Jesus' words became, causing more and more to fall away, including some who were already disciples, until only the truly faithful were left.[5] In fact, the text suggests that Jesus deliberately made increasingly provocative remarks to get his audience to show their true colors, to make either a positive or negative decision about him.

While many have been tempted to read this whole chapter in light of the reference to the nearness of the Passover in v. 4, and of v. 51, "The bread that I will give for the life of the world is my flesh," and in light of the discussion of consuming Christ's flesh and blood which follows v. 51, this is not a major issue before the end of the public dialogue, when Jesus makes his most controversial remarks, and even there the significance of the remarks is debatable.

Prior to v. 51 the Old Testament story chiefly alluded to is the feeding of the multitudes in the wilderness with manna, the bread that came down from heaven. That story, as this one, has a large group of Jews who benefit from the manna, and a smaller group among them who continue to murmur and complain, as "the Jews" do at vv. 41 and 52 in our text. There is, furthermore, nothing eucharistic about a meal of bread and fish, and the crowd is not depicted as receiving sacramental-sized portions.[6] Rather, they ate their fill, and there were leftovers afterward. Nor is Jesus said to break the bread before it is distributed. Nor is there anything eucharistic about the discussion of the meal in the dialogue that follows the miracle up to v. 51.

Most importantly, even in vv. 51ff. the point is that if those in the audience wish to have eternal life it is Jesus and his death that they are required to "swallow," and it is precisely Jesus' divine claims and his death that they can't stomach. The issue is not whether they can accept participating in a ritual meal, or a new Christian form of Passover that conveys life. It is Jesus, not the Passover or the Lord's Supper, and in particular Jesus through his death,[7] that is seen as the source of eternal life. Were the point sacramental, we might have expected this story to immediately precede the account of the Last Supper in John 13. Strikingly, even there the evangelist shows no interest at all in developing the Last Supper story's eucharistic overtones.

The chief symbolic associations this story *does* have is with the various Jewish manna traditions, where Torah or Wisdom is called or alluded to as manna/bread from God that feeds God's people. The wisdom traditions are especially important in light of the degree of sapiential reading of the Jesus story we have already found in John 1—5.[8] For example, Wisdom in Sir. 24 says, "Come to me. . . . Those who eat of me will hunger for more, and those who drink of me will thirst for more" (vv. 19, 21), and Prov. 9:5 reads, "Come, eat of my bread and drink of the wine I have mixed."[9] In *Exodus Rabbah* 25:7, this verse in Proverbs is linked to Ex. 16:4—"Because I will cause to rain bread from heaven," the former text in Proverbs being seen as the explanation of the latter. Philo is more explicit. In commenting on Ex. 16:4 he remarks: "Of what food can he rightly say that it rained from heaven, save of heavenly Wisdom?" In short, there were plenty of examples before, during, and after the time of Jesus for a sapiential reading of the manna story. Here in John 6 when Jesus is speaking of eating of his flesh and drinking of his blood, immediately after referring to himself as the bread that came down from heaven, he and/or the evangelist is drawing on wisdom texts like Prov. 9:5, Sir. 24, and the wisdom reading of Ex. 16:4 in order to imply that Jesus is God's divine wisdom that feeds God's people. When one takes wisdom in, one receives eternal life.[10] In this regard there are close parallels between John 4, which surely has no eucharistic overtones, and John 6, as Painter remarks: "In one there is the offering of life-giving water and in the other the offer of the life-giving bread. Here we have the two fundamental and universal symbols of the sources of life which have universal appeal. The symbols also have a particular resonance for Judaism."[11] Though Painter goes on to say that both water and bread are well-known symbols for the law, it is equally true that water and bread are symbols for wisdom, which could be identified with Torah, as in Sirach, but more often had a broader range of meaning. The Fourth Evangelist is taking these traditions and depicting Jesus as greater than the law, which merely enshrines God's wisdom, for Jesus is Wisdom in the flesh. In other words, John 6 is another text about revelation of the truth about Jesus, not about nurture of those who are already disciples.

Thus, the discussion here is christologically, not ecclesiologically or sacramentally, focused, as is clearly shown by the way the evangelist ends the discussion—with Peter's confession of who Jesus is, after Jesus has explained that people become true disciples and people of God only as God has drawn them to Christ. The issue in John 6 is true faith in Jesus, true discipleship, and the benefits thereof, but this entails the even larger issue of *who* provides eternal life and where one can obtain it. The evangelist's answer is Jesus—both by his coming to earth as the living bread from heaven, and by his dying and making the sustenance he *is* available to all who will offer the true confession as Peter does. This is apt discussion in a book intended to help Johannine Christians lead others to Christ.

I. The Historical Horizon

A. A Tale of Two Miracles (John 6:1–24)

6:1   After this Jesus went to the other side of the Sea of Galilee, also called the Sea of Tiberias. [2]A large crowd kept following him, because they saw the signs that he was doing for the sick. [3]Jesus went up the mountain and sat down there with his disciples. [4]Now the Passover, the festival of the Jews, was near. [5]When he looked up and saw a large crowd coming toward him, Jesus said to Philip, "Where are we to buy bread for these people to eat?" [6]He said this to test him, for he himself knew what he was going to do. [7]Philip answered him, "Six months' wages would not buy enough bread for each of them to get a little." [8]One of his disciples, Andrew, Simon Peter's brother, said to him, [9] "There is a boy here who has five barley loaves and two fish. But what are they among so many people?" [10]Jesus said, "Make the people sit down." Now there was a great deal of grass in the place; so they sat down, about five thousand in all. [11]Then Jesus took the loaves, and when he had given thanks, he distributed them to those who were seated; so also the fish, as much as they wanted. [12]When they were satisfied, he told his disciples, "Gather up the fragments left over, so that nothing may be lost." [13]So they gathered them up, and from the fragments of the five barley loaves, left by those who had eaten, they filled twelve baskets. [14]When the people saw the sign that he had done, they began to say, "This is indeed the prophet who is to come into the world."

15 When Jesus realized that they were about to come and take him by force to make him king, he withdrew again to the mountain by himself.

16 When evening came, his disciples went down to the sea, [17]got into a boat, and started across the sea to Capernaum. It was now dark, and Jesus had not yet come to them. [18]The sea became rough because a strong wind was blowing. [19]When they had rowed about three or four miles, they saw Jesus walking on the sea and coming near the boat, and they were terrified. [20]But he said to them, "It is I; do not be afraid." [21]Then they wanted to take him into the boat, and immediately the boat reached the land toward which they were going.

22 The next day the crowd that had stayed on the other side of the sea saw that there had been only one boat there. They also saw that Jesus had not got into the boat with his disciples, but that his disciples had gone away alone. [23]Them some boats from Tiberias came near the place where they had eaten the bread after the Lord had given thanks. [24]So when the crowd saw that neither Jesus nor his disciples were there, they themselves got into the boats and went to Capernaum looking for Jesus.

The narration of this sign begins with a mention of its location: it transpired on the east side of the Sea of Tiberias. The use of this name for the Sea of Galilee suggests three things: (1) The evangelist is writing to an audience outside of Israel, at least some of whom were more likely to know the lake in Galilee by the Roman name it came to have after Herod Antipas in about A.D. 20 built and named a city on its banks after the Emperor Tiberius; (2) this name connects our author with the author of the epilogue in John 21, where it is also called the Sea of Tiberias (v. 1); there is no need to conjure up a later editor or redactor as author of John 21—the same person who put together the whole Gospel gave us John 21; (3) the name may well suggest some Gentiles in addition to Jews in the audience, for Gentiles would be more familiar with Roman geographical designations than with Jewish ones.

John 6:2 says that the crowd kept following Jesus because they saw the signs Jesus was doing for the sick. Since this is a Galilean crowd this could refer to the second Cana miracle, but in any case the evangelist alludes here to a longer Galilean ministry about which he records very little. The miracle transpires on the hills near the lake. The lake is in a depression, with considerable hills rising all around it. This geographical feature leads to swirling winds and very choppy water on the lake when there is a storm.

In the Johannine telling of this story, Jesus is the focus of attention—it is he rather than the disciples who distributes the bread and fish (v. 11), whereas the Synoptics tell us that the disciples played a role.[12] Jesus uses the occasion to test one of the disciples, Philip. Here as elsewhere in this Gospel the disciple fails the test, and thinks only on a mundane level of the money required to buy enough bread to feed each in the crowd just a little. Two hundred denarii, or about 6 or 7 months' wages of a day laborer, would be insufficient to give each only a mouthful. Andrew draws attention to the fact that a boy has five barley loaves and two fish, but adds, "What are they among so many people?" Clearly neither disciple, despite Jesus' previous signs, has any inkling of what Jesus is about to do, or faith in his satisfying such a large crowd. We are reminded of the similar portrait in John 4, of the slow-witted disciples returning from the village with material food and failing utterly to grasp what Jesus is doing or talking about. It is a striking feature of this Gospel that with rare exception, such as the confession of Peter at the end of this chapter, the Twelve come off rather more like the dirty dozen than the illustrious and illuminated inner circle. Other characters in the drama, the Samaritan woman and the Samaritans, and the blind man in John 9, are depicted as more spiritually perceptive than they.[13]

Only the Fourth Gospel mentions that the loaves were barley loaves, and this has been seen by many scholars as an allusion to the story of Elisha feeding a hundred people with twenty barley loaves, after which they had some left over (2 Kings 4:42–44). If this is alluded to here, the point would be that Jesus far outstrips the Old Testament prophet in his deeds—behold, one greater than Elisha is here![14]

Verse 11 tells us that the people were given fish "as much as they wanted." It does not say that they were satisfied with a sacramental-size portion. We are to think here of a hearty repast, perhaps even a depiction of the messianic banquet, when many would come from the east and the west and eat with Messiah (cf. Luke 14:15–24). Verse 12 provides another insight found only in the Fourth Gospel's version of the story—the fragments were to be gathered up so nothing might be lost. This resulted in the astounding outcome that after eating they finished with more bread than they started with![15]

The sign leads some in the crowd to say, "This is indeed the prophet who is to come into the world." This seems likely to be an allusion to Deut. 18:15–19, and thus to the eschatological prophet like Moses. It is not clear to what degree speculation about this shadowy figure had advanced in Jesus' day. In the Qumran community there was the expectation of a prophet to accompany the two messiahs (priestly and kingly), and there the text Deut 18:18 is alluded to (1QS 9:10–11; 4QTest 5–8), but the function of this prophet is not made clear. Perhaps equally important is the evidence provided by W. A. Meeks that Moses was seen by many early Jews as the ideal king and prophet par excellence, in particular among the Samaritans.[16] It is in light of this background that we must read v. 15, which tells us that Jesus realized that the crowd would seek to make him king by force, and so he withdrew.

This raises the issue of what sort of view Jesus had of the role of messiah or the king of the Jews. I have discussed this matter elsewhere at length and have argued that Jesus, while not refusing to use force on some occasions, deliberately avoided any attempts to have foisted on him the role of zealot messiah, dedicated to the political overthrow of the Romans and the restablishment of self-rule and the monarchial borders of the land.[17] As both the Synoptics and the Fourth Gospel suggest, Jesus did *not* reject all messianic acclaimation of him by others, *but* always sought to define or redefine things in his own terms.[18] His own preferred language of self-reference involved the phrase the Son of man. Jesus' caution in this regard was necessary, for there were many different ideas about messiah and the eschatological age in early Judaism.

Jesus' withdrawal is followed by the disciples' rowing across the Sea of Galilee toward Capernaum in the evening. A strong wind arose when they were about three miles out in the lake, and things got very rough. We are then told they saw Jesus walking on the water and coming toward them, and they were terrified. Jesus calmed their fears by letting them know it was he, not to be afraid, and then when they tried to take him into the boat, immediately the boat reached the land, at the appropriate destination. Some scholars have suggested that this entailed two miracles—walking on water, and the boat miraculously and suddenly arriving at land shortly after it was in the middle of the lake.

Beasley-Murray has plausibly suggested that the miracle recorded in John 6:16–21 should be read in light of Ps. 77:16, 19, which speaks of how God came to his people in the exodus—"The waters saw you, O God, they saw you and writhed. . . . Your path was through the sea."[19] Thus, it may be that we are meant to see the feeding followed by a second exodus experience for God's people, with Jesus seen as God or God's agent coming to deal with his people's distress. If this is correct, then the people are portrayed very much like the lost wilderness-wandering generation, who focused on material things and some of whom murmured over the slightest difficulties.

What are we to make of these two miracle stories? In both, the miraculous element is made clear but is not dwelt on. In both, Jesus is the central figure and the disciples respond with obtuseness at best, and lack of understanding and fear at worst. Jesus in these two miracles is portrayed as the master of nature, able to make all sorts of material things, simple bread and fish or water and a boat, do his bidding. In the first and second stories Jesus is not who the audience thinks he is. He is not the sort of king the crowd had in mind, and he is not some ghost or terrifying nighttime apparition that the disciples apparently feared he was (cf. Mark 6:4).[20] In both stories Jesus satisfies the audience, but only temporarily, and so the story of lack of understanding on the part of the crowd and the disciples goes on. What these miracles reveal is not only who Jesus is, but how spiritually obtuse his audience is seen as being.

There is a brief transitional passage in John 6:22–24, where it is explained that the next day when the crowd realized that both Jesus and the disciples were gone, at least some of them got into boats and went to Capernaum looking for Jesus.[21]

B. The Dialogues with Outsiders (John 6:25–59)

6:25   When they found him on the other side of the sea, they said to him, "Rabbi, when did you come here?" [26]Jesus answered them, "Very truly, I tell you, you are looking for me, not because you saw signs, but because you ate your fill of the loaves. [27]Do not work for the food that perishes, but for the food that endures for eternal life, which the Son of Man will give you. For it is on him that God the Father has set his seal." [28]Then they said to him, "What must we do to perform the works of God?" [29]Jesus answered them, "This is the work of God, that you believe in him whom he has sent." [30]So they said to him, "What sign are you going to give us then, so that we may see it and believe you? What work are you performing? [31]Our ancestors ate the manna in the wilderness; as it is written, 'He gave them bread from heaven to eat.' " [32]Then Jesus said to them, "Very truly, I tell you, it was not Moses who gave you the bread from heaven, but it is my Father who gives you the true bread from heaven. [33]For the bread of God is that which comes down from heaven and gives life to the world." [34]They said to him, "Sir, give us this bread always."

35   Jesus said to them, "I am the bread of life. Whoever comes to me will never be hungry, and whoever believes in me will never by thirsty. [36]But I said to you that you have seen me and yet do not believe. [37]Everything that the Father gives me will come to me, and anyone who comes to me I will never drive away; [38]for I have come down from heaven, not to do my own will, but the will of him who sent me. [39]And this is the will of him who sent me, that I should lose nothing of all that he has given me, but raise it up on the last day. [40]This is indeed the will of my Father, that all who see the Son and believe in him may have eternal life; and I will raise them up on the last day."

41   Then the Jews began to complain about him because he said, "I am the bread that came down from heaven." [42]They were saying, "Is not this Jesus, the son of Joseph, whose father and mother we know? How can he now say, 'I have come down from heaven'?" [43]Jesus answered them, "Do not complain among yourselves. [44]No one can come to me unless drawn by the Father who sent me; and I will raise that person up on the last day. [45]It is written in the prophets, 'And they shall all be taught by God.' Everyone who has heard and learned from the Father comes to me. [46]Not that anyone has seen the Father except the one who is from God; he has seen the Father. [47]Very truly, I tell you, whoever believes has eternal life. [48]I am the bread of life. [49]Your ancestors ate the manna in the wilderness, and they died. [50]This is the bread that comes down from heaven, so that one may eat of it and not die. [51]I am the living bread that came down from heaven. Whoever eats of this bread will live forever; and the bread that I will give for the life of the world is my flesh."

52 The Jews then disputed among themselves, saying, "How can this man give us his flesh to eat?" [53]So Jesus said to them, "Very truly, I tell you, unless you eat the flesh of the Son of Man and drink his blood, you have no life in you. [54]Those who eat my flesh and drink my blood have eternal life, and I will raise them up on the last day; [55]for my flesh is true food and my blood is true drink. [56]Those who eat my flesh and drink my blood abide in me, and I in them. [57]Just as the living Father sent me, and I live because of the Father, so whoever eats me will live because of me. [58]This is the bread that came down from heaven, not like that which your ancestors ate, and they died. But the one who eats this bread will live forever." [59]He said these things while he was teaching in the synagogue at Capernaum.

The dialogue with the crowd begins with a question about the time of Jesus' arrival in Capernaum. Jesus does not respond to their spoken question, but rather to what he knows is on their heart: "You are looking for me, not because you saw signs, but because you ate your fill of the loaves." Jesus is pursued as the ultimate provider of a free lunch! In other words, the reason for pursuing him was purely material and selfish; there was no altruism or spiritual seeking really involved. Apparently they hadn't even discerned that Jesus was performing symbolic acts that pointed to a larger reality and meaning than mere physical sustenance. Since Jesus did, after all, perform the miracle of the loaves and fish, it is not as if he is despising physical things or food, but rather that he wishes to use them to point to a food that is more sustaining, crucial, indeed, a food that endures to eternal life. The two-level discussion once more comes into play, but Jesus is portrayed as being willing to provide both physical and spiritual food, not just the latter. It is not, then, very helpful to talk about the Johannine Christ as being *purely* interested in spiritual things, nor is it helpful to simply call this the "spiritual" Gospel, not the least reason being because it is the Gospel that most clearly focuses on the incarnation. Rather the physical is meant to be seen as an icon of the spiritual, a window on a larger truth, a means to a greater end. No doubt this is a difficult lesson to learn for poor and hungry people who do not know the source of their next meal.

John 6:27 provides us with another Son of man saying. It is as Son of man that Jesus provides the more enduring food, and it is on the Son of man that God has set his seal—a probable allusion to the discussion in John 1:32, and perhaps 1:51 and 3:13 as well. This verse uses agency language—the Son of man is the one upon whom God has set his seal of approval and authorization, to act on the Father's behalf to provide the food that does not perish.[22]

In John 6:29, belief is said to be the work of God. In view of 6:28, the main focus here seems to be on faith's being the one "work" or activity human beings must do in response to God's action on their behalf. In this case the work in question involves faith in the one God sent, a willingness to recognize Jesus as God's apostle, God's sent one. The dim-wittedness of the crowd is stressed in v. 30, where they ask for a validating sign to be given so that they may believe Jesus' claim. They ask what work Jesus is performing, and they attempt to act as theologians, alluding to Ps. 78 and its reference to the manna story of Ex. 16. The dialogue then revolves around the exegesis of Ps. 78, with Jesus correcting the crowd's understanding of that text, particularly vv. 24ff. What follows is a contrast between what the people thought they got through Moses and what is available through Jesus, with the aim of portraying Jesus as one greater than Moses.[23]

It was not Moses, but God, who provided the bread from heaven. Furthermore, what was provided in the time of Moses was mere physical sustenance. There is some evidence, though it postdates the New Testament era, that some rabbis believed that the latter-day Moses figure would bring down manna from heaven as Moses did (cf. *Eccl. Rab.* 1:28: "As was the first Redeemer so is the latter Redeemer, . . . as the first Redeemer brought down manna, so also will the latter Redeemer").[24] Jesus is responding that true sustenance, true bread, is to be found only in him, and not just in the material signs he performs. This leads to the famous "bread of life" saying in John 6:35, which must be set in the context of the other "I am" sayings.

EXCURSUS: THE "I AM" SAYINGS AND THE DISCOURSES

Any study of Johannine theology will necessarily have to deal with both the "I am" sayings and the discourse material, both of which contribute to the distinctiveness of this Gospel. It has often been argued that there are seven "I am" sayings, which are to be matched up with the seven discourses in the book. There are some reasons to doubt that a clear correlation can be made in every case. For example, while the connection between the "I am the bread of life" discourse and the feeding miracle in John 6 is very evident and the two are closely juxtaposed within the same chapter, it is difficult to see what the waters of life discourse has to do with the healing of the royal official's son in John 4. As Carson points out, the discourse in John 8:12–59, while it begins with the theme "I am the light of the world," which corresponds to the giving of sight to the blind in John 9, quickly moves in another direction.[25] In short, while there may be seven discourses (actually there seem to be more), and there are seven "I am" sayings that take a noun as an object, the two groups of material cannot always be easily correlated.

Before we examine the seven sayings, a few words are in order about other sorts of "I am" sayings in this Gospel. The Greek phrase *ego eimi* is a perfectly ordinary one, with a basic meaning of "It is I," a simple way of identifying oneself to someone else or to a group who may be in doubt about the identity of the person they are seeing or to whom they are speaking. I suspect that we have an example of this kind of usage in John 6:20 during the walking on the water incident. Jesus calms the disciples' fears by simply saying, "Don't be afraid, it's me." There are other incidents, however, of the absolute use of *ego eimi* in this Gospel that seem to have clearly theological overtones. In John 8:58 Jesus says, "Before Abraham was, *ego eimi*," and this surely seems to be a claim to preexist Abraham; and one might also cite John 13:19. In these sorts of texts Isa. 43:10 ("that you may know . . . and understand that I am he")[26] may lie in the background, suggesting a divine claim is being made. Thus, sometimes the phrase when used absolutely seems to entail an implicit claim to a divine or eternal status. Whether it is ever an intended direct echo of the name by which God revealed the divine character to Moses in Ex. 3:14 is more debatable because the Hebrew phrase there involves imperfect tense verbs and is more likely to be translated "I will be what I will be," than "I am that I am."

In any event, the seven "I am" sayings that are qualified by a noun object deserve to be studied in and of themselves, for they are predicating something *about* Jesus, not simply making an identity statement, though the two things intertwine. These seven sayings are as follows:

1. I am the bread of life (6:35; cf. vv. 41, 48, 51)
2. I am the light of the world (8:12; cf. vv. 18, 23, which clearly refer to actions, not identity)
3. I am the gate (of the sheep) (10:7, 9)
4. I am the good shepherd (10:11, 14)
5. I am the resurrection and the life (11:25)
6. I am the way, and the truth, and the life (14:6)
7. I am the true vine (15:1, 5)

It is evident immediately that these sayings are not evenly distributed in the Gospel. They do not begin until the Gospel is a fourth over (the crucial Galilee miracle story), and they end in the middle of the farewell discourses. Primarily these sayings are of two natures: (1) Most are associated with a particular miracle, though sometimes the saying follows the miracle, sometimes it precedes it. (2) However, the fifth and sixth above statements are of the nature of summary statements. They make evident that the essence of all the signs is to reveal that Jesus is the true life of and for humanity, the revealer of that life, and the way to obtain that true (eternal) life. They also make clear that Jesus is the true light, or truth, of God as well. What is striking about all this is that light and life are the two chief things that Wisdom, which is another way of referring to God's divine Word, is said to bestow on the devotee in Jewish wisdom literature. Besides the texts cited previously, note that in Wisd. Sol. 7:25–26 Wisdom is said to be a pure emanation of the glory of the Almighty—a reflection of God's eternal light. In Wisd. Sol. 8:8 it is said she "knows the things of old, and infers the things to come"; she understands turns of speech and solutions of riddles; she has foreknowledge of signs and wonders and of the outcome of seasons and times. All these attributes are also predicated of Jesus in this Gospel. It is also said of Wisdom that giving heed to her word is the assurance of immortality (Wisd. Sol. 6:18), that while remaining in herself she renews all things (7:27), that she was sent from on high, from the throne of God's glory (9:10), and the people were taught what pleases God and were "saved by wisdom" (9:18). In Wisd. Sol. 11:4 it is said that it was Wisdom who provided the Israelites with water in the wilderness when Moses struck the rock. When one also bears in mind texts like Sir. 24, where Wisdom speaks in the first person and says, "Like the vine I bud forth delights" (v. 17) or, "Come to me, you who desire me, and eat your fill of my fruits" (v. 19); or like Prov. 9:5, where Wisdom says directly, "Come, eat of my bread," it is hard to doubt that in these "I am" sayings Jesus is presented as God's divine Wisdom. He is offering the light and life, the revelation and salvation in himself that was previously said to be available in and through God's wisdom, which in Sir. 24 is said to be found in Torah. Jesus can offer these things because he is an expression of the one true God, God's Word and wisdom. Of Jesus now, as previously of Wisdom, it can be said, "Whoever finds me finds life . . . ; but . . . all who hate me love death" (Prov. 8:35–36).

As a final remark, note that the seven "I am" sayings bind together the public ministry and the private teaching of Jesus into a thematic unity, making clear that these two divisions of the Gospel ultimately go back to the same creative mind of the Beloved Disciple. They begin to appear at the crucial juncture when Jesus starts to reveal very openly who he is, both to the public and to the disciples in Galilee. These sayings make clear that a major, if not *the* major, function of both ministry narration and farewell discourses is to reveal clearly who Jesus is and what he bestows on those who receive him. In other words, they show the christological and soteriological character of this whole Gospel.

John 6:37 seems to be a statement involving some kind of idea of election. It is in order to point out, however, the text says, "all of *it*" not "all of *them*" (NRSV: "everything"),[27] which suggests the verse is referring to an elect group, not elect individuals. It is true to say that none come to Jesus unless the Father draws them, but we are not told on what basis or for what reason God draws or leads some and not others in this way. By contrast, when the author speaks about the human response he speaks of individuals, not a group: "Anyone who comes to me I will never drive away." God's will is that Jesus lose none of those the Father has given him, but rather raise them up on the last day. That is God's will clearly enough, but we are not told here that someone God draws, or even Jesus chooses, may not commit apostasy or rebellion. Indeed, in this same text we are told that while Judas Iscariot was one of the Twelve, he turned out to be a devil (v. 70). It must always be borne in mind that God does not will sin, any more than he desires for human beings to be judged, and thus even though the Fourth Gospel has a strong view of God's sovereignty, it also recognizes that there are things that happen that are *contrary* to God's desires and will.

It seems unlikely that one can derive a doctrine of eternal security from a passage like John 6:37ff.[28] It is one thing to say that Jesus will not turn away anyone who comes to him; it is another to suggest he will force them to stay or be faithful against their will. Both God's sovereign grace and human response play a role in human salvation, but even one's human response is enabled by God's grace. God's role in the relationship is incomparably greater than the human one, but the fact remains that God does not and will not save a person without the positive human response, called faith, to the divine leading and drawing.

At vv.41ff. the issue of Jesus' true identity comes to the fore, and as we have seen in our discussion of the prologue and other texts the key to understanding who Jesus truly is, is understanding where he has come from and where he is going. In short the key to understanding his character and identity is understanding that he is God's wisdom in the flesh, pursuing the course of life and the trajectory that the earlier scriptures predicated of Wisdom. The "Jews" (i.e., Jewish leaders or Torah zealots) within the crowd murmur and argue as follows: Jesus can't be the bread that comes down from heaven because (1) we know where he came from; (2) he's Joseph's son. The irony is thick at this point in the dialogue, and it may reflect the evangelist's knowledge of the fact that Jesus had one only human biological parent, Mary. The issue here, however, is probably that the Jews are thinking on a purely human level, rather than about Jesus' ultimate eternal origins.

At v. 46 Jesus makes the claim that he has seen God, implying his origins in heaven. Then at v. 48 he makes clear that certain kinds of doctrines of election are incorrect. God's elect and chosen people were led out of Egypt and into the Sinai peninsula, but because of the rebellion of the many they were judged and died in the desert. It was only the faithful that either saw or entered the Promised Land. "Your ancestors ate the manna in the wilderness, and they died." That bread, the sort offered during the tenure of Moses, did not provide eternal life. Jesus alone offers and is the bread of heaven, which provides eternal life. He is the living bread (v. 51). Yet, in a paradoxical twist in the argument, the dying Jesus is bread as well, for no eternal life can be provided unless Jesus dies. "Flesh and blood" is a phrase that can represent Jesus as living or Jesus as dying. Verse 51b suggests humanity can partake of eternal life only if they partake of or accept the death of Jesus. It is not surprising, in light of the extreme aversion Jews had to drinking blood and to cannibalism, that the Jews are portrayed as completely offended by Jesus' increasingly graphic remarks. We cannot tell where the scene shifts into the synagogue, but v. 59 indicates that what has been going on here is a synagogue debate, which perhaps was of special relevance for Johannine Christians, who likely were still witnessing in such contexts.

C. The Private Dialogue with Disciples
(John 6:60–71)

6:60 When many of his disciples heard it, they said, "This teaching is difficult; who can accept it?" [61]But Jesus, being aware that his disciples were complaining about it, said to them, "Does this offend you? [62]Then what if you were to see the Son of Man ascending to where he was before? [63]It is the spirit that gives life; the flesh is useless. The words that I have spoken to you are spirit and life. [64]But among you there are some who do not believe." For Jesus knew from the first who were the ones that did not believe, and who was the one that would betray him. [65]And he said, "For this reason I have told you that no one can come to me unless it is granted by the Father."

66 Because of this many of his disciples turned back and no longer went about with him. 67So Jesus asked the twelve, "Do you also wish to go away?" 68Simon Peter answered him, "Lord, to whom can we go? You have the words of eternal life. 69We have come to believe and know that you are the Holy One of God." 70Jesus answered them, "Did I not choose you, the twelve? Yet one of you is a devil." 71He was speaking of Judas son of Simon Iscariot, for he, though one of the twelve, was going to betray him.

Following as it does hard on the heels of the public discussion in the synagogue with "the Jews," the complaining of the disciples mentioned in v. 61 could be seen as similar to the murmuring of the Jews, especially since the evangelist tells us that "Jesus knew from the first who were the ones that did not believe, and who was the one that would betray him." This reflects not only what is about to be said about Judas in v. 71, but also what is said in v. 66 about many of the disciples turning back and no longer traveling with Jesus. The disciples complained that the teaching about consuming Jesus was a hard and unacceptable teaching. Jesus in reply suggests that were they to see the Son of man ascend to where he was before, they might be even more scandalized. One of the keys to the whole discourse is mentioned in v. 63b— that which gives spirit and life is Jesus' *words,* not some sacramental action. The issue here is salvation through revelation and the transformation it brings.

In an editorial remark we are told that Jesus knew supernaturally from the outset who did and did not believe in him. What Wisd. Sol. 8:8 says of Wisdom is now applied to Jesus—he knows the things of old and infers the things to come, including having foreknowledge of signs and wonders and the outcome of the times. The Twelve, however, remain loyal at least for the moment, and as if to test them Jesus asks, "Do you also wish to go away?"[29] after the other disciples have left. Simon Peter, speaking for the disciples in a moment of revelation, says, "Lord, to whom can we go? You have the words of eternal life.[30] We have come to believe and know that you are the Holy One of God." One might have expected at this point an affirmative response by Jesus, but in fact he replies, "Did I not choose you, the twelve?[31] Yet one of you is a devil." Scholars have long pondered the relationship of this confession to the one Peter is said to have made at Caesarea Philippi (in Mark 8:29–30 and par.). Is it simply the Johannine adaptation of Peter's confession to another setting? There is certainly some similarity between John 6:69–70 and the Matthean form of the Synoptic confession (Matt. 16:13–23). Both have a confession followed by a response of Jesus which includes calling one of the disciples a or the devil. In John, however, it is Judas, not Peter, who is alluded to in these negative terms.

While it is possible that this is the Johannine version of Peter's great confession,[32] it is just as possible that the Fourth Evangelist has substituted a different tradition at this juncture, since the differences in the two accounts are substantial,[33] unlike the relatively minor differences between the accounts of the feeding of the five thousand in John 6 and Mark 6. In fact, I will argue that the content of the confession is so different that it cannot be said to be an alternative way of calling Jesus Christ the Son of the living God.

In an important article W. R. Domeris has demonstrated the following points about the confession "Holy One of God": (1) Its background lies partially in the Old Testament traditions that refer to God as the Holy One of Israel (cf., e.g., Isa. 43:14–15), as the agent and representative who speaks on behalf of Israel in the heavenly council; (2) but perhaps more interesting, though less relevant, is the fact that when this title appears elsewhere in the New Testament it appears on the lips of demons (cf. Mark 1:24; Luke 4:34);[34] (3) the context of this confession is critical: various disciples have just rejected and abandoned Jesus, and so "the events of John 6 therefore resemble an enacted parable in which there are some who find Wisdom, and others who reject it."[35] Therefore Domeris concludes that the overtones of the whole chapter suggest that Peter is here responding to Jesus as the incarnate Wisdom, the one who has the words of life (cf. Prov. 8:35). As such this represents a true insight into who Jesus is, but at the same time Peter's remarks reflect overconfidence that all the disciples have such an insight.[36] This title distinguishes how a true disciple should view Jesus, as opposed to the crowd who would make Jesus the wrong sort of king. As a sapiential title it is entirely appropriate, for about Wisdom it is said, "There is in [Wisdom] a spirit that is intelligent, holy" (Wisd. Sol. 7:22), "In every generation she passes into holy souls" (7:27), she comes "forth from the holy heavens" (9:10), she gave Joseph "knowledge of holy things" (10:10). Wisdom leads Israel out of Egypt, prompting "hymns, O Lord, to your holy name" (10:20), and Wisdom is even at one point said to be God's "holy spirit" sent from on high (compare 9:17 to Wisd. Sol. 1:6). The point is, in light of this wisdom tradition, which closely associates wisdom with the holy, the title "the Holy One of God" is perhaps the most appropriate title for one portrayed as Wisdom come in the flesh to earth, both rejected by his own and received by a few to whom he gave eternal life, and then ascending again to heaven (cf. *1 Enoch* 42).

One final note about Judas Iscariot is in order. It has been suggested that Iscariot is a variant of Sicarii, which means dagger men, and might imply that Judas had been part of the Zealot movement, working for the revolutionary overthrow of the Roman rulers and their Jewish collaborators. It is possible to support this conjecture by noting another (former?) Zealot among the Twelve, namely, Simon the Zealot. This might explain why Judas became disillusioned with Jesus after he refused to allow the Galileans to force him to be king, and then failed to follow up the advantage he had when he had cleansed the Temple. In that state of disillusionment, he decided to betray Jesus, since it became clear that he was advocating a "kingdom not of this world," one not brought in by human revolutionary movements. From a human and historian's perspective, this makes good sense of the Judas traditions. It is also very possible, however, that Iscariot means "man of Kerioth," as a reference to a place of origin.[37]

II. Bridging the Horizons

This text will in some respects be easier to preach from in settings where hunger and starvation regularly haunt the individual or the group involved, than in places where food has mainly a secondary sense of entertainment or recreation ("going out to eat"), since eating enough to survive is not a pressing personal issue.

A word of caution is in order in the way the latter half of the chapter is used. There should be no scandal but the scandal of the Gospel itself. This material is deliberately polemical, forged in the heat of a hostile and at times dangerous situation, and it is meant at some points to be a provocation, at other points to be a rebuttal to the arguments of some of the early Johannine Christians' dialogue partners. Sometimes material like 6:41ff. has been taken as providing a warrant for being obnoxious and arrogant for the sake of Jesus. A much better approach to evangelism is that of one beggar showing another where the true bread is. There is a place for polemics and apologetics, but they should be reserved for when the faith is under attack, or badly misrepresented, or maligned, as was apparently the case when the Johannine epistles and Gospel were written.

It may be worth stressing that traditions like John 6:1–15, coupled with various of the Passion traditions of Jesus' entering Jerusalem on an animal that connoted peace, not revolutionary action, provide strong evidence that Jesus was no revolutionary or Zealot. This is not to say that his teaching did not have some social content and intent, nor to say that his ministry did not have some rather radical social consequences and effects, especially for women and those ostracized from society due to sin or sickness.[38] It is simply to say that Marxist liberation theology will find no support or solace in texts like these.

One further caveat is in order. Many interpreters have made and do make the mistake of reading the dialogue material in John 6:35ff. in the very way that the evangelist would not want it to be read—at the material and earthly level. By turning this material into a discussion about the Eucharist and eucharistic elements, rather than about the One to whom all signs, including the sacraments, point, one has read this material on a mundane level when it shouts out, "Come up higher, brother and sister." As Milne puts it:

> The eating of his flesh and the drinking of his blood would appear a vivid, even shocking, illustration of what "believing" in him implies. In its "earthiness," however the image is ideally suited to the materialistic mindset of his audience. . . . It is perhaps to the point to note that "everlasting life" is attributed to faith in verse 47, and to eating and drinking in verse 54, an implicit pointer to the latter as a picture of the former; cf. Augustine, "Believe and you have eaten." Interpreting the passage in this

way, however, does not preclude our recognizing that Jesus' imagery came to life in a new way in the later experience of the church as it shared the meal Jesus instituted.[39]

This is aptly put. While the passage has implications for seeing the sacraments as *signs* that point away from themselves and do not in themselves provide eternal life any more than the eating of the physical bread and fish by the five thousand provided eternal life, it is not about the sacraments, but rather about receiving Jesus. "It is the spirit that gives life; the flesh is useless" (v. 63).

Obviously this material is very appropriate to use for preaching and teaching on a Sunday when there will be a collection for famine relief, World Vision, Bread for the World, or other worthwhile relief agencies. Yet it is even more a text that reminds us that the social gospel of itself is not the whole gospel and not an adequate response to human need, a message many churches need to hear. "One does not live by bread alone" (Matt. 4:4).

Another equally important theme in this chapter is the warning about pursuing Jesus, or religion in general, simply for the material benefits one can get out of it. Some have found it profitable to go to church in order to make business contacts or political connections. Jesus offers a stern rebuke to this sort of self-serving approach to things. It may be in order to preach on seeking Jesus, and not merely his benefits. Some people also attend a certain church simply for what they can get out of it, rather than what they can give.

An even more profound message could be derived from this text based on why people eat in the first place. The most basic reason people eat is that they wish to go on living. Notice how a depressed person or a terminally ill person often refuses food, for the very good reason that he or she does not wish to go on living. In the Western world of course, there are some people who actually live to eat, rather than just eating to live, mistaking the means of living for the ends of living. There are also others who binge and purge, or splurge and diet ("sin in haste, repent at leisure"), because they do not wish to be careful about their diet but also do not want to suffer the consequences of high cholesterol, hypertension, obesity, and the like. It has been estimated that in Western Europe and North America we have perhaps 20 percent of the world's population, but we use and consume over 60 percent of the the world's resources. This text, especially where it refers to the gathering up of the leftovers, serves as a good reminder that God will hold us accountable for our gross waste of the bounty and blessings he provides. Yet we must not overlook the overriding christological theme: that if one wants to go on living eternally, one must imbibe—one must take Christ into one's life. Jesus, if taken into one's life, not only brings immediate spiritual satisfaction, but brings a source of spiritual nourishment forever. If physical hunger is symptomatic of the human hunger for life itself, our passage reminds us that Jesus is the source of the only sort of life that lasts forever. "I came that they may have life, and have it abundantly" (10:10). Just as earlier chapters have pointed the audience to look from birth to Birth, and from water to Water, here we are led to look from bread to Bread,[40] and from life to Life.

11. Temple Discourses and Healing (John 7:1–10:42)

By the time the reader reaches John 7, Jesus has left Galilee behind for good and will be in or near Judea for the remainder of his ministry. That this material has been joined together by the evangelist's omitting much interim material is shown by the fact that the narrative begins with Jesus' going up to the Feast of Booths, a fall festival, and it concludes with Jesus at the Feast of Dedication in the wintertime (cf. 10:22). There is little action in this middle section of the Gospel, save for the account of Jesus' going up to the first of these feasts and the memorable story of the healing of the blind man, which could be seen as a self-contained unit, but is also about a happening in or very near Jerusalem (cf. 9.7). In the main, the story goes forward through dialogues and discourses, and many of the themes already discussed resurface here with some new nuances: (1) Jesus as God's agent; (2) the Sabbath controversy; (3) the origins and character and destiny of Jesus and "the Jews"; (4) Jesus' testimony and the issue of judgment. There is also an extended *mashal,* or parable, in John 10 about Jesus as the good shepherd, which introduces some new material.

There is one subunit that some later manuscripts place in this section, which in all likelihood does not belong here—the beloved story of Jesus and the woman caught in adultery (John 7:53–8:11). While these verses are present in most of the medieval Greek manuscripts, they are absent from almost all the early Greek manuscripts of the Gospel of John, with the exception of the Western manuscript D, which is idiosyncratic in other respects as well. These verses are also absent from the earliest Coptic and Syriac Gospels and from many other old manscripts (Old Latin, Old Georgian, and Armenian ones). The testimony of the church fathers is even more striking. None of them comment on these verses, even when they are making comments seriatim on the Gospel of John—they skip from 7:52 to 8:12 in such commentaries. None of the Eastern (including Greek) fathers mention the passage before the tenth century A.D. Furthermore, while some manuscripts place these verses after John 7:52, others place them after John 7:44; John 7:36; John 21:25, and even after Luke 21:38. The text of this Gospel reads quite smoothly if one skips from 7:52 to 8:12. The reference to some going home in 7:53 does not fit the context. In short, it was a free-floating tradition, and conservative scribes were looking for a place to insert it into the Gospel text.[1]

The evidence mentioned above leads to the conclusion that these verses, although there is no reason to doubt that they may preserve an authentic story about an encounter Jesus had, were not part of the original Gospel of John as drafted by the Fourth Evangelist. This is why most modern translations if they include these verses do so either in a footnote or in square brackets, to indicate they were not likely part of the original text. It is not even clear that these verses represent a Johannine tradition, in view of the vocabulary and style of the material. They may be Lukan in origin. Accordingly, we will comment further on these verses in an appendix. This author's own views are that what the inspired author wrote and originally placed in his Gospel, not later additions, should be accepted as the canonical text. For this reason, I suggest that this story be treated as an extracanonical text likely preserving a historical memory about Jesus, which may be used with other material that is *not* part of scripture to inform oneself and others about early views of Jesus and his deeds, but should not be preached on *as* a portion of Holy Writ.[2] One must remember, as the Fourth Evangelist tells us in John 20:30, that there were many other historical things Jesus did and said that were not recorded in the canonical Gospels. John 7:53–8:11 is surely one such tradition.

I. The Historical Horizon

A. *Trying Times Again*
(John 7:1–8:59)

7:1 After this Jesus went about in Galilee. He did not wish to go about in Judea because the Jews were looking for an opportunity to kill him. [2]Now the Jewish festival of Booths was near. [3]So his brothers said to him, "Leave here and go to Judea so that your disciples also may see the works you are doing; [4]for no one who wants to be widely known acts in secret. If you do these things, show yourself to the world." [5](For not even his brothers believed in him.) [6]Jesus said to them, "My time has not yet come, but your time is always here. [7]The world cannot hate you, but it hates me because I testify against it that its works are evil. [8]Go to festival yourselves. I am not going to this festival, for my time has not yet fully come." [9]After saying this, he remained in Galilee.

10 But after his brothers had gone to the festival, then he also went, not publicly but as it were in secret. [11]The Jews were looking for him at the festival and saying, "Where is he?" [12]And there was considerable complaining about him among the crowds. While some were saying, "He is a good man," others were saying, "No, he is deceiving the crowd." [13]Yet no one would speak openly about him for fear of the Jews.

14 About the middle of the festival Jesus went up into the temple and began to teach. [15]The Jews were astonished at it, saying, "How does this man have such learning, when he has never been taught?" [16]Then Jesus answered them, "My teaching is not mine but his who sent me. [17]Anyone who resolves to do the will of God will know whether the teaching is from God

or whether I am speaking on my own. [18]Those who speak on their own seek their own glory; but the one who seeks the glory of him who sent him is true, and there is nothing false in him.

19 "Did not Moses give you the law? Yet none of you keeps the law. Why are you looking for an opportunity to kill me?" [20]The crowd answered, "You have a demon! Who is trying to kill you?" [21]Jesus answered them, "I performed one work, and all of you are astonished. [22]Moses gave you circumcision (it is, of course, not from Moses, but from the patriarchs), and you circumcise a man on the sabbath. [23]If a man receives circumcision on the sabbath in order that the law of Moses may not be broken, are you angry with me because I healed a man's whole body on the sabbath? [24]Do not judge by appearances, but judge with right judgment."

25 Now some of the people of Jerusalem were saying, "Is not this the man whom they are trying to kill? [26]And here he is, speaking openly, but they say nothing to him! Can it be that the authorities really know that this is the Messiah? [27]Yet we know where this man is from; but when the Messiah comes, no one will know where he is from." [28]Then Jesus cried out as he was teaching in the temple, "You know me, and you know where I am from. I have not come on my own. But the one who sent me is true, and you do not know him. [29]I know him, because I am from him, and he sent me." [30]Then they tried to arrest him, but no one laid hands on him, because his hour had not yet come. [31]Yet many in the crowd believed in him and were saying, "When the Messiah comes, will he do more signs than this man has done?"

32 The Pharisees heard the crowd muttering such things about him, and the chief priests and Pharisees sent temple police to arrest him. [33]Jesus then said, "I will be with you a little while longer, and then I am going to him who sent me. [34]You will search for me, but you will not find me; and where I am, you cannot come." [35]The Jews said to one another, "Where does this man intend to go that we will not find him? Does he intend to go to the Dispersion among the Greeks and teach the Greeks? [36]What does he mean by saying, 'You will search for me and you will not find me' and 'Where I am, you cannot come'?"

37 On the last day of the festival, the great day, while Jesus was standing there, he cried out, "Let anyone who is thirsty come to me, [38]and let the one who believes in me drink. As the scripture has said, 'Out of the believer's heart shall flow rivers of living water.' " [39]Now he said this about the Spirit, which believers in him were to receive; for as yet there was no Spirit, because Jesus was not yet glorified.

40 When they heard these words, some in the crowd said, "This is really the prophet." [41]Others said, "This is the Messiah." But some asked, "Surely the Messiah does not come from Galilee, does he? [42]Has not the scripture said that the Messiah is descended from David and comes from Bethlehem, the village where David lived?" [43]So there was a division in the crowd because of him. [44]Some of them wanted to arrest him, but no one laid hands on him.

45 Then the temple police went back to the chief priests and Pharisees, who asked them, "Why did you not arrest him?" [46]The police answered, "Never has anyone spoken like this!" [47]Then the Pharisees replied, "Surely you have not been deceived too, have you? [48]Has any one of the authorities or of the Pharisees believed in him? [49]But this crowd, which does not know the law—they are accursed." [50]Nicodemus, who had gone to Jesus before, and who was one of them, asked, [51] "Our law does not judge people without first giving them a hearing to find out what they are doing, does it?" [52]They replied, "Surely you are not also from Galilee, are you? Search and you will see that no prophet is to arise from Galilee."

8:12 Again Jesus spoke to them, saying, "I am the light of the world. Whoever follows me will never walk in darkness but will have the light of life." [13]Then the Pharisees said to him, "You are testifying on your own behalf; your testimony is not valid." [14]Jesus answered, "Even if I testify on my own behalf, my testimony is valid because I know where I have come from and where I am going, but you do not know where I come from or where I am going. [15]You judge by human standards; I judge no one. [16]Yet even if I do judge, my judgment is valid; for it is not I alone who judge, but I and the Father who sent me. [17]In your law it is written that the testimony of two witnesses is valid. [18]I testify on my own behalf, and the Father who sent me testifies on my behalf." [19]Then they said to him, "Where is your Father?" Jesus answered, "You know neither me nor my Father. If you knew me, you would know my Father also." [20]He spoke these words while he was teaching in the treasury of the temple, but no one arrested him, because his hour had not yet come.

21 Again he said to them, "I am going away, and you will search for me, but you will die in your sin. Where I am going, you cannot come." [22]Then the Jews said, "Is he going to kill himself? Is that what he means by saying, 'Where I am going, you cannot come'?" [23]He said to them, "You are from below, I am from above; you are of this world, I am not of this world. [24]I told you that you would die in your sins, for you will die in your sins unless you believe that I am he." [25]They said to him, "Who are you?" Jesus said to them, "Why do I speak to you at all? [26]I have much to say about you and much to condemn; but the one who sent me is true, and I declare to the world what I have heard from him." [27]They did not understand that he was speaking to them about the Father. [28]So Jesus said, "When you have lifted up the Son of Man, then you will realize that I am he, and that I do nothing on my own, but I speak these things as the Father instructed me. [29]And the one who sent me is with me; he has not left me alone, for I always do what is pleasing to him." [30]As he was saying these things, many believed in him.

31 Then Jesus said to the Jews who had believed in him, "If you continue in my word, you are truly my disciples; [32]and you will know the truth, and the truth will make you free." [33]They answered him, "We are descendants of Abraham and have never been slaves to anyone. What do you mean by saying, 'You will be made free'?"

34 Jesus answered them, "Very truly, I tell you, everyone who commits sin is a slave to sin. [35]The slave does not have a permanent place in the household; the son has a place there forever. [36]So if the Son makes you free, you will be free indeed. [37]I know that you are descendants of Abraham; yet you look for an opportunity to kill me, because there is no place in you for my word. [38]I declare what I have seen in the Father's presence; as for you, you should do what you have heard from the Father."

39 They answered him, "Abraham is our father." Jesus said to them, "If you were Abraham's children, you would be doing what Abraham did, [40]but now you are trying to kill me, a man who has told you the truth that I heard from God. This is not what Abraham did. [41]You are indeed doing what your father does." They said to him, "We are not illegitimate children; we have one father, God himself." [42]Jesus said to them, "If God were your Father, you would love me, for I came from God and now I am here. I did not come on my own, but he sent me.[43]Why do you not understand what I say? It is because you cannot accept my word. [44]You are from your father the devil, and you choose to do your father's desires. He was a murderer from the beginning and does not stand in the truth, because there is no truth in him. When he lies, he speaks according to his own nature, for he is a liar and the father of lies. [45]But because I tell the truth, you do not believe me. [46]Which of you convicts me of sin? If I tell the truth, why do you not believe me? [47]Whoever is from God hears the words of God. The reason you do not hear them is that you are not from God."

48 The Jews answered him, "Are we not right in saying that you are a Samaritan and have a demon?" [49]Jesus answered, "I do not have a demon; but I honor my Father, and you dishonor me. [50]Yet I do not seek my own glory; there is one who seeks it and he is the judge. [51]Very truly, I tell you, whoever keeps my word will never see death." [52]The Jews said to him, "Now we know that you have a demon. Abraham died, and so did the prophets; yet you say, 'Whoever keeps my word will never taste death.' [53]Are you greater than our father Abraham, who died? The prophets also died. Who do you claim to be?" [54]Jesus answered, "If I glorify myself, my glory is nothing. It is my Father who glorifies me, he of whom you say, 'He is our God,' [55]though you do not know him. But I know him; if I would say that I do not know him, I would be a liar like you. But I do know him and I keep his word. [56]Your ancestor Abraham rejoiced that he would see my day; he saw it and was glad." [57]Then the Jews said to him, "You are not yet fifty years old, and have you seen Abraham?" [58]Jesus said to them, "Very truly, I tell you, before Abraham was, I am." [59]So they picked up stones to throw at him, but Jesus hid himself and went out of the temple.

The material in John 7—8 reveals Jesus once again on trial, and as Harvey has noted, the evangelist shows considerable understanding of the Jewish judicial procedures and the legal ramifications of some of Jesus' remarks.[3] Furthermore, we have now moved farther along in the judicial proceedings from what we saw in John 5, so that now not only do we hear charges against Jesus, and his defense in response, but also we are told that some were convinced enough of Jesus' culpability in the matter of blasphemy as well as Sabbath violation that they were prepared to carry out the sentence of stoning, but Jesus managed by the providence of God to escape their clutches, "because his hour had not yet come."

Some scholars have objected to this entire portrayal, on the basis of a later rabbinic definition of blasphemy based on Lev. 24:15–16 which states: "Anyone who curses God shall bear the sin. One who blasphemes the name of the LORD shall be put to death." The later rabbinic explanation of this text states that blasphemy in the form that counts as a capital offense requires the pronouncing of the divine Name (Yahweh). This, however, as Harvey shows, is a later and narrower view.[4] In the New Testament era we have the clear statement of Philo that "any unseasonable uttering of God's name," including the sort usually regarded as trivial, amounts to naming the Name and is punishable by death (*De vita Mosis* 2.206). Josephus seems also to know of a broader definition of blasphemy during the New Testament era (cf. *Ant.* 4.202). In other words, the emotionally charged scene depicted in John 7—8 that leads to some Jews' attempting to punish Jesus for blasphemy on the spot is historically plausible.

The charge of blasphemy seems to come as a result of Jesus' claim to be God's agent on earth, acting and speaking for the Father on earth[5] in various forms including "the Father and I are one" (10:30), which surely does not amount to an identity statement, but rather a claim that Jesus, due to his spiritual union and unity in character and in purpose with the Father, is acting and speaking as the Father would speak and would have him do. The claim to preexistent and divine origins such as Wisdom also factors into the accusation of blasphemy when Jesus says, "Before Abraham was, I am." Understanding John 7—8 requires that we realize that Jesus is really already on trial for his life at this point, and must defend himself using, among other tactics, polemics. The legal process is clearly defined: (1) utterance of words taken to be blasphemy; (2) challenging of such words; (3) further utterance of such remarks; (4) attempt to seize or punish Jesus; (5) an unexpected obstacle of divine origins placed in the path of the execution of the sentence at this juncture. "No other New Testament writer presents Jesus in a long drawn-out legal action provoked in the first place by certain of his words and deeds. But equally, no other writer offers such a compelling account of why Jesus was brought to trial by his fellow-Jews: the sequence of events in John's Gospel seem rooted in the normal and necessary observance by Jews of their own legal system."[6]

The sticky point, however, was that on the one hand it was impossible for Jesus to *prove* the claims that he was God's agent or Wisdom in the flesh. The sort of miracles he performed had for the most part been performed by prophets before, who made no such grandiose claims about themselves. Human witnesses, even John the Baptist, could only provide possible corroboration based on things Jesus said or did, but they could not present compelling proof that Jesus was the light of the world. To be sure, if Jesus made false claims, he was guilty of blasphemy, but on the other hand if these claims were true, and if Jesus was willing to swear to them on oath, that meant that only God in heaven by direct intervention could validate or invalidate the claims. It further meant that if Jesus was God's agent and he were attacked, it would also be an attack on the Father who sent him. Exodus 22:8–9 was clear enough that if someone swore such an oath falsely, God was brought into the process and would judge the person. On the Jews' reading of things, this is precisely what happened when Jesus died on the cross. God would not allow a good or righteous man to die a slave's or a rebel's death on the cross. On the contrary, various Jews believed that persons who died on a cross were cursed by God (cf. Deut. 21:23).[7] This judicial setting hovers over these Temple discourses.

They are, however, discourses at least ostensibly set in a Temple and feast framework. We have already noted on various occasions in this commentary how the evangelist stresses that Jesus replaces or fulfills, and thus makes obsolescent, the institutions of Judaism. The Feast of Tabernacles or Booths was a fall harvest festival and, among other things, it involved a prayer for rain. One of the ceremonies that took place on each of the seven mornings of the feast was a procession down the hill from the Temple to the Gihon spring, which supplies the pool of Siloam (cf. John 9:7). There a priest filled a laver full of water, carried it back up the hill, passing through the Water Gate returning to the altar, where he poured the water into a funnel which dispersed it into the ground. Certain key scriptures were associated with this feast; for instance, Isa. 12:3 apparently was sung during the drawing of the water—"With joy you will draw water from the wells of salvation."[8] Zechariah 9—14 seems to have also been read, which discusses the day of the Lord (*yom Yahweh*) in the context of this feast, involving three key assertions: (1) In Zech. 9:9 we hear of the triumphal entry of the king riding on an ass into the holy city; (2) 12:10 speaks of God pouring out a spirit of compassion and supplication on Jerusalem; and (3) at 14:8 we are told of living waters that flow out from Jerusalem into the Mediterranean and Dead Sea. In the Court of Women on the first day of this feast there was a ceremony where the golden candlesticks were lit, and there were torchlight dances in the evening. This is the setting of John 7—8, and gives it pregnant meaning. What was offered and depicted in the feast, Jesus now claims to give—water and light to God's people.[9]

Though further adventures in Galilee are not described, clearly 7:1 indicates the evangelist knows of such. Yet he is more concerned with why Jesus did not go up to the feast in Jerusalem. It was because some Jews were already seeking to kill him.[10] At 7:3 Jesus' brothers enter the discussion for the first time, and clearly they do not represent a group of his faithful followers.[11] They are, rather, portrayed as baiting Jesus to go up to Jerusalem if he wants to establish a reputation as one "widely known," as a doer of miraculous deeds. Their attitude seems either to be one of jealousy of Jesus, or they viewed Jesus as on some sort of ego trip. The evangelist states flatly,

"For not even his brothers believed in him" (v. 5), and we may be meant to think again of the prologue: "His own people did not accept him" (1:11). This, of course, did not mean that they did not believe Jesus could perform miracles—the text suggests they did. From the evangelist's point of view, however, this does not amount to true faith in Jesus. What is most interesting about their remarks is the suggestion that Jesus' chief group of disciples could be found in Judea (v. 3), not Galilee.

The repeated emphasis in this Gospel of Jesus' fulfilling the feasts, and the obvious knowledge of such feasts reflected in the narrative, lead to a conjecture worth reflecting on. If the Beloved Disciple was a Judean or even Jerusalem disciple of Jesus, perhaps we should identify him with the "other" disciple referred to in John 18 as going with Peter to the high priest's house when Jesus appeared before him and was questioned. We are told that this "other" disciple was known to the high priest, hence his access to the priest's courtyard (cf. 18:15–16).[12] This raises the distinct possibility that the Beloved Disciple had some sort of role in the Temple, perhaps as a priest or Levite. This would explain the keen interest in this Gospel to portray Jesus as the true Temple, the true locus of proper worship, the fulfillment of all the feasts, the Passover lamb, to mention but a few examples.

Jesus' response to his brothers is that his time or the right time has not yet fully come, and that he is therefore not going to the festival. The world already hates Jesus because he testifies against it that its works are evil, so there is certainly no incentive due to the size of the crowds at the feast to be in a hurry to go up to Jerusalem.[13] The discussion concludes at v. 9 with the flat statement: "After saying this, [Jesus] remained in Galilee." And yet the very next verse turns 180 degrees and says that Jesus did go up to the festival, only secretly, not publicly. How are we to reconcile these statements?

One possibility would be to say that Jesus' "right time" did finally come, shortly after the brothers left for Jerusalem, and therefore Jesus went up to the feast, under orders from the Father.[14] What he had said to the brothers he sincerely meant, but he received a late word from God shortly thereafter that changed his plans. Probably here, as in John 11, we are meant to see Jesus acting as God's agent. He cannot go and do anything at the bidding of anyone other than the Father. Not his mother (John 2) nor his brothers (John 7) can be allowed to direct his paths and times of coming and going. Jesus is a man under authority and must act accordingly. Jesus has resolved to act only as and when the Father directs him to do so (cf. 5:19ff.).[15]

Notice that in vv. 11–13 there is a clear distinction made between the Jews who are seeking Jesus with malicious intent and the crowds who are divided about Jesus. The Jewish authorities are pursuing a quest in regard to Jesus, but it is a negative one, and thus is frustrated by divine providence.[16] Verse 13 makes clear the distinction. The crowds would not speak openly about Jesus because of fear of the Jews (i.e., Jewish authorities opposed to Jesus).

Verse 14 tells us that Jesus went up to the Temple and taught at about the middle of the festival. The Jews respond, "How does this man have such learning when he has never been taught?" They are astonished and impressed with the depth and profundity of his teaching, but not convinced and converted.[17] Jesus' response is the response of the agent—he is just delivering the message of his Father who sent him (v. 16). Jesus stresses that he is not seeking his own glory, but the glory of the one who sent him. It is interesting that Jesus says on the one hand that anyone who resolves to do God's will, will know if he is speaking the truth (v. 17), but he also turns around and says none of the "Jews" keep the revealed will of God in the Mosaic law (v. 19). At this point the dialogue becomes exceedingly vitriolic. Jesus is accused by the crowd of having a demon, and they indicate surprise at the charge that someone is trying to kill Jesus.

Various scholars have suggested that at least vv. 22–25 belong with the Sabbath discussion in John 5. This may be correct, but in any case it provides a good defense of Jesus' actions on the Sabbath. If Jewish authorities were willing to say that the obligation to circumcise on the eighth day supersedes the obligation to rest on the Sabbath when the two times coincide, why then should they be angry with Jesus because he healed on the Sabbath? This portion of the dialogue also makes clear that the evangelist does not see astonishment, either at works or teachings, as a sign of true faith.

John 7:25 opens a new subsection of this ongoing dialogue. The crowd begins to wonder, since the authorities have not laid hands on Jesus, if perhaps the authorities really know Jesus is the Messiah. Verse 27 again makes clear that to understand who Jesus is, one must truly understand where he comes from, "but when the Messiah comes, no one will know where he is from." There were many different traditions about messiah in early Judaism, and Justin's *Dialogue with Trypho* 8.4–7 refers to this belief held by some Jews, though obviously there were other traditions that suggested that messiah would come from Judea, and in particular from the Davidic city of Bethlehem. The dialogue is thick with irony at this point, because the real origins of the Son as a preexistent One who came forth from heaven were unknown to the crowds and authorities. Yet, adding irony to irony, Jesus says they really do know where he is from: he is God's apostle, God's sent one, but they just don't want to accept it. The real problem, says Jesus, is that they do not know the One who sent Jesus; otherwise they would recognize his Son and agent. There follows an unsuccessful attempt to arrest Jesus, unsuccessful because the hour for him to go up to Golgotha has yet to come. The evangelist makes clear that it is God who is really in control of these events. Verse 31 stresses that many in the crowd believed in Jesus, or at least believed in his signs. This verse seems to reflect a certain expectation that when messiah came he would do the sort of miracles Jesus was known to have performed. Verse 32 refers to the Pharisees and chief priests' sending Temple police to arrest Jesus, another attempt that fails, and reveals that once again it is not all Jews, but some Jews, that are after Jesus.[18]

Beginning at v. 33 Jesus begins to announce his departure: he will depart in a little while, and people will search for and not find him. This remark is intended on one level, but is heard on another. The Jews ask if perhaps Jesus intends to go and instruct the Greeks in the Diaspora. There is considerable debate as to whether this is a reference to Gentiles or to Greek-speaking Jews in the Diaspora. The use of the term "Dispersion" (Diaspora) suggests Jews outside of Israel were being alluded to. Further support for the latter suggestion is the reference at 12:20 to the Greeks who have gone up to the feast to worship in Jerusalem and seek an audience with Jesus.[19] This is an important point. If the Johannine community is still witnessing to Greek-speaking diaspora Jews, this discourse, or at least the material in John 12:20ff., becomes a powerful tool to be used in such a witness. Such Jews should indeed seek Jesus.

The text of John 7 at this point may also allude to the fact that Jesus' witness in the Diaspora was now bearing more fruit than it had among the Jewish authorities and crowds of Judea and Jerusalem. If, however, it is right to suggest that the evangelist is directing this material in such a way that it will be useful in the Diaspora mission in and around Ephesus, then it is surely a misreading of the text to suggest that the references to being cast out of the synagogue (cf. below) indicate that the Johannine community no longer has any witness in the synagogue. What it indicates, rather, is that the community is experiencing opposition and even expulsion due to such a witness, but these Christians take it as part of their missionary mandate to continue such a witness, even if they experience the sort of reaction Jesus did in the Temple. The Greeks (Greek-speaking Jews) must be allowed to seek and find Jesus.

The next two subsections of the ongoing Temple dialogue (7:37–52; 8:12ff.) may emphasize how Jesus is the fulfillment of what the festival celebrated, the giving of water (rain) on the last day of the feast, and the celebration of lights on the first day of the feast. Alternatively, it is possible to take the setting of the material in John 8 as being the Festival of Dedication, or Hanukkah, the festival of lights celebrating the Maccabean victories and the retaking of the Holy City (cf. 10:22), in which case the saying about Jesus being the light of the world in John 8, the giving of sight to the blind in John 9, and the discussion in John 10 that includes mention of Hanukkah all belong together. I favor the latter view, and suggest the material in John 7:37ff. concludes the discussion of Jesus as the fulfillment of the Feast of Booths, bringing it to a dramatic climax on the last day.

The event described at 7:37 may take place on the seventh day of the feast, or more likely on day eight, when the booths were being taken down and there was some final celebrating before departure. Jesus offers the people something the feast could not give—a permanent source of thirst quenching, a permanent satisfying of one's essential needs. Verse 38 is one of the most problematic verses in the entire Gospel. Not only is the source of the quotation uncertain, but so is its meaning.[20] The source is likely a now-lost sapiential saying which Sirach also knows of and reflects in Sir. 24:30–32, where Ben Sira says of himself, "As for me, I was like a canal from a river, like a water channel into a garden. I said, 'I will water my garden and drench my flower-beds.' And lo, my canal became a river, and my river a sea. . . . I will again pour out teaching like prophecy, and leave it to all future genera-tions." This is all stated immediately after the discussion of Wisdom/Torah being a source of a river of wisdom.

Does the Johannine saying refer to water coming forth from Jesus, which would seem to make good sense in light of 7:37 and of the general portrait of Jesus as Wisdom in this Gospel, or is it water that comes forth from the one who believes in Jesus? On balance, it seems likely to be the latter, which comports with what Jesus says in John 4 about Jesus providing his listener with a source of water that will be with believers forever, which would make superfluous and supersede all such seeking of water at this festival. The NRSV, in similar fashion to the NIV, is right to translate "Out of the believer's heart shall flow rivers of living water." The point, then, is that one can be-come a reservoir of water and no longer need to seek it. Indeed one can be-come a dispenser of water when one believes in Jesus, the ultimate source of living water.[21] This is an appropriate remark in a Gospel meant to be used as a missionary tool.

Water here, as the parenthetical remark of the evangelist in v. 39 shows, refers to the Holy Spirit, which Jesus would not be able to bestow until Je-sus was glorified (i.e., crucified, risen, and exalted).[22] The evangelist thus in-dicates why the Spirit could not yet be given—Jesus' earthly ministry must be successfully concluded first.[23] There is no allusion here to baptism, but only to the Spirit, as the source of eternal life. It is worth mentioning again Sir. 24:21b where Wisdom/Torah says that those who drink of her will thirst for more. The implication is that Wisdom/Jesus offers a greater thirst quencher than Torah.

The response to Jesus' words on the last day of the feast is mixed. Some said, "This is really the prophet" or "Messiah," but others once again ques-tion Jesus' origins as being from Galilee, rather than Bethlehem. Once again Jesus' remarks divide the crowd, with some wishing to believe, others wish-ing to arrest Jesus. Painter is likely right that at this point we are meant to think of the crowd as having been infiltrated by the "Jews," who are trying to influence the discussion.[24]

According to v. 45 the Temple police return to the authorities and indi-cate they are impressed with the way Jesus speaks. The crowd is said by the authorities to be accursed because they do not know the law, another sign of the distinction between the crowds and the authorities. Nicodemus, who is one of these authorities, objects to arresting Jesus without giving him due process, in the form of a hearing. Their response amounts to a strong rebuke in the form of the statement that Jesus' Galilean origins rule out his even be-ing a true prophet.

At 8:12 we get the preliminary announcement that Jesus is the light of the world, picking up one of the themes of the prologue and preparing for the story of giving sight and so light to the blind in John 9. Light, of course, has many symbolic associations. In the Old Testament it can be associated with the act of creation itself in Gen. 1—2, the first thing God made. Or it can refer to the knowledge of God or a knowledge from God that illuminates one's way through a dark world (cf. Ps. 119:105). Light in various Old Testament stories refers to the dazzling presence of God when God appears on earth to his people (a theophany, such as at Sinai). Light is also associated in this Gospel, at Qumran, and in other early Jewish literature with truth. We have also already seen how Wisdom is described as light in Wisd. Sol. 7:22ff. (cf. above). Probably in this context light has a soteriological content—light as the transforming revelation that changes and saves a person's life. Notice the second half of John 8:12, which stresses that following Jesus means never having to walk in darkness, but rather having the light of life.

John 8:13–20 continues the legal discussion of whether Jesus should or can testify on his own behalf, and thus whether his testimony is valid.[25] Jesus is in the position of being the only human being who can adequately testify to himself, and thus the authorities must decide on the basis of his own testimony whether to believe him or not, as in a case when a murder is committed but there is only one surviving witness. Jesus indicates that it was not his intention to come and judge, but since his testimony, which is also the testimony of God, is not believed, he has no choice but to judge, for whoever rejects the testimony and will of God will be judged. Calling "God to witness is equivalent to swearing a solemn oath. If his opponents disbelieve that, they will have condemned themselves. It was as dangerous to disbelieve a statement on oath as to make a statement on oath that was not true."[26]

Jesus indicates again (cf. vv. 14, 21ff.) that the key to understanding his character is understanding his origins and destiny and the fact that he is God's agent. His association with the world above leads to an understanding of his nature, authority, and mission below. Like the discussion in John 6, Jesus' remarks become more and more offensive, until those in the audience are forced to show their true colors and/or make a decision about Jesus. Not only does Jesus say the interlocutors will die in their sins if they do not believe in him, but he even says that this must amount to believing *ego eimi* ("I myself am," or "I am he," or simply "I am"). Here at 8:24 we have the absolute use of *ego eimi*, which likely is drawing on Isa. 41:4ff. and on God's self-designation, involving a possible play on the manner God revealed himself to Moses in Ex. 3:14.[27] Notice, however, that this does not amount to a claim to *be* the heavenly Father, or to exhaust the Godhead, as v. 28 makes evident. It may be seen, then, as a claim to divine status or eternal existence, which thus warrants the use of the divine name of Jesus as well as the Father. Jesus is eternal but not self-existent; he is dependent on the Father and, while on earth as his agent, in a subordinate role to him.

Verse 28 involves another use of *ego eimi*, but here it seems to mean that when Jesus is lifted up on the cross the audience will realize that Jesus is that divine Son of man referred to in Dan. 7, who is the representative of both God and God's people.[28] This knowledge of who Jesus is, however, is not fully available until the Son of man is lifted up. This is why none of the potential converts portrayed in this Gospel up to the crucifixion are portrayed as models of Christian faith and confession but as those who are on the way to a fully adequate faith in Jesus—which is possible only when they incorporate the lifting up/exalting of the Son of man into the equation, a lifting up that involves his death, resurrection, and exaltation. Bultmann remarks that the Jews

> do not suspect that "lifting him up" they themselves make him their judge. The double meaning of "lifting up" is obvious. They lift up Jesus by crucifying him; but it is precisely through his crucifixion that he is lifted up to his heavenly glory as the Son of Man. At the very moment when they think they are passing judgement on him, he becomes their judge.[29]

Knowledge of the full mystery of who Jesus is, and thus the possibility of truly Christian faith in him, is not possible before the crucifixion, resurrection, and Spirit bestowal by Jesus. Thus the portraits, including the compelling ones of the blind man in John 9 and Mary and Martha in John 11, are not meant to be prototypes of Christian faith, but rather of those on the way to a more fully adequate faith in Jesus. In short, they are portraits appropriate for a document intended for use with seekers and religious questers.

At 8:28 Jesus also affirms that he speaks what the Father instructs him to speak, and that the Father has not abandoned him but rather is always with him because Jesus always does what pleases God. Thus, at v. 30, the response to this is some sort of faith in him on the part of many, but its content is not further specified.

Verse 31, however, suggests this faith is had by some of the "Jews." His word of advice to them is the famous "If you continue in my word, you are truly my disciples; and you will know the truth, and the truth will make you free." Notice that this speaks of a process: continuing in Jesus' word leads not only to true discipleship but to knowing the truth, which in turn leads to being set free. Jesus does not suggest that those who believe in part in him, yet know the full truth, are set free. It is appropriate at this juncture to ask Pilate's question—"What is truth?"

EXCURSUS: TRUTH IN THE FOURTH GOSPEL

In a detailed and helpful study, I. de la Potterie has shown that the background to the use of the term *aletheia* in this Gospel lies in the late Jewish wisdom and apocalyptic literature, not the Greek world or even just the earlier Jewish literature. Generally speaking, the term "truth" in late Jewish wisdom and apocalyptic literature has the sense of *revealed truth,* the *teaching of wisdom* or insight that has a moral significance.[30] As Wisd. Sol. 3:9; 6:22 indicates, having wisdom, knowing the truth, means knowing God's secret divine plan for humankind and its salvation. Knowing the truth refers to knowing the mysteries of the way God has chosen to deal with humankind and offer salvation. Thus the appropriate question to be asked about a text like John 8:31–32 or 8:40 is, Where is the divine plan of salvation revealed?

and the answer is in the career of Wisdom/Son of man, who came from above and returns to above, disclosing that revelation and salvation come to the world from the Father, but through his agent, the Son. Truth has a human face in this case, and speaks of the pilgrimage and incarnation of divine Wisdom. Truth here has a very specific sense: "This verse [8:40] proves that for John 'truth' does not denote the typically Greek idea of divine reality but the word of God, the revelation Jesus comes to impart to [hu]mankind."[31] And that revelation is Jesus himself and his career—he is both revealer and the revelation, for in him the divine plan of revelation and salvation is unveiled and comes to fruition. While in early Judaism it was Torah that was truth, and studying it made a person free (cf. Ps. 119; *Pirke Aboth* 3:5),[32] here the claim is that believing in Jesus and his story has this effect.

The response of the Jews in v. 33 is to the effect that they are Abraham's descendants and have never been slaves to anyone. But both their words and their conduct will reveal their true parentage. The irony, of course, is that the response in v. 33 completely leaves out of the discussion the period of time when the Israelites were slaves in Egypt after the time of Abraham, *and* the present, when they are in servitude to Rome! However, they are perhaps thinking of a different sort of slavery, but so is Jesus. His point is that they are slaves to sin—they do not keep Moses' law. They act as slaves, not servants in God's house. In a bold move, Jesus begins to assert not only that the Jews are not truly Abraham's descendants, but that he has precedence over Abraham in any case, since he existed before Abraham. Furthermore, the audience is eventually even said to be the children of the devil (v. 44).

Again it must be remembered that the polemics we hear in vv. 39ff. came in a context of the attempt to kill Jesus, and Jesus is here depicted as exposing the audience for what they truly were. The hyperbole reveals the true and deep-seated feelings of the audience, about Jesus and about themselves. The truth about what one is, is revealed by what one does, and in this particular case by what one does about or with Jesus.[33] "It is the interior reality of the opponent's alienation from God underneath the exterior appearances that the author is attempting to expose."[34]

When Jesus says in v. 39 that if they truly were Abraham's children they would do what Abraham did, he is likely alluding to the story of Abraham's reception of the divine messengers in Gen. 18. There is also evidence that it was said in early Judaism to be the hallmark of the descendant of Abraham that one was humble rather than proud (*Pirke Aboth* 5:22), and that one was merciful rather than vengeful toward one's fellow human beings (*b. Beşa* 32b). These are two traits notably lacking in the Jews facing Jesus at this point, but the overriding complaint is that if they truly knew the Father, they would recognize his Son and agent. Failure to recognize the latter indicates they do not in fact know the former.

At v. 41 the interlocutors offer an angry retort—"At least we are not illegitimate." Scholars have suggested that this may reflect the Jewish polemic that Jesus *was* illegitimate, a polemic that is clearly seen in Origen's famous

work *Against Celsus,* in which Celsus makes the accusation that Jesus was illegitimate, the product of a union of Mary with someone who was not her
husband.[35]

The polemic becomes increasingly vehement. The portrait of the devil is
as though he were the evil opposite to Jesus. Both are described as being
from the beginning, but Jesus is life (cf. 14:6), has life in himself, gives life,
while the devil is a murderer. Jesus is and speaks the truth, but the devil is
false and does not have the truth in him. "So for the author the devil is the
personification of what is exactly the opposite of Jesus." [36] The author makes
clear that the devil is evil through and through. Jesus begins by talking about
his activity—he is a murderer—then says he is alienated from truth's sphere,
and then says that truth is not in him. He is false to the core; thus it is hardly
surprising that he is called a liar and the father of lies. Notice that while the
devil speaks from himself, this is the opposite of what Jesus does—he speaks
what the Father gives him to say.[37] The devil is likely said to be a murderer
from the beginning and the father of lies because the stories of Adam and
Eve, the lies in the garden, and Cain and Abel, the murder once out of the
garden, are in mind. Our author does not explain, any more than Genesis
did, where evil first came from. He simply existed even as early as the time
of the founders of the human race.

Throughout this whole discussion, the underlying assumption is that
one's origins determine one's character. Jesus' true source, and likewise his
opponents' true source, determine their respective characters. The desire to
kill Jesus shows that the opponents are in tune with the will of their parent,
the devil, who has always been a murderer. "It is because their rejection [of
Jesus] is based on what is deepest within them that the author asserts that at
heart they are not related to God at all but to the devil."[38]

In response to Jesus' charges, the opponents answer with their own
charges in v. 48—Jesus is demon-possessed or an unclean Samaritan, probably a frequent charge about Jews who came from the north who were considered suspect. Jesus then claims that whoever keeps Jesus' word will never
taste death. This, of course, is seen as ludicrous by the audience and as proof
that Jesus had a demon. Jesus says that it is not his intent to glorify himself,
but in order to support his claim of giving eternal life he must make clear
that he has it in himself; hence the dialogue comes to a dramatic and crash-
ing halt with Jesus' claim in v. 58—"Before Abraham was, I am." This produces the response one would expect when devout Jews believe they have
heard a clear example of blasphemy: they seek to stone Jesus, but Jesus mys-
teriously slips away and leaves the Temple. Thus ends the first act of the
three-act drama of the middle section of this Gospel that centers in the Temple. The second act follows in the story of the blind man and in turn is followed by the good shepherd discourse and its fallout, both of these being
connected with the festival of Hanukkah, the celebration of the liberation of
Jerusalem by the Maccabees. Only now Jesus will offer a new sort of liberation or light, as a new sort of shepherd for God's people.

B. Gaining Sight and Insight
(John 9:1–41)

9:1 As he walked along, he saw a man blind from birth. [2]His disciples asked him, "Rabbi, who sinned, this man or his parents, that he was born blind?" [3]Jesus answered, "Neither this man nor his parents sinned; he was born blind so that God's works might be revealed in him. [4]We must work the works of him who sent me while it is day; night is coming when no one can work. [5]As long as I am in the world, I am the light of the world." [6]When he had said this, he spat on the ground and made mud with the saliva and spread the mud on the man's eyes, [7]saying to him, "Go, wash in the pool of Siloam" (which means Sent). Then he went and washed and came back able to see. [8]The neighbors and those who had seen him before as a beggar began to ask, "Is this not the man who used to sit and beg?" [9]Some were saying, "It is he." Others were saying, "No, but it is someone like him." He kept saying, "I am the man." [10]But they kept asking him, "Then how were your eyes opened?" [11]He answered, "The man called Jesus made mud, spread it on my eyes, and said to me, 'Go to Siloam and wash.' Then I went and washed and received my sight." [12]They said to him, "Where is he?" He said, "I do not know."

13 They brought to the Pharisees the man who had formerly been blind. [14]Now it was a sabbath day when Jesus made the mud and opened his eyes. [15]Then the Pharisees also began to ask him how he had received his sight. He said to them, "He put mud on my eyes. Then I washed, and now I see." [16]Some of the Pharisees said, "This man is not from God, for he does not observe the sabbath." But others said, "How can a man who is a sinner perform such signs?" And they were divided. [17]So they said again to the blind man. "What do you say about him? It was your eyes he opened." He said, "He is a prophet."

18 The Jews did not believe that he had been blind and had received his sight until they called the parents of the man who had received his sight [19]and asked them, "Is this your son, who you say was born blind? How then does he now see?" [20]His parents answered, "We know that this is our son, and that he was born blind; [21]but we do not know how it is that now he sees, nor do we know who opened his eyes. Ask him; he is of age. He will speak for himself." [22]His parents said this because they were afraid of the Jews; for the Jews had already agreed that anyone who confessed Jesus to be the Messiah would be put out of the synagogue. [23]Therefore his parents said, "He is of age; ask him."

24 So for the second time they called the man who had been blind, and they said to him, "Give glory to God! We know that this man is a sinner." [25]He answered, "I do not know whether he is a sinner. One thing I do know, that though I was blind, now I see." [26]They said to him, "What did he do to you? How did he open your eyes?" [27]He answered them, "I have told you already, and you would not listen. Why do you want to hear it again? Do you also want to become his disciples?" [28]Then they reviled him, saying,

"You are his disciple, but we are disciples of Moses. [29]We know that God has spoken to Moses, but as for this man, we do not know where he comes from." [30]The man answered, "Here is an astonishing thing! You do not know where he comes from, and yet he opened my eyes. [31]We know that God does not listen to sinners, but he does listen to one who worships him and obeys his will. [32]Never since the world began has it been heard that anyone opened the eyes of a person born blind. [33]If this man were not from God, he could do nothing." [34]They answered him, "You were born entirely in sins, and are you trying to teach us?" And they drove him out.

35 Jesus heard that they had driven him out, and when he found him, he said, "Do you believe in the Son of Man?" [36]He answered, "And who is he, sir? Tell me, so that I may believe in him." [37]Jesus said to him, "You have seen him, and the one speaking with you is he." [38]He said, "Lord, I believe." And he worshiped him. [39]Jesus said, "I came into this world for judgment so that those who do not see may see, and those who do see may become blind." [40]Some of the Pharisees near him heard this and said to him, "Surely we are not blind, are we?" [41]Jesus said to them, "If you were blind, you would not have sin. But now that you say, 'We see,' your sin remains."

Obviously this is a crucial narrative for the Fourth Evangelist, for he not only gives it full treatment, but there is evidence of great care taken with and literary structuring of the material into several scenes, with the drama shifting rapidly from one scene to the next: (1) introduction and narration of the miracle—9:1–7; (2) neighbors and relatives of the blind man talk with him—vv. 8–12; (3) first interrogation by the Pharisees of the cured blind man—vv. 13–17; (4) interrogation of the parents of the man—vv. 18–23; (5) second interrogation of the cured blind man, resulting in his expulsion from the synagogue—vv. 24–34; (6) theological conclusion: the faith of the cured man and the blindness of the Pharisees—vv. 35–41.[39] "The care with which the Evangelist has drawn his portraits of increasing insight and hardening blindness is masterful. Three times the former blind man, who is truly gaining knowledge, humbly confesses his ignorance (vv. 12, 25, 36). Three times the Pharisees, who are really plunging deeper into abysmal ignorance of Jesus, make confident statements about what they know of him (vv. 16, 24, 29). The blind man emerges from these pages in John as one of the most attractive figures of the Gospels."[40]

By way of background, it is crucial to bear in mind that there is no story of giving sight to the blind anywhere in the Old Testament. Nor do we find such a miracle attributed to any of Jesus' followers during his ministry. Acts 9:17ff. provides a partial parallel from after the time of Jesus. Yet it is very striking that among the miracles of compassion there are more miracles of giving sight to the blind recorded of Jesus than of any other sort of miracle (cf. Matt. 9:27–31; 12:22f.; 15:30f.; 21:14; Mark 8:22–26; 10:46–52; Luke 7:21f.; and John 9). In the Hebrew scriptures the giving of sight to the blind is associated with God's own activity (Ex. 4:11; Ps. 146:8), or with that of his chosen one (cf. Isa. 29:18; 35:5; 42:7), but with no one else. It is thus very likely that by recording this miracle the evangelist is attempting to say something special about Jesus' messianic, and perhaps also his divine, status. It is worth pointing out, however, that tales of the restoration of sight were known from the Greco-Roman world, including a famous story in the inscriptions of a blind Roman soldier named Aper, who was told (apparently by the god Asclepius) to go rub his eyes with an eye salve made of a concoction of honey and cock's blood; he did rub these together into an eye salve and apply it to his eyes, after which he received his sight (cf. *Syll.* 1173.15–18); or the famous story of Vespasian in Alexandria, where spittle is used to bring eyesight to the blind (Tacitus *Histor.* 4.81). Spittle was widely thought of as having medicinal qualities; many early Jews thought this (*y. Shabb.* 14, 14d, 17f.). In short, this story if heard by a Gentile audience would have singled out Jesus as a very special person and miracle worker; if heard by a Jew, as probably the Messiah, and definitely one uniquely endowed with divine power.

As is true with the other miracle stories in this Gospel, not much if any time is spent discussing the mechanics of the miracle itself, because it is the sign quality of the event in which the evangelist is most interested. The miracle is spoken of in matter-of-fact, nonflamboyant terms. Despite this fact, it creates a storm of protest, a detailed investigation amounting to further judicial proceedings, and finally a rejection of both the cured man and the one who cured him. The story is in many ways an apt exegesis of John 1— "In him was life, and the life was the light of all people. The light shines in the darkness, and the darkness did not overcome [understand] it. . . . He came to what was his own, and his own people did not accept him."

> On the one hand, he is the giver of benefits to a humanity which apart from him is in a state of complete hopelessness: "It was never heard that one should open the eyes of a man born blind" (v 32). The illumination is not presented as primarily intellectual . . . but as the direct bestowal of life or salvation. . . . On the other hand, Jesus does not come into a world full of [people] aware of their own need. Many have their own inadequate lights (e.g. the Old Testament 5.39f) which they are too proud to relinquish for the true light which now shines. The effect of the true light is to blind them, since they wilfully close their eyes to it. Their sin abides precisely because they are so confident of their righteousness.[41]

One of the more surprising aspects of the whole discussion of light in John 8—9 is that it is interwoven with the theme of judgment. This is not because, as Craddock colorfully puts it, God gets some sort of fiendish delight in turning on the light in a cellar full of cockroaches, for the light's purpose in coming was not judgment but illumination.[42] Light's *effect*, however, on those who refuse to recognize or adjust to its presence is to blind and to show up one's flaws, and this is precisely what happens to Jesus' opponents in this story.

Since this chapter provides the chief grist for an influential scholarly mill, one further preliminary comment is in order. I am referring to the theory of

Martyn that this story must be read on two levels, and that it is primarily *about* the situation of the Johannine community, which had been cast out of the synagogue like the blind man in the story.[43] While I have no doubt that the Fourth Evangelist is applying this story from the Jesus tradition to his own audience, in other words is doing the sort of hermeneutics any good preacher or teacher would do, one must ask what this story is really telling us. In the first place, it is not a story about a person who is a model of, or for, those who are *already* Christians. The blind man knows and affirms nothing about the lifting up of the Son of man, or Jesus as God's divine Wisdom. This is a story of a person coming to an increasingly more adequate understanding of and faith in Jesus, like so many other stories in this Gospel. We are told that the end result of that spiritual pilgrimage is that he is cast out of the synagogue.

If the story had a contemporary application in the Fourth Evangelist's day, one would expect it to be addressed to those who were contemplating a fuller commitment to Christ, perhaps those in the synagogue who were doing so. The point would be that they should know and count the cost before going ahead with such a commitment. The message would *not* likely be addressed to the Johannine community, which was already a separate entity and already had expressed full faith in the Son of man. In other words, the application would be appropriate to a group actively involved in Christian mission. If it had a message for the Johannine community itself, it would be to expect rejection of the message when they went and tried to share it in the synagogue, and to expect that those new converts they did make from that setting would pay a heavy price for recognizing the Son of man. In short, there is no reason to see in the story an allegory of a past trauma in the Johannine community dealing with the *community's expulsion from the synagogue.* We have no historical evidence that the Johannine community was ever attached to, or an integral part of, or ever met in a diaspora synagogue.

The first scene of this drama includes various key features. It is right to compare this story with John 5, especially because the evangelist once again reserves the information that this miracle transpired on the Sabbath until after the relating of the miracle itself (cf. v. 14), and once again Jesus takes the initiative in this act of compassion. The evangelist is preparing to explain once again how the judicial processes against Jesus arose, despite the fact that he was engaged in a work of compassion. Like the story in John 5, the issue of the relationship of suffering and sin once more arises, as does the issue of work on the Sabbath. Various early Jews firmly believed there was no death without sin (on the basis of Ezek. 18:20) and no punishment or suffering without guilt (on the basis of Ps. 89:33).[44] Jesus, however, does not accept this simple equation—he denies that the man born blind is in that condition because of either his own or his parents' sin.[45] Notice it is the disciples who ask the initial question. They are not yet illuminated on this subject. The question to be raised about 9:3 is whether we are being told that the man was born blind for the *purpose* of revealing God's work in his life, or that he was born blind and the *result* of this is that God has chosen to reveal his work in this man's life. I suspect that the latter, which is grammatically quite possible, is meant here, in which case we are not being told that God *caused* a person to be born blind just to use him as an illustration of divine power later in life.[46] The man's blindness will be made to serve God's larger purposes; it will be the occasion for God to reveal his works. One should compare what is said of the case of Lazarus in John 11:4.

Verses 4 and 5 make clear that Jesus feels it incumbent upon him to take advantage of the time he has to shed light in the world, for "night is coming when no one can work." The dark/light symbolism permeates the whole Gospel, but is especially prevalent here.

Notice that we are not told that the miracle occurred when Jesus spread clay and spittle on the man's eyes, but rather when he went and washed in the pool of Siloam, a pool on the southwest slope of the old city hill now known as the City of David.[47] As Schnackenburg says, there is no intent here to suggest that saliva has magical properties, since the healing transpires at the pool. More importantly, mixing paste, in this case in the form of clay with spittle, is among the listed actions prohibited on the Sabbath (cf. *m. Shabb.* 7:2). While Jesus is seizing the moment to do good works, he must also know that his deed would be interpreted once more as a deliberate violation of the Sabbath. The evangelist also tells us that the Hebrew word Siloam means Sent, which apparently he deems appropriate, since it is where Jesus sent the man to wash. As in the similar story in John 5, nothing is said in the miracle story itself about the man in question's having faith in Jesus, or of faith being a prerequisite for such a miracle.

The second scene, in vv. 8–12, validates that the man was healed, for naturally enough he goes to his neighbors and those who knew him before to share the news about his new condition. Even in this setting, however, the audience is divided as to whether this could possibly be the same man whom they knew before as a blind beggar. Verse 11 reveals that the man already knows the name of his healer—"the man called Jesus." He is already farther along than the paralytic portrayed in John 5.

The third scene shows the formerly blind man appearing before the Pharisees, and we are told he was "brought to" them by his previous inquisitors. In other words, informal judicial proceedings of the inquiry-stage sort were being initiated against this man, because it was suspected that the Sabbath had been violated. The Pharisees are portrayed as divided, as was the original crowd (v. 16), only this time the division is over whether Jesus could be a man from God or not. On the one hand, it appeared Jesus violated the Sabbath. On the other hand, it is asked, "How can a man who is a sinner perform such signs?" Notice in v. 17 that the Pharisees at this stage do not deny a miracle could have happened, and at this stage the man makes a step in the right direction by saying of Jesus, "He is a prophet" (v. 12).

Verse 18 begins scene four, and here the "Jews" are described as divided over the matter, and Jews here can only mean the Pharisaic leaders previously mentioned. The parents are called into the proceedings, and they vouch both that the man is their son and that he was born blind, but they disavow any knowledge of how the miracle has happened. Instead they direct the inquiry back to their son, who can answer for himself, since he is of age (v. 21). The evangelist in v. 22 makes an editorial remark that shows that he sees this response as an act of fear—they were afraid of being put out of the synagogue, because "the Jews" had already imposed a ban on those who confessed Jesus to be Messiah.[48]

Scene five, beginning at v. 24, involves the recall of the man born blind by the officials, but this time the tactic is to get the man to repudiate Jesus and give glory to God. Jesus is here called a sinner by them, doubtless due to his action on the Sabbath. The man professes not to know whether Jesus is a sinner[49]—he only knows he has received his sight. The officials request again the details of *how* Jesus healed him, and the man gets exasperated, asking if they want to become Jesus' disciples.

Their response to this rhetorical question is to revile the man and call him a disciple of Jesus, while they claim to be Moses' disciples. Then with irony, speaking more truth than they realize, they say that they do not know where Jesus comes from, while Moses' origins are clear (v. 29). This, of course, is precisely the problem—not knowing Jesus' origins and destiny leads to inevitable misunderstanding of Jesus and his work. In one of the most dramatic and effective retorts in this Gospel, the man, perhaps with some sarcasm, says in effect that though these officials do not know where Jesus came from they are ready to condemn him, and yet he had opened the man's eyes; and surely God does not provide miracle-working power to people who are sinners, but rather to those who worship and obey God.[50] Verse 32 stresses the point that no one had ever done this sort of thing before, and surely this must mean that if Jesus was not from God, he could do nothing. To this his angry interlocutors can only revile the man as one who must have been born in sin (as proved by his blindness), and thus be unsuitable to teach the teachers of the Jews. He is then expelled from their presence.[51]

A sixth and final scene occurs between the man and Jesus, with some Pharisees listening in nearby, doubtless gathering more data against Jesus. This scene may be meant to instruct Johannine Christians in how to bring about closure, how to lead a religious seeker to a more adequate faith in Jesus. Notice that we are told that Jesus not only sought the man out but also gave him a chance to develop and articulate his faith by asking, "Do you believe in the Son of Man?" (v. 35).[52] The response of the man reflects ignorance but also respectfulness.[53] The man *desires* to be informed so he may believe in him. Jesus identifies himself as this self-same Son of man, and the response is a confession of faith: "I believe,"[54] followed by prostration.[55] Though in terms of the larger narrative this conclusion jumps the gun, since the Son of man has yet to be lifted up, nonetheless it is an important preview or foretaste of what the evangelist is wishing to be the outcome of the pilgrimage of faith (cf. John 20:28)—an adequate confession and worship of Jesus. This story then could be used as a paradigm to reveal the progress of a soul and so lead others in the same direction. It is also a negative paradigm about how *not* to respond to Jesus and his deeds, and the Pharisees play the negative role.

Jesus' response to the man's falling down before him is to explain that his coming into the world as light promotes sight among the blind or provokes blindness among those who claim to see, and this is what he means by judgment. The decision for or against Christ not only reveals one's character but determines one's present relationship with God—either in a state of eternal life beginning in the present, or in a state of judgment, likewise beginning in the present. Thus the episode closes on a rather dark note. The Pharisees ask, "Surely you're not suggesting we are blind?" What is surprising is that Jesus does not say yes to this question. He says that their sin is culpable and remains because they claim to see—"If you were blind, you would not have sin." This in turn leads to the conclusion that there is a difference between spiritual blindness and deliberate spiritual perversity or obtuseness, a refusal to accept the light, a calling good evil and vice versa.[56] The story, then, serves as a powerful appeal for faith, but also as a powerful indictment of the willfully disbelieving, who know but refuse to accept what they have heard and seen. The Pharisees have enough spiritual knowledge and insight to be held responsible for rejecting Jesus. Their sin remains, for they did not act on their best insights but acted like the blind. Like a person who witnesses a crime being committed and knows the right thing to do is to report it but turns a blind eye, they have chosen darkness rather than light.

C. The Good Shepherd and the
Bad Sheep (John 10:1–42)

10:1 "Very truly, I tell you, anyone who does not enter the sheepfold by the gate but climbs in by another way is a thief and a bandit. ²The one who enters by the gate is the shepherd of the sheep. ³The gatekeeper opens the gate for him, and the sheep hear his voice. He calls his own sheep by name and leads them out. ⁴When he has brought out all his own, he goes ahead of them, and the sheep follow him because they know his voice. ⁵They will not follow a stranger, but they will run from him because they do not know the voice of strangers." ⁶Jesus used this figure of speech with them, but they did not understand what he was saying to them.

7 So again Jesus said to them, "Very truly, I tell you, I am the gate for the sheep. ⁸All who came before me are thieves and bandits; but the sheep did not listen to them. ⁹I am the gate. Whoever enters by me will be saved, and will come in and go out and find pasture. ¹⁰The thief comes only to steal and kill and destroy. I came that they may have life, and have it abundantly.

11 "I am the good shepherd. The good shepherd lays down his life for the sheep. ¹²The hired hand, who is not the shepherd and does not own the sheep, sees the wolf coming and leaves the sheep and runs away—and the wolf snatches them and scatters them. ¹³The hired hand runs away because

a hired hand does not care for the sheep. [14]I am the good shepherd. I know my own and my own know me, [15]just as the Father knows me and I know the Father. And I lay down my life for the sheep. [16]I have other sheep that do not belong to this fold. I must bring them also, and they will listen to my voice. So there will be one flock, one shepherd. [17]For this reason the Father loves me, because I lay down my life in order to take it up again. [18]No one takes it from me, but I lay it down of my own accord. I have power to lay it down, and I have power to take it up again. I have received this command from my Father."

19 Again the Jews were divided because of these words. [20]Many of them were saying, "He has a demon and is out of his mind. Why listen to him?" [21]Others were saying, "These are not the words of one who has a demon. Can a demon open the eyes of the blind?"

22 At that time the festival of the Dedication took place in Jerusalem. It was winter, [23]and Jesus was walking in the temple, in the portico of Solomon. [24]So the Jews gathered around him and said to him, "How long will you keep us in suspense? If you are the Messiah, tell us plainly." [25]Jesus answered, "I have told you, and you do not believe. The works that I do in my Father's name testify to me; [26]but you do not believe, because you do not belong to my sheep. [27]My sheep hear my voice. I know them, and they follow me. [28]I give them eternal life, and they will never perish. No one will snatch them out of my hand. [29]What my Father has given me is greater than all else, and no one can snatch it out of the Father's hand. [30]The Father and I are one."

31 The Jews took up stones again to stone him. [32]Jesus replied, "I have shown you many good works from the Father. For which of these are you going to stone me?" [33]The Jews answered, "It is not for a good work that we are going to stone you, but for blasphemy, because you, though only a human being, are making yourself God." [34]Jesus answered, "Is it not written in your law, 'I said, you are gods'? [35]If those to whom the word of God came were called 'gods'—and the scripture cannot be annulled— [36]can you say that the one whom the Father has sanctified and sent into the world is blaspheming because I said, 'I am God's Son'? [37]If I am not doing the works of my Father, then do not believe me. [38]But if I do them, even though you do not believe me, believe the works, so that you may know and understand that the Father is in me and I am in the Father." [39]Then they tried to arrest him again, but he escaped from their hands.

40 He went away again across the Jordan to the place where John had been baptizing earlier, and he remained there. [41]Many came to him, and they were saying, "John performed no sign, but everything that John said about this man was true." [42]And many believed in him there.

It has been argued above that the discussion of what Jesus said and did at the Feast of Dedication likely begins in chap. 8, but as Beasley-Murray reminds us the blending together of stories about the Feast of Tabernacles and the Feast of Dedication is not at all surprising, since Jews viewed the latter and later festival as *another* feast of Tabernacles, but celebrated in the winter (cf. 2 Macc. 1:9).[57]

If this message was delivered at a Feast of Dedication, it would have had a peculiarly appropriate character. In the midst of celebrating the military victory of the Maccabees and the recovery of the Holy City, Jesus delivers a discourse indicating that true leadership does indeed mean laying down one's life for the sheep, as some of the Maccabees had in fact done. Only now, instead of many heroic shepherds, Jesus speaks of only one true shepherd for God's people; and when he speaks of his death, he is talking about not only a martyr's self-sacrificial act but a death that amounts to both the lifting up of the Son and his return to the glory from whence he came.[58] These sorts of claims in their original setting would have had both a social and a political implication, for they implied that the existing or preexisting leadership in Jerusalem was illegitimate, involving robbers, thieves, and hirelings. This is especially clear when one reads this text in light of its Old Testament background in Ezek. 34, which speaks not only of Israel's false shepherds but of God as the true shepherd of Israel, and of David, God's anointed and appointed agent, who will be set up to feed God's flock.

There has been considerable debate as to whether what we have in John 10 is properly called a parable. The Hebrew word *mashal* can refer to a wide range of metaphorical speech, and the Greek word used here is *paroimia*, which in light of such texts as Sir. 39:3 should likely be seen as a synonym for *parabolos*. From John 16:25, 29 we learn that Jesus had spoken in *paroimiai* throughout his ministry, but that soon (after Easter) he would speak to his disciples openly. It seems clear for this sort of discussion (cf. the parallel in Mark 4:11ff.) that the terms involved refer to the fact that Jesus spoke in various form of wisdom speech, using figurative discourse, parables, riddles, aphorisms, and the like, a form of speech that both conceals the truth from the obtuse and reveals it to the spiritually open and partially enlightened.[59] In John 10 it appears, in fact, that we are dealing with two parabolic images that have been combined here, one having to do with Jesus as the good shepherd, and one having to do with Jesus as the door, or gate, for the sheep. A more detailed discussion will shed light on these images, which are introduced in vv. 1–10, and then their christological implications are drawn out as the chapter progresses.

The chapter begins with the double "Amen" saying, strongly affirming the truthfulness of what follows. It is important to bear in mind the metaphorical quality of what follows as the images shift rapidly—one moment Jesus is portrayed as the shepherd who enters through the proper gate to the sheep, the next he is seen as the proper door to the pasture through which the sheep must enter. We should not look for consistency in the development of the images. Despite protests from scholars, in early Jewish wisdom literature there was a sliding scale between parable and allegory. Parables often had more than one point and could have some allegorical elements.[60]

The probable reason for using such material is, as C. H. Dodd once suggested, to tease the audience into active thought and contemplation.[61]

It should be seen from the general tone of this material that this teaching is directed to a situation where there are competing claims about who is the true leader and *way* for God's people. Such competitive claims were being made not only during Jesus' ministry but, obviously enough from the Johannine epistles, during the time of the Johannine community as well. This material would be apropos in either of these settings, and in many since then as well where there is a crisis of leadership. It should be seen, however, that the material does not suggest a purely defensive and in-house situation (a flock is being raided by outsiders), but suggests competition for the same sheep *and* a situation where Jesus and his followers are still reaching out for "other sheep" not of this fold. In other words, it will not do to interpret this material without due attention to its missionary overtones.

Verse 1 contrasts the true shepherd, whose approach to the sheep is correct, as opposed to the thieves and robbers, who climb in by another way. The true shepherd's voice is recognized by his sheep, and he calls them by name. The naming of sheep was not unknown in Palestinian sheepherding. In fact the practice still continues today in the Holy Land, especially among those who have only a few precious sheep to care for.[62] The point of mentioning this here is not, however, to discourse on such customs but to make clear that Jesus' approach to evangelism is a personal one—he calls them by name, not by form letter or by appeal to an unknown television audience! In the Fourth Gospel this practice is seen coming vividly to light in the story of Mary Magdalene in John 20 (cf. below). By contrast, the sheep do not recognize and thus do not follow the voices of strangers.[63] We are told at v. 6 that the audience did not understand this figurative speech Jesus was using, and so Jesus offers another and different way of speaking of the matter. Throughout the whole discussion the illegitimacy of the current leadership of God's people (apart from Jesus) is stressed.

The second "parable," beginning at v. 7, portrays Jesus as the door or gate for the sheep, through which they must pass in order to get to the proper pasture—an image that has clear soteriological import. It implies the same exclusive claim as the saying "No one comes to the Father except through me." A contrast is made with "all who came before me," but this can hardly refer to all the previous leadership of Israel including Abraham, Moses, various good kings, and all the great prophets, including John the Baptist. It must surely refer to all previous false shepherds (compare Ezek. 34 to Zech. 11:4–9), including those who had been leading before and now during Jesus' day with whom Jesus was in a controversy at present. The application in the evangelist's day would be to the long-standing leadership of the local synagogue(s), who were competing for some of the same potential converts. We learn at v. 9 that this second parable at least is about salvation or, as v. 10 puts it, abundant life. The issue here, then, is not just good leadership versus poor leadership, but salvation versus lostness. In the second parable we are told that the competitor not only is a thief but has as his goal stealing, killing, and destroying. It is clear enough that the evangelist thinks the very spiritual lives of God's people are at stake.

At v. 11 the explanation of the parable(s) begins to be unveiled by a clear identification of Jesus with the good shepherd. Yet this material goes on to add something new to the discussion, namely, that the shepherd will lay down his life for the sheep. Though God is described in numerous places in the Old Testament as a shepherd (cf. Ps. 23; 80:2; Isa. 40:11; Jer. 31:9) and God's people are called sheep at times (Ps. 74:1; 79:13; 95:7; 100:3), more relevant for our purposes are the places where David is called the people's shepherd (cf. Ps. 78:70–72; Ezek. 37:24; Micah 5:3), or Moses (Isa. 63:11 LXX). What is being implied about Jesus in John 10 is at the very least his messianic status, or status as the true leader of God's people.

There is in the Fourth Gospel an apologetic approach to Jesus' death, attempting to show it was part of God's plan for Jesus' life and a fulfillment of scripture (cf. 2:17; 3:14; 13:18; 15:25; 19:24, 28, 36, 37).[64] In addition there is stress in John 10 and elsewhere on the fact that Jesus' life is not taken from him by force, but rather that he willingly lays it down at the appropriate time (his "hour"). Even more amazing is the claim that Jesus has the power and will take his life back up again (vv. 17–18).[65] This is part and parcel of the attempt of the evangelist to portray Jesus as a divine agent of God who has eternal life in himself, the sort of life that cannot be brought to a halt by physical death.

In vv. 11–13 Jesus contrasts himself with the hired hand, who does not have the same existential concern for the sheep as a shepherd, since they are not his own. The hired hand leaves the sheep in the lurch when a wolf comes. In the context of its application in the Johannine community, this may allude to those false leaders who went out from but were not of the Johannine community (cf. 1 John 4:1–6; 2 John 7–11).[66]

Verse 14 speaks of the shared knowledge of Jesus and his own. They know one another intimately, a sort of mutual knowledge that is analogous to the way the Father and the Son know each other (v. 15; cf. 1:10; 6:69). This latter saying is similar to the so-called Johannine thunderbolt in Matt. 11:27, and makes clear that what we have in the Fourth Gospel is a making explicit for missionary purposes of what is at least implicit and sometimes even clear in the Synoptic tradition. As Barrett stresses, it is clear that the evangelist with his mutual-knowledge language does not intend to suggest that the lesser person is absorbed by the greater—human beings are delivered, not deified. Their knowledge of God in Christ comes in a moral context of a loving relationship between distinct persons. Thus the concept of salvation and knowing God here is rather different from that of various ancient pagan cults, where union with the god involved a sort of apotheosis or deification of the human individual.[67]

At v. 16 we learn that Jesus has other sheep not of this fold. This likely is a reference to Gentiles (cf. 1:10; 4:42; 12:32), and thus an allusion to an eventual Gentile mission. Though during his earthly ministry Jesus was sent to the lost sheep of Israel and did not engage in an active recruitment of

Gentiles, nonetheless he responded to Gentiles who sought his aid, and he alluded at several points to the possibility of Gentiles' replacing some misbehaving Jews in the kingdom.[68] If, as we have argued throughout, this Gospel is meant to be used as an evangelistic tool, then this is a crucial verse, as many hearers of this Fourth Gospel would likely have been Gentiles, who would have heard texts like this one as referring to themselves.[69] Thus the ultimate vision held out here is for one flock to be produced of both Jewish and Gentile believers in Christ, a vision very similar to what we find in Pauline texts like Gal. 3:28 or Eph. 2. Verse 16 makes evident that the idea of two peoples of God was considered a nonstarter in the Johannine community—there was one flock and one shepherd. "For John the unity of the one flock is not a given unity naturally existing, but a unity created in and by Jesus."[70]

Though on one level it may seem surprising, we are told at v. 17 that just as one who loves Jesus keeps Jesus' commandments and is loved for doing so, so too Jesus is loved by the Father for carrying out the divine plan even unto death on the cross. Verse 17b suggests one of two possible translations. Does Jesus give up his life for the purpose of taking it back again, or with the result that he will take it back again through resurrection? It is a possible interpretation to suggest that Jesus died in order that he might be raised to a more powerful form of life, which he then could convey to others. The important point in any case is that Jesus intended to submit to death, but never intended for that to be the end of his story. Death would not have the last word about him, for he was the eternal Word/Wisdom of God. For a nonbelieving audience, it was crucial to convey the point that Jesus was the master of his own fate—his death and its form was deliberately planned and its timing chosen. Crucifixion did not happen to Jesus by accident.

The overall image here is of Jesus as a powerful and deeply caring shepherd who can provide for, protect, and even rescue his sheep. It is the image of a universal shepherd, whose ambition is to have one flock made up of Jewish and Gentile sheep. Only Jesus is the good shepherd, only he knows his sheep, only he is the gate through which they must pass to enter into salvation, into the green pastures. All other shepherds are false ones, of whom the sheep should beware. Thus we see again how universalism and particularism are combined in neat fashion in this Gospel.[71]

The sequel to the good shepherd discourse, in vv. 22–41, is the encounter and dialogue between Jesus and "the Jews" in Solomon's Portico in the Temple, in which the true sheep are contrasted with the Jews who are not Jesus' sheep. Again, the phrase "the Jews" when used in a pejorative context in this Gospel refers to certain Jewish leaders and those zealous for Torah who totally rejected Jesus' claims, not to be confused with many other Jews who believed in Jesus to one degree or another (cf. v. 42).

Jesus is confronted by the Jews and asked to tell them plainly if he is Messiah. Jesus' response is that he has already done so (cf. the above good shepherd discourse). Verses 28–29 say not only that Jesus' sheep are granted eternal life, and so will never perish, but also that "no one will snatch them out of . . . the Father's hand." This speaks to the matter of being "stolen" by outside forces or false shepherds, not to the matter of personally chosen apostasy.[72]

At v. 30 Jesus claims clearly, "The Father and I are one." It is clear from the context that this means one in intent, one in purpose, one in power, one in authority, one in works (cf. v. 25).[73] Jesus is God's true and faithful agent, carrying out the Father's designs. Yet there is in such a claim also an implicit message about who Jesus truly is. Thus the response in v. 31 by the Jews that Jesus is speaking blasphemy, claiming to actually make himself God while being only a human being (v. 33), is a claim ironically enough that is at once both true and false. The Jews are right that there is an implicit or even explicit divine claim in Jesus' words, but they are wrong that he is a mere human being, acting like Adam and so trying to make himself into a god. The hearer of the story of the Fourth Gospel will know that the Word/Wisdom of God was God from before the foundation of the universe; divinity was not something the Word had to attain at some point. The Jews, however, explain that they are not going to stone him for the good deeds he does, but for his christological claims. This whole dialogue may suggest that some Johannine Christians had also been in grave danger because of the claims they were making about Jesus in the diaspora synagogue and elsewhere.

Verses 34–36 are intriguing. The reference here is to Ps. 82:6 (LXX), and stresses that those to whom God's word had come could in some sense be said to be gods on the earth, presumably because they have knowledge of divine things revealed to them in God's Word. Jesus says then, a fortiori, if even ordinary Jews could be said to be in some sense gods, how much more the one whom God sanctified and sent into the world, the one who is God's Son. The term translated "sanctified" here surely has its normal biblical sense of being set apart or dedicated to God,[74] and thus the whole sentence indicates that the Son was set apart and sent on a divine mission as God's agent on earth. There is some irony in this remark, for what better time for the Dedicated One to reveal himself to God's people than at the Feast of Dedication?[75]

What is said here of Jesus, and throughout this chapter, has echoes in Wisd. Sol. 7—9, where Wisdom is given a similar characterization: (1) Wisdom is sent forth from the holy heavens (9:10) and is holy or set apart in herself (7:22); (2) she understands and gives understanding of parabolic speech (8:8; 9:11); (3) she rescues humanity, saving them (9:18); (4) she sits by the throne of God (9:4); (5) she is an associate or partner in all God's works (8:4); (6) she has the qualities and character traits of God (7:23ff.). Jesus finally in v. 38 appeals to the Jews to believe his works even if they will not believe his words, for this may at least be a starting place to understanding the Son and who he is. Yet the response to even this more modest request is negative, because it is joined to an astounding claim.

The divine claim is made clear at the climax of the dialogue (v. 38b), where Jesus says plainly that the Father is in him and vice versa, a claim that leads to another foiled attempt to arrest Jesus. Jesus escapes across the

Jordan to the place where John had previously been baptizing. His hour had not yet come.

II. Bridging the Horizons

There is such a great deal of rich material in John 7—10 that one could easily teach or preach from the material for weeks. It is wise in handling the text to break it down into manageable-sized units, or to deal with certain themes that surface time and again (e.g., truth); otherwise one quickly becomes overwhelmed by such material.

There will inevitably be a tendency to skip some of the more polemical sections of these chapters, or to domesticate them. My counsel is to let one's audience feel the fury and full force of the text when it is read, but then to explain the context in which the charges and countercharges were made in these dialogues.

John 9 is perhaps as good a place as any to deal with the subject of a person's growing in moral insight in regard to who Jesus is and what he can do, as well as with the opposite process—of the disintegration of spiritual perceptivity. On the latter topic one should read Charles Williams's gripping novel *Descent into Hell* to gain a real feel for what it is like to go spiritually blind.

A powerful message could focus on what exactly amounts to darkness in our own time.

> It is also darkness to refuse to hear the truth and to tolerate no teacher or preacher or politician who tells it. It is to avoid certain sections of town so as not to be disturbed by the conditions in which some have come to live. It is to avoid any book or any speaker who shatters my illusions of innocence in this evil world. It is not to ask questions at work, at home, or at church because I prefer to let sleeping dogs lie. It is to persuade myself that problems in the church, in the schools, in the neighborhood, in society at large are really none of my business. No wonder, then, that sermons on God's love for the world come into such darkness as judging light.[76]

Another manageable-sized issue that has current relevance is the issue of to what degree our origins determine our nature and destiny. The discussion in the text about being the true descendant of Abraham or the true Son of God could be bounced off the current discussions about the influence of parents on children, not only in terms of nurture but also in terms of nature. This in turn raises the question of in what sense one can pass on one's Christian heritage to one's children, and in what sense and how they must appropriate it for themselves.

A good exercise that makes the text come to life for children as well as adults is dramatizing the activities that went on during the various Jewish festivals such as the Feast of Booths or Hanukkah. Also a visit to the local synagogue, if the rabbi is willing, during the celebration of a feast can help bring understanding of the reason that Jesus made claims about water and light in the contexts of the two festivals mentioned above.

One of most important keys to enabling preaching or teaching to be compelling is aiding the audience to identify with one or another of the characters in the story. One effective way, then, to use John 9 is to ask a series of rhetorical questions at the end of the sermon as to who the audience does identify with in the story: (1) The blind man? (2) The neighbors? (3) The parents? (4) The Pharisees? (5) Jesus himself? (6) The narrator/evangelist?

The parable of the good shepherd lends itself naturally to a storytelling form of sermon, and it would not be inappropriate to draw an analogy with what the local church looks for in its leadership, and what leaders should expect of those in the pews. More of a stretch but still valuable would be a comparison between what we see as the essential qualities we look for in a senator, congressman, or President and the sort of traits spoken of in John 10 about the good shepherd. People are looking for leaders who feed their flock, not graze upon or fleece them! Perhaps the most important reminder is that the parable(s) of the good shepherd are not full-blown allegories, and allegorizing or looking for a hidden meaning in every single detail of the text is unwarranted. The main function of these vignettes is to bring out Jesus' positive role by contrasting it with others, and at the same time to make clear what is appropriate behavior for his followers and the benefits of faithful following.

The bondage of sin, as opposed to free service given to God, can be discoursed on at length, with numerous possible analogies with other sorts of bondages—addiction to drugs, to sex, codependency in the family, and the like. One of the most profound analyses of the fallenness of the human condition in the twentieth century was written by Reinhold Niebuhr in his classic work *Moral Man and Immoral Society*. Like Jesus' opponents in the text, human beings reveal an infinite capacity for rationalization and for belief in the goodness of their own actions and attitudes despite all evidence to the contrary. A powerful sermon could be preached on the peeling back of the layers of the self, to reveal the human core as it truly is—selfish and self-centered. As C. S. Lewis puts it:

> All this is flashy rhetoric about loving you.
> I never had a selfless thought since I was born.
> I am mercenary and self-seeking through and through:
> I want God, you, all my friends, merely to serve my turn.
>
> Peace, reassurance, pleasure are the goals I seek,
> I cannot crawl one inch outside my proper skin:
> I talk of love—a scholar's parrot may talk Greek—
> But self-imprisoned, always end where I begin.
>
> Only that now you have taught me (but how late) my lack.
> I see the chasm. And everything you are was making

My heart into a bridge by which I might get back
From exile, and grow man. And now the bridge is breaking.

For this I bless you as the ruin falls. The pains
You give me are more precious than all other gains.[77]

Analyzing the human heart as in this exercise would be painful but also very revealing, and my guess is that true healing happens only when the thorn is pulled out of the flesh and revealed for what it is.

One last warning as one is bridging from back then to our own context. John 7:37–39 is most appropriately used during the season of Pentecost, or perhaps during an evangelistic service, since it is discussing what the church received only after Jesus departed to heaven, and which individuals receive once they experience the new birth. It is not a text about Jesus as the ongoing fount from which we drink.

One of the major stresses in literature about the church in recent years has been the stress on the church suffering from a kind of amnesia, not remembering what it is, in part because it has forgotten whose it is. It is a fact that many churches continue to carry on long after they have lost any sense of where they have come from, who they are, and where they are going. The deep irony that is evident in the material in John 7—8 is well expressed by F. Craddock:

> The community of faith had gathered for that festival celebrating their history as a pilgrim people, living in tents, having no abiding city, with no compass but trust in God. These people whose past was nothing, who were no people, slaves in Egypt; these people whose future was uncertain save for the certainty of trust; *these are the people who will evaluate Jesus only in terms of his past and future.* These people who had neither unless they claim God as their past and future, now reject Jesus because he claims God as his past and future. Jesus says he comes from God . . . , they say he comes from Galilee and that is not an adequate past. Jesus says he is going again to God . . . they say he must be going to live among the Gentiles . . . and that is an inadequate future. The one who epitomized what Tabernacles memorialized, pilgrimage from God to God, was not recognized by those assembled for the weeks remembering.[78]

If one is doing a sermon focused on personalities in the Fourth Gospel, then an exercise in textual comparison might be in order. A. Culpepper has suggested that close attention be paid to the similarities and differences between the portrayal of the lame man and the blind man. Consider the following chart:[79]

The Lame Man	The Blind Man
1. The man's history is described (38 years; 5:5)	1. History is described (from birth; 9:1)
2. Jesus takes initiative to heal (5:6)	2. Jesus takes initiative to heal (9:6)

3. The Bethesda pool has healing powers for some	3. The man washes in Siloam and is healed (9:7)
4. Jesus heals on Sabbath (5:9)	4. Jesus heals on the Sabbath (9:14)
5. Jews accuse the man of Sabbath violation (5:10)	5. Pharisees charge Jesus with Sabbath violation (9:16)
6. Jews ask who healed him (5:12)	6. Pharisees ask how the man was healed (9:15)
7. Man doesn't know where or who Jesus is (5:13)	7. Man doesn't know where Jesus is (9:12)
8. Jesus finds him and invites belief (5:14)	8. Jesus finds him and invites belief (9:35)
9. Jesus may imply a relationship between sin and suffering (5:14)	9. Jesus rejects specific connection between sin and suffering (9:3)
10. The man goes to tell the Jews (5:15)	10. The Jews cast the man out (9:34)
11. Jesus must work, as his Father works (5:17)	11. Jesus must do the works of the One who sent him (9:4)

Despite the many similarities, of course there is the obvious salient difference between the portrait of one man growing in faith, and another showing no signs of faith at all. The former story, at least, could be taken as an implicit rebuttal of the arguments that miracles necessarily require or produce faith, while the blind man's story shows that a miracle can open a person up to a growing knowledge of and relationship with Jesus.

12. Family Affairs (John 11:1–12:11)

The stories recorded in John 11—12 are some of the most familiar in all of this Gospel, and also those which unfortunately raise the most historical questions for scholars and others who read the Gospels with a historian's eye. This commentary is not of the scope or genre that a detailed argument for the historicity of this material can be presented here, but I have presented such an argument for part of the material elsewhere[1], and Murray Harris offers a strong argument for the historical substance of the account of Lazarus's raising.[2]

I have already suggested, following the argument of R. Brown,[3] that the placement of this story is likely to owe more to the evangelist's theology than to chronology. It is an especially fitting foreshadowing of what would happen to Jesus on Easter, and it is likely for this reason the evangelist has placed an originally independent narrative here. If this deduction is correct, and this story was but one of a number of stories of Jesus' raising the dead that were told and retold in the early church as self-contained narratives, there is no compelling reason why the Synoptic writers would have had to include the Lazarus story if they knew it. If, on the other hand, the Lazarus narrative was known to other evangelists and this episode was in fact *the* event that triggered the events that led to Jesus' death and resurrection, it is very difficult to see how the Synoptic writers could possibly have afforded to omit the story. One cannot argue that the Synoptic writers knew nothing of Mary and Martha and Bethany, for Luke 10:38–42 makes very clear that at least Luke had access to such traditions, and Mark 14/Matt. 26 show that the Bethany anointing story was also widely known. There is one further reason why the story of the raising of Lazarus may have been placed here at John 11—it was grouped together with the other Bethany tradition the Beloved Disciple knew, which *was* a story about an event, an anointing that happened shortly before Jesus' death.

I. The Historical Horizon

A. An Heir-Raising Tale (John 11:1–57)

11:1 Now a certain man was ill, Lazarus of Bethany, the village of Mary and her sister Martha. [2]Mary was the one who anointed the Lord with perfume and wiped his feet with her hair; her brother Lazarus was ill. [3]So the sisters sent a message to Jesus, "Lord, he whom you love is ill." ⁴But when Jesus heard it, he said, "This illness does not lead to death; rather it is for God's glory, so that the Son of God may be glorified through it." ⁵Accordingly, though Jesus loved Martha and her sister and Lazarus, ⁶after having heard that Lazarus was ill, he stayed two days longer in the place where he was.

7 Then after this he said to the disciples, "Let us go to Judea again." ⁸The disciples said to him, "Rabbi, the Jews were just now trying to stone you, and are you going there again?" ⁹Jesus answered, "Are there not twelve hours of daylight? Those who walk during the day do not stumble, because they see the light of this world. ¹⁰But those who walk at night stumble, because the light is not in them." ¹¹After saying this, he told them, "Our friend Lazarus has fallen asleep, but I am going there to awaken him." ¹²The disciples said to him, "Lord, if he has fallen asleep, he will be all right." ¹³Jesus, however, had been speaking about his death, but they thought that he was referring merely to sleep. ¹⁴Then Jesus told them plainly, "Lazarus is dead. ¹⁵For your sake I am glad I was not there, so that you may believe. But let us go to him." ¹⁶Thomas, who was called the Twin, said to his fellow disciples, "Let us also go, that we may die with him."

17 When Jesus arrived, he found that Lazarus had already been in the tomb four days. ¹⁸Now Bethany was near Jerusalem, some two miles away, ¹⁹and many of the Jews had come to Martha and Mary to console them about their brother. ²⁰When Martha heard that Jesus was coming, she went and met him, while Mary stayed at home. ²¹Martha said to Jesus, "Lord, if you had been here, my brother would not have died. ²²But even now I know that God will give you whatever you ask of him." ²³Jesus said to her, "Your brother will rise again." ²⁴Martha said to him, "I know that he will rise again in the resurrection on the last day." ²⁵Jesus said to her, "I am the resurrection and the life. Those who believe in me, even though they die, will live, ²⁶and everyone who lives and believes in me will never die. Do you believe this?" ²⁷She said to him, "Yes, Lord, I believe that you are the Messiah, the Son of God, the one coming into the world."

28 When she had said this, she went back and called her sister Mary, and told her privately, "The Teacher is here and is calling for you." ²⁹And when she heard it, she got up quickly and went to him. ³⁰Now Jesus had not yet come to the village, but was still at the place where Martha had met him. ³¹The Jews who were with her in the house, consoling her, saw Mary get up quickly and go out. They followed her because they thought that she was going to the tomb to weep there. ³²When Mary came where Jesus was and saw him, she knelt at his feet and said to him, "Lord, if you had been here, my brother would not have died." ³³When Jesus saw her weeping, and the Jews who came with her also weeping, he was greatly disturbed in spirit and deeply moved. ³⁴He said, "Where have you laid him?" They said to him, "Lord, come and see." ³⁵Jesus began to weep. ³⁶So the Jews said, "See how he loved him!" ³⁷But some of them said, "Could not he who opened the eyes of the blind man have kept this man from dying?"

38 Then Jesus, again greatly disturbed, came to the tomb. It was a cave, and a stone was lying against it. [39]Jesus said, "Take away the stone." Martha, the sister of the dead man, said to him, "Lord, already there is a stench because he has been dead four days." [40]Jesus said to her, "Did I not tell you that if you believed, you would see the glory of God?" [41]So they took away the stone. And Jesus looked upward and said, "Father, I thank you for having heard me. [42]I knew that you always hear me, but I have said this for the sake of the crowd standing here, so that they may believe that you sent me." [43]When he had said this, he cried with a loud voice, "Lazarus, come out!" [44]The dead man came out, his hands and feet bound with strips of cloth, and his face wrapped in a cloth. Jesus said to them, "Unbind him, and let him go."

45 Many of the Jews therefore, who had come with Mary and had seen what Jesus did, believed in him. [46]But some of them went to the Pharisees and told them what he had done. [47]So the chief priests and the Pharisees called a meeting of the council, and said, "What are we to do? This man is performing many signs. [48]If we let him go on like this, everyone will believe in him, and the Romans will come and destroy both our holy place and our nation." [49]But one of them, Caiaphas, who was high priest that year, said to them, "You know nothing at all! [50]You do not understand that it is better for you to have one man die for the people than to have the whole nation destroyed." [51]He did not say this on his own, but being high priest that year he prophesied that Jesus was about to die for the nation, [52]and not for the nation only, but to gather into one the dispersed children of God. [53]So from that day on they planned to put him to death.

54 Jesus therefore no longer walked about openly among the Jews, but went from there to a town called Ephraim in the region near the wilderness; and he remained there with the disciples.

55 Now the Passover of the Jews was near, and many went up from the country to Jerusalem before the Passover to purify themselves. [56]They were looking for Jesus and were asking one another as they stood in the temple, "What do you think? Surely he will not come to the festival, will he?" [57]Now the chief priests and the Pharisees had given orders that anyone who knew where Jesus was should let them know, so that they might arrest him.

The material in John 11:1–12:11 is used by the evangelist to neatly provide a transition from the telling of the story of Jesus' public ministry to the story of the Passion narrative. The raising of Lazarus foreshadows what will happen to Jesus on Easter, and the anointing of Jesus is portrayed as a proleptic burial ritual. This in turn means that the material in John 12:12–50 in fact introduces the Passion narrative with the triumphal entry, being followed by one last quest story (the Greeks), a summary of Jesus' public teaching, the last meal that Jesus shared with the disciples, and the farewell discourses. This sort of portrayal of the matter makes good sense in a Greco-Roman biography, for meals were the proper occasion for teachers, philosophers, and rhetoricians to discourse and lead discussions, after the supper itself, on interesting, entertaining, or important subjects.[4] Jesus, then, in John 11—12, but also in the beginning of the Passion material in John 13, is continuing to be portrayed as the sage instructing seekers and disciples.

The technique of presenting the raising of Lazarus story differs from earlier miracle stories in this Gospel in that instead of presenting the miracle first followed by dialogue and monologue, the latter comes first in the narrative and the miracle provides the climax of the story. It is also important to understand the substance of the story in John 11. While it is certainly the case that Lazarus is portrayed as truly dead and thus truly raised from the dead, the end result of what happens to Lazarus is not identical to what happens to Jesus on Easter. There are telltale signs in the narrative that this is so. For one thing, Lazarus's resurrection is not like Jesus', for he is still wrapped up in the grave clothes (compare John 11:44 to John 20:7) and must be helped to get loose.[5] For another thing, Lazarus does not receive a resurrection body like Jesus, but rather returns to life in the body he had before, only now without his former illness. In other words, while he is raised and returns to earthly life, he does not experience resurrection in the sense that Jesus did. His is a return to former health, not a moving forward into a body that is immune to disease, decay, and death, or into a body that can appear and disappear in various locales instantaneously.[6] Inscriptions on ancient burial boxes (ossuaries) found in Bethany in 1873 bear the names Mary, Martha, Lazarus, and Simon (cf. Mark 14:3), which at the very least shows that various early Christians believed that Lazarus, like other members of his family, went on to die—only in his case it was for a second time.[7]

If we are to read John 11 correctly, we should bear in mind the pattern we have already noted in many stories in this Gospel. Even those people presented in a generally positive light as potential or actual followers of Jesus are not portrayed as full-fledged Christians. Thus in this story Martha clearly enough believes in Jesus, in particular in his healing power and messianic character, but she does not yet understand that Jesus *is* the resurrection and the life, who can give life even in the present. Her objection to Jesus' command to roll away the stone before the tomb clearly reflects a lack of adequate faith and understanding, and earns something of an exasperated response by Jesus (vv. 39–40). This story, then, once more portrays the progress of a soul toward a more adequate faith in who Jesus is, and as such is a fine tool to be used in missionary work with seekers and those of good will who already accept some truths about Jesus.[8]

The characterization of Martha and Mary is striking, not least because it so closely matches the portrayal in Luke 10:38–42—of Martha as the outgoing and vocal sister, while Mary is the quieter one, less likely to take the lead but portrayed nevertheless as the more devout of the two, always found at Jesus' feet (compare John 12:3 to Luke 10:39). The story also reveals something important about Jesus' modus operandi during his public ministry. It reveals that he had not only traveling disciples, but also followers who remained in one place and offered Jesus and the disciples hospitality when they were in the area. This is an important point, because it means that Jesus did not require all his true followers to leave home and family in order to meet the demands of discipleship.[9] It cannot be argued, in view of Luke 8:1–3, that female disciples were required by Jesus to stay at home. We must reckon with several forms of following Jesus that existed during his public ministry, *none of which were gender specific.* What was radical for Jesus' setting and day was allowing women to be disciples, even traveling disciples, of a great Jewish sage.

Another important social dimension of the text is the fact that Jesus had followers who were reasonably well off, and who did not give up all their property in order to follow Jesus. The relatively high status of Mary, Martha, and Lazarus is shown by: (1) the many Jews who come from Jerusalem to mourn Lazarus's death (11:19, 45); (2) the fact that they are able to serve a banquet for at least fifteen in their dining area, suggesting a house of some size (John 12:1–2)—Greco-Roman dining areas normally accommodated somewhat less than this number;[10] (3) the expensive ointment, pistic nard, of which Mary uses a large quantity to anoint Jesus, reflecting the family's high status (John 12:3);[11] (4) the tomb with a rolling stone, though this seems to have been simply a cave tomb, as 11:38 suggests, which was not uncommon in Judea. All in all, the profile of the Bethany family painted not only here but also in Luke 10:38–42 suggests a family of some means who provided hospitality for Jesus and the disciples when they were in the Jerusalem area. Since Mary and Martha are portrayed in John 11 as those who are on the way to being full-fledged disciples of Jesus without leaving home, this text has social implications about not only the status but also the mode of discipleship assumed by some of Jesus' followers, at least in Judea. In view of this text and Luke 8:1–3 it will not do to simply portray Jesus as being interested in, recruiting from, or being followed by the poor and outcasts of society, though he gave the marginalized and oppressed his special attention, gaining a reputation as a friend of sinners and other despised persons such as tax collectors.

John 11:1–44 is the longest continuous narrative in the Fourth Gospel before the Passion narrative. This is not without reason, for in the Johannine schema of things it is the climactic and most miraculous episode in the series of signs that the evangelist presents prior to the telling of the even greater miracle of Jesus' death and resurrection. In many ways this story parallels the first sign, in John 2, and serves to bring together and reemphasize some of the evangelist's chief themes. The message Martha and Mary send in 11:3 is similar to the open-ended suggestion of Jesus' mother in 2:3. Furthermore, Martha's remark in 11:22 about "whatever you ask" resembles Mary's statement in 2:5. In both scenes the hope is held that Jesus will act despite the seeming impossibility of the situation. The theme of glory is also found in both stories (cf. 11:4, 40; 2:11). In this story, as in John 2 and 7, Jesus can act only as the Father wills, not at the request of his mother, brothers, or friends. As the best is saved for last in John 2, so here the best sign is saved for last at the close of the telling of the public ministry. In John 2

Jesus came and brought new life and joy to the celebration of the union of two lives, while in John 11 he brings new life and reunion to a family he has dearly loved. Finally, both narratives portray women who are in the process of learning Jesus' true nature and so becoming his true disciples. Mary and Martha, like Jesus' mother, believe in Jesus' miracle-working power, but in both cases this faith and knowledge is inadequate to plumb the depths of Jesus' identity. They do not realize that Jesus can bring life because he *is* the resurrection and the life. If in John 9 Jesus was revealed as the divine Son of man, here he is revealed as the divine Son of God, one who has life and light (cf. 11:10) in himself. Jesus will not stumble into his fate, he will work it out resolutely at the proper time, knowing God's plan for his life.

At John 11:1 Lazarus is introduced as a new character in the story. This does not rule out the possibility that he might be the Beloved Disciple, since the latter figure has not been formally introduced in those terms up to this point in the story, and since this document was not written primarily for the Johannine community, who needed no introduction to the Beloved Disciple.[12] Lazarus is the only male disciple singled out by name in this Gospel as one whom Jesus loved, hence the conjecture that he might have been the Beloved Disciple. This conjecture could also be supported by John 21, since Lazarus's resurrection would explain why some in the community might have thought he would not die before Christ's return. Finally, if John 12 and 13 were meant to be read together, Lazarus's having the seat of the host in John 12 could suggest an identification with "the one whom Jesus loved" in John 13 (compare 12:1–2 to 13:23). As Culpepper says, however, this identification of Lazarus with the Beloved Disciple is not made clear in the text, and thus probably was not intended by the evangelist.[13]

The story as it is presented is mainly about Mary and Martha and their faith response, or lack thereof, to Jesus. It involves a request, not a quest story, and thus is truly parallel to what we find in such narratives as John 2.[14] Lazarus is merely acted on and does not speak. The bulk of the material is taken up with Jesus' dialogue, first with his disciples, then with the sisters.

We are not told what sort of illness Lazarus suffered from, but it proved to be terminal. In John 11:2 Mary is introduced for the first time, *prior* to the telling of the anointing story. This need not point, however, to the Johannine community's being the primary audience of this Gospel material, but may serve as a simple reminder of Mary's identity to the Christians who would be using this Gospel as a missionary tool to bring outsiders to Christ.[15] John 11:2 does suggest, however, that the evangelist is not addressing a group of Judean Christians, who would have needed no such reminder about Mary's famous act.

A messenger was sent to Jesus to inform him that Lazarus was ill. Jesus' response is cryptic: "This illness does not lead to death; rather it is for God's glory, so that the Son of God may be glorified through it." Carson points out that the term glory (*doxa*) here and elsewhere in this Gospel means not "praise," as if the illness will serve for the praise of God, but rather revelation. This illness and the way Jesus handles it will serve to reveal God and God's Son for who they are—the authors of life.[16] This verse should be compared to John 9:3, and here again the point is the function the illness and death will be made to serve in God's large scheme of things. It is not suggested that God made Lazarus terminally ill in order to turn him into an object lesson and demonstration of divine glory.

It is clear from vv. 1–5 in general that Jesus' not going to help Lazarus immediately does not reflect a callous disregard for the sisters' concern, but rather Jesus knows in advance how the matter will turn out, and furthermore, here as elsewhere in this Gospel, he can act only when the Father gives him the signal to go and to do, for he is God's agent. Jesus remains two more days where he is, before setting out for Bethany.[17]

Jesus' sudden resolve to go back into Judea at v. 7 is met with surprise and dismay by the disciples, for they were deeply concerned about the threats against Jesus' life by the "Jews" (cf. John 10:31). Jesus' reply in vv. 9–10 amounts to saying that his ministry is not over yet, and he must continue his work while there is still time to do so. Jesus has the light within him, and he knows in advance when the darkness will descend on him.

In v. 11 Jesus explains his reason for going. He plans to awaken Lazarus from sleep. Sleep was a common Jewish euphemism for death (cf. Job 14:11–12; 1 Thess. 4:13ff.), and the disciples, still thinking on one level while Jesus speaks on another, assume he means that Lazarus is literally only asleep (vv. 12–13).[18] Here, as in Mark 5:39, Jesus would seem to call death sleep because it is something that in his hands has no more than temporary power over its victim. It is something one comes back from alive and well, because of Jesus' power. Jesus must speak plainly to the disciples and explain that Lazarus is in fact dead (v.14), and from the point of view of the disciples this is a good thing, for they are about to witness an event which, if properly understood, could strengthen their faith and act as a parable of what would yet happen to their Master. How one should read v. 16 has been often debated, but in view of the dim-wittedness of the disciples already displayed in these same verses, I doubt that this verse should be seen as an expression of courage. It sounds more like fatalistic resignation to what seemed inevitable.[19] This conclusion comports with the later portrait of Thomas, in John 20, as skeptical and doubting.

Wherever Jesus was, he was a good two days' walk away from Bethany, for v. 17 tells us that he arrived when Lazarus had been in the tomb for at least the better part of four days. This may be of some significance, because there are early Jewish traditions that suggested that the spirit of the deceased remained near the corpse for three days and then departed. After three days, then, it was thought there was no hope of resuscitation.[20]

The proximity of Bethany to Jerusalem (within two miles) is stressed at v. 18 to explain why many Jews were able to come up from Jerusalem to mourn with the family. Jewish burial and mourning customs are interesting in various regards. For one thing, Jews did not know the Egyptian arts of embalming, and so used spices and ointment to conceal the odor of the corpse during the period of mourning, which often went on for a week. When Jesus arrived the corpse would already be decaying significantly, and so would stink (cf. v. 39). Second, the obligation of the community to grieve with the mourners was strongly felt in early Judaism, and there is nothing in this story to suggest that the many Jews were insincere in their attempts to empathize and console. The term Jews is not used in a pejorative sense in 11:1–44.

There would be a period of loud lamentation immediately after death, followed by a period of public weeping and consolation.[21] Every family was obligated to hire at least two flute players for mourning, and women might also be hired to weep at the grave.[22] As was the case with most ancient Middle Eastern cultures, grieving was not viewed as a private matter, and extended public display of one's grief was expected.

Martha goes out to meet Jesus, and her first words to Jesus seem to be a mixture of faith and accusation—"If you had been here, my brother would not have died." Yet she adds, "Even now I know that God will give you whatever you ask of him." It is clear from the sequel (v. 39) that this does not include a belief that Jesus might ask for and receive Lazarus back from the dead then and there. Jesus' assurance that Lazarus will rise is taken to mean that he will rise on the last day (v. 24).[23] Jesus then responds that he is the resurrection and the life.

Verses 25b–26 may explicate these two attributions in reverse order—Jesus' being the life means that he gives eternal life, which begins in the present life and continues beyond death, while Jesus being the resurrection means that, in a larger sense of the term, a person who believes in him will never die (i.e., go on to experience eternal death), for he or she will be raised. Jesus asks if Martha believes this, to which she responds with the least inadequate confession yet in this Gospel—Jesus is Messiah, Son of God, and, most crucially, the One coming into the world.[24] Yet this does not mean that she believes that Jesus will at the present moment raise Lazarus. She believes truly, but still inadequately.

Mary is summoned and goes to meet Jesus as well, and offers in v. 32 much the same complaint as Martha had. She too does not understand that Jesus *is* already the resurrection and the life. Verse 33 is a crucial verse for understanding this passage, and one that has often been misread. Jesus sees both Mary and the consoling Jews weeping, and this produces a very strong emotional reaction in Jesus. The key Greek word, *embrimaomai*, invariably has the sense of anger, outrage, or indignation when it is predicated of a human being.[25] The grief and weeping of Jesus, then, comes from anger within, and the translation "moved with indignation in spirit" is close to the mark.[26] The question is, indignation at what? Since we are told that what sparks this reaction in Jesus is the weeping of Mary and the Jews, the most natural conclusion is that Jesus is upset at their lack of faith, for they mourned as people without hope for Lazarus's immediate future, while they were in the presence of One who was both resurrection and life. Thus when the Jews are moved to say of Jesus, "See how he loved him!" when Jesus himself begins to weep, there is a certain irony in their words, for while they were right that Jesus loved Lazarus, they were wrong to interpret his tears as an expression of that fact. Verse 37 confirms this interpretation, for it suggests that the Jews think that Jesus seems impotent in the face of death, though he was able to cure a blind man.[27] Verse 37 is also important because it indicates that the evangelist believes that Jesus' raising of Lazarus is an even more stupendous miracle than giving sight to the blind.

Jesus' reaction to the verbal expression of the Jews is equally strong. Verse 38 indicates he was greatly disturbed.[28] Probably we are to think of Jesus reflecting on the fact that he was coming to the close of his ministry, and yet not only those who had seen miracles like the healing of the blind man, but even his close friends and disciples, *still* did not yet adequately understand and believe in who he was. After the command to roll away the stone, Jesus responds to Martha's objection with, "Did I not tell you that if you believed, you would see the glory of God?" (v. 40). This is peculiar, because it is only to the Twelve (v. 4) that Jesus had said anything of this sort, unless one counts Jesus' words in vv. 23–26, which do not mention glory.

In any event, the scene is concluded by Jesus praying, not to be heard, but rather giving thanks that he has now been and always was heard by the Father. The prayer is said for the benefit of the crowd, "that they may believe that you sent me." Here again, when one compares this prayer to what Jesus says in vv. 23–26, we see the interplay between Jesus as having life in himself, and Jesus as radically dependent on the Father for direction. The Fourth Evangelist wishes to stress that both things are true of Jesus, and he is able to bring these two concepts together by using the language of agency. Jesus is the one the Father sent, his authorized and empowered agent on earth, who is given specific guidance on when and where to act.[29]

Jesus calls Lazarus by name, and he comes forth bound up in the burial shroud and wrappings (v. 44). We may be meant to see in this a preliminary fulfillment of the teaching that the dead would respond to the Son's voice and come forth from their graves (cf. 5:25–29). The point is that Jesus already has this power prior to his death and resurrection, and can both give life and overcome death because he already *is* the resurrection and the life. Jesus commands that Lazarus be unbound and set free. Not even death was stronger than God's Son. He, not death, would have the last word about human life for those who loved him.

The response to Jesus' mighty miracle was mixed. Many Jews believed at least in Jesus' miraculous power, while others went and reported him to the Pharisees. The text does *not* say that the authorities were reacting to Lazarus's raising in particular, but rather to the fact that "this man is performing *many signs*" (emphasis added). In other words, it was a judgment that was arrived at not because of one event but because of a whole series of events.

The authorities were concerned about the political implications of Jesus' acts if people believed in Jesus because of them: " 'Belief' . . . would not have been simply a matter of religious faith: it would have meant accepting Jesus as an authoritative agent of God and therefore as the leader and ruler of the people."[30] This in turn would have meant rejecting the present leadership as invalid, and thus also would have implied a rejection of the Roman overlords who sanctioned the current Jewish authorities, in particular the high priest. In short, it was Caiaphas and the Sadducees as well as other members of the Sanhedrin, including its Pharisaic members, who had the most to lose if Jesus was recognized as the Jews' messianic leader. The words in vv. 47ff. must be evaluated in this light: "If we let him go on like this, everyone will believe in him, and the Romans will come and destroy both *our holy place and our nation*" (emphasis added). This is a most revealing statement. It indicates that the authorities called the Temple "our place," rather than God's place.[31] Caiaphas responds harshly to such a complaint, for he has what he takes to be a clear solution to the problem: "It is better for you to have one man die for the people than to have the whole nation destroyed."

Here at v. 50 we have reached the height of irony. Caiaphas is thinking of what is expedient to preserve the status quo and remain in power, while, as the evangelist says in v. 51, it was God who prompted him to prophesy more than he realized. Jesus would indeed be the one who died so that the nation and, indeed, also the dispersed children of God might be saved, though not from the wrath of the Romans but rather from the wrath of God. Salvation entailed gathering all God's children into one flock.

The portait here of Caiaphas as a blunt, cynical, and self-serving figure is only confirmed by what Josephus says about the Sadducees as leaders in general (*War* 2.166). It must also be remembered that the Sadducees did not believe in resurrection (cf. Mark 12:18; Acts 23:8), and thus they would have regarded the promise of Jesus' resurrection, or even a resurrection of the dead in general, as idle speculation. In their way of thinking, if they could get rid of Jesus now, they wouldn't have to deal with him or his followers any longer.

Caiaphas was high priest from A.D. 18 to 36. "In a beautiful stroke of sarcasm, the Evangelist calls Caiaphas 'high priest that year' (vv. 49, 51). In Jewish tradition the high priest was such for life, but now, under Rome, a breath could make or unmake a high priest. Those who sit so uneasily place political expedience above the word of God. He was not God's man; he was not even his own man; he was Rome's man."[32]

If at least the anointing of Jesus in Bethany transpired during Jesus' third Passover since he began his ministry (cf. 3:24; 6:4), and the first of these Passovers was forty-six years after Herod began to build the Temple (cf. 2:20) this places the death of Jesus at about A.D. 30.[33] The signs of Jesus precipitate the official decision to have Jesus put to death (v. 53). This is important because up to this point Jesus had been subject only to informal trial by his peers, and possible stoning, but now the Jerusalem authorities were prepared to act against him as well.

Verse 54 indicates once again that Jesus had supernatural knowledge or informed sources[34] about the plans of the authorities, so we are told he no longer walked about openly among the Jews, but chose to go to the remote town of Ephraim near the Judean wilderness, remaining there for some undisclosed length of time.[35]

Verses 55–57 must be seen as transitional. The Passover of the Jews is again mentioned in a way that suggests an audience for the Gospel, including at least some Gentiles. The days of purification that preceded the Passover are mentioned. This was normally a period of a week, in which ritual preparations were made so that a person could partake of the Passover in good faith and in a proper ritual condition.[36]

The speculation among the crowds is given. Various people were of the opinion that Jesus would not show up for the festival because of the danger involved. Notice that it is the Pharisees who are said to give orders in v. 57 that Jesus' whereabouts should be reported to them so he could be arrested. The picture we gain from the last ten verses of John 11 is that a concerted effort of the leaders of the Sadducees and Pharisees was involved in the trial and arrest of Jesus, which in turn suggests that he was seen as a considerable political threat, since these two groups often did not see eye to eye. *Mishnah Sanh.* 7:10 records a procedure for capturing by stealth someone who leads the Jewish people away into idolatry.

B. An Annoying Anointing (John 12:1–11)

12:1   Six days before the Passover Jesus came to Bethany, the home of Lazarus, whom he had raised from the dead. [2]There they gave a dinner for him. Martha served, and Lazarus was one of those at the table with him. [3]Mary took a pound of costly perfume made of pure nard, anointed Jesus' feet, and wiped them with her hair. The house was filled with the fragrance of the perfume. [4]But Judas Iscariot, one of his disciples (the one who was about to betray him), said, [5] "Why was this perfume not sold for three hundred denarii and the money given to the poor?" [6](He said this not because he cared about the poor, but because he was a thief; he kept the common purse and used to steal what was put into it.) [7]Jesus said, "Leave her alone. She bought it so that she might keep it for the day of my burial. [8]You always have the poor with you, but you do not always have me."

9   When the great crowd of the Jews learned that he was there, they came not only because of Jesus but also to see Lazarus, whom he had raised from the dead. [10]So the chief priests planned to put Lazarus to death as well, [11]since it was on account of him that many of the Jews were deserting and were believing in Jesus.

The second episode involving the Bethany family is related in John 12:1–11, and the introduction of the story (six days before the Passover) is meant to convey the impression that this event happened sometime later than the raising of Lazarus. Indeed, the narrative is told as though it were originally a self-contained unit, as it needlessly reminds the reader in 12:1b that Lazarus is the one whom Jesus raised.[37] We are told that a dinner was given for him (presumably for Jesus, not Lazarus), and that Lazarus sat at table with him.[38] Just as Jesus' ministry in a sense began with a banquet celebrating a wedding and new life at Cana (John 2), so it ends with a banquet celebrating the new life of Lazarus. Yet over this latter meal hovers the shadow of death, and the tone is much more somber as it will foreshadow the Master's end.[39]

This story raises numerous historical questions about the relationship of this story not only to Mark 14:3–9/Matt. 26:6–13 but also to Luke 7:36–50. Since I have dealt with these matters at some length elsewhere,[40] I must simply summarize my conclusions here: (1) There were originally two stories of Jesus' being anointed by a woman, Luke 7:36–50 being a separate tradition from the story found in Mark, Matthew, and John; (2) the fact that Luke omits the story found in Mark 14:3–9 and includes the other story proves no more than that Luke was attempting to avoid repetition, since the two stories are similar in various important ways; (3) in the telling of the two anointing stories at the stage of oral tradition there may have been some cross-fertilization of some details, but these details may also be explained in terms of the historical and theological purposes of the respective evangelists[41]—in the case of the Fourth Evangelist, the anointing of the feet symbolizes Jesus' being glorified in death,[42] while the Markan account with the anointing on the head indicates Jesus' kingly character; (4) the story rests on good historical tradition. As even Bultmann says, it is no ideal scene, but in the strictest sense biography.[43] In terms of historical probabilities, it seems more likely that the Bethany episode preceded the triumphal entry as the Johannine account has it, rather than the order we find in Mark.

The story contains very typical Johannine irony, in that the place where Jesus gave life to the dead (12:1) becomes the very place where "[s]eated beside Lazarus, whom he 'called out of the tomb' (xii.17), He is anointed as one would anoint a corpse."[44] Though comparisons can easily be made between the way Martha serves in Luke 10:38–42 and in John 12, there are differences as well. Here she serves quietly without complaint, and is not rebuked by Jesus. It is possible to see her hospitality as an example of her taking on the role of a servant at an all-male feast, a role that normally was reserved for slaves. Freedom in Christ is not only freedom from customs that restrict love, but also freedom to take a lower place, to humble oneself to serve, as Jesus himself will do in John 13.

Mary also seems to be assuming the role of a servant, for it was the servant's task to anoint the master's feet when he came off the dusty highways of Judea. As Luke 7:46 makes evident, anointing with oil to prevent feet or scalp from cracking is of a different order from anointing a person with expensive perfume. It is the latter sort of extravagance that is being objected to in this story, not the former functional sort of anointing. *Myron*, which Mary pours on Jesus' feet, is not oil, but perfume. Nard was a well-known aromatic, and expensive, Eastern perfume.[45] Such perfume was used in small quantities for cosmetic purposes,[46] but it was also used for burial rites, and Jesus interprets this act in light of the latter use.

The extravagance of the gesture is stressed by mentioning that she used a whole pound of the fragrance, and the smell of it filled the entire house. A plausible explanation of Mary's act of wiping Jesus' feet with her hair is the ancient practice of diners' wiping excess oil or other potable substances from their hands onto a servant's hair.[47] In other words, it would be another gesture of lowly service done in devotion to Jesus the Master.

Jesus' response to the objection of Judas[48] that this act was a waste of money amounting to a year's wages of a day laborer has been debated by scholars. Probably the proper translation is "Let her alone; let her keep it" with "it" referring to the burial ritual, not the keeping of the ointment or the keeping of something in mind.[49] If this translation is correct, then the words of Jesus in the Fourth Evangelist's account have essentially the same meaning as Mark 14:6 and 8, except that they are given in a much more shortened form.[50] Mary will not have the opportunity to prepare Jesus for burial later; therefore she is allowed to do so at this juncture. It has been suggested, but is unprovable, that the reference to the fragrance filling the house may also be a symbolic way of saying what the Synoptic writers relate that Jesus said at the conclusion of their account of this event: "Truly I tell you, wherever the good news is proclaimed in the whole world, what she has done will be told in remembrance of her" (Mark 14:9 and par.).

The saying about the poor always being with us is found in both the Johannine and Synoptic accounts of this story, and must not be taken out of context, or used as an excuse to avoid helping the poor simply because the problem of poverty seems to be insurmountable and everlasting. What Jesus is talking about is a matter of priorities. While he was still with his disciples, for only a short while, such extravagant gestures of devotion were not out of order, even though Jesus was very concerned for the plight of the poor (cf. Matt. 25:31–46). We are told by the evangelist not only that the objector was Judas, but that his objection was far from altruistic. Verse 6 indicates that he was the keeper of the disciples' common purse, and that he was a thief, dipping into the purse for his own ends on occasion. This is not the first reference to Judas and his character in the Gospel (cf. 6:70–71), and he is always portrayed in an even more negative light in this Gospel than in the Synoptics. He is seen as a true child of darkness and wickedness, whom Satan will finally possess at the Last Supper and force to betray Jesus (cf. 13:27). It may be, too, that we are meant to think that the money offered for betrayal of Jesus, which after all was a considerable sum, was (humanly speaking) the factor that finally led Judas to do what he did.[51] It is possible too that the reference to the purse that Judas carried for the Twelve was in fact to an alms bag, from which the poor would be aided by Jesus and his followers.

The narrative closes in vv. 9–11 with a reference to both the crowd of the Jews[52] and the authorities finding out the whereabouts of Jesus and Lazarus and coming to see them. We are then told that the chief priests determined that Lazarus needed to be executed as well, since it was on account of his being raised from the dead[53] that many Jews were deserting the traditional Jewish fold to become followers of Jesus.[54] There is a certain air of desperation conveyed in these verses, and they neatly provide a transition from the anointing story to the account of the Passion narrative, which properly begins at John 12:12.

II. Bridging the Horizons

The careful study of these texts in their original historical context reveals some avenues for using these texts, as well as some warning signs that show us how they ought not to be used. For one thing, the portrait of Martha and Mary, while more salutary in some respects than that of the disciples or other of Jesus followers, nonetheless does not present us with a picture of people with a fully developed Christian faith. Even Martha's good and true confessions in 11:22–27 fall short of the sort of faith the evangelist is trying to inculcate in his audience—a faith that includes a belief that Jesus can give life to the dead, both physically and spiritually here and now, for he is the resurrection and the life. We must also beware of portraying "the Jews" in John 11 as the bad guys, as the term is not used in a pejorative sense in this text, and there is no cause to doubt that their grieving and concern was anything but sincere. We are even told in the end that many of them believed in Jesus as a result of the raising of Lazarus (11:45).

Another caution worth urging is that unless one makes clear that the ongoing portrayal of Jesus in this Gospel is of one who can only act when the Father gives the go-ahead, Jesus will appear quite callous to many who simply read or hear John 11 in isolation from its larger Johannine context. It is also worth stressing that we must not minimize Jesus' anger at the unbelief that is manifested by those who grieve "as others who have no hope." In other words, sermons about Jesus' weeping with those who weep, while true enough to the spirit of the compassionate Christ, likely do not find a basis in this text. Jesus was weeping for a very different reason. He had come to the end of his public ministry and even some of his closest friends and followers still did not understand who he truly was and what he could do.

The anointing story is suggestive in many regards and can be used as an example of self-forgetful devotion and generosity, which can be contrasted with the avaricious character of Judas. Both the anointing act and the words of Caiaphas promote reflection on analogous occasions in our own lives when we have said or done more than we realized.

The Johannine portraiture of the chief characters in the drama of Jesus' life tend to follow the sort of principles Rembrandt followed in his famous paintings where bright light is set over against dark shadow for the sake of emphasis, the stressing of certain aspects of a life or an act. Furthermore the Gospel portraits are painted with twenty-twenty hindsight, not simply as things may have appeared at the moment when they occurred. The Fourth Evangelist is simply following universal principles of drama and communication. These sort of texts call for the comment that we do not have well-rounded portraits of any of these Gospel characters, with the possible exception of the central character, Jesus himself. Nonetheless, we may assume that what the evangelist does reveal of these characters is not mere caricature, but rather reveals something true and characteristic of these persons.

Another word of caution is in order in dealing with all the complex proceedings that led up to Jesus' crucifixion. One needs to understand certain key factors, such as the tenuousness of the positions of Jewish officials under the yoke of Rome, as well as the enormous threat Jesus seems to have posed to the status quo, to understand why things turned out as they did. Caiaphas may well have really believed that what he was doing would most likely spare the country a larger disaster. Nevertheless, when one starts acting on the basis of expediency almost any human behavior can seem justified. In our own century, expediency was often cited as the rationale for the treatment of Jews in Germany during World War II.

We must stress once more that John 11 is not an Easter story, but a ministry story which only foreshadows Easter. Lazarus must not be taken as exhibit A of the resurrection, if by the latter term we mean what Jesus experienced on the third day after his crucifixion.

Mourning and burial customs vary considerably throughout the world and over the course of history, and to a real extent understanding John 11—12 depends on understanding the ancient Jewish customs. This leads to the plea that whether one is teaching or preaching this material, one must inform one's audience how very different from our own and yet in other respects how very similar to ours the ancient reactions to death were.

There is in our midst another religion which we all serve unawares. Its temples are sparkling hospitals, its priests are doctors, its symbol a blue cross (and shield) or a serpent and a staff (the symbol of the ancient Greek god of healing, Asklepios), and the sacrifices it requires of us are much more than a tithe. Besides money, there is also a credo that goes along with this modern religion—"This life is all there is; it must be preserved *at all costs.*" Against this whole philosophy of life stand the words of Jesus, "I am the resurrection and the life. Those who believe in me, even though they die, will live," to which we may add the poignant words of the missionary Jim Elliot, who gave up his physical life while witnessing to South American Indians: "He is no fool who gives away what he cannot keep in order to gain what he cannot lose."

Without wishing to belittle or demean the important and wonderful work that doctors and nurses do, it is crucial to stress that the ideology that stands behind a good deal of the rationale for the way modern medicine is practiced is in some important respects untrue and unchristian. Our culture is in a profound state of denial about death and dying, which results in brain-dead people being kept from finishing the process of dying, endless rounds of debilitating radiation treatments even when the prognosis of recovery is minimal or nonexistent, and, perhaps worst of all, people dying in sealed rooms, bristling with tubes stuck in them, far removed from family, friends, and home during the closing stages of life. The creed that says "This life is all there is; it must be preserved at all costs," leads inevitably to such scenarios. We have set up a system whereby we not merely prolong the living, we also, paradoxically enough, prolong the dying. We do our best to keep the stench and sight of death hidden from our eyes and out of our lives, except when it can be witnessed from a safe distance on TV or at the movies. Even the ways our funeral homes prepare the body of the deceased reflect an effort to make it appear as though the person has never died. Frequent comments at visitation hours are "He looks so good" or "She looks as if she's merely asleep."

Yet it must be said that there is something natural and even biblical about this reaction to death, this profound attempt to run from or hide from it. It reflects an instinct that says death is the antithesis of life, the antithesis of all that is good and true and beautiful in this world. This much at least is right. As Paul puts it, death is indeed the last enemy to be conquered (cf. 1 Cor. 15). It is the ultimate wages of sin.

In preaching on John 11—12 one would be well served to avoid denying the ugly reality and power of death, or denying the shadow it casts over our world. The Christian answer to death is not denial, but affirming that there is a yet greater power already extant in the world today. It is only when one stares death in the face and sees it for all it is, that one gains a full grasp and appreciation of life and all its abundance that Jesus came to offer. Furthermore, the story of Lazarus is no permanent answer, for he went on to die again. It is only the greater story Lazarus's tale betokens that provides the real answer to death's dilemma. It is also crucial to bear in mind that the answer Jesus ultimately gives is not just about life *beyond* the grave, but about life *back from* the grave. God wishes to be sovereign and have the victory over every part of our being, redeeming not merely the human spirit but also the human body.

Another and entirely different approach to John 11—12 would be to do first-person presentations of some of the major characters in these stories— one Sunday on Martha, another on Mary, another on Jesus, another on Caiaphas and the Jewish leaders, another on the disciples and in particular Judas. One would have to fill in some of the gaps in the story, but if this is done carefully it can help one's audience identify with the characters in the story.

Finally, John 11—12 reveals a great deal about feelings and the motives for which people do things. We are told why Jesus does not go immediately to the side of an ailing Lazarus. We are told how Jesus reacts to unbelief and to a grieving without hope. We are informed about Caiaphas's motive for proceeding against Jesus, and Judas's motive for his protest against Mary's extravagant act. In each case certain actions reveal the person's heart and concerns. There are endless analogies in the modern setting which could appropriately be related to this material: (1) the Christian who protests lavish spending on some optional item in the church budget ostensibly for the sake of frugality, but really because he has designs on using the money for something else; (2) the individual in a position of power and influence, whether in government or the business world, who compromises his or her ethics because of the tyranny of the expedient; (3) the believer who trusts in Jesus for the future, but has a hard time praying for and trusting God to act now, in the present, as well; (4) the follower of Jesus who mistakes fatalism for courage.

But if there really is a Savior who came back from the dead in a deathless body, then we can no longer go on playing the game of life as if it were a matter of business as usual, with death dictating our every maneuver. At some point faith must win out over fear in the believer's life, and then she or he becomes free to live and to die without undue concern about the "valley of the shadow," free to risk his or her life for the sake of Christ. D. Bonhoeffer put it well when he said that when Christ calls us, he bids us to come and die.[55] But he also bids us to come and live eternally, not as though time was running out or life could be snuffed out. If we do that, then indeed "death shall have no dominion" (Dylan Thomas; Rom. 6:9).

Another possible application of John 12 is to use it to talk about the joy but also the strain of family reunions, and couple it with a discussion of the ultimate family reunion—the messianic banquet in the kingdom of God. One could draw analogies between the awkwardness of this occasion, with Lazarus present, and the awkwardness of a family reunion when someone unexpected or long out of touch with the family shows up. What does one say over dinner to someone just back from the dead like Lazarus? What does one say to someone one hasn't talked to in years who seems to have little in common with the rest of the clan? If our vision of the kingdom of God is that we will finally get back together with all the people we feel comfortable with or feel friendly toward, we are going to be in for a big surprise. There will be people there with whom we may not have gotten along at all during this life. There will be people there whom we would regard as enemies of our country, and on the other hand there will likely be some people we expect to see at the final family reunion who will not be there at all. Jesus paints such a picture of the final family reunion in Luke 13:29–30 and elsewhere, suggesting that some of the people we would least likely expect in the kingdom will show up for the banquet and be given a place at the head of the table. In fact it will be the most cosmopolitan of all meals, with people present from all sorts of different places, cultures, and ages, including Abraham, Isaac, Jacob, and the prophets (Luke 13:28). It will not, in other words, be a cozy little gathering of our well-known and respectable Christian friends, any more than heaven will be that way.

Lazarus, according to John 12:10, was a marked man due to his having been raised and his association with Jesus. Many Christians have experienced this sort of situation. I remember well hearing the testimony of a Russian Baptist minister in the late 1970s telling of how the KGB burst into a secret and illegal Christian wedding, taking some captive and killing others for daring to want to bear the name of Christ in their relationships. Our text is full of irony because Lazarus had already been dead once and Jesus had remedied that problem, and yet the priests assumed they could still stifle belief in Jesus by killing Lazarus! They did not know they were up against the author of life, whose work could not be deterred or halted even by death. Indeed, generation after generation of Christians have shown that "the blood of the martyrs is seed for the church." For Christians death is not an end, because God is greater than death and can bring us back from it or take us through it to eternal life.

Part IV. The Passion Narrative:
Phase One (John 12:12–17:26)

13. The Return of the King and His Last Audience (John 12:12–50)

In the remainder of John 12 we have a variety of traditions, including a brief account of the triumphal entry of Jesus into Jerusalem; the quest to meet Jesus of some "Greeks," either Greek-speaking (diaspora?) Jews or God-fearing Gentiles, since they are in town to worship during the festival; and a brief summary of Jesus' final public teaching and the unbelief that persisted despite Jesus' self-revelation. On any showing, the Johannine account of the events that lead up to the passion of Christ is notably different from the Synoptic accounts, though there are certain key events, such as the entrance into Jerusalem, that all the accounts have in common. This is significant, since scholars widely hold the view that it was the Passion narrative that achieved a relatively fixed form and was written down first of all the Gospel material. As D. M. Smith has shown, even in the material in John 12:12ff. held in common, such as the triumphal entry, there is no need to posit that the Fourth Evangelist knew, or if he knew them used, the Synoptic accounts.[1] This is an independent testimony to these events. The fact that the Gospel accounts share some of the same Old Testament citations (Ps. 118:25 appears in all four accounts; Zech. 9:9 in Matthew and John) likely points to an earlier Christian collection of texts (a *testimonium*) used by the various evangelists to demonstrate that the surprising climactic events in Jesus' life were a fulfillment of scripture.[2] The other possibility is that the Beloved Disciple was for some long time after Jesus' death and resurrection a part of the Jerusalem community where the Passion narratives were likely composed, and may even have been part of the process of seeking out and applying Old Testament texts to the story of Jesus, before he moved to Asia Minor sometime before A.D. 70. If this conjecture is plausible, then the Johannine text may reflect the earlier and more primary stage of the use of the Old Testament to interpret the Passion material, and the Synoptics, especially Matthew, may reflect a later stage in the process.[3] On the other hand, it may have been the Fourth Evangelist who added these scripture citations to the testimony of the Beloved Disciple from a *testimonium*.

In any case, one cannot fail to notice that the Fourth Evangelist's account of the Passion narrative has some notable omissions and additions compared to the Synoptic accounts: (1) Missing in John 13 is any discussion of Jesus' Last Supper with the disciples as a Passover meal per se, with ramifications for the later celebration of the Lord's Supper. There is no interpretation of the elements of the meal in John at all. (2) Likewise missing is any account of Jesus' final temptation in the Garden of Gethsemane, though it is widely thought that John 12:27–28 seems to reflect a knowledge of the Gethsemane traditions. (3) Instead of such traditions we have a lengthy selection of farewell discourses to the disciples in John 14–17, which are not found or even suggested in the Synoptic accounts.[4] These discourses are presented in the format of the after-dinner discussions (*symposia*) that characterized Greco-Roman meals and were led by a philosopher, sage, or rhetorician.

In other words, the evangelist means for these discourses to be seen as the continuation of what happened at the meal setting referred to in John 13. They are not simply awkward intrusions into the Passion narrative. They are part of the evangelist's overall efforts to portray Jesus as the great sage, and even as Wisdom, who does not leave this world without giving final advice to his followers. This is especially clear when one compares texts like John 13:1–20 to Ben Sira's advice (Sir. 32:1–2) about proper Jewish behavior at a Greco-Roman banquet: "If they make you master of the feast, do not exalt yourself; be among them as one of their number. Take care of them first and then sit down; when you have fulfilled all your duties, take your place. . . ."[5] Equally clearly, the discussion of Jesus' parabolic speech in John 16:25–30 and what follows relates to Ben Sira's description (Sir. 39:1–11) of the great sage: "He seeks out the wisdom of all the ancients, and is concerned with prophecies; he preserves the sayings of the famous and penetrates the subtleties of parables; he seeks out the hidden meanings of proverbs and is at home with the obscurities of parables. He serves among the great and appears before rulers." Ben Sira then goes on to conclude about the great sage: "If the great Lord is willing, he will be filled with the spirit of understanding; he will pour forth words of wisdom of his own and *give thanks to the Lord in prayer*. . . . His memory will not disappear, and his name will live through all generations" (emphasis added). In this showing, the high-priestly prayer in John 17 should be seen as the last great act of the sage before God and on behalf of his disciples, which helps preserve his memory among his followers. Thus we may divide up the first two major portions of the Passion narrative into two parts: (1) the final public stage of the sage, still sought by questers and still offering public dialogue and discourse (John 12:12–50); (2) the private meal, last discourses, and prayer of the sage (John 13—17).

12:12   The next day the great crowd that had come to the festival heard that Jesus was coming to Jerusalem. [13]So they took branches of palm trees and went out to meet him, shouting,

"Hosanna!
Blessed is the one who comes in the name of the Lord—
the King of Israel!"

[14]Jesus found a young donkey and sat on it; as it is written:
[15]"Do not be afraid, daughter of Zion.
Look, your king is coming,
sitting on a donkey's colt!"

[16]His disciples did not understand these things at first; but when Jesus was glorified, then they remembered that these things had been written of him and had been done to him. [17]So the crowd that had been with him when he called Lazarus out of the tomb and raised him from the dead continued to testify. [18]It was also because they heard that he had performed this sign that the crowd went to meet him. [19]The Pharisees then said to one another, "You see, you can do nothing. Look, the world has gone after him!"

20 Now among those who went up to worship at the festival were some Greeks. [21]They came to Philip, who was from Bethsaida in Galilee, and said to him, "Sir, we wish to see Jesus." [22]Philip went and told Andrew; then Andrew and Philip went and told Jesus. [23]Jesus answered them, "The hour has come for the Son of Man to be glorified. [24]Very truly, I tell you, unless a grain of wheat falls into the earth and dies, it remains just a single grain; but if it dies, it bears much fruit. [25]Those who love their life lose it, and those who hate their life in this world will keep it for eternal life. [26]Whoever serves me must follow me, and where I am, there will my servant be also. Whoever serves me, the Father will honor.

27 "Now my soul is troubled. And what should I say—'Father, save me from this hour'? No, it is for this reason that I have come to this hour. [28]Father, glorify your name." Then a voice came from heaven, "I have glorified it, and I will glorify it again." [29]The crowd standing there heard it and said that it was thunder. Others said, "An angel has spoken to him." [30]Jesus answered, "This voice has come for your sake, not for mine. [31]Now is the judgment of this world; now the ruler of this world will be driven out. [32]And I, when I am lifted up from the earth, will draw all people to myself." [33]He said this to indicate the kind of death he was to die. [34]The crowd answered him, "We have heard from the law that the Messiah remains forever. How can you say that the Son of Man must be lifted up? Who is this Son of Man?" [35]Jesus said to them, "The light is with you for a little longer. Walk while you have the light, so that the darkness may not overtake you. If you walk in the darkness, you do not know where you are going. [36]While you have the light, believe in the light, so that you may become children of light."

After Jesus had said this, he departed and hid from them. [37]Although he had performed so many signs in their presence, they did not believe in him. [38]This was to fulfill the word spoken by the prophet Isaiah:

"Lord, who has believed our message,
    and to whom has the arm of the Lord been revealed?"
[39]And so they could not believe, because Isaiah also said,
    [40]"He has blinded their eyes
        and hardened their heart,
    so that they might not look with their eyes,
        and understand with their heart and turn—
        and I would heal them."
[41]Isaiah said this because he saw his glory and spoke about him. [42]Nevertheless many, even of the authorities, believed in him. But because of the

Pharisees they did not confess it, for fear that they would be put out of the synagogue; [43]for they loved human glory more than the glory that comes from God.

44 Then Jesus cried aloud: "Whoever believes in me believes not in me but in him who sent me. [45]And whoever sees me sees him who sent me. [46]I have come as light into the world, so that everyone who believes in me should not remain in the darkness. [47]I do not judge anyone who hears my words and does not keep them, for I came not to judge the world, but to save the world. [48]The one who rejects me and does not receive my word has a judge; on the last day the word that I have spoken will serve as judge, [49]for I have not spoken on my own, but the Father who sent me has himself given me a commandment about what to say and what to speak. [50]And I know that his commandment is eternal life. What I speak, therefore, I speak just as the Father has told me."

I. The Historical Horizon

The Johannine portrayal of the entry of Jesus into Jerusalem has several unique features: (1) the suggestion that part of the crowd in Jerusalem went out to meet him; (2) that the branches waved were *palm* branches; (3) the lack of understanding by the disciples of at least some aspects of this event; (4) the mention of some of the crowd (from Bethany?) who had been with Jesus when he raised Lazarus; (5) the concluding reaction of the Pharisees to this event in John 12:19. By comparison to the Synoptic portrayal, there is much less pomp and circumstance in the Johannine portrait of this event, and there is an air about the Johannine narrative that suggests things aren't as they may seem on the surface of things. Though there are crowds prepared to acclaim Jesus and bestow on him lofty titles like "the King of Israel," the disciples do not understand the real significance of what is happening, and Jesus himself acts in a fashion to *correct* the acclamations and actions of the crowd. The crowd is not an example of those who have clear insight into Jesus' character.

To understand the scope of things at the Feast of the Passover, one may compare the account in Josephus's *War* 6.422–25 of its celebration some thirty years later. Josephus says that 2.7 million pilgrims came to the feast, not even counting foreigners or ritually unclean persons who may have been present. Even allowing for a certain amount of exaggeration, this still gives us an idea of how popular this festival was, and why Jewish officials might become understandably paranoid if many in the crowd believed that a great prophet, wonder-worker, or even messianic figure was entering the city at this time. Historically speaking, the actions taken against Jesus may in part be explained by the time that Jesus chose to enter the city, coupled with the fact that the Jerusalem officials knew that Jesus had a history of controversial actions, not only at feasts but also on ordinary Sabbaths.

If the mere presence of Jesus was likely to have made officials edgy, the waving of *palm* branches can only have heightened the tension and concern. There is some debate as to whether there were palm trees in Jerusalem during Jesus' day as there are today, but Pseudo-Aristeas 112 says that dates were a product of Jerusalem in that era. For our purposes what is important is that palm branches had come to be associated with the triumphs of the Maccabees and their triumphal entry into Jerusalem, which was celebrated at the Feast of Dedication (Hanukkah).[6] It is said of Simon Maccabee that when he drove the Gentile forces out from the citadel of Jerusalem he then "made his entry with a chorus of praise and the waving of palm branches . . . with hymns and songs, to celebrate Israel's final riddance of a formidable enemy" (1 Macc. 13:51). One may also point to other passages that associate palms and the triumph of kings (cf. Rev. 7:9; 2 Macc. 10:7; cf. *Test. Naph.* 5). Furthermore, at the Feast of Tabernacles the Hallel psalms (Pss. 113—118) were sung every morning, and when the words of Ps. 118:25–26 were reached ("Hosanna . . . Blessed is the one who comes in the name of the LORD") every male in the Temple was to shake the *lulab* in his hands, consisting of a bunch of willow and myrtle tied *with palms*. The *lulabs* actually came to be called hosannas because of this association.[7] While the Hallel psalm Ps. 118 had originally been sung as a greeting to pilgrims entering the city during a feast, there is some evidence that it had come to be applied particularly in early Judaism to the coming of Messiah to the city (cf. *m. Tehillim* [*Midrash on Psalms*] 244a). If one puts this together with the additional phrase "the King of Israel," and bears in mind that the Galileans had already tried unsuccessfully to force Jesus to be their political leader and king (John 6),[8] there can be little doubt that the evangelist is telling us that the crowds were proclaiming Jesus to be the political Messiah they had been looking forward to since at least the demise of the Maccabean rule in the land.

It is *against* this sort of messianic acclamation, not as a ringing endorsement of it, that the Fourth Gospel portrays Jesus choosing to ride into Jerusalem, not on a warhorse but on a young donkey, conjuring up the image of a very different sort of messianic figure—a peaceful and merciful shepherd-king. The fuller context of Zech. 9:9 deserves to be cited: "Rejoice greatly, O daughter Zion! Shout aloud, O daughter Jerusalem! Lo, your king comes to you; triumphant and victorious is he, humble and riding on a donkey. . . . He will cut off the chariot from Ephraim and the war horse from Jerusalem; and the battle bow shall be cut off, and he shall command peace to the nations; his dominion shall be from sea to sea." The evangelist is making clear that Jesus did not come to conform to this crowd's desires for a political solution to the bondage to the Roman overlords, but rather to meet the need for a universal Savior who would bring peace to all nations. By his own means he would have a dominion extending from sea to shining sea. The crowds do not understand Jesus any better than the disciples do, and we are told specifically that the disciples understand only after Jesus' death and resurrection.

One should compare the editorial comment in 12:16 to the very similar one in John 2:17, 22. Some scholars have rightly pointed out that this connection strongly suggests that the story of the Temple cleansing belongs with this and other Passion narratives, where a concerted effort is made to show how Jesus fulfilled various scripture passages through the traumatic and climactic events of the last week of his life, an emphasis that is notably absent in the evangelist's presentation of the events of the public ministry *prior* to Palm Sunday.[9] If it is true, as the Synoptics suggest, that Jesus cleansed the Temple only once, after having made a triumphal entry into Jerusalem, it is hard to avoid the conclusion that the Jewish officials would have taken these symbolic acts as political gestures making some sort of messianic claim.[10] Though the Fourth Evangelist makes clear that these officials misunderstood what Jesus meant by such actions, it is clear enough that Jesus was surely making some sort of messianic claim. Jesus interpreted his life in the light of the Hebrew scriptures, but for him the crucial text in this case is Zech. 9:9–10. Yet even the gesture of riding into Jerusalem on a donkey in the charged atmosphere of the Passover Feast could have been taken to be threatening to status-quo approaches to power, politics, and the person of the messiah.

Furthermore, we are told that the crowd who had seen some of Jesus' remarkable signs continued to testify (v. 17) to his power and person, and this in turn led various of the Jerusalem locals to go out and meet Jesus as he entered the city (v. 18). This too could only upset Jesus' powerful opponents. The Pharisees somewhat forlornly remarked about this whole scene "You see, you can do nothing. . . . The world has gone after him!" This of course was another exaggeration out of the mouths of Jesus' opposition, but it is also an example of typical Johannine irony, for in due course it would prove to be true. Jesus was a universal Savior whom all sorts of people would flock to, as this Gospel has been repeatedly telling us and will continue to tell us in the immediately following verses (vv. 20–26).

The importance of the evangelist's including v. 19, which is not found in the Synoptics, is that it reflects on and aptly addresses the situation for which this Gospel was written—a missionary situation in which all sorts of people, both Jewish and otherwise, were coming to Christ and inquiring about him. It is not accidental in such a situation that the Fourth Evangelist stresses that Jesus was fulfilling Zechariah's oracle about such a universal and nonbelligerent savior. Part of his goal was to fully portray the power of Jesus, while at the same time downplaying the potentially politically volatile implications of his actions. Jesus was indeed the King of Israel, but his kingdom was not of this world (cf. below).

"Faced with the nationalistic politicization of the messianic title as he had been in Galilee (cf. 6.15), Jesus again takes corrective action. In Galilee he withdrew into the hills, in Jerusalem he mounts a donkey! . . . Jesus deliberately demilitarizes their vision and declares the nature of his messianic rule: a rule of peace, gentleness, and universal tolerance. 'Nothing further from a Zealotic view of Messiah could be imagined.' "[11] Jesus did not come to meet his people's expectations; he came to meet their needs.

If we are right that the cleansing of the Temple was the next passage in the original Johannine outline, then the approach of the Greeks in 12:20ff. to Jesus could be seen as a response to his action in the Temple, which surely took place in the Court of the Gentiles. But who are these Greeks? Some have suggested they are Greek-speaking diaspora Jews, but it must be admitted that *Hellenes* is not the normal word to describe any sort of Jewish person, and thus it is perhaps more likely that what is meant is Gentiles who are God-fearers or perhaps proselytes.[12] Though these "Greeks" are mentioned in vv. 20–21, thereafter they disappear entirely from the discussion, and we are not told the outcome of their quest to see Jesus.[13] The alert reader will recognize here, however, the direction the future of the Jesus movement will go, in view of the rejection of Jesus by most of his fellow Jews. The death of Jesus signals a new direction or a new primary target audience for the missionary-minded followers of Jesus.

The suitability of much of the material in John 12 for use in missionary efforts is evident not only because of the implicit reference in the Zech. 9:9 quote to a universal Shepherd, but also because of the reference to the Greeks, the reference to Jesus' death bearing much fruit, the reference to the death of Jesus being the cause of "all people" being drawn to him (v. 32), and the reference to Jesus' coming to save, not condemn, the world (v. 47). In addition, the discussion of Jesus' followers' possibly having to endure the same fate as their Master (vv. 25–26) is especially appropriate if this document was intended for missionary use by those in the Johannine community, who are encountering considerable resistance and persecution because of their witness.[14]

The Greeks are said to approach Philip of Bethsaida (v. 21), asking to see Jesus. Perhaps they approached him because he is one of two disciples with a Greek name,[15] perhaps because Philip was from a city where there may have been many Greek-speaking God-fearers. Josephus confirms that such people liked to frequent Jerusalem during the feasts, even if they were not allowed to fully participate in some parts of the Temple worship, as, for instance, sharing in the Passover lamb (cf. *War* 6.427). Whatever the reason for their approach to Philip, later Christian tradition says that Philip became involved in missionary work with Gentiles in Asia Minor and that he died in Hierapolis, not far from Ephesus (cf. Eusebius, *H.E.* 3.31.3; 5.24.2–3).[16] What is important to notice is that the evangelist is not interested in narrating the outcome of this particular quest to see Jesus; it is simply a foil to stress the universal scope of Jesus' work, and the missionary direction the work of his followers would take *after* the Son of man was glorified.

Verse 23 tells us that Jesus' hour has finally come—his hour to be glorified, paradoxically by means of his crucifixion.[17] The parabolic saying in v. 24 indicates that Jesus' life cannot bear much fruit unless it is consummated in his death. It is the latter that will cause his ministry to bear much fruit.[18] Verse 25 seems to be the Johannine version of a saying also found in Mark 8:35. Jesus begins to speak of his followers as his servants who will act as he does, loving their mission more than their own lives. Here the language of agency is applied to the disciples. They will be where Jesus is, and they will

be honored by the Father, because of their service for Christ. Jesus' followers, then, will be extending the ministry of Christ to new audiences like the
Greeks.

Jesus does not face the prospect of his death without emotion and concern. We are told at v. 27 that he is inwardly troubled by the prospect. Verses
27–28 have been called the Johannine version of Jesus' hour of anguish, said
in the Synoptics to transpire in Gethsemane. There is some debate whether
v. 27b should be seen as a statement or a question. Most probably it should
be seen as a statement—"Father, save me from this hour," after the question
"What should I say?" However deeply troubled by the prospect of his
death[19] Jesus was, he desires even more deeply to fulfill his mission in life,
to have his "hour" on the cross, which paradoxically would glorify his Father's name as he himself is glorified. At this juncture, for the only time in
this Gospel, a voice from heaven speaks and says: "I have glorified it [pre-
sumably through the life and signs of Jesus], and I will glorify it again
[through Jesus' death, resurrection, and exaltation]." The response of the
crowd at this point reveals their spiritual obtuseness. The more impercep-
tive said it sounded like thunder,[20] some said it was the voice of an angel,
but they could not understand what was said, and they assumed it was addressed to Jesus. Jesus, however, paradoxically says it was spoken for the
crowd's sake. This means that Jesus assumes that the voice from heaven and
the crowd's lack of understanding should reveal to the crowd their spiritual
state—that they stand in danger of judgment. This makes the connection
with v. 31a understandable: "Now is the judgment of this world."

Verse 31b speaks of the "ruler of this world" being driven out, by means
of what is about to happen to Jesus on the cross. This presumably refers not
to his being driven out from heaven (but cf. Luke 10:18; Rev. 12), but rather
his being ejected from his role as ruler of this world, a role Jesus will assume
as a result of and by means of his glorification.[21] Not only in Johannine tradition but also in Pauline tradition (cf. Col. 2:15) Christ's death is viewed as
the crucial turning point in the war against the powers of darkness. Both Augustine and Thomas Aquinas were on the right track when they interpreted
our text to mean that Satan can no longer rule within believers, though he
is still active and has power in the world in general.[22] Paul says that the supernatural powers are disarmed by Christ's action on the cross, but again he
is speaking of the benefit of Christ's death for believers. It will be worthwhile
to note a few things about what the Fourth Evangelist has to say about Satan and the powers of darkness, compared to early Jewish beliefs and the
larger New Testament witness.

EXCURSUS: SATAN AND THE POWERS OF DARKNESS

The Fourth Evangelist, like other New Testament writers and Jesus himself,
believed in the reality of powerful evil supernatural beings in the universe,
both demons and a devil, both powers and a ruler of this world (cf. 14:30;
16:11). These figures were not considered mere myths by most of the an-

cients, as they are by many modern persons, including various New Testament scholars.[23] Indeed, Satan was considered a very powerful being, as the title "ruler of this world," or in 2 Cor. 4:4 "the god of this world," indicates. The references to a belief in Satan and his minions are widespread in early Christian literature (cf. Eph. 2:2; 6:12; Matt. 4:8–9/Luke 4:6–7; Ignatius, *Ephes.* 17.1; 19.1; *Magn.* 1.3; *Trall.* 4.2; *Ascension of Isaiah* 1:3; 10:29; *Martyrdom of Isaiah* 2:4). But equally widespread was the belief that Christ's death meant Satan's eventual defeat, not his victory. This belief distinguished early Christians from early Jews. Furthermore, the Fourth Evangelist believed that the Holy Spirit further limited what remaining power evil had, at least in the lives of believers (cf. John 16:11). Satan had been judged and condemned.

Nothing suggests that early Christians believed that followers of Jesus could be possessed by demons. Rather, Christ was Lord of their lives, and the Spirit dwelt within them. There was not room for other lordships in the believer's life. Nevertheless, the New Testament writers are equally clear at various points that Christians could be misled, deceived, pestered, persecuted, and even physically afflicted by the powers of darkness (cf. 1 Cor. 5:5; 2 Cor. 2:11; 12:7; 1 Tim. 1:19–20; 1 Peter 5:8). The Christian, therefore, had defenses against Satan, but had to consciously avail himself or herself of these defenses, for Satan was viewed as deceptive and not without power (cf. Eph. 5:11–18).

Basically the older view of O. Cullmann aptly sums things up.[24] Cullmann argued that many early Christians believed that they stood between D-day, the decisive turning point in the war against the principalities and powers, and V-day. Christ's death represented D-day, and his return, Victory Day. In between these parameters, Satan and his minions were still powerful but fighting a losing battle, a rear guard action. Since "greater is he who is in you, than any forces in the world," it was believed that Christians not only had defenses against evil, but some Christians at least were gifted with the ability, like Jesus before them, to exorcise demons from those who were possessed, (cf. Acts 16:16–20; 19:11–20). Christians were indeed engaged in spiritual warfare, but since the armor described in Eph. 5 is depicted as defensive armor, and since the exorcisms depicted in Acts are responses to crises, not a planned part of missionary work, nothing suggests that early Christians believed they should go on the offensive against the powers of darkness. Rather, they believed that such large tasks as binding the "strong man," or limiting his scope of operations, should be left to God and God's agents such as Christ or angels (cf. Mark 3:26–27; Rev. 20:1–3).

Verses 32–33 speak of Christ's death and allude to its mode—by means of crucifixion. As has been the case throughout this Gospel, Jesus is seen as one who has a certain sort of spiritual magnetism, who draws seekers and requesters to himself. His death is seen as only accelerating this process.

The crowd once again fails to understand Jesus' words. Verse 34 speaks of a belief in a messiah who remains forever, as opposed to one who dies on a cross. The belief in a messiah who abides forever is well attested in early

Judaism (cf. *1 Enoch* 49:1; 62:14; *Orac. Sib.* 3:49–50; *Ps. Sol.* 17:4). This was not, however, the only belief in early Judaism, but the belief in a messiah who is defeated and destroyed before the consummation comes from a somewhat later period (cf. *4 Ezra* 7:28–29).[25] Jesus' interlocutors have no idea who the Son of man is. Yet Jesus is giving this audience one last chance to see, recognize, and be in the light. Time is running out, not for Jesus who will have his hour and be glorified, but for "the Jews" and the crowds who stand in darkness. This appeal, in the context of this Gospel, must be seen as the sort of thing Johannine Christians would have been likely instructed to say when witnessing to Jews, either in or out of the synagogue. Despite all the polemics, there is no indication that the community had given up its witness or some hopes of its success even in the synagogue, despite rejection, ejection, and persecution. Jesus and his followers still longed for all sorts of people to be drawn to the Christ and so become children of light.

There are two major subsections to the remaining verses in John 12. Verses 37–43 summarize the state of unbelief Jesus found in Judaism and offers an explanation, and this in turn is followed by a succinct summary of Jesus' teaching given during the public ministry in vv. 44–50, which Jesus, who has now departed and hidden from the crowds (v. 36b), is said to cry out or shout to a world that by and large isn't listening.[26] Perhaps we may see an intended contrast here. While Isaiah predicted Israel's unbelief, nonetheless Jesus proclaimed (shouted out) his good news to the world, and at least some listened.[27]

Perhaps the first thing to notice about v. 37 is that it echoes Deut. 29:3–4: "You have seen all that the LORD did before your eyes in the land of Egypt, ... the great trials ... , the signs, and those great wonders. But to this day the LORD has not given you a mind to understand, or eyes to see, or ears to hear." In other words, the reaction to Jesus and his words shouldn't have been unexpected in view of Israel's track record.[28]

The use of Isa. 6:9–10 in early Christianity to explain the reaction of the majority of Jesus' contemporaries to his ministry is found not only here but in Mark 4:11–12 as well, and the sense of the passage here also comports with what we hear elsewhere in Paul's discussion in Rom. 9—11.[29] Far from Israel's unbelief in her Messiah catching God by surprise, we are told that it fulfilled the Isaian prophecy. Her unbelief had been incorporated into God's plan all along. The quotation of Isa. 6:10 in v. 40 is closer to the Hebrew text than to the LXX, but probably the evangelist is quoting from memory here. Verse 41 is quite explicit that Isaiah said this because he saw Jesus' glory (i.e., his death) and spoke about him. Isaiah 53 may be lurking in the background here as well.[30] The point is that just as Jesus' death was part of God's plan, and a fulfillment of scripture, so too was the rejection of Jesus by many of his fellow Jews, including many of the authorities. Indeed the latter (the rejection) is what brought about the former (the death), humanly speaking.

The Fourth Evangelist does not go on to say, as Paul does, that the hardening of the Jews was a temporary expedient so that the Gentiles may come into the kingdom, but the discussion of the search of the Greeks in the immediately preceding section may point in this direction. Yet the evangelist is also eager to point out that this was not some blanket or blind predestinarian scheme that consigned all Jews to even temporary unbelief, much less permanent rejection of Jesus. In our same passage (v. 42) we hear that even many of the Jewish authorities believed in Jesus. We later learn this includes Nicodemus and Joseph of Arimathea (cf. John 19). We must thus conclude that we are being told that Jewish unbelief at the time was the foreordained means by which God fulfilled his plan for his Son to be glorified by being lifted up on the cross. Isaiah's words had to be fulfilled, and so "they could not believe" (v. 39a) at that time.

It is worth pondering the possibility that once again Jesus is being portrayed as Wisdom, who "raise[s] her voice. . . . At the entrance of the portals she cries out: . . . [cf. John 12:44] 'Hear instruction and be wise. . . . For whoever finds me finds life and obtains favor from the LORD; but those who miss me injure themselves; all who hate me love death' " (Prov. 8:1, 3, 33, 35–36). Yet, like Wisdom, Jesus is rejected and must return to the One who sent him (cf. *1 Enoch* 42). Furthermore, the wisdom tradition says that in the end one can only learn God's counsel if God gives wisdom and sends the spirit from on high, and then one indeed is saved by wisdom (Wisd. Sol. 9:17–18). It is not likely accidental that this is very similar to what the Fourth Evangelist will go on to stress in the farewell discourses. God has already sent wisdom, but now God must send the Spirit so the followers of Jesus may understand wisdom and his teaching and thus be truly saved by him.

Despite rejection, Jesus cries out to the world that he was God's agent, and belief in the one entailed belief in the other, just as rejection of the one implied the rejection of the One who sent Jesus. Jesus came into the world as light in the darkness, not to judge the world but to save it. Yet the very words of good news will stand in witness against those who reject them on the last day. What God commanded Jesus to proclaim was eternal life, not judgment and death, yet necessarily the one who rejects eternal life has chosen death, condemnation, judgment for himself. It is interesting that the summary in vv. 44–50 has close parallels not only with what precedes but also with the farewell discourses (compare 12:45 to 14:9; 12:50 to 14:31).[31] More than a mere epilogue to the public ministry,[32] it thus serves as an apt bridge between the account of the public ministry, which ends at 12:50, and the account of the final private sessions between Jesus and his closest followers.

II. Bridging the Horizons

In view of the commentary above, several implications need to be brought to light that should guide how we use John 12:12–19. Although the interpretation of Jesus' actions with the Zechariah text provide no encouragement for those who would attempt to use the story of Jesus to advance some kinds of liberation theology, it may equally be said that this story does not

encourage Christians to assume that it has no social or political implications. Rather, the implications are that Christians, like their Master, are
called on not only to be peacemakers, but to be those who live in such a way
that rest and restoration (*shalom*) is brought to those around them. The mil-
itaristic interpretation of Jesus' actions by the crowd is rejected by Jesus, but
their vision is replaced by another one—a vision of a Messiah who establishes his kingdom throughout the world by peaceful means, and in fact
abolishes the use of weapons in the Holy Land and presumably elsewhere.
There is in this text an implicit criticism of the attempt to use military or violent solutions to solve the problems of God's people. This cuts not only
against those who would needlessly and violently end an unborn child's life,
but also against those who would kill doctors who perform abortions and
firebomb abortion clinics. It also cuts against those who would argue for liberal gun-control laws in a fallen world, and those who would insist that one's
patriotic duty to kill a nation's enemies overrides one's Christian obligation
to act in a peaceful manner like Christ and love our enemies. In view of Jesus' rejection of the political implications of the waving of the palms, one
also wonders how appropriate it is for us to continue to glibly perpetuate
such practices on Palm Sunday without understanding the action's original
meaning. Perhaps the practice can be depoliticized, but not without adequate explanation of its original significance and our choice to make the gesture mean something else.

Something should be said about the need to recognize the cumulative effect of what has gone before these climactic scenes at the end of the public
ministry of Jesus. It is not an accident that only here we have a voice from
heaven confirming and in essence praising what Jesus has done and will do,
binding together what has gone before and what will come. The casual
reader of a section here or there of this Gospel will not note the distinctive
character of these final scenes in John 12 and how they bring things to a close
with the end of Jesus' travels, a final quest by seekers, a final word from
heaven, and a final proclamation shouted by Jesus to the world.

The stress on the fulfillment of scripture, both remarked on and alluded
to, becomes increasingly important from now on in this Gospel, and in order to relate this material to our own setting it will be crucial to speak with
one's audience about what the nature of biblical prophecy is—for example,
what the difference is between clear prediction and fulfillment of even some
things that are not presented as predictions in the Old Testament.[33] Likewise critical is explaining the sort of apologetic purpose that is being undertaken in these chapters, namely, the attempt to show that the conclusion
of Jesus' life was no mistake or mere tragedy, but a part of a divine plan for
humankind. The evangelist clearly assumes and relies on the acceptance of
the idea that the Old Testament is a holy book that is prophetic in the broad
sense of the term, something even a Gentile who was familiar with oracles
like that at Delphi, or the books of Sibylline oracles in Rome, could understand and accept.

Palm Sunday is without doubt one of the more celebratory days in the church calendar. Yet it is in order to suggest that the joy and excitement usually associated with this day should be perhaps tempered with the recognition that Jesus was meaningfully and purposely rejecting the acclamations of the crowd, at least in part by riding into town on a donkey. Jesus did not ride into town like Clint Eastwood prepared to kill the bad guys—he rode into town prepared to die for others. In other words, some of our most basic American cultural myths about how we should solve the problem of evil and injustice in this world go *against* the grain of the Gospel story of Palm Sunday and other Gospel stories. In an important book titled *The Politics of Jesus,* John Howard Yoder has presented a compelling argument that we as Christians are called to emulate Jesus' nonviolent appproach to the human dilemma; otherwise we end up siding with the Caiaphases of this world, for whom political expediency is used as an excuse to justify violent behavior.

If there is one lesson to be learned by the ongoing struggles in the Holy Land, it is that violence only begets more violence, and the recent efforts at peacemaking between the Israelis and the Palestinians is to be applauded, not least because various of the Palestinians are Christians, who have as much right to live in peace as free citizens in Israel as anyone else. The man who rode into Jerusalem on a donkey, and proclaimed a universal reign of peace where war weapons would be abolished, would surely have approved.

As Milne eloquently says of our text, "There is no sanction here for nationalistic visions in our own day which limit global obligations, or which glorify our national heritage to the exclusion of the nations beyond our borders, of whatever colour, race, creed for whom the King has come, died, and risen."[34] The universal Savior calls his followers to a more global vision of what is best for humankind, not merely what is best for one's own kin and nation.

Any use of what the Fourth Evangelist says about Satan and the powers of darkness must take into account not only the immediate Johannine context, but the larger thought world of early Judaism and early Christianity. Modern deliverance ministries often seem to operate on the basis of an inadequate understanding of what the New Testament actually says about things like demon possession. A good, thorough teaching on this sort of material can prevent many misunderstandings and misguided, even if well-intentioned, practices. Though books like Frank Peretti's series of novels on the supernatural (*This Present Darkness,* and others) helpfully dramatize the reality of supernatural evil in this world, they also leave the rather misleading impression that Christians should look for demons under every rock, and that human beings, at least outside Christ, are always being manipulated by forces beyond their control and against their will. This hardly comports with the balance of the New Testament witness, which stresses human responsibility for human actions and attitudes, both when people respond to and when they reject Christ and the light. Satan and his minions will indeed be judged, but human beings will also be held responsible for their sins. A balanced perspective is required to incorporate the whole of the biblical witness on these matters.

A very fine series of sermons could be constructed based on the presentation of Jesus as God's wisdom in the Fourth Gospel, which begins in John 1 and appears again and again in the narrative. Jesus is indeed the revelation, and one can even say the correct exegesis, of God. The close connection between revelation, Word, wisdom, and salvation in this Gospel needs to be stressed. The concept of God's wisdom helps one see how Christ relates to both God (sent by the Father, sending the Spirit) and humankind (rejected by many but offered to all), and how Christ can be at once the object, and so content, of our faith as well as the author of our faith.

14. A Farewell Dinner (John 13:1–30)

Scholars have long had difficulty in assessing various features of the material in John 13—17 precisely because these chapters seem so different from the Synoptic accounts of the Last Supper. For instance, there is no clear indication at all in these chapters that Jesus is celebrating a Passover meal. Rather, we are told that this event transpired not only before Passover day but "before the festival of the Passover" (13:1), and the speculation of the disciples about Judas leaving to buy things for the festival (13:29) also suggests a meal prior to the Passover.[1] The time reference in 13:1 may be compared to the one in John 12:1—"six days before the Passover." This could mean that this meal is depicted as occurring even before Jesus was anointed by Mary, but in all probability we are meant to think of it as occurring *sometime* during the week before the actual celebration of Passover, *not necessarily on the eve of Passover*.

The vast majority of scholars of all theological stripes, including more conservative ones,[2] have recognized that we do not have just one theological discourse in John 13:31–17:26 but several, combined here in all probability to indicate the sort of in-house teaching Jesus offered to the disciples at the close of his ministry when he was preparing them for his departure. Some of this teaching seems to have been offered on one occasion and some on another, for certainly 14:31 indicates that the discourse is over, and the natural sequel to 14:31 is 18:1. I would suggest that perhaps this teaching was offered on successive nights of the Passover feast leading up to Good Friday, and the Fourth Evangelist has put the material into his own idiom and combined it to convey the gist of these occasions. Clearly enough, from 13:21–30 it includes some Last Supper traditions as well as other material. The more important question is why the evangelist has presented the material as he has done, and what the significance of it is. Is it really true that John 13:1–30 is only loosely connected to what follows it? My basic suggestion is as follows: (1) The Fourth Evangelist is portraying the disciples sharing a farewell dinner with Jesus; (2) this dinner is *not* portrayed as a Passover meal, which is shown not only by the time reference in 13:1, but by the lack of any discussion of or reinterpretation of the Passover elements in any of these chapters. This may be because, as F. Craddock puts it, "Jesus does not *eat* the Passover, he *is* the Passover,"[3] and will be portrayed as dying as the Passover lamb at the appropriate time in John 19:31–37;[4] (3) instead of a Passover meal, what we have in these chapters is a portrayal of a Greco-Roman banquet complete with a closing *symposium*, in which Jesus acts as the sage who offers the teaching, and the religious rites associated with such meals. This is not unlike what we find in 1 Cor. 11—14, where Paul describes a worship event that involves a meal, a *symposium,* and closing religious acts. So that we may see this, a few remarks are in order about Greco-Roman meals and the Jewish celebration of them.[5]

EXCURSUS: GRECO-ROMAN MEALS AND
THEIR JEWISH PRACTICE

The normal Greco-Roman banquet in the first century A.D. involved a meal and a *symposium* (teaching, dialogue, or entertainment period following the meal but during the drinking party). The *symposium* in particular tended to be an all-male affair, any women who had been present at the meal politely excusing themselves before the *symposium.* In a Jewish setting this was all the more likely to be the case. A formal transition was usually made between the meal and the drinking party or *symposium* by a wine ceremony, where wine was poured out to the god. After the transition (cf. Plato, *Symposium* 176A), a hymn or a chant would be sung to the god, perhaps a calling upon a god as savior (cf. Athenaeus, *Deipnosophistai* 15.675b–c). The drinking party could then continue with entertainment, or, for the more sober-minded, conversation, which was considered an essential feature of the *symposium.* Plutarch, writing shortly after Paul's time, says the proper conversations at such an occasion could involve talking about history, current events, lessons on philosophy, lessons on piety, or exhortations to charitable or brave deeds (cf. Plutarch, *Quaestiones Conviviales* 697E). The conversation often was prompted by a guest teacher or a Sophist.[6] In many ways meals were an occasion for gaining or showing social status. They reflected in microcosm the aspirations and aims of the culture as a whole. In 1 Cor. 11—14 we can see Paul's attempt to deconstruct the social stratification that was occurring at the Lord's meal in Corinth, an action that went directly against the tendency of such meals. I will suggest in a moment that Jesus is in part depicted as doing the same thing in John 13. For Paul, the function of reciting the sacred tradition about the Last Supper in 1 Cor. 11 is to encourage social leveling, overcome factionalism created by stratification and its expression at meals, and create unity and harmony in the congregation. The same may be part of the intent of the foot washing episode in John 13, coupled with the prayer in John 17 for the unity of Jesus' followers.

We know for a fact that early Jews, including even the more religiously conservative among them, had by Jesus' day adopted and adapted the customs of Greco-Roman dining to suit their own ends and religious practices. A good example of this can be seen in Luke 7:36–50 where Jesus is portrayed as "reclining at table" (the Greco-Roman practice) with one Simon the Pharisee. It is clear from the discussion in Luke 7:44ff. that Jesus expects foot washing to be a regular act of hospitality of the host for the guest, at the beginning stages of the meal, something he missed when Simon did not provide such services.[7] Putting the above things together, we can now provide an in-depth and coherent analysis of the structure of John 13—17 as follows:

1. The meal depicted in John 13 is definitely a meal in the Greco-Roman style, as is shown by the remark in John 13:23, 25 that the Beloved Disciple was *reclining next to Jesus.*[8]

2. The act of foot washing by Jesus depicts him as the host of this banquet, who quite extraordinarily is assuming the role the host's slave or other family members would normally perform for the guest in Israel. The act is portrayed as a typical Johannine sign act, but the point is that it was a regular part of hospitality at the Jewish celebration of a banquet in the Greco-Roman style. Here this opening act, coupled with the closing prayer, in part serves the purpose of creating unity among the inner circle of disciples, especially in view of the coming betrayal, denial, and general desertion of Jesus. It works against social stratification within the inner circle.[9]

3. The mention of the common purse in John 13:28–30 is reminiscent of Greco-Roman meals held by *collegia* or trade associations where there would be a sort of treasurer's report and where charitable acts or future spending would be discussed.[10]

4. Jesus provides discourses, with some dialogue, after the meal, as was common for a sage or a Sophist to do at a Greco-Roman banquet. The fact that a good deal of this material is like other farewell discourses or "testaments" of those about to die found in the Bible and elsewhere in early Jewish literature (cf. below) should not obscure that this material is said to be conveyed in the meal setting. In other words, John 13:31–16:33 is the appropriate sequel to the meal mentioned in 13:1–30.

5. Jesus' closing or "high-priestly" prayer was an appropriate closing act at such a meal, although sometimes this act would happen at the transition between the meal and the *symposium* (cf. above).[11] Notice the similar closing prayer for and exhortation to the sage's disciples in Sir. 51:13–30. The character of this prayer may suggest that the situation of the Johannine community is or has recently been the one described in the Johannine epistles, where some factionalism has happened. Like Judas in John 13, some have gone out and betrayed the Christ (cf. 2 John 7–11).

6. Jesus is portrayed as not just any kind of great teacher in the discourses but as a Jewish sage (16:25–27) who speaks parabolically and explains his figures of speech to his disciples in this sort of setting. More important, he is portrayed as Wisdom in these discourses. Like Wisdom in Prov. 9, who built her house and then called her disciples, including the simple and immature, to a feast saying, "Come, eat of *my* bread and drink of *my* wine, live and walk in the way of insight" (9:5–6), so Jesus once more before his rejection and departure calls his disciples to hear and heed the voice of Wisdom (cf. *1 Enoch* 42), even though as the "simple" they do not spiritually perceive what is going on between Jesus and his betrayer in 13:28–29.[12]

7. The reason that Jesus' last meal with his disciples is portrayed as a Greco-Roman banquet, instead of bringing out its associations with the Jewish Passover meal, is that this material is now a part of a missionary document. While Jesus is portrayed as a Jewish sage and as Wisdom in John 13—17, the portrayal here is presented in a fashion that highlights the

more universal aspects of his character, ministry, and mission, the traits that would appeal to Gentiles as well as to some Diaspora Jews among the potential converts. In other words, Jesus is portrayed as offering teaching and sharing fellowship in a setting that anyone in the Greco-Roman world could identify with—at a Greco-Roman banquet. It is to be noticed as well that these chapters conclude with words and allusions to the ongoing missionary work of Jesus' disciples (cf. 15:16; 17:21, 23). In short, these chapters are not written so much *about* the Johannine community and its communal history and development; rather, they are written to encourage the Johannine community to continue their missionary work, proclaiming him who is a universal Savior and Wisdom, even though they face persecution for their witness when they enter synagogues and other places to witness (cf. 15:18ff.; 16:1; 17:4), and there are divisions within the Christian community.

13:1   Now before the festival of the Passover, Jesus knew that his hour had come to depart from this world and go to the Father. Having loved his own who were in the world, he loved them to the end. [2]The devil had already put it into the heart of Judas son of Simon Iscariot to betray him. And during supper [3]Jesus, knowing that the Father had given all things into his hands, and that he had come from God and was going to God, [4]got up from the table, took off his outer robe, and tied a towel around himself. [5]Then he poured water into a basin and began to wash the disciples' feet and to wipe them with the towel that was tied around him. [6]He came to Simon Peter, who said to him, "Lord, are you going to wash my feet?" [7]Jesus answered, "You do not know now what I am doing, but later you will understand." [8]Peter said to him, "You will never wash my feet." Jesus answered, "Unless I wash you, you have no share with me." [9]Simon Peter said to him, "Lord, not my feet only but also my hands and my head!" [10]Jesus said to him, "One who has bathed does not need to wash, except for the feet, but is entirely clean. And you are clean, though not all of you." [11]For he knew who was to betray him; for this reason he said, "Not all of you are clean."

12   After he had washed their feet, had put on his robe, and had returned to the table, he said to them, "Do you know what I have done to you? [13]You call me Teacher and Lord—and you are right, for that is what I am. [14]So if I, your Lord and Teacher, have washed your feet, you also ought to wash one another's feet. [15]For I have set you an example, that you also should do as I have done to you. [16]Very truly, I tell you, servants are not greater than their master, nor are messengers greater than the one who sent them. [17]If you know these things, you are blessed if you do them. [18]I am not speaking of all of you; I know whom I have chosen. But it is to fulfill the scripture, 'The one who ate my bread has lifted his heel against me.' [19]I tell you this now, before it occurs, so that when it does occur, you may believe that I am he. [20]Very truly, I tell you, whoever receives one whom I send receives me; and whoever receives me receives him who sent me."

21   After saying this Jesus was troubled in spirit, and declared, "Very

truly, I tell you, one of you will betray me." [22]The disciples looked at one another, uncertain of whom he was speaking. [23]One of his disciples—the one whom Jesus loved—was reclining next to him; [24]Simon Peter therefore motioned to him to ask Jesus of whom he was speaking. [25]So while reclining next to Jesus, he asked him, "Lord, who is it?" [26]Jesus answered, "It is the one to whom I give this piece of bread when I have dipped it in the dish." So when he had dipped the piece of bread, he gave it to Judas son of Simon Iscariot. [27]After he received the piece of bread, Satan entered into him. Jesus said to him, "Do quickly what you are going to do." [28]Now no one at the table knew why he said this to him. [29]Some thought that, because Judas had the common purse, Jesus was telling him, "Buy what we need for the festival"; or, that he should give something to the poor. [30]So, after receiving the piece of bread, he immediately went out. And it was night.

I. The Historical Horizon

At the outset we note the parallels between the story in John 12:1–8 and in 13:1–30. In the former, Jesus is anointed on the *feet,* and it is interpreted as a symbol of his coming burial. In John 13, Jesus himself washes the feet of his disciples, and this is seen as foreshadowing two things: (1) the coming death of Jesus by which all those who believe in him will be made clean; and in particular (2) the cleansing of Peter foreshadows his future need for cleansing once he betrays his Master. Peter then is depicted as fallible but redeemable, but Judas is portrayed as one who by contrast becomes possessed by Satan and chooses darkness over light. When he goes forth to do his dastardly deed, it is suddenly said to be night (v. 30). John 13:1–30 then has links both with what has come before and with what is yet to come in the narrative of this Gospel.

If we are right that the evangelist is *not* interested in speaking about the disciples taking part in the specifically Jewish celebration of Passover with Jesus and may even be suggesting that this non-Passover meal took place earlier in the week than Thursday, but *rather* that he is interested in portraying this meal as a Greco-Roman banquet that leads to discourses after the meal proper, then all speculation attempting to relate the account in the Fourth Gospel to the accounts of the Last Supper Passover in the Synoptics is pointless and will prove fruitless.[13]

The account of the foot washing begins in 13:1 not only with a time reference, "before the festival of the Passover," but with an indication that Jesus knew his time was up or, better said, that his hour to culminate his ministry had come. It is important to the evangelist to portray Jesus being in control every step of the way, even to the point that he orders Judas to get on with his treachery (v. 27b), a feature not found in the Synoptic accounts of the Last Supper. Verse 1 is in fact a long, unwieldy sentence in the Greek which climaxes with the assertion that Jesus loved his disciples *eis telos,* which here likely means "unto the end" (of his life) rather than as the NIV has "to the full extent." The evidence of Jesus' love for his disciples to the very end is going to be shown in the material that follows not only in the foot washing and in the farewell discourses but in Jesus' testamentary dispensations for his mother and the Beloved Disciple even while he hangs on the cross (cf. below on John 19:25–27).

By contrast with Jesus' love is the evil the devil had put into the heart of Judas that led him to betray Jesus (v. 2). The shocking character of this meal lies not just in the announcement that one of the inner circle would betray Jesus but that the decision to betray would take place at a fellowship meal and furthermore would involve the one who was sitting near to Jesus, a place of honor. Irony is piled on irony when we are told that the very one to whom Jesus gave a "choice morsel" at that moment decided to betray Jesus. Thus Judas's act violates a basic rule of ancient hospitality that one does not break fellowship with one's host while one is sharing in a meal with him, regardless of the animus one may bear for that host. Jesus gave Judas a sign of friendship, Judas chose that occasion to decide to get on with betraying him (vv. 26–27).[14]

Verse 3 tells us that Jesus chooses to perform a dramatic act during the meal, knowing that he had come from and would soon go back to God, and knowing furthermore that the Father had delivered into his hands his own fate.[15] We are told that Jesus not only chose to perform a task reserved for those at the lower end of the social spectrum in the household but that he even strips himself down to the spartan attire of a slave, disrobing and tying a towel around himself.[16] It is sometimes overlooked that Jesus washes not merely Peter's feet but the feet of at least some of the other disciples as well, apparently including Judas. Jesus washed their feet with water from a basin and then wiped them with a towel.

At vv. 6 and 8 we are told that Simon Peter questions and then rejects this shocking behavior of his Master. This was a role reversal for which he was not prepared, for it might have been appropriate for a pupil to do this for his teacher, but not the other way around. Verse 7 is very important, for it indicates that Peter will only later understand the real significance of this act, which points us forward to Peter's denials of Christ in John 18, and perhaps also the story of his restoration now found in John 21. Jesus responds, "Unless I wash you, you have no share with me." The language is that of having a kind of inheritance and is further developed in 14:3 and 17:24. Jesus himself is seen as the disciple's promised land, his or her prized possession.[17]

Peter responds in v. 9 with his typical impulsiveness and exuberance: "Well then, Lord, wash my hands and head as well." Verse 10 has sometimes been thought to refer to both baptism and the later Christian rite of foot washing, but as D. A. Carson says, the focus here is christological, not sacramental.[18] It is Jesus, not some rite, that cleanses in particular by his death, as is symbolized in this act of foot washing. The disciples are said to be clean, "though not all of you." The evangelist once again clarifies matters for the listener in v. 11, making clear that Jesus knew who would betray him. Such an explanation would hardly be necessary for a Christian in the Johannine community, but it makes sense if this narrative was written to be used with outsiders for missionary purposes. Having performed this symbolic act, Jesus dons his robe again and returns to the table (v. 12). How are we to evaluate this act? Does it have any bearing on later Christian practices?

In the first place, it must be seen as very doubtful that the act has any bearing on the practices of Christian baptism or the Lord's Supper. If it were meant to symbolize baptism, we would hardly expect the feet to be the prime object of attention, and more to the point, we would definitely not expect the rejection by Jesus of the pouring of water on the head and hands, as if Jesus were an advocate of an anti-immersion form of baptismal practice!

The foot washing rite points forward to the actual cleansing work of Christ on the cross, not to later sacraments such as baptism which look back retrospectively on Christ's cleansing death. Even R. Schnackenburg, who once held a baptismal view of the significance of the foot washing story, came in due course to reject such a view as implausible.[19] He says "the washing of the disciples' feet is interpreted in the Christological and soteriological sense as a symbolic action in which Jesus makes his offering of himself in death graphic and effective, not in a sacramental manner, but by virtue of his love, which his disciples experience to the extreme limit (see v. 1)."[20]

In regard to the connection of this rite to the Lord's Supper, if the conclusions that we offered at the outset of the discussion of this chapter are correct, then *even if* this act took place at the Last Supper, the evangelist makes *nothing* of any connection of it to the Lord's Supper ritual. Washing someone's feet can hardly be a symbol parallel to the bread and wine and the words of institution of the Lord's Supper, for the latter refers to partaking of Christ, while foot washing symbolizes the cleansing necessary *before* one can have a part in Christ.[21]

Jesus then proceeds to interpret the act he has just done. He is indeed the teacher and Lord of his disciples, and this act should have taught them something about their need and his provision of cleansing. He suggests that they ought to wash one another's feet, doing as he has done. The question then becomes, Does this mean follow the ritual I have just instituted? Or does it mean, Practice the forgiveness of and cleansing from sins that I have just symbolically depicted? In view of this Gospel's lack of interest in sacraments in general,[22] I suspect that the point here is not to institute a new rite but to insist on the practice of what the rite symbolizes. Here as elsewhere in this Gospel, one is encouraged to read the story at a level beyond the material one and to look for the spiritual significance behind or within them. Jesus asks, "Do you know what *I* have done to you?" not, "Do you understand now how to perform this rite?"

Jesus sees his followers as his agents and messengers sent out into the world to do what he has just symbolically done—offer cleansing from sin through Christ. They are blessed if they do the same sort of loving and forgiving acts as Jesus performed. They, like Jesus, are called to be servants performing self-sacrificial deeds.

Verse 18 refers to the fact that there is one who, while chosen by Jesus to be one of the Twelve (cf. 6:70), nonetheless is no longer properly called one of the chosen, for he will betray Jesus. Yet even Judas's act of betrayal is seen as part of the plan and drama, the means by which the will of God will be accomplished. Judas's treachery was incorporated into God's plan, and in fact it is likened to the treachery that David experienced and expressed in the Psalms.[23] Verse 18b quotes Ps. 41:9 in a form closer to the Hebrew than to the LXX text and refers to a gesture that suggests extreme insult and a breach of good faith to a person with whom one has shared the most intimate fellowship.[24] It may be related to the idea of shaking the dust off one's feet onto another person as one departs from the person.[25]

Verse 19 says that Jesus explains this to the disciples so that when the time comes they will learn something crucial about his identity. *Ego eimi* here[26] could mean "I am he," that is, the one about whom scripture spoke, or it could be seen as a claim to deity or eternality, in which case one should translate it "I am." The former suggestion makes better sense of the verse in its context in view of the scripture citation. On the other hand, the language of agency in v. 20, which follows, has persuaded some that the translation "I am" is appropriate. Yet it is hard to see why this is the case, since it speaks of the agency of Jesus' followers for him in the same terms that it speaks of Jesus' agency for the Father, and certainly the title "I am" is not appropriate here for the disciples. More important, the missionary note about the reception of Jesus' emissaries meaning the reception of Jesus himself should not be overlooked, as it prepares for the missionary theme in the farewell discourses that follow in John 13:31–16:33.

Once again in v. 21, and for the last time in this Gospel, we are told that Jesus is deeply troubled in his spirit, and this time it is evident that his agitation is over his betrayal by one of his close disciples. Unbelief here, as in John 11, deeply upsets Jesus.[27] The disciples are dumbfounded by this public announcement, even though Jesus had hinted at it before (cf., e.g., 13:11).

Verse 23 provides us with the first clear reference in the Gospel to "the one whom Jesus loved."[28] It is said that he reclined on the bosom of Jesus. This is likely to be an allusion to John 1:18 where Jesus as God's Word and Wisdom is said to be in the bosom of the Father. "The Evangelist introduces the Beloved Disciple as standing in analogous relation to Jesus as Jesus to the Father with respect to the revelation he was sent to make known; behind this gospel is the testimony of the one who was 'close to the heart' of Jesus."[29] This sentence then is making a claim about the authenticity of the witness of the Beloved Disciple—he understood the mind and meaning of the Word/Wisdom of God.

It is also worth stressing at this point that the person in question, if he is *introduced* here, is by no means clearly identified, and certainly there is no hint that he is John the son of Zebedee. The outsider hearing this tale would never have guessed such was the case. What is suggested by the story is not only the closeness of this disciple to Jesus but also his Judean provenance, since this is the first place he is *clearly* mentioned in the Gospel. His position at the head of the table next to Jesus may in fact suggest that it was his house in which this banquet was held. Notice too that the Fourth Gospel says nothing about this meal being confined to Jesus and the Twelve.

In regard to the usual assumption that the meal portrayed in the Synoptics must be the same meal described in John 13, *even if* this is so, it is in order to point out that Mark 14:17 does *not* say only Jesus and the Twelve were present at this meal. It says, rather, that Jesus came *with* the Twelve to this meal, and it is appropriate to ask, At whose house? It cannot have been at the house of any of the Galilean disciples, including John the son of Zebedee, but it may have been at the house of a Judean disciple such as the Beloved Disciple.[30] Greco-Roman meals, at least in the second stage of the banquet, tended to be all-male affairs, but nothing either in the Synoptics or in John requires us to believe that the meal was limited to the Twelve.

The portrayal of the betrayal scene in vv. 21–30 has a few additional interesting features. Although Peter and Judas are the two most featured disciples throughout the first thirty verses of this chapter, it is the Beloved Disciple who is depicted as sitting closest to Jesus, as is shown by the fact that Peter inquires through the Beloved Disciple whom Jesus has in mind. Nothing in the first twelve chapters suggests this sort of prominence of a heretofore unnamed disciple. We might have expected Peter, Andrew, Philip, or one of the other named disciples to assume such a place of honor at the meal by Jesus, *unless* the Beloved Disciple is a Judean disciple who first clearly appears at this point and has this place of prominence not only because of his intimacy with Jesus but because he is providing the venue for this meal. Normal protocol in a meal taken in the Greco-Roman style would call for a placing of the guests in a certain order around the table, with the host and the guest of honor reclining at the head of the table. Note that, in view of v. 24, Peter seems to have been ranked next to the Beloved Disciple. The side to the right of the host was the more favored side at such meals, while the left-hand side was less favored and sometimes even had negative associations, and it is on this side, apparently just to the left of Jesus, that Judas seems to have been positioned.[31] Despite this, Jesus treats Judas with great favor, not only giving him a piece of bread but dipping it for him in the dish with the sauce or, more likely, fruit puree.[32] Satan enters Judas after Judas receives the bread, Jesus then commands Judas to get on with his task, and finally we are told that after this Judas immediately left the house, the other disciples wondering what he was going to do.

II. Bridging the Horizons

We have already spoken to this text's possible bearings on a discussion of the sacraments, but a few other points are in order in discussing how we bring this text into the present. One possible avenue of approach would be to use W. Wangerin's wonderful short story about Christ as the Rag Man operating in the slums of a big city. Another possibility would be to focus on what we learn about the character of the four major figures in this story—Jesus, Judas, Peter, and the Beloved Disciple. Yet another is the approach suggested by Craddock.[33] This is a story that dashes spiritual arrogance, false pride, and triumphalism which has always plagued the church. We see a Peter resistant to foot washing, just as many of us are frequently resistant to the idea of repenting and seeking forgiveness and cleansing. Yet this story calls us to remember that even if a Peter can deny Jesus, if even a Judas, one of the Twelve whom Jesus highly favored, can betray Jesus, and if the chief model of virtue other than Jesus is an unnamed disciple (!), this ought to cause us soberly to evaluate ourselves to see what sort of work the Lord still needs to do in our lives in order to remove arrogance and other un-Christlike traits.

Finally, a word of caution is in order in dealing with the character of Judas. A careful reading of this story shows a Judas whom Satan had to enter so that Judas could finally be compelled or propelled into betraying Jesus. This does not exonerate Judas, not least because the story suggests that Judas had been contemplating some act of treachery for a while, otherwise Jesus' words, "What you are about to do . . ." would have made no sense to him. Certainly the story in John 12:1–8 shows that Judas was a greedy individual prior to this occasion, but remember that this Gospel shows other disciples' shortcomings as well, especially Peter in John 13 and in the denial scene. We must keep in mind that "there but for the grace of God go I" when we contemplate Judas.

With a typical twist of Johannine irony, Judas, rather than Jesus, is being depicted here as the real victim of the powers of darkness, while Jesus, who deliberately chooses his every move in this Passion narrative, is depicted as one who deliberately stoops to conquer, deliberately takes up the cross to overcome the powers of darkness, outwitting them. In short, the ultimate bad guy in this story is Satan, not Judas, and it may even be that we are being told that at the end Judas became a victim of demon possession. While this should not be taken as a sympathy plea for poor old Judas, especially since human responsibility and decision making are not denied here or elsewhere, it is a plea to see the *complexity* of this story, with the interaction of forces both human and divine determining both Judas's and Jesus' destinies.

There are many powerful points of departure for the modern use of John 13:1–30, such as the cleansing work of Christ, the example of self-sacrificial service, the misunderstanding and even treachery of disciples, but perhaps one of the most powerful messages has to do with humility. In the West we are used to thinking of humility as an attitude in one's heart, just as we think of love in that fashion, but in the New Testament both humility and love are action words. Since Christ is presented again and again in the New Testament as *the* example of humility (cf. John 13 to Phil. 2:5–11), this "virtue" can surely have nothing to do with a person's having a low self-image or an inferiority complex. Sometimes a message is unconsciously conveyed that we are all called to be Milquetoasts or doormats for Jesus, but surely there was no one with more ego strength and surety about what he could accomplish in life than Jesus. Jesus is the last person I would ever think of as having an inferiority complex. It follows from this that humility in the biblical vein can surely have nothing to do with low self-esteem. It is rather the *action* of a person who knows what she or he has and is willing to give and give up for the sake of others. In point of fact, this takes tremendous character strength to accomplish. Jesus is no more an example of false modesty than he is of false pride. This is not to say that we are not to have an accurate understanding of our limitations and shortcomings—even Jesus was limited or limited himself to doing what the Father directed him to do. Thus, while humility does have something to do with our own self-concept, it has nothing to do with feelings of no or low self-worth. In fact, it has a lot more to do with our attitude toward others than our attitude about self. If humility is willing self-sacrificial service for others, then it is essentially an other regarding, not self-regarding act. The model for all such action is Jesus, the one who washed the disciples' feet.

What we may learn from the foot washing episode is that any task is ennobled, however menial or seemingly low, if it is done in service to the Lord and to God's people. If even Jesus can wash feet, then surely any Christian, including ministers, can and should set an example of doing whatever sort of service is required to better the people of God and accomplish the tasks of ministry, evangelism, and the like.

Perhaps two small illustrations in closing will put flesh on these bones. In my denomination (United Methodist), most of the larger churches have what is called an every member canvass, or stewardship campaign, to get all the church members to contribute a fair share to the church's budget. Inevitably some give a little and some a lot. In one particular campaign, one of the canvassers, a rather successful young lawyer, was called upon to visit an elderly woman who was basically shut in and living on a small fixed income. When he saw the house and its condition he resolved in advance, feeling somewhat ashamed to ask her for money, that he would just visit with the lady. After a nice chat, the young executive gathered his things and prepared to leave without asking for any money, but the elderly woman told him to hold on, that she had her pledge ready. The young man responded: "That's all right, ma'am, you don't have to." To this the woman replied: "Don't you dare take away my chance to make a sacrifice and participate, at least a little, in the ministry of Christ." Not only did she have the strength of character to make sacrifices, she considered it an honor to do so.

The British Methodist Reginald Mallett tells the compelling story of a brilliant scientist whose laboratory discovered a new wonder drug that helped cure a previously incurable disease. The announcement of the cure came while this scientist was lecturing in London, and the *Times* and other papers trumpeted the man's accomplishment. Yet one reporter found it somewhat odd that the scientist wasn't more forthcoming in explaining how and when the cure was discovered. He thus set out to the scientist's laboratory to interview the man's staff. It soon became apparent that it wasn't the scientist at all who had made the discovery but some of his staff working hard and experimenting until the cure was happened upon. The reporter was eager to give credit where credit was due, and so he tracked down the individuals who actually had made the discovery and asked them how they felt that the "great man" had grabbed all the headlines but they had done all the hard work. Their response was memorable: "It does not matter who gets the credit, if those in need get the cure."

Some of the most memorable work ever done for Christ and his kingdom has been done anonymously, or by individuals subordinating themselves and seeking no credit of their own, in order to accomplish a larger good. If even Christ can take on the role of a Gentile slave to show how he cleanses us, then it is not possible for us to stoop *too low* to lift another up. It takes character, strength, and fortitude to do such things—Christian humility has nothing to do with feelings of inadequacy.

The symbolic action of foot washing by Jesus in this passage was meant to have a practical consequence for the relationships that existed between his disciples. His command for them to wash each other's feet was an attempt to lead them to act in such a way that social divisions, pride, and other all-too-human factors would not stand in the way of the unity of the fellowship. Once one has washed another's feet, it would be hard, if not impossible, to take a superior attitude toward that person. In a similar fashion, it is difficult, after having confessed one's own sins, to partake of the Lord's Supper without being willing to forgive others present from whom one may feel alienated. Symbolic action and role playing can break down barriers between people; it can humble the proud, and, on the other hand, it can reassure those who feel of little worth. Jesus knew this and so he encouraged his disciples to follow his example.[34]

It is possible to see in the foot washing episode a symbol of Jesus' coming death—stripped of his clothes, he performs an action that will cleanse his followers from sin. Indeed, he assumes the position of a slave, just as in his death he dies a rebellious slave's death. Philo, in his discussion of Passover, says that the ultimate Passover is when one passes through death to eternal life from all that is passion to the divine (*De congressu* 106). In a similar fashion this narrative begins at 13:1 by speaking about Jesus passing from this life through death back into the Father's presence.[35] In other words, the text is about rites of passage, and Jesus is inviting his followers to follow in his footsteps, even if it leads to death, for he will go before them and prepare their place in heaven. There is great comfort in knowing that even our worst nightmare, even the worst thing that we could possibly go through in this life, an extremely painful death at the hands of those who should have loved us, has already been endured by Jesus. He has already walked this path, shown us the way through death, and prepared a place for us in the presence of God. No prospect in this life is unfaceable if Life rather than Death will have the final say about our existence. Because of Christ's sacrifice and triumph over the grave, a Christian can be a person with an unconquerable spirit who can say with Paul, "We are afflicted in every way, but not crushed; perplexed, but not driven to despair; persecuted, but not forsaken; struck down, but not destroyed; always carrying in the body the death of Jesus, so that the life of Jesus may also be made visible in our bodies" (2 Cor. 4:8–10).

No task is too great or arduous if the one who leads us to and through it has already taken on the form of a servant and paved the way for our actions. A Christian can also take on any task however menial and do it to the glory of God, realizing that one's worth and status in God's eyes are not affected by how the world evaluates the task one does. Whether we do something or not should be determined not by what the neighbors will think but by what Jesus will think and what he would have done.

15. The Farewell Discourses (John 13:31–17:26)

To say the material in the farewell discourses is difficult to analyze is to understate the case. Nevertheless, for our purposes certain positive things can be said. As we have already argued in the immediately preceding section of this commentary, these discourses are presented as the "after-dinner speech," if you will, at a banquet in the Greco-Roman style. Just as it appears that John 13:1–30 may reflect the conflation of narratives of two meals Jesus shared with his disciples during Passover week, we have in 13:31–17:26 the editing together of several discourses that in all likelihood were originally separate.[1] It may be that this material was delivered on successive nights during Passover week, and it is possible, but unlikely, that the material in John 15—16 was offered prior to the material in John 13:31–14:31 and John 17.

The reason for such a theory is that there is a clear break at 14:31 where the first discourse is brought to an end, and at this point we could easily skip to 18:1, where the command to "Rise, let us be on our way" (14:31) is carried out. Notice that the material in John 15—16 contains considerable repetition of various major themes also found in John 13:31–14:31.[2] Even more telling is the fact that in 13:36–38 Peter raises the very question about where Jesus is going that Jesus upbraids the disciples for *not* raising in 16:4b–6! This has led to various compositional theories about these discourses, including the view that the material in 16:4b–6 must have been part of an earlier discourse than the material found in 13:31–14:31. The simplest solution is to notice that 13:31–14:31 certainly makes up one discourse, while 15:1–16:33 seems to be a composite of several discourses, and all of this is followed by the prayer in 17:1–26 that brings to a climax and rounds off this whole subsection of the Gospel. The evangelist has welded all of this material into a whole with a regular marker in the text that indicates subdivisions or at least that a particular discussion is coming to a close ("I have said these things to you"—14:25; 15:11; 16:1, 4a, 6, 25, 33).

The most convincing discussion of both the parts and the whole of our material is F. Segovia's recent study, and we will be basically following his outline of the material's subdivisions, which is as follows:

1. Discourse (or Part) One (13:31–14:31)—"Yet a Little While I Am with You!"
2. Discourse Two (15:1–17)—"Abide in Me! Abide in My Love!"
3. Discourse Three (15:18–16:4a)—"The World Will Hate You!"

4. Discourse Four (16:4b-33)—"It Is Better for You that I Leave!"[3]
5. Epilogue/Closing Prayer (17:1–26)[4]

Two more important matters need to be addressed before we can reflect on the exegetical particulars of the text. First, the material in these chapters shares many traits in common with other ancient farewell discourses both in the Bible (e.g., cf. the farewell of Jacob in Gen. 49 or Elijah's in 2 Kings 2:1–12, or David's speech to Solomon in 1 Chron. 28—29, or Paul's Miletus speech in Acts 20:17–38, but perhaps especially Moses' farewell in Deuteronomy) and in the Greco-Roman world where we have accounts of the farewells of various statesmen and philosophers in which the meaning of death and other subjects are broached.[5] What is important for our purposes is that in both cases the *function* of such speeches is the preservation and handing on of wisdom and lessons from one's life to the next generation shortly before death or departure.[6] Surely the main reason for including this material in this Gospel is that it contributes nicely to the overall portrait of Jesus as a great sage and teacher. Again we see that perhaps *the* explanation for the salient differences between this Gospel and the Synoptics can be put down to the attempt of the evangelist to portray Jesus as a sage and as Wisdom. But he is not being portrayed as just any sort of great teacher or sage.

What we find in the farewell discourses is that Jesus is portrayed as a *Jewish* sage addressing his pupils a final time. He speaks of things such as a great commandment, the true vine, and other Jewish forms of discourse. Thus it is not surprising that he resorts to various forms of metaphorical and puzzling speech, including the extended metaphor in John 15:1ff. as well as the explanation of such figures of speech in 16:25ff. Notice what the collector and/or editor of the material of another great sage, Qoheleth, says about his master at the end of Ecclesiastes (12:9–14):

> Besides being wise, Qoheleth [or, the Teacher] also taught the people knowledge, weighing and studying and arranging many proverbs. The Teacher sought to find pleasing words, and he wrote words of truth plainly. The sayings of the wise are like goads, and like nails firmly fixed are the collected sayings that are given by one shepherd. . . . The end of the matter; all has been heard. Fear God, and keep his commandments; for that is the whole duty of everyone. For God will bring every deed into judgment, including every secret thing, whether good or evil.

The contacts of this material with the content of the farewell discourses can be seen at various points: (1) teaching in wisdom forms of speech (cf. John 16:25–29); (2) words of truth (15:26; 16:12–15; 17:17); (3) coming judgment (cf. 16:8–10); (4) good and evil (cf. 15:22–26); (5) keeping commandments (15:10–17); (6) the concept of a collection of the Teacher's wise sayings, as here we have a collection of discourses; and (7) the intent to pass on this sapiential material to the world (cf., e.g., the references to missionary purposes and work: 13:35; 15:5, 8, 16; 16:2; 17:21, 26).

Yet the call to abide "in me," among other features of the text, makes equally clear that a higher claim is being made, namely, that Jesus *is* divine Wisdom—"for whoever finds me finds life and obtains favor from the LORD" (Prov. 8:35). The disciples are called to abide in Jesus/Wisdom in similar fashion to the description of Solomon's relationship with Wisdom in Wisd. Sol. 7—8. With this information, we can begin to examine the text itself.

I. The Historical Horizon

A. Discourse One: "Yet a Little While"
(John 13:31–14:31)

13:31   When he had gone out, Jesus said, "Now the Son of Man has been glorified, and God has been glorified in him. [32]If God has been glorified in him, God will also glorify him in himself and will glorify him at once. [33]Little children, I am with you only a little longer. You will look for me; and as I said to the Jews so now I say to you, 'Where I am going, you cannot come.' [34]I give you a new commandment, that you love one another. Just as I have loved you, you also should love one another. [35]By this everyone will know that you are my disciples, if you have love for one another."

36   Simon Peter said to him, "Lord, where are you going?" Jesus answered, "Where I am going, you cannot follow me now; but you will follow afterward." [37]Peter said to him, "Lord, why can I not follow you now? I will lay down my life for you." [38]Jesus answered, "Will you lay down your life for me? Very truly, I tell you, before the cock crows, you will have denied me three times.

14:1   "Do not let your hearts be troubled. Believe in God, believe also in me. [2]In my Father's house there are many dwelling places. If it were not so, would I have told you that I go to prepare a place for you? [3]And if I go and prepare a place for you, I will come again and will take you to myself, so that where I am, there you may be also. [4]And you know the way to the place where I am going." [5]Thomas said to him, "Lord, we do not know where you are going. How can we know the way?" [6]Jesus said to him, "I am the way, and the truth, and the life. No one comes to the Father except through me. [7]If you know me, you will know my Father also. From now on you do know him and have seen him."

8   Philip said to him, "Lord, show us the Father, and we will be satisfied." [9]Jesus said to him, "Have I been with you all this time, Philip, and you still do not know me? Whoever has seen me has seen the Father. How can you say, 'Show us the Father'? [10]Do you not believe that I am in the Father and the Father is in me? The words that I say to you I do not speak on my own; but the Father who dwells in me does his works. [11]Believe me that I am in the Father and the Father is in me; but if you do not, then believe me because of the works themselves. [12] Very truly, I tell you, the one who believes

in me will also do the works that I do and, in fact, will do greater works than these, because I am going to the Father. [13]I will do whatever you ask in my name, so that the Father may be glorified in the Son. [14]If in my name you ask me for anything, I will do it.

15 "If you love me, you will keep my commandments. [16]And I will ask the Father, and he will give you another Advocate, to be with you forever. [17]This is the Spirit of truth, whom the world cannot receive, because it neither sees him nor knows him. You know him, because he abides with you, and he will be in you.

18 "I will not leave you orphaned; I am coming to you. [19]In a little while the world will no longer see me, but you will see me; because I live, you also will live. [20]On that day you will know that I am in my Father, and you in me, and I in you. [21]They who have my commandments and keep them are those who love me; and those who love me will be loved by my Father, and I will love them and reveal myself to them." [22]Judas (not Iscariot) said to him, "Lord, how is it that you will reveal yourself to us, and not to the world?" [23]Jesus answered him, "Those who love me will keep my word, and my Father will love them, and we will come to them and make our home with them. [24]Whoever does not love me does not keep my words; and the word that you hear is not mine, but is from the Father who sent me.

25 "I have said these things to you while I am still with you. [26]But the Advocate, the Holy Spirit, whom the Father will send in my name, will teach you everything, and remind you of all that I have said to you. [27]Peace I leave with you; my peace I give to you. I do not give to you as the world gives. Do not let your hearts be troubled, and do not let them be afraid. [28]You heard me say to you, 'I am going away, and I am coming to you.' If you loved me, you would rejoice that I am going to the Father, because the Father is greater than I. [29]And now I have told you this before it occurs, so that when it does occur, you may believe. [30]I will no longer talk much with you, for the ruler of this world is coming. He has no power over me; [31]but I do as the Father has commanded me, so that the world may know that I love the Father. Rise, let us be on our way.

Verses 31–35 should be seen as transitional. Although the betrayal of Judas means that night and darkness have come, it also means that the bright light of the Son's glorification is about to shine forth in the crucifixion, which reveals both evil at its worst and God in God's most loving mode at one and the same time. Jesus immediately warns the disciples that he will be with them now for only a short time longer (13:33). Jesus is going to a place where neither the disciples nor the Jews can come, at least at present. It is hard to escape the impression that Jesus means that when he dies he goes immediately to the Father to prepare a place for the disciples, even before the resurrection. Jesus then leaves the disciples with a new commandment—to love one another as Christ has loved them. This will be the chief evidence to the world that the disciples are Jesus' disciples.[7] Notice here that love is commanded. Jesus is not referring to a warm mushy feeling, he is referring to an action. In particular he is referring to the sort of loving self-sacrificial action that is foreshadowed in the foot washing and preeminently modeled in Jesus' death for others.

The farewell discourses really begin at 13:36 with the question of Peter about where Jesus is going. R. Michaels points out the close parallels between this discourse and the discussion with the Jews in John 8:12–20.[8] Especially at 8:14 we find the matter of where Jesus came from and where he is going. This theme actually is spread out throughout the Gospel and relates to the theme of the sending of the Son by the Father (cf. 3:16). As we have stressed before, the clue to understanding where Jesus came from and is going is to know who Jesus is—namely, the perfect image and revelation of the Father, who has come from God and will return to God. Notice that in John 20 understanding why Jesus must go away and where he is going depends on knowing who Jesus is. Even the disciples do not know Jesus' origins and destiny, and this is a sign that they do not really know him very well.

C. K. Barrett stresses the parallels between the first farewell discourse and the extended one in John 15—17. In both places we have discussion of some of the same matters: Jesus' relation to the Father; his departure to the Father; his coming again; his revelation of the Father; prayer in his name; keeping his commandments; the Paraclete; the peace Jesus gives; and judgment of the world or devil.

As a result of these parallels, Barrett suggests that we have here alternate versions of the same discourse.[9] Against this, however, repetition is a common feature in Jewish teaching, especially sapiential teaching, and frequently involves looking at one subject from various angles.[10] It is also a feature of Johannine style, and so skillful an editor is unlikely simply to lump together two tellings of the same material. The better explanation is that we are dealing with successive discourses given in a short span of time on related themes. It is clear enough, however, that the first discourse is the most unified and reveals the clearest logical progression, having three major parts: (1) 13:31–38 is on the meaning and consequences of Jesus' glorification; the departure is announced and its negative consequences enumerated; (2) 14:1–27 presents the fundamental meaning and *positive* consequences of the departure for the disciples, including a call to courage and faith; and (3) 14:28–31 presents the purpose of the present revelations to the disciples, and the mode and positive consequences of the departure are stressed.[11] In view of the repetition, we will spend more time on this discourse and less on some of the others.

Verses 36–37 indicate that the disciples are troubled by Jesus' talk of leaving them, and Jesus in this discourse wishes to allay their fears and show that his leaving will in fact work to their advantage. The "meaning of the departure and its consequences for the disciples can be designated as the overarching theme of the unit."[12] Faith rather than fear is the called-for response at this juncture. In all likelihood the verb *pisteuo* in 14:1 is in the imperative form and means "trust" with the Greek preposition *eis* ("in"). "Trust in God, trust also in me." John 14:2 speaks of "my Father's house," and here the reference, unlike John 2:16, is to heaven, not to the temple. Jesus says that in heaven there are plenty of dwelling or abiding places. "Mansions" is not a good translation, for we are talking about room or rooms within a place, not separate heavenly condominiums. The point here is that there is plenty of room for all who abide in Jesus. Jesus, then, is going to prepare the way and a place for believers. He was God's agent on earth, he is the believer's agent in heaven.[13]

Of course Jesus' means of journeying to the Father is through death. There is some ambiguity throughout this discourse when Jesus speaks of returning—is he referring to his return from death on Easter, or is he speaking of the parousia, or is he speaking of a more individual coming for a believer, at his or her death ushering the person into the eternal home? We must also bear in mind, however, that in a sense Jesus *is* the dwelling place of the believer, and the believer dwells or abides in him. The evangelist is able to say this about Jesus because he sees Jesus as divine Wisdom, and hence capable of omnipresence. He is not merely discussing the idea of the disciples adhering to or being faithful to Jesus when he is gone, as is shown by the analogous language about the Son being in the Father and vice versa. This incorporation is made possible because Jesus dies, rises, and goes to the Father so that, like the Father, he may be everywhere at once. The Johannine community then viewed itself as already in heaven in the sense that they were already abiding in the Son and experiencing even in this life the fruit of that abiding—eternal life. Heaven begins on earth for believers, according to Johannine theology.[14]

At 14:4 the discussion turns from where Jesus is going to the way to get there. Here again the disciples do not yet know the way. They are not portrayed in the farewell discourses as any more spiritually perceptive than they were in the earlier parts of the Gospel, but at least a partial rationale for this obtuseness will also be provided in these discourses—they had not yet received the Paraclete who would lead them into all truth. Notice that in this discourse there are four questions or requests by the disciples to Jesus in response to which we have four parts to Jesus' answer: (1) 13:36—Where are you going? (2) 14:4—How can we know the way to get there? (3) 14:8—Show us the Father and we will be satisfied; and (4) 14:22—Why do you reveal yourself to us and not to the world? Around these questions the answers are structured. Notice that the four questions are asked by four different disciples: Peter, Thomas, Philip, and Judas, indicating that it was not just one but all of the disciples who failed to understand these things at this juncture.[15]

Jesus proclaims himself as both the way and in one sense the end or goal for the disciples. Not only does this mean that one can get to the Father and to heaven only by means of the Son; it appears also to mean that Jesus' life pattern, including being faithful unto death, is the way believers must follow. The shadow of death hovers over both Jesus and the disciples.

To say that Jesus is the truth and the life is in part just another way of saying that Jesus is the way. Since God is the source of all truth and life, and Jesus is the way to God and the one who embodies God and all his gifts to us, Jesus is also the truth and the life. It is interesting that while "life" may be said to be the key term in the first half of the Gospel (thirty-one times in John 1—12, only four thereafter), "truth" is the characteristic theme in John

13—21 (twelve instances). I would suggest that the reason for this is the missionary character of this document. It was especially crucial that the listener get the story straight and know the truth about the climax of Jesus' life, including his death and resurrection. The signs and ministry discourses mainly reveal Jesus as the source of new life, while the farewell discourses and what follows them reveal not only the truth about Jesus and the end of his earthly career but Jesus as the Truth.

At this point in the narrative the disciples as yet know Jesus only in part, but it has not yet dawned on them that to know Jesus is to know the Father. The request in 14:8 seems astounding, but it gets an equally amazing response—the one who has seen Jesus *has* seen the Father. Here again the point is not that Jesus *is* the Father but that he is the perfect likeness and exegesis of the Father as his unique Son, as God's Wisdom, the expression of the very mind and character of God.

At 14:11ff., Jesus begins to speak about his works and those of his disciples, alluding to their missionary deeds and accomplishments, not to miracles. That miracles are not likely in view is shown by the fact that the word for "work" here is *erga* ("works"), not *semeion* ("sign"). The disciples will go beyond what Jesus did in evangelizing the world and bringing about its salvation. But this great commission to the church will be quite impossible unless Jesus goes to the Father, for unless Jesus dies and returns to the One who sent him, there can be no sending of the Paraclete, nor can Jesus respond to the believers' prayers for help unless he is in heaven. The greater works of mission are possible only if Jesus hears prayers for help and sends the Spirit. In 14:13 the phrase "Ask in my name" probably means "Ask, invoking my name," which involves asking in accord with the character and will of Jesus.

In 14:15–16 we have a conditional statement, in which all depends on the believer's loving Jesus. Notice the juxtaposition of loving and keeping Jesus' commandments, which leads to his sending the Paraclete. If one does the former, Jesus will send the latter and it will remain a permanent possession just as it was for Jesus (cf. 1:32 to 14:16). For reasons about to be enumerated in the following excursus, the term "Paraclete" should be translated "Advocate" and it connotes someone's agent in a judicial situation. In our text it conveys the idea that the Spirit is the representative of Jesus who equips the believer to face whatever trials, persecution, or expulsions they may face in the course of their missionary work, as well as equipping them with the knowledge and power for effective witnessing in other cases where there is a positive response. In addition, the Spirit's presence comforts and consoles the disciples, bringing them peace and joy even though Jesus has departed.

EXCURSUS: THE PARACLETE—JESUS' AGENT, THE DISCIPLE'S ADVOCATE

There are five Paraclete sayings in the Gospel of John, all of them occurring within the farewell discourses (14:26; 15:26; 16:7–11, 12–15).[16] It follows from this observation that since this section of the Gospel is especially directed to disciples, and is to be seen as an attempt to prepare and equip them for their roles as Christian witnesses and disciples once Jesus has departed, the Spirit's role must have something to do with the essential condition and function of disciples after Jesus' lifetime.

Jesus promises to send to his disciples one called in the Greek *parakletos*, and more to the point is said to be *another parakletos*, which intimates that Jesus was the first one. The meaning of this Greek term in this context has been much debated, with suggestions ranging from Counselor to Comforter to Advocate. Whatever it means about the Spirit it must mean in the case of Jesus as well, otherwise the comparison "another *parakletos*" would be meaningless. It suggests that the Spirit will have the same agenda and functions and power that Jesus previously had, at least in some respects. It is at this point that we remember the language of agency that appears over and over again in this Gospel and is applied to Jesus.[17] Here, this same sort of language is applied to the Spirit,[18] and it will in somewhat similar fashion be applied to the disciples as Jesus' missionaries in 15:18–27 (cf. below). If we examine all the passages in the farewell discourses in which the Spirit is referred to, we see that the Spirit has in the main a threefold task: (1) to indwell the believer and convey the divine presence and peace, including Jesus' presence to the believer (14:17–20, 27); (2) to teach the believer and to guide the believer into all truth and to testify to the believer about and on behalf of Jesus (14:26; 15:26); (3) to enable the disciples to testify about Jesus to the world and by means of the Spirit's guidance and power convict the world about sin, righteousness, and judgment (15:26–27; 16:8–11). The language of agency is used quite clearly of the Spirit and of Jesus in 16:13–15—"for he will not speak on his own, but will speak whatever he hears, and he will declare to you the things that are to come. He will glorify me, because he will take what is mine and declare it to you. All the Father has is mine. For this reason I said that he will take what is mine and declare it to you."

There is a very close association of Wisdom and the Holy Spirit in the Wisdom of Solomon—there they are virtually equated. Wisdom of Solomon 1:4–6 says, "Wisdom will not enter a deceitful soul, or dwell in a body enslaved to sin. For a holy and disciplined Spirit will flee from deceit. . . . For Wisdom is a kindly Spirit, but will not free blasphemers from the guilt of their words; because God is a witness of their innermost feelings, a true observer of their hearts." The text goes on to say that this Wisdom or Spirit fills the world and makes inquiry into the counsels of the ungodly and makes a report of their words to God "to convict them of their lawless deeds" (1:9). Elsewhere in the same book it is said, "Who has learned your counsel unless you have given Wisdom, and sent your Holy Spirit from on high? And thus the paths of those on earth were set right, and people were taught what pleases you, and were saved by Wisdom" (9:17–18). This material is relevant not only because the relationship of Wisdom and Spirit in this document has close analogies with the description of the relationship of Jesus and the Spirit but also because of the way it describes the role of the Spirit. The Spirit teaches believers but also investigates, testifies, and convicts the world of sin. In short, the portrayal of the Spirit, like the portrayal of Jesus in this Gospel, is deeply indebted to the Jewish sapiential tradition.

Furthermore, judicial language is used of the Spirit's role in both documents, and the "history of the term [*parakletos*] in the whole sphere of known Greek and Hellenistic usage outside the New Testament reveals the clear picture of a legal adviser or helper or advocate in the relevant court. The passive form does not rule out the idea of the *parakletos* as an active speaker 'on behalf of someone, before someone.' "[19] The word is in fact a verbal adjective and has basically the same thrust as the word *ho parakeklemenos* ("one called alongside"). In secular Greek it was especially used of one who helps another *in court*, although it never becomes a technical term like the Latin *advocatus*.[20] The related terms *parakalein* and *paraklesis* both refer to prophetic Christian preaching elsewhere in the New Testament (cf. Acts 2:40; 1 Cor. 14:3), which again strongly suggests a translation of *parakletos* that focuses on the Spirit's public and missionary roles carried out through the disciples.[21] "The Paraclete is the Spirit of Christian paraclesis."[22]

I would suggest then that (1) in view of the clear evidence of the use of agency language of the Spirit in these discourses; (2) in view of the use of judicial language about the Spirit's role here and in earlier wisdom literature; (3) in view of the missionary function of this document, addressing Gentiles among others, who certainly would have understood the term *parakletos* in its predominant Greek sense; and finally (4) in view of the use of judicial language and the portrayal of Jesus being on trial throughout most of this Gospel, we must translate the term as "Advocate."

The Spirit is Jesus' agent on earth, just as Jesus has been the Father's agent. The Spirit will equip the disciple with the presence of Jesus, and the understanding of Jesus' teaching, as well as with the power to convict and convert when witnessing to the world, not to mention equipping the disciple to face whatever persecution or trials or expulsions from the synagogue the disciple may face in the course of his or her mission work. The Spirit is the surrogate of Jesus when he leaves the earth, and the closeness of Jesus and the Spirit is much like the closeness or near-identity of Wisdom and the Spirit in earlier Jewish sapiential literature. Also like that latter portrayal, the ultimate goal of the Spirit is salvific, involving the sanctification of the believer in the truth and salvation of at least some from the dark world.

The disciples are indeed being comforted with the knowledge that when Jesus departs, the divine presence will not be withdrawn from them but will return to them in the form of the Advocate, the Holy Spirit. But comfort and consolation are not the Spirit's only, or perhaps primary, role, as a reading of all the Paraclete sayings together will show. The Spirit empowers the disciple with the presence, knowledge, and authority of Christ to do even greater works of mission than Christ was able to do. The Spirit becomes Advocate both for Christ and of the disciple in the witnessing situation, attempting to convict the world of sin, or defend the disciple if necessary when the disciple is under fire.

The Spirit is basically not an innovator; rather, the Spirit leads the disciples into the truth the Son has already conveyed, by reminding them of Jesus' teaching (14:26). The repeated reference to the disciples remembering in this Gospel (cf. 2:22; 12:16) is a testimony to the fact that *after* Jesus departed, they had indeed received the Holy Spirit. Remembrance came when the Spirit reminded. The Spirit, however, does not only speak about the past but also conveys the message of Jesus about the future (16:13), presumably the disciples' future. Thus the Spirit is seen as a source of continuing revelation for the disciples, but that revelation is seen as ultimately going back to the exalted Jesus and is not confused with the role of reminding the disciples what Jesus had said during his earthly ministry.[23] The words of the exalted Jesus are basically *not* conveyed in the farewell discourses, they are only promised as something the Spirit *will* bring when the Spirit comes to the disciple.[24]

The Spirit may be said to be a major player in the Fourth Gospel, unlike in Matthew and Mark where mention of the Spirit is infrequent. The Fourth Evangelist's perspective is that Jesus during his ministry is the bearer of the Spirit, on him the Spirit descended and remained (1:33), and he is the one who eventually will give the Spirit to disciples after his resurrection and exaltation (cf. on John 20:22 below). Unlike the case with the Old Testament prophets, the Spirit abides on Jesus continually. Thus Jesus has continual power to do signs and know God's will. At 3:5 we were told that the Spirit is necessary for rebirth, and at 6:63 that only the Spirit gives life, which in turn must mean that the disciples before Jesus' resurrection have neither of these, hence their constant misunderstanding and lack of spiritual perceptivity during the ministry. The disciples are all portrayed as on the way to becoming full-fledged followers of the Christ, but none arrive at that destination before Easter.

As Barrett points out, the rudiments of a doctrine of the Trinity are indeed already found in this Gospel, for Father, Son, and Spirit all act as divinity, all bear the divine presence and power, and all are deeply personal.[25] Even the Spirit is not seen as an it—the term *parakletos* is masculine, not neuter. This is also affirmed in the same breath with the affirmation that there is a functional subordination of the Son to the Father and of the Spirit to the Son. The Spirit then stands on the side of the Creator rather than on the side of the created or creature.

Jesus then leaves not only his teaching with the disciples through his agent the Spirit, he leaves his *shalom,* the very presence of God and the peace that brings, with them through the gift of the Spirit. This presence leads to both courage and joy despite the Master's bodily absence from the community. Jesus' peace referred to in 14:26 does not refer to the absence of turmoil or activity but rather to the presence of God even throughout all trials and temptations, sufferings and sorrows, diseases and even death.

This first farewell discourse ends with the affirmation both that Jesus is going away and that in another sense he is coming to them. He tells this to the disciples in advance so they will be prepared when it happens. The ruler of this world is about to come and do his worst with Jesus, but he really has no ultimate power over Jesus, for Jesus has chosen to act in this fashion anyway. Jesus is acting as the Father commanded, not as Satan demanded. The discourse closes with the command, "Rise, let us be on our way" (14:31), and one senses it is time to go to Gethsemane (cf. 18:1ff.) In conclusion, Segovia is right to suggest about this last section of the first farewell discourse that "the description of Jesus' departure as both act of love for the Father and an encounter with 'the ruler of the world' again introduces the possibility of a similar encounter with the world and its ruler on the part of the disciples in the course of their own mission in and to the world. . . . Such veiled warnings provide a counterbalance to both the didactic and consolatory functions of the unit."[26]

B. Discourse Two: "Abide in Me"
(John 15:1–17)

15:1 "I am the true vine, and my Father is the vinegrower. [2]He removes every branch in me that bears no fruit. Every branch that bears fruit he prunes to make it bear more fruit. [3]You have already been cleansed by the word that I have spoken to you. [4]Abide in me as I abide in you. Just as the branch cannot bear fruit by itself unless it abides in the vine, neither can you unless you abide in me. [5]I am the vine, you are the branches. Those who abide in me and I in them bear much fruit, because apart from me you can do nothing. [6]Whoever does not abide in me is thrown away like a branch and withers; such branches are gathered, thrown into the fire, and burned. [7]If you abide in me, and my words abide in you, ask for whatever you wish, and it will be done for you. [8]My Father is glorified by this, that you bear much fruit and become my disciples. [9]As the Father has loved me, so I have loved you; abide in my love. [10]If you keep my commandments, you will abide in my love, just as I have kept my Father's commandments and abide in his love. [11]I have said these things to you so that my joy may be in you, and that your joy may be complete.

12 "This is my commandment, that you love one another as I have loved you. [13]No one has greater love than this, to lay down one's life for one's friends. [14]You are my friends if you do what I command you. [15]I do not call you servants any longer, because the servant does not know what the master is doing; but I have called you friends, because I have made known to you everything that I have heard from my Father. [16]You did not choose me but I chose you. And I appointed you to go and bear fruit, fruit that will last, so that the Father will give you whatever you ask him in my name. [17]I am giving you these commands so that you may love one another.

If one of the major themes of John 14 was Jesus as the way and means to relationship with the Father, here in John 15 the focus is on the end product of such a relationship, the *abiding* results of relating to Jesus that way. Nevertheless, the issue here is not just abiding in Christ but bearing fruit for Christ. At 15:1 we have yet another of the "I am" sayings, and as was true in various of the previous examples we have the "I am" announcement twice for emphasis (vv. 1 and 4). The basic structure of this material is that in vv.

1–4 Jesus identifies himself in relationship to the Father and in vv. 5–8 in relationship to the disciples. While the other "I am" sayings may be said to focus on coming to Jesus, this one speaks to those who have already come and thus the focus is on remaining or "abiding," a word that occurs ten times in vv. 4–10, as well as on bearing fruit, making clear the basic theme of this subsection.[27] As we have argued all along, this document is intended to be used for missionary purposes. Within this broader description we must note that while other portions of this Gospel seem to be intended to be used by Christians directly with a non-Christian audience, the farewell discourses in their present setting and function are directed more toward the missionaries themselves, preparing them for their roles as witnesses. This is not incongruous, since this document is not simply a tract to be handed out directly to strangers but rather a tool for Christians to use with outsiders and also to prepare themselves for evangelism.

The understanding of the full significance of this passage hinges on understanding the background and the way the function and reference of metaphor are altered from their traditional usage. In the Old Testament, Israel is described as the vine (Jer. 2:21; 12:10ff.; Isa. 5:1–7; 27:2ff; Ezek. 15:1–8; 17:5ff.; 19:10–14; Ps. 80:9–16). In Sir. 24:17–21, Wisdom is described as having planted herself in the midst of God's people and she remarks: "Like the vine I bud forth delights, and my blossoms become glorious and abundant fruit. Come to me you who desire me and eat your fill of my fruits. For the memory of me is sweeter than honey, and the possession of me sweeter than the honeycomb. Those who eat of me will hunger for more, and those who drink of me will thirst for more." It is also in this same passage only two verses later that Ben Sira identifies Wisdom with Torah (Sir. 24:23). The question then becomes: In the evangelist's use of this metaphor is Jesus being identified as the people of God, or the locus where the true people of God dwell, or is he being identified as God's true revelation, the locus of God's Wisdom superseding the claims in the Wisdom tradition that Torah was that locus? On the one hand, as J. W. Pryor has pointed out, every Old Testament text in which Israel is mentioned as the vine, it is always in the context of judgment for unfaithfulness (cf. Mark 12:1–9).[28] While this might make some sense of the warnings in our text about branches being cut off, the predominant character of 15:1–17 is not negative but positive. The main issue in our text is not God's judgment on Jesus *or* on Jesus' followers. This suggests that we ought to look elsewhere for the provenance of the vine metaphor in this text. There are several clues that help us decide this issue.

First, the issue being addressed in the farewell discourses as a whole is the preparation of the disciples for Jesus' departure and the promise that Jesus will equip them with the Advocate not only to remain faithful but to continue to carry out the evangelistic tasks to which God has called them, bearing much fruit, despite resistance and rejection. In other words, the primary issue here is not *where* is the true people of God (in Jesus now, in Israel before) but rather *how* can the true people of God remain faithful and continue to function properly despite a hostile environment.

Second, nowhere else in this Gospel does Jesus claim to *be* Israel; rather, he claims to stand on the side of God and to reveal the Father to the world and to God's people. We have heard much about Jesus fulfilling and in essence superseding the institutions of Judaism in this Gospel, including Torah in the very first chapter. Jesus is God's Word/Wisdom—while the law came through Moses, grace and truth came through Jesus Christ (1:17). In such a context it would be natural to have a metaphor about Jesus being the true Word, the true locus of God's revelation.

Third, this Gospel, despite claims by some scholars, is not suggesting that the Jews have simply been replaced by Gentiles or others as the true people of God. Throughout this Gospel we have seen that some Jews have responded positively to Jesus, while others have rejected him. "The Jews," when the term is used pejoratively in this Gospel, refers chiefly if not solely to Jewish officials and authorities and perhaps other Torah-observant Jews who opposed Jesus.[29] This Gospel is not interested in pitting the Christians over against the Jews as the true people of God. Indeed, it states clearly at John 4:22 that salvation is of the Jews, and it is manifestly clear that throughout this Gospel it is seen as for Jews, even Jewish officials such as Nicodemus and Joseph of Arimathea as well as for others. The point is that the focus and the locus of God's revelation are now in Christ, and he is calling forth a more *intentionally* inclusive people of God that includes both Jews and many others (Samaritans, Greeks, etc.) by means of a more universally accessible proclamation. It is not that Jews have been rejected and Christians selected, but that Jews no longer have any *exclusive* claims to be the people of God or to have God's revelation, because salvation comes through and in the Son, God's Wisdom who came into the world to save the world, both Jew and Gentile. Like Paul, the Fourth Evangelist sees as the true community of God, Jew and Gentile united in Christ, while still recognizing that Jesus was a Jew and that the new community began with faithful Jewish followers of Jesus and continues to have some Jewish adherents. Salvation comes from the Jews, in particular the Jew Jesus, but it is for everyone.

Fourth, notice that immediately at the beginning of this passage we are told that the faithful and abiding branches have been "cleansed" by the word that Jesus has spoken to them (v. 3). The issue is not just abiding *but also* bearing fruit. The lopping off of branches comes when one does not bear fruit, and even the fruit-bearing branches are pruned or cleansed (cf. below) to make them bear more fruit. The point is not just staying faithful or staying in the community, but acting in a way that causes fruit bearing. This latter task is enabled by the cleansing that comes through Jesus' word.

Fifth, the Greek word *alethinos* surely means authentic as opposed to inauthentic, not true as opposed to false here.[30] One must ask then, What does it mean to say Jesus is the authentic vine? I would suggest that it is not a matter of contrasting a true versus a false people of God but rather a positive statement about where the authentic source of nourishment, strength, and empowerment for ministry lies. It lies in Jesus, the Wisdom of God, not in Torah or other possible sources. When one is cleansed by Jesus' word one is enabled to share the Word with others successfully, bearing much fruit. It seems plausible to see the reference to pruning as a reference to the suffering and difficulties one undergoes while witnessing in a hostile environment. One must then remain in, abide in, the true Wisdom/Word of God. This Gospel is no sectarian tract meant to anathematize all the world except the saved community. It engages in polemics only with those who oppose the Word, precisely because the Johannine community continues to reach out to seek and save the lost from all other communities.

Finally, as R. Bultmann long ago argued, and J. Ashton has recently reconfirmed, the major category for understanding this Gospel is revelation, including John 13—17.[31] Put another way, the major issue in this Gospel is Christology and soteriology, not ecclesiology. The Fourth Gospel primarily raises and answers questions about the means of salvation, and the way to the Father. It is not an accident that the disciples play such a small role in the narrative in this Gospel and Jesus bestrides the stage as God, to paraphrase E. Käsemann. This is only what one would expect in a christologically focused document meant to be used for missionary purposes. Bearing this in mind, we are now prepared to interpret the details of the vine metaphor.

The vine was one of the most prized of all ancient plants in Israel because it provided something to drink for a relatively low cost in manual labor in a land where water came and went because of the rainy seasons alternating with the long, hot summers when there would not be any rain. Thus here the vine stands as a symbol for an especially prized and fruitful source of nourishment and strength. Incorporation into, and then abiding in, the Christ as the vine provides the believer with the means not only to love one's fellow believers but also to bear fruit in one's witness to the world.[32]

That this interpretation of bearing fruit is correct is seen from the fact that already in John 4:36 fruit bearing is mentioned in the context of mission outreach and in 12:24 as well in the context of reaching the Greeks. Finally, as Pryor points out, the command to "go" and bear fruit at the climax of this discourse in v. 16 would be passing strange if the allusion was not to bearing witness to the world.[33]

While 15:1–17 can be said to focus mainly on the inward life of the community of Christ, and 15:18–16:4a focuses on the outward relationship to the world (cf. below on this material), there is a relationship between the two sections or discourses and thus it is not surprising that many scholars take 15:1–16:4a as one unit.[34] Abiding in Christ is not simply an end in itself, nor just a means of maintaining unity in the community, it is also the necessary prerequisite to effective evangelism in a hostile world.

There was in early Judaism a wide range of forms of metaphorical wisdom speech. The term *mashal*, or in the plural *meshalim*, covered a wide range of things from aphorisms/proverbs to riddles to parables to what we would view as a form of allegory. There was not a hard-and-fast distinction between what amounted to parable and what amounted to allegory,[35] and thus it is not surprising or implausible that Jesus should use even allegory at some points in his teaching of the public and of the disciples. He was, after all, a Jewish sage using the conventional means that sages used to speak to their Jewish audience.[36]

Here the subordination of the Son to the Father is made clear again. While Jesus is the vine, the Father is the vinedresser or gardener who planted the vineyard and the one who prunes the good branches and lops off the fruitless ones. Since it is Jesus who is the vine, and not Israel, and since the issue is abiding in Jesus' love, which amounts to abiding in and being cleansed by his word, the issue here has to do with the followers of Jesus, not with Jews in general. Apostate or unfruitful believers are envisioned who are cut off the tree because they do not bear fruit. Nothing is said here to suggest that these branches were not truly part of the vine originally or that they were not a growth from the authentic vine. Rather, the point is they did not do what branches were expected to do—bear fruit. Verse 6 is quite clear. This being cut off is not seen as happening to those who have never been a part of the authentic vine but to those who "do not *remain* in me." This of course presupposes that at one point they were authentically joined to Jesus but did not stay the course because of pressures and problems created by a hostile world.

The application of this teaching during the time of the Johannine community can be seen in 1 and 2 John (cf. especially 2 John 7–11). In the epistles the issue is clearly christological, having to do with faithfulness to the true confession of Christ and living by his word, and the parallels with our passage here are especially close. In view of the strong similarities between the farewell discourses and 1 and 2 John there is good reason to think that the epistles were written at a time very close to, perhaps shortly before, the composition of the Fourth Gospel, and, more to the point, that these letters were written at the *same time* that the Beloved Disciple was orally or in writing conveying teaching such as John 15 to his community.

What does remaining in Christ involve? As Barrett stresses, it means hold on loyally to Christ, obeying him, giving the service of self-sacrificial love within the community, but I would add that it also involves bearing fruit outside the community, since following Christ entails not only being and remaining a disciple but also making disciples.[37] Christ as vine is the source of the disciples' words of witness, he cleanses the disciples with his word, and as the Word/Wisdom that reveals the very mind of God he is what the disciple must ponder and abide in. Notice that the verb *menein* in vv. 4ff. is in the present and continual tense. "Remaining" is an ongoing, not already completed, process. The Christian is unable to bear fruit outside Jesus, just as a branch that is severed from the vine is cut off from its source of life and hence its ability to bear fruit.

Verse 7 speaks of the word remaining in believers, and in the larger context we are given some clue as to what this "word" is. We have a commandment of Jesus, not unlike the commandments of Moses, only now Jesus rather than Torah is the source of life and enlightenment. The commandment is not merely to love one another. That in itself would be hard enough.

Rather, the commandment is to love one another as Christ has loved his followers (v. 12). Indeed, the relationship of the Son to the Father, the former abiding in the latter, is to provide a model for the relationship of the disciple to Jesus. Jesus has kept his Father's commandments and now he gives his own commandments to the disciples, expecting them to keep them. This obedience is possible only if one abides in Christ's word and in his love.

This context of abiding in Christ's word and love is the proper context out of which one must interpret vv. 7 and 16. Asking "whatever you will" "in Jesus' name" presupposes that one will ask only for things that are in accord with Jesus' will and with continuing to abide in Christ and in his word. If one is going to sign Jesus' name to a prayer to the Father, one had better be sure that it is the sort of prayer Jesus would himself endorse and sign his name to in the first place. Asking "whatever you will" presupposes abiding in and by Christ's will and word. In v. 10 abiding is even said to be contingent upon obedience to Jesus' word. It is not something the believer may take for granted. Clearly enough, it requires ongoing effort on the part of the believer as well as on the part of Christ and the Spirit.

Here as elsewhere in this Gospel is a close relationship between love and obedience. Since love is an activity, self-sacrificial actions like those of Christ (cf. above), it can be commanded. Believers abide in Christ's love *by loving as Christ loves.* The vertical relationship to Christ is affected by the horizontal relationship to others. This is why, in another context, we are told in the Lord's Prayer that we may pray for forgiveness of sins only as we are forgiving others. Christ's love in believers' lives is meant to be shared with others. It is not meant to be kept as a private possession. Christ remained in the Father's love by keeping the Father's commandments, and, *mutatis mutandis,* the same applies in the relationship of the disciples to Christ.

Notice that in v. 12 the word "commandment" becomes singular. Here as in the Synoptics (cf. Mark 12:31 and par.) we find that love of God and others can be seen as bound together, and the love commandment summarizes or encapsulates the whole of God's and Christ's demand on the disciple. Verse 13 refers to the fact that one can do nothing greater for a friend than die for the friend.[38] The word *philos,* rather than translated as "friend," can and probably should be translated here in vv. 13 and 14 as "those he loves."[39] Believers are Jesus' friends (i.e., those he loves) *if* they obey him and keep his commandments, which can be summarized by the exhortation to love. V. Furnish has aptly said that Christian love is not like a heat-seeking missile that directs itself to something inherently attractive in the object of love.[40] Rather, it is directed even and perhaps especially to the unlovely and those who see themselves as unlovable. Taking on the role of a servant means doing what Jesus has done without making conditions or demands, not saying things such as "I will love if . . ." or "I will love when . . ." or "I will love until . . ."

Beginning at v. 15 the analogy between slave and master is made. Notice that the difference between a slave and a friend ("one whom Jesus loves") is that the "friend" knows and understands what the Master is doing. The one whom Jesus loves is not in the dark about who Jesus is, what his will is, and why one should do what he commands. The Son does not call for blind obedience but for willing assent to God's design as it is revealed in Christ. At v. 16, however, any thought that believers are free to do as they please with the knowledge given us by Jesus is rejected. Rather, believers, like Jesus, are people under authority, agents of a higher power.[41] Believers are chosen, although of course they must respond to the choice, and if they do not continue to respond positively and bear fruit, they can be broken off by the Father. Believers have been chosen, not as an end in itself, but in order that they might bear much fruit, contribute to the mission of the Christian community. Moreover, this fruit is fruit that should endure. Any prayer for the work of mission, any prayer that is in accord with God's plan that disciples bear much fruit will be heard and answered affirmatively.

Abiding in Jesus, the authentic Vine, the authentic Word/Wisdom of God is "the essential condition for the disciples' fulfillment of that activity proper to them as disciples of Jesus, the bearing of fruit."[42] But this bearing of fruit can not be confined to just loving one another. Loving one another within the community does not lead to the self-sacrificial death of the disciple. The disciple dies for other disciples, both potential and actual, when she or he bears witness in a hostile world, a matter discussed more fully in the next farewell discourses.

C. Discourse Three: "The World Will Hate You" (John 15:18–16:4a)

15:18   "If the world hates you, be aware that it hated me before it hated you. [19]If you belonged to the world, the world would love you as its own. Because you do not belong to the world, but I have chosen you out of the world—therefore the world hates you. [20]Remember the word that I said to you, 'Servants are not greater than their master.' If they persecuted me, they will persecute you; if they kept my word, they will keep yours also. [21]But they will do all these things to you on account of my name, because they do not know him who sent me. [22]If I had not come and spoken to them, they would not have sin; but now they have no excuse for their sin. [23]Whoever hates me hates my Father also. [24]If I had not done among them the works that no one else did, they would not have sin. But now they have seen and hated both me and my Father. [25]It was to fulfill the word that is written in their law, 'They hated me without a cause.'

26   "When the Advocate comes, whom I will send to you from the Father, the Spirit of truth who comes from the Father, he will testify on my behalf. [27]You also are to testify because you have been with me from the beginning.

16:1   "I have said these things to you to keep you from stumbling. [2]They will put you out of the synagogues. Indeed, an hour is coming when those who kill you will think that by doing so they are offering worship to God. [3]And they will do this because they have not known the Father or me.

⁴But I have said these things to you so that when their hour comes you may remember that I told you about them.

In view of the evangelistic overtones of the previous discourse, or section in that discourse, it is not surprising that we now turn to a warning about the cost of discipleship when one is a member of a witnessing community. There is a strong contrast here between the world, which hates Jesus and his followers, and the community of faithful followers. Disciples have been chosen out of the world and do not belong to it; therefore they are hated by those who do belong to the world. Since servants are not greater than their masters, disciples should not expect better treatment than Jesus received at the hands of the world.

It is not just that the fate of the disciple may be similar to the fate of the master, even to the point of speaking of the "hour" of the disciple when she or he is called upon to die for what she or he believes in (16:2), just as Jesus has his "hour." The point is that Jesus has spoken and done things in the midst of the world that now make the world culpable both for not knowing that God has sent Jesus *and* not knowing God who did the sending. In fact, he had done things no one else had done before him (v. 24), such as giving sight to the blind man (John 9). To whom more knowledge and experience is given, more accountability is required. Those who hate the Son hate the Father, and, *mutatis mutandis,* those who hate the disciples hate both the Son and the Father. This reaction is without a justifiable cause and amounts to inexcusable sin. In fact, this reaction amounts to a fulfillment of scripture: "They hated me without a cause." This quotation seems to be drawn from either Ps. 35:19 or Ps. 69:4. In all likelihood it is the latter, since that psalm was thought in early Judaism to have messianic overtones.[43] The point is that such a reaction should not surprise the disciples; it was foreseen in scripture, and God has worked it into the divine plan. The fact that it is said to come from "their Law" reveals that the world here is chiefly associated with the Jewish opposition to Jesus, as becomes abundantly clear by the reference to the synagogue in 16:2.[44]

Verses 26–27 refer once more to the Advocate (cf. above), also called the Spirit of truth, who will testify on Jesus' behalf. The Advocate comes from the Father but is sent by the Son to the believers. The disciples will likewise be called upon to testify. A. E. Harvey admirably summarizes the scenario:

> The standard and most comprehensive activity of any advocate [is] to bear witness, or give evidence. But instead of giving favourable evidence about the followers of Jesus in the heavenly court (which is the function of the *paraclete* in 1 John 2:1) this *paraclete* will give evidence about Jesus in the earthly court—as is made absolutely clear by the following sentence: "And you give evidence, because you have been with me from the beginning" (15:27). The *paraclete* and the disciples each have the same function: to be witnesses. The dependability of the *paraclete* derives from the fact that he is sent straight from God; of the disciples, that they have been eyewitnesses—have known it all first hand—"from the beginning."

The court is any occasion when Jesus' claim to be Son of God and Messiah is denied by the enemies of the Christian community.[45]

Much of this Gospel has portrayed Jesus as already on trial long before Caiaphas ever laid eyes on him, and in this regard it relates more adequately to the experience of the disciples who are on trial every time they sally forth to witness about Jesus in the synagogue or elsewhere in the world. It is striking that this material is very similar to what is said in the Synoptics about disciples witnessing, being on trial and in danger, and being enabled to testify truly by means of the Spirit (cf. Mark 13:9–13; Matt. 10:17–25; Luke 12: 2–9).[46]

The final paragraph of this discourse is found in 16:1–4a where we learn that the reason for mentioning these things is so the disciples will not stumble when they are put out of the synagogues or, worse, killed. This had direct bearing for the Johannine community, which continued to witness in the synagogue, even though it was not part of the synagogue but rather had its own community life.[47] This is one of the warnings Jesus offered that he was counting on the Spirit bringing to their minds at the relevant hour (v. 4a).

In view of the Synoptic parallels to this teaching, which do not reflect the Johannine idiom but have the same substantive message, from a historical point of view it appears very probable that Jesus did warn his disciples in this fashion before his death. If the language seems extreme when it argues that those who kill the disciples will see it as an act of worship, remember that Paul himself before his conversion seems to have seen such actions as a religious duty and a way of showing zeal for God and God's law (cf. Gal. 1:13–14). Jesus says that the ultimate reason for such actions is that the persecutors know neither God nor God's Son. Here as throughout this Gospel the ultimate issue is truly knowing Jesus and the Father, the issue is revelation and its proper reception.

D. Discourse Four: "It Is Better for You that I Should Leave" (John 16:4b–33)

16:4b   "I did not say these things to you from the beginning, because I was with you. [5]But now I am going to him who sent me; yet none of you asks me, 'Where are you going?' [6]But because I have said these things to you, sorrow has filled your hearts. [7]Nevertheless I tell you the truth: it is to your advantage that I go away, for if I do not go away, the Advocate will not come to you; but if I go, I will send him to you. [8]And when he comes, he will prove the world wrong about sin and righteousness and judgment: [9]about sin, because they do not believe in me; [10]about righteousness, because I am going to the Father and you will see me no longer; [11]about judgment, because the ruler of this world has been condemned.

12 "I still have many things to say to you, but you cannot bear them now. [13]When the Spirit of truth comes, he will guide you into all the truth;

for he will not speak on his own, but will speak whatever he hears, and he will declare to you the things that are to come. [14]He will glorify me, because he will take what is mine and declare it to you. [15]All that the Father has is mine. For this reason I said that he will take what is mine and declare it to you.

16 "A little while, and you will no longer see me, and again a little while, and you will see me." [17]Then some of his disciples said to one another, "What does he mean by saying to us, 'A little while, and you will no longer see me, and again a little while, and you will see me'; and 'Because I am going to the Father'?" [18]They said, "What does he mean by this 'a little while'? We do not know what he is talking about." [19]Jesus knew that they wanted to ask him, so he said to them, "Are you discussing among yourselves what I meant when I said, 'A little while, and you will no longer see me, and again a little while, and you will see me'? [20]Very truly, I tell you, you will weep and mourn, but the world will rejoice; you will have pain, but your pain will turn into joy. [21]When a woman is in labor, she has pain, because her hour has come. But when her child is born, she no longer remembers the anguish because of the joy of having brought a human being into the world. [22]So you have pain now; but I will see you again, and your hearts will rejoice, and no one will take your joy from you. [23]On that day you will ask nothing of me. Very truly, I tell you, if you ask anything of the Father in my name, he will give it to you. [24]Until now you have not asked for anything in my name. Ask and you will receive, so that your joy may be complete.

25 "I have said these things to you in figures of speech. The hour is coming when I will no longer speak to you in figures, but will tell you plainly of the Father. [26]On that day you will ask in my name. I do not say to you that I will ask the Father on your behalf; [27]for the Father himself loves you, because you have loved me and have believed that I came from God. [28]I came from the Father and have come into the world; again, I am leaving the world and am going to the Father."

29 His disciples said, "Yes, now you are speaking plainly, not in any figure of speech! [30]Now we know that you know all things, and do not need to have anyone question you; by this we believe that you came from God." [31]Jesus answered them, "Do you now believe? [32]The hour is coming, indeed it has come, when you will be scattered, each one to his home, and you will leave me alone. Yet I am not alone because the Father is with me. [33]I have said this to you, so that in me you may have peace. In the world you face persecution. But take courage; I have conquered the world!"

The fourth discourse, which is really the last one, since John 17 provides a closing prayer by Jesus, returns to various of the themes of the first discourse found in 13:31–14:31. Yet it is by no means a mere duplicate of that discourse, and in view of the triumphant climax and conclusion that the discourse leads to in 16:32–33 it is best to see this as the intended last discourse in the sequence and not opt for the suggestion that John 15—16 might be better placed before the discourse in 13:31–14:31. How, then, do we explain

16:5, "Yet none of you asks me, 'Where are you going?' " in light of 13:36? I would suggest that the most plausible explanation is that the discourse in 13:31–14:31 was given on one occasion, that in 16:4b–33 on another and later occasion, perhaps on successive nights during Passover week. Thus the remark of Jesus in 16:5 pertains to another occasion than the question in 13:36. The evangelist has simply grouped a collection of discourses together in the farewell discourses.

Although the basic themes of the first discourse, including the departure and return of Jesus, reappear in this discourse but with a difference, here the focus is on the meaning and consequences, in particular the positive consequences of this departure for the disciples.[48] In 16:4b–15 the discussion of the consequences focuses on the Advocate, while in vv. 16–33 the discussion of consequences focuses on Jesus himself.

The contrast between the disciples and the world continues in this discourse as does the focus on teaching and the tone of consolation. What is noticeably different here is the increased emphasis on Jesus' approaching hour and that he must face it, coupled with the increased failure of the disciples to understand what Jesus is saying.[49] The disciples have more to say in this discourse than in previous ones. There is also an increased emphasis on the promises and their expansive nature, as compared to the first discourse. This final discourse ends with Jesus speaking more plainly and with less figurative language than in the previous discourses, but it also ends with the disciples still not fully understanding what has been said.[50] Full and clear knowledge, as the evangelist stresses, is not possible before Easter, and thus the judgment on the disciples' lack of perceptivity during this pre-Easter period is not as harsh as it might otherwise be. This discourse can be seen as an artistic and coherent whole, and we will treat it as such.[51]

The discourse begins with Jesus affirming in 16:4b that he had not disclosed these sorts of things about his departure from the beginning, because he planned to be with the disciples for a while. In other words, farewell discourses are only appropriate shortly before leaving. The language of agency recurs in 16:5—Jesus returns to the one who sent him. Jesus is depicted as knowing that his disciples are sorrowful over his departure, and so he must explain to them the advantage it will be for them if he departs. The advantage is first stated negatively: "If I do not go away, the Advocate will not come to you" (v. 7).

Here the role of the Advocate is clearly stated in forensic or legal terms. The verb *elencho* has legal overtones and has a range of meanings, especially in classical Greek, including convict, accuse, cross-examine, and put to shame.[52] It is hardly convincing to argue that the verb in this context means "prove the world wrong about sin."[53] This is certainly not what *elencho* with the preposition *peri* ("concerning") means in John 8:46. The point is not that the world simply holds wrong opinions about Jesus and sin and the like. Just as in John 8:46 the sense is "Can any of you convict me of sin?" so here the sense is that the Advocate, through the disciples, will convict the world concerning sin, because the world does not believe in Jesus (v. 9).

The world will also be convicted about righteousness, the righteousness of Christ, because he will go to the Father.[54] The Father's vindication of Jesus demonstrates his righteous character. Lastly, the Advocate convicts the world concerning judgment because Satan stands condemned as a result of Jesus' death and vindication. Christ's death was indeed a judgment, but not on Jesus and the validity of his ministry. Rather, the judgment turns out to be on sin, on the world, and on the prince of this world. The point here is that the world, in its judgment of Jesus, is allied with Satan, who provoked such an evaluation. Its judgment of Jesus is not only incorrect, it is immoral. Thus, when Satan is condemned, any judgment, such as the world's evaluation of Jesus, that ultimately comes from Satan is likewise condemned.[55] "All false judgment is related to him who was a liar from the beginning, whose children we are if we echo his values (8:42–47)."[56]

Verse 12 makes clear that Jesus realizes that the disciples not only cannot understand many things before Easter, they cannot bear some things Jesus might tell them prior to Easter. The Advocate will come to the disciples after Easter and lead them into all truth that they need to know. The Spirit, as Christ's agent, speaks for Jesus. It appears we are being told that the Spirit will convey the words of the exalted Jesus to the disciples after Easter. It does not follow from this that we have such words in the Fourth Gospel, although it appears we do have Spirit-inspired commentary and further extrapolations on Jesus' historical words at various points.[57] Although D. M. Smith and others appeal to the words of the exalted Jesus in Rev. 1—3, it should be noted that those words are portrayed as words of Jesus from heaven, not words of Jesus during the ministry.[58] The evidence for retrojecting words of the exalted Jesus back into the mouth of Jesus as he speaks in the narrative of the ministry is lacking.[59]

The disciples of course do not understand about the "little while," and Jesus freely admits that during the first little while the world will rejoice while the disciples will have pain, will weep, and will mourn. But this too will pass. Their pain will turn to joy at Easter. The analogy is made in v. 21 with a woman in labor who is temporarily in anguish but then is overwhelmed with joy at having brought a human being into the world. Notice again that Jesus is portrayed here as a sage, not quoting the prophets or saying "thus saith the Lord," but using analogies from everyday life, as was the tendency of Jewish sages.[60] Verse 22 speaks then of the reunion at Easter when the disciples will see Jesus again. Then there will be no more questions, only joy and the dawning of full understanding.

Verses 25–33 bring the discussion to a close with Jesus affirming that his normal *modus operandi* was to speak in a sapiential mode during the ministry, using figures of speech, metaphors, riddles, parables, aphorisms, and the like. These verses are crucially placed, for they come at the very end of Jesus' final discussion with his disciples and provide a key clue to how we should read the portrayal of Jesus in this Gospel. He is seen as both sage and Wisdom at once, as both revealer and the content of revelation, as both means and ends of salvation. Jesus says, however, that a time will come when he will speak plainly of the Father. As this passage unfolds, it becomes clear that he means he will provide clear understanding through the Spirit, once he has returned to the Father, and the disciples can pray in Jesus' name.

There is considerable debate in regard to the phrase "a little while," which appears twice in v. 16. I agree with Michaels that it is likely that the first "a little while" is the interval until Jesus' death and that the second "little while" is the interval between Jesus' death and the resurrection, not the interval between Jesus' death and the second coming.[61] The Fourth Evangelist says very little about the return of Christ and shows no obvious interest in speculating about the timing of the second coming. This in turn means that the hour or time of gladness and joy is seen as the present time of the church, including first and foremost the time of the Johannine community. It is not a reference to the final joy of the eschaton.

This conclusion is especially clear because, as Michaels shows, vv. 23–24 indicate that the time of joy is still a time of praying for the followers of Jesus.[62] The church age is seen as the time of answered prayer and of the joy of knowing Christ's presence through the Advocate. If the Old Testament age was the age of the Father, and the ministry was the age of the Son on earth, the church age is the age of the eschatological Spirit. It is an age in which the prince of this world is already judged, and Jesus has already overcome the world. This does not mean that the disciples will not have trouble in this world, but it means that whatever trouble they face cannot snuff out their faith and will not have the ultimate word about either the fate of the disciples or the future of the world.

Verses 26–28 affirm that the Father loves the disciples because they recognize properly that Jesus came from God and they have loved Jesus. Verse 28 makes as clear as it can be made that the key to understanding who Jesus is, is understanding his origins and destination, from and to the Father.

Although the disciples say they believe that Jesus knows all things and that he came from God in v. 29, it is clear from Jesus' reply to the disciples that they clearly do not understand well enough, and here finally at v. 32 we have a connection forward to the conclusion of the Passion narrative: "You will be scattered, each one to his home, and you will leave me alone."[63] Yet the Father will be with Jesus during his walk down the road to Golgotha, even if the disciples won't be.

Jesus has said all these things to his disciples so they might not give way to despair but rather would have some peace. But this promise is also directed to the later disciples in the Johannine community who face persecution (v. 33). The disciples are not to let the world get them down, for Christ has overcome the world. They must have courage in the face of stiff resistance to their witness.

E. The Sage's Prayer
(John 17:1–26)

17:1 After Jesus had spoken these words, he looked up to heaven and said, "Father, the hour has come; glorify your Son so that the Son may glorify you, [2]since you have given him authority over all people, to give eternal life to all whom you have given him. [3]And this is eternal life, that they may know you, the only true God, and Jesus Christ whom you have sent. [4]I glorified you on earth by finishing the work that you gave me to do. [5]So now, Father, glorify me in your own presence with the glory that I had in your presence before the world existed.

6 "I have made your name known to those whom you gave me from the world. They were yours, and you gave them to me, and they have kept your word. [7]Now they know that everything you have given me is from you; [8]for the words that you gave to me I have given to them, and they have received them and know in truth that I came from you; and they have believed that you sent me. [9]I am asking on their behalf; I am not asking on behalf of the world, but on behalf of those whom you gave me, because they are yours. [10]All mine are yours, and yours are mine; and I have been glorified in them. [11]And now I am no longer in the world, but they are in the world, and I am coming to you. Holy Father, protect them in your name that you have given me, so that they may be one, as we are one. [12]While I was with them, I protected them in your name that you have given me. I guarded them, and not one of them was lost except the one destined to be lost, so that the scripture might be fulfilled. [13]But now I am coming to you, and I speak these things in the world so that they may have my joy made complete in themselves. [14]I have given them your word, and the world has hated them because they do not belong to the world, just as I do not belong to the world. [15]I am not asking you to take them out of the world, but I ask you to protect them from the evil one. [16]They do not belong to the world, just as I do not belong to the world. [17]Sanctify them in the truth; your word is truth. [18]As you have sent me into the world, so I have sent them into the world. [19]And for their sakes I sanctify myself, so that they also may be sanctified in truth.

20 "I ask not only on behalf of these, but also on behalf of those who will believe in me through their word, [21]that they may all be one. As you, Father, are in me and I am in you, may they also be in us, so that the world may believe that you have sent me. [22]The glory that you have given me I have given them, so that they may be one, as we are one, [23]I in them and you in me, that they may become completely one, so that the world may know that you have sent me and have loved them even as you have loved me. [24]Father, I desire that those also, whom you have given me, may be with me where I am, to see my glory, which you have given me because you loved me before the foundation of the world.

25 "Righteous Father, the world does not know you, but I know you; and these know that you have sent me. [26]I made your name known to them, and I will make it known, so that the love with which you have loved me may be in them, and I in them."

The farewell discourses close with an intercessory prayer on behalf of himself (vv. 1–5), for his disciples (vv. 6–19) and their converts (vv. 20–23), and for the perfection of all believers in the glory of Jesus (vv. 24–26).[64] As the number of verses devoted to each subject suggests, the emphasis is on prayer for the disciples. It should be noted that the concern for christological purity and unity in vv. 17–23 mirrors a similar concern in the Johannine epistles and again suggests that these documents all presuppose the same sort of situation and time frame for the Johannine community.[65] This prayer clearly belongs with the farewell discourses because it reiterates and sums up various of the themes found in these discourses: (1) the departure of Jesus (vv. 11, 13); (2) the joy of the disciples (v. 13); (3) the hatred of the world (v. 14); (4) the division of the world and the disciples (v. 16); (5) the truth (v. 17); and (6) the indwelling of Christ in the believers (v. 23).

Scholars have urged that this prayer takes the place of the Gethsemane prayer in the Synoptics. Yet we have noted that 12:27–28 seems to be a nearer parallel, and certainly there is nothing here about Jesus being troubled or asking for a cup to pass and the like. I would suggest that this prayer should be seen as the proper prayer that concludes the discourse and discussion period at the *symposium* and portrays Jesus as a sage who has left his legacy with his disciples and now leaves them, having entrusted them to God's care. This is the pattern we find in Sirach, which closes with a final prayer of the sage in Sir. 51:1–12, followed by some final words to and on behalf of his disciples in 51:13–30, which concludes with a benediction in v. 29.[66]

What we have here is not so much a "high-priestly" prayer[67] but a prayer of dedication and consecration of both Jesus and his followers. Jesus is dedicated or set apart for his final missionary act of death on the cross, while the disciples are set apart and consecrated not only *in* the truth but *for* the task of witnessing to the world, even if such witness should lead to the same conclusion as Jesus' life. This makes analogies with some of the earlier and contemporary Jewish farewell prayers (cf. Deut. 33; 4 *Ezra* 8:19b–36; *Jub.* 1:19–21; 10:3–6) rather remote.

Like the prayer in John 11, this prayer should be seen as a didactic and public prayer, meant for others to hear and learn from. It is not meant to be seen simply as an example of the private prayer life of Jesus. It is also not simply a prayer that reflects Jesus' state before Good Friday, as v. 24 makes clear. While in some important ways the prayer reflects the time before Jesus goes to the cross, it also reflects a time when Jesus can say that he longs for the disciples to see his glory and *be* where he is (i.e., in a heavenly state— v. 24). These are words that a risen Jesus could speak after Easter.[68] In other words, the evangelist has made this prayer appropriate for use in the post-Easter situation, even though much of it is also appropriate to the time just before Jesus went up to Golgotha. The prayer is, however, generally remote from the Gethsemane prayer in the Synoptics, but it can be seen as an expansion of the Johannine petition at the close of the public ministry (12:28): "Father, glorify thy name."[69] The keynote of the prayer has to do with the glorification of the Father, the Son, and even of the disciples, in the sense that the latter are consecrated, set apart, sanctified, or made holy for their task of mission.

The passage begins with the indication that Jesus looked up to heaven, indicating an attitude of prayer (cf. 11:41). That Jesus prays meaningfully to someone other than himself indicates his humanness and his distinction from God the Father. That he always prays within and knowing the Father's will indicates his divine knowledge and union with the Father. Verse 1 indicates that the Father is glorified in the glorification of the Son, and already here there is an allusion to Christ's death as *the* means of the glorification and exaltation of the Son. Christ should be glorified, since he has been given authority over "all flesh," an authority that allows him to dispense eternal life to those who have been given to him by the Father, those who have faith and believe in the Son.

We should probably see v. 3 as an editorial comment of the evangelist, stating a basic confession of the Johannine community. In important ways it is similar to the confession we find in 1 Cor. 8:6 where God the Father is confessed along with and yet distinguished from the Lord Jesus Christ. This confession in 1 Corinthians reflects the expansion of the Shema (cf. Deut. 6:4–5), caused by reflecting on Jesus in light of the Wisdom tradition that placed preexistent Wisdom at God's very side and as one who came to earth to save those who believe.[70] As R. Schnackenburg points out, the reference to the "only true God" is missionary language, the sort of expression used with outsiders (cf. 1 Thess. 1:19), and points us forward to the essential character of this prayer, setting the disciples as well as Jesus apart for their missionary tasks.[71] Christ is confessed here as God's agent, his apostle, his sent one, a particularly Johannine and sapiential way of confessing Jesus. This confession is similar and should be compared to the one in 1 John 5:20.

Verse 4 could be said to look back on the finished work of Christ on the cross (cf. John 19:30), especially in view of the phrase "on earth," and thus once again we have this ambivalence that the one praying this prayer seems at one moment to be the exalted Jesus and at one moment the Jesus about to be lifted up. The prayer has been written by the evangelist with both the benefit of hindsight and the use of foresight, so it would be relevant to the situation of his audience. Verse 5, however, makes equally clear that the dominant posture of Jesus throughout this passage is of one about to die, about to say farewell to this earthly life. Verse 5 is also important because it suggests that the Word/Wisdom gave up at least a goodly portion of his glory when he came to earth and looks to reassume it when he returns to heaven. This makes all the more likely the suggestion that John 1:14 reflects the voice of the community speaking of what they saw during the resurrection appearances, not primarily during the ministry.

In Semitic thought the name of a person reveals something essential about that person's nature or character. Thus, when we hear in 17:6 that Jesus has made known the name of the Father, he means he has revealed God's essential character to the disciples, who are characterized as "those who have kept your word" or those who know that God has sent Jesus.

As v. 9 makes evident, this prayer is specifically for the disciples, not directly for the world, but as the conclusion of the prayer makes evident, this is not because Jesus does not care about the world. If the disciples are being consecrated for the task of witnessing in the world, this can hardly be the correct conclusion. Jesus, then, is not inculcating here a strictly sectarian community that would withdraw from and simply anathematize that world from within the safe confines of the Christian group. Indeed, the very reason the disciples need this prayer, and the consecrating and equipping it speaks of, is that they will and must continue to go out to a largely hostile world and bear witness about Christ. The dualism here between disciples and world is not absolute, since some of the world is expected to be recruited for discipleship.

In v. 11 we again have indications of the dual perspective of the prayer. Jesus is no longer in the world, and yet he is, according to v. 13. He is at the point of returning to the Father and can speak as if he were already gone. Jesus entrusts the disciples into the care of the Father, that he will protect them and keep them unified. Verse 12 indicates that Jesus had guarded them, and yet one was lost—the son of destruction, a clear reference to Judas. The allusion to scripture being fulfilled is likely once again to Ps. 41:9, as in John 13:18 (cf. above). Chosenness did not preclude apostasy in the case of Judas.

In v. 13 Jesus is said to speak these things while he is still in the world, so the disciples' joy may come to completion, presumably at and after Easter. The disciples are in the world but are not of it, do not belong to it. Christ does not pray that the disciples be removed from the sphere of the world, like the sectarian community at Qumran, but rather that they be guarded from the evil one, while they are still operating in the world.

Verses 17–19 become confusing when *hagiason* and related cognates are translated "sanctify." The issue here is not the Christian doctrine of sanctification or even cleansing by means of God's word, as is made clear by the fact that Jesus is said to *hagiazo* himself in v. 19. The translation of this verb here should surely be "set apart," "consecrate" (cf. Jer. 1:5; Ex. 28:41). The disciples are to be set apart in the truth, just as Jesus sets himself apart, or consecrates himself in the truth. The language of sacrifice seems to be in the background here where an animal is consecrated or set apart or dedicated to God in preparation for the actual act of sacrifice. In Deut. 15:19, 21 the term "consecrate" is in fact synonymous with "sacrifice." Christ's dedication unto death "is made in order that they too [the disciples] may be dedicated to the same task of bringing the saving sovereignty to the world *in like spirit as he brought it.*"[72]

It has been said that Christ has no hands on earth save those of the disciples, no legs but those of his followers, no voice but that of the Christian community. There is a goodly measure of truth in this. The Christian community is dedicated here to the task of acting and speaking for Christ on earth, an awesome task.[73] The disciples, to be like Jesus, must be sent into the world.

Verse 20 has often been debated, but it surely refers to at least the partial success of the mission of the original (and later the Johannine) disciples.[74] It also indicates a need to pray for the unity of the original disciples and those who come to believe through their word. This would be an especially apt prayer in light of the divisions and disunity evident in the Johannine epistles, especially 2 John. But unity among believers must also be grounded in unity with or dwelling in the Father and Son. Verse 22 speaks of Jesus having passed on his glory to the disciples so they may be one. The meaning seems to be that Jesus has conveyed to them the divine presence and life so that they can be spiritually united with each other and with God. One purpose of such unity if it is real and manifest is so "the world may know that you have sent me and have loved them" (v. 23).

Christ concludes the prayer in vv. 24–26 with a wish that the disciples not only be guarded on earth but arrive safely in the presence of the heavenly Christ and may see his glory. D. A. Carson argues that we must not overlook the eschatological element here, of seeing Christ's glory when he returns (cf. 5:28–29; 6:39–40; 14:2–3).[75] But the reference to "where I am," coupled with all the language in this prayer of returning to the Father, surely makes clear that the focus is on heaven here, unlike 1 Cor. 13:8–13 where the "now"/"then" contrast is clear. Believers, when they die, will be with Christ and see his heavenly glory, which he had before and after his earthly career. It was a glory given by the Father "because you loved me before the foundation of the world" (v. 24b). Like Wisdom, who is said to be a pure emanation of God's glory (Wisd. Sol. 7:25), and one who comes forth from God's glorious throne in heaven (Wisd. Sol. 9:10), the Son partakes of the very qualities of the Father and derives them from the Father.

The language of consecration consummates with a reference to the righteous Father. God's Son and God's people must be set apart because God the Father is distinct and set apart from all else in the universe. He is righteous in character and actions. Christ has made his character known and, through the Spirit, will continue to do so, so that the love shared by Father and Son may also be shared by the children of God. The goal of the knowledge of God is the love of God, and knowledge here is seen as an indispensable means of having the love of God in the community and its individual members. Revelation, here as elsewhere in this Gospel, is the key to everything—salvation/eternal life, eternal love, eternal light, true community and unity with God and with God's people.

The life, power, character direction, and purpose of God's people should not be worldly in nature, any more than Jesus or his kingdom was "of this world." The saying is attributed to Bultmann that the church's task is to be a place on earth where the world is annulled within the world. Yet it is also so that the church is set apart precisely to serve and reach out and save those who are in the world. At 20:31 we will hear more of this missionary purpose, the purpose of being Christ bearers to and in the world, but for now it is crucial to recognize that this was Jesus' last word to and for his disciples—to be sent ones as he was.

II. Bridging the Horizons

The material in the farewell discourses and in the concluding prayer in John 17 is complex and requires careful handling as one attempts to bring it forward into a modern context. For example, this material is not really very good source material for a minister to use in preaching a farewell sermon to a congregation she or he is leaving after a fruitful time of service. This is so because of course the minister is not Jesus, and the leaving of the minister by no means has the same consequences as Christ's return to heaven. A more apt and usable analogy can be found in Paul's farewell speech in Acts 20:17–38. I myself have tried this latter approach and found it to be a plausible way to deal with a situation of leaving.

Many have been tempted to take a thematic approach to the material in these chapters, since certain basic motifs recur throughout John 13—17. This is a manageable approach, but one should avoid the "word study" approach because terms such as "glory" in these chapters *develop* in meaning in these chapters or, better said, have more than one nuance, depending on the context.

F. Craddock suggests a gradual preaching through this material in its sequential order, without repeating themes unnecessarily, by picking distinctive verses in each discourse to focus on. The question that he urges us to ask of these texts in general is, "What does the departing Christ say to the church?"[76] It is appropriate to add that these chapters may be used to prepare and "steel" disciples for mission and ministry, but they are not intended to be used directly as evangelistic material—their primary audience is disciples, unlike much of the rest of the Gospel.

Another possible approach by which we can get from the first century to our setting is that of asking what concerns or problems are addressed in these texts that the church still must face. These would include the problem of disunity, the problem of evil and the need for protection from the evil one, the problem of knowing and then doing the truth, the problem of love, the meaning of dwelling in God and God dwelling in the church, and the problem of a hostile world resistant to the gospel.

Obviously another point of contact can be found in a meaningful series of sermons of teachings on the Paraclete, the Advocate. Here is not the place to discuss spiritual gifts in the mode of 1 Cor. 12—14. Rather, focus should be on the following roles of the Spirit: (1) The Spirit brings to mind in the believer what one needs to know to understand the Jesus tradition and to be an effective witness; (2) the Spirit through the believer can convict the world of its sin; (3) the Spirit does not draw attention to self but rather to Christ; (4) the Spirit does not offer so much new revelation as further understanding and a teasing out of the meaning of the old revelation; and (5) the Spirit is the conveyor of the divine Christ's presence to and in the believer.

If I am right in my exposition of the meaning of John 15:1–11, this material should *not* be used as fodder for polemics against Judaism, as the subject is not who are the true people of God but where is the locus of authentic revelation, namely, in Jesus who is said to be the authentic vine. A sober discussion of what branches being cut off might mean in terms of apostasy from the truth is also in order. The vine metaphor still works in our culture, since viticulture remains a major industry in this country. Nevertheless, it is good not to get sidetracked into long discussions of what the growing of grapes is actually like, for here the analogy is used as a mere taking-off point to discuss a very different subject—abiding in Christ by means of abiding in his word. The image of bearing fruit, however, has a certain amount of resilience to it as an image of successfully bearing witness as a means of "making disciples."

Particularly if one is dealing with John 14:1–2 a fruitful discussion could be engaged in comparing ancient and modern visions of what heaven is and will be like. In some ways this Gospel has more to say on that subject than any other book in the New Testament except perhaps Revelation. The image of Christ going to heaven to prepare a place for his followers is a pregnant one. Yet caution must also be urged, for it is as important what the text does not say as what it does say. For one thing, it does not really tell us much about what believers shall be doing in heaven. It also does not suggest a universalistic view of who will end up there. That there is plenty of room does not mean that Christ will have an equal number of takers on his offer of eternal life. Indeed, the contrast between the world that represents the majority and the believers who are a distinct minority suggests the contrary.

The cost of discipleship today is little different from what it was in the first century for the Johannine community *if* one lives in a place where Christians are a persecuted minority—for instance, in China or North Korea or in some predominantly fundamentalist Islamic countries today. But even apart from such settings the world's hatred of God's truth about human fallenness and the human need for redemption can be experienced in a variety of other settings as well.

Another cost of discipleship comes in the willingness not only to experience rejection due to one's witness but also to experience sorrow caused by the absence of Christ's bodily presence on earth. There are surely times when all of us have been in the position of reiterating the words of Martha, "Lord, if only you had been here, my —— would not have died." The life of faith then as now amounts to believing without seeing. The good news, however, is that this means, as John 20:29, the last blessing of the Gospel, affirms, that those who came to faith after the life of Jesus are more blessed with faith and spiritual strength than the first disciples needed to be. The danger of the first disciples ever assuming that they were just dreaming was much less great than it is for those of us who not only have never seen Jesus in person but have no clue what he looks like.[77]

Another fruitful sermon can be preached drawing on ancient Jewish and modern conceptions of what peace really amounts to, perhaps using the sort of peace talks that perennially go on in the Middle East as a jumping-off point. What sort of peace does Jesus leave his disciples and how does it differ from the peace the world can give?

Finally, the concept of glory that is found especially in the first and the last discourse, and its connection with dying, could be examined. The related concept of consecration and dedication could also be explored. How and in what contexts are glory and death intertwined in modern culture? How does Christ's vision of what amounts to glory differ?

One way that the material in this chapter has been used is in the ecumenical discussions about church unity and reunification. Jesus, however, is not here talking about the merger of denominational institutions but rather the spiritual unity between believing peoples. G. R. Beasley-Murray rightly stresses:

> Christians from Pentecost on are called to give expression to their unity in Christ, as truly as they are called to give expression to their new life in Christ, and in both cases this has to happen before the eyes of the world. . . . In the light of the divisions that have arisen between Christian churches through the centuries, it was inevitable that a movement should arise to call the churches to reverse the trends of the centuries and to seek to experience and express anew their unity in Christ. It was equally natural that this movement should begin within the missionary agencies of the churches . . . , since the divisions were hindering the carrying out of the missionary task; the nations frequently saw the reconciling power of the gospel less clearly than its divisive power. That the World Council of Churches in process of time has made mistakes, and at times even adopted policies that have alienated Christians rather than brought them closer together, is a reminder that churches are composed of sinners saved by grace, and sometimes the sins are more apparent among them than the grace. For this the churches and their agencies need to repent— again, and again, and again. But they also need to listen to the prayer of Jesus—again, and again, and again![78]

It is to be noticed that Christ prays for the spiritual unity of believers, he does not assume it is a given. It is something God-created and Spirit-sustained, but it can be put asunder by divisions, rivalries, factionalism, caucuses, and church splits.

Sometimes the first law of American Protestant ecclesiology seems to have been "Thou shalt divide and multiply." This is not by any means necessarily a good thing. There is always a tension in the church between unity among believers and truth as it is understood and held by believers. Protestantism has tended to hold up Truth, with a capital *T*, while intoning unity with a lowercase *u*, with the end result that Protestant churches and denominations have proved endlessly divisive and factious. On the other hand, Catholicism and Orthodoxy have held up Unity with a capital *U*, and at least from a Protestant viewpoint this has been at the expense of Truth. In other words, no part of the church has adequately gotten the balance between truth and unity right, it would seem. It is indeed a poor witness to the truth when the churches cannot even get their act together enough to agree on the fundamentals of what the truth in and about Christ amounts to. If one finds one particular denominational version of the gospel too unsettling, one may choose from a smorgasbord of other interpretations and approaches. The material in the farewell discourses encourages us to wrestle once more with what really amounts to truth and unity in Christ and what we as the people of God who must bear witness to the world with one accord and one voice should say.

These discourses also raise disturbing questions of whether the theology of denominationalism, which, after all, is a late invention caused originally by the Protestant Reformation, is biblically valid and whether the modern ecumenical movement is the way to bring about church unity. Or should a more grassroots movement inspired by the Spirit be encouraged from the local church level up rather than from the top of the institutional church down? Perhaps a small parable is in order.

I was once sitting at an annual conference meeting of my denomination at Lake Junaluska, North Carolina. While the discussion was being carried on in the open-air auditorium about church growth and unity and elaborate plans that were being made to build new churches, I noticed a man rowing a sailboat down the lake, for there was not a breath of wind. Too often that seems to be the church's approach to efforts at growth or church unity. We are like a boater with no wind in his sail who has resorted to paddling out of frustration. It is assumed that if we just plan hard enough and work hard enough, the ends we desire will be achieved. It seems to me that we should first have held some prayer meetings and consecrated ourselves to the task and received power from on high for its implementation.

Jesus here resorts to prayer and to imploring God as both Father and Spirit to bring about the ends he desires for his disciples. Historically too, most great revivals have begun with extensive, sometimes even worldwide commitments to wrestling in prayer with God to discern the divine will and call down the divine power and activity into our midst.[79] Here at least is the proper place to start, although it does not mean that we should end there without planning and human efforts to carry out God's will. "Prayer is the price of power, and the church of Jesus Christ is not likely to recover its lost authority until this basic biblical truth is recovered."[80]

In the end Jesus' farewell turns out to be a wish that the disciples will fare well, not so much a final parting or good-bye. This is so because, as the discourses make clear, Christ comes to us again, only now in and by means of the person of the Holy Spirit. He has not left us orphaned in the world, or at the mercy of this world's ruler. Rather, he has overcome the world's great threat and power—the power of death. Those who know that death does not stop eternal life can live as people with unconquerable spirits.

Since the narrative of the life of Jesus is drawing to a close, it is appropriate for us to notice that God does not call us, any more than he called Jesus, to do everything for the world or for the church. Ministers are apt to run around trying to be all things to all people, and to do all the ministry, rather than to equip other saints for ministerial tasks and to hone in on what God has given one to do in particular. Jesus knew what it meant to have single-minded devotion to a particular task.

Geographically his whole career was confined within the [general region of] Palestine. He never saw Rome, or Athens, or Alexandria, to say nothing of the further flung lands of the globe. His ministry was circumscribed also in terms of his life experience. He never knew the intimacies of marriage, the struggles of parenthood, the challenges of middle age, or the limitations of aging. Even within the sphere of his teaching and healing ministry, there were multitudes of his needy contemporaries in Palestine to whom he never ministered, whether in word or deed. Yet his ministry was perfect and whole, because he did, with complete and single-minded dedication, "all that he has given me to do." . . . A similar limitation rests on every disciple. . . . There is a specific work for us to do, and in finding and doing that specific thing to the limits of our powers lies our fulfillment, and our peace.[81]

The issue of sectarianism always arises in the discussion of John 13—17, and it is appropriate to say something about it at this juncture. Clearly enough from the Johannine epistles, the Johannine community was a minority group that experienced internal problems having to do with Christology and matters of leadership. It seems equally likely that John 13—17 is written in a context where Jesus' warning about future persecutions was coming true for the Johannine Christians. In such a milieu it is hardly surprising that a certain "we" versus "they" mentality is reflected in this material. Nevertheless, the material, especially toward its conclusion in John 16 and in the prayer in John 17, reflects the fact that the Johannine community understood that it was of necessity part of a missionary movement and that it must carry on the missionary task *without giving up its essential christological identity.*

When we examine modern sectarian communities we notice that there are some characteristics that they share in common with the Johannine community, in particular the "we" versus "they" mentality. However, when we are using this text today, remember that the antagonism reflected in the text is due to persecution, *not to the belief structure of the group.* In the case of modern christological heresies such as the beliefs of Jehovah's Witnesses, it is the belief structure itself that creates the "we"/"they" mentality, not personal suffering. By contrast, the belief structure of early Johannine Christianity basically was inclusive rather than exclusive in character, not only because it was missionary in nature but also because it understood that God sent Christ to manifest divine love for the world. The important conclusion for the modern church is: There is no reason why it cannot adopt and adapt the belief structure manifested in this document, the Christocentric view of God coupled with a missionary view of discipleship, *without becoming a sectarian group of its own devising,* in any negative sense of the term "sectarian." A Johannine sort of sectarianism may and does happen to the modern church when it endures ongoing persecution for its faith from the dominant culture. We are not called upon to inculcate a hatred for the world in this literature, but on the other hand we are warned that such may happen to us in a world increasingly hostile to orthodox Christianity.

Part V. The Passion Narrative
Phase Two (John 18:1–19:42)

16. The Arrest and Trial
of Jesus (John 18:1–19:16a)

When we arrive at John 18 we return to the narrative of the events of Passion Week. It is crucial from the outset to stress that if it had been a major agenda to fix blame almost solely on the Jews for the crucifixion of Jesus, the material we are about to investigate would have been presented very differently. In the Johannine presentation of things no trial before the Sanhedrin is mentioned at all; rather, the pretrial hearing(s) before Annas and then Caiaphas is followed by the delivery of Jesus over to Pilate for judgment. Not only so, but it is in *this* Gospel that we are told plainly that the "Jews" admitted "We are not permitted to put anyone to death" (18:31). Attempts to present this Gospel as an anti-Semitic tract founder on the hard rocks of the Passion narrative. In this Gospel, as in the Synoptics, while it can be argued that some Jews, particularly some priestly officials, precipitated a Roman trial and strongly lobbied for Jesus' execution (cf. 19:15–16), it seems clear enough even in this Gospel that Jesus is executed by Romans (cf. 19:16, 23, 25). Crucifixion was not a Jewish means of punishment. Perhaps because a trial before the Sanhedrin did not in fact decide the issue, while the trial before Pilate did, the evangelist has simply left out the earlier trial.

It is understandable in a Gospel meant to be used for missionary purposes, including use with Gentiles in Asia Minor, that an explanation had to be given as to how the Gentile authorities ended up executing Jesus. The portrait painted is that of a Pilate under severe duress, indeed, according to 19:12, in danger of losing his favored status as an *amicus Caesaris* ("friend of Caesar") if another complaint was lodged against him by those whom he ruled, and thus acting in his own best interests in executing Jesus. In short, the portrait is of a miscarriage of Roman justice, which thereby exonerates the system, while indicating the weakness of the particular official. Jesus is portrayed as being no obvious threat to Rome's territorial claims—his kingdom is not of this world. This sort of portrait was not likely to get a Christian witness in trouble with the authorities in Asia Minor, as the corruption of various officials from time to time was a recognized fact of life. The evangelist's overriding concern is to portray Jesus' arrest and trial as something that Jesus himself and/or the Father is ultimately in charge of.

EXCURSUS: PILATE AND THE ROMAN TRIAL

Pontius Pilate became prefect of Judea in A.D. 26. His proper title, as a Caesarea Maritima inscription shows, was prefect, not procurator. Pilate was an appointee of Tiberius, but no doubt through the advice of Sejanus, the regional Roman official who pursued a clearly anti-Jewish policy. Josephus tells us two stories that strongly suggest that Pilate himself had no great sensitivity to Jewish religious sensibilities. The first is the story of Pilate attempting to install images (Roman standards with images of Caesar) in Jerusalem (cf. Josephus *Ant.* 18.3.1; *War* 2.9.2–3). He refused to remove them when the Jewish protest came, until it became clear that the people were willing to die rather than have the images in the Holy City in apparent violation of the Ten Commandments. Later in his tenure, Pilate took money from the Corban fund in the Temple to build an aqueduct. This time when a protest arose he had his men beat the opposition into submission with clubs. Luke 13:1 in addition mentions the slaughtering of Galileans by Pilate apparently when they were sacrificing in Jerusalem. None of this suggests a man likely to be very sympathetic to Jewish concerns.

Pilate's position when Jesus came to trial may have been more tenuous than in earlier days, because of the demise of Sejanus, his ally. This may explain why he was susceptible to the *amicus Caesaris* cry finally. After the demise of Sejanus, Tiberius seemingly no longer sanctioned an openly anti-Semitic policy. Pilate knew the Jewish authorities could send a delegation to the emperor and get him in hot water. Josephus tells us that Pilate inflicted the punishment of the cross on Jesus (*Ant.* 18.63–64). It is uncertain whether the original text of Josephus also had the bit about "on the indictment of our chief men," in view of the evidence of Christian interpolations elsewhere in Josephus.

Pilate as the prefect of a Roman province possessed what was called the full *imperium,* which included criminal, jurisdictional, and military authority, and the power to levy taxes. His jurisdiction was directly from the emperor and could not be delegated in capital cases. The only limitation on his power was the Roman law against extortion. Pilate's power in a criminal case was called *coertio* if it dealt with certain public crimes (e.g., adultery, forgery, murder, bribery, and treason). Anything that fell outside this list came under what was called personal *cognitio,* and the punishments inflicted under the latter were *extra ordinem.* A. N. Sherwin-White argues that in the case of Jesus the latter procedure was involved.[1] In Roman trials there were no juries, but there were counselors or advocates. There had to be a formulation of charges by accusers, and then by the judge who also formulated the penalties. The judgment could be handed down publicly *pro tribunali,* as in the case of Jesus, or privately in chambers. Matthew 27:19 indicates that Pilate sat on the *bema* (judgment platform and seat) to pronounce judgment in Jesus' case. In a Roman trial the accusers would allege facts, and the judge would attempt to see what to make of them in part by inquiring of the accused in regard to various matters. There were no lawyers or witnesses for the defense for such a trial. When the accused was found guilty, one or another degree of beating/scourging normally accompanied the main punishment, but it was not usually considered a punishment in and of itself.

The portrayal of Pilate in the Gospels is of a cynical and vacillating official who on the one hand strongly suspects an ulterior and false motive on the part of those who were trying to get Jesus crucified, and who, perhaps because of his dislike for the Jewish officials, tries to get Jesus off with little or no punishment other than a light scourging. J. Blinzler suggests that both Philo and Josephus are rather too strongly negative in their portrayal of Pilate but that nonetheless Pilate probably tried to be fair to Jesus just to gall or frustrate the designs of the high priest and the hierarchy.[2] Evidently he did not like being used. The Fourth Evangelist, in typical Johannine fashion, presents us with a lengthy dialogue between Jesus and Pilate. It may well be that the restraint in the portrayal of Pilate in the Gospels is in part due to the attempt not to inflame Romans against the already suspect religion of Christianity.

In view of the dialogue between Jesus and Pilate, and especially the first question he asks Jesus in all four Gospels, "Are you the King of the Jews?" (Mark 15:2 and pars.), it appears clear that Pilate had been informed by the chief priests and elders that this was the accusation against Jesus. They had couched it in these terms so that a political and capital crime would appear to be at issue. Such a charge, if it could be made to stick, would amount to high treason and would be likely to lead to execution. Only Luke 23:2 gives us details of the Jewish charges that were presented to Pilate. The first two, stirring up the people and forbidding the paying of taxes to Caesar, are not taken up in what follows. The crucial charge is about being King of the Jews.

It would seem that Pilate was somewhat baffled by Jesus' failure to defend himself, which was normally the only way an accused would be defended. In what follows we see a series of moves by which Pilate tries to avoid or delay giving the Jewish authorities what they press for. Pilate finally gives in only when the crowd cries for Jesus' execution.

There are several aspects of the trial before Pilate, at least in its last stages, that have been thought to be suspect. One is the offer of release of a prisoner at feast time, and the other is the acceding to the crowd's wishes in a capital matter. In regard to the former matter, Blinzler points to *m. Pesah.* 8:6a, where it may suggest that it was a custom to release a prisoner at feast time just before the Passover meal would be eaten.[3] Perhaps more apt is the parallel in *P. Flor.* 61:59ff. (A.D. 85) in which the Roman governor of Egypt says to a certain prisoner that instead of scourging him he will give him to the people.

In Roman law there were two possible forms of amnesty, the *abolitio*, releasing a prisoner not yet condemned, and the *indulgentia*, giving amnesty to a condemned criminal. It appears that the former would apply in Jesus' case. All four Gospels mention this paschal amnesty custom, and so it should not be quickly dismissed as unhistorical. Once Pilate had consulted the crowd about the amnesty, it was a natural, if irregular, sequel to ask them what to do with Jesus, since he had expected them to clamor for Jesus' release. Even then Pilate tries to forestall the cry of the crowd (which apparently had been stirred up by the Jewish officials, or perhaps consisted of their entourage and dependents), but finally to no avail. The cry of *amicus Caesaris* is quite believable and may have been the final straw that broke down Pilate's resistance to executing Jesus.

As a theological footnote it should be clear that Pilate did not think Jesus was guilty of the crime of high treason. Thus his death is rightly termed a judicial murder, not merely a just execution of a criminal. That Jesus claimed that his kingdom was not of this world to Pilate was in itself ambiguous. It probably meant that it had not come from this world, not that it did not exist in this world or did not have this-worldly implications and effects. This may be Johannine theologizing, but it is possible on Jesus' lips. Jesus himself gave no encouragement to Pilate to condemn him.

One further matter to be considered is the troops to whom Pilate finally handed Jesus over. John 19:23 suggests that Jesus was handed over to a centurion with four of his underlings. Prefects did not have any regular Roman troops at their command, no legions but only auxiliary troops, recruited from the non-Jewish inhabitants of Palestine (i.e., Samaritans and Syrians in the main, people definitely at odds with the Jews). This raises the question of whether the centurion at the cross might have been a Samaritan who knew Jewish traditions about Messiah and might have been in a position to really utter something such as "Surely this was the Son of God." This sort of cry is surely much more likely on Semitic lips than on the lips of a Gentile pagan soldier, unless Luke's wording is the original here: "Surely this was a righteous man."

Pilate remained in office in Palestine until A.D. 37, when he was recalled because of mishandling yet another religious incident, this time involving Jews and Samaritans. None of the extant sources suggest a flattering picture of Pilate, or a picture of a man sensitive to other people's religious convictions. The Johannine characterization of this man is aptly summed up by A. Culpepper: "Like other characters caught between the Jews and Jesus (principally Nicodemus, the lame man, and the blind man), Pilate is a study in the impossibility of compromise, the inevitability of decision, and the consequences of each alternative. In the end, although he seems to glimpse the truth, a decision in Jesus' favor proves too costly for him. In this maneuver to force the reader to a decision regarding Jesus, the evangelist exposes the consequences of attempting to avoid a decision. Pilate represents the futility of compromise."[4] In other words, Pilate is yet another object lesson in this Gospel, meant to make the uncommitted commit themselves. This narrative too reflects a missionary agenda.

18:1 After Jesus had spoken these words, he went out with his disciples across the Kidron valley to a place where there was a garden, which he and his disciples entered. ²Now Judas, who betrayed him, also knew the place, because Jesus often met there with his disciples. ³So Judas brought a detachment of soldiers together with police from the chief priests and the Pharisees, and they came there with lanterns and torches and weapons. ⁴Then Jesus, knowing all that was to happen to him, came forward and asked them, "Whom are you looking for?" ⁵They answered, "Jesus of Nazareth." Jesus replied, "I am he." Judas, who betrayed him, was standing with them. ⁶When Jesus said to them, "I am he," they stepped back and fell to the ground. ⁷Again he asked them, "Whom are you looking for?" And they said, "Jesus of Nazareth." ⁸Jesus answered, "I told you that I am he. So if you are looking for me, let these men go." ⁹This was to fulfill the word that he had spoken, "I did not lose a single one of those whom you gave me." [10]Then Simon Peter, who had a sword, drew it, struck the high priest's slave, and cut off his right ear. The slave's name was Malchus. [11]Jesus said to Peter, "Put your sword back into its sheath. Am I not to drink the cup that the Father has given me?"

12 So the soldiers, their officer, and the Jewish police arrested Jesus and bound him. [13]First they took him to Annas, who was the father-in-law of Caiaphas, the high priest that year. [14]Caiaphas was the one who had advised the Jews that it was better to have one person die for the people.

15 Simon Peter and another disciple followed Jesus. Since that disciple was known to the high priest, he went with Jesus into the courtyard of the high priest, [16]but Peter was standing outside at the gate. So the other disciple, who was known to the high priest, went out, spoke to the woman who guarded the gate, and brought Peter in.[17]The woman said to Peter, "You are not also one of this man's disciples, are you?" He said, "I am not." [18]Now the slaves and the police had made a charcoal fire because it was cold, and they were standing around it and warming themselves. Peter also was standing with them and warming himself.

19 Then the high priest questioned Jesus about his disciples and about his teaching. [20]Jesus answered, "I have spoken openly to the world; I have always taught in synagogues and in the temple, where all the Jews come together. I have said nothing in secret. [21]Why do you ask me? Ask those who heard what I said to them; they know what I said." [22]When he had said this, one of the police standing nearby struck Jesus on the face, saying, "Is that how you answer the high priest?" [23]Jesus answered, "If I have spoken wrongly, testify to the wrong. But if I have spoken rightly, why do you strike me?" [24]Then Annas sent him bound to Caiaphas the high priest.

25 Now Simon Peter was standing and warming himself. They asked him, "You are not also one of his disciples, are you?" He denied it and said, "I am not." [26]One of the slaves of the high priest, a relative of the man whose ear Peter had cut off, asked, "Did I not see you in the garden with him?" [27]Again Peter denied it, and at that moment the cock crowed.

28 Then they took Jesus from Caiaphas to Pilate's headquarters. It was early in the morning. They themselves did not enter the headquarters, so as to avoid ritual defilement and to be able to eat the Passover. [29]So Pilate went out to them and said, "What accusation do you bring against this man?" [30]They answered, "If this man were not a criminal, we would not have handed him over to you." [31]Pilate said to them, "Take him yourselves and judge him according to your law." The Jews replied, "We are not permitted to put anyone to death." [32](This was to fulfill what Jesus had said when he indicated the kind of death he was to die.)

33 Then Pilate entered the headquarters again, summoned Jesus, and asked him, "Are you the King of the Jews?" [34]Jesus answered, "Do you ask this on your own, or did others tell you about me?" [35]Pilate replied, "I am not a Jew, am I? Your own nation and the chief priests have handed you over to me. What have you done?" [36]Jesus answered, "My kingdom is not from this world. If my kingdom were from this world, my followers would

be fighting to keep me from being handed over to the Jews. But as it is, my kingdom is not from here." [37]Pilate asked him, "So you are a king?" Jesus answered, "You say that I am a king. For this I was born, and for this I came into the world, to testify to the truth. Everyone who belongs to the truth listens to my voice." [38]Pilate asked him, "What is truth?"

After he had said this, he went out to the Jews again and told them, "I find no case against him. [39]But you have a custom that I release someone for you at the Passover. Do you want me to release for you the King of the Jews?" [40]They shouted in reply, "Not this man, but Barabbas!" Now Barabbas was a bandit.

19:1   Then Pilate took Jesus and had him flogged. [2]And the soldiers wove a crown of thorns and put it on his head, and they dressed him in a purple robe. [3]They kept coming up to him, saying, "Hail, King of the Jews!" and striking him on the face. [4]Pilate went out again and said to them, "Look, I am bringing him out to you to let you know that I find no case against him." [5]So Jesus came out, wearing the crown of thorns and the purple robe. Pilate said to them, "Here is the man!" [6]When the chief priests and the police saw him, they shouted, "Crucify him! Crucify him!" Pilate said to them, "Take him yourselves and crucify him; I find no case against him." [7]The Jews answered him, "We have a law, and according to that law he ought to die because he has claimed to be the Son of God."

8   Now when Pilate heard this, he was more afraid than ever. [9]He entered his headquarters again and asked Jesus, "Where are you from?" But Jesus gave him no answer. [10]Pilate therefore said to him, "Do you refuse to speak to me? Do you not know that I have power to release you, and power to crucify you?" [11]Jesus answered him, "You would have no power over me unless it had been given you from above; therefore the one who handed me over to you is guilty of a greater sin." [12]From then on Pilate tried to release him, but the Jews cried out, "If you release this man, you are no friend of the emperor. Everyone who claims to be a king sets himself against the emperor."

13   When Pilate heard these words, he brought Jesus outside and sat on the judge's bench at a place called The Stone Pavement, or in Hebrew Gabbatha. [14]Now it was the day of Preparation for the Passover; and it was about noon. He said to the Jews, "Here is your King!" [15]They cried out, "Away with him! Away with him! Crucify him!" Pilate asked them, "Shall I crucify your King?" The chief priests answered, "We have no king but the emperor." [16]Then he handed him over to them to be crucified.

I. The Historical Horizon

There is no escaping the impression that the Fourth Evangelist's source material is very different from that of the Synoptic writers, and there are some small telltale signs that suggest an eyewitness account (cf. below). Nevertheless, there are also some features of the account of the arrest and trial that make them very difficult for many scholars to accept as a historical account. Particularly difficult is the idea that two hundred or even six hundred Roman soldiers came to arrest Jesus, when no Roman soldiers are mentioned in the Synoptics, and one would think this would be hard to omit or overlook. Also difficult is the idea that the soldiers fell to the ground when Jesus said, "I am." We will deal with these difficulties when we come to them in the text, but for now it is sufficient to point out that we have already seen this evangelist's flair for drama and the dramatic portrayal of the life of Jesus, and this may in part explain such features.

The following distinct omissions of the arrest narrative should be kept in mind: (1) there is no betrayal with a kiss; (2) there is no agony in the Garden of Gethsemane; (3) there are no sleepy disciples; (4) there is no healing of the servant's ear (cf. Luke); and (5) there is no hint that Jesus was tempted not to go the route of the cross. Instead, in v. 11 we have a saying indicating that Jesus recognized he must drink the cup. The overall impression of the arrest scene is of a divine Jesus who overwhelms his supposedly powerful adversary by a mere repetition of the divine name. Jesus is not at the mercy of the Romans but in control of his own destiny, and he is even able to rescue his disciples from a similar fate by commanding his foes to "let these men go." Without question, the Fourth Evangelist has chosen to emphasize the divine Jesus at this juncture, while the Synoptics reveal Jesus at his most human here, asking for the cup to pass if possible.

One of the most interesting facts we learn from the presentation in this Gospel is that these events very likely happened in late winter. We are told at 18:18 that it was cold at night, hence the charcoal fire, but even more telling is that at 18:1 we are told they crossed "the winter torrent of the Kidron," a brook that has water only during the rainy winter season.[5] Only the Fourth Gospel tells us there was a garden the disciples entered with Jesus, and it is only in the Fourth Gospel that we are told how Judas knew where to find Jesus and the disciples—it was a place where they frequently met together. This suggests a frequency of Jesus and the disciples in Jerusalem not hinted at in the Synoptics.

At 18:3 we get the impression that Judas is the instigator of this attempt to capture Jesus, although, as R. E. Brown says, the text may mean only that he was the guide to the garden.[6] Who came with him? Two groups of people are mentioned—the temple police of the priest and the Pharisees but also a band of soldiers. *Speiran* normally means a cohort, the tenth part of a Roman legion, or six hundred men. Occasionally the term *speiran* refers to as few troops as a maniple, or two hundred men. The term *speiran* is not a synonym for "the police"; it is a technical military term for a specific number of Roman troops. Brown suggests that Pilate, being edgy and fearing an insurrection during the feast, may have sent a large contingent of troops. This is plausible if this event happened shortly after Jesus' triumphal entry and cleansing of the Temple, both of which would have been seen as political actions.[7] Acts 23:23 suggests that sometimes Romans could use a large number of troops for a small task, perhaps because they did not know the magnitude of the task or of Jesus' following. There is, however, another explanation.

The Fourth Evangelist may be trying to dramatize the magnitude of the forces of darkness set against Jesus. Notice that they come carrying torches in the darkness, something mentioned only in the Fourth Gospel. The opposition was large, in the dark, but it was they who were about to be overwhelmed by the words of the Word.

At v. 4 we are told that Jesus knew very well what was about to transpire. Whatever other limitations there may have been to Jesus' knowledge, this Gospel stresses that Jesus knew his destiny well before it transpired (cf. 13:1, 3; 19:28). He is not caught by surprise by the timing and manner of his death. In this same verse we are told that Jesus takes the initiative. He comes forward and asks twice, "Whom do you seek?" When they respond, "Jesus of Nazareth," Jesus says, "*Ego eimi*," which means either "I am he" or "I am." We have seen both of these meanings for this phrase earlier in the Gospel.[8] Here some aspects of the context suggest the same thing that John 8:24, 28, 58 does—that a theophanic or divine formula is involved. Only so can the reaction of the soldiers be explained. They backed up and fell to the ground. This may also be said to be a pictorial fulfillment of Ps. 27:2: "When evildoers assail me to devour my flesh—my adversaries and foes—they shall stumble and fall." In view of the stress on the fulfillment of scripture elsewhere in this Passion narrative, this allusion is quite possible. On the other hand, the same phrase, *ego eimi* in v. 8, used again in *response* to the information that they are seeking Jesus of Nazareth, appears to mean "I am he." Perhaps the usage here is yet another example of Johannine double-entendre.

At v. 9 we find a striking phenomenon. A formula quotation used elsewhere in the Gospels only to introduce a quotation from the Old Testament is now used to introduce the words of Jesus, which have already been quoted earlier in this Gospel in the sage's prayer (cf. John 17:12). We will find this same phenomenon again at John 18:32. What this surely implies is that by the time this Gospel was being assembled in the last decade of the first century Jesus' words were already put on a level with the Word of God. It is hardly surprising that we find this phenomenon in this Gospel where Jesus is portrayed as God's Word and Wisdom, the very expression of the mind of God. Notice that already in John 1:17 Jesus' words are said to surpass Torah, and elsewhere that they come from God (17:8).

Jesus rescues his disciples from suffering a fate similar to his by both boldly surrendering and then telling his adversaries to let the disciples go, again a clear sign that he is in charge of this whole affair. Jesus' intention to surrender to the foe is misread or not accepted by Peter, who lops off the ear of the slave of the high priest. Only in this Gospel are we told that his name was Malchus and that it was Peter who did this act. Redaction critics have taken this as a sign of the lateness of this material, based on the assumption that early Christian scribes and writers tended to add names to the nameless as the tradition was handed down. While this tendency is sometimes in evidence in the handling of the Gospel tradition, the generalization of some more specific narratives is also seen in the tradition, as E. P. Sanders has demonstrated.[9] In other words, that we have names in the Johannine account but not in the Synoptic account of this story cannot necessarily be put down to a tendency to give names to the nameless. This may be a telltale sign that we have here an eyewitness account of the Beloved Disciple, who, we learn in v. 16, is known to the high priest and thus could have known his servant's name. Jesus tells Peter to put his sword, or more likely dagger, back into its holder. Jesus must drink the cup the Father wishes him to drink. Thus far, the account would seem to have a rather clear significance especially for Gentiles concerned to see how Jesus related to the governing Roman authorities in the empire. We see a Jesus who respects their authority, and authorities who are impressed by and even fall down before Jesus when he identifies himself. Equally clear is the message that Jesus does not condone the use of force against any authorities or their representatives, even against the high priest's slave. We will shortly hear of the head Gentile authority and how he tries repeatedly to avoid doing away with Jesus.

According to v. 12, Jesus is arrested, bound, and taken first to Annas, the father-in-law of Caiaphas the high priest, who may be thought of as the power behind the authority of Caiaphas. He had been the high priest between A.D. 6 and 15,[10] and he remained powerful because all of his five sons eventually became high priests. This family was noted for its greed, its wealth and power, and recent archaeological reports from Jerusalem inform us that the family tomb, including the burial location of Caiaphas himself, has been found. It is important to bear in mind that a high priest, even out of office, retained his obligations and a certain amount of his respect and authority,[11] especially because in Jewish thinking, although Romans might remove someone from office, a person was appointed high priest for life. This of course makes all the more deliberately ironic the remark found again here as well as before in 11:49 that Caiaphas was high priest "that year." This reflects the tenuousness of Jewish power under Roman rule and may be a not so subtle put-down of the Jewish authorities behind the plot to have Jesus executed, who saw themselves as powerful people but in fact were also under someone else's thumb. This impression that the evangelist is being ironic here is only confirmed by the later cry of the crowd in 19:15, "We have no king but Caesar." In other words, for Jewish officials and people to get their way in such a matter they had to renounce their own hegemony over the land and its people.

Verse 14 reminds the reader that Caiaphas was the one earlier spoken of as making a prophetic announcement about the necessity of Jesus' death (cf. 11:50–51). This reflection backward in the text suggests an audience not readily familiar with the cast of characters in the story, perhaps an audience that will not have heard *this* story at the same sitting at which they had heard the story in John 11 that involved Caiaphas, and finally it may also be that this is a hint that this Gospel was written to be read as well, with reminders in the text to first-time readers to think back to what they had earlier read.

In John 18:15–27 we have the technique called intercalation, where one piece of story is inserted between two pieces of a related story.[12] We are told of Peter and one "other disciple."[13] In light of John 20:2 where the identification of the other disciple is made clear, it is likely that here as well the anonymous disciple is none other than the Beloved Disciple. Several points are in order here. If he was a Judean and even a Jerusalem disciple of Jesus known to the high priest, it is likely that he knew the location where the high priest lived as well as other important locations in Jerusalem, such as where the family garden tomb of Joseph of Arimathea would be. This would explain Peter's following him to the tomb and going with him to the courtyard of the high priest. They would be representatives of the Galilean and Judean disciples respectively, with the Beloved Disciple being more familiar with the area. Then too, the presence of the Beloved Disciple as the only male disciple said to be at the death of Jesus may suggest connections in Jerusalem, because normally only family members were likely to be allowed near the guarded cross of an executed man (cf. below). One gets the feeling, especially from John 13 on, that we are being told the story by an eyewitness with a Judean and Jerusalem perspective, and it is no accident that it is not until John 13 that the Beloved Disciple clearly emerges in the text. From then on, the rest of the story until the epilogue is clearly situated in Jerusalem.

The other disciple is even said at v. 15 to go into the courtyard of the high priest *with* Jesus, while Peter stands outside the gate. The other disciple speaks to the woman guarding the gate and brings Peter in, again suggesting both familiarity and some recognized authority in this situation in Jerusalem. Is it really plausible that a Galilean fisherman would have had this sort of intimacy with the high priest and respect among his household servants?[14] We may perhaps read some reluctance on Peter's part to come this close to the authorities in this portrayal, not least because he had just attacked the high priest's slave. Verse 17 suggests that the other disciple was known to be a follower of Jesus, for the woman asks Peter, "You are not *also* one of this man's disciples, are you?" The response provides the first denial by Peter. His "I am not" may be seen as the opposite of Jesus' "*Ego eimi.*" Jesus affirms his own identity in defense of his disciples, while Peter denies his own identity in defense of himself.[15] Verse 18 groups Peter with the slaves and temple police warming himself by a charcoal fire in the courtyard because it was cold that night. This may contribute to the symbolic quality of the narrative—Peter is in the dark and the cold associating with Jesus' captors and denying his own identity and allegiance to Jesus.

The second scene in this miniature drama is found in vv. 19–24 and consists of Jesus' dialogue with Annas. If the Beloved Disciple was present or nearby, he may have overheard this exchange. We are told that Jesus is first questioned about his disciples and about his teaching. Note that Jesus says nothing about his disciples, perhaps to protect them.[16] Jesus' response is that he has given his basic teaching in public places such as synagogues and the Temple: Do nothing in secret. So he suggests they ask those who had heard him. This is taken to be a flippant or disrespectful remark, and so

Jesus is slapped by one of the "temple" police who remarks rhetorically, "Is that how you answer the high priest?" In fact, if these proceedings were proper Jewish ones, the defendant would not be the one questioned but rather the witnesses, for this was the normal Jewish trial procedure. Jesus says that if he has spoken wrongly, then testimony should be presented about this wrong. The language of a trial is used here, even if this is but a pretrial hearing. On the other hand, says Jesus, "If I have spoken rightly, why have you struck me?" This leads to Jesus' being bound and sent off to the de facto high priest, Caiaphas. Of the conversation with the latter we hear nothing. The point the evangelist seems to be making is that these exchanges with the Jews settled nothing, and thus they are not given more space.

This episode is followed by a return to the denials by Peter, where Peter again denies being one of Jesus' followers, and then he is confronted by a relative of Malchus who seems to have seen Peter in the garden, and this time Peter denies having been with Jesus. It is at this juncture, and only at this juncture, that we are told the cock crowed. Jesus confronts his critics denying nothing, Peter wilts before his inquisitors denying everything.[17]

The trial narrative proper begins at 18:28 and carries on until 19:16. It is on this sequence of events that the evangelist wishes to place the major stress. The presentation of the dialogue between Jesus and Pilate is masterful and can be divided into seven scenes (cf. below), alternating between scenes inside and scenes outside. Great care has been taken in the presentation of this material. Many scholars have pointed out that this account seems to manifest the most clear understanding of the pre-70 A.D. power and authority structures that operated in Judea and gives the most plausible rationale for Roman authorities' being the ones who ended up executing Jesus. "John's account of the trial is the most consistent and intelligible we have. Only John makes it clear why Jesus was brought to Pilate in the first place and why Pilate gave in and had Jesus crucified."[18] We are told that the encounter between Jesus and Pilate took place at the Praetorium, which seems more likely to have been not at or next to the Antonia Fortress but rather at the Herodian palace on the western hill near the modern Jaffa Gate. We are told that, to avoid uncleanness, the Jews do not enter this locale. Pilate must come out to deal with the matter, and he asks what accusation is brought against Jesus (v. 29). It appears that the Jewish authorities assumed that Pilate would cooperate and simply execute this man without further delay or due process of law, because their response is defense and has overtones of irritation: "If he were not a wrongdoer, we would not have delivered him to you." This claim of mere wrongdoing in itself was hardly sufficient in Pilate's mind to warrant his action.[19] The Jewish authorities for their part take umbrage that their condemnation and judgment of Jesus are seemingly not enough to get Pilate to proceed directly to the desired execution.[20]

The irony in this series of scenes becomes thicker and thicker. These Jewish officials have no scruples about doing away with an innocent man and morally defiling themselves, especially a man who turns out to *be* the

Passover lamb for humankind, but they are very particular about avoiding ritual uncleanness so that they may partake of the Passover. Jesus is even slaughtered on the day the Passover lambs were to be slaughtered. The term the "Jews" normally refers to Jewish authorities, but on the lips of Pilate when he uses the phrase "the King of the Jews" it has a more normal generic sense.

The story indicates that only some Jews were involved in this miscarriage of justice, although 18:35 indicates that an official action had taken place— the nation and the Jewish officials, including the high priest, had handed over Jesus to the Roman authorities. The fact that no witnesses are called by Pilate, among other factors, suggests to most scholars that despite the fact that the Fourth Evangelist does not tell us this, Jesus has already been officially condemned by the Jewish authorities and so stands before Pilate as a culprit, an already judged felon.[21] The course of Pilate's dialogue with Jesus also suggests this, for he alludes to an earlier discussion before the Jewish authorities and the accusations raised in that context (cf. 18:33b).

Pilate is clearly not interested in being enmeshed in a purely religious squabble, but if Jesus' claims are such that they have clear implications of a political nature, namely, if his claiming to be King of the Jews has a social and political component, then Jesus could be charged with treason, a conspiring against the existing ruling powers, including Tiberius Caesar himself. One possible reading of the data in all the Gospels is that in the Jewish trial the issue became whether Jesus not merely acted against the heart of the law (circumcision, ritual purity laws, keeping of the Sabbath, the Temple and its apparatus) but also claimed to be messiah/*christos* in some blasphemous way.[22] When he was condemned by that body for such a claim, the results of such a trial were then couched in terms that suggested a strong political claim—Jesus claimed to be a *basileus*, a king of the Jews, as, for instance, Herod the Great was at the time of Jesus' birth.[23] There would be a certain naturalness in this way of proceeding, since messiah was widely expected to be "great David's greater Son," and thus a king of some sort (cf. *Pss. Sol.* 17). "If, then, there is a connection between the Sanhedrin investigation and the one carried out by Pilate, the link must be found in the question with which the Roman prefect, according to the reports of all four Gospels, started his interrogation, the question of Jesus's kingship."[24] Notice that Jesus only indirectly admits his kingship. At v. 37 he says, "You say I am a king," although he has previously admitted to having a kingdom (v. 36).

It was normal procedure in Roman jurisprudence for the defendant to defend himself. A confession would be invoked, and it can be seen in the proceedings in John 18—19 that Pilate is trying to make Jesus give an innocent interpretation to the charge against him. Jesus' fundamental silence about the main issue puzzles Pilate, because it was the normal procedure for a person to do all he could to exonerate himself, since there were no attorneys for the defense. Pilate attempts to hand Jesus back over to the Jewish authorities and have them judge him. They reply that they do not any longer have the power of capital punishment,[25] which is historically believable considering that the Romans liked to have the control of executions in their territory.[26]

Jesus' asking Pilate in v. 34 whether he was prompted to ask about Jesus' being a king by someone else or whether it was his own idea is important. Jesus here is following normal and expected Jewish procedure. If Pilate says he heard this from Jewish authorities, which he does (v. 35), then Jesus as a loyal Jew was expected to say nothing against his fellow Jews in a Gentile court (cf. 1 Cor. 6:1ff.). Even at the brink of death, Jesus shows more concern for others than for himself, even for the Jewish authorities as well as for his own followers.

Notice that in vv. 34–35 the inquisitor becomes the one put on trial, on the spot. Pilate's response, "Am I a Jew?" sounds like the words of an exasperated man who thought he was in charge and now things are getting out of hand. He is not really personally but only officially interested in the answer of whether Jesus is indeed the King of the Jews. As such, he is portrayed as a Gentile giving the wrong sort of response to the Christ and the witness about Jesus.

The defense of the disciples in v. 36a is also a crucial element in the story. Jesus is stressing that they are not revolutionaries and would not fight for his kingdom. This may have been an especially important testimony to avoid prosecution against the disciples, in particular against Peter for the action taken against Malchus. It is also possible to see Jesus' claim that his "kingdom is not from this world" as an attempt to protect his disciples from charges rather than to exonerate himself.

Verse 36 is also important because it reveals something about Jesus' kingdom. Jesus is *not* saying that his kingdom is not *in* this world. Rather, he is speaking about the source and thus about the nature of his kingdom. It is not a worldly political kingdom in origin or character. That it is not "of this *kosmos*" means it has not been dreamed up or built up by humanity, and since *kosmos* in this Gospel generally means fallen humanity organized against God,[27] the meaning is likely to be that Jesus' kingdom and movement are not another political scheme of fallen human beings to establish their own sovereignty in the world. It is not surprising, then, that Jesus' response to any direct question about being King of the Jews is evasive. Indirection was in any case typical of a Jewish sage like Jesus.

It will be seen from Jesus' reply in v. 37 that he is not much interested in the title of king; rather, he prefers to speak of himself as a sent one or the agent of God born to bear witness to the truth, not born to make worldly claims about himself. Such claims were at the very least not wholly appropriate, because of the way they would ordinarily be understood. The height of irony in the story is reached when Jesus is in fact crucified as "King of the Jews" (cf. below).

At this juncture Pilate seems to assume that the conversation has turned philosophical and so he asks, "What is truth?" The question may or may not reflect the cynicism of Pilate about this whole proceeding, or perhaps about

Jewish messianic claims. We are then led to think that this more philosophical turn in the dialogue has led Pilate to conclude that Jesus is surely no
threat to society, and not worthy of execution: "I find no fault [i.e., nothing
legally blameworthy] in him" (v. 38). Pilate is shown not to be a real truth
seeker; indeed, the real irony is that he does not perceive truth with a capital *T* when he is standing right before him in the flesh. The question, "What
is truth," should have been, "Who is the truth?"[28] Apparently Pilate concludes that Jesus is a deluded quack whom he can banter with but not take
seriously. This in turn leads to the mockery of Jesus in short order.

After this exchange Pilate offers a choice between Jesus and Barabbas (v.
39). "The suggestion is only meaningful if the two persons were understood
to represent different aims and stand-points."[29] In other words, in Pilate's
eyes Jesus was surely no revolutionary, unlike Barabbas. The historical likelihood of the custom referred to in v. 39 of releasing a prisoner at the feast
has been endlessly debated by scholars. As E. Bammel says, this custom
makes good historical sense—"one prisoner is released in remembrance of
Israel's salvation from Egypt."[30] It may be related to the Jewish practice that
we do have some record of elsewhere of Jews buying their fellow Jews out of
bondage during Passover as a way of tangibly commemorating the Passover.[31] It also makes general sense in light of the custom of Roman authorities' dispensing amnesty of various sorts at feasts.[32] Pilate, however, mis-
gauges the mood of the "Jews," perhaps here the Jewish officials and a crowd
of their adherents, for they clamor for Barabbas.

Pilate then has Jesus scourged, perhaps hoping this will placate the audience (18:40b). It was a vain hope, not least because Pilate also mocked their
messianic hopes by dressing Jesus up in a royal purple robe and a mock
crown, made of thorns, and derisively hailing Jesus King of the Jews. Jesus
is also struck in the face, adding further insult to injury. It is generally
thought that the severe scourging of Jesus, probably with a cat-o'-nine-tails,
which had hooks and would rip the flesh off a person, is what caused him to
expire so quickly on the cross.[33]

If there was sarcasm and irony before, this is all the more so by the time
we reach John 19. Pilate a second time goes forth to say he finds no fault in
Jesus, making all the more clear that the scourging was not seen as a prelude
to further punishment but was meant to bring this charade to an end. Pilate
intones "*Ecce homo,*" "Behold the man" (v. 5). The irony is particularly thick
at this point because Pilate means, Behold, this pitiful man is your king; this
is the sort of specimen you deserve as king. Pilate is not merely mocking
Jesus, he is mocking the Jews as well. On the level of the Fourth Evangelist's
theology, however, we must remember that we have been told throughout
this Gospel that Jesus must suffer and be glorified as the Son of man.[34]

Throughout this drama Pilate is depicted as a pawn, not merely manipulated by "the Jews" but ultimately as Jesus will say given authority to do what
he is doing by God. Not only does he say more than he realizes about Jesus,
he does more than he realizes as well. Thus *Ecce homo* from another point of
view becomes here the announcement that the representative human being

will die for all, including Gentiles such as Pilate himself as well as Jews. Like Peter, Pilate three times denies the Jews what they ask for, saying he finds no fault in Jesus, no basis for the "supreme penalty" (18:38; 19:4, 6).

Pilate's parody backfires, however, for the chief priests and their officials are set into a frenzy when they see Jesus in royal attire. "Crucify him! Crucify him!" they shout. Seeing Jesus as their King was precisely the opposite of what they wanted. Pilate is so fed up and disgusted that he retorts, "Oh, crucify him yourself." He is not implying that they have the right to do so, only that he wishes to have nothing to do with this sordid affair.

At v. 7 the real bone of contention comes to light. What really stuck in the craw of these officials was that Jesus "made himself out to be the Son of God." This is an important point, as it comports with the evidence from the Synoptics about Jesus' trial before the Sanhedrin that it was finally blasphemy that was the ground of Jesus' condemnation by the Jews.[35] The Talmud also reflects that this is what Jesus was condemned for (*b. Sanh.* 43a). Jesus' claim to a special, indeed even a unique, relationship with the Father proves to be the real sticking point, and it still is in the dialogue between Jews and Christians.

To Pilate this suddenly becomes a very different ball game. For a Gentile, a son of the gods was at the least some sort of messenger from the gods. It may be thought that Pilate, like many pagans, was superstitious enough to be fearful of getting on the wrong side of the gods. If this man was more than a pitiful all too human Jew, if he was, rather, a divine messenger incognito, the matter took on a much more serious air. We are thus told at v. 8 for the first time that Pilate was afraid and withdrew into the Praetorium for one further parlay with Jesus. At this point he does indeed ask the question that this Gospel sees as *the right question*: "Where are you from?" To this, Jesus responds with stony silence, although he had indirectly answered this before by speaking of the origins of his kingdom. Obviously Pilate is on the hot seat rather than the judgment seat, and he is soon to realize how much is at stake. Note the close parallels between 10:18 and 19:10.[36] No one will take Jesus' life from him, he will give it away. Not Pilate but Jesus and the Father are in charge of this drama.

Jesus' final response to Pilate in 19:11 is that Pilate would have no authority or power over him if it had not been given from above. Pilate's sin is seen as less grave than that of the Jewish officials, apparently because he is acting without really knowing whom he is dealing with, and acts very unwillingly under duress, while the Jewish officials act willingly and freely. Indeed, we are told even as late as 19:12 that Pilate is still trying to set Jesus free.

Verse 12 also brings to light the "friend of Caesar" remark (cf. above). The Roman historian Tacitus tells us that whoever was a close friend of Pilate's overseer and crony Sejanus was a friend of Caesar.[37] What we know about Sejanus is that he was extremely anti-Semitic and that Pilate behaved just the way Sejanus did. Sejanus, however, lost his own status in Syria in A.D. 31, leaving Pilate to justify his own policies for the remainder of his rule.

The main point is that if Pilate harbored, favored, or released someone who claimed to be a king in defiance of the claim of Caesar, he could expect to lose his most treasured status. Thus, the appeal to self-interest finally works. The irony is again heavy. Pilate fails the test in the presence of the real divine king in order to maintain his status with a merely human king who claimed divinity.

Pilate then by v. 13 has resolved to judge Jesus, however reluctantly, and so he brings Jesus forth and sits down on his judgment seat. Yet he cannot resist adding a further insult to Jesus' tormentors, and so this time he says, "Here is your King." This sitting for judgment transpired at a place called the Pavement.[38]

Verse 14 tells us that this transpired about the sixth hour on the day of the Preparation for the Passover. If this is reckoned according to Jewish ways of counting, the hour would be noon. However, it is possible, indeed likely, in view of the provenance and primary audience of this Gospel that a Roman form of reckoning is being used, in which case the sixth hour is near dawn, at six in the morning. The Romans were known for dealing with such matters first thing in the morning, and Pilate is likely to have followed the same practice.[39] This in turn means that Jesus' pretrial hearing and trial before the Sanhedrin likely took place at night and into the early hours of the morning, as the Synoptics suggest. The reference to the day of Preparation means that Jesus is crucified on the day the Passover lambs were sacrificed in preparation for the feast. It is important to note that Friday was normally called Preparation day by the Jews, although what was alluded to was preparation for the Sabbath. If in this year the Sabbath and the Passover coincided, then Preparation day would be sundown on Thursday to sundown on Friday, and preparation for both events would be made on the same day. Theories of Jesus' being crucified before Friday are quite unnecessary and have no real basis in the text.

The cry goes up again to have Jesus crucified, and Pilate asks one last time, "Shall I crucify your King?" To this the Jews respond that only Caesar is their king. What we have seen in these proceedings is that the Jews must renounce what is most precious to them, their independence and indeed their own Jewishness, for only God and God's messiah could truly be said to be their ruler,[40] if they are to get their way in regard to Jesus, while ironically Pilate must let Jesus go in order to hold on to what is most precious to him—his status as friend of Caesar. In both cases the acceptance of Jesus' claim would require their giving up the religious and political status quo, which neither party was prepared to do. They both wished to retain what power and authority they had, even at the cost of the emasculation of their own integrity. In the hour of decision, Jesus' hour, the true thoughts of all hearts, Jew and Gentile, are revealed for what they are. The evangelist wishes to make very plain that how one reacts to Jesus will tell the tale of whether one is finally judged or justified, vanquished or vindicated, lost or liberated. Jesus in being judged becomes the one who is the judge.

In yet one more ironic twist the narrative is deliberately ambiguous at v. 16—Pilate delivered Jesus to "them" to be crucified and they took Jesus and led him away. Who can this be? It could be an allusion to the Jewish officials, presumably accompanied by the Roman soldiers and the temple police who accompanied them when Jesus was arrested. More likely it simply refers to the soldiers who are mentioned clearly at vv. 23–25. The scene has been set for the crucifixion of the King.

II. Bridging the Horizons

As one attempts to bring the Johannine text into the twentieth century, sometimes negative examples are as helpful as positive ones. Thus, an example of bad contextualization is in order. On several occasions I have received from *Time* magazine a subscription renewal letter in which the computer was to type in my name every so often. Unfortunately the computer read "Ben Witherington III" and assumed that III was my last name. Hence the letter read, "Dear Dr. III: We know what a caring *person* you are, and how you long to keep abreast of current affairs in the world. Thus, Dr. III, we are sure we can count on you once again to renew your subscription to our great American newsweekly. Sincerely, Time Inc." I was tempted to write them back, "Dear Inc." My point is that an impersonal approach to being personal will not work when one tries to apply the Gospel of John, especially when this is the Gospel in which we are told that Jesus as the Good Shepherd calls us all by name! An effective word is a word in season, a word on target, a word intentionally directed to an audience that not only the Holy Spirit but also you know well and know how to relate to.

This having been said, this Gospel also intones the merits of "distance" in evaluating the truth and the meaning of something. We are constantly hearing in this Gospel that the disciples only later understood this or that action or saying of Jesus. Notice that in this unit of material even Jesus' words are treated as sacred tradition that may be quoted as classic words from the past. In other words, our author encourages us to bridge the horizons but not fuse and confuse them. A certain distance of time and space, as well as the new factor of the Holy Spirit, was required before the disciples could understand what happened to Jesus and to themselves. This is often true of us as well. Any number of times we catch ourselves saying, "If I had only known then what I know now," but the point is precisely that understanding came later only when there was opportunity for reflection. This whole Gospel is in one sense an exercise in theological reflection after the fact on the meaning of the Christ event for the world the evangelist addresses.

Perhaps one of the grossest misuses of the Johannine Passion narrative is the attempt to see it as a basis for anti-Semitic actions. On the basis of the misreading of the data, Adolf Hitler's official church theologians painted Jews as Christ killers and thus as cursed by God. The sad irony of all of this, of course, was that Mussolini and his followers were allies of Hitler in the Axis powers and also contributed to this travesty, and yet it was ultimately Romans who executed Jesus. Equally unhelpful, however, at the other end of the spectrum, although part of a generally laudable attempt to compensate and even atone for the sin of anti-Semitism, has been the attempt to suggest that no Jews, and especially no Jewish officials, had or could have had any responsibility for Jesus' death. The evidence as we have it, even allowing for a certain amount of polemics, suggests otherwise. Some Jews were surely involved in having Jesus brought before the Roman authorities, condemned, and executed. The late J.A.T. Robinson has the balance right when he says that the evangelist is "concerned from beginning to end to present the condemnation of Jesus, the *true* king of Israel, as the great betrayal of the nation by its own leadership. Their motivation is exposed as unashamedly collaborationist, and it could be said that the most un-Jewish remark in the Gospel, indeed in the Bible, is one which is placed on the lips not of the evangelist but of the chief priests: 'We have no king but Caesar' (John 19:15)."[41]

We may go farther than this. In view of how Jews such as Philo and Josephus paint the family of Annas and Caiaphas, it is not hard to believe that such immoral and unscrupulous leaders could have played a role in Jesus' death. I must insist, however, that the Jewish people as a whole could not then, and cannot now, be judged on the basis of a few bad leaders, any more than all Americans would want to be branded as xenophobic and racist simply because we have had our Joseph McCarthys and J. Edgar Hoovers among the top echelons in the halls of power. Lord Acton was right that all power corrupts and absolute power corrupts absolutely, especially when we are talking about fallen human beings. Great care must be taken in bridging the horizons that we understand that the Johannine narrative provides no justification for anti-Semitism. How could that be so when the author was a Jew, and his main subject, Jesus, is presented as the King of the Jews, and when the Jewish trial of Jesus is completely omitted in this Gospel?

A plausible and profitable point of contact between these stories and our modern world would be to talk about the issue of justice and the miscarriage of justice both then and now. Jesus in our story confronts Annas and in essence demands a just trial, with a calling of the witnesses as would be normal in a Jewish trial.[42] How does it happen that the innocent are sometimes executed? What should we think of a system of justice that favors the rich who can buy better lawyers? What should we think of trial by judge as opposed to trial by jury in a capital case? Is there a case to be made for capital punishment in a world that is not only dark and dangerous but also full of fallible jurors and judges? What should Christians think about the attempt to solve all our problems in a court of law? Why is it that America is the most litigious society on earth today, just as Roman society was in antiquity? In the Roman system of justice, incarceration while waiting trial was common, but not incarceration as a means of punishment. Why should we see imprisonment as the chief solution to crime? Are there other analogies between the Roman Empire and America as a global power that need to be examined when the issues of a proper Christian view of power and authority are raised? Without turning John's Gospel into a brief for lawyers, the trial language and atmosphere that pervade the whole Gospel should be explored and used to probe deeply into our own psyche and ask hard questions about what our judicial system says about our character and morality. In a more general vein, the story of the trial of Jesus can be used as a taking-off point for the discussion of the heavy-handed misuse of power in a number of realms, including the church, schools, and government.

A further crucial issue to plumb the depths of is what it means to say that Jesus' kingdom is not of this world today in comparison to what it meant then. It is clear enough that Jesus is *not* talking about a kingdom without social and moral dimensions but rather one that is not humanly generated or simply human in character. What, after all, is the relationship between the kingdom of God and the institutional church?

A further simple way to bridge the gap between the text and today would be to dramatize the story. One way to do this would be to portray the different major characters—Judas, Jesus, Pilate, Peter, the Beloved Disciple, Annas and Caiaphas—in a series of sermons or teachings. If the message of the text is to come to life, the text's characters must take on flesh for the audience. Another way to do this would be to have a Passion play, as is still done at Oberammergau and elsewhere. This practice has a long history in the church and is especially suitable for a generation of visual learners such as our television generation. Dorothy Sayers's series of plays published under the title *The Man Born to Be King* provides excellent resources for such an attempt.

A word of caution is in order. When one is teaching and preaching this material it is tempting to get bogged down in some of the particulars of the text and miss some of the larger message. An archaeological sermon or teaching about the places mentioned in the text can be beneficial, perhaps with the aid of some good slides,[43] but not if the message of what happened and why in these locations is lost.

Finally, ministers sometimes get martyr or Jesus complexes. It will serve the congregation well if one preaches and teaches on the distinctive character of Jesus' sacrifice and the importance of his death. Some facts in the text are without modern analogy, and they should simply be proclaimed.

In a memorable movie about cross-cultural missions called the *Peace Child*, we hear the story of a young Midwest couple who went to Africa to bring the gospel to a tribe that had been as yet unreached. The couple knew very little about their target audience when they went, and very little of their language or culture until they had been on site for a considerable period of time. Imagine their surprise when they learned that all the while they had been telling the story of Jesus' death and resurrection, the audience had assumed that Judas was the hero of the story, because their culture saw trickery and betrayal as a way of life to be admired and emulated. This led the couple in due course to a rephrasing of the message when they discovered that the tribe in question and the neighboring tribes with whom it was regularly fighting had a custom of making peace by giving up a son of a tribal leader to the opponents' leader to seal the peace pact. The child was called a peace child. The missionaries learned to tell the story of Jesus as the coming of the peace child whom God was giving to humankind, his enemy, to reconcile the two parties.

The most salient reason for telling this story is that one must know one's audience as well as one's Bible to relate the one to the other. It is reported that Karl Barth said that every good minister should prepare his sermons with the newspaper in one hand and the Bible in the other. This means not only that one must keep abreast of current affairs but also that one must take pains to know one's parishioners. This takes time, indeed often it takes several years. One cannot presume to know what they need to and are able to hear until one knows them.

Sometimes we get frustrated with our politicians because they seem wishy-washy, always trying to compromise, always trying to please everybody instead of standing on principle. Yet at the same time we get angry with our representatives when they take a strong stand on an issue and stick by it, even though we and others strongly object to their stance. Pilate is caught squarely in the midst of trying to please the Jews and yet trying to be true to his sense of Roman justice in the case of Jesus. Pilate knew well "the daily compromises, the prudential balancing of forces, the application of ruthless power, that half-light world of greys and polka dots where people grope wearily for truth and the soul shrivels and dies."[44] He does a tap dance between trying to please the public and trying to heed the inner voice that tells him something is awry. This tap dance is portrayed in the seven artfully presented scenes as follows:

Scene 1. Pilate is outside. He tries to discern the charge against Jesus and would like to pass the buck back to the Jews to handle this hot potato. (18:29–32)

Scene 2. Pilate is inside. He questions Jesus about the nature of kingship and truth. He is sarcastic and philosophical but does not understand Jesus. (18:33–38a)

Scene 3. Pilate is outside. He declares Jesus innocent, and offers his release according to the paschal custom, but the Jews ask for Barabbas. (18:38b–40)

Scene 4. Pilate is inside. Jesus is scourged and mocked. (19:1–3)

Scene 5. Pilate is outside. He displays the beaten but royally attired Jesus. But this mockery does not satisfy the "Jews." Indeed, it only increases the clamor for Jesus' crucifixion. (19:4–7)

Scene 6. Pilate is inside. Pilate is frightened and takes the position of a bully, waving his power and authority in Jesus' face, but Jesus calmly says Pilate has only what power God has given him. (19:8–11)

Scene 7. Pilate is outside. A last attempt to release Jesus fails, and Pilate is pressured into officially decreeing execution while the Jews are maneuvered into renouncing their heritage. (19:12–16).[45]

Needless to say, the above scenario gives new meaning to the term "shuttle diplomacy." Pilate goes back and forth like a yo-yo, and finally acts only when his own status and position are threatened. What this whole scene does is raise the crucial issue of *when* compromise is a good thing and when compromise is a betrayal of certain crucial and fundamental principles. Too often ministers tend to confront crises or important decisions with a "take it or leave it" attitude when they ask boards or congregations to make a decision, assuming that in every decision-making situation some eternal principle must be upheld at all costs. This is by no means always the case. Whether the pulpit is on the left or the right side of the chancel or in the middle is of no eternal significance, although where one places it may be of some symbolic significance. One must learn how to distinguish between absolutes and contingencies that are negotiable. F. Craddock puts it well when he says: "None of us is exempt from decisions hammered out under extreme pressure, decisions which demand of us not only wisdom and insight but penitence and moral courage."[46] In other words, we must ask, if we had been in Pilate's place in danger of losing a job we desperately wanted to keep, would we have acted any differently? Identifying with Pilate in the story may not make us comfortable, but it may be closer to the mark, considering how often we all act in selfish and self-seeking ways.

One could also preach a splendid sermon along the "straining at a gnat but swallowing a camel" line dealing with how the Jewish authorities do not hesitate to do in an innocent man but are very picky about not getting ritually unclean and so missing out on eating Passover. Craddock gives the wonderful illustration of a felon who refused to sing in a prison choir because his church did not believe in singing with instrumental accompaniment, and yet he was willing to commit a capital crime![47]

Throughout this Gospel we have seen a wide variety of people who may in some sense be called truth seekers. They come to Jesus by night or day, looking for answers, and receive responses that often make them very uncomfortable. The problem with truth seeking is that we may find out things about ourselves and others that make us uneasy or that may even require of us significant change. So often when people ask the question, What is truth? they are not serious about the question, or they are looking for a truth that they can swallow easily that will not require them to change their life or lifestyle. If Pilate was really interested in truth at all, it was only the "comfortable" sort of truth he was likely to embrace.

Sometimes one of the most discouraging aspects about being a teacher is that one gets few truth seekers and many degree seekers. So many students view education as just one more necessary hurdle they have to jump over in order to get a job. Sadly, this is even sometimes true of seminary students. Some even resent having to come to seminary. They believe they already know and have the truth, and they are irritated when someone tries to stretch their categories. If we are really honest as Christians, however, we must admit that we all have a lot to learn, even about the essentials of our faith. We must ask ourselves whether it will really be valuable to us if we receive or believe a truth that requires no changes in our lives, even though we are fallen human beings. A. Solzhenitsyn, the great Russian Christian, has said, "One person speaking the truth has more power than a whole city living in falsehood."[48]

It has been said that it is the task of preachers to comfort the afflicted and afflict the comfortable. This seems to be the opposite of what we sometimes get in the pulpit. Preachers dispense truth in bite-size portions that almost anyone can swallow without needing to pause to reflect seriously on one's life or think of truth's implications for one's lifestyle. Too often the message turns out to be little more than "God bless us and help us maintain our standard of living." So many ministers are caught up in trying to please their people and help out God, not realizing this is the opposite of their real job. They must please God, and help the people, even if it means stepping on some toes along the way.

If we analyze the Jewish officials in John 18—19, they seem convinced that they already know what the real truth is, even about Jesus, and believe they know what will best please themselves and the people in the long run—"It is necessary that one man die." The story reminds us to be wary of any and every attempt to sacrifice someone *else's* life or dreams for the sake of the status quo or one's *own* vision of normality. Like the Christian who when called to be a missionary said, "Here I am, Lord, take my sister," we are often more than ready to sacrifice things that are important for others, so that we may go on doing and being what we are already doing and being.

It would be well for us to ask ourselves with some regularity not merely, "What have I given to the cause of Christ lately?" but "What have I given *up* for the sake of Christ lately?" The hymnist beckons us to "let goods and kindred go, this mortal flesh also." In other words, if we wish to be real Christians in a world full of hunger, thirst, homelessness, poverty, and despair, we will necessarily have to give up certain things in order to keep Christ and the name Christian. The alternative is to sacrifice Christ and his call upon our lives, as various of the characters do in this story, in order to keep what we have. The latter option means that we silence the voice that says, "Inasmuch as you have not done it to the least of these my brothers and sisters, you have not done it unto me."

A moving message can be centered around the theme, "Who is it that you seek?" It involves telling again the story of Jesus in the garden deliberately going out to meet those who would come and take him captive. When they meet him, however, they are bowled over by his presence. This is not the Jesus they expected to find, a Jesus they could exercise authority over and control, a Jesus who fit in with their vision of what a rabble-rouser must be like. This is in fact the way Jesus confronts a fallen and dark world. He does not set out to meet their expectations but rather to meet their needs. The Jesus the world seeks is not the same as the Jesus the world finds if it really en-counters him. "Thus the forces of evil in that sinister confederacy—personal treason in the person of Judas, corrupt religion expressed by the temple po-lice, political ruthlessness embodied in Roman soldiery, and behind all, the malignant form of the prince of this world—all fall back before this meek monarch who offers himself up to their will."[49] Yet strangely and wonder-fully it was not merely their will that ended up being done when Jesus was sacrificed, but God's as well. God can even use the wrath of human beings for good, indeed ultimate and life-transforming good.

The story of Peter's denials, as grim as they may be in showing how even one who truly loves Jesus can under pressure be led to renounce him, also has another message to convey to us. Peter's denials did not place him be-yond the realm of divine rehabilitation. The story of Peter in John 18 should not be told without at least mentioning its sequel in John 21 where Peter is restored and recommissioned. The analogy to our own situation should be obvious. There will be people we meet, even in our church, who will say they do not believe this or that. They may even renounce allegiance to Christ at some point, perhaps because they have never truly known or encountered him in the first place. The story of Peter reminds us that we must not write such people off as hopelessly lost. Even if they are backsliding Christians un-der some kind of duress, we must seek them out and attempt to restore them and recommission them. It is painfully true that "John has constructed a dramatic contrast wherein Jesus stands up to his questioners and denies nothing, while Peter cowers before his questioners and denies everything."[50] "How many Christians live with a continual sense of failure because of their inability, or unwillingness, to stand clearly for Christ in their public lives! Like Peter, we find ourselves drawn step by step into ever deeper compro-mise until existence is a continuous denial, and worship with God's people on a Sunday, instead of renewing and invigorating us, serves only to under-line the hypocrisy of our lives."[51] It is also true, however, that denial is not the end of the story for Peter. As the Lukan version of the story makes more clear, Jesus had prayed for Peter, knowing that Satan would sift him, and he says to him, "When once you have turned back, strengthen your brothers" (Luke 22:32).

The reader will recognize that this author believes that following Jesus in-volves a commitment to peacemaking, although it may also involve a com-mitment to civil disobedience and nonviolent resistance when the basic principles of Christian faith and life are infringed upon. What it does not in-volve is a taking of swords into one's hands and acting violently, as Peter does. An excellent teaching could be centered around the theme of how the world from time to time clamors, "Give us Barabbas." Indeed, some in the church, in the form of some liberation theologians, seem to have also clam-ored, "Give us Barabbas," preferring a revolutionary option to a Jesus whose kingdom refuses to resort to worldly ways of handling corruption and the abuse of power. Yet violence only begets more violence, and it is the oppo-site of the ethic of the one who taught us to love our enemies, pray for our persecutors, and turn the other cheek. The ethic of Jesus not only calls into question the idea of a revolutionary Christianity, it also calls into question the assumptions of any society with a Rambo mentality that assumes that might makes right or that we can finally solve world problems through an overwhelming display of military might. It appears that the lessons of Vietnam and more recently of Somalia are still to be learned.

In a Gospel meant to elicit from the audience a true confession of who Jesus was, Pilate is depicted as one who raises some of the right questions but for all the wrong reasons. Although he sounds like a truth seeker when he asks Jesus whether he is the King of the Jews, and when he asks what truth is, in fact as the narrative makes evident he is prompted to ask about Jesus' identity only because someone else had prompted him to ask about Jesus' kingly status. Jesus accordingly does not respond to the question in 18:33 as if Pilate were an honest seeker; rather, Jesus forces Pilate to reveal that he is not one, with his probing remark, "Are you saying this of your own accord, or have others been telling you about me?" Pilate is unmasked in his response to this question, "I am no Jew!" In short, he has no interest in Jewish messiahs.

This illuminating interchange in which Pilate had to reveal who he was and what his values were, tells us a great deal about when witnessing is likely to be fruitful and when it is not. When people are seeking and asking their own questions they do not react as Pilate does in this story. When in this Gospel, however, they ask their own questions and sincerely seek to know Jesus, he does not hesitate to give them a full answer, and neither should we. Pilate is portrayed as one who is not a sincere seeker but rather a self-server caught up in an unpleasant affair and seeking to escape with the least personal harm or obligation. Also, in matters of eternal importance one cannot merely mouth someone else's questions or pat answers, one must seek out the truth and grasp it for oneself. I cannot enter the kingdom by resting on the laurels of my parents, or merely mouthing the formulas they passed along to me. One must make the Christian faith one's own.

17. The Death and Burial
of Jesus (John 19:16b–42)

The study of Jesus' death and burial should not be done in isolation from what we know about the Roman practice of crucifixion, for much light is shed, especially on the Johannine narrative, by examining the first-century evidence outside the Christian canon. Accordingly, we will begin this section with an excursus for those who need refreshing or want more detail about the nature and significance of crucifixion in the first-century world.

EXCURSUS: THE CRUCIFIXION OF JESUS

If there is one thing that almost all New Testament scholars of all stripes agree on, it is that Jesus was crucified in Jerusalem during the rule of Pontius Pilate (A.D. 26–36). Even the Roman historian Tacitus (A.D. 55–100) in his *Annals* (15.44.2–8) records this event, saying: "Christus . . . suffered the extreme penalty during the reign of Tiberius at the hands of one of our procurators, Pontius Pilate." It behooves us, then, to understand the practice of crucifixion and what sort of person normally received this punishment. It used to be thought that only Romans practiced crucifixion in the Mediterranean crescent, and so it was assumed that Jesus was executed by Romans. There is, however, some evidence of Jews' practicing crucifixion as well.

This evidence, however, points, for example, to the Hasmonaean period and figures such as Alexander Janneus (cf. Josephus, *Ant.* 13.14.2, also referred to in 4QpNah 3–4.i.7–8). It is possible that col. 64, ll. 6–13, of the *Temple Scroll* from Qumran (11QTemple) instructs Jews to practice crucifixion in the case of a traitor who informs against his people, but the crucial line reads, "You shall hang him on a tree and he shall die . . . he shall be put to death, and they shall hang him on the tree." It is clear this is an exposition of Deut. 21:22–33 which probably did not originally refer to crucifixion but to the displaying of the corpse by hanging it on a tree after execution, or possibly to death by hanging. Yet in the New Testament era the Deuteronomy text was apparently understood to refer specifically to crucifixion (cf. Gal. 3:13; Acts 5:30; 10:39). The most that we could derive from the two Qumran passages is that the Qumranites practiced or envisioned practicing crucifixion for treason/betrayal to the enemy. There is not a single example in Josephus of the practice of crucifixion during the reign of Herod the Great. He apparently eschewed such a practice, nor is there any hard evidence of Jews (particularly the Sanhedrin or other Jewish officials) using this practice *during* the lifetime of Jesus. The material in the later Targums (Targums on Num. 25:4; Lev. 19:26, Ruth 1:17) is probably too late to be of direct relevance. I

303

agree with J. Fitzmyer that while it is possible that some *Jews* crucified Jesus (and this *has* been argued on the basis of John 19:16), Luke 23:25 probably interprets the matter correctly. Although Pilate delivered Jesus up to the *will* of the Jewish authorities, the latter did not execute him.

The question then becomes, How did someone like Jesus get himself executed by Romans and by a form of punishment normally reserved for the extreme elements of society, namely, rebels, bandits, runaway slaves? The two *lestai* whom Jesus was crucified with were probably, like Barabbas, not mere thieves but revolutionary bandits. M. Hengel has made abundantly clear that there is no evidence for a positive evaluation of crucifixion in the ancient world.[1] It was not seen as a noble way to die, it was not viewed as a good route to go even for a person who wanted to be a martyr. This is clear from a Roman graffito found in the catacombs that portrays a man bowing before a donkey that is being crucified, with the subtitle "[personal name] worships his God." This surely was an attempt to mock the early Christian belief and reveals what one suspects was a prevalent initial reaction to Christian preaching of the crucified Jesus in the Greco-Roman world.

In a Jewish context, the Qumran evidence as well as the New Testament evidence mentioned above makes clear that Jews could not possibly see crucifixion in a positive light in view of Deut. 21. Rather, it was seen as a sign that one was cursed by God. In early Judaism, being crucified (cursed by God) and being Messiah (God's anointed) would surely have been seen as mutually exclusive ideas. This surely means that crucifixion might have been seen by some of Jesus' enemies as a good way to make clear that Jesus *wasn't* the Messiah, but it is unlikely that either Jesus or his disciples would have assumed during the ministry that going to Jerusalem and getting crucified by Romans would be a way to prove one *was* the Messiah.

The disciples going down the road to Emmaus in Luke 24:21 assume that Jesus' crucifixion made clear that he was *not* the one to redeem Israel. Bear in mind that prior to Jesus there is no evidence, unless the new finds at Qumran produce some, that anyone envisioned Messiah as being a suffering servant figure. Daniel 7 might suggest such, but it is very vague on whether the Son of man figure had previously suffered before appearing before the Ancient of Days, much less dying on a cross. Furthermore, the record of the tradition of Jesus' passion prediction in Mark 8:31; 9:31; and 10:34 simply says the Son of man will be "killed." It does not mention crucifixion as the means of death. There is no evidence in the Synoptics that Jesus predicted death by *crucifixion* (cf. Mark 10:45; Luke 9:44). If one wanted to squelch the rumors that Jesus might be Messiah, crucifixion was the way to exorcise those ideas.

As a result of the excavations at Giv'at ha-Mivtar near Jerusalem in 1968–70 we now have some rather clear information about execution by crucifixion during the first century A.D. First, nails could be and were used in some cases, driven through the wrists (not hands) and through the ankles. In the crucified remains found at Giv'at ha-Mivtar, both ankles were nailed together to the cross with one nail. This may have also been the case with Jesus. The normal Roman procedure once death by crucifixion had been decided upon was to scourge or flog the victim severely, usually with a *flagellum* (cat-o'-nine-tails) prior to making him carry the crossbar to the spot of execution.

In Jesus' case, the flagellation had apparently happened earlier during the Roman trial when Pilate had hoped to inflict this sort of punishment on Jesus and then release him. Thus the punishment was not repeated shortly before execution. The *flagellum* could in fact and often did kill the victim, ripping out flesh right down to the bone with the hooks and bits of broken rock tied to the thongs.[2] In Roman law, unlike Jewish law, there was no maximum number of lashes; it just depended on the degree of malice of the inflicter. If Jesus was severely scourged, as is suggested by both the fact that he was unable to carry the crosspiece all the way to Golgotha and that he died soon after being nailed to the cross, he would have been in great pain well before being nailed to the cross. This suits well the prediction of suffering many things at the hands of human beings (cf. Mark 8:31; 9:31; 10:33–34).

It is not perfectly clear whether Jesus died on a cross shaped like a capital "T" with a slot in the top or on the "t" shape we are most familiar with. It was not the practice to carry the whole cross to the spot of execution, only the crosspiece. Normally there would also be a *sedecula,* a small block of wood on which one could rest one's rear end, to prevent collapse and prolong the agony. If the executioners were in a hurry, they might break the legs to hasten death with a *coup de grâce.*[3] Jesus, however, died before any such expedient was needed.

There is no general medical agreement as to the actual cause of Jesus' death when he was crucified. It could perhaps have been suffocation, caused by inability to hold oneself up on the cross and breathe. This might explain the Markan reference to a great cry just before death. Jesus may have been gasping for breath. It is also possible that Jesus died from traumatic shock or from heart failure. The gush of blood and water could have come from the piercing with the lance of the pleural cavity, where the fluid had collected after heart stoppage.

Normally one was executed in the nude as a further element of humiliation, and this may have been true in Jesus' case. It is also possible, because of Jewish sensibilities, that the victim was allowed to wear a loincloth. It is true that according to Roman law the executioners were allowed to keep the clothes of the victim (cf. *Digest* 48.20).

There are other details about Jesus' death on the cross that match what we know from other sources about such matters. For instance, the offer of myrrhed wine (Mark 15:23) as a narcotic to lessen the pain is known from Jewish sources, in which it is said that respected Jerusalem Jewish women gave such to the victim prior to death.[4] Also the offering of *oxos,* wine vinegar, to Jesus while on the cross was not likely an act of malice. It was the normal thirst-quenching beverage (the equivalent of Gatorade) of the time, which day laborers drank (cf. Mark 15:36 and par.).[5] E. Stauffer has also produced some evidence that a dying man could make testamentary dispensations from the cross, as we see happening in John 19 in the case of Mary and the Beloved Disciple (cf. below).[6]

The so-called *titulus,* the placard attached to the cross, was to display the crime of the one crucified. The Gospels vary somewhat as to the words on the *titulus* (in black or red letters on a white background, in three languages—John 19:20—Aramaic, Latin, and Greek).[7] The oldest extrabiblical sources mention actually a *tabula* carried by the criminal to the spot of execution. Public crucifixion was practiced as a deterrent by the Romans, and although law did not require it, they did in notable cases display the supposed reason for execution. The story of Jesus' death thus has numerous elements in it that are historically plausible.

The *titulus* did not necessarily indicate the juridical verdict (i.e., what Jesus was actually found guilty of), but the public reason for execution. E. Bammel suggest that there could be a bit of mocking involved in the *titulus* in Jesus' case. The four Gospels differ a bit in the wording of the *titulus* (Mark 15:26—"The King of the Jews"; Matt. 27:37—"This is Jesus, the King of the Jews"; Luke 23:38—"This is the King of the Jews"; and John 19:19—"Jesus of Nazareth, the King of the Jews").

What is important to understand is that the charge then would have read *malka, rex,* and *basileus* of the Jews, not *mashiach, christus,* and *christos*.[8] This means that Jesus, so far as the Roman end of things is concerned, was executed as a political criminal, guilty of high treason for claiming to be a king when there is no political king in the Roman Empire but Caesar, or those underlords whom he might endorse. The Romans would surely not have executed Jesus simply for claiming to be a nonpolitical Jewish messiah or a prophet.

There is a somewhat parallel case, involving the story of Jesus bar Hanan, the prophet of woe who predicted the fall of Jerusalem and the Temple. He was scourged until his bones showed and was then released by the procurator Albinus in A.D. 62 during the Feast of Tabernacles.[9] "Messiah" after all was primarily a religious claim. Yet religion and politics could not be neatly separated in antiquity. There were political implications to claiming to be Messiah in Jesus' day, and on the other hand there were religious implications to claiming to be a king as well.[10] We must not be guilty of trying to impose modern secular/sacred, religious/political distinctions on ancient documents that are not appropriate to that era.

19:16b   So they took Jesus; [17]and carrying the cross by himself, he went out to what is called The Place of the Skull, which in Hebrew is called Golgotha. [18]There they crucified him, and with him two others, one on either side, with Jesus between them. [19]Pilate also had an inscription written and put on the cross. It read, "Jesus of Nazareth, the King of the Jews." [20]Many of the Jews read this inscription, because the place where Jesus was crucified was near the city; and it was written in Hebrew, in Latin, and in Greek. [21]Then the chief priests of the Jews said to Pilate, "Do not write, 'The King of the Jews,' but, 'This man said, I am King of the Jews.' " [22]Pilate answered, "What I have written I have written." [23]When the soldiers had crucified Jesus, they took his clothes and divided them into four parts, one for each soldier. They also took his tunic; now the tunic was seamless, woven in one piece from the top. [24]So they said to one another, "Let us not tear it, but casts lots for it to see who will get it." This was to fulfill what the scripture says,

"They divided my clothes among themselves,
   and for my clothing they cast lots."

25And that is what the soldiers did.

Meanwhile, standing near the cross of Jesus were his mother, and his mother's sister, Mary the wife of Clopas, and Mary Magdalene. 26When Jesus saw his mother and the disciple whom he loved standing beside her, he said to his mother, "Woman, here is your son." 27Then he said to the disciple, "Here is your mother." And from that hour the disciple took her into his own home.

28 After this, when Jesus knew that all was now finished, he said (in order to fulfill the scripture), "I am thirsty." 29A jar full of sour wine was standing there. So they put a sponge full of the wine on a branch of hyssop and held it to his mouth. 30When Jesus had received the wine, he said, "It is finished." Then he bowed his head and gave up his spirit.

31 Since it was the day of Preparation, the Jews did not want the bodies left on the cross during the sabbath, especially because that sabbath was a day of great solemnity. So they asked Pilate to have the legs of the crucified men broken and the bodies removed. 32Then the soldiers came and broke the legs of the first and of the other who had been crucified with him. 33But when they came to Jesus and saw that he was already dead, they did not break his legs. 34Instead, one of the soldiers pierced his side with a spear, and at once blood and water came out. 35(He who saw this has testified so that you also may believe. His testimony is true, and he knows that he tells the truth.) 36These things occurred so that the scripture might be fulfilled, "None of his bones shall be broken." 37And again another passage of scripture says, "They will look on the one whom they have pierced."

38 After these things, Joseph of Arimathea, who has a disciple of Jesus, though a secret one because of his fear of the Jews, asked Pilate to let him take away the body of Jesus. Pilate gave him permission; so he came and removed his body. 39Nicodemus, who had at first come to Jesus by night, also came, bringing a mixture of myrrh and aloes, weighing about a hundred pounds. 40They took the body of Jesus and wrapped it with the spices in linen cloths, according to the burial custom of the Jews. 41Now there was a garden in the place where he was crucified, and in the garden there was a new tomb in which no one had ever been laid. 42And so, because it was the Jewish day of Preparation, and the tomb was nearby,they laid Jesus there.

I. The Historical Horizon

The story of Jesus' death and burial is full of striking differences from the Synoptic accounts in regard to who carries the cross, what Jesus says, who stands beneath the cross, the spear thrust, and the story of the burial. If we begin at 19:16b–17, we notice immediately that we are told that Jesus carried the cross by himself and that he went out to Golgotha, which in Aramaic means Skull. The location of this spot has been much debated by archaeologists, but the balance of the evidence strongly favors the traditional location somewhere within the precincts of the Church of the Holy Sepulchre, not at

Gordon's Calvary. The old city walls in Jesus' day were at a different spot from where they were in the Middle Ages or are today.[11] There is no mention of Simon of Cyrene in the Johannine account, probably because the Fourth Evangelist again wishes to stress that Jesus is in control of his own fate. It was the Roman custom that the victim would carry his own cross.[12]

Nothing is made of the fact that Jesus is crucified with two others; it is mentioned only in passing at v. 18. A good deal, however, is made of the placard, or *titulus,* that was put on the cross and indicated that Jesus the "Nazorean" was king of the Jews.[13] The reference to Jesus' hometown may be significant, since it could be taken as an insult to Judean Jews, who certainly did not believe that the Messiah would come from Galilee.[14] We are told at v. 20 that many Jews read and objected to the *titulus,* because Jesus was crucified *near to the city.* We are also informed that the inscription was written in the three primary languages of this part of the Roman Empire— Latin, Greek, and Hebrew or Aramaic—so all could read it. The chief priests are said at v. 21 to have asked Pilate not to write the inscription as he did but to put "This man said, I am King of the Jews." Pilate refused, saying that what he had written, he had written and that was that. No doubt he was tired of being wheedled and manipulated.

As R. Michaels points out, we really have four vignettes in vv. 23–37: (1) the episode with four Roman soldiers (vv. 23–24); (2) Jesus and the two (vv. 25–27); (3) Jesus alone (vv. 28–30); and (4) the results and the witness (vv. 31–37).[15] Three of these four episodes are punctuated with the assertion that they fulfill scripture. The most probable reason for this, since this is not a major stress elsewhere in the Gospel, is that in a missionary document addressed to Jews as well as to Gentiles a defense of the close of Jesus' life was felt to be necessary. It had to be shown that what happened to Jesus was in accord with a divine plan, as revealed in Holy Writ. Thus the most difficult and scandalous aspects of the story receive the most scriptural grounding. Only the episode about Mary and the Beloved Disciple beneath the cross does not receive this sort of attention.

First, there is the business about the soldiers dividing up Jesus' clothing, including the seamless tunic he wore. It was Roman practice for the executioner to assume possession of the victim's effects. On the surface of things, it would appear that the seamless tunic is mentioned to explain how it was that the casting of lots came about, and thus how the scripture (Ps. 22:18) was fulfilled. Many commentators, however, have seen a deeper symbolic significance here, and in due course the seamless garment of Christ came to be a symbolic way of talking about the unity of the universe, or of humanity, or of Christ with his people, or of the body of Christ, that is, the church, which not even the pagan world could tear asunder. The latter may be the most probable of these possible allusions in view of the scene in vv. 25–27, but none are totally convincing.

A seamless tunic was not unusual for a Jew, since he was not to wear a garment made of two sorts of material or that mixed two sorts of thread. Thus the mentioning of this detail here, which is not found in the Synoptics, could be seen as a way of emphasizing that Jesus was a good Jew. If there is a further symbolic allusion, it could be to the fact that the high priest is said in Ex. 39:27 to have worn a garment woven of one piece,[16] but the problem with this suggestion is that Jesus was wearing a tunic, not the sort of outer garment the priest wore. It is perhaps best not to overpress all the details of the text here. The image of Jesus as high priest is evident in the letter to the Hebrews, but not so clear in the Fourth Gospel,[17] even though it would be effective to allude to Jesus' being both sacrifice and sacrificer here.

What is clearer is that Jesus is seen even on the cross as in control and completing the work his Father gave him to do. He makes provision for his male and female disciples, he gives up his spirit before the soldiers can take it from him, and he presents his work as a finished product to the Father with last words appropriate to the occasion. Jesus is seen in these vignettes as the Passover lamb, as the references to hyssop, unbroken bones, mingled blood, and testimony all suggest.

Without a doubt John 19:25–27 is a crux in the Johannine problem. Not only do the Synoptics say that all of the Twelve deserted Jesus in the garden,[18] and are nowhere to be found in the crucifixion stories, but we are also told that while women observed Jesus' death, they did so from afar (cf. Mark 15:40–41 and par.). Furthermore, while there is overlap in all four Gospels between the women listed as being present, Jesus' mother is not mentioned as one of the women there in the Synoptics, despite the fact that Luke especially had an interest in Mary, including an interest in her later role in the church (cf. Luke 2; Acts 1:14).[19] These problems are somewhat alleviated if, as we have argued, the Beloved Disciple was a Judean disciple and not one of the Twelve. In fact, it appears that the Johannine list of women said to have been eyewitnesses of this event may have only one name in common with the Synoptic list—Mary Magdalene. Historically speaking, there is nothing improbable about a few grieving women, especially relatives, being allowed near the cross of a loved one, especially if it was guarded, as was true in Jesus' case.

Stauffer has shown that it was possible for those being crucified to make a sort of last will and testament from the cross.[20] Historically then, this scene could have been about Jesus making provisions for the ongoing security of his mother. True to his principles (cf. Mark 3:31–35 and par.), and perhaps especially since his brothers did not believe in him (John 7:5), Jesus apparently preferred to have his mother cared for by a member of the family of faith rather than by his own physical family, for "his own received him not." Even the phrases "Behold your son" and "Behold your mother" suit the language of Jewish family law where someone is legally entrusted to another.[21] Whatever the full historical facts about this event, the Fourth Evangelist has transformed this scene into a powerful statement about male and female disciples standing beneath the foot of the cross. Indeed, these verses could even be seen as a symbolic depiction of the new Adam and Eve standing beneath the tree, only this time they obey the divine command and community rather than strife results.

On any showing, this story about Jesus' mother and the Beloved Disciple should probably be seen as the climax of the Passion narrative in this Gospel. Commentators have often remarked on the fact that neither of these persons is named here, perhaps because they are being presented as paradigms so that the unbelieving audience may follow their examples. There may also be something of a message here about the resolution of the tension between Jesus' family and the family of faith, a tension that we see in John 2 and 7. The two families are brought together finally in the context of Jesus' hour.

It is historically significant that women are mentioned in all four Gospels as the chief believing witnesses of Jesus' death, apart from the Beloved Disciple who is mentioned only in this Gospel. It was women, not the Twelve, who stayed with Jesus until the end, and they were the ones who could later vouch for this article of the Creed: "crucified under Pontius Pilate."

Here, as in John 2, Jesus is depicted as addressing his mother as "woman" (*gynai*).[22] I would suggest that the evangelist chose to use this term in both stories, not just because Jesus had disengaged from his mother in her parental authority, but because she represents women in their pilgrimage toward full faith in Jesus. We see Mary making progress from believing in Jesus as a wonder-worker, but remaining with her physical family, to joining the family of faith. There is a sense in which Jesus resolves the tension in his mother's two roles as mother and disciple, by indicating that she must relate to him as a woman, not as his mother. "As she loses Jesus both in a physical and spiritual sense, she gains a new family, the Beloved Disciple being her first 'son' in the faith."[23] Discipleship then must be the larger context in which Mary's role must be defined. She can be a spiritual mother in the church, but she is not depicted here as the mother of the church, for the Beloved Disciple's discipleship to Jesus precedes hers, and only he is called "the disciple" in this scene. Nonetheless, both are addressed and both receive a commission from Jesus at this juncture. The dignity of woman is restored beneath this tree, as she is portrayed as one who can become a full disciple of Jesus. "The Fourth Evangelist's vision of male-female equality in the Christian community entails an incorporation of the physical family into the family of faith, and a reinterpretation of physical family roles in light of the priorities of the family of faith."[24] Having achieved the reconciliation of the physical family and the family of faith, the Fourth Evangelist suggests that Jesus had basically completed his work, for the story is directly followed by the words, "After this, when Jesus knew that all was now finished . . ." (v. 28).

At v. 28 we are also told that Jesus said "I thirst" in order to fulfill scripture. The point may be that Jesus is conscious of trying to do everything in accord with God's plan and will. Psalm 69:21 is the scripture, and perhaps one reason to mention it is to show Jesus' true humanness. If this is correct, then there is a certain irony here, since in John 4 Jesus was portrayed as the one who could meet any human thirst. Sour wine-vinegar was indeed a common thirst-quenching beverage drunk especially by the poor (cf.

excursus above). The Gentile reader or hearer would likely see this as an act of kindness, not cruelty, on the part of the soldiers.

Unlike Mark's Gospel, in which we have the cry of God-forsakenness, here Jesus is calm and aware that he has completed the work his Father had given him. At v. 30 we are told that Jesus bowed his head and gave up his spirit, surely a reference to his human spirit, indicating that he was truly human and truly died.

We are told at v. 31 that this is the day of Preparation and that the coming Sabbath is a "high day," that is, a feast day. The Jews wished for the legs of these three on the crosses to be broken, so that they would not be left on crosses during the Sabbath and certainly not during a great feast day.[25] Breaking the legs would cause almost immediate suffocation. This Jewish plan, however, was thwarted in Jesus' case because he was already dead and there was no need to break his legs. Psalm 34:20 and Zech. 12:10 are the two scriptures said to be fulfilled here. C. K. Barrett notes that the evangelist seems to follow the Hebrew Old Testament not the LXX, in these partial citations,[26] which points to a Jewish-Christian author.

Perhaps as a final act to make certain that Jesus is dead he is pierced in the side. It is in fact anatomically possible for blood and a clear fluid to spurt forth from a pierced dead person if the person has only recently died. This particular act seems to be of great importance to the evangelist, for he takes great pains to insist that this act was witnessed, likely by the Beloved Disciple, if v. 27b doesn't indicate he had already departed. The act was important because it proved that Jesus was no apparition on the cross but rather fully human. Some have seen in the mention of blood and water a reference to the two sacraments that spring forth from the death of Christ and symbolize it. This is unlikely on several counts: (1) We have already seen that this evangelist shows no interest in the actual baptizing of Jesus by John and makes no mention of the elements of the Passover meal in his description of the Last Supper. There is no special focus on the sacraments in this Gospel. (2) Blood by itself is never a symbol for the Lord's Supper, any more than bread and fish are.[27] More likely Barrett is right that the theological point is that Jesus' death and our life paradoxically come together. The blood shed symbolizes his life poured out in death; the water, as elsewhere in this Gospel, symbolizes the life that comes from Jesus to his followers.[28] Jesus had to die so others might have life and have it abundantly. Since this is the Gospel that has eternal life as a chief theme, and Jesus' death is seen as its indispensable source, it is not surprising that the author stresses that this act is witnessed and a fulfillment of scripture, in accord with God's plan.

The story of Jesus' burial, which begins at v. 38, is both interesting and strange. Joseph of Arimathea appears for the first time as a sort of secret follower of Jesus, and it may be implied that Nicodemus is as well.[29] If Nicodemus is some sort of follower of Jesus, he is one who still lives with fear, but again this scene, like all the others in this Gospel, must be judged on the basis of the fact that the resurrection has not yet happened, the Spirit was not yet given, and thus full-fledged discipleship is not yet possible. It was not un-usual for criminals crucified by the Romans to be left on public display as a deterrent. Criminals executed by Jewish authorities would be provided with a burial place by the Sanhedrin. Joseph and/or Nicodemus could have been claiming the prerogatives of the Sanhedrin when they requested the body.[30] Verse 31 tells us, in any case, that Pilate was allowing the Jews to remove bodies, so it is likely he simply saw these two Jews as part of the party who made the original request for the execution and disposal of the body. The listener is reminded at v. 39 that Nicodemus was the one who came to Jesus at night, a fact that may suggest that this Gospel was also meant to be read by those being led into the Christian faith, read by those who had already learned about Nicodemus in John 3. There is also possibly some symbolism here—Nicodemus is coming out of the darkness to do something for Jesus, taking a personal risk, whereas before he had come to Jesus under the cover of darkness. This could be taken as a sign of spiritual progress toward being a full-fledged disciple.

The amount of spices used can be said to be overdoing things by an enor-mous amount. Seventy-five pounds of myrrh and aloes amounted to extra-vangance in the extreme, as was the case of Mary's anointing of Jesus in John 12.[31] Jewish burial practice did not involve embalming, which was an Egyp-tian art, but rather the placing of spices in the winding sheet or burial shroud of the corpse to retard odor during the week or more when the gravesite would be visited by the mourners. It has been pointed out, however, that in royal burials enormous amounts of spices could be used (cf. 2 Chron. 16:14); thus this scene perhaps should be read as an example of a burial fit for a king.[32] One might also conjecture that perhaps these "secret disciples" were trying to make up in death for their neglect of Jesus or their lack of courage to support his cause while he was alive.

The Jewish burial custom involved the use of linen cloth. Much conjec-ture and study has gone into the claim that the Shroud of Turin is Jesus' original burial shroud, as the ghostly negative imprint of a crucified body suggests. Recent carbon dating of the Turin shroud would seem to count against this possibility, but since the shroud was burned once in the Middle Ages, the carbon dating may reflect this later scorching rather than the time when the body imprint was originally made.[33] There is nothing in the Jo-hannine account to rule firmly against such a possible identification, al-though the evidence in favor of it is less than compelling.[34] In any case, the Jewish custom was that the spices would be mixed with an oil to make an ointment to rub on the body, which would leave a stain of some sort on the cloth.

Verse 41 leads us to believe that the garden tomb was quite near to the cross, but unfortunately we cannot be sure how close or where this may have been. Joseph and Nicodemus seem to have been in a hurry and got Jesus into a nearby convenient tomb, presumably with a round stone that could be rolled into place in the trench in front of its entrance. It is interesting that with all the emphasis on the fulfillment of scripture we are not told that

Jesus' being laid in a rich man's tomb is an example (cf. Isa. 53:9). What is stressed is that this tomb had never been used by anyone. Thus there was no excuse for mistaking it for someone else's tomb, nor was it likely that anyone would visit this tomb by accident. The sequel to this silent and somber scene is as dramatic as this one is melancholy, as we shall soon see. The Passion narrative ends quietly, not with a bang.

II. Bridging the Horizons

The stories surrounding Jesus' crucifixion in the Fourth Gospel are such that the danger is in saying too little about their significance rather than too much. It is important, however, to let the Fourth Evangelist have his own say and for us to follow his lead when we are using the text with a present-day audience rather than reading the Passion narrative in light of the Synoptics. We do not have in this Gospel a Jesus who cries out about his God-forsakenness on the cross; rather, we have a Jesus who is in control from start to finish and who finishes his life's work from the cross by creating the new community of his followers as represented by Mary and the Beloved Disciple. Male and female are united before and by the crucified Jesus into one new community of faith.

One way of honoring this Gospel's distinctiveness is by concentrating on the uniquely Johannine elements in the story, for example, the emphasis on Jesus' dying as the Passover lamb, as is hinted at by the mention of his legs not being broken (cf. Ex. 12:46; Num. 9:12), and the mention of hyssop which was used for the sprinkling of the doorposts with blood at Passover (cf. Ex. 12:22), as well as the mention of his dying on the day the lambs were to be slaughtered. Naturally if one is going to paint a picture of Jesus as the unblemished Passover lamb, it will be necessary for the teacher or preacher to have a rather clear idea how much the audience knows about Passover, both the events of the exodus, including the first Passover, and the later ritual celebration of Passover. We have seen a regular theme throughout this Gospel of demonstrating that Jesus replaces the institutions of Judaism with himself or with something he has to give that those institutions only give in part or only foreshadow. This story is a further development of that Johannine theme.

Another major theme of this Gospel is that Jesus is a universal savior. This theme is reiterated in this Gospel by the stress of Jesus' being proclaimed the King of Jews in all the major languages of that part of the empire—the legal language of the rulers (Latin), the *lingua franca* of the empire (Greek), and the holy language of the Jews (Hebrew). This theme is also seen in the fact that names are not assigned to the two major figures standing beneath the cross—they are simply a woman and a beloved male disciple, perhaps even representing the new humanity created by Christ from the tree.

It will be well to be very cautious in the handling of the cross itself as a theme. Our own culture has successfully trivialized the cross by turning it into a mere article of jewelry without pausing to think that the modern equivalent of wearing a cross would be wearing a little golden electric chair around one's neck. Today the cross can be worn as costume jewelry without making any statement of faith whatsoever by doing so. But the scandal and offense of the cross cannot be removed by these attempts at domestication.

It is no accident that even to this day religious Muslims assert that Jesus did not die on the cross. They see neither the necessity nor the appropriateness of the act, only its scandalousness, for how could a loving or just God allow such a thing to happen to so good and just a son as Jesus? Let it be made clear in your preaching and teaching that *unless* Jesus' death was absolutely necessary for human salvation, the forgiveness of sins, and life everlasting, then God is in no sense a loving God. What parent would condemn his only son to such a death unless that death was seen as the only necessary and sufficient means of salvation? At issue here is whether salvation and atonement for sins are going to be seen as God-centered and grace-engendered acts or whether redemption is just another human self-help program.

One's reaction to the cross is one of the ultimate tests of whether a person really understands and accepts Christianity or not. It is not our task to make the cross less offensive but rather to let it speak for itself in a plain and unvarnished way. In the Johannine portrayal of the crucifixion Jesus' divine dignity and power are made clear—his life was not taken, it was given up freely by a person in control of his fate. Nevertheless, Jesus' true humanness and the reality of his death are also stressed by the spear thrust, the blood and water pouring out, and the giving up of his spirit. Doubtless this was originally stressed to combat docetism of the sort argued against in the Johannine epistles. The Johannine community seems to have been plagued with those who denied that Jesus came and died in the flesh.

There is sometimes a danger of Docetism in conservative churches because the divinity of Christ is so emphasized that his humanity is not given its due. The fact is that there would be no salvation without the incarnation. Unless Jesus had become truly and fully human, he could not have died for the sins of the world. The cross stands foursquare against any attempts to rid the gospel of a fully human Jesus or to ignore God's demands for justice and atonement for sin.

Another possible way of bridging the horizons would be to focus on the subject of life's ironies. For example, there is profound irony in Pilate's insistence on portraying and labeling Jesus as king of the Jews, which he not only is caricatured as but really is, especially at the moment of his death on the cross. Even further irony is added to the story because the means chosen by Jesus' adversaries to do away with him in fact proves to be the very means by which he is exalted and which will provide salvation to those who accept him. "Those who had insisted that the imposter be crucified unwittingly have enthroned him."[35]

Burial customs vary considerably from one culture to another, and one possible way of handling the burial story would be to analyze and draw analogies between the way Joseph and Nicodemus chose to honor the beloved dead one and the way we do it today. There is, however, irony in this story as well, for these two Jews, perhaps feeling a little guilty and trying to compensate for earlier failures to act, show more respect for the dead Jesus than they appear to have done to the living one. He is buried like a king, but he was not served like one while living.

The burial of Jesus is also a fundamental article of the Christian creed (cf. 1 Cor. 15:4 and the Apostles' Creed). It stresses that Jesus truly died, that no swoon theory will account for his resurrection. The burial story also acts as the necessary prerequisite to stories of Jesus' resurrection which must be from the grave and from the dead. In other words, it is not enough to emphasize Jesus' death and resurrection at Easter. His burial needs to be stressed as well, for the sake of the empty tomb stories especially.

In his now classic study *The Crucified God,* J. Moltmann stressed the importance of seeing God's involvement and presence in and on the cross. The issue here is a profound one and includes such questions as: If Jesus' divine nature was not involved in the death on the cross, in what sense would his death have a universally atoning scope or in what way could his death provide eternal life? How would we distinguish Jesus' death from that of the martyrs if his divine nature is not involved, or, to make a more extreme case, how would it have differed from the death of Adam, if Adam had chosen, *before he sinned,* to offer himself for Eve and her fallen future progeny? Yet another question would be: How could there be any meaning in the claim "God died for us" if Christ's divine nature or the divine presence did not in some sense participate in what happened on the cross? How could the Father feel our suffering and know our pain, if God in God's divine nature is immune to suffering, sorrow, and the like? While it may be going too far to speak of the death of God, if we cannot speak of the suffering of God with us and on the cross for us in some sense, it is hard to see how this act can be seen as a divine one done on behalf of humanity by God. Moltmann puts it as follows:

> We cannot therefore say here in patripassian terms that the Father also suffered and died. The suffering and dying of the Son, forsaken by the Father, is a different kind of suffering from the suffering of the Father in the death of the Son. Nor can the death of Jesus be understood in theopaschite terms as the "death of God." To understand what happened between Jesus and his God and Father on the cross, it is necessary to talk in Trinitarian terms. The Son suffers dying, the Father suffers the death of the Son. The grief of the Father here is just as important as the death of the Son. The Fatherlessness of the Son is matched by the Sonlessness of the Father, and if God has constituted himself as the Father of Jesus Christ, then he also suffers the death of his Fatherhood in the death of the Son.[36]

Even with these qualifications, Moltmann is right that unless God is involved and present at Calvary in the person of the Son, it is hard to see how redemption is divine in its source, since redemption comes to us through and in the cross. The ultimate expression of the incarnation and divine self-sacrifice comes at the cross.

The theme of eyewitness is stressed in this account of Jesus' death, especially at v. 35 where Jesus' death is demonstrated by the spear thrust. Jesus' death was witnessed by no less than the Beloved Disciple himself, the one whose memoirs have been preserved and edited in this Gospel. The story raises the question about the value and validity of eyewitness testimony, both then and now. Eyewitness testimony is still highly prized in our society, especially when something illegal happens and a trial ensues. The stress on such testimony presupposes not only that there is a real world of facts which can be perceived, known, and properly interpreted but also that truth is a value our society prizes above most others values.

A helpful message could be developed around the theme of what sort of world we live in and what happens when truth is revealed in a dark and hostile environment. For example, what happened to the German psyche when the truth about the death camps during World War II was revealed? Some people went into and remain in denial, writing revisionist history. Some accepted this heavy burden and have sought to get beyond these horrors by seeking forgiveness and working to make sure it never happens again. Others have seen that we cannot even begin to atone for such atrocities. What is done is done. However, Christ's death can atone and has atoned for the sins of the world. Paradoxically, the answer to Auschwitz is found at Golgotha, not in modern *mea culpas*.

In a fallen world, living the truth is in many ways much easier than living a lie. Living a lie requires that we constantly strive to get our story straight, strive for consistency, always having to remember what we said and did before, lest we are caught in our lie. It often also requires secrecy to a degree that no human being can finally have. Eventually our sins will find us out. Living the truth, on the other hand, does not require us to put up a front or be overly cautious about our words. It does, however, require that we be prepared to accept the consequences of living the truth, which often involves rejection, vilification, persecution, and suffering. Fallen people do not like too much light, when they are used to wearing moral sunglasses. They do not like being reminded of things they are at least in part ashamed of. In short, they are not interested in looking in an accurate mirror; they prefer the sort that one finds at the circus, which everyone knows is a deliberate distortion. Jesus the truth in part died because he made others see the lie they were living.

Some people are even willing to kill rather than to have to give up the lie they have created and have fallen in love with. Recently a woman who had been involved in the anti-Vietnam movement turned herself in to the authorities in Boston, because she had driven the getaway car in a bank robbery in which an officer was killed. She stated in the trial that after two decades she could no longer live the lie of a fake identity and a life that denied that she had done what she had done. She said she would rather state the truth and accept the consequences so she could live with herself the rest of her life. Truth has a way of setting people free from the web of deceit and denial, even if it comes at a heavy price.

What does it say about human beings that we shout Alleluia on Palm Sunday and crucify Jesus on Good Friday? What does it say about us that we crucified the way, the truth, and the life? The ultimate mirror of what fallen humanity is like and is capable of is the cross. After the cross, even the atrocities of centuries of wars should not surprise us. History is the record of human fallenness and degradation repeating its bloody acts over and over again. The cross stands at the crossroads and offers us a way to break the cycle of violence.

J.R.R. Tolkien in a number of his writings has discussed the concept of what he calls eucatastrophe, a fortunate disaster. The death of Christ is seen as the chief example of this sort of event. Although there are many ironies and peculiar turns to the story of Jesus, none is more strange than the way this story ends. Considering the first-century view of crucifixion, it is both amazing and surprising that the Fourth Evangelist boldly presents the death of Jesus as a form of exaltation, of being lifted up. His near-contemporary Cicero had said that crucifixion was the most cruel and terrible punishment, incapable of description, and Josephus likewise called it the most wretched way to die.

So then is the Fourth Evangelist guilty of gilding the lily, of putting a brave face on about an event that was a terrible tragedy? The answer to this can only be no, *if* the death of Jesus is seen in the light of its sequel, the resurrection. In other words, the death of Jesus has no redeeming qualities, in both senses of that phrase, unless Jesus also rose from the dead. However perfect a sacrifice Jesus may have offered, and however much he may have been like a Passover lamb in that respect, if the story ends with John 19, Jesus is but one more example of how in a fallen world the good die young, one more example of a life that ends in a horrible bloody mess.

The Fourth Gospel, more than any other, allows the light of Easter to affect the way the whole story is told, all the way back to John 1, for already there we hear that the community of the faithful has seen Jesus' glory. Does this amount to coating the story with a varnish that obscures the truth, or does it amount to a clearer reading of the life of Jesus because of the benefit of hindsight and insight? The Fourth Evangelist believes it is the latter, and he does so because the Beloved Disciple bore witness not just to Jesus' death but also to the empty tomb *and* resurrection. Even the empty tomb story proves nothing, and is capable of numerous explanations such as grave robbing (cf. below on John 20), unless that event is framed by both the death and the resurrection of Jesus.

The Fourth Evangelist's portrayal of these events requires the reader to see them in the light of the sequel in John 20 and, by doing so, see in a disaster a eucatastrophe. The death of Jesus should not be preached in isolation from its glorious sequel in the view of this evangelist. Indeed, the sequel causes this evangelist not to dwell on the darker side of Jesus' death. He does not dwell on any of the more gruesome or disturbing aspects of the story, unlike Mark, since he is not trying to produce gut-wrenching feelings in his audience but rather faith in and reverence for Jesus. Gone are most of the taunts, the darkness at noon, the earthquake, the uncomprehending multitudes who gawk, the splitting of the Temple veil, and, most of all, gone is the cry of dereliction: "My God, my God, why have you forsaken me?" In short, the Fourth Evangelist's version of Jesus' death is intended to produce different emotions and reactions in the audience than Mark's portrayal. I would suggest again that this is because this Gospel is written essentially for a nonbelieving audience.

We must not forget that we have four portrayals of Jesus' death, and if we blend them all together, we lose the intended effect of any one of these writers. This is not to say that there is not a place for a harmony of the Gospels that tries to figure out exactly what happened, in what order, and why, but such an effort is more appropriate in a teaching setting and in a traditional commentary. The job of the minister in the pulpit, however, is proclamation, not speculation, and thus the minister is required to tell the story as one or another Gospel tells it, and let the evangelist have his say. Preaching is, after all, an attempt to offer inspiration and to cause transformation, not just a matter of offering information.

The Fourth Evangelist is trying to present the story in a fashion appropriate to the mission of the church, in a fashion for an unchurched audience. He thus focuses on the issues of Christology and revelation and tries to present as positive a portrayal of Jesus' life and death as honesty will allow. There are some difficult things that one may discuss with one's family that one will not necessarily need to or feel free to air in public. The Fourth Gospel, then, concentrates on the public face of Jesus, and even more narrowly on the winsome side of that public face in order to "draw all to him." In this evangelist's view, a glorious, powerful, divine and yet fully human Jesus who acts as the perfect Son and agent of God, and has both a heavenly origin and destiny, was more likely to win Gentiles and Jews to Christ in the environment in which he operated than some other presentation of Jesus.

What this amounts to is a heavy concentration on one side of Jesus' story and character. Jesus truly was glorious in many ways, but that is not the whole story. Other portrayals that drew on other aspects of the authentic Jesus tradition would be in order with other audiences and other purposes in mind. In short, the Christ of faith was a larger-than-life figure, at least larger than any *one* life of the man could possibly hope to convey in one telling of the story. Thus we must tell the tale over and over in many different ways, depending on time, audience, needs, and a host of other factors. At the heart of the story in each case, however, must be the eucatastrophe of Jesus' death, burial, resurrection, empty tomb, and resurrection appearances.

In what is, in many ways, his most powerful and poetic book F. Buechner speaks of the effect of gazing on the many faces of Jesus, as he has been portrayed down through the ages. He says:

Yet whatever our religion or lack of it, we tend to shrink from beholding him and play our game instead with Shakespeare's face or Helen of Troy's because with them the chances are we could survive almost anything— Shakespeare's simper, say, or a cast in Helen's eye. But with Jesus the risk is too great; the risk that his face would be too much for us if not enough, either a face like any other face we see, pass by, forget, or a face unlike any other face, so unlike any other that we would have no choice but to remember it always and follow or flee it to the ends of our days and beyond. . . . With part of ourselves I think we might avoid meeting his real eyes, if such a meeting were possible, the way at certain moments we avoid meeting our own real eyes in mirrors because for better or worse they threaten to tell us more than we want to know.[37]

The Fourth Evangelist believed that Jesus had an unforgettable face, a face in which, if one beheld it, one not only could see his glory but could also be transformed by the act of gazing upon it. He calls all men and women as potential disciples to come stand beneath the cross and look up at Jesus, not look down on him because he was crucified. It is remarkable how often through the ages this evangelist's appeal and story have been heeded, with life-changing effects similar to the sort of thing that happened to those first two witnesses, Mary and the Beloved Disciple. It is our task to unleash the power and glory of this Gospel for another generation of those who live in deep darkness.

Part VI. The Resurrection Narratives: Including the Epilogue (John 20:1–21:25)

18. The Presence of His Absence (John 20:1–10)

The Gospel accounts are in agreement that women were last at the cross and first at the empty tomb. It is not surprising in these circumstances that at least two Gospels (Matthew and John) present women as not only the first to see the empty tomb but also the first to see and bear witness to the risen Jesus, carrying the Easter message to the male disciples. This sort of portrayal has all the earmarks of authenticity, in view of the low view of women's witness held in many quarters in the ancient world which had one degree or another of a patriarchal bias against women, depending on which subculture one was a part of (cf. *m. Rosh.* 1:8).[1] We must turn our attention first to the empty tomb traditions in the Fourth Gospel and study the significance of the absence of Christ's presence in the tomb.

20:1 Early on the first day of the week, while it was still dark, Mary Magdalene came to the tomb and saw that the stone had been removed from the tomb. ²So she ran and went to Simon Peter and the other disciple, the one whom Jesus loved, and said to them, "They have taken the Lord out of the tomb, and we do not know where they have laid him." ³Then Peter and the other disciple set out and went toward the tomb. ⁴The two were running together, but the other disciple outran Peter and reached the tomb first. ⁵He bent down to look in and saw the linen wrappings lying there, but did not go in. ⁶Then Simon Peter came, following him, and went into the tomb. He saw the linen wrappings lying there, ⁷and the cloth that had been on Jesus' head, not lying with the linen wrappings but rolled up in a place by itself. ⁸Then the other disciple, who reached the tomb first, also went in, and he saw and believed; ⁹for as yet they did not understand the scripture, that he must rise from the dead. ¹⁰Then the disciples returned to their homes.

I. The Historical Horizon

The resurrection narratives begin with the assertion that very early on the first day of the week, Mary Magdalene, who had been present and had witnessed Jesus' crucifixion (19:25), and probably some other women,[2] went to the tomb in the dark. The latter note probably has some symbolic significance. The followers of Jesus are still in the dark about his nature and destiny. The stress on this happening on the first day of the week in all four Gospels is striking. We might have expected the accounts to specify that this event happened on the third day after the crucifixion.[3] Perhaps the reason for the first day emphasis is that the evangelists all wrote for or as a part of communities that worshiped on the first day of the week (Sunday). The Christian community is the community of the resurrection, and worship habits change in light of the climactic events that end the Gospel story.

We are simply told that Mary Magdalene saw that the stone had been rolled away from the tomb and ran to tell Simon Peter and the Beloved Disciple. Her immediate assumption is that an act of grave robbing has transpired. This was a very common practice in antiquity, especially if the tomb was a wealthy person's. Indeed so prevalent was the act that the Emperor Claudius (A.D. 41–54) made a decree prohibiting this activity on pain of capital punishment, a copy of which decree has been found in Nazareth![4]

This report in turn brings Peter and the Beloved Disciple on the run, the latter one reaching the tomb first (v. 3). The Beloved Disciple bends down and looks into the tomb and sees the linen strips of cloth lying on the platform where the body would have been laid. He does not, however, go into the tomb. Peter, when he arrives, does not hesitate to go in. He sees what the Beloved Disciple had seen—the linen strips of cloth were in one place, and the cloth that had been wrapped around Jesus' head was rolled up and in a place by itself. After this the Beloved Disciple enters and we are told he "saw and believed." We are not, however, told *what* he believed. What we *are* told is that as yet neither he nor the other disciples understood the scripture that he must rise from the dead. This section of the narrative concludes with the affirmation that the disciples returned again "to their own"—to their own homes is implied (cf. Luke 24:12).[5]

A variety of points from this narrative are important. First, the narrative itself comports in a general way with what we are told about the visit of Peter to the tomb in Luke 24:12, which is said in that Gospel to have been prompted by the report of some women about an empty tomb. Second, we are not told that either Peter or the Beloved Disciple saw anything supernatural when they visited the tomb, not even any angels. Third, there is no basis in this text for the older allegorical conjectures that we are meant to see some sort of rivalry depicted here between Johannine and Petrine churches or between Jewish and Gentile forms of early Christianity.[6] Peter and the Beloved Disciple come together and leave together in this episode, and whatever the Beloved Disciple may have believed, it does not result in the sort of behavior that one would expect of a person who now has Easter faith. He does not go forth and proclaim the Lord is risen—he, like Peter, simply goes quietly home, and so far as we can tell, he says nothing to anyone! In other words, this is hardly much of a picture of the superiority of Johannine Christianity over other forms.

We must focus our attention more closely on vv. 8–9. Although traditionally it has been assumed that the Beloved Disciple is being depicted here as believing in the resurrection on the basis of the evidence of the empty tomb, thus revealing his superior spiritual perceptivity over that of Peter's, this interpretation must be seen as extremely doubtful. For one thing, as G. R. Beasley-Murray stresses,[7] it is likely that if the disciples understood Jesus' prediction of his resurrection at all before the resurrection appearances, it would *not* have been understood to mean that he *alone* was going to be raised but rather that he would be raised with at least all of the righteous as the kingdom dawned. They were not looking for an isolated resurrection in the midst of human history. Furthermore, as P. Minear rightly stresses, the text explicitly says they did *not* understand from scripture that Jesus had to rise from the dead.[8] Then too, we have seen various examples where the verb *pisteuo* ("to believe") can mean a true but inadequate faith in Jesus, a faith that falls short of belief in or understanding of Jesus as a crucified and risen messiah (cf. 2:23–24; 12:42–43; 20:8).

It is perfectly possible, then, that the Beloved Disciple believed, on the basis of what he saw in the empty tomb,[9] that Jesus' life was brought to an orderly conclusion and that God had probably taken Jesus up into heaven bodily, much as the prophet Elijah or even Moses. Had not Jesus previously spoken about being lifted up as the Son of man? This could be understood in several ways. I thus must conclude that there is no hard evidence of Easter faith, even in the case of the Beloved Disciple, prior to the appearances of the risen Jesus. That the Beloved Disciple believed more than Mary at this juncture, and more than Peter, does not mean that even his pilgrimage of faith was over yet. To reject the theory of grave robbing and believe that God had done something on behalf of Jesus amounts to less than Easter faith.

What we must learn from this story is that these two key disciples, one of whom could be said to represent Galilean disciples and one of whom could be said to represent Judean ones, both confirmed the report of Mary about the empty tomb. Yet an uninterpreted empty tomb was subject to several possible interpretations both positive and negative, two of which are manifested in this story.

II. Bridging the Horizons

This story makes evident that eyewitness testimony in and of itself is no guarantee of correct interpretation of the facts. Mary Magdalene was right enough that the tomb was empty, but her inference, "*They* have taken the Lord out of the tomb, and we do not know where *they* have laid him," was all wrong. On the positive side, this story, *when coupled with those that follow it in John 20,* confirms that Jesus' resurrection was a bodily one. This text then can be used to show the character of Jesus' resurrection and reveal that it was not merely a spiritual event. The neatly rolled up grave clothes also suggest that we should compare this story to that of Lazarus, where the latter comes hobbling out of the tomb bound and gagged. What happened to Jesus was seen as something more than what happened to Lazarus. One must then beware in one's teaching or preaching of claiming too much or too little about the empty tomb. It is an effective deterrent to a docetic or purely spiritual view of Jesus' resurrection, but only when it is closely linked with the rest of John 20.

This story also shows that seeing the visible evidence of the empty tomb and that something had happened to Jesus' body was not enough to produce insight into the scriptures about resurrection. Perhaps our author had certain texts in mind as foreshadowing Jesus' resurrection, such as Hos. 6:2; Ps. 16:10; or Lev. 23:11. The understanding of Jesus' resurrection required the understanding of the scripture he fulfilled, and the understanding of the latter came only when the disciples received the Holy Spirit, sent by Jesus from heaven (cf. below). Remembering with insight came when the Reminder came to dwell within the believer.

In view of the fact that this story shows that belief in an empty tomb is a necessary but insufficient belief in what happened to Jesus after crucifixion, it would be possible to draw analogies with contemporary pilgrimages to the Holy Land. Many devout Christians go every year, hoping to walk where Jesus walked and so draw closer to their Lord. They hope that seeing will lead to a deepening of believing. The truth is that this may or may not be the outcome of such a pilgrimage. Many come back disillusioned, not merely by all the commercialism, but by the fact that archaeologists cannot firmly pinpoint beyond reasonable doubt where the upper room was or where precisely Jesus was crucified or where the empty tomb may have been. Much has been lost in the shifting sands of time, and faith in the risen Lord is not dependent on the conjectures of scholars about this or that locale. Many of the most devout Christians have never seen the Holy Land and yet have believed fervently in the risen Lord.

The question that this and the succeeding stories raise, especially the Thomas story, is: Do we need a tangible Jesus today? Is it necessary to see, to feel, to touch in order to believe in our generation? Must we insist on a "seeing leads to believing or deepening faith" approach? I think that the Fourth Evangelist would tell us this is not the case. Indeed, I think he is telling us that those who believe without seeing are in a sense more blessed and have a stronger faith. We are required to have the eyes of faith to see and understand the risen Lord, not the eyes of a tourist on pilgrimage. The pilgrimage of faith takes place within the human heart and has to do with matters of spirit and truth. This is not to say that it does not involve matters of history, for this is certainly the case, and also matters of the authenticity of testimonies about history by the Beloved Disciple and others. What it does not require is the confirmation of sight, or even of scholarly opinion in our day, to be proved true. Historical facts, not the ever-changing tides of scholarly opinions about those facts, are the basis of Christian faith.

True worship transpires wherever God is worshiped in spirit and in truth. Jesus is a universal savior, not one confined to a particular land or age, and he has sent forth a Spirit that is universally accessible. It is the Spirit, not the tour guide, that may be called upon to lead the believer into all truth and deeper faith, although of course this process can sometimes be aided by visual reminders such as the remains and rocks found today in the Holy Land. It can also be aided, it is hoped, by good and faithful commentators who have labored long to understand the text of scripture.

One must, however, distinguish between what may be helpful and what is necessary. The empty tomb reminds us that seeing the place that marks the presence of Jesus' absence is not the same as encountering his presence. Even the unbeliever's dawning recognition of the absence of his presence in his or her life is more important than discovering the spot that marks the absence of his presence. Whether our experience and testimony is that of Mary's or that of the Beloved Disciple's, neither amounts to a full-fledged encounter with the risen Lord or a witnessing thereto. It is more important to understand and believe in *who* moved the stone than to know exactly *where* the stone lies.

Finally, it is worth stressing to our audiences that these stories bear all the earmarks of authenticity. Not only because they openly tell us that women were first at the tomb but also because they indicate that the first witness thought the body was stolen and because not even the key male disciples leave the empty tomb with full understanding or Easter faith, these stories reveal that they are not cunningly devised fables. Early Christians would not have made up such stories about the witnesses to the foundational events of their faith. The stories are self-authenticating, and even the silences and absences in these stories speak louder than many words. The witnesses did not go looking for a stone rolled back, an empty tomb, a close encounter with angels, or a risen savior. They were people in mourning, as the story shows. One must posit something dramatic to explain the change in these people. The explanation in John 20 speaks for itself.

19. Mary, Mary, Extraordinary (John 20:11–18)

The story of Mary Magdalene as presented in John 19–20 is a moving drama of the progress of a soul on the way to full faith in the risen Lord.[1] She moved from a state of abject sorrow and preoccupation with the body of the dead Jesus to a state of sudden euphoria which involved clinging to Jesus' physical nature in a way that limited her "grasping" of what had happened to Jesus to a state of understanding so that she was enabled to leave her preoccupations behind and become an apostle to the apostles, carrying and then proclaiming the message of Easter faith.

This narrative is in all likelihood the same as that mentioned only in summary form in Matt. 28:9–10, and it forms the logical sequel to the women discovering the empty tomb. The Fourth Evangelist has chosen to focus on the experience of a particular individual, even though he is aware that other women likely were present on this occasion (cf. 20:2, "*we* do not know where"). This comports with his technique elsewhere, which primarily focuses on the reactions of individuals to Jesus, such as the Samaritan woman or Nicodemus or Caiaphas. It will be critical to recognize when illumination comes for Mary in this story, for it provides a clue to understanding how this text is meant to function.

It is also critical to bear in mind the great restraint shown in all the canonical Gospels when they are dealing with Jesus' resurrection. Nowhere is the actual resurrection of Jesus described, and no human being is said to have witnessed it. What was seen was the *result* of resurrection, namely, the risen Lord. Furthermore, the Gospel accounts stress that it was Jesus' disciples who saw the risen Lord, not strangers. The resurrection, then, can be seen as an event that confirms or renews or brings to full flower the faith of those who already believed in Jesus, but it is not presented as an event that took place in such a manner that it coerced nonbelievers into faith, unless we should see Thomas as an example of this. Even in the case of Thomas, however, we are dealing with a doubting disciple, not with an opponent of Jesus or with someone who has never heard or seen Jesus and his works before. The interest, then, in the resurrection is not in *how* it happened, nor in the event of resurrection as something that in itself forces those into faith who despise or are ignorant of Jesus, but rather in its *effect* on the community of Jesus' followers. They became Christians in the full sense, and missionary-minded ones, because they had seen, been restored by, and been commissioned by the risen Lord. Resurrection has to do with vindication: (1) the vindication of Jesus, his claims, and cause; and (2) the vindication and renewal of the faith and trust the disciples had placed in Jesus during the earthly ministry.

We must also notice how very different all the resurrection traditions are. In Luke we have appearances only in Jerusalem, in Matthew appearances only in Galilee to the inner circle of male disciples after one appearance in Jerusalem to women, and in the original text of Mark we have the proclamation of resurrection by the angel but no account of resurrection appearances, for the earliest and best Greek manuscripts do not include Mark 16:9–20.[2] In this latter case, the absence of resurrection appearances is likely because the original ending of Mark is lost, not because the author intended to end the story abruptly at 16:8 with fright and flight from the tomb by the women. The Fourth Gospel has appearances both in Jerusalem and, in the epilogue, in Galilee, both to women and to men. The story of the appearance to Mary Magdalene is as distinctive to this Gospel as the Emmaus road story is to Luke's account.[3] We believe C. H. Dodd was right to say about the account in John 20:11–18 that there "is something indefinably firsthand about it. . . . There is nothing quite like it in the gospels. Is there anything quite like it in all of ancient literature?"[4]

These stories, though there are differences in the telling even where the Gospel accounts overlap, nonetheless bear all the earmarks of authenticity. If it is difficult to believe that early Christians would make up a story about an appearance to otherwise unknown disciples while failing to give any significant attention to appearances to the key disciples (Luke 24), it is quite impossible to believe in the patriarchal climate of the eastern part of the Roman Empire that early Christians would invent stories about resurrection appearances to women, especially women of the background of Mary Magdalene (cf. Luke 8:1–3). Christianity already labored under the burden of trying to explain the idea of a crucified Messiah. It is implausible that they made things doubly difficult by conjuring up appearance stories to witnesses that outsiders would be disposed to doubt from the outset.

20:11 But Mary stood weeping outside the tomb. As she wept, she bent over to look into the tomb; [12]and she saw two angels in white, sitting where the body of Jesus had been lying, one at the head and the other at the feet. [13]They said to her, "Woman, why are you weeping?" She said to them, "They have taken away my Lord, and I do not know where they have laid him." [14]When she had said this, she turned around and saw Jesus standing there, but she did not know that it was Jesus. [15]Jesus said to her, "Woman, why are you weeping? Whom are you looking for?" Supposing him to be the gardener, she said to him, "Sir, if you have carried him away, tell me where you have laid him, and I will take him away." [16]Jesus said to her, "Mary!" She turned and said to him in Hebrew, "Rabbouni!" (which means Teacher). [17]Jesus said to her, "Do not hold on to me, because I have not yet ascended to the Father. But go to my brothers and say to them, 'I am

ascending to my Father and your Father, to my God and your God.' "
[18]Mary Magdalene went and announced to the disciples, "I have seen the
Lord"; and she told them that he had said these things to her.

I. The Historical Horizon

From the very beginning of this story in v. 11, we can perceive a gradual
process of revelation to Mary, which goes for naught until the crucial moment of recognition and the even more crucial teaching that follows it. A
certain similarity between Mary's activity in v. 11 and Peter's in v. 5 should
be recognized, except that evidently Mary is more spiritually perceptive, for
not only does she see the grave clothes, she sees two angels sitting like book-
ends on the slab where Jesus' body had been laid. The point of this was surely
to signal, as angels normally do, that divine activity was involved in this
emptiness between them. There is indeed a void, but it is not devoid of
meaning. They signal that Jesus' body is no longer in the tomb and thus one
should no longer focus on the past—on either his death or his body.

The virtual silence of the angels in this version of the story, in contrast to
the proclamation of the angels in the Synoptic account, is striking. Here the
mere asking of a question prepares the way for the dialogue to follow. Even
though this revelation is more positive than the one that Peter or the
Beloved Disciple received, neither the empty tomb nor the presence of the
supernatural is sufficient to change Mary's mournful mood. It is likely that
the evangelist wants us to think that nothing less than Jesus himself could
accomplish that feat. In this regard she is like Thomas (cf. 20:25). The angels attempt to draw Mary out of her sorrow by asking, "Woman, why are
you weeping?" Without question, Mary's problem is that her mental horizons are fixed on the past, and significantly it is only when she turns *away*
from the empty tomb that she sees Jesus.

In v. 15 Jesus opens his dialogue with Mary by reiterating the question of
the angels: "Woman, why are you weeping?" It is not, however, until Jesus
calls her by name that she recognizes Jesus, and thus the knowledgeable
reader will recognize in this a paradigm of what Jesus had earlier said (cf.
10:3–4). Jesus is approaching Mary as the gentle shepherd leading his sheep
away from preoccupation with death and the past. If in the case of Jesus'
mother we saw a progression from her being called woman to her becoming a mother in the church (cf. above on John 19:25–27), here we see a progression from "woman" to "Mary" as the revelation becomes more personal. Mary Magdalene is being favored even more than Jesus' mother, for
here she is portrayed as the first to see the risen Lord.

By including the question, "Whom are you looking for?" Jesus is implying that Mary's focus should be on someone, not on something (i.e., a
corpse). She wants to know where *it* is, and Jesus responds by speaking
about a living person. Yet Mary's thoughts are still so riveted on the past and
on the body that she makes the colossal and ironic error of mistaking Jesus

for the gardener who may have moved the body. Her lack of spiritual perceptivity at this point could hardly be made clearer. On the other hand, it seems characteristic of first appearance stories that Jesus is not immediately recognized (cf. the Emmaus story in Luke 24). G. R. Beasley-Murray has conjectured that the glorified Jesus made himself sensibly recognizable only to his disciples but that in his transfigured condition he would not have been distinguishable from other supernatural beings such as an angel.[5] The problem with this suggestion is that Mary confuses Jesus with a gardener, but she certainly does not confuse him with the angels in the tomb.

Even when Jesus calls Mary by name, her pilgrimage is not over. In her initial reply she calls Jesus *Rabbouni* (my master), which suggests that she still thinks of Jesus in terms of her past relationship with him, as her teacher. This is verified by the translation the evangelist gives to the term—Teacher (v. 16). At this juncture it becomes clear that it is no longer adequate to relate to Jesus as a great sage.[6] He must now be seen as more than just a conveyor of Wisdom. Her reaction is of course natural and also involves her clinging to Jesus.

The Greek phrase *me mou haptou* has been translated variously as "Do not touch me" or "Stop touching (clinging to) me." It is very probable that it has the latter meaning here, but in any case it implies that Mary is trying to approach Jesus in a particular physical way that Jesus must put a stop to. He is not interested in renewing relationships with his disciples on the same old terms, for he is no longer the same Jesus. He is now well and truly on the way to the Father. Beasley-Murray suggests that the ascension had begun at the resurrection and is not completed until Jesus is back in heaven.[7] However, from the evangelist's perspective there is a sense in which the ascension began when Jesus was lifted up on the cross. In any event, Jesus is portrayed as not wishing for Mary to depend on what will only be a temporary state of affairs. Jesus must soon return to the Father,[8] and so it is time to recognize that clinging to the past will no longer do.

There are two major keys to understanding this story. The first is to see how it compares and contrasts with the Thomas narrative that follows it in 20:24–31. Both narratives focus on a special appearance by Jesus for the sake of an individual, and in both the one receiving the appearance has a strong conviction that Jesus is not alive. This engenders a strong preoccupation with the past (Mary with Jesus' body, Thomas with Jesus' wounds). In both stories there is a need to touch or hold on to Jesus. In both stories Jesus also appears suddenly, in order to lead the individual to overcome his or her doubts and believe in Jesus in the right way (cf. 20:17–27). We may see in these two narratives the evangelist's attempt to indicate Jesus' desire to recover both his sisters and his brothers. Finally, both Mary and Thomas are led in the end to make professions of faith that are seen as reflecting full Christian faith, a faith possible only on or after Easter, and thus the Gospel is brought to a climax.

There are, however, crucial differences in the two stories. In one story there is a prohibition of clinging, in the other a command to touch. This is to be explained in part by the differences in the two situations, no doubt. Thomas had heard of previous resurrection appearances and still had not believed, whereas Mary had only knowledge of Jesus before his death to guide her response. This is why there is no recognition motif in the Thomas story, unlike Mary's tale. Thomas's unbelief is more entrenched and reprehensible than Mary's and so would seem to require a more radical remedy. Mary, having once touched Jesus, does not need to cling to him but rather can be commissioned to undertake an apostolic task. Thomas by contrast must be bidden to touch and he is not given an apostolic task as Mary is. In other words, this sister comes off better in these stories than either Peter and the Beloved Disciple mentioned before her as examining the empty tomb or the cynical Thomas mentioned after her.

The second major key to understanding this narrative is the journeying motif. Throughout this Gospel we have seen references to Jesus' having come from the Father and returning to the Father (cf. 7:33; 13:3; 14:12, 28; 16:28). The key to understanding Jesus comes from knowing where he comes from and where he is going. It is similar with Jesus' disciples.[9] The key to self-understanding is knowing who has sent the disciple and where he has commissioned the disciples to go. Mary's initial concern is with where the body of Jesus is. She is seeking Jesus in the wrong sense. The evangelist is suggesting that it is not knowledge of where Jesus was at that moment that was the key to understanding him but rather where he was going. Only the latter leads to having a firm "grasp" of and on Jesus. Until Jesus ascends, he cannot be where all his disciples can equally have access to him. Until Mary understands this, her own pilgrimage cannot come to a successful conclusion.

The evangelist, however, indicates that Mary finally does understand once Jesus explains the matter to her and that she completes her own faith pilgrimage by journeying to the disciples and bearing witness to the male disciples about the risen Lord. "Knowledge of Jesus' true destination gives her the freedom to play a part in revealing the destiny of Jesus and his followers. Just as Jesus must journey to the Father before his disciples can journey to the nations, so too Mary must learn of Jesus' journey to the Father before she can journey to the disciples."[10]

That Jesus calls the male disciples his brothers, and speaks of a shared faith in the Father, indicates the sort of family relationships he wishes to exist in the community of faith, as does John 19:25–27. This family is brought back together in part because "Mary went proclaiming (*angellousa*) to the disciples" (20:18). These words reveal that Mary is no longer fixated on the past but is focused on the task before her. Jesus had spoken to her about spiritual relationships in the present tense, which meant that her relationship with Jesus would continue, although on a higher plane. Ironically, Jesus has begun to reestablish fellowship with his brothers by first reestablishing a relationship with one of his sisters.

There is little doubt that the evangelist, by devoting more space to the story of Mary Magdalene than to the story of any of the male disciples individually, wishes to portray this Mary as important to the story and the witness about it. Indeed, her story is given more space and detailed attention than even Jesus' own mother and the Beloved Disciple. It is very likely that the reason Mary Magdalene is mentioned first in all the witness lists of the women[11] is that early on the tradition became firmly fixed that she had been the first to see and proclaim the risen Lord. The Fourth Evangelist draws on this fact in order to portray to his audience of potential converts what real faith in the risen Lord entails and does not entail.

Here witness and mission come together finally, and it is made clear that one is saved to serve, called by name in order to be sent out proclaiming to others. Here we have as positive a portrayal of the value and validity of a woman's witness to Jesus as one will find anywhere in the Gospels. It should not surprise us that this Gospel closes with the paradigmatic testimony of one woman and one man. It is intended as a tool for witness to all people both male and female, both Greek and Jew, both slave and free. Mary's lack of spiritual perceptivity at the beginning of the story is not covered up any more than her bold witnessing to the risen Lord at the end of the story to the inner circle of male disciples is glossed over. The portrayal is meant to be realistic, showing how far true faith in Jesus can bring a person. Even now, the church has not fully grasped what it means for men and women to both confess the risen Lord boldly and proclaim him equally boldly in the believing community and in the world.

II. Bridging the Horizons

Obviously this story can be used to show how one person can come to full-fledged faith in Jesus. Since the Gospel of John has a wide variety of other pilgrimage stories, this story should not be dealt with in isolation from the others. It only presents *a way* that Christian faith comes about.[12]

It is not surprising, in a Gospel meant for missionary work with those who have never seen or heard Jesus in the flesh, that having physical contact with Jesus or seeing him is downplayed as a crucial factor in full Christian faith, while *hearing* his calling of a person by name, and then receiving his teaching, is accentuated as the means of recognizing who Jesus is and what he would have a person to do to be his follower. "Neither the empty tomb nor the vision of Jesus lifted the veil for Mary Magdalene, only the words of Jesus."[13] Here it is equally clear that fuller understanding both enables and makes one responsible for witnessing to one's faith.

One way of bridging the gap between now and then would be to focus on the serendipity of the Gospel—how it often produces results that are the opposite of what we might expect, or even want. We may have expected either Peter or the Beloved Disciple to go and proclaim the risen Lord to the other male disciples, but instead it is Mary Magdalene.

Another avenue of approach would be to discuss how distance in time and space from the historical Jesus is seen in this text as a help for discipleship in these closing stories. Analogies could be drawn with other relationships, such as the relationship between parents and some adult children which actually are helped by establishing a healthy distance, which promotes greater understanding and prevents a clinging to the past and a reliance on the past way of doing things when one was not fully mature. Thomas Wolfe was right that there is a sense in which when you grow up, you can never really go home again.

There is also the matter of spiritual development or pilgrimage that could be mined from this text to various good ends. For example, it is not adequate to confess Jesus as a great teacher or sage, when one has come to know him as the risen Lord. This Gospel is full of true confessions that are nonetheless inadequate if and when one has encountered the risen Lord. The earlier chapters of this Gospel must not be used as presenting models of Christian faith. Rather, they depict people on the road to full Christian faith, a faith not possible until after Easter, when seekers finally become finders and finders become keepers, oddly enough by letting go of the old way of relating to Jesus.

Finally, it is wrong to make too much of Mary's misunderstanding of the meaning of the empty tomb and lack of recognition of Jesus at first. The latter is characteristic of first appearance stories, as Luke 24 shows, and reveals that the disciples were not looking for the Easter events that transpired. Further, this Gospel stresses that full understanding is not possible without the Holy Spirit in any case, and so prior to Easter none of the disciples should be judged too harshly, and even during the Easter events but before the coming of the Spirit one should not expect full spiritual perceptivity on the part of the characters in the story.

One of the most serious problems for many struggling churches today is that of clinging to their past in a way that is neither healthful nor helpful. Like Mary Magdalene, they long for the good old days, they long to carry on with things as they had been before, and they strive mightily to preserve things as they were—preserve the appearance of the altar, preserve the order of worship, preserve the type of Sunday school teaching they used to have, preserve the way money had been always handled in the church. All too often rather than preserving the life of a church, this approach squeezes what little life is left right out of the church. We are the people of the resurrection, and because of this, old things keep passing away and we must not cling to them. We may learn from the past, we may even carry over many of the values of the past, but we cannot live in the past. If we attempt to do so, we become a glorious anachronism like the Amish, making the mistake of assuming that Christianity must have *a particular cultural expression or form* in order to be true Christianity. If the Fourth Gospel teaches us anything, it is that we have a universal Savior and a faith that can and must be incarnated in a thousand different sorts of cultural expressions.

When I was growing up in the South, I often saw signs that said "Turn back to the Bible" or "Turn back to God." I would say that the real problem, if our God is a God of resurrection, is not finding God in the past, much less dwelling there, but rather catching up with a God who has so far outdistanced us and our obsolescent ways of thinking.

Sometimes it is a matter of what we find comfortable in a secular society that emphasizes the separation of church and state, which is taken also to mean the separation of religion/ethics and state as well as the separation of the spiritual and the physical. Witnessing in such a society makes many people uncomfortable, as if they were in violation of the Constitution when they propagate their faith. Sometimes it is much more comfortable to sequester ourselves within the cozy walls of our churches and enjoy the presence of Christ and the beauties of the worship of God and do so in a way that allows us to negate or forget about the outside world, at least for a while. I agree with B. Milne when he says, "Tragically, over the centuries the Christian community has shown a far greater interest in sitting at Jesus' feet, holding on to him amid the comfort of his presence, than in going out to the world to share the good news with broken, needy hearts who have as valid a claim to know of him as we."[14]

The churches in the West have become a group of nurture organizations that have an occasional missionary committee or a sponsored missionary rather than being essentially a missionary organization that also does nurture, which was the character of much of the early church. In other words, to a very large extent we have placed the emphasis on the wrong syllable when we spend $95 of every $100 on nurture and maintenance of the existing structures, including our buildings, compared to only $5 or less on missions. It is of course easier and more comfortable to cling to Jesus than to heed his demand to go and tell others, but this is what we are called upon to do.

Another form of thinking in the church that has echoes in this story is the futile desire to play first-century church. We hear from time to time, "Oh, if only we could be like the early church." This would be all right if what we meant by that was, If only we could have the faith that some early Christians had and bore witness to, but all too often it seems to mean, If only we could arrange the church in the way it was arranged then, with the same sort of leadership structure and the like. The problem with this is that we would have to ask: Which church would we want to emulate? Should we emulate First Church Corinth, with all its problems and possibilities? How about First Church Galatia? Would we be willing to sell all our church buildings and simply meet in homes, because first-century Christians had no church buildings? What would we do about the problem that we have no more apostles in our midst, for as Paul indicates in 1 Cor. 9 and 15, the criterion for being an apostle was "having seen the risen Lord" (cf. Acts 1)? My point is this: Although we may learn from the church in the past, it was as flawed as is the modern church, and as often as not, we will have to say to the modern church, "Go and do otherwise." There are, of course, some principles and practices that may be carried on and carried over from the first century unto all ages of the church. Nevertheless, as the church of the resurrection, it is incumbent on us always to ask: What new thing is God doing, and what would he have us do to be effective witnesses for Christ in our own age and place?

Another subject that the story of Mary Magdalene may help us to address is the subject of grieving. It has often been said that Christians are not to grieve as people without hope. Certainly that is how Mary is grieving at the empty tomb. She is asked repeatedly why she is crying by supernatural beings who needed no explanation. The question, then, must be seen as the first step in drawing Mary out of her sorrow, to a new vision of life. "From the perspective of heaven nothing is more incongruous than tears at the empty tomb of Jesus. If there is one place in space and one moment in time when tears are least appropriate it is at the empty tomb of Jesus on Easter morning!"[15] Yet of course Mary does not yet see the incongruity until Jesus calls her by name. People must be drawn away from their sorrow by an experience or encounter with God that is at least as powerful as their encounter with the death of a loved one. Otherwise, they will indeed continue to grieve as people without hope.

Grieving overly much can be a form of self-indulgence and, when it goes on too long, feeling sorry for oneself. I am not suggesting that Christians are called to be stoics and grit their teeth and pretend that their hurts do not hurt. I am suggesting that if we focus on the risen Christ in our grief, joy will come back in the morning and tears of sadness will turn to tears of gladness and then to smiles and peace. A Christian funeral should be a joyful occasion, if we really have the condition of the deceased in view. For to be absent from the body is to be present with the risen Lord, and that is a far better condition than being in this vale of tears, especially if one is suffering a terminal illness.

The story is told about a Christian man who lived in the Pacific Northwest in the shadow of beautiful mountains. From the time when he first discovered he had a terminal illness, and then went through endless rounds of treatment without remission of the disease, he was despondent. Then one starry moonlit night when he was sitting out in the shadow of his favorite mountain and near his favorite stream and thinking about how much he would miss these things, the following thought came to him: "Long after this mountain crumbles into dust, I will still be alive, for I am in Christ. Long after this river ceases to flow to the sea, I will still be alive in Christ. Long after the stars fall from the sky, I will still be vibrantly alive, for Christ has given me abundant and eternal life." The Christian faith does not deny the reality of disease or death, suffering or sorrow, it simply asserts that "Greater is the one who is in me than any of these worldly forces."

In evangelical circles there is always and rightly a lot of emphasis on the historicity and concrete reality of the resurrection and the resurrection appearances of Jesus. The fact remains that alternate explanations of how a dispirited, denying, and deserting bunch of disciples were transformed into dynamic witnesses for Christ, willing to give up their lives for their faith in the risen Lord, fall well short of being convincing.

The theory that the body of Jesus was stolen by the authorities or their allies will not work, for then they would surely have produced the body when the Easter message began to be proclaimed publicly in Jerusalem. The continued existence of the Jerusalem Christian community is quite unthinkable under such circumstances.

Equally unthinkable is the view that Christians stole the body, not just because there was likely a guard set on the tomb (cf. Matt. 27:62–66), but because the transformation of the disciples was too absolute to be explained by fraud. The Gospels, on their own showing, present the disciples as abandoning ship when Jesus was arrested, and the resurrection stories are full of evidence of the doubting of the reports of the empty tomb and/or of Jesus' resurrection *even by the believers,* and in some cases they even doubted *after* they saw the risen Lord (cf. Luke 24:11; Matt. 28:17; John 20:24ff.). This is hardly the sort of report one would expect from those conjuring up a resurrection myth in order to keep the Jesus movement going. No, resurrection had to be more than a myth or a metaphor to work this sort of transformation of so many human lives.

"If Christ has not been raised, then our proclamation has been in vain and your faith has been in vain. We are even found to be misrepresenting God, because we testified of God that he raised Christ. . . . If for this life only we have hoped in Christ, we are of all people most to be pitied" (1 Cor. 15:17–21). Christianity is not a philosophy of life. It is not even a religion in the ancient sense, for first-century churches had no temples, no altars, no sacrifices, no priests. Christianity is a faith centered in and on the historical fact that Jesus rose from the dead, leaving the tomb empty, and appeared to various of his followers. It is a faith which believes that this event requires us to interpret the cross and the life of Jesus differently, and our own lives differently, from the way we otherwise would.

The interesting thing about a historical religion is that we have a heritage that no one can take from us. No one can erase the death and resurrection of Jesus from history if these things actually happened. Scientists might be able to prove a scientific theory to be untrue. Philosophers might be able to show the internal inconsistencies in a particular philosophy of life. But when we are dealing with historical facts, no amount of human rationalizing or explaining can explain these things away, although myriads have tried.

If the historical foundation of Christianity is its vulnerable point, it is also its strength, for if these things are true, then life cannot go on as if it were a matter of business as usual, with death casting its shadow over all. If life has the final word, then death has no more dominion, and we must live as people of the resurrection.

Mary learned this at Easter, and she left her grieving behind to go forth and proclaim the risen Lord. Strikingly it is Mary, not the Beloved Disciple,

who is depicted as undertaking this task. If ever there was a sufficient warrant for women being commissioned to proclaim the liberating Easter message in the church, it is found in this story in John 20. If Jesus could send
Mary forth to proclaim to the apostles the Easter message, who are we to
refuse to go and do likewise?[16]

20. Preserving Appearances behind Closed Doors (John 20:19–31)

In the twentieth and climactic chapter of this Gospel, we see the pilgrimage of faith finally brought to its climax in the proclaiming by Mary of the risen Lord and in the confession of Jesus as "My Lord and my God," and finally in the blessing bestowed on those who believe, even without seeing. As we have seen, this Gospel is a tale of less and less inadequate types of faith and confessions. Here we have a representative woman of God who comes to full faith, and finally we also see even the most skeptical of the men come to truly believe as well. There is little doubt that Thomas is seen as representative of more than just himself. He is a type (cf. Luke 24:11; Matt. 28:17). There were those even after Easter who doubted, some even *after* having seen or heard about the risen Lord. Furthermore, in a missionary document such as this one it would be important to have a character like Thomas, for there would be many skeptical about the Christian witness both in the synagogue and elsewhere, who, like Thomas, would need convincing before true faith in Jesus would be possible. The pilgrimage of Thomas could be taken as an example of how such a person could become not only a nominal Christian but even one who makes a full and robust confession about Jesus.

It is not an accident that it is only in the Fourth Gospel that Thomas plays any sort of role (cf. 11:16; 14:5; 21:2). Only here do we get any inkling of his personality. We have seen at 11:16 how he represents the fatalistic sort of person.[1] At 14:5 he simply admits his spiritual obtuseness and says he does not know where Jesus is going. The story in John 20 is certainly in character with one whose horizons are fixed on earthly matters and a worst case scenario. Thomas is not going to believe until he sees. Indeed, he says he will not believe until he feels the reality of the risen Lord.

We have in the two scenes in vv. 19–29 a clear attempt to show that these events are the fulfillment of what was spoken about in the farewell discourses, including Jesus' warning about being off the scene for a while and then "yet a little while and you will see me again." Consider the following chart:

Promise	Fulfillment
Jesus will come back to disciples (14:18, 23, 28)	Jesus came and stood in their midst (20:19, 26)
"You will have peace" (14:27; 16:33)	"Peace be with you" (20:19, 21, 26)

339

"I will see you again and you will rejoice" (16:22)	The disciples were filled with joy at seeing him (20:20)
The Spirit will be sent (14:16–17, 26; 15:26; 16:7–15)	"Receive the Spirit" (20:22)[2]

If these parallels are closely examined, it becomes clear that the events recorded in John 20 are seen as providing the fulfillment of the promises made in the farewell discourses, at least in part.[3]

This in turn raises difficult questions about the relationship of this material to the Pentecost narrative in Acts 2. Did Jesus really bestow the Holy Spirit twice, or is this the Johannine portrayal of that scene in the upper room?[4] If it is the latter, it must be admitted that it is a very different telling of the story from the one we find in Acts 2. In John 20, Jesus is present, in Acts 2 he is absent when the Spirit falls on the disciples. Some have even suggested that Jesus ascended between the visit with Mary Magdalene and the visit with what was left of the Twelve.

To this writer, the approach that causes the least difficulties is the one that argues that John 20:22 portrays a prophetic sign act or parable on a par with the sort of gesture we saw Jesus perform in John 13 when he washed the disciples' feet. The gesture then does not entail an actual bestowal of the Holy Spirit at that moment. Several things point in this direction.

First, after this episode the disciples are still portrayed as being behind closed doors in Jerusalem, not out converting the world (cf. v. 26). Indeed, in the epilogue in John 21 the disciples have returned to Galilee and have gone fishing, and it did not involve fishing for followers! Besides the unpromising sign that the disciples are still behind closed doors in Jerusalem after John 20:22–23, in John 21

> the disciples are sidling back to their old employment (21:1–3), sorting out elementary reconciliation with the Master (21:15–19), and still playing "let's-compare-service-record" games (21:20–22). All this is not only a far cry from the power, joy, exuberant witness, courageous preaching and delight in suffering displayed by early Christians after Pentecost in Acts, it is no less distant from the same virtues *foretold in John's farewell discourse, where the promise of the Spirit receives such emphasis.* If John 20:22 is understood to be the Johannine Pentecost, it must be frankly admitted that the results are desperately disappointing, and the promises of John 14–16 vastly inflated.[5]

Second, this Gospel is full of signs of various sorts, as we are reminded at v. 30. The gesture of breathing is clearly symbolic, making evident that the Spirit would come to the disciples directly from Jesus when he ascended and that the Spirit would be the Spirit of Christ. The gesture does not immediately transform the disciples from fearful followers hiding behind closed doors to dynamic missionaries, but the coming of the Spirit would accomplish this.

Third, Jesus had said it was necessary for him to be away from the disciples in order for the Spirit to come to them. The contrast in 14:25–26 between Jesus being with the disciples and the Father sending the Advocate when Jesus is absent is clear enough, and even more explicit is 16:7: "It is to your advantage that I go away, for if I do not go away, the Advocate will not come to you; *but if I go, I will send him to you.*" The sending of the Spirit transpires when Jesus is away, not when the risen Jesus is still with the disciples. Lastly, this approach resolves the problem that Thomas misses out on the bestowal of the Spirit, if the Spirit was given in the upper room while he was not present.

Thus in John 20:19–29 we have commissioning scenes in preparation for mission, but the Spirit was only later bestowed, enabling that mission to take place. The evangelist wished to make clear that the actual mission work did not begin until *after* Jesus had finally departed from earth; hence the Gospel closes twice (in John 20 and 21) without the portrayal of mission work but with the portrayal of two highly figurative stories that *foreshadow* the equipping for ministry (20:22) and *foreshadow* the actual mission work (21:4ff.).[6]

20:19   When it was evening on that day, the first day of the week, and the doors on the house where the disciples had met were locked for fear of the Jews, Jesus came and stood among them and said, "Peace be with you." [20]After he said this, he showed them his hands and his side. Then the disciples rejoiced when they saw the Lord. [21]Jesus said to them again, "Peace be with you. As the Father has sent me, so I send you." [22]When he had said this, he breathed on them and said to them, "Receive the Holy Spirit. [23]If you forgive the sins of any, they are forgiven them; if you retain the sins of any, they are retained."

24 But Thomas (who was called the Twin), one of the twelve, was not with them when Jesus came. [25]So the other disciples told him, "We have seen the Lord." But he said to them, "Unless I see the mark of the nails in his hands, and put my finger in the mark of the nails and my hand in his side, I will not believe."

26 A week later his disciples were again in the house, and Thomas was with them. Although the doors were shut, Jesus came and stood among them and said, "Peace be with you." [27]Then he said to Thomas, "Put your finger here and see my hands. Reach out your hand and put it in my side. Do not doubt but believe." [28]Thomas answered him, "My Lord and my God!" [29]Jesus said to him, "Have you believed because you have seen me? Blessed are those who have not seen and yet have come to believe."

30 Now Jesus did many other signs in the presence of his disciples, which are not written in this book. [31]But these are written so that you may come to believe that Jesus is the Messiah, the Son of God, and that through believing you may have life in his name.

I. The Historical Horizon

The setting for the events recorded in John 20:19–23 is said to be the evening of Easter day, whereas the event recorded in 20:26–29 is said to take place a week later.[7] It would appear that Mary's announcement of the good news was insufficient to transform the mood of these male disciples (cf. Luke 24:11). They are locked behind closed doors "for fear of the Jews" (v. 19), which surely means here the Jewish authorities responsible for doing away with Jesus.

Jesus comes and suddenly appears in their midst. Although the Fourth Evangelist does not engage in speculation about the matter, he clearly portrays Jesus in all the Easter stories as having differing properties from those he had before the crucifixion. He is seen as still a physical human being, but one who is also much more, and can appear in or disappear from a room without using a door. The one who could pass through the grave clothes and leave a neat pile behind would not find locked doors any obstacle.

Jesus' first symbolic gesture is to offer the normal Jewish greeting *shalom*, "Peace be unto you." In fact, the gesture is offered twice, and only the second time, after Jesus had shown his disciples his hands and side, did the disciples rejoice and recognize the Lord. It will be his signature greeting again a week later (v. 26). Whether the disciples recognized it at the time, Jesus was beginning to fulfill his promises to the disciples, which gave good reason for hope that he would continue to do so after he had ascended.

Verse 21 provides a Johannine commissioning of the disciples for mission. Jesus makes clear that his disciples are his agents, just as he was the Agent of the Father.[8] He is authorizing them and will go on to symbolically promise them empowerment to carry out their commission. Notice that in this Gospel the disciples are just sent without any content being specified as to the task.[9] Nevertheless, everything in this scene, including the giving of peace, is meant to remind the disciples (and the audience of this Gospel) of what had been said in the farewell discourses, where the tasks of mission are spelled out somewhat. The disciples are to go out into the world and make more disciples (17:18). The commission, however, should be closely linked with the gesture of showing Jesus' wounds. Jesus is calling his disciples to take up a costly task, one that may even require that they give their lives (cf. 16:2), but Jesus was standing in their midst showing them that even if that is so, there would be victory beyond the grave. In both the case of this gathering of the disciples and the case of Thomas later it is seeing that leads to fuller faith, in particular seeing Jesus' wounds that demonstrated beyond cavil that it was "this same Jesus." Their faith is depicted as weak and needing this kind of visual confirmation.

Probably we should see v. 22 as an echo of the story of creation where God breathed life into Adam, the first human being. Thus, we are to see this scene as a sort of starting over, the beginning of the creation of a new humanity.[10] The theme of life in this Gospel comes to a climax as we see Jesus now able to truly bestow eternal life and power once he returns to the Father who sent him. When Jesus breathes out, he is not only emulating the original role of the Creator, he is also, as C. K. Barrett points out, communicating and committing himself to his disciples, in the person of the Spirit.[11] It is his own resurrection life that he will bestow on them, something he could not do before Easter, and before he returned to the Father, having truly completed his earthly work.

There are certain key parallels between this story and what is said elsewhere about Wisdom. In Prov. 8:30, Wisdom appears to be portrayed as having an active role in creation.[12] In John 1 the same thing is said about the Logos. In Wisd. Sol. 15:11, after the portrayal of the sending of the Spirit as the sending of Wisdom (9:17–18), we hear about idolaters: "They failed to know the one who formed them, and inspired them with active souls, and breathed a living spirit into them." The giving of the Spirit means the giving of life. Importantly, in Wisd. Sol. 7:22ff. we hear: "For Wisdom the fashioner of all things taught me. There is in her a spirit that is intelligent, holy . . . and penetrating through all spirits. . . . For she is a *breath of the power of God* and a pure emanation of the glory of the Almighty . . . and while remaining in herself she renews all things; in every generation she passes into holy souls and makes them friends of God and prophets." Solomon goes on to pray in Wisd. Sol. 9:1–4: "O God of my ancestors and Lord of mercy who have made all things by your word, and by your Wisdom have formed humankind, . . . give me the Wisdom that sits by your throne."

Jesus in our text is being portrayed as Wisdom and as the giver of wisdom, as one who, like the Father, can create human beings anew by a mere breath, as the one who goes to dwell at the right hand of God's throne after having been on earth and who can come again to the faithful in the form of the Holy Spirit (cf. also *1 Enoch* 42), as the one who, once entering the believer, makes them friends of God, sent by God with a prophetic mission of proclamation.[13] At this point, the disciples are being promised enlightenment, and a commission, for once one has received wisdom one is commissioned. Later they will be given empowerment and wisdom from on high when Wisdom returns to glory in the presence of the Father. Yet as Barrett stresses, what the Spirit will convey to the disciples is not just power or insight but the very presence of Christ. As the texts cited above show, Wisdom conveys herself when the spirit of life passes into a believer.[14]

The disciples will most definitely need the wisdom Jesus gives, for in v. 23 we are told they will be called upon to perform an awesome task—the forgiving and retaining of sins. The similarities of this saying to the ones in Matt. 16:19 and Matt. 18:18 are often noted, but their differences are perhaps more important. In Matthew the discussion is about church discipline; here the discussion is about being commissioned for evangelism. Although the text may sound harsh at first, forgiving or retaining sins is simply a natural component of the calling of people to repentance and the offering of forgiveness in Christ.[15] Those who reject the Gospel are still in their sins, as earlier texts in this Gospel stress (cf. 9:41).

The second episode in this drama is necessitated because Thomas was not with the ten others when Jesus appeared to them.[16] Although the other disciples shared the Easter message ("we have seen the [risen] Lord") with him, Thomas refuses to believe until he sees and feels the tangible evidence personally. He wishes to put his fingers into the print of the nails in Jesus' wrists and in his spear-pierced side.[17] The underlying theme here is that no testimony, no dead body, no apparition would have satisfied some disciples after the shattering event of the crucifixion. Some required, and got, tactile and tangible proof that Jesus rose from the dead. It seems likely that part of the purpose of relating this story is to combat docetic tendencies that seem to have plagued one or another of the Johannine communities (cf. 1 John 1:1; 6:6; 2 John 7) during the same general time period this Gospel was being assembled. It was important to stress in such a context that Jesus' resurrection involved a real, tangible body.

It is implied here that Thomas's faith is extraordinarily weak at this point, if not nonexistent, as the final blessing of Jesus in v. 29 will make clear. Those who do not need to see, and yet believe, have stronger faith. In Thomas's defense even he, when confronted with the risen Christ, apparently does not have to resort to touching Jesus, even though Jesus offers him the opportunity. The text does not say he touched Jesus. Indeed, Jesus' response suggests that he did not: "You believe because you see," not "You believe because you touched." He was not utterly cynical and faithless, for his faith did not require the most extreme form of confirmation.

Whatever his spiritual status before seeing Jesus, once he had seen, Thomas is urged to be a full-fledged Christian, believing in all that Jesus is and does. Thomas's response constitutes the climactic confession in a Gospel that provides a series of less and less inadequate confessions leading up to this one. Notice that only here in this Gospel do we find the words *apistos* ("unbelief") and *pistos* ("faith," "belief"). This is because we have reached the climax of the many pilgrimages of faith in this Gospel. Thomas is called upon to show that he does believe, and he responds outwardly and visibly, having seen a visible risen Lord.

The confession "My Lord and my God!" recapitulates some of the claims about God's Son/Wisdom made in the prologue in John 1. Jesus is not just the believer's Lord but also the believer's God, and so an appropriate object of worship, even before the ascension. "It is Thomas who makes clear that one may address Jesus in the same language in which Israel addressed Yahweh. . . . It is no wonder that Thomas' confession constitutes the last words spoken by a disciple in the Fourth Gospel (as it was originally conceived, before the addition of John 21). Nothing more profound could be said about Jesus."[18] The term *theos* is only very rarely used of the Son in the New Testament (cf. John 1, here; Rom. 9:5; Titus 2:13), but there are plenty of other ways that the divinity of Christ is affirmed in the New Testament (cf. Phil. 2; Col. 1).[19] The context shows that this confession does not mean Jesus is the Father, and so we are witnessing here an example of the early Christian expansion of what the concept of monotheism amounted to, namely, that it involved more than one person in the Godhead. That this confession is made without strain in this Gospel is partly due to the fact that throughout Jesus is portrayed as God's divine Wisdom. The attributes formerly predicated of Wisdom in early Judaism are now predicated of Jesus. Such a confession was in principle possible very early on in the first century A.D., indeed as soon as Jesus was seen as the fulfillment of all that had previously been said about Wisdom.

With John 20:28 we have come full circle in this Gospel. The Word who was God is finally seen to be God by those who believe and receive the power to become children of God. With the coming of the Spirit, the presence, power, and work of Christ is placed in the hands of his disciples, who become his agents. Notice that Thomas confesses Jesus to be *his* Lord and God, acknowledging his sovereignty over his own life and the personal relationship that this betokens.

The evangelist is not, however, satisfied with leaving such confessions in the past. At least the last half of v. 29 is in a sense directed to the audience who hears or reads this Gospel at whatever time and in whatever place. Although it might have been glorious to see Jesus, such a mountaintop experience is not necessary to have faith in and confess Jesus as Thomas does. There is a sense in which those who have not seen, and yet have believed, are more blessed, for their faith must be greater.

As Barrett urges, we should see in these upper room stories another pregnant sign.[20] We have here most or all of the elements of early Christian worship—the first day of the week, a meeting of the gathered community in a disciple's house, the passing of the peace (three times!), the bestowal of the Spirit, the mention of the forgiving or retaining of sins, the confession of faith, and finally the act of worship, with Jesus in the midst. Here then at the end of this Gospel we have a picture for outsiders not only of what true confession should amount to but what true worship entails as well. The message to the Johannine community is also clear. Let doubters come into the presence of Christ among his people, so even they may be led to say "My Lord and my God."

The Gospel concludes with vv. 30–31 and indicates that the evangelist has seen all of the words and deeds of Jesus as being pregnant with deeper meaning, as having sign and symbolic character. This is hardly surprising in a Gospel in which Jesus is repeatedly portrayed as a sage who speaks in the figurative language of Wisdom speech,[21] and indeed speaks as God's divine Wisdom in the flesh. The life of Jesus was a storehouse of wisdom and wondrous signs. The evangelist, knowing the wisdom tradition, is ending his Gospel in an analogous fashion to the way Ecclesiastes ended. "The sayings of the wise are like goads, and like nails firmly fixed are the collected sayings that are given by one shepherd. . . . Of making many books there is no end" (Eccl. 12:11–12). When the evangelist added the epilogue, he once again turned to a sapiential way of drawing things to a close: "But there are also many other things that Jesus did; if every one of them were written down, I suppose that the world itself could not contain the books that would be written" (21:25).

The striking difference of course between the Fourth Evangelist and the disciple of Qoheleth who collected and edited his wise sayings is that the evangelist is not worn out by the study of Jesus' words and deeds but rather is invigorated by the act. He has much more he could and would share.

Readers who love this Gospel ever since have wondered what more he would tell were he still alive, and have longed to hear the telling.

Since we have dealt in detail with John 20:31 in the Introduction,[22] it is only necessary to reiterate here that the translation "But these things are written so that you may come to believe that Jesus is the Messiah . . ." is the most likely rendering. We should see this statement of purpose as signaling the missionary character of this document, although it could and should also be used with disciples, especially the material in John 13—17, which prepares disciples for witnessing in a world where Jesus no longer dwells in the flesh.

The Gospel ends, however, not merely with a statement that these things are written to engender faith but that they are written so the hearers or readers may have life and have it abundantly. Faith without eternal life would be a groping in the dark. It would be blind faith. Eternal life without faith, however, is equally unthinkable, for Jesus is seen as the way to receive this sort of life, as the truth about this life. One must believe in him to have such life. Christ is seen as both the means and the end of life and light, just as the Gospel began by telling us he was the beginning of life and light. The story of Christ transfigures, and in some degree prefigures, the story of his followers.

II. Bridging the Horizons

It will be seen from the exegesis above that it is probably an unwarranted move to see our text either as the Johannine version of Pentecost or as warranting the notion that the Spirit was dispensed twice by Jesus. The highly symbolic character of this Gospel must be kept squarely in view and also the immediate context of John 20:22. The context does not suggest a group of disciples empowered by the Holy Spirit, and neither does the epilogue in John 21. The problem of relating John 20 to Acts 2 is a problem that arises only *after* the canon has been assembled in the second century A.D., unless of course one wants to argue that the Fourth Evangelist knew and is deliberately and drastically altering the Pentecost story. The option argued for above not only makes better sense of the Gospel of John but also creates fewer problems for those who take seriously the need to piece together the history of the early church using all the relevant data.

Sometimes the particulars of a text make a large difference in interpretation. For example, if one pays attention to the fact that the text *does not* say Thomas actually touched Jesus, we may see him as one who in the end, having seen the risen Jesus, did not need the strongest form of confirmation that Jesus was alive. In other words, even Thomas was not wholly devoid of faith, or at least was not unwilling to believe when he saw Jesus, unlike some characters portrayed in this Gospel. "Thomas enters the story as a clear-eyed realist who knows that following Jesus back to Judea means risking death. He calls others to go with Jesus even if it means dying with him (11:16), but

Thomas does not understand that Jesus' death will be his exaltation. He does not understand where Jesus is going . . . (14:5). He cannot comprehend an appearance of the risen Christ . . . (20:25). Realist more than doubter, Thomas stands in for all who, like Mary Magdalene, embrace the earthly Jesus but have yet to recognize the risen Christ."[23] This assessment may need some modifying, since it appears that Thomas also is presented as one whom some of the non-Christian audience could identify with. The Fourth Gospel gives us well rounded enough portraits of some of the disciples such as Mary Magdalene, Thomas, Judas, Peter, and the Beloved Disciple that one way of handling the text would be to relate these characters to certain personality types of those who are fledgling Christians or on the way to being such.

A further word of caution is in order about drawing strong contrasts between Mary and Thomas. Although Mary, unlike Thomas, does not express open unbelief, her mind is so fixed on the Jesus of the past that it requires nothing less than an epiphany to bring her around. Thomas and Mary were in different circumstances, and this explains in part the differences in Jesus' response to each one of them. What it would take to rehabilitate them differed in each case. Nonetheless, Thomas is portrayed as the one who has weaker or even no faith, for he will not believe even after the stories of Jesus' appearances are conveyed to him by fellow members of the Twelve. It must also be kept in mind that Thomas had been with Jesus all through his ministry and had been privy to things such as the farewell discourses, and this probably to some extent distinguishes him from Mary.

It has been argued in this commentary that this document's intended purpose is to lead people to an adequate faith in Jesus Christ and so to have eternal life. This is not to deny its usefulness in helping those who are already Christians grow in the faith as well, but it is a Gospel mainly addressed to the seeker and quester, and we have true finders in the full sense of the term only in John 20—21. It is important to notice how a biblical book is intended to be used, or to function, when we are making decisions about how we shall use it. Sometimes a book or a passage has a significance for us that goes beyond the literal or intended meaning of the text, indeed may draw out a significance that is no part of the original meaning, although it may be seen as on the same trajectory of meaning. A personal example is perhaps in order.

When my wife and I lived in England during my years of doctoral study, and we were expecting our first child, my wife's blood pressure rose too high and she was placed in the hospital and confined to bed. One day a doctor came in and decided that he was going to have to induce my wife into an early delivery because of her blood pressure. This upset us both, for we had gone through the natural childbirth classes and were looking forward to a drug-free delivery. The night before this was to transpire, Ann and I were reading through the book of Ezekiel, and we came to some rather gloomy portions, but in the midst of them we heard the assurances, "I will multiply your kindred . . . , I will keep you safe, you will come home soon . . . and you will know that I am the Lord" (Ezek. 36:8–15). My wife and I knew of course that these words were not written for us by Ezekiel but rather were addressed to the Israelites in exile in Babylon in the sixth century B.C. Yet I was convinced that God had spoken to us through those words. I went home from the hospital convinced that our first child was going to be born the next day without the need for the use of drugs. Sure enough, our Christian friends rang me up and delivered me to the hospital the next morning, for Christy was on the way into this world. By ten thirty we had a healthy daughter born with a head full of hair. I tell this story to show the difference between the meaning of the text and the larger significance it had for my family. Our situation in many regards was very different from that of the Israelites in exile, and yet there was enough continuity and analogy that the promise of progeny, safety, and of going home rang out as if they had been addressed to us in the first place.

A great deal of good preaching involves drawing out the significances of the text for audiences vastly different from those originally addressed. This does not provide a warrant for making the text say whatever we would like it to say, for the starting point must always be, What did it mean in its original context? The later significances must be seen to be moving in the same direction as the text's original meaning or drawing out its possible implications. Otherwise we lose contact with the original intent and purposes of the inspired author and the Bible becomes an ink blot into which we can read whatever we please with impunity.

Throughout this Gospel we have seen people on a pilgrimage seeking out Jesus and struggling to have an adequate faith in and understanding of him. Faith in this Gospel is not seen as something static but rather as dynamic and having the potential for growth and change. As Craddock puts it, "There is faith based on signs and faith that needs none; there is faith weak and faith strong, faith shallow and faith deep, faith growing and faith retreating. Faith is not in this Gospel a decision once and for all, but a decision anew in every decision."[24] It would be better to say that faith is not only a decision once and for all in this Gospel. What we have stressed repeatedly is that before Easter, true Christian faith was not really possible and thus the characters in the drama are presented as paradigms of those on the way to having full Christian faith but having not yet arrived. In John 20 this changes with the examples of Mary and Thomas confessing a faith in the risen Lord, in the one who is "my Lord and my God."

This strongly suggests that for our evangelist a definite christological and soteriological content was required for faith to be truly Christian faith. This fact is confirmed by what we read in the Johannine epistles. Notice that Thomas in John 20 can be said to be *apistos*, "unbelieving," until he comes to full Christian faith. Journeying in faith is not sufficient. In the evangelist's mind one must eventually arrive at the proper destination for faith to truly be called Christian faith.

I once heard a memorable Easter sermon, based on the Thomas story, entitled "Late for the Holy Spirit." The point was made repeatedly and forcefully to the largest crowd of the year that by not gathering together with God's people, it is possible to miss out on the presence of Christ and the blessings that go with him. How true this is. One never knows in advance what light will break forth from God during a particular worship experience. The message may be better than anticipated, the music may be more moving than it ever was previously, we may be better attuned to what God is saying and doing on a particular Sunday, the Lord's Supper may be served in a manner in which we finally find healing and forgiveness for some sin or sorrow that has been plaguing us for ages.

In the last two decades of the first century, the emperor Domitian accepted the address "*Dominus et Deus noster,*" which means "Our Lord and God." In other words, at about the time this Gospel was being written the same claim was being made about the emperor as here is made about Jesus.[25] It is hard to doubt that the evangelist, living in Asia Minor where Domitian was highly revered, especially in Roman colony cities such as Ephesus, knew of this fact and is here highlighting an alternate confession of faith. Perhaps the most reliable test of whether what one confesses about one's object of worship is true or not is to examine whether anything or anyone is changed by what one confesses and whether anything of enduring worth comes from such a confession. Domitian has long since been dead, and there exists no cult of emperor in the twentieth century. Christianity by contrast is alive and well and has millions of adherents in the late twentieth century. As a religion it has not merely stood the test of time but has eclipsed many other ancient religions that made absolute claims.

Truth claims that do not stand the test of human experience, as well as the scrutiny of great minds over a long period of time, are likely to be just that—claims about the truth, and nothing more. The record of millions of people who have accepted certain truth claims about Jesus, have made the good confession of a Thomas and have been changed into more loving, joyful, peace-filled, sacrificial people, is not to be sneered at.

Our modern world exudes the attitude that the Christian religion is a crutch for the weak and those of low intellect but that it has no real substantive basis in truth. This arrogance is in part engendered by the assumption that only tangible things, things that can be quantified, measured, or tested in a laboratory can possibly be certified as true in a scientific age. Of course the very premise "Only things we can see, smell, taste, touch, or hear are real, and only experimental conclusions based on these things are true" is itself *not* verifiable or falsifiable by any scientific test. Everyone lives life on the basis of certain faith premises.

The commuter gets into his car and believes it will start when he sticks the key in the ignition. He has not done scientific tests in advance to be sure this is the case; he simply trusts that it will do so based on his own and others' previous experience. A student sits down in a chair in a first-period class, having faith that the chair will hold her up. The scientist believes, but cannot prove, that there is a real objective world beyond his or her own sensory perception that can be studied and understood. The musician believes and feels that tiny dots on a page are somehow related to the sound a human soul hears and then translates into notes, and that with enough practice and skill and devotion and the proper instruments, a moving human experience can be created by playing those notes. Yet the musician cannot explain why human beings normally prefer harmony to dissonance, variety to endless repetition, why some performances move one person and not another. Why is it that playing a piano concerto for a human audience is an exercise in faith and trust, whereas playing before a stand of trees is not?

My point is simply this. Every day in every human life a myriad of things are taken on faith, and faith decisions are made. Christian persons likewise makes faith decisions based on what they have found to be true in their own experience. Had Thomas not had his experience of the risen Christ, he would never have been able to make the confession he made. Christians should *not* accept on faith the argument that what they believe is simply a matter of subjective opinion, whereas what a scientist believes, say about the theory of relativity, is grounded in objective fact.

The truth is that Christian faith, like any good scientific theory, must stand up to the tests of human experience and reflection, and both are grounded in something objective. Scientific theory is grounded in the repeatable occurrences of the natural world. Christian theory is grounded ultimately in unrepeatable historical events and must stand up to historical scrutiny, but it is also tested and is verified over and over in the lives and experiences of millions of Christian people.

When Jesus said, "Blessed are those who have believed without seeing" he was not encouraging blind faith. He offers himself up to us for scrutiny through the scriptures and through the lives of believers all the time. This Gospel was written on the premise that a persuasive presentation of the story of Jesus can change people's lives for the better, even provide them with eternal life if they accept the truth enshrined in the story. John does not call us to an unreflective faith, but rather one that is led to worship after a good hard look at the life and works of Jesus, and after one has actually encountered this risen Lord. Faith in the Fourth Gospel is not the opposite of knowledge. It is, rather, the means of gaining it, just as the scientist's faith in and use of his scientific method is the indispensable means of obtaining results.

This Gospel above all others bids the hearer to put Jesus to the test, to place him on trial in one's thoughts and life, to "taste and see that the Lord is good." It is a call that many have heeded, and it helped them immeasurably. Jesus Christ is not our crutch, he is our total foundation, for he is our Lord and our God, whether we recognize him as such or not.

The Johannine version of the Great Commission found in John 20:21–22 is often overlooked. This is unfortunate because there are some distinctive lessons that can be drawn from this text. For example, M. Arias and A. Johnson rightly point out that incarnational Christology is shown to be the basis of the commission. The experience of the human Jesus ("he showed them his hands . . .") and the divine Christ who passes through locked doors shows the disciples not only the basis of their mission but also the content of their proclamation. Furthermore, they are sent out as agents just as Jesus was, and sent to perform essentially the same kind of ministry, offering forgiveness of sin and eternal life through Jesus the way. The stress on the Spirit as equipping the disciples for ministry is clear here in a way that is not the case in Matt. 28.[26] The sequence of the text suggests that receiving of the Spirit is what makes possible the forgiving of sins. Also notable is what is *not* mentioned in the Johannine commission, namely, that the making of disciples involves baptizing in the name of the Trinity. This comports with the overall orientation that takes a nonsacramental approach and concentrates on the things that such signs symbolize. The usefulness of the Johannine commission in a mission setting should be apparent. What is crucial is conveying the heart of the Gospel about the God-man Jesus, about forgiveness of sins and eternal life, and making clear that disciples are sent ones, they are saved to serve. This the Johannine account does better than any other Gospel.

21. Breakfast by the Sea (Epilogue) (John 21:1–25)

When we turn to the epilogue in the Fourth Gospel we find ourselves in an odd set of circumstances. John 20 might have led us to expect that the disciples would be out evangelizing the world, but instead we are told that some seven of them are back in Galilee fishing, seemingly as if nothing had happened in Jerusalem. Furthermore, we are told that this is the third resurrection appearance, but three have already been recorded in John 20, and it hardly seems feasible to fit it in between the two appearances in the upper room which transpire only a week apart.[1]

We may also wish to ask why this appearance seems to be an account of a first appearance, for the disciples do not immediately recognize Jesus, as was also the case with Mary and with the disciples on the Emmaus road in Luke 24. To all of this we may add that there are numerous words (some twenty-eight) and phrases in this chapter that are not found elsewhere in the Fourth Gospel. For example, the disciples are called "young men," and here alone we have a reference to the sons of Zebedee.[2] When we couple all of this with the obvious closure that John 20:30–31 brings to this Gospel, the suggestion that this was originally a free-floating tradition that the evangelist placed here after having written the Gospel seems most likely. It is a credit to his sense of narrative that he did not try to force this tradition into the midst of John 20. I would suggest that the Fourth Evangelist has added this material to the Gospel, probably because the Beloved Disciple died shortly after the first draft of most of the Gospel had been compiled from his memoirs.[3] This chapter was added to clear up some problems caused by the Beloved Disciple's death among other things, perhaps just before the Gospel was published.[4]

21:1 After these things Jesus showed himself again to the disciples by the Sea of Tiberias; and he showed himself in this way. [2]Gathered there together were Simon Peter, Thomas called the Twin, Nathanael of Cana in Galilee, the sons of Zebedee, and two others of his disciples. [3]Simon Peter said to them, "I am going fishing." They said to him, "We will go with you." They went out and got into the boat, but that night they caught nothing.

4 Just after daybreak, Jesus stood on the beach; but the disciples did not know that it was Jesus. [5]Jesus said to them, "Children, you have no fish, have you?" They answered him, "No." [6]He said to them, "Cast the net to the right side of the boat, and you will find some." So they cast it, and now they were not able to haul it in because there were so many fish. [7]That dis-

ciple whom Jesus loved said to Peter, "It is the Lord!" When Simon Peter heard that it was the Lord, he put on some clothes, for he was naked, and jumped into the sea. [8]But the other disciples came in the boat, dragging the net full of fish, for they were not far from the land, only about a hundred yards off.

9 When they had gone ashore, they saw a charcoal fire there, with fish on it, and bread. [10]Jesus said to them, "Bring some of the fish that you have just caught." [11]So Simon Peter went aboard and hauled the net ashore, full of large fish, a hundred fifty-three of them; and though there were so many, the net was not torn. [12]Jesus said to them, "Come and have breakfast." Now none of the disciples dared to ask him, "Who are you?" because they knew it was the Lord. [13]Jesus came and took the bread and gave it to them, and did the same with the fish. [14]This was now the third time that Jesus appeared to the disciples after he was raised from the dead.

15 When they had finished breakfast, Jesus said to Simon Peter, "Simon son of John, do you love me more than these?" He said to him, "Yes, Lord; you know that I love you." Jesus said to him, "Feed my lambs." [16]A second time he said to him, "Simon son of John, do you love me?" He said to him, "Yes, Lord; you know that I love you." Jesus said to him, "Tend my sheep." [17]He said to him the third time, "Simon son of John, do you love me?" Peter felt hurt because he said to him the third time, "Do you love me?" And he said to him, "Lord, you know everything; you know that I love you." Jesus said to him, "Feed my sheep. [18]Very truly, I tell you, when you were younger, you used to fasten your own belt and to go wherever you wished. But when you grow old, you will stretch out your hands, and someone else will fasten a belt around you and take you where you do not wish to go." [19](He said this to indicate the kind of death by which he would glorify God.) After this he said to him, "Follow me."

20 Peter turned and saw the disciple whom Jesus loved following them; he was the one who had reclined next to Jesus at the supper and had said, "Lord, who is it that is going to betray you?" [21]When Peter saw him, he said to Jesus, "Lord, what about him?" [22]Jesus said to him, "If it is my will that he remain until I come, what is that to you? Follow me!" [23]So the rumor spread in the community that this disciple would not die. Yet Jesus did not say to him that he would not die, but, "If it is my will that he remain until I come, what is that to you?"

24 This is the disciple who is testifying to these things and has written them, and we know that his testimony is true. [25]But there are also many other things that Jesus did; if every one of them were written down, I suppose that the world itself could not contain the books that would be written.

I. The Historical Horizon

We are not told precisely when these events transpired. Several of the disciples have returned to fishing in the Sea of Tiberias (i.e., the Sea of Galilee).[5]

Apparently it is the Galileans who have returned to their home region—Peter, James, John, Nathanael, Thomas, and two unnamed disciples. Since this is not the Twelve, it is unlikely that v. 14 means that this is the third time Jesus had appeared to this particular group. Two other such appearances to the seven are not recorded in this Gospel. It is an interesting fact that the Fourth Gospel, before John 21, does not include any of the Synoptic material about Peter or others being fishermen. Nor is there any mention of Jesus making them fishers of people in this Gospel. Yet knowledge of such traditions seems to be presupposed here. Here then is a tradition that seems to have circulated in the Johannine community and was originally written for knowledgeable Christians, not for unbelievers. Only they were likely to appreciate the symbolism of this tale, and only they would be concerned about the restoration of Peter, the explanation of what Jesus really said about the Beloved Disciple's life span, and the concern of Jesus with the nurturing of the Christian flock, as well as the missionary task.[6] If the Gospel in the main is christologically and soteriologically focused, this chapter is ecclesiologically focused.[7]

The story begins in earnest by telling us that Peter decides to go out fishing at night, supposedly the best time to catch fish. The others go with him, but it is a fruitless venture. Sunrise comes and there is someone standing on the shore, but the disciples are not aware of who it is. He asks whether they as *paidia* (children, young men) have caught any fish. When they respond in the negative he tells them to cast the net on the right side. Suddenly their catch is so great they can't even haul in the net, yet, unlike the similar tale in Luke 5, the net doesn't break.[8]

There is a stereotypical reaction of the two major characters other than Jesus. The Beloved Disciple, depicted as the spiritually more perceptive one already in this Gospel, is first to realize what this miraculous catch means: "It is the Lord."[9] Peter, the one who thinks with his feet, acting first and asking questions only later, wraps his outer garment around him, tucking it in so he can swim.[10] They were only a hundred yards from shore, and so they towed the huge catch of fish in. Peter at v. 11 is depicted as one with enormous strength, possibly equal to the other six who had towed the nets into the boat, for he alone drags ashore the net full of fish.

Arriving on shore, they see that Jesus already has a fire and a meal of bread and fish going. Their fish, then, would seem to be unnecessary for eating at this point, except that v. 10 may suggest that Jesus needed a few more. This meal that they share is not a eucharistic meal. There is no mention of a cup or drinking, of breaking bread or giving thanks. Rather, this is to be seen as a fellowship meal, a family reunion of a sort. Jesus is the one who gives them the bread and fish, and R. Michaels is right to point to the parallel story of the feeding of the five thousand in John 6:1–13.[11] There the fish is mentioned in passing and the focus is on the bread. Here it is the reverse. In both cases the point is that the Lord provides the sustenance the disciples need. The disciples are fed by Jesus and will be sent forth to feed his sheep.

What, then, are we to make of this narrative with its obvious symbolism?

This is not merely a symbolic or allegorical tale, and we should not try to find a hidden significance in every little detail. There is, however, some symbolism. The disciples are seen as fishers of human beings but as merely working in the dark without results unless they cast their nets where and when Jesus guides them. The point then will be that they can do no successful mission work without Jesus. John 15:5 says, "You can do nothing without me." However, with Jesus' guidance the results can be large. It is hard to say whether 153 is to be seen as a symbolic number or simply a piece of historical reminiscence, or both. If it is symbolic, it could symbolize the numerous different kinds and certainly also the large number of people that could come into the community of Jesus through evangelism. There is some evidence to suggest that some ancient zoologists thought there were about 153 kinds of fish in the world.[12] If this is alluded to, then it suggests that there would be converts from all different kinds of people. Missions would be a large success among the various peoples of the world.

The net not breaking likely does not symbolize church unity but rather the fact that Jesus can enable the disciple to bring in even a large catch of disciples without losing any (remembering the theme in the Gospel of Jesus' not losing one). In a sense we have here two stories in one. The former signifies the mission, the latter the ongoing fellowship with Jesus. The latter makes the former possible. It is through union with Christ and being fed by him that disciples are enabled to go out into the world and fish. Thus, here we see the church scattered for witness but gathered for fellowship and feeding. Notice too that the recognition theme follows the success of the disciples in fishing only after they have obeyed Christ's command.[13]

Verse 12 is interesting because it too suggests that this is a first appearance story. The disciples are on pins and needles and are afraid to ask Jesus things. They can hardly believe their eyes, although they know it is he. Possibly we are to think of this appearance as occurring much later, and so it rekindles the old excitement. Then too it happens unexpectedly and not in Jerusalem but in Galilee.

Here then we see a parable of the church in its twofold thrust—outward mission coupled with inward feeding and fellowship. Through it all Jesus is the one guiding the mission and providing the food, although it is expected that the disciples will bring some fish to him. They must do their part.

The next major subsection in this chapter is found in vv. 15–19. It must be remembered that the first and longer section of the chapter dealt with the role of disciples in general, and only here does the evangelist focus more particularly on two of the inner circle of believers—Peter first and then the Beloved Disciple. The chapter, then, is not primarily about the primacy of Peter or a possible rivalry between the Petrine and Johannine communities. Indeed, it is doubtful that any rivalry is depicted in these narratives at all. What we do find in vv. 15–19 is the story of the restoration of Peter's relationship with Jesus and a renewed commission to teach the Christian community.

G. R. Beasley-Murray is right that entirely too much has been made here of the two words for love, *phileo* and *agapao*, since the two terms seem to be interchangeable in this Gospel.[14] The distinction here, then, in all likelihood is purely a matter of stylistic variation (cf. below on the preaching implications).[15] It is possible that this recommissioning scene involving Peter may have actually occurred when Jesus first appeared to Peter (cf. 1 Cor. 15:5; Luke 24:34) and has been inserted here to make clear what happened to Peter after his denial of Christ, namely, that his sins were forgiven, not retained, and that in fact he went on to be a great leader who had the honor of dying in a fashion similar to Jesus (vv. 18–19).

There is considerable question about the meaning of "Do you love me more than these?" Is Jesus asking whether Peter loves Jesus more than the other disciples do, or is he asking whether Peter loves Jesus more than Peter loves these other disciples, or, finally, is he being asked whether he loves Jesus more than he loves these things (i.e., fishing and the like)? The grammar does not favor the last suggestion, and the context favors the second of these possibilities. Jesus is not encouraging Peter to compare his love with that of other disciples;[16] rather, "Jesus was asking Peter to leave behind attachments to other people and follow him."[17]

As has often been noted, the threefold questioning of Peter's love parallels his earlier threefold denial. It could suggest Jesus' dissatisfaction with Peter's first two answers, but more likely, since the third answer is the same as the first two, the point is that Jesus is sifting Peter to the core to see whether he has the courage and perseverance to assume a shepherding role. Here Peter is being portrayed as a sage who teaches disciples, just as Jesus has been earlier in John 10.[18] The text does not say, however, that Peter should be seen as the first among equals. This text does not rule out other shepherds, such as the Beloved Disciple, being appointed, perhaps over other Christian communities. Note that Peter needs a fresh commissioning and the Beloved Disciple apparently does not. There is here no attempt to elevate Peter over the Beloved Disciple or vice versa but rather to stress that they had differing roles and destinies in Jesus' plans for them.

Jesus the sage chooses to use a common proverb to address the issue of Peter's future. The proverb contrasts the freedom of youth with the limited possibilities of old age, although here the application is made to Peter being constrained to undergo crucifixion. It is probable that the church tradition that Peter died in the mid-60s A.D. during the reign of Nero is correct, and this chapter is written with benefit of that knowledge. The editorial comment in v. 19 makes this evident.

In the reference to the stretching out of his hands, which is a common metaphor for crucifixion, it is likely that we are being told not only how Peter would die but how Peter did die, some twenty-five to thirty years before this Gospel was published, at least in its present form. The later traditions about Peter being crucified upside down are too late, and too poorly grounded in the biblical text, to be given a great deal of credence, although such a form of death is not impossible or unknown.[19] Peter then would also be deprived of his freedom, led away, and crucified like Jesus, and so would glorify God both in his life and in his death, as his Master had done. Verse 19 concludes with the exhortation "Follow me," which is repeated at v. 22. Here it surely has the double sense of "Be a faithful follower" and also "Your life's journey and end will be patterned after mine."

At v. 20 the Beloved Disciple enters the picture and is said to be following along behind Peter and Jesus. The description of who the Beloved Disciple is clearly links him with the person mentioned as reclining next to or on Jesus in John 13. This parenthetical explanation is typical of the Fourth Evangelist's technique,[20] and it probably suggests that this tradition circulated separately from John 19—20, since the Beloved Disciple is prominent in those chapters.

Peter at v. 21 asks Jesus about the Beloved Disciple and his fate, and Jesus answers a question with a rhetorical question: "If it is my will that he remain until I come, what is that to you?" This remark and its explanation in v. 23 have several important features. First, it alludes to the second coming as an idea with which the Johannine community was well familiar and makes evident that the Fourth Evangelist has no difficulties with such ideas. Second, the question involves a conditional remark (if . . .), and in Koine Greek a mere possibility is affirmed, not a certainty or likelihood.[21] The reply in fact basically means, it is none of Peter's business. He must concentrate on what God has in mind for him. The evangelist explains the saying because of the misunderstanding within the Johannine community about the Beloved Disciple's life span, which on any showing had already been considerable. The explanation suggests perhaps some considerable dismay in the community that the Beloved Disciple had died before Jesus returned.

The epilogue concludes with the reminder in vv. 34–35 that it was the Beloved Disciple who had testified to these things and in fact had them written down in some form.[22] The "we," however, of v. 24 makes highly probable that he is not writing this verse but rather that the Fourth Evangelist, who was likely one of his disciples, was doing so.[23] The Gospel concludes in a sapiential fashion (cf. Eccl. 12 and above on John 20:30), alluding to Jesus' many other deeds which, if written down, could fill the world with books. It is interesting that Ben Sira, when he reflects on his lifelong pursuit of Wisdom, says that he was amazed when he came to share it that there was a much more vast quantity of wisdom than he had expected:

> As for me I was like a canal from a river, like a water channel into a garden. I said "I will water my garden and drench my flower-beds." And lo, my canal became a river, and my river a sea. I will again make instruction shine forth like the dawn, and I will make it clear from far away. I will again pour out teaching like prophecy, and leave it to all future generations. Observe that I have not labored for myself alone, but for all who seek Wisdom (Sir. 24:30–34).

A similar sort of claim is being made for Jesus at the end of this Gospel, for he is Wisdom incarnate, and an endless flow of wisdom comes from him.

This word is meant as an encouragement to a community who no longer had eyewitnesses to consult. The evangelist reassures them that through this Gospel, and doubtless through other resources such as the Johannine epistles, the stream of wisdom will continue to flow; indeed there was still much more that could be said. In a strange sense this last verse has come true about this Gospel itself, for the Christian community and scholars down through the centuries have written endless numbers of tomes on this great narrative of the good news.

II. Bridging the Horizons

Because of the highly symbolic and figurative character of especially the first part of John 21 it is easy to let imagination run riot and turn this material into a full-scale allegory. I would urge restraint in this matter and a focusing on the major issues addressed in the chapter, the issues of discipleship and leadership in the church and the character of each. E. C. Hoskyns was right to say that "a Christian gospel ends properly, not with an appearance of the risen Lord to his disciples, and their belief in him, but with a confident statement that this mission to the world, undertaken at his command and under his authority, will be the means by which many are saved."[24] This is especially the case in this Fourth Gospel, which is essentially a document written for missionary purposes. It is appropriate to note that even in the chapters in which the focus is on the disciples, such as John 13—17 and John 21, the substance of the discussion revolves around preparing these disciples for mission once Jesus is gone and providing them with the resources to carry on.

A further word of caution is in order in regard to turning John 21 into a discussion about dueling apostles, or personality clashes. The text certainly reflects personality differences, but there does not seem to be any agenda to put Peter in the Beloved Disciple's shade or vice versa. Both are seen as revered Christian leaders, and neither one is really seen as being above, or having authority over, the other. The task of both men will be that of feeding and tending the sheep, and although they may go about this differently—for instance, the Beloved Disciple by writing a good deal more than the evidence suggests Peter did (although cf. 1 Peter)—they both are serving the same Master and are called upon to follow him *in the way that suits Christ's plan for their respective lives*. As much as we might like to spend our ministry working with our friends, God's call to each one of us is individual. Many of my closest college and seminary friends, with whom I still have contact from time to time, are spread all over the globe from Zimbabwe to Singapore to Brazil to Australia to the United States. We seldom see each other, yet we write and support each other in prayer. We know that we have been called to individual ministries and must follow in Jesus' footsteps, not in each other's.

The early part of this chapter makes evident how important fellowship meals were to early Christians. It is not an accident that we hear in Luke 24 that the disciples recognized Jesus when he broke the bread. In the ancient Near East, table fellowship was one of the main signs, if not the main sign, of human intimacy and sharing, for an ordinary person seldom had other things that she or he could give to or share with friends. We may draw an analogy with church fellowship meals not only in Acts or 1 Corinthians but even today. The text allows us to ask hard questions about how we inculcate the bond of fellowship in a way that is equally effective as the meal was in antiquity. It should be noted that Jesus allows the disciples to contribute to this meal, and the meal is an opportunity not just for eating but for meaningful reflection on important times.

Some of my earliest church memories are of my family attending pancake suppers during the week in the basement of our church, where we would eat, sing the hymns of the faith, and discuss gospel or church matters. Too often today in the church the meal becomes an end in itself and not a means to Christian fellowship. We would do well to contemplate this text and see how this might be rectified.

John 21 can be used especially effectively even today in a leadership workshop where one raises questions about the expectations that ministers have about their jobs, the essential tasks on which they should concentrate their attention, the loyalty to Christ required to do the job well, and the promises Christ makes about our individual futures. The focus should dwell on the exhortations about following Jesus, feeding, tending, and minding one's own business, among other things.

The chapter may also be used at a missions conference to make clear that when we are closely following Christ's guidance, there is good prospect for results. "The church in the western world has never had such an array of helps, resources, and methodologies as at present. The psychological and sociological sciences, as well as the fruits of the technological and communications revolution, have been plundered for secrets of successful mission."[25] Without minimizing the importance of availing ourselves of all helpful tools and techniques, this chapter is about the nature of the essential task, not the technique. There is great danger in assuming that if we just use the right techniques, church growth is inevitable. In our story, that is rather like the fishermen when they cast their nets on the wrong side of the boat. There was nothing wrong with the nets, the fishermen just needed to follow Jesus' guidance about where and when to cast them. In our own situation this requires of us more time with the Lord in prayer than time with Lyle Schaller (on church growth) in the library. The means must not be mistaken for the ends, nor assumed to be a foolproof method for achieving such ends.

A very fruitful message can be developed from the material in John 21 on the problems of comparing oneself and one's future with other Christians. A good title might be "Mind Your Own Business," for this is in essence what Jesus said to Peter. "Christians are not to compare and contrast themselves with each other as though they were being graded on the curve."[26] If one wishes to have another Gospel text that could also illustrate the principle, one might draw on the parable of the Pharisee and the tax collector in Luke 18:9–14. There is almost an inevitable tendency of human beings not only to compare themselves to others but to model themselves on some of these others, or alternately to elevate their own sense of self-worth by putting others down, as in the parable in Luke 18. Peter is not guilty of the latter in John 21. He may in fact be showing some genuine concern for the Beloved Disciple, but the context suggests otherwise.

It has often been said, and it is true, that we become like those whom we admire, whether it is parents, teachers, sports figures, pastors, or others. Jesus in this passage insists more than once that the task of each Christian is to follow him, not be a follower of other human beings. The cult of personality is highly developed in our society, indeed so much so that we still have numerous people running around imitating Elvis Presley two decades and more after his death. People are desperately looking for someone whom they can look up to and model themselves after. Jesus in his discussions with Peter indicates that his life will indeed become an example of the imitation of Christ, even in the way it ends. This is not just his fate, it is also his task to intentionally follow in the footsteps of Jesus. "The ministries of Peter and John would be different. Peter would be the shepherd, John the seer; Peter the preacher, John the penman; Peter the foundational witness, John the faithful writer; Peter would die in the agony and passion of martyrdom, John would live on to a great age and pass away in quiet serenity."[27]

If, as I think likely, Peter wrote 1 Peter, it would appear that he not only took Jesus' advice, or, better said, heeded his imperatives, but passed them along to others. In 1 Peter 5:1–4 he urges:

> Now as an elder myself and a witness of the sufferings of Christ, as well as one who shares in the glory to be revealed, I exhort the elders among you to tend the flock of God that is in your charge, exercising the oversight not under compulsion but willingly, as God would have you do it—not for sordid gain but eagerly. Do not lord it over those in your charge, but be examples to the flock. And when the chief shepherd appears, you will win the crown of glory that never fades away.

Another helpful message could be developed along the lines of what one does after a mountaintop experience. After Easter, Peter's answer was "Let's go fishing." F. Craddock helpfully draws an analogy with what inevitably happens in churches after Easter Day. One cannot sustain that level of emotional and spiritual excitement constantly. But the answer to the dilemma was not the one Peter took. This text neither calls us to return to business as usual nor even to go on vacation. Rather, Peter is called to get on with ministry—to feed and tend the Christian flock. It was this day-to-day task that was to define his life's work, not the occasional mountaintop experiences.

Jesus, in addressing Peter, quotes what is in all likelihood a common proverb: "In youth a person is free to go where he will; in old age a person must allow himself to be taken where he does not will." Jesus was a sage who most often conveyed his message through the use of proverbs, parables, and the like. This should cause us to reflect on our own preaching and teaching styles, and it could also lead to a series of fruitful discussions on how much people in our culture, even Christian people, live on the basis of conventional wisdom such as "A penny saved is a penny earned" or "Early to bed and early to rise makes a person healthy, wealthy, and wise." It is indeed surprising how often advice dispensed in such forms seems to stick with a person and is called upon to guide the person through difficult times in life. A pastor could get a lot of mileage out of discoursing on the difference between common sense and Christian sense.

The particular proverb that Jesus applies to Peter and his future can also meaningfully relate to how our culture treats senior citizens. They are often placed in nursing homes and have no freedom of movement, diet, choice of activities, or choice of friends. They often tend to revert to their childhood in their imagination when they did have freedom and possibilities before them. One must ask whether this sort of ending to life is inevitable for us all, or whether there may be a better way, in which senior citizens are allowed to live out their lives at home as long as that is physically possible, and are allowed to have meaningful service in the church after they are retired. In a context where few are martyred for the faith, we need to address the constraints our society puts on its older members, for our culture is producing an ever larger percentage of people over the age of sixty-five.

Appendix

The Woman Caught in Adultery
(John 7:53–8:11)

The beloved story of the woman caught in adultery is a clear example of a free-floating tradition that various early Christian scribes loved so much they tried to find a home for it in at least two different Gospels (Luke and John). For our purposes what is crucial to point out is that, as even so conservative a commentator as Don Carson stresses,[1] the textual evidence is squarely against this story being an original part of the Fourth Gospel. Although we have dealt with this problem to some degree at the appropriate point in the text,[2] a brief rehearsal of the data is in order: (1) These verses are absent from almost *all* of our earliest Greek manuscripts, including ones of widely differing places of origin and character, although they are present in later medieval Greek manuscripts. (2) The exception to the rule is the Western uncial D which is well known for its idiosyncratic and independent handling of numerous texts. (3) These verses are also missing from the earliest Syriac and Coptic Gospels and from numerous Old Latin, Armenian, and Georgian manuscripts. (4) All the earliest church fathers in commenting on the Fourth Gospel pass directly from John 7:52 to 8:12, omitting these verses as if they were never present. (5) Not a single Eastern church father cites these verses before the tenth century A.D.[3] (6) Even many of the manuscripts that do include these verses mark them off with asterisks or obelisks indicating strong doubts about their authenticity and right to be placed in this Gospel. (7) Perhaps most telling is that these verses are found not only at John 7:53–8:11 in some manuscripts but that some place them after Luke 21:38 and others after John 7:36; 7:44, or even at the very end of the Gospel at John 21:25.[4] We may gather from this that most scribes thought this was a Johannine tradition of some sort, but the evidence as we have recited it above must prove fatal to the assumption that these verses were an original part of this Gospel.

If original text should determine what should be in the canon, then these verses do not belong in the canon. This by no means, however, requires us to think of this story as an inauthentic or unhistorical tradition; perhaps it is even a Johannine story, and so we have chosen to comment on it. If it is a Johannine story, we should remember that the evangelist warned us that there were many other traditions of the Beloved Disciple he could have conveyed but chose not to (John 20:30), and so this could be one of them.

Several factors in this story favor its authenticity. There is first the fact that the portrayal of Jesus, as one who had compassion but with a balancing of justice and mercy, rings true to what we know of him elsewhere in the Gospels. Second, since the Jewish practice of stoning seems to have been replaced after the first century with strangling as a form of punishment, this story surely originated in a first-century milieu[5] and one that was cognizant of Jewish law and how it was practiced at the time. Third, there must have been strong reasons in the second century for assuming that this was an authentic story about Jesus; otherwise it is very difficult to explain why scribes tried so hard to insert the story into various places in the Gospels.

Some have seen this story as likely a Lukan story on the basis of the use of certain terms. For example, the term *orthros* ("dawn") is found elsewhere in the New Testament only in Luke 24:1 and Acts 5:21. The terms *paraginomai* and *laos* are rare in John but common in Luke-Acts. Finally, the content of John 8:2 is seen to be close to that of Luke 21:38.[6] This evidence must be said to be slender, especially since only the term *orthros* is not found elsewhere in the Fourth Gospel. The tone of the story, however, and the way its controversy setting is handled seem much nearer to the Johannine style, a chief feature of which is the presenting of Jesus as being constantly on trial at the hands of the adversaries but repeatedly eluding their grasp until he wishes to be taken. Then too, Jesus is depicted here as in control of the situation even though he is put on the spot, another Johannine trait. I would suggest that this story depicts a scene during the general time frame of the material in John 7—10, during one of the visits of Jesus to Jerusalem. Its insertion at John 7:53 by numerous scribes reflects an understanding of the text's kinship with a good deal of the surrounding material. Accordingly, we will treat this story as a Johannine one, reflecting the Judean ministry of Jesus and its atmosphere of controversy that led up to the events of Passion Week.

[7:53   Then each of them went home,
8:1   while Jesus went to the Mount of Olives. ²Early in the morning he came again to the temple. All the people came to him and he sat down and began to teach them. ³The scribes and the Pharisees brought a woman who had been caught in adultery; and making her stand before all of them, ⁴they said to him, "Teacher, this woman was caught in the very act of committing adultery. ⁵Now in the law Moses commanded us to stone such women. Now what do you say?" ⁶They said this to test him, so that they might have some charge to bring against him. Jesus bent down and wrote with his finger on the ground. ⁷When they kept on questioning him, he straightened up and said to them, "Let anyone among you who is without sin be the first to throw a stone at her." ⁸And once again he bent down and wrote on the ground. ⁹When they heard it, they went away, one by one, beginning with the elders; and Jesus was left alone with the woman standing before him. ¹⁰Jesus straightened up and said to her, "Woman, where are they? Has no one condemned you?" ¹¹ She said, "No one, sir." And Jesus said, "Neither do I condemn you. Go your way, and from now on do not sin again."]

I. The Historical Horizon

The setting for this story is the Temple, in the women's court. Scribes and Pharisees suddenly burst into the court bringing with them a woman caught in the very act of adultery. There is no good reason to doubt that a married woman is envisioned here, although there was a provision in the law for stoning both partners involved in such a sexual act when the woman was a betrothed virgin (cf. Deut. 22:23–24). Jewish law required that a person be caught in the very act, if the very serious penalties were to apply. Hearsay testimony would not do. Furthermore, witnesses were required to warn persons caught in the act of adultery, which would give them at least one chance to repent and not persist in such behavior. Thus the writer presents a very suspicious scene. Where is the woman's partner in crime? If a husband had suspected his wife of adultery, he could have her undergo the ordeal of the bitter waters (*m. Soṭa* 1:1ff.).

The scribes and the Pharisees confront Jesus, saying that Moses prescribed stoning, and ask, "What then do you say?" Jesus is being invited to set himself against Moses, or against the Roman law which prohibited Jews from exercising capital punishment.[7] Jesus seems to avoid the issue by stooping down and drawing with his finger in the dust. There are many possible interpretations of this act, but we simply do not know what Jesus wrote. It may be the act itself rather than something Jesus drew or wrote, and an act of avoidance of a direct response, which is typical of Jesus, carried its own message. The gesture seems to suggest that Jesus does not wish to be dragged into this sordid affair, nor does he wish to step into a legal trap. If it was true that only Mosaic law prescribed stoning for such an act, but only the Romans could pass the death sentence, then Jesus could be said to be between a rock and a hard place. If he fails to pronounce judgment, he will seem to be rejecting the Mosaic law; if he pronounces judgment, he will be usurping Roman privilege.

It should be noted that Jesus does not refrain from judgment. Indeed, by implication he judges the woman when he says, "If anyone is without sin . . ." This last phrase alludes to Deut. 13:9 (cf. 17:7) and makes clear that the issue is anyone without sin in this particular matter. Jewish law required that the witnesses to a crime be the first to throw the stones against the guilty party, and they must not have any guilt in or legal responsibility for this particular crime themselves. Jesus then is questioning the motives of these men, for as leaders of Jewish society they had a moral responsibility to uphold the moral integrity of their community. In this case, neither the scribes nor the Pharisees are morally free from blame, for they are trying to use this woman as a tool to trap Jesus, the one person who *is* morally qualified to judge this matter. Thus, what Jesus does is spring the trap that he and this woman are being asked to step into, by passing judgment but in a manner that makes the execution of the punishment impossible.

The Jewish leaders appear to understand the implications of Jesus' "Let anyone among you who is without sin [in this matter] . . . ," so one by one they silently slip away, leaving the woman standing alone in the presence of Jesus. The hunters have lost not only their prey but also their bait.

The woman finally tells Jesus that no one has condemned her, when Jesus asks. Jesus replies emphatically, "Neither do *I myself* condemn you." I would suggest that Jesus here is rejecting a procedure that was inherently prejudicial and biased against the woman. In view of Matt. 5:27–30, it is clear that Jesus does not approve of any procedure where a woman's sin is taken more seriously than a man's. His action is a condemnation of a double sexual standard. Notice also that Jesus does not condone the woman's behavior but ends the encounter by saying, "From now on do not sin." Her sin is not pronounced forgiven, for she is not said to have repented. Jesus shows the woman the balance of justice and mercy intended to lead the woman away from a sinful life in the future.

In this story we have seen an implied critique of religious leaders who fail to reflect the sort of moral character that would set them apart from this woman and set them up as moral exemplars in society. Jesus also rejects stereotypes that make women scapegoats in a more complex social situation.

II. Bridging the Horizons

Since it is not likely that this story is part of the original text of any of the canonical Gospels, I do not encourage ministers to preach on this as a "Gospel text." It may, however, appropriately be used as an illustration of the character of Jesus when one is preaching on another Gospel text, much as we will use other sorts of illustrative material in a sermon. I would also not encourage starting with this text when one wishes to deal with how Jesus handled the problem of adultery but rather begin with material the textual authenticity of which is not in doubt and then bring in this story as further confirmation of one's point. In one's teaching and preaching one must be able to distinguish between the inspired canonical text and illustrative material that may well be historically true, as this story likely is, but that should not have the status or normative role of scripture.

Jesus' views on human sexuality and marital relations are not really a topic for much discussion in the Fourth Gospel (although cf. John 2 and 4), unlike the case with the Synoptics (cf. Mark 10 and par.; Matt. 5 and par.). This being the case, it may be more appropriate to bring this material up when one is discussing the relevant Synoptic material.

This text raises three main ethical issues: (1) social stereotyping and scapegoating and its unfairness; (2) the responsibility of religious leaders to live exemplary lives; and (3) the handling of judgment so that a balance of justice and mercy is shown.

In regard to this last matter, the story we are examining shows that in a fallen world moral situations are often more complex than we realize. When judgment is recorded and sometimes even rendered in the media, rather than in the courtroom, the nuances of a case are often overlooked. Americans tend to want instant justice and instant restitution, forgetting that judges and juries, unlike God, are not omniscient and that evidence must be sought out and evaluated. In the advocacy system of justice, it is not the lawyer's job to present a balanced perspective but rather to interpret the evidence in the light most favorable either to the defense or to the prosecution of the accused. It is the jury and/or the judge that must be impartial. This text also raises questions about vigilante justice which often is a pretext to grind some personal ax or express some personal bias. I doubt that Jesus would be pleased either with modern attempts to prosecute people in the media or with efforts at vigilante justice by private citizens, or with a good deal of what passes for jurisprudence in our courts today. What is legal is by no means necessarily ethical, and when the distance between the two is great, a society often becomes cynical about its justice system.

Of late, we have had a rash of scandals involving televangelists and some other church leaders. Chaucer once remarked, "If gold ruste, what shal iren do?" The need for religious leaders with character and moral integrity is critical in a world full of fallen people just looking for opportunities to point fingers at the church. Unfortunately, too often pulpit committees and boards of ordained ministry are wowed more by personal charisma than by moral character. The criteria by which Christian leaders should be chiefly measured are not the criteria normally applied to salespersons, or, politicians, or, for that matter, any other public figures. They are the sort of criteria enunciated in 1 Tim. 3, where character takes precedence over giftedness as a standard of measurement.

Our culture has reacted, some would say overreacted, to the male bias of our culture affecting all aspects of life in a generally patriarchal culture. We now are called upon to follow the dictates of political correctness. While some may grumble about this, there is some justice in the pleas for equality. Jesus had no time for male bias when it came to matters of religion or justice. He believed that men and women were equal in the eyes of God and should be treated equally, especially in the application of God's law. Jesus did not care for sexual stereotyping or scapegoating. There must be no double standard in the Christian community. Every sin is a sin for which Jesus had to die, and every sin must be taken seriously regardless of who committed it. If the community of Christ wishes to bear witness to Jesus, it must model the attitudes Jesus reflected in dealing with men and women and the issues of justice and fairness.

Notes

Introduction: The Background and Foreground of the Fourth Gospel

1. G. R. Beasley-Murray, *John*, xxxii.
2. See E. Käsemann, *The Testament of Jesus: A Study of the Gospel of John according to John 17*, 22ff.
3. R. Bultmann's judgment was formative for a whole generation of scholars; cf. R. Bultmann, *History of the Synoptic Tradition*, 372ff.; J. Painter, *The Quest for the Messiah*, 75.
4. See my discussion of this matter in my dissertation "Women and Their Roles in the Gospels and Acts," 47ff.
5. R. Burridge, *What Are the Gospels?* This work eclipses previous efforts by C. Talbert and others, which were somewhat flawed in that they sometimes drew on documents that were not ancient biographies. Burridge is well grounded in both the classics and the New Testament, a prerequisite for undertaking this sort of analysis properly.
6. On the matter of chronology one may compare Tacitus's *Agricola*, which does have an interest in broad chronological concerns but not in precision about particular details unless they are crucial to the narration.
7. Burridge, *What Are the Gospels?*, 226.
8. On the question of whether and when the Gospels appeared in codex or book form, cf. M. Hengel, *The Johannine Question*, 2ff. I think it is likely that the Gospels may have first appeared in codex form when the four Gospels were first gathered together in one collection, perhaps early in the second century A.D.
9. Burridge, *What Are the Gospels?*, 256.
10. Ibid.
11. R. Kysar, *The Fourth Evangelist and His Gospel: An Examination of Contemporary Scholarship*, 191.
12. Burridge, *What Are the Gospels?*, 55–67.
13. See ibid., 251–53. It should be stressed that modern distinctions between the implied author and the real author are not really appropriate with a document that manifests the genre of an ancient biography. While such distinctions might be helpful in the analysis of ancient apocalypses where we are dealing with the problem of pseudonymity, this is not the case with a formally anonymous document like the Fourth Gospel, which is not analogous to the modern novel.
14. See S. S. Smalley, *John: Evangelist and Interpreter*, 192ff.
15. Burridge, *What Are the Gospels?*, 247.
16. On the hymn of homage to the emperor at the outset of a play, cf. R. C. Beacham, *The Roman Theater and Its Audience*, 169.
17. On the use of hyperbole and hyperdramatic conflicts in Roman drama, cf. ibid., 154.

18. See the sort of exalted language even used in edicts in R. K. Sherk, *The Roman Empire: Augustus to Hadrian*, 145ff.; cf. below on John 20:28.

19. Cf. the discussion of the whole issue now in D. M. Smith, *John among the Gospels.* Smith argues that even if the Beloved Disciple knew other Gospels such as Mark "it does not necessarily follow that he would have felt constrained by them" (193).

20. Ibid., 180.

21. It is this last part I am most skeptical about, while I think the literary critical task can produce some soundly based conclusions.

22. A. Culpepper (*Anatomy of the Fourth Gospel*, 3) rightly notes how in the literary critical approach the meaning of the Gospel is derived from the way it is related to the reconstructed history of the text, which has of course been built up out of the text itself.

23. As does J. L. Martyn, *History and Theology in the Fourth Gospel.*

24. Cf. my dissertation, "Women in the Gospels and Acts," 50ff., and my article "Principles for Interpreting the Gospels and Acts," *Ashland Theological Seminary Journal* 19 (1987): 35–70.

25. C. K. Barrett, *The Gospel according to St. John*, 42–54.

26. C. H. Dodd, "The Framework of the Gospel Narratives," in his *New Testament Studies*, 1–11.

27. Ibid., 11.

28. Barrett, *John*, 44–45.

29. D. M. Smith, "Johannine Christianity," 11.

30. Cf. the English version: R. Bultmann, *The Gospel of John: A Commentary.*

31. R. T. Fortna, *The Fourth Gospel and Its Predecessors.*

32. Painter, *Quest for the Messiah*, 82–83.

33. Ibid., 405n8.

34. Ibid., 86.

35. See the discussion below.

36. I would suggest that John 20:30–31, as we now have it, is a statement written by the Fourth Evangelist about the function of this biography itself and not just a relic of his source material (although the Beloved Disciple may have made some such remark about the sign narratives he wrote down which he had used in evangelism), and that it appears that the Beloved Disciple died *while* this Gospel was being completed, making necessary the addition of John 21 as an explanatory epilogue. John 21 then would be the last thing added to the Gospel before its initial publication. This comports with the textual evidence, for there is no real evidence that John 21 was ever *not* part of this Gospel.

37. I have modified my earlier judgments on this matter found in *Jesus the Sage*, 368–70, where I argue that the Gospel was directed to Christians to help them further grasp the significance of Jesus.

38. Though M. Hengel, *Studies in the Gospel of Mark*, 66–84, has suggested that the title was attached from the outset, in this case presumably by the Fourth Evangelist. P66 and P72 are early papyri written in Greek with portions of the Fourth Gospel on them.

39. See the discussion in Hengel, *Johannine Question*, 75: "The form of the title *euaggelion kata Ioannen* imitated the titles of earlier Gospels according to Mark, Luke and Matthew which were already quite widespread around 100 CE." In fact, however, we do not know that these Synoptic Gospels had this particular form of title prior to the second century. More likely the form of the title implies a distinction *in a context where the Fourth Gospel was going to be compared with the Synoptics*, in other words, when they were collected together.

40. Compare Hengel, *Johannine Question*, 1ff., to D. A. Carson, *The Gospel according to John*, 23ff.
41. Though there is much to be gained from Culpepper's discussion of the Fourth Gospel using modern literary theory in his *Anatomy of the Fourth Gospel*, some of it is simply not applicable to first-century biographies. In particular the distinction between the implied author in the text and the actual author of the text, while it may be of some use in analyzing ancient pseudepigraphical documents, is not very helpful in studying an ancient biography like this one. The Fourth Evangelist is not interested in misleading his audience about who he is and what he knows, but he is interested in distinguishing himself from his source and giving credit to his source for the substance of this Gospel. This means that the text should provide us with some clues as to: (1) who the Fourth Evangelist was not (namely, the Beloved Disciple) and (2) who the Beloved Disciple was (namely, the originator of these traditions). This distinction is a rather different one from the modern distinction between implied and actual author.
42. See Painter, *Quest for the Messiah*, 29–39.
43. See my discussion in *The Christology of Jesus*, 34–56.
44. See the discussion in the commentary itself, pp. 226ff. below. I do not, like some, think these texts are the key to the provenance of this Gospel, not least because the Synoptics also suggest that Jesus and his first followers sometimes had synagogue controversies, and Luke 4 suggests that Jesus himself was expelled from at least one synagogue. It is a mistake to underestimate the hostility Jesus and his first followers sometimes generated in the volatile atmosphere of early Judaism, which had more than its share of zealots and messianic pretenders and contenders, all of which were perceived to be a threat by those who had something to lose by a change in the status quo.
45. There were of course some of Jesus' adherents, like Mary, Martha, and Lazarus, who were not peripatetic.
46. Cf. above, and note the anonymous disciple mentioned in John 1:35 who is not Andrew, and the stress on the Baptist's importance in John 1 and 3 as the first major witness to Jesus.
47. On all this compare the discussion in W. G. Kümmel, *Introduction to the New Testament*, 245.
48. J. W. Pryor, *John: Evangelist of the Covenant People*, 3. Carson, *John*, 24ff., still maintains the view that John son of Zebedee is the author.
49. The tradition that Papias in fact wrote down the Fourth Gospel is found in the anti-Marcionite prologue, and it comes down to us only in a late corrupt Latin text, and so nothing should be based on it.
50. See Hengel, *Johannine Question*, 80ff.
51. But cf. Carson, *John*, 77.
52. See my discussion in *Jesus the Sage*, chap. 8.
53. Cf. pp. 47–58 above.
54. C. H. Dodd, *The Interpretation of the Fourth Gospel*, 285.
55. Culpepper, *Anatomy of the Fourth Gospel*, 226, is right that John sets limits on Christian Logos speculation by giving the Logos a narrative interpretation in the form of casting Jesus even during his ministry as the Logos. It is likely true that the relationship of Jesus and the Word, or Jesus and Wisdom, was a matter of significant discussion in the Johannine community and thus the evangelist felt it necessary to provide parameters for that discussion.
56. Culpepper, *Anatomy of the Fourth Gospel*, 106.

57. Hereafter Wisdom of Solomon will be abbreviated as Wisd. Sol. This book was likely written somewhat before or less probably during the time of Jesus, but in any case it existed well before the time the Fourth Gospel was written.
58. Painter, *Quest for the Messiah*, 256ff.
59. The V pattern refers to the fact that the Son preexists in heaven, comes to earth (the bottom of the V), and returns to the Father's side in heaven.
60. See Prov. 8; Sir. 24; *1 Enoch* 42, among other texts, and my discussion in *Jesus the Sage*, 36–49.
61. On the plot of this Gospel, cf. Culpepper, *Anatomy of the Fourth Gospel*, 83ff.
62. See the more detailed discussion in *Jesus the Sage*, 370–75.
63. It may be that the addition "who is in heaven" found in some mss. is original, in which case the whole sentence should be seen as the evangelist's parenthetical remark to his audience for whom the ascending as well as the descending is in the past. Cf. Barrett, *John*, 213.
64. H. R. Moeller, "Wisdom Motifs and John's Gospel," 95.
65. B. Witherington, III, *Women in the Earliest Churches*, 177ff.
66. Culpepper, *Anatomy of the Fourth Gospel*, 33–34, calls this perspective on Jesus which author and audience share in the light of the Logos hymn stereoscopic: "The gospel narrative therefore portrays Jesus as the one who continued the creative work of the divine *logos* by creating eyes for the man born blind, restoring the dead to life, and breathing life into spiritless disciples. The narrator also knows that Jesus will be exalted to the Father so he prepares the reader to understand Jesus' death as exaltation rather than humiliation. These entrance and exit points . . . condition the Johannine narrator's stereoscopic view of the ministry of Jesus." This is as much as to admit that the presentation of the ministry is thoroughly conditioned by the Logos hymn.
67. Despite the different way of putting it, both texts seem to be saying basically the same thing. The point in John is that once one partakes of the living water one will not thirst for anything else and this is probably the point in Sirach as well. Cf. Beasley-Murray, *John*, 60–61.
68. Bultmann, *John*, 218ff.
69. G. Ziener, "Weisheitbuch und Johannesevangelium."
70. Ziener's argument that the sequence of signs in John follows the sequence in Wisd. Sol. 11ff. is not fully convincing, but cf. Ziener, "Weisheitbuch," 405.
71. Bearing in mind that in the light of Wisd. Sol. 9:1–2 Word and Wisdom seem to be basically two ways to speak of the same thing in this book. Just as Wisdom is personified or even hypostatized in Wisd. Sol. 7, so also in Wisd. Sol. 18:15 one hears "your all-powerful Word leaped from heaven from the royal throne, into the midst of the land that was doomed, a stern warrior carrying the sharp sword of your authentic command." Cf. Heb. 4:12.
72. See my discussion in *Jesus the Sage*, 106–7.
73. But cf. above, pp. 18ff., on Job 19.
74. J. E. Bruns, "Some Reflections on Coheleth and John," has rightly pointed out that John's conception that physical life and death do not provide meaning for human existence seems to owe something to Qoheleth's discussion of these matters.
75. Dodd, *Interpretation of the Fourth Gospel*, 281–82, 306.
76. Ibid., 306.
77. Moeller, "Wisdom Motifs," 95.
78. R. E. Brown, *The Gospel according to St. John*, 1:cxxiv.
79. Ziener, "Weisheitbuch," 60, finally concludes that both authors are drawing on a common late wisdom tradition.

80. Brown, *John,* 1:cxxiii.
81. On John's use of the sources, cf. Fortna, *The Fourth Gospel and Its Predecessors,* 1ff.
82. I would not rule out the suggestion that *this* John might well have been John son of Zebedee, which would further explain the confusion of the second- and third-century churches on this matter. The Greek of the book of Revelation might well be within the scope of a Galilean fisherman who mainly used Greek in oral contexts for business purposes prior to moving to Asia. If two Johns migrated from Israel to Asia and worked together to form the Johannine community, and if one was exiled to Patmos by the Romans, perhaps for his polemics about the emperor, Rome, and empire, while the other lived to a ripe old age in Asia and was *never called John* but rather the Beloved Disciple or the Elder to distinguish him from John of Patmos, it is understandable why the two might later be readily confused.
83. Barrett, *John,* 123ff.
84. Cf. Kümmel, *Introduction to the New Testament,* 450.
85. Cf. the discussion of W. Horbury, "The Benediction of the *minim* and Early Jewish Christianity."
86. Hengel, *Johannine Question,* 114–15.
87. Cf. Painter, *Quest for the Messiah,* 53n68.
88. Burridge, *What Are the Gospels?,* 236.
89. Cf. ibid., 237.
90. See G. D. Fee, "On the Text and Meaning of John 20:30–31."
91. Ibid., 2199.
92. See the discussion of Fee, 2203.
93. We will say more about John 11:27 and its relationship to John 20:31 in the commentary.
94. See Painter, *Quest for the Messiah,* 129ff.
95. Burridge, *What Are the Gospels?,* 236–37.
96. Carson, *John,* 87ff. Notice that the discussion revolves around preparing for persecution in John 15:18ff., something that comes as a result of aggressive missionary efforts, and in John 14:12 the disciples are expected to do even greater works than Jesus, aided by the Paraclete.
97. Cf. Pryor, *John: Evangelist,* 91: "His whole purpose in writing has been soteriological."
98. See G. Van Belle, "Les parenthèses johanniques."
99. One could point to 2:17 as well, which is part of a pericope which was likely originally part of the Beloved Disciple's remembrances about and telling of the Passion narrative, and has been moved here for theological purposes by the Fourth Evangelist.
100. See Van Belle's conclusion, 1915.
101. See the important study by C. J. Bjerklund, *Tauta Egeneto: Die Präzisierungssätze im Johannesevangelium,* esp. 133–45.
102. Whether the Fourth Evangelist knew about the Synoptic Gospels is another matter. Possibly he knew about them, but was determined to present the distinctive testimony of the Beloved Disciple.
103. Morris, L. *Studies in the Fourth Gospel,* 70.
104. I am thinking of course of C. H. Dodd's classic work, which came at the end of his career, *Historical Tradition in the Fourth Gospel.*
105. Barrett, *John,* 142.
106. Cf. Dodd, *Interpretation of the Fourth Gospel,* 9.

107. See H. Schürmann, "Die vorosterlichen Anfänge der Logien-Versuch eines Formgeschichtlichen Zugangs zum Leben Jesu," in *Traditions-geschichtliche Untersuchungen zu den Synoptischen Evangelien,* (Düsseldorf: Patmos Verlag, 1968), 39–65. Schürmann is of course mainly discussing Synoptic logia but his arguments have clear implications for our discussion here.
108. H. Riesenfeld, *The Gospel Tradition and Its Beginnings: A Study in the Limits of "Formgeschichte,"* 63.
109. Cf. Martyn, *History and Theology in the Fourth Gospel.*
110. Smith, "Johannine Christianity," 35.
111. See my discussion in *Christology of Jesus,* 56ff.
112. For the discussion of the likely authenticity of at least some of this material, cf. my *Christology of Jesus,* 132ff. The Markan material in 6:10–11 may be the most primitive form of the charge.
113. Note the point made by Smith, "Johannine Christianity," 20–21, that claims such as "We have seen his glory" in John 1 point us back to the testimony of an eyewitness of various of the crucial events in Jesus' life. Glory here may be a reference to Jesus' exaltation through death (cf. below, pp. 248ff.).
114. Or perhaps when those who had attended the synagogue along with the church began to share more openly about Christ.
115. Cf. D. Rensberger, *Johannine Faith and Liberating Community,* 130ff.
116. But see W. Meeks, *The Prophet-King,* and his "The Man from Heaven in Johannine Sectarianism."
117. See Rensberger, *Johannine Faith,* 144ff.
118. J. Neyrey, *An Ideology of Revolt.*
119. Ibid., 205.
120. Ibid., 209.
121. See Brown, *John,* 1:cxxxvii ff.
122. Morris, *Studies in the Fourth Gospel,* 70.
123. My suggestion would be because it has been taken from the Passion narrative and was not designated as such there.
124. G. Mlakuzhyil, *The Christocentric Literary Structure of the Fourth Gospel,* 17ff.
125. I would suggest John 12, not John 11—12, is the bridge section.
126. I would still say there are three major sections really, with prologue and epilogue making five sections in all.
127. Mlakuzhyil, *Christocentric Literary Structure,* 346.

1. The Prologue to the Fourth Gospel (John 1:1–14)

1. See pp. 4–5 above.
2. Cf. E. Hoskyns, *The Fourth Gospel,* 1:130: "The prologue, like other literary introductions, is not so much a preface to the gospel as a summary of it." This requires some qualification, as we shall see.
3. I have basically followed Brown's division of the hymn with minor modifications; cf. Brown, *John,* 1:3ff.
4. More words could be added; cf. J. Painter, "Christology and the History of the Johannine Community in the Prologue of the Fourth Gospel," 462, citing among other words *photizei, eskenosin, exegesato.*
5. M. Scott, *Sophia and the Johannine Jesus,* 28ff., makes much of the gender issue of Wisdom (since *sophia* is a feminine noun) in the Fourth Gospel, but

unfortunately for him the evangelist chose to use the term *logos* rather than *sophia*, and thus Scott overpresses the gender issue in ways that probably do not comport with the intentions of the author (cf. below).

6. Painter, "Christology," 463–64, notes that vv. 1–5, 10–12b, 14a–c are markedly poetic, and adds that while the poetry is basically in vv. 1–14, the peculiar or unique vocabulary is basically in vv. 14d–18.

7. J. T. Sanders, *The New Testament Christological Hymns*, 20–21.

8. Some of the material that follows here in the discussion of the *logos* hymn appears in a somewhat different form with more discussion of scholarly opinion in my book *Jesus the Sage*, 282–94.

9. That Pliny is referring to hymn singing seems clear in the light of the way Tertullian interprets the text in *Apol.* 2.6.

10. In what follows I am indebted to M. Hengel's seminal essay "Hymns and Christology."

11. Cf. above what Pliny says about Christians singing at dawn.

12. J. A. Sanders, "The Psalms Scroll of Qumran Cave 11."

13. Cf. *Jesus the Sage*, 16–49.

14. I agree with E. Schweizer ("Paul's Christology and Gnosticism," 115–23) that the parallels between the Gnostic use of hymns and wisdom and Paul's use diverge in important ways. The hymns in Paul and elsewhere in the New Testament do not devalue creation nor do they stress the idea of a redeemer figure who in essence passes through the intervening layers of creation separating God and humanity, escaping the taint of the material universe. Indeed, in the christological hymn fragments in the New Testament not only is creation seen as good but the Redeemer has a hand in making it. "While Gnosticism took up and radicalized a notion which had, perhaps, been at the root of Jewish Wisdom literature, the idea of a divine order inherent in all things and particularly in man's mind, Christianity, on the contrary, did so with the typically Jewish idea of Wisdom as a gift of God to his elect people, manifest . . . definitively, 'eschatologically' (Heb. 1:2) in Jesus Christ" (120).

15. Another text pointing to early evidence of christological hymn singing is Ignatius, *Ephes.* 4.1–2, which speaks not only of singing through Christ to God but also of Jesus Christ being sung.

16. Cf. the important article by M. Hengel, "Psalm 110 und die Erhöhung des Auferstandenen zur Rechten Gottes." The attempt to argue that the hymns were originally thanksgiving hymns on the basis of what comes before Col. 1:15–20 seems strained at best. As E. Schüssler Fiorenza ("Wisdom Mythology and the Christological Hymns of the New Testament," 25) points out, a standard psalmic thanksgiving formula is not used in connection with these hymns, and furthermore, the psalms of thanksgiving do not seem to have been the main quarry used to construct these hymns.

17. R. P. Martin, "Some Reflections on New Testament Hymns."

18. Schüssler Fiorenza, "Wisdom Mythology," 19. Cf. also the new preface to the revised edition of R. P. Martin, *Carmen Christi: Philippians 2:5–11*, xi ff.

19. Cf. pp. 20ff. above.

20. Cf. the discussion of this material at pp. 22–23 above.

21. This supports the contention that we are dealing with hymn material in John 1, drawing water from Jewish wells to create it. The translation cited is that of G. Vermes, *The Dead Sea Scrolls in English*, 93.

22. R. Schnackenburg, *The Gospel according to St. John*, 1:165ff.

23. Sanders, *New Testament Christological Hymns*, 35, and n. 1.
24. Barrett, *John*, 154: "Philo's Logos, broadly speaking, takes the place Sophia had occupied in earlier Hellenistic Judaism, and in particular exercises a cosmological function."
25. I would not rule out that the hymn may originally have spoken of *Sophia* rather than *Logos*, but this is simply an unsupportable conjecture.
26. H. Gese, *Essays on Biblical Theology*, 198.
27. It is not really so puzzling that the *Logos* is nowhere specifically identified by name in the hymn with Christ, and J. Ashton ("The Transformation of Wisdom: A Study of the Prologue of John's Gospel," 172ff.) tries to make more of this than he should. Had he studied all the christological hymns together he would have realized that the absence of a named subject is a characteristic of these hymns. J. Jeremias ("Zum Logos-Problem") suggests that the absolute use of *ho logos* in John 1:1, 14 suggests the audience knew this title already before reading the Gospel. The author was referring to "the (well known) *logos*."
28. J.D.G. Dunn, *Christology in the Making*, 239ff.
29. On the concept of fullness applied to Wisdom, cf. Wisd. Sol. 7:24, 27 and 8:1.
30. M. Harris, *Jesus as God: The New Testament Use of Theos in Reference to Jesus*.
31. M. D. Hooker, "The Johannine Prologue and the Messianic Secret."
32. P. S. Minear, " 'We Don't Know Where . . . ' John 20:2."
33. The phrase "We have seen his glory" perhaps hints at the second half of the hymnic pattern of exaltation; however, it can be argued that Jesus, being divine, manifested God's glory (i.e., presence) throughout his ministry (cf. John 2:11).
34. Schnackenburg, *John*, 1:271–73.
35. Painter, "Christology," 470.
36. See Barrett, *John*, 164–65.
37. In this case the subject is ontology, not primarily status or prerogatives as was true in the Philippian hymn. This fact as well may suggest this hymn is a later development than the one in Phil. 2.
38. The "we" here would seem to refer to the eyewitness testimony of the Beloved Disciple and his fellow eyewitnesses, which strongly suggests this hymn may go back to him ultimately as the basis of even this portion of the Fourth Gospel. As such, this "we" could be distinguished from the "we" of John 21:24. On the other hand, if the community saw itself as in continuity with the Beloved Disciple and his witness, the ones passing on his testimony, the "we" here might mean the Beloved Disciple and his community, including of course the Fourth Evangelist who gathered and arranged the testimony of the Beloved Disciple.
39. E. D. Freed, "Theological Prelude and the Prologue of John's Gospel," 266.
40. Some have seen in these verses an allusion to the virginal conception of Jesus, particularly if the variant reading "was born" rather than "were born" is accepted. Cf. the discussion in Hoskyns, *Fourth Gospel*, 1:167–68. Whether there is an intentional allusion to the virginal conception or not, there is surely an analogy in these verses that can be drawn between what is true of the children of God and what was true of the Child of God. The idea of incarnation seems to require some such idea as a virginal conception in order to show that the Son came into the world by means of God's will alone and not that of two human beings. Cf. Barrett, *John*, 164.
41. Hoskyns, *Fourth Gospel*, 1:132.
42. This is true even in the case of the blind man, or Martha, as we shall see.
43. See F. Mussner, *The Historical Jesus in the Gospel of St. John*, 40ff.

44. Meditation no. 15, last two lines J. Donne, *Complete English Poems* (London: Penguin, 1971), 315.

2. A Cloud of Witnesses (John 1:6–9, 15–51)

1. A. E. Harvey, *Jesus on Trial: A Study in the Fourth Gospel*, 15. As J. Ashton (*Understanding the Fourth Gospel*, 228) rightly points out, the strength of Harvey's case lies in the material that begins in John 5, but I would suggest it is not absent even in the first chapter if (1) there is at least a somewhat polemical edge to the prologue and (2) the motive for presenting John as the first great witness to Jesus is to convince those who are still his followers.
2. M. Hengel, *Crucifixion.*
3. See my *Christology of Jesus*, 34–56.
4. This, like John's baptism, was an unrepeated ritual.
5. Witherington, *Christology of Jesus*, 35–36.
6. See the discussion in the Introduction, pp. 11–18.
7. Ashton, *Understanding the Fourth Gospel*, 234.
8. Harvey, *Jesus on Trial*, 23–24.
9. See Beasley-Murray, *John*, 12. If this is correct, this text has nothing to say in favor of the Wesleyan idea of every person receiving illumination or prevenient grace from God at birth.
10. Cf Painter, *Quest for the Messiah*, 121 "Such a denial, 'he was not that light,' makes sense only if there were those who claimed that he was."
11. Ibid., 139ff.
12. In general I am in agreement with the following conclusions of E. D. Freed ("John 1:19–27 in Light of Related Passages in John, the Synoptics, and Acts," 1943) when he says that John 1:19–27 is composed "to show the subordination of the Baptist to Jesus and to stress the Christological views of the author. John wrote to convince his readers to believe that Jesus was the Christ, the Son of God (20:31). This is the first clue for studying any aspect of the Fourth Gospel."
13. See my *Christology of Jesus*, 129ff.
14. See Brown, *John, I–XII*, 78: "That the disciples did not attain such an insight in two or three days at the very beginning of the ministry is quite obvious from the evidence of the Synoptics. For instance, only halfway through Mark's account (8:29) does Peter proclaim Jesus as Messiah, and this is presented as a climax. Such a scene would be unintelligible if, as narrated in John, Peter knew Jesus was the Messiah before he ever met him. The Fourth Gospel itself subsequently insists on the gradual evolving of the disciples' faith (6:66–71; 14:9); and indeed John is the most insistent of all the Gospels that full understanding of Jesus' role came only after the resurrection (2:22; 13:7). Thus, we cannot treat John 1:35–51 *simply* as a historical narrative. . . . John has placed on their lips at this moment a synopsis of the gradual increase of understanding that took place throughout the ministry of Jesus and after the resurrection. John has used the occasion of the call to summarize discipleship in its whole development" (emphasis added). The only other alternative I can see to this suggestion is the view that all these disciples were suddenly inspired with prophetic insight, as the Baptist is portrayed here. But the text does not suggest such a thing about the disciples. Indeed, the later part of the Gospel suggests that the disciples did not receive the Spirit and the insight he brought until after the resurrection.

15. Ashton, *Understanding the Fourth Gospel,* 158. Cf. John 18:3, 12.
16. There is certainly no point after A.D. 70 of stressing the opposition of chief priests or Levites to Jesus since the Temple was destroyed and their power base ceased to exist, *unless there really is some interest on the part of the evangelist in getting the historical facts straight about the opposition to Jesus.* Were the primary focus here on those who were opposing the Johannine community we would have expected more reference to Pharisees or synagogue rulers of various descriptions. This document is intended to be an interpretation of the life of Jesus in the form of a biography, with implications of course for the later Christian community. It is not primarily about the Johannine community's struggles with "the Jews." Excessive reading between the lines for hints about the traumas and trials of the Johannine community can lead to a skewing of the data and a misunderstanding of its proper function. Since this is a missionary document, there is a good reason to make clear that the focus of the opposition to Jesus was by a limited group of leaders which was in large part defunct when the Gospel was written, and thus need not hinder other ordinary Jews from following Jesus when the Johannine Christians shared their faith with those outside the Christian community. We will have more to say on this matter when we get to the three references to expulsion from the synagogue, which does suggest by the insistence on this point that this was a problem the Johannine community had been or was facing in its witnessing about Jesus.
17. See Barrett, *John,* 173.
18. On this matter see D. Daube, *The New Testament and Rabbinic Judaism,* 266ff.
19. Carson, *John,* 147.
20. Ibid., 148.
21. I am following the Greek rather than the Armenian text here, which in general seems free of Christian influence up until 19:11. Cf. H. C. Kee's translation of and commentary on the *Testament of Joseph* in *The Old Testament Pseudepigrapha* (New York: Doubleday, 1983), 1:824, and note b.
22. Cf. Ashton, *Understanding the Fourth Gospel,* 259.
23. Notice the word "Israel," not "the Jews," is used here.
24. Hoskyns, *Fourth Gospel,* 1:172.
25. There is considerable debate among scholars as to whether the designation "the Son" carries the same meaning as the phrase "the Son of God." Conceivably the former phrase could be taken as just a relational term that usually occurs when reference is made to the Father as in 1:18. The problem with this suggestion, at least insofar as the Fourth Evangelist's usage is concerned, is that in 1:18 it not only is qualified by *monogenes,* which may mean only or unique, but also probably should read, "It is God the only Son, who is in the bosom of the Father" (cf. the NRSV). If so, Son by itself probably has more than merely relational overtones. Ironically, however, it is the phrase Son of God which probably did not have divine, but only messianic overtones. Early Jews were not looking for a divine messiah, son of God, but rather a divinely endowed human one.
26. Thus if Son of God was a messianic designation (cf. Ashton, *Understanding the Fourth Gospel,* 260), it is not beyond the realm of possibility that historically John could have used such a phrase of Jesus, since he was looking for a Coming One, and would likely have conceived of him in terms that were possible and normal in early Judaism.
27. Notice the close association of the two ideas in John 20:31.
28. Cf. Barrett, *John,* 189–90.
29. Painter, *Quest for the Messiah,* 131. Cf. the entire discussion in vv. 129–31.

30. And thus these persons are not portrayed as completely adequate models for those who are already Christians to follow. This Gospel is primarily meant to reach out to questers and seekers.
31. J. L. Staley, *The Print's First Kiss: A Rhetorical Investigation of the Implied Reader in the Fourth Gospel*, 80.
32. There is some evidence from ossuary inscriptions that the term "rabbi" was used as a synonym for teacher even before A.D. 70. Cf. Brown, *John*, I–XII, 74.
33. See the discussion in the Introduction, pp. 32–35.
34. See Brown, *John*, 1:79.
35. Cf. ibid., 73.
36. It was not uncommon in ancient biographies for strict chronology to be sacrificed to serve the larger purposes of the work (cf., e.g., some of the lives of the Caesars by Plutarch). In this case theological and missionary purposes are dictating the placement of various Gospel sayings and narratives.
37. Roughly translated, Bethsaida means Fishertown, an appropriate place for fishermen to be from. The Synoptics, however, tell us that Peter and Andrew lived in Capernaum, which is farther along the northeast shore of the Sea of Galilee. Perhaps the former was where they were from, but Capernaum was where at least Peter resided as a married adult (cf. Mark 1:21ff.).
38. Cf. Carson, *John*, 157–58.
39. Hoskyns, *Fourth Gospel*, 1:175.
40. Barrett, *John*, 184.
41. See Harvey, *Jesus on Trial*, 36.
42. See Schnackenburg, *John*, 1:317.
43. See my *Christology of Jesus*, 233ff.
44. Ashton, *Understanding the Fourth Gospel*, 340.
45. Ibid., 347.
46. See Schnackenburg, *John*, 1:320.
47. Especially in the light of John 1:32 it is unlikely that the focus here is on Jesus being the way up to heaven and the way down from it. Rather, the point is he is the locale at which these things come together.
48. See Brown, *John*, 1:77.

3. The New Wine of the Gospel (John 2:1–12)

1. See Scott, *Sophia and the Johannine Jesus*, 177ff.
2. Whether Mary can be said to recognize Jesus as Wisdom in this narrative, because she knows he can provide the wine, is more difficult to discern. Cf. Scott, *Sophia and the Johannine Jesus*, 179. If this is so, the evangelist makes little of it, and in fact it is not said at the end of the story that she "believed in him" as the disciples did.
3. See Painter, *Quest for the Messiah*, 154.
4. Nathanael may well have not been one of the Twelve, as he fails to appear in any of the Synoptic lists of the Twelve (cf. Mark 3:16–19 and par.). The Fourth Evangelist shows little or no interest in the Twelve as a particular unit, or as apostles for that matter.
5. Painter, *Quest for the Messiah*, 156.
6. See my *Women in the Ministry of Jesus*, 80–83.
7. But see Dodd, *Historical Tradition in the Fourth Gospel*, 225.
8. Cf. A. W. Argyle, "Wedding Customs at the Time of Jesus"; J. Jeremias, *The Parables of Jesus*, 171–75.

9. It is quite improbable that the toastmaster at a Jewish wedding in antiquity would ever exclaim, "But you've saved the best (nonalcoholic) grape juice until last." The whole point of the remark is that the best wine was properly served first before the senses were dulled, and while it could still be appreciated.

10. On the whole matter of Jesus' and early Christianity's eschatological views, cf. my *Jesus, Paul and the End of the World*.

11. As C. S. Lewis once remarked, "When the author comes on the stage, the play is over," and the Son has already been shown in John 1 to be at least the coauthor of creation and thus of the human drama.

12. It reads literally "What to me and to you?"

13. See my *Women in the Ministry of Jesus*, 84.

14. Ibid.

15. See the discussion in Ashton, *Understanding the Fourth Gospel*, 269–70, and n. 60.

16. In favor of this rendering is that in the New Testament in all other instances where *oupo* is preceded by a question (Matt. 16:9; Mark 4:40; 8:17), it introduces a further question. Against it is that elsewhere in this Gospel Jesus' hour seems to refer rather exclusively to his passion (cf. John 12:27; 17:1).

17. Cf. Ashton, *Understanding the Fourth Gospel*, 268: "So the mother of Jesus occupies a mediating position, ranged in the first place with the hosts and guests, associating herself with their need, and eliciting, by her plea on their behalf, a sharp retort that contains a charge of misunderstanding; and in the second place with the servants, who are waiting to do Jesus' bidding. This mixture of incomprehension and compliance is surely part of the *meaning* of the story. . . . In the context of an appeal to Jewish readers and listeners to come forward and declare themselves for Christ, the significance of Jesus' mother . . . is as a representative of those who do just that, *those for whom misunderstanding is not a permanent obstacle to discipleship*."

18. Ibid., 271.

19. Ibid., 273.

20. The saying of course exaggerates the charge, but the point is that it must have been based on some evidence that Jesus ate and drank wine with sinners and tax collectors.

21. See my discussion of this material in *Christology of Jesus*, 71–73.

22. B. Milne, *The Message of John: Here Is Your King!*, 65, provides a salutary caution: "The accumulated human misery in every corner of the earth which results directly or indirectly from the immoderate use of alcohol puts the burden of proof on those who would advocate anything other than abstinence as the Christian stance in the late twentieth century."

23. F. B. Craddock, *John*, 26.

24. Milne, *Message of John*, 66, quoting W. Temple.

4. Cleaning House (John 2:13–25)

1. Craddock, *John*, 23–24.

2. See Painter, *Quest for the Messiah*, 157–60.

3. This is the suggestion of Schnackenburg, *John*, 1:344.

4. Carson, *John*, 176ff., is an exception.

5. This point, however, can be vitiated if Jesus' action was very small in scale and basically an acted parable, not an actual cleansing out of any major portion of the Temple precincts.

6. On the basic historicity of the story of the Temple cleansing, see my *Christology of Jesus*, 107–16.
7. Unconvincing is the argument of Carson (*John*, 176) that the term *Ioudaios* is used here in a geographical sense, for what sense does it make to speak of a Judean Passover or a Passover of the Judean Jews, when the feast is clearly portrayed in this Gospel as for all Jews, including Galileans like Jesus who attend? Passover was not just a regional festival but one celebrated by all Jews.
8. So Beasley-Murray, *John*, 39.
9. See Josephus, *Ant.* 15.380.
10. The fifteenth year of Tiberius, cf. Luke 3:1.
11. The *flagellum* was a Roman implement of torture that often had bits of metal tied to the ends of the barbs in order to rip the flesh of those who were being flogged. This Latin word had also come to be used of the whip used to drive animals and probably has the latter sense here.
12. Cf. Schnackenburg, *John*, 1:346.
13. See my discussion in *Christology of Jesus*, 109–10. Nothing in the Johannine account suggests that Jesus is angry because of some sort of robbery or extortion taking place through these economic activities.
14. Cf. V. Eppstein, "The Historicity of the Gospel Account of the Cleansing of the Temple."
15. The "all" here, like some of the large numbers and hyperbolic actions (such as the whole Roman cohort falling down in John 18:3–6), is likely part of the attempt of the evangelist to dramatize the significance of the event. In this case, the point is that Jesus' desire was for the whole of the Temple precincts to be cleansed. Alternatively, one could argue that the "all" refers just to the sheep and cattle, but even so, we must be talking about considerable numbers of animals. Notice that neither the Synoptic nor the Johannine narrative suggests that Jesus was using some sort of supernatural power here or that a miracle was involved.
16. See Mussner, *Historical Jesus*, 40.
17. Harvey, *Jesus on Trial*, 46ff.
18. One has to ignore or explain away the apologetic aspect of this Gospel, if one insists it is mainly directed toward Christians, who already accept the paradox that Jesus was both Christ and crucified.
19. Cf. the similar request in the Synoptics in Mark 8:11, and esp. Matt. 12:38–40 and par.
20. Cf. my discussion of the sage speaking in Ecclesiastes and some of the material in Proverbs in *Jesus the Sage*, chaps. 1–2.
21. The "two levels of meaning" approach, with the deeper meaning understood only after the resurrection, does not justify the conclusion that the story at the second level is then especially about or addressed to the Johannine community and its problems (*pace* Ashton, *Understanding the Fourth Gospel*, 414ff.). What it means is that the listening audience must rely on the testimony of the Johannine witnesses who pass along the memories of the Beloved Disciple to gain the correct understanding of the original Jesus story. This narrative is about two stages in the revelation of the truth (pre- and post-Easter) about the one story of Jesus, not about two stories, that of Jesus and that of the Johannine community.
22. The verb is the same (*episteuein*) in both cases, but with slightly differing nuances. Cf. Carson, *John*, 184.
23. The driving of the money changers out of the Temple amounted to an objection to the exchange of coins in these Temple precincts where worship was supposed to transpire. There is no evidence that the money changers charged exorbitant fees

(apparently only 1 or 2 percent commission), and Jesus was certainly not object-
ing to putting money into the Temple treasury, something elsewhere he commends, even when the act is undertaken by someone nearly destitute (cf. Mark
12:41–44 and par. and my discussion in *Women in the Ministry of Jesus,* 16ff.).

5. Nicodemus and Nativities (John 3:1–21)

1. As Pryor, *John: Evangelist,* 18, points out, the word *anthropos* (human being)
   connects 2:25 to 3:1. Nicodemus is the human being who will serve as an example of the sort mentioned in 2:25.
2. See Beasley-Murray, *John,* 46.
3. See the discussion in Painter, *Quest for the Messiah,* 161ff.
4. This narrative, which is neither a sign narrative nor part of the farewell discourse, demonstrates that it is not adequate to argue that the missionary orientation of much of this early part of the Gospel can be confined to the agenda of
   those who put together the sign source. John 1:12–13 and 3:1–12 show that it is
   also the intent of the evangelist who put this Gospel together in its final form.
5. Culpepper, *Anatomy of the Fourth Gospel,* 135.
6. Thus Meeks, "The Man from Heaven," 144–50. As John 19:39 shows, Nicodemus's coming at night is taken to characterize the man. Furthermore, his appearance (19:39) with one hundred pounds of spices shows that he is devoted
   but has totally failed to understand that the Son of man must be lifted up. On
   the theologically loaded sense of darkness and night, see John 1:5; 13:30b.
7. Here I am rejecting one of the major theses of Martyn's stimulating and influential book *History and Theology in the Fourth Gospel,* 121ff.
8. Bultmann, *John,* 131.
9. Cf. Josephus, *Ant.* 14.37.
10. See Milne, *Message of John,* 76.
11. See Barrett, *John,* 205.
12. Contrast Staley, *The Print's First Kiss,* 92, who sees Nicodemus as the butt of a
    joke or pun here.
13. See Barrett, *John,* 206.
14. Cf. Apuleius, *Metamorphoses,* 11.
15. See my *Jesus, Paul and the End of the World,* 59–72.
16. See pp. 62–67 above.
17. See my "The Waters of Birth: John 3:5 and 1 John 5:6–8."
18. See the more detailed discussion in ibid., 159.
19. See my *Christology of Jesus,* 186–89.
20. The double Amen appears twenty-five times in this Gospel.
21. Brown, *John,* 1:132.
22. See Brown's discussion in ibid.
23. See the discussion in Ashton, *Understanding the Fourth Gospel,* 348–56.
24. Hoskyns, *Fourth Gospel,* 1:220.
25. I suspect it is the latter.
26. Though there are certain helpful hints in the text: (1) the change from singular
    to plural addressee; (2) the shift to third-person speech about Jesus.
27. Anyone who felt this way would hardly have needed to worry much about pre-
    serving or carefully passing on the testimony of the eyewitness, the Beloved Dis-
    ciple, as this evangelist obviously is concerned to do.
28. Milne, *Message of John,* 77.

29. Note especially the parallels between v. 15 and v. 16c.
30. Thus the evangelist believes in realized eschatology of both sorts.
31. It is notable that it is when sin becomes brazen and blatant and out in the open in the Bible that it most receives divine condemnation; cf. Gen. 6, 11, 19.
32. See Ashton, *Understanding the Fourth Gospel*, 515ff. While I would not go so far as Bultmann did in maintaining that the only thing that Jesus has to reveal in this Gospel is that he is the revealer, this fact is clearly central to the message of this Gospel—Jesus reveals himself through his words and deeds, and those words and deeds, while clearly self-referential, are not contentless. To put it another way, had Jesus not done what he did, he could not have revealed himself to be who he was—the Son sent from heaven to redeem the world. The being, doing, and speaking of Christ are inexorably linked together in this Gospel; there is not one without the others.
33. Ibid., 406.
34. Craddock, *John*, 28.
35. Ibid., 28–29.
36. Which is not to belittle the work of James Fowler and others on the stages of faith, but simply to say that this text is not the proper venue for that sort of analysis.
37. Cf. Milne, *Message of John*, 79.
38. Cf. ibid., "We are either one or the other, born again, or dead in sins. . . . There is no middle ground. We may not necessarily recall the details of our regeneration. That is not the primary issue, which is that we are now living in constant dependence on Jesus Christ as our living Lord and Saviour."
39. It may be worth noting the negative corollary to the discussion here, namely, that Nicodemus needed to be converted *from* at least some aspects of the Jewish faith he currently held.
40. Hoskyns, *Fourth Gospel*, 1:221.

6. John, Jesus, and the Waterworks (John 3:22–36)

1. Cf. Brown, *John*, 1:159ff.
2. Ibid., 154.
3. Cf. Beasley-Murray, *John*, 55.
4. Meeks, "The Man from Heaven," 150.
5. See Carson, *John*, 208ff.
6. Cf. Josephus, *War* 2.129; *Life* 11; *t. Yad.* 2:20.
7. In view of John 7:39, it is equally clear that the subject is not Spirit baptism.
8. See Schnackenburg, *John*, 1:411–12.
9. Witherington, *Christology of Jesus*, 54.
10. On the Markan saying, cf. my *Christology of Jesus*, 212.
11. That the evangelist would include such a parable in turn suggests that he did not feel he was writing in a period when a witness to Jews, and a union between Jesus and Jews, was out of the question and should not be pursued.
12. Note that Paul claims this role in 2 Cor. 11:2.
13. Cf. Jeremias, *Parables*, 52–53; Schnackenburg, *John*, 1:416–17.
14. See my *Christology of Jesus*, 53ff.
15. Cf. Brown, *John*, 1:158.
16. God's love for the Son can be expressed using either the verb *agapao* as here or *phileo* as in 5:20, and this leads to the conclusion that no dramatic differences in meaning are intended in texts such as John 21:15ff. (see below on this text).

17. This is not a matter of realized eschatology as opposed to future eschatology, as we shall see; rather, this author is combining the earlier confidence in the wisdom literature in the moral structure that God enforces in the here and now, with the later wisdom perspective of Wisdom of Solomon, where life beyond death and judgment beyond the grave are also and in addition contemplated. This seems to have been Jesus' approach as well, affirming a partially realized view of kingdom, blessing, judgment here and now without that eclipsing the future dimension entirely. See my *Jesus, Paul and the End of the World*, 51ff.
18. See Craddock, *John*, 33.
19. Milne, *Message of John*, 82.

7. A Savior in Samaria (John 4:1–42)

1. However, H.G.M. Williamson ("Samaritans") argues that 2 Kings 17 should be discounted in the discussion of Samaritan origins since the reference is to some who live near Samaria, not to the later Samaritan group who centered themselves in Shechem and whom Josephus's source calls "Shechemites" (*Ant.* 11.340–47; 12.10).
2. For critical analysis of this passage and its composition, cf. my *Women in the Ministry of Jesus*, 57–63.
3. See also Ruth 2:1–23; 1 Sam. 9:11–12.
4. See the interesting discussion in Staley, *The Print's First Kiss*, 96–101.
5. Cf. R. Alter, *The Art of Biblical Narrative*, 51–62.
6. Staley, *The Print's First Kiss*, 102.
7. Notice that the Qumran community also use water and well imagery of Torah as a source of life (CD 3:16f.; 6:4–11; 19:34). It is not beyond the realm of possibility that Jacob's well is seen as a type in this narrative of Torah, to which one must return time and time again to slake one's thirst. Cf. Pryor, *John: Evangelist*, 22.
8. Scott, *Sophia and the Johannine Jesus*, 194ff.
9. G. W. McRae, *Faith in the Word—the Fourth Gospel*, 38.
10. See my *Women in the Ministry of Jesus*, 2ff.
11. See Barrett, *John*, 232–33.
12. On Jewish customs about men not speaking with unrelated women in public, cf. *b. Kid.* 49b; *m. Abot* 1:5; *b. Shabb.* 152a; Philo, *On Drunkenness*, 58–59.
13. But see Scott, *Sophia and the Johannine Jesus*, 191.
14. An obvious exaggeration in the moment of excitement.
15. Craddock, *John*, 37.
16. This is one of the few instances in the Fourth Gospel where Jesus is presented as telling something like a parable, the gist of which is seize the day, the fields are ripe for harvest. This suits the realized eschatological message of this Gospel very well.
17. Witherington, *Women in the Ministry of Jesus*, 63.
18. See Milne, *Message of John*, 85–86.

8. The Second Sign at Cana (John 4:43–54)

1. This saying which Jesus surely used was apparently a traditional proverb, for it is also found in *P. Oxy.* 1.
2. Barrett, *John*, 244–46.

3. See Brown, *John*, 1:xi.
4. See Craddock, *John*, 40.
5. Painter, *Quest for the Messiah*, 171.
6. A device called *inclusio.*
7. Here I follow Carson, *John*, 237.
8. This is true even of various more conservative scholars such as Beasley-Murray, *John*, 71; and Pryor, *John: Evangelist*, 24.
9. See my article "Principles for Interpreting the Gospels and Acts," *Ashland Theological Seminary Journal* 19 (1982): 35–61.
10. Found in *b. Ber.* 34b.
11. Herod Antipas, whom Jesus called a "fox," was of course not technically a king but tetrarch of Galilee from 4 B.C. to A.D. 39, but he was popularly considered a king and seems to have viewed himself in that light (cf. Mark 6:14).
12. See A. H. Mead, "The *basilikos* in John 4:46–53."
13. It may be that this conversation actually did transpire in Greek, if this man was a Roman soldier. On Jesus' knowledge of Greek, see the forthcoming essay by J. A. Fitzmyer, delivered at the August 1993 meeting of the Society for New Testament Studies.
14. When Jesus later prays at the Lazarus raising (11:42), it appears clearly for the benefit of those around him, not because this is how he obtained power at that moment. Jesus was one on whom the Spirit descended and remained during the ministry, yet paradoxically he can use that power only if and when the Father gives the go-ahead.
15. Craddock, *John*, 41.
16. Another way to approach this text is to focus on Jesus' challenge to a stronger and greater faith, one that acts on the basis of a promise and trusts the promise, or one could focus on the emotions displayed in the text—the persistence and desperation of the man, the frustration and yet compassion of the Master.

9. Sabbatical Work (John 5:1–47)

1. Pryor, *John: Evangelist*, 25, notes the four major differences between John 2:1–4:54 and John 5ff.: (1) Jesus makes explicit claims by word and deed that are an affront to Judaism (John 5, 6, 8, 9). (2) Jesus claims a relationship with the Father that far exceeds anything said in John 2—4. (3) Opposition between Jesus and some Jews becomes intense. (4) Jesus begins to turn accusations back on his adversaries (John 5, 7, 9), even to the point of denying them covenantal status (John 8).
2. See Painter, *Quest for the Messiah*, 178n11.
3. Beasley-Murray, *John*, 80.
4. In short, the Fourth Gospel is a larger exercise in evangelistic hermeneutics.
5. See Painter, *Quest for the Messiah*, 175.
6. See Beasley-Murray, *John*, 71. Notice that the Synoptic non-Sabbath healings also generally require a prior demonstration of faith. So Pryor, *John: Evangelist*, 26.
7. Various scholars have argued that the two stories are in fact variants of one story, but both the setting (one in Capernaum, one in Jerusalem) and various other differences in the stories suggest we may be dealing with separate incidents.
8. See my discussion of this last option, and Jesus' approach to the Sabbath in general in my *Christology of Jesus*, 66–71.
9. Harvey's whole discussion is important for all the material in John 5—10. Cf. his *Jesus on Trial*, 18ff.

10. Ibid., 47.
11. Ibid., 55.
12. One conjecture is that it was at the Feast of Pentecost, which would explain the reference to Moses and the discussion of the law, for the giving of the law on Sinai was celebrated at that feast. Cf. Brown, *John*, 1:206.
13. The Greek reads *Hebraisti*, which could mean Hebrew, but more likely refers to Aramaic, the spoken language of most Palestinian Jews.
14. There are a variety of variant readings here. Probably the Hebrew name *Beth* (house) *esda* (of outpouring) is what the Greek text is trying to transliterate. We now have evidence from the Copper Scroll from Qumran for the dual form of this same expression.
15. The fact that the text says "There is in Jerusalem a pool . . ." probably does not suggest that the evangelist is writing prior to A.D. 70. The Fourth Gospel is the testimony of someone who lived both before and after 70, and it is natural in telling the story to do so in a manner that comports with the reliving of the event in one's mind.
16. On the archaeology of this site, cf. J. Jeremias, *The Rediscovery of Bethesda*.
17. Cf. Craddock, *John*, 43.
18. This would include of course the Pharisees.
19. Carson, *John*, 246.
20. Notice that the evangelist does not deny that technically Jesus was doing so. The basic early Jewish rule was that if a person was not in a life-threatening situation, helping or healing him should wait until after the Sabbath was over. Cf. my *Christology of Jesus*, 66–71, and *b. Yoma* 85B.
21. See the discussion of W. Meeks, "Equal to God," in *Studies in Paul and John*, 309–21.
22. The basic Jewish data are helpfully assembled in P. Borgen, "God's Agent in the Fourth Gospel."
23. The agency concept also helps us to grasp why Jesus tells the disciples they will do even greater works than he has done—but only of course under his authorization and with his power.
24. We will discuss later (see pp. 250–252 below) whether and in what sense the Holy Spirit is also seen as Christ's agent and advocate while on earth.
25. See the discussion of A. E. Harvey, "Christ as Agent."
26. See my discussion in *Christology of Jesus*, 213–15, 224–25.
27. On the meaning of the title "the Holy One of God" in John 6:69, cf. below where it will be argued that it refers to Jesus' being God's Wisdom in the flesh and thus his agent on earth. Unfortunately the most important study on agency in the Fourth Gospel is not available in English. Cf. J. A. Bühner, *Der Gesandte und sein Weg im 4. Evangelium*.
28. See above on John 1:51.
29. See the helpful discussion in Ashton, *Understanding the Fourth Gospel*, 357–63.
30. Cf. above on the discourse in John 3, and below on John 19.
31. N. A. Dahl ("Do Not Wonder! John 5:28–29 and Johannine Eschatology Once More") suggests that the future eschatology, which a Jewish audience was more likely to accept as true, is used to provide a warrant for the present eschatology in this discourse. It must be kept in mind, however, that the likely reason for the focus on present eschatology in this Gospel is its missionary purpose, focusing as it does on the individual (and the universal implications of the Gospel for all individuals, whether Jewish or not) and his or her being born anew through faith in Christ.

32. As I have pointed out in *Jesus the Sage*, the use of Father language of God first comes to prominence in early Judaism in the sapiential literature such as Wisdom of Solomon. This is one hint that not only Jesus but the Beloved Disciple and the Fourth Evangelist are steeped in this literature, and this in part accounts for the rather unique character and language of this Gospel. The Beloved Disciple used sapiential language, which was part of Jesus' way of speaking about himself, to flesh out the real significance and meaning of who Jesus was and what he did.

33. Notice that the Spirit is not mentioned at this juncture for the very good reason that the audience of this material is outsiders, whereas when one gets to the farewell discourses the Spirit is discussed, because the original audience of that material was believers who already had the Spirit which could lead them into all truth. In John 5, Jesus must appeal to witnesses he and his accusers had both knowledge of and access to.

34. This cross-reference makes apparent that "the Jews" here are a particular group of Jewish authorities zealous for Torah, and not any or all Jews.

35. Barrett, *John*, 265.

36. See Craddock, *John*, 43ff.

37. Milne, *Message of John*, 101.

38. C. S. Lewis, *Mere Christianity*, 55–56.

39. See the discussion in Neyrey, *An Ideology of Revolt*, 9ff., on John 5.

10. Food for Thought, Bread on the Waters (John 6:1–71)

1. I do not agree with the view of Schnackenburg (*John*, 2:1–9) that the order of chaps. 6 and 5 should be reversed to make sense of the text. As Carson (*John*, 267) points out, this hardly helps the flow of the text from John 6 to John 7 because in the latter text one is back in Galilee, and if it was originally preceded by John 5 it would still have entailed a leap from Judea and Galilee.

2. Cf. Schnackenburg, *John*, 2:12: "Attempts at critical surgery on the grand composition of Chapter 6 are undesirable."

3. Notice that v. 59 appears to draw the story to a closure, but in fact it is only the end of the public discussion, while private discussion continues with the disciples.

4. As Painter (*Quest for the Messiah*, 227) points out, in 6:22–35 there are two references to the crowd; in 6:41–59 there are two references to the Jews; in 6:60–66 there are two references to the disciples; and in 6:67–71 there are two references to the Twelve.

5. Here as in places like Luke 8:1–3 it becomes clear that at various points Jesus had more disciples than just the Twelve, and some even traveled with Jesus and the Twelve, including some women.

6. See Carson, *John*, 270: "John portrays this as a miracle, not as a eucharistic mouthful, still less an ethical lesson on how to shame people into sharing their lunches."

7. The source of eternal life is Jesus as the true Passover lamb, though nothing is made of that image at this juncture.

8. See pp. 47–147 above.

9. See above on John 2.

10. See the entire helpful discussion in P. Borgen, *Bread from Heaven*, 154ff.

11. Painter, *Quest for the Messiah*, 242.

12. A fact only possibly hinted at when we are told twelve basketsful of fragments are left over (v. 13).

13. The tandem of Philip and Andrew occurs in John 1:44; 12:21–22 (cf. 14:8), but very notable by its absence is the tandem so familiar and important in the Synoptics—James and John sons of Zebedee. This surely must count strongly against the argument that the Beloved Disciple should be identified with John of Zebedee, a suggestion that the text of the Fourth Gospel itself nowhere seeks to make. Both the personal absence of John in the narrative and the absence of the most telling stories involving him that are recorded in the Synoptics (raising of Jairus's daughter, transfiguration, request for seats in the kingdom) strongly speak against the traditional view of the authorship of the Fourth Gospel.

14. See Schnackenburg, *John*, 2:15–16.

15. See Bultmann, *John*, 213.

16. Compare the discussion of Samaritans above, p. 117, and Meeks, *The Prophet-King*.

17. See my *Christology of Jesus*, 98–104.

18. Sometimes, as in John 6:15, when Jesus knew that the messianic ideas did not match his own self-understanding he withdrew, or did not encourage a true acclamation to be made public, because it would lead to misunderstanding, not to enlightenment (cf. Mark 8:30).

19. Beasley-Murray, *John*, 89.

20. It is worth pointing out that in the ancient Near East water was often thought to be the dwelling place of spirits and demons, and for persons who believed this, being out on the water at night could quite naturally bring to the surface all sorts of unconscious fears, which Jesus seeks to allay.

21. Is this yet another hint that Capernaum was widely known to be Jesus' Galilean home during the ministry?

22. See Carson, *John*, 284.

23. On this whole passage, see Barrett, *John*, 281ff.

24. This text, however, can be dated no earlier than A.D. 340, since it is associated with Rabbi Berechiah.

25. See the whole discussion in Carson, *John*, 274.

26. *Ani hu* in the Hebrew.

27. *Pas* is in the neuter gender.

28. My own reading of the matter is that the New Testament suggests that one is not eternally secure until one is securely in eternity. Short of that, there is the possibility of apostasy or rebellion against God by one who has believed in Christ. Apostasy, however, is not to be confused with the notion of accidentally or unconsciously "falling away." Apostasy is a conscious, willful rebellion against God, a wrenching oneself free from the firm grip of God on one's life. Unless one commits such an act of apostasy or rebellion, one need not worry about one's salvation, for God has a firm grip on the believer.

29. These words would be especially apropos if, as I have argued, when the Fourth Gospel was written there had already been the internal crisis in the Johannine community recorded in the *earlier* Johannine epistles, where some had gone forth from the community.

30. Notice again the connection between *words* and eternal life, not signs or sacraments.

31. The Twelve are mentioned by number as an entity only here in John 6 and at John 20:24. The evangelist shows little interest in them as a group that amounted to Jesus' inner circle, and no interest at all in the inner circle within the inner

circle of Peter, James, and John. This is passing strange if John the son of Zebedee is the source of this Gospel, but understandable if it comes from a Judean disciple who was not among the Twelve or the three.

32. See Barrett, *John*, 301ff.
33. The differences include: (1) the location of the confession; (2) what is confessed; (3) who is criticized by Jesus in response; and (4) the question Jesus asks of the disciples which prompts the confession.
34. The demons' confession of Jesus as the "Holy One of God" appears as the first thing any being confesses Jesus to be in Mark's Gospel.
35. W. R. Domeris, "The Confession of Peter according to John 6:69," 163.
36. Note Peter's "we."
37. See my discussion in *Christology of Jesus*, 98.
38. See my *Women in the Ministry of Jesus*, passim.
39. Milne, *The Message of John*, 113.
40. As Craddock (*John*, 53) points out.

11. Temple Discourses and Healing (John 7:1–10:42)

1. See the discussion in B. M. Metzger, *A Textual Commentary on the New Testament*, 219–23.
2. It could, however, fruitfully be used as an illustration in a sermon.
3. See Harvey, *Jesus on Trial*, 52ff.
4. Ibid., 78ff.
5. On agency, see pp. 140–41 above.
6. Harvey, *Jesus on Trial*, 58.
7. This law was originally about a dead person who was hung on a tree, not someone crucified alive, but by Jesus and Paul's time apparently various Jews took it to apply to the crucified as well (cf. Gal. 3:13).
8. On this whole matter, cf. Brown, *John*, 1:326ff.
9. On the twin themes developing in these two chapters of the rising tension with the Jews and Jesus fulfilling the feast, cf. Pryor, *John: Evangelist*, 35.
10. The discussion of the Fourth Evangelist's use of the term "Jews" by P.J. Thomson, "The Names Israel and Jew in Ancient Judaism and the New Testament," 281–83, is unconvincing. This evangelist often uses words in a way that is unconventional or distinctive (cf. now the discussion in N. R. Petersen, *The Gospel of John and the Sociology of Light*, 81ff., though calling it an anti-language is stretching things a bit far). It is clear enough at various key points that "the Jews" is not always used in a pejorative sense in this Gospel, and that when it is, it is referring to a certain group of Torah-observant Jews, in particular some Jewish authorities, but as Nicodemus demonstrates, not even all of them were seeking to do Jesus in.
11. Nothing said here suggests that these brothers were anything other than Jesus' actual brothers through Mary, rather than cousins. Cf. my discussion in *Women in the Ministry of Jesus*, 89ff.
12. The identification of this disciple with the Beloved Disciple seems natural in view of the fact that the Beloved Disciple is mentioned as being involved in these final events in Jesus' life at John 19:26 and the tandem of the "other" disciple and Peter show up together again on Easter morning and go to the tomb (John 20:2–8). The evangelist clearly believes that the Beloved Disciple was an eyewitness of these climactic events in Jerusalem and has testified about them, and so it is natural to see the other disciple and "the disciple whom Jesus loved."

13. Notice how the term "world," and the term "Jews" blend into one in this discussion (cf. vv. 7–11). The Jews are the representative examples of those of the world that hate Jesus.
14. Staley, *The Print's First Kiss,* 103–5, thinks the evangelist is deliberately trying to victimize the reader, in order to demonstrate that she or he does not yet truly understand the depths of Jesus' character and mission. This is perhaps barely possible, but seems to be too modern a literary strategy to predicate of the author of this document.
15. See the helpful discussion in Carson, *John,* 308–9.
16. See Painter, *Quest for the Messiah,* 255f.
17. Cf. the similar reaction to Peter and John in Acts 4:13.
18. It may be that the authorities mentioned in v. 32 are the same as "the Jews" in v. 35. The evangelist knows that the Pharisees had a role in Jesus' demise, as the Synoptics stress, and mentions them here, though the combination of Pharisees and chief priests is an odd one (cf. John 1:19).
19. See Painter, *Quest for the Messiah,* 255n40.
20. Cf. Barrett, *John,* 326–27.
21. Ashton, *Understanding the Fourth Gospel,* 422 and n.26, may be right that both Jesus and the believer are meant as the source of this water.
22. The three events are joined together in this Gospel as one act of the lifting up of Jesus, his exaltation.
23. On the sending of the Spirit, see below on 14:16, 26 and 15:26.
24. See Painter, *Quest for the Messiah,* 249ff.
25. The Greek word *alethes* could be translated "true," as opposed to false, but the forensic context of this discussion shows that it is about the validity of Jesus' witness. Cf. Harvey, *Jesus on Trial,* 56–57.
26. Ibid., 58.
27. See pp. 156–58 above for a discussion of its meaning.
28. Cf. the discussion in Ashton, *Understanding the Fourth Gospel,* 364–66.
29. Bultmann, *John,* 350.
30. I. de la Potterie, "The Truth in Saint John," esp. 54–55.
31. Ibid., 55.
32. Cf. Barrett, *John,* 344–45.
33. See the discussion in R. Whitacre, *Johannine Polemic,* 69–71.
34. Ibid., 70.
35. One form of the polemic says the father was a Roman named Pantera. Cf. one of the earliest forms of the polemic in *m. Yebam.* 4:13.
36. Whitacre, *Johannine Polemic,* 73.
37. Ibid.
38. Ibid., 76.
39. Here I follow Schnackenburg, *John,* 2:239.
40. Brown, *John,* 1:377.
41. Barrett, *John,* 324.
42. Craddock, *John,* 64.
43. See Martyn, *History and Theology in the Fourth Gospel,* 37ff., and our discussion of the matter in the Introduction.
44. See *b. Shabb.* 55a.
45. The use of the phrase "blind from birth," as opposed to the Semitic phrase "blind from the mother's womb," may provide yet another clue that the audience is predominantly Gentile, not Jewish. Cf. Brown, *John,* 1:371.
46. Cf. the use of *hina* as result in 5:2 and cf. Barrett, *John,* 356.

47. On this pool, cf. 2 Chron. 32:30 and the Copper Scroll at 3Q15 10, 15–16.
48. Notice that it is here *not* the blind man but his family that fear expulsion, and clearly his family is not depicted as a Christian one. This is surely another clue that Martyn is on the wrong track with his analysis of this story.
49. This is another sure sign that the evangelist is not portraying the man born blind as a model Christian.
50. Again these remarks show that the man does not yet fully understand who Jesus is—Jesus is not merely one who worships God.
51. The text does not say he was formally expelled from the synagogue, only cast out of the hearing, though the former may be implied.
52. Notice that three times in this Gospel the title Son of man is used to supplement or make more adequate a confession of faith: 1:51; 9:35; 12:34. Cf. Ashton, *Understanding the Fourth Gospel*, 181.
53. *Kyrie* (vocative) means something like "respected sir," not "divine Lord," and was a common form of address to one's superiors.
54. It is difficult to tell whether "lord" here is meant to be seen as having its more pregnant sense, but perhaps not.
55. This is probably to be taken as an act of worship, but the verb simply means to prostrate oneself.
56. Notice that in Rom. 5:13, in similar fashion to here, people are not condemned for their ignorance of the truth, but they are held responsible if they willfully *ignore* or reject the truth.
57. See Beasley-Murray, *John*, 148.
58. See Neyrey, *An Ideology of Revolt*, 64: "Jesus' death is no mere heroic apotheosis but actually constitutes his return to the glory he had with God before the creation of the world (17:5, 24)."
59. See the discussion of Schnackenburg, *John*, 2:280–86.
60. See my discussion in *Jesus the Sage*, 370–76.
61. See C. H. Dodd, *The Parables of the Kingdom* (New York: Charles Scribner's Sons, 1961), passim.
62. Cf. Schnackenburg, *John*, 2:282.
63. This suggests that perhaps one reason some individual Christians and congregations are so easily led astray is that they have never been taught how to recognize the distinctive voice and message of Jesus.
64. See the discussion in Neyrey, *An Ideology of Revolt*, 63–64.
65. Compare this to the Synoptic and Pauline portrait where it is the Father that raises Jesus from the dead: Mark 16:6; Acts 5:30; 1 Cor. 15:4; and so on.
66. Here is yet another piece of evidence that it is wrong to suggest that the epistles were written after the Gospel, depicting a later crisis in the Johannine community.
67. See Barrett, *John*, 375–76.
68. On the whole subject of whether Jesus could have foreseen a Gentile mission, cf. J. Jeremias, *Jesus' Promise to the Nations*.
69. John 7:35 likely refers to diaspora Jews; see p. 173 above.
70. Barrett, *John*, 376.
71. Cf. Ashton, *Understanding the Fourth Gospel*, 238ff.
72. It is notable that in texts like this, and in Rom. 8:38–39, the one thing or person that is *not* excluded as a possible source of severing an individual from the Father or Christ is the person himself or herself. Both John 10:28 and Rom. 8:38–39 are texts meant to reassure that no outside force or being can snatch one out of the firm grasp of God. They do not address the issue of apostasy.
73. See Milne, *Message of John*, 154.

74. See Barrett, *John*, 385.
75. See Milne, *Message of John*, 155.
76. Craddock, *John*, 64.
77. C. S. Lewis, *Poems* (New York: Harcourt, Brace & World, 1964), 109–10.
78. Craddock, *John*, 61.
79. From Culpepper, *Anatomy of the Fourth Gospel*, 139.

12. Family Affairs (John 11:1–12:11)

1. See my discussion in *Women in the Ministry of Jesus*, 103–14, and the notes.
2. See the discussion in M. Harris, "The Dead Are Restored to Life: Miracles of Re-vivification in the Gospels."
3. Brown, *John*, 1:429–30.
4. See my discussion on Greco-Roman meals in my *Conflict and Community in Corinth*, 191–95.
5. See Culpepper, *Anatomy of the Fourth Gospel*, 141.
6. See Harris, "Revivification," 320: "Before Jesus' resurrection, it could be said only that 'the dead are restored to life' (. . . Mt. 11:5; Lk. 7:22). After his resurrection it can be said 'the dead will be raised immortal' (. . . 1 Cor. 15:52)."
7. On these traditions cf. Carson, *John*, 404 and n. 2.
8. Cf. Brown, *John*, 1:433: "Throughout the incident involving Martha we see that she believes in Jesus but inadequately. In vs 27 she addresses him with lofty titles . . . yet 39 shows that she does not yet believe in his power to give life. She regards Jesus an intermediary who is heard by God (22), but she does not understand that he is life itself (25)."
9. See my discussion in *Women in the Ministry of Jesus*, 116ff.
10. See my discussion in *Conflict and Community in Corinth*, 191–95.
11. There is evidence that nard was a plant grown in India, not in Israel, and so it was an expensive imported fragrance. Cf. Milne, *Message of John*, 175.
12. Contra Painter, *Quest for the Messiah*, 315n10.
13. Culpepper, *Anatomy of the Fourth Gospel*, 141 and n. 84.
14. Painter, *Quest for the Messiah*, 313ff.
15. See Carson, *John*, 405.
16. Ibid., 406.
17. It may be significant that the sisters knew where to send for Jesus, which suggests he was in a location that was a familiar haunt of his when he was in the Judean region. John 10:40–41 suggests that he was associated with the areas where John the Baptist had formerly performed his ministry. John 10:40–41 does not conclude the public ministry, but it does serve as a reminder of the earlier witness of the Baptist to Jesus, and its truth.
18. The lack of spiritual perceptivity of the disciples in general is a constant feature of this Gospel, right up to the time of Jesus' death and resurrection and even beyond as John 20 shows.
19. Thomas is called Didymus, which means the twin, though we have no idea whose twin he was.
20. Cf. Brown, *John*, 1:424; Gen. Rabbah 100 (64a).
21. Cf. Schnackenburg, *John*, 2:328ff.
22. Cf. *m. Ketub.* 4:4 and my *Women in the Ministry of Jesus*, 74–75, and n. 176.
23. As Carson (*John*, 412n1) notes, only the Fourth Evangelist uses the expression "the last day" (cf. 6:39–40, 44, 54; 12:48), as opposed to the more common "last days" which refers to the days just before the end (cf. Acts 2:17; 2 Tim. 3:1).

24. We have seen already how knowing where Jesus came from and is going is the key to understanding his identity; cf. pp. 53–54 above.
25. See Beasley-Murray, *John*, 193; Schnackenburg, *John*, 2:335.
26. Cf. Hoskyns, *Fourth Gospel*, 2:472.
27. Notice they speak of Jesus' keeping Lazarus from dying, not raising Lazarus.
28. Cf. 12:27; 13:21 on this verb.
29. See the excursus on pp. 140–41 above.
30. Harvey, *Jesus on Trial*, 98.
31. Cf. *2 Ezra* 14:7; Acts 6:14.
32. Craddock, *John*, 89.
33. See the discussion in Carson, *John*, 424.
34. See John 18:16—is this the Beloved Disciple?
35. Probably this is the city today called Et-Taiyibeh near Bethel, and so some distance from Jerusalem. Cf. Barrett, *John*, 408.
36. See Josephus, *War* 1.229; 6.290. This goes back to Num. 9:6–12, as it is interpreted in Jewish tradition (cf. *m. Pesah.* 9:1).
37. This strongly points to the material in John 11 and John 12 *not* being originally connected chronologically. Had they originally been paired together, neither the reminder about Mary in 11:2 nor the reminder about Lazarus in 12:1 would have really been necessary.
38. Ancient Christian commentators speculated on what might have been the conversation at the dinner. After all, what does one say to a person recently back from the dead? The juxtaposition of one just raised and one yet to be raised in this story was too much for some early Christian allegorists to pass by without extended speculation. Cf. Origen's commentary on the Gospel of John ad loc. Even modern commentators seem unable to refrain from such an approach; cf. Culpepper, *Anatomy of the Fourth Gospel*, 142: "Martha represents the ideal of discerning faith and service, Mary unlimited love and devotion, and Lazarus the hope of resurrection life. Together they are almost a Johannine characterization of the Pauline virtues—faith, hope, love."
39. See Milne, *Message of John*, 175.
40. See my *Women in the Ministry of Jesus*, 53ff. and 110ff. I remain very unconvinced of the argument that the version in the Fourth Gospel is simply a redaction of the Synoptic version, but cf. M. Sabbe, "The Anointing of Jesus in John 12:1–8 and Its Synoptic Parallels."
41. For example, both the Markan and Lukan stories identify the anointing as taking place at the house of a man named Simon, while the Fourth Gospel places it at Lazarus's house. Mark and Matthew have the anointing taking place on the head, while John and Luke speak of an anointing on the feet.
42. In the Markan account these two events are in the opposite order. Barrett argues that it is important that Jesus be anointed for burial before his triumphal entry into Jerusalem in the Johannine account because in the Johannine scheme of things the dying Jesus must be presented before the triumphant Jesus, indeed the dying of Jesus is his means of triumph and exaltation (cf. Barrett, *John*, 409). It can, however, be argued that Mark has located this story after the triumphal entry in order to place it close to the Lord's Supper story. The anointing of the feet prior to the Johannine narrative of the washing of others' feet may also signal the servant character of Jesus (cf. below on John 13).
43. See my discussion of the arguments of M. Dibelius and Bultmann in *Women in the Ministry of Jesus*, 111ff. and the notes.
44. Dodd, *Interpretation of the Fourth Gospel*, 370; cf. 369.
45. See my *Women in the Ministry of Jesus*, 193n203, for references.

46. Women sometimes wore small flasks of nard around their necks, which they could use to freshen up from time to time.
47. See Petronius, *Satyricon*, 27.
48. The identity of the objector(s) is not made clear in the Synoptic version of the story, as it is in the Fourth Gospel.
49. But see Barrett, *John*, 414, for the possibility that the second command means "let her remember it" on the day of my burial. As Barrett admits, *terein* does not normally have the sense of "remember," but it does have the sense of "keep."
50. This story provides an excellent test case to see to what degree an evangelist could alter the words of his source in the service of making the story his own in style and diction, as well as his own in terms of his theological and social agendas, and yet still convey essentially the same message and meaning in both the narrative and sayings material used.
51. See Milne, *Message of John*, 176.
52. Here as in all of John 11, the term "Jews" does not have a pejorative sense, and does not refer to the authorities.
53. The meaning of the phrase here is not raised from death but raised from the realm of the dead ones, which in the Old Testament is called Sheol and in Greco-Roman literature is called Hades. This latter term did not mean to pagans hell or a place of eternal punishment but simply a place where the dead spirits go after death. Hell, whether called Hades, Gehenna, or something else (cf. Luke 23 for Hades = Hell), was a distinctively Judeo-Christian concept.
54. We are not told that these Jews' faith in Jesus was adequate, and thus their quick deserting of his cause later is not surprising; cf. Schnackenburg, *John*, 2:370. Notice that they seem to have a hunger for seeing the miracle man, the one who came back from the dead, as well as the miracle worker.
55. D. Bonhoeffer, *The Cost of Discipleship*, 99.

13. The Return of the King and His Last Audience
(John 12:12–50)

1. See D. M. Smith, "John 12:12ff. and the Question of John's Use of the Synoptics."
2. The considerable effort in all the Gospels to stress that these concluding events in Jesus' life did not happen by accident and were not a result of God's curse on Jesus' life, but rather were part of God's long-standing plan for his anointed one as revealed in scripture, reflects the needs of early Christians to provide a defense (*apologia*) of the conclusion of Jesus' life. Apparently, few if any early Jews or synagogue adherents before or during Jesus' era were expecting a crucified messiah, although there may now be some scant evidence from Qumran, just now coming to light, that a few sectarian Jews may have entertained the possibility of a pierced or suffering messiah. The point is that evidence is lacking that early Jews interpreted such texts as Isa. 53 as speaking of messiah, unless the new Qumran material provides such evidence. Even if this should prove to be the case, we would not be able to talk about a widespread expectation of a crucified messiah in early Judaism. It appears that Jesus and his followers were offering a new interpretation of the role of messiah to their fellow Jews.
3. Matthew clearly follows and draws on Mark, and it may be that Mark was indebted to Peter, as the Papias traditions suggest, for his account of the Passion material. On the other hand, it is also very possible that John Mark, whom Acts

associates with the Jerusalem church, himself derived the Passion material already with its use of the Old Testament from the Jerusalem community, as the Beloved Disciple may have done. As for Matthew's use of the Zechariah text, which is also found in John but which is *not* in Mark, here the suggestion of a *testimonium* used by Matthew and possibly the Fourth Evangelist (if the Beloved Disciple's testimony did not include such scripture citations) is plausible.

4. One may, however, point to Luke 22:24–30, 35–38 as possible historical evidence that Jesus had some extended discussion at the last meal with his disciples about their trials and roles after his death, among other subjects.

5. Cf. also the closely similar material in Luke 22:27, which also depicts the last meal of Jesus and his disciples as being like a Greco-Roman banquet with dialogues with and discourses by the great teacher following the meal.

6. Cf. pp. 217–20 above.

7. The word "Hosanna" from the Hebrew *hosi'a na'*, which means "save now," had become by Jesus' day a general exclamation of joy, much like our "hooray."

8. Cf. the discussion at pp. 152–54 above .

9. Cf., e.g., Schnackenburg, *John*, 2:377: "The similarity of the commentary allows us to assume that the evangelist found Jesus' entry into Jerusalem and the cleansing of the Temple in fairly close association."

10. See my discussion in *Christology of Jesus*, 104–16.

11. Milne, *Message of John*, 181. He is quoting Beasley-Murray, *John*, 209.

12. Cf. Mark 7:26, where the same Greek word refers not to a native of Greece but to a Syro-Phoenician woman who spoke Greek.

13. On the quest motif here, cf. Painter, *Quest for the Messiah*, 322–23.

14. The reference to sympathizers in the synagogue (vv. 42–43) may also point to such a context.

15. The other is Andrew, who is constantly coupled with Philip in this Gospel. Cf. 1:40, 43–46; 6:5, 7; 14:8–9.

16. Though Polycrates, whom Eusebius is quoting, seems to have confused Philip the apostle with Philip the evangelist referred to in Acts 6:5; 8:4–13, 26–40; 21:8–9.

17. Up to this point it had always been referred to as something in the future. Cf. 2:4; 4:21, 23; 7:30; 8:20.

18. Schnackenburg, *John*, 2:383.

19. The Greek word here signifies revulsion, anxiety, horror, agitation. Cf. Carson, *John*, 440.

20. Cf. Acts 9:7; 22:9.

21. Cf., however, Beasley-Murray, *John*, 213.

22. Cf. Augustine, *In Johann.* 52.7ff.; Aquinas, *Lect.* 5.7.

23. I am unconvinced by the attempts to demythologize supernatural evil in the Bible.

24. This view of Cullmann was first enunciated in his *Christ and Time.*

25. It is hard to say what scriptural text is in mind when "the Law" is referred to in v. 34. Cf. Isa. 9:7; Ezek. 37:25; Ps. 72:17.

26. The explanation of Dodd (*Interpretation of the Fourth Gospel*, 382) that what *ekraxen* means is "this is the content of the kerygma" is ingenious.

27. See Ashton, *Understanding the Fourth Gospel*, 543. Carson, *John*, 451, suggests that vv. 44–50 is the evangelist's own summary of Jesus' teaching and he is likely right.

28. See Brown, *John*, 1:485.

29. Cf. Acts 28:26–27; Mark 8:17–18.

30. See Carson, *John*, 448ff.

31. See Barrett, *John*, 433.
32. But cf. Ashton, *Understanding the Fourth Gospel*, 541ff.
33. See my treatment of prophecy in *Jesus, Paul and the End of the World*, in the Appendix.
34. Milne, *Message of John*, 182.

14. A Farewell Dinner (John 13:1–30)

1. Carson in *John*, 475, speculates that the Feast of Unleavened Bread is in view, but the only feast mentioned in this passage (13:1) is the Passover Feast, and in view of how intrusive the evangelist is into the text of this Gospel it is difficult to believe he would not explain if another feast were referred to. On the other hand, the reference to giving something to the poor has been taken to allude to the custom of giving alms to the poor on Passover night (cf. J. Jeremias, *The Eucharistic Words of Jesus*, 54), but in view of the sources cited by Jeremias the issue is whether this was a known practice as early as Jesus' day.
2. Cf. Beasley-Murray, *John*, 240ff.; Pryor, *John: Evangelist*, 58ff.
3. Craddock, *John*, 100.
4. A clear hint that the evangelist would move in this direction is found in the exclamation of the Baptist in John 1:36.
5. What follows can be found in much fuller form in my *Conflict and Community in Corinth*, 204–10.
6. Nero's regular practice was to call in the teachers of *sophia* after dinner to amuse the guests, which could include philosophers and rhetors. Cf. R. MacMullen, *Enemies of the Roman Order*, 59.
7. It is understandable why this custom would be assumed to be a necessary and regular part of hospitality in the Middle East in view of all the dust and dirt that covered one from traveling on roads during the nonrainy seasons, roads that for the most part had not been laid or "repaved" by the Romans.
8. These sorts of remarks are not found in the Synoptic portrayal of the Last Supper in Mark 14 and par. Only Luke's brief remark that the cup of wine came *after supper* (Luke 22:20) points in the direction of a Greco-Roman meal.
9. It is intriguing that Luke portrays the Last Supper as including a discussion by the disciples of who is the greatest, and Jesus' reiteration of his own servant leadership as a pattern for the disciples to follow in Luke 22:24–27, in a similar fashion to what we find in John 13. This suggests that they are both drawing on common tradition about this sort of closing meeting and teaching session.
10. On the guilds and trade associations, including burial associations, see my discussion in *Conflict and Community in Corinth*, pp. 243–47. Here, again, the Johannine similarity to material in Luke 22, this time in vv. 35–38, is striking, where the issue of money and purse is raised 243–47.
11. Notice that the Last Supper is depicted as ending with a religious act, a hymn (Mark 14:26 and par.).
12. In other words Jesus is portrayed as Wisdom, while the disciples are portrayed as the simple and spiritually immature, as in Prov. 9.
13. But see the discussion in Carson, *John*, 455–58; Brown, *John*, 2:555ff.
14. See Beasley-Murray, *John*, 238.
15. Notice that once we get to the Passion narrative, Jesus controls the action and no longer suggests he must wait for the Father's go-ahead or for his hour to

arrive. Jesus will lay down his life at a time and under the circumstances of his own choosing.

16. Mekilta no. 1 on Ex. 21:2 says that Jewish slaves should not even be required to perform this menial task; rather, it should be reserved for Gentile slaves, or for women, children, and pupils of a great teacher.

17. Cf. Luke 15:12; Matt. 24:51; Rev. 20:6 for the language; and Beasley-Murray, *John*, 234.

18. Carson, *John*, 462ff.

19. Cf. Schnackenburg, *John*, 3:19–20.

20. Ibid.

21. This makes especially problematic the practice of those who wish to perform foot washing at the end of celebrating the Lord's Supper. If the rite is going to be performed, it should surely transpire *before* partaking of the bread and wine. Cleansing must precede receiving the other benefits of Christ's death.

22. See above, pp. 148ff. on John 6, and pp. 92ff. on John 3.

23. One may distinguish between prediction and fulfillment. Judas's act is a fulfillment of what scripture says, even if the act David or the psalmist referred to was originally an event in the lifetime of the son of Jesse.

24. Cf. Schnackenburg, *John*, 3:26.

25. See Barrett, *John*, 445.

26. Cf. the discussion above on this phrase, pp. 156–58.

27. See above pp. 203–4.

28. "The one whom Jesus loved" may be alluded to earlier in John 1. Cf. pp. 69ff. above.

29. Beasley-Murray, *John*, 238.

30. The description of the arrangements made by the disciples for the Passover meal in Mark 14:13–15 have always struck readers as odd, unless we are to think of this being another example of Jesus' prophetic foreknowledge. Several factors bear closer scrutiny: (1) It is assumed that the owner of the house will have a guest room ready for the meal, but, more important, it is assumed that he will know who "the Teacher" is! (2) A man bearing a jar of water is in itself a rather odd sight and is perhaps why Jesus mentions it. He would be easy to spot if he were the only man among many women carrying a jar of water, for this was normally a woman's task, as remains the case in many villages in Israel today, including Nazareth (cf. John 4). (3) Point 2 thus suggests that we may be dealing with a prearranged signal, a man carrying water, that will tip off the disciples and guide them to the proper house. This sort of secretive arrangement is very believable if Jesus wished to avoid apprehension after having cleansed the Temple, but before sharing the Passover meal with his disciples. (4) Again, if prophetic foresight is *not* what Jesus is exhibiting in these key verses, then the text suggests that Jesus not only knows about these advance arrangements but also knows the house where they will have this meal, as he describes the upper room. This suggests it belongs to a Jerusalem disciple of Jesus who knows "the Teacher" and in whose house Jesus may have been before, during a feast perhaps. (5) If this house's owner is a disciple or at least a sympathizer, it would be very strange indeed for him not to participate in such a meal in his own house, for under all normal circumstances the owner of the house is the host for such a meal in antiquity.

I would suggest, then, that there are two possible households that we know of who may have provided such a guest room in Jerusalem: (1) the household of the Beloved Disciple, who is apparently known to the high priest (John 18:15), a fact that favors his being a Jerusalem native; or (2) the household of John Mark (cf. Acts 1:13; 12:12). I favor the former suggestion.

31. The left side often had sinister associations in ancient Near Eastern thinking. Notice, for example, that in Matt. 25:31–46 the sheep are on the right-hand side and the goats on the left, the saved on the right and the lost on the left.
32. Cf. Beasley-Murray, *John*, 238.
33. Craddock, *John*, 102.
34. See R. L. Kinast, *If Only You Recognized God's Gift*, 99–102.
35. M.-E. Boismard, *Moses or Jesus: An Essay in Johannine Christology*, 20–22.

15. The Farewell Discourses (John 13:31–17:26)

1. An analogy might be the Sermon on the Mount, which most scholars, including conservative ones, recognize is a composite of elements from various of Jesus' sermons and teachings, as is shown by the fact that a good deal of the material found together in Matt. 5—7 is scattered throughout Luke's Gospel (cf. Luke 11—14 for elements of Matt. 6—7).
2. This feature of repetition could be attributed to the fact that Greco-Roman style discourses on religion or philosophy often saw it as a virtue to treat material in this fashion. It was taken as a sign of sublimity. Cf. F. Thielman, "The Style of the Fourth Gospel and Ancient Literary Critical Concepts of Religious Discourse."
3. F. Segovia, *The Farewell of the Word: The Johannine Call to Abide*, esp. 49ff.
4. On this division of the material, see also Beasley-Murray, *John*, 223.
5. Cf. W. S., "Luke 22:14–38 and Greco-Roman and Biblical Farewell Addresses," *Journal of Biblical Literature* 104 (1985): 251–68.
6. See Segovia, *Farewell of the Word*, 17.
7. Notice the concern here and elsewhere in these discourses about the witness to the world. These discourses are not in-house teaching for a group that has anathematized the world, given up on evangelism, and is almost solely concerned with its own internal problems.
8. J. R. Michaels, *John*, 243ff.
9. Barrett, *John*, 449ff.
10. Cf., for instance, the notable repetitiousness not only in the proverbs and riddles in Prov. 10ff. but also in the earlier discourses or meditations in Prov. 1—9.
11. Here I am following Segovia, *Farewell of the Word*, 68.
12. Ibid., 69.
13. On the concept of agency in this Gospel, cf. pp. 140–41 above.
14. Notice the similar concept in Paul of the believer being "in Christ" *and* of Christ being in the believer, which then becomes the believer's hope and assurance of glory—the completion of the eschatological process.
15. Cf. Michaels, *John*, 143–47.
16. The amount of literature on the Paraclete in the Fourth Gospel is staggering. Among many others, cf. G. Burge, *The Anointed Community: The Holy Spirit in the Johannine Tradition*, and E. Franck, *Revelation Taught: The Paraclete in the Gospel of John*.
17. On this, see pp. 140–41 above.
18. The *parakletos* is clearly identified as the Holy Spirit at 14:26.
19. J. Behm, art. "*parakletos*."
20. See the discussion in Beasley-Murray, *John*, 256, whom I am basically following.
21. Cf. Barrett, *John*, 462.

22. Ibid.
23. One may, for instance, point to the inspired commentary of the Beloved Disciple and/or evangelist in John 3 on the teaching of Jesus about new birth, drawing out their meaning (cf. pp. 99–106 above). The Spirit is seen not only as pedagogue, reminding of the former teaching of Jesus, but the Spirit enables the disciple to be both exegete of the Jesus tradition and applier of that tradition to a new setting, spinning out its ongoing implications. In other words, the evangelist and probably the Beloved Disciple believed in pneumatic hermeneutics.
24. The function of this material as farewell material must be taken seriously. When the Fourth Evangelist wrote this Gospel, the Johannine community had long since received the Spirit and remembered the Jesus tradition. The basic promises that are found in this material had long since been fulfilled. The function of this material is not to offer new teaching of the exalted Jesus but in part to reassure Christians under fire that they should and can continue with their witness and that the Spirit will give them divine presence, power, and utterance to testify. As the Christian missionaries use this material, *they* will be strengthened in their witness as they use the rest of the Gospel material with outsiders.
25. Barrett, *John*, 456ff.
26. Segovia, *Farewell of the Word*, 120.
27. Michaels, *John*, 257.
28. Pryor, *John: Evangelist*, 64.
29. Cf. the discussion at pp. 64–65 above.
30. Cf. 176–77.
31. See now Ashton, *Understanding the Fourth Gospel*, 381ff.
32. Here I would depart from Segovia, *Farewell of the Word*, 125ff., who seems to assume that bearing fruit simply amounts to loving one another and/or abiding in Christ.
33. Pryor, *John: Evangelist*, 64.
34. Cf. Schnackenburg, *John*, 3:91–94; Painter, *Quest for the Messiah*, 349ff.
35. See my discussion in *Jesus the Sage*, 183–92.
36. I have argued at length in *Jesus the Sage*, 147–208, that since Jesus did not go around proclaiming, "Thus saith Yahweh," but rather spoke on his own authority using wisdom speech, that he chiefly presented himself as—and would have been viewed primarily as—a great sage and teacher.
37. Barrett, *John*, 473–75.
38. The matter of love of enemies is not at issue here since the primary focus in this section is on internal matters in the community.
39. Cf. Brown, *John*, 2:664.
40. Cf. the fine book by V. Furnish, *The Love Commandment in the New Testament*, 60.
41. See above, pp. 140–41, on agency language in this Gospel.
42. Segovia, *Farewell of the Word*, 142.
43. See Carson, *John*, 527.
44. The term "Law" here is used in the general sense that Torah was a general label for all the Old Testament, not just the Pentateuch. Cf. Segovia, *Farewell of the Word*, 195.
45. Harvey, *Jesus on Trial*, 112–13.
46. See the discussion in Pryor, *John: Evangelist*, 65.
47. A second possibility would be that some Jewish Christians in the Johannine community continued to go to synagogue while also being part of the Christian community, and they were being warned that they could expect to be "unsynagogued," as the term literally means in 16:2. The text reads literally "to make you unsynagogued." Cf. Segovia, *Farewell of the Word*, 203n54.

48. See ibid., 216.
49. Ibid., 217.
50. See D. M. Smith, *John*, 50–51.
51. See Segovia's conclusions in his *Farewell of the Word*, 276–82.
52. Cf. Carson, *John*, 534.
53. Ibid., 535.
54. Notice that in the Greek there is no "the" before any of these three errors. The subject is sin in general, righteousness in general (here is the only place in this Gospel where the word *dikaiosyne* appears), and judgment in general.
55. The implication is not that the world is incapable of making moral judgments but that without the Spirit to enlighten the conscience its decisions are always going to go awry.
56. Carson, *John*, 538. In the entire discussion of these difficult verses I am indebted to Carson's lucid analysis.
57. Cf. above on John 3, pp. 92ff.
58. See Smith, *John*, 48.
59. The role of the Spirit is not to speak of himself but to glorify Jesus. Smith, *John*, 48, argues that John 16:15 shows that "revelations of the Spirit which are authentically God-given are also from Jesus." This is not, however, what the text actually says. The point is that all of what is God's has now been placed in the hands of the glorified Christ, who assumes most of the Father's roles during the eschatological age. This does not warrant the leap Smith makes. The logic is, "Everything from the Spirit is from Jesus, for all things have been given to Jesus by the Father and the Spirit is Jesus' agent." The logic is not, "Anything from God can appropriately be predicated of Jesus."
60. Cf., e.g., Prov. 10:26.
61. Michaels, *John*, 270–71.
62. Ibid., 271.
63. This word is found in a somewhat different form in the Synoptics in Mark 14:27 and par. and involves a quote of Zech. 13:7. Notice that it involves *all* of the Twelve deserting and scattering. The Johannine version speaks of "each one" being scattered. This word, however, if directed to the Twelve (or, better said, the Eleven), would not include the Beloved Disciple, if my reading of the evidence is correct and the Beloved Disciple was a Johannine disciple not among the Twelve. Thus there is no incongruity between this Johannine prediction and the later portrayal of the Beloved Disciple standing beneath the cross in John 19. There may also be a secondary allusion to John 20:10 where Peter and the Beloved Disciple again return to their own homes not knowing Jesus was risen (cf. below on this text).
64. On this division of the material, cf. Schnackenburg, *John*, 3:168–69; Pryor, *John: Evangelist*, 68.
65. Cf. Pryor, *John: Evangelist*, 70.
66. Notice the similar attempt at closure in Eccl. 12:9–14. Notice how the discourses in Prov. 1—9 are concluded with Wisdom's Feast (9:1–6) and contrasted with Folly's Dinner (vv. 13–18).
67. The designation "high-priestly prayer" appears to go back to David Chytraeus, a Lutheran theologian in the sixteenth century.
68. It seems to me that the only way around this conclusion about at least v. 24 is to assume that the statement is proleptic. Jesus is so sure of completing his work and being exalted to glory in heaven that he speaks as if it has already happened.
69. See Beasley-Murray, *John*, 294.

70. I have discussed this at some length in *Jesus the Sage*, chap. 6.
71. Schnackenburg, *John*, 3:172.
72. Beasley-Murray, *John*, 301.
73. The language of sacrifice and being set apart is similar to what we find in Rom. 12:1–2, only there the appeal is for the disciples to present themselves as a living sacrifice.
74. See Beasley-Murray, *John*, 302.
75. Carson, *John*, 570 and n. 1.
76. Craddock, *John*, 104–5.
77. It might also be worth asking, since chosenness did not protect Judas from apostasy, and since Jesus prays for the disciples to be guarded from the evil one, what sort of view of eternal security of disciples is conjured up by these discourses.
78. Beasley-Murray, *John*, 307.
79. See the discussion above about the characteristics of revival in church history, pp. 270–71.
80. Milne, *Message of John*, 237.
81. Ibid., 242.

16. The Arrest and Trial of Jesus (John 18:1–19:16a)

1. See A. N. Sherwin-White, *Roman Society and Roman Law in the New Testament*, 27ff.
2. J. Blinzler's *The Trial of Jesus* is the classic study on this subject. One will also wish to consult *Jesus and the Politics of His Day*, ed. E. Bammel and C.F.D. Moule, 353ff.
3. Blinzler, *Trial of Jesus*, 207ff.
4. Culpepper, *Anatomy of the Fourth Gospel*, 143.
5. The dating of Easter in the spring is traditional, in part to replace a pagan spring festival, but of course it was linked to when the celebration of Passover would be in a given year, sometimes in spring, sometimes somewhat earlier than that.
6. Brown, *John*, 2:807.
7. Ibid., 808.
8. Cf. the discussion of this phrase above, pp. 156–57.
9. See E. P. Sanders, *The Tendencies of the Synoptic Tradition*, 96ff.
10. Cf. Josephus, *Ant.* 18.2.1.
11. Cf. *m. Hor.* 3:1–4.
12. This is sometimes called the sandwich technique and is seen frequently in Mark. Cf. Mark 3:20–21, 31–35, and 22–30, and Mark 5:21–24a, 35–43, and 24b–34.
13. Or "another" disciple. Some later scribes added the Greek article "the" to make clear the Beloved Disciple was in mind.
14. Both the Markan account and the Johannine one mention this servant girl who confronts Peter the first time (cf. Mark 14:66, 69 and par.).
15. See Brown, *John*, 2:824, on this ironic twist. Notice that Peter's threefold denial takes a somewhat different form in the Synoptics (cf. Mark 14.66ff. and par.).
16. Cf. Carson, *John*, 584–85.
17. Cf. Brown, *John*, 2:842.
18. Ibid., 861.
19. It is likely that the agreement on Pilate's part to send Roman auxiliaries to help round up Jesus was seen by him as simply a precautionary measure in view of the huge crowds at the feast and the potential volatility of any possible political

claims under the circumstances during a Passover feast. After all, Passover was about deliverance from bondage of foreign overlords in Egypt, and Rome now ruled in both Egypt and Israel.

20. Perhaps we are meant to see here latent anger about the fact that they cannot execute Jesus themselves, and they despise having to rely on someone as callous and religiously insensitive as Pilate.

21. Cf. E. Bammel, "The Trial before Pilate," 415–51.

22. Not just any claim to being messiah could have led to this sort of condemnation by the Sanhedrin. It had to be a claim that suggested blasphemy against the name and nature of God and against the heart of the *practice* of early Jewish religion. For example, many messianic pretenders existed before and after Jesus' day, but only those whose claims seemed to compromise or pervert Jewish monotheism or the essence of Jewish life (monotheism, Torah, Temple, Sabbath, circumcision, keeping kosher) were likely to face prosecution by the Great Sanhedrin.

23. Josephus says this title was applied to Herod. Cf. his *Ant.* 16.10.2.

24. Bammel, "Trial before Pilate," 418.

25. An exception seems to have existed in the case of a Gentile violating the sanctity of the Holy of Holies. Warnings were posted outside the Holy of Holies to the effect that such violation could end in a speedy execution. One of these warnings has now been found by archaeologists and is confirmed by Josephus (*War* 5.193–94; 6.124–26). Josephus, however, also says that the right of capital punishment in other circumstances had been taken away from the Jews and was invested in the Roman appointed governor of Judea (cf. *War* 2.117). This was standard operating procedure for the Romans for whom "the capital power was the most jealously guarded of all the attributes of government" (Sherwin-White, *Roman Society and Roman Law;* cf. 24–26).

26. Michaels, *John*, 300, is likely wrong that the issue is that Jesus has not been formally condemned by a Jewish court and thus could not be executed under Mosaic law without violating the Mosaic commandment against murder.

27. Cf. above on John 1.

28. Cf. above, pp. 156–57, on the "I am the truth" pronouncement.

29. Bammel, "Trial before Pilate," 420.

30. Ibid., 427.

31. This is the custom referred to in *m. Pesah.* 8:6.

32. Cf. Blinzler, *Trial of Jesus*, 205ff.

33. See Beasley-Murray, *John*, 336.

34. Cf. 3:14; 8:28; 12:23, 34; 13:31.

35. This charge is referred to earlier in the Johannine account. Cf. 5:17–18; 10:30–39, which presents the vast majority of the ministry as an example of Jesus on trial.

36. Michaels, *John*, 304.

37. Cf. Tacitus, *Annals*, 6.8.

38. Gabbatha is a word meaning "height" or "ridge." That the evangelist needs to explain this reveals something of the Gentile character of his audience, although diaspora Jews in many cases may not have known Aramaic either, though the evangelist clearly does. The term *hebraisti* does not likely mean Hebrew here but rather refers to the related Semitic dialect of Aramaic, for Gabbatha is not a Hebrew but an Aramaic word.

39. What may be significant is that this particular Roman form of recognition was used in official documents and for legal purposes. We have seen the interest of this evangelist throughout in presenting the story of Jesus as "Jesus on trial" and

there is a certain fitness to have it close with a sort of time marker used in Roman legal proceedings.

40. Cf. Michaels, *John*, 306.
41. J.A.T. Robinson, *The Priority of John*, 273–74.
42. See Beasley-Murray, *John*, 325.
43. For example, Holy Land slide sets are available from *Biblical Archaeology Review*.
44. Milne, *Message of John*, 267.
45. This analysis is adapted from Craddock, *John*, 133.
46. Ibid., 135.
47. Ibid., 134.
48. Quoted in Milne, *Message of John*, 262, source unnamed.
49. Ibid., 254.
50. Brown, *John*, 2:842.
51. Milne, *Message of John*, 260.

17. The Death and Burial of Jesus (John 19:16b–42)

1. See Hengel's classic study *Crucifixion*.
2. Cf. Philo, *In Flaccum* 10, par. 75; Josephus, *War* 2.21.5, par. 612—scourged until the entrails were visible; *War* 2.21.5, par. 304—scourged until bones showed.
3. This was the case of Johanan, the crucified man found at Giv'at ha-Mivtar.
4. Cf. *b. Sanh.* 43a; Tertullian, *De jejuniis* 12.
5. Cf. Ruth 2:14 and the Jewish midrash on Ruth 2:14.
6. E. Stauffer, *Jesus and His Story*.
7. Cf. p. 306.
8. Cf. C.F.D. Moule, *The Origin of Christology*, 33.
9. Cf. Josephus, *War* 6.5.3, par. 304.
10. As R. A. Horsley rightly points out in Horsley and J. S. Hanson, *Bandits, Prophets, and Messiahs: Popular Movements at the Time of Jesus*.
11. The garden tomb of course provides a good visual image of what the burial site of Jesus may have been like, and the old cemetery adjacent to it on top of a skull-like hill behind the bus station near Damascus gate provides a much better visual likeness of what Golgotha may have looked like in Jesus' day.
12. Cf. Plutarch, *The Divine Vengeance* 554 A/B.
13. Cf. the excursus above on the *titulus*. Nazorean presumably was understood to mean a person from Nazareth.
14. The Fourth Gospel, of course, does not tell the story of Jesus' birth in Bethlehem.
15. Michaels, *John*, 313–14.
16. Cf. Josephus, *Ant.* 3.161: "This garment consists not of two parts, so that it would be sewn around the shoulders and at the side, but it is woven from a single length of thread."
17. Cf. pp. 267–70 above on John 17, the so-called high-priestly prayer.
18. The Fourth Gospel also seems to bear witness to this tradition of the desertion of the Twelve. Cf. John 16:32; 20:10.
19. For a more detailed discussion of this passage, see my *Women in the Ministry of Jesus*, 92–98.
20. Stauffer, *Jesus and His Story*, 136–38.
21. See ibid., 138.
22. See the discussion of John 2, pp. 76–84 above.

23. Witherington, *Women in the Ministry of Jesus*, 95.
24. Ibid., 97.
25. Cf. Deut. 21:22ff.
26. Barrett, *John*, 550ff.
27. See the discussion on John 3, p. 92ff. above.
28. Cf. Barrett, *John*, 556–57.
29. But cf. above on John 3, pp. 92ff.
30. Note the mention of Nicodemus's rank in John 3:1.
31. Robinson, *Priority of John*, 283, notes that if spices were to be packed around the entire body including underneath it, following Jewish procedure, a very large amount might be used.
32. Josephus, *Ant.* 17.199, says that Herod the Great's burial procession involved five hundred slaves carrying the spices!
33. Cf. Brown, *John*, 2:941–42, and the enormous amount of literature on the subject cited there.
34. If *othonia* does indeed mean linen "strips" here, this would seem to count against such a possibility. Cf. Beasley-Murray, *John*, 360.
35. Craddock, *John*, 137.
36. J. Moltmann, *The Crucified God*, 243.
37. F. Buechner, *The Life of Jesus*, 9.

18. The Presence of His Absence (John 20:1–10)

1. Cf. my *Women in the Ministry of Jesus*, 9ff., on the validity or invalidity of women's testimony in the first-century world.
2. Note the "we" in John 20:2.
3. See Carson, *John*, 635.
4. Cf. C. K. Barrett, *The New Testament Background: Selected Documents*, 15.
5. This is not unimportant and may be taken as yet one further small bit of confirmation that the Beloved Disciple was a Judean disciple who had not only relatives but a home in Jerusalem to which he could return.
6. Cf. Bultmann, *John*, 685ff.
7. Beasley-Murray, *John*, 373ff.
8. Cf. Minear, " 'We Don't Know Where . . .' John 20:2."
9. The rolled-up head cloth would suggest purposeful activity, and certainly not the activity of thieves, who if they were interested in stealing the body would hardly pause to roll up the grave clothes before leaving!

19. Mary, Mary, Extraordinary (John 20:11–18)

1. See my detailed discussion of this narrative in *Women in the Earliest Churches*, 177–82.
2. Cf. the better commentaries on this point. This conclusion is borne out even by very conservative scholars such as R. Gundry in his fine new commentary on Mark (*Mark: A Commentary on His Apology for the Cross* [Grand Rapids: Eerdmans, 1993]) and W. L. Lane in his classic commentary (*The Gospel according to Mark* [Grand Rapids: Eerdmans, 1974]).
3. It is likely that the reason the Passion narratives in the four Gospels are much more similar than the resurrection narratives is threefold: (1) The narration of

certain key events in a certain order was necessary to make any sense of how Jesus came to be crucified. For example, Jesus' appearance before the Jewish authorities had to precede his final appearance before Pilate. (2) The resurrection appearances happened at a variety of times to a variety of people in a variety of places. The cast of characters and the locale vary considerably. It is thus not surprising that the four Gospels select certain appearance stories and omit others, according to their purposes. (3) There was no number or sequence of appearances that *had* to be recorded to make sense of the story. The evangelists could afford to be selective and arrange the accounts as best suited their agendas.

4. Dodd, *Historical Tradition in the Fourth Gospel,* 148.
5. Beasley-Murray, *John,* 374–75.
6. On this cf. above, pp. 60ff.
7. Beasley-Murray, *John,* 377–78.
8. If the verb had been in the present tense of *anabaino* in v. 17a, the meaning could be "I am not yet (fully) ascended to the Father," but in fact it is in the perfect tense—"I have not yet ascended." This favors the view that ascension properly speaking has yet to happen. The present tense of *anabaino* in 17b then must be interpreted in the light of the earlier use of the verb—a future certainty is expressed by means of a present tense verb.
9. See Minear " 'We Don't Know Where . . . , ' " 132.
10. Witherington, *Women in the Earliest Churches,* 180–81.
11. Except of course in John 19:25. Cf. Mark 15:40 and par.; 16:1 and par.
12. See the discussion above, pp. 92–96, on John 3 and the new birth.
13. Culpepper, *Anatomy of the Fourth Gospel,* 144.
14. Milne, *Message of John,* 293.
15. Ibid., 291.
16. The hypocrisy of suggesting that it is all right for women to go and be missionaries in a foreign land and proclaim the word there, but not to be ordained to do so in our own country, simply shows what happens when a church treats certain cultural preferences as if they were biblical absolutes.

20. Preserving Appearances behind Closed Doors
(John 20:19–31)

1. See p. 202 above.
2. This chart is taken from Michaels, *John,* 331.
3. This makes quite clear not only that the Fourth Evangelist wrote both of these sections of this Gospel but that the restoration of the inner core of male disciples was seen as essential to the initial mission of the church (cf. below). In other words, our reading of the function of the farewell discourses as preparation not only for restoration but for mission is correct. This is hardly surprising in a Gospel intended as a tool for missionaries to use.
4. A variant of the first option would be to argue that Jesus bestowed the Spirit on the inner circle first and then on the larger group of disciples, including on the women.
5. Carson, *John,* 653.
6. This view of the text in the early church was taken by so brilliant an exegete as Theodore of Mopsuestia, although it was condemned at the Second Council of Constantinople in A.D. 553.

7. In both cases well before the Jewish celebration of Pentecost, and well before the time Acts says Jesus ascended and then sent the Spirit (cf. Acts 1:3). It is difficult to believe that the Fourth Evangelist was not aware of the Pentecost events and when they transpired, so crucial were they to the early church. It is next to impossible to believe that the Beloved Disciple, a Judean disciple who probably lived in Jerusalem and in whose house may have been the upper room (cf. pp. 11–18 above), and whose memoirs are recorded in this Gospel, was ignorant about the matters recorded in Acts 1—2.

8. Cf. pp. 140–41 above on the agency concept in this Gospel.

9. Cf. M. Arias and A. Johnson, *The Great Commission*, 81.

10. Here is another good reason why the evangelist did not wish to portray people during the ministry as full-fledged Christians. The new humanity or, better said, the new human community of Jesus' followers was created only after Jesus rose.

11. Barrett, *John*, p. 570.

12. See my *Jesus the Sage*, pp. 43–45.

13. On Jesus being portrayed as Wisdom throughout this Gospel, cf. pp. 18–29, above.

14. Carson, *John*, 652, argues that the Greek text simply says Jesus breathed (i.e., exhaled), not that he breathed *on* the disciples. This is true enough, but in the light of the parallels with both the story of Adam and the wisdom material it is surely clear enough that we are meant to think of *something* being conveyed, namely, the wisdom to discern when to forgive and when to retain sins.

15. Cf. J. Marsh, *The Gospel of St. John*, 641–42.

16. The evangelist once again introduces Thomas as Didymus "the twin" (cf. 11:16), though we do not know the twin of whom, here. This shows surely that this Gospel would be used in parts, and likely used for missionary purposes with those who needed such explanations or reminders (i.e., with potential and new converts).

17. The text of course speaks of the marks in Jesus' hands, but there is no attempt here to be anatomically precise. The wrist could be seen as part of the hand. Anyone nailed in the palms of the hand would not be held up on a cross. Only if one were nailed in the cavity which can be felt at the base of the back of the hand, or even at a spot below the wrist, would one have the necessary bone support to be held up on a cross.

18. Brown, *John*, 2:1047–48.

19. Cf. Harris, *Jesus as God: The New Testament Use of Theos in Reference to Jesus*, 124ff. This book is an excellent resource on the whole subject of Christ's divinity.

20. Cf. Barrett, *John*, 573.

21. Cf. pp. 11–18 above.

22. Cf. pp. 29–31 above.

23. Culpepper, *Anatomy of the Fourth Gospel*, 124.

24. Craddock, *John*, 144.

25. Cf. Suetonius, *Domitian* 13.

26. Cf. Arias and Johnson, *Great Commission*, 80ff.

21. Breakfast by the Sea (Epilogue) (John 21:1–25)

1. It is perhaps likely that the evangelist means that this is the third appearance to the inner circle of male disciples, *but* we do not have the Eleven in this scene, and

it is even possible that the meaning is that this is the third appearance to the seven mentioned in this text.

2. See the entire list in Barrett, *John*, 576. Whatever else one may say, this story makes clear that the Fourth Evangelist associated the Zebedees with fishing and the Sea of Galilee, and he groups them together. He does not separate out one of them and call him the Beloved Disciple in a way that makes clear that the Beloved Disciple must be one of these two brothers. There is also nothing here to suggest he associates the Zebedees with a house in Jerusalem.

3. That this is a Johannine narrative is shown not merely by the presence of the Beloved Disciple throughout the chapter but by the technique of composition used, where we have a miracle tale followed by a dialogue section, which is characteristic of some of the earlier sign narratives. Cf. pp. 133ff. above.

4. If this is correct, there is no need to posit two editions of this Gospel, although I would not rule that possibility out. One must, however, reckon with the fact that no manuscript evidence supports the view that this chapter was added to a later edition of this Gospel. If it is an afterthought, it must have occurred to the Fourth Evangelist very near to the time when the Gospel was first published, perhaps just before he was ready to circulate it. For an interesting though not entirely convincing argument supporting the view that John 21 is not an afterthought or epilogue at all, cf. W. S. Vorster, "The Growth and Making of John 21," 2207–21.

5. The mention of the name for this lake that Gentiles were more likely to use, the Sea of Tiberias, may tell us something about the primary audience for this tradition.

6. In other words, this tradition did not *fit* in a missionary Gospel, and so it is added here as an epilogue meant to help Christians get beyond certain problems. Perhaps it is addressed especially to those Johannine Christians who would be using the Fourth Gospel to bear witness to the world, and needed these matters cleared up so they could get on with the task at hand.

7. Precisely because it is an epilogue, it would be wrong to try to judge the character and function of the bulk of the Gospel from this one chapter.

8. Some scholars think John 21:1–13 is another version of the story in Luke 5, but this seems unlikely since some of the main features of this narrative (the recognition motif, and the reticence to ask questions) hardly comport with an original call narrative. Cf. G. R. Osborne, "John 21: Test Case for History and Redaction in the Resurrection Narratives," 294–95, on the similarities and differences between these two narratives.

9. If indeed this story does presuppose various Synoptic stories like the one in Luke 5, then it is in order to note that this story is an example of *déjà vu* in at least two regards: (1) At the end of Jesus' appearances the disciples have an experience similar to when he first called them to be disciples. (2) Peter is restored in threefold fashion while sitting at a charcoal fire, and the only other time such a fire is mentioned in this Gospel is at the scene of his threefold denial in 18:17–27. I owe this suggestion to my colleague Luke Keefer.

10. Apparently Peter had no undergarment on save perhaps a loin cloth, and did not wish to come out of the water stark naked, or nearly so.

11. Michaels, *John*, 340–41.

12. Though Jerome cites Oppian as listing 153 kinds of fish, actually Oppian's list seems to have included 157 species. Cf. Carson, *John*, 672.

13. Osborne, "John 21," 299.

14. Compare 3:16 to 16:27 of God's love for humankind; 3:35 to 5:20 of God's love for the Son; 11:3 to 11:5 of Jesus' love for persons, 13:34 to 15:19 of love between

human beings; and finally 8:42 to 16:27 of the love of people for Jesus. Cf. Beasley-Murray, *John*, 404ff.

15. Osborne, "John 21," 308–09, disputes this conclusion on the basis that two words are used for Peter's task, feeding and tending, which are not identical in meaning but rather complementary. This conclusion may stand for the use of the task terms, but it is unconvincing as an argument about the use of the love verbs (cf. the previous note).

16. Notice the rejection of comparisons later in the chapter.

17. Osborne, "John 21," 308.

18. Cf. pp. 26–27 above and cf. Eccl. 12:11.

19. Cf. *Acts of Peter* 37–39; and Eusebius, *History of the Church* 3.1. On upside-down crucifixion, cf. Seneca, *Consolation to Marcia* 20.

20. Cf. pp. 32–33 above.

21. Cf. Osborne, "John 21," 313. *Ean* with the subjunctive means "If, as may or may not be the case."

22. The parallel in John 19:19 may prove instructive where the same form of the verb means "he caused the words to be written" (cf. also Rom. 15:15).

23. Cf. the Introduction, pp. 13–14, on these verses.

24. Hoskyns, *Fourth Gospel*, 2:656.

25. Milne, *Message of John*, 312.

26. Craddock, *John*, 148.

27. Milne, *Message of John*, 319.

Appendix: The Woman Caught in Adultery (John 7:53–8:11)

1. Carson, *John*, 333.

2. Cf. pp. 164–65 above.

3. Didymus the Blind does cite this story in a different form at an earlier date, but it is not the form of the story as we have it in the Fourth Gospel.

4. Cf. Metzger, *Textual Commentary on the New Testament*, 219–22.

5. See my discussion in *Women in the Ministry of Jesus*, 21.

6. Cf. Carson, *John*, 334.

7. Cf. Witherington, *Women in the Ministry of Jesus*, 22.

Bibliography

Commentaries

Barrett, C.K. *The Gospel according to St. John.* 2d ed. Philadelphia: Westminster Press, 1978.

Beasley-Murray, G.R. *John.* Waco, Tex.: Word, 1987.

Brown, R.E. *The Gospel according to St. John,* I–XII; XIII–XXI. 2 vols. Garden City, N.Y.: Doubleday & Co., 1966–70.

Bultmann, R. *The Gospel of John: A Commentary,* trans. G.R. Beasley-Murray. Oxford: Basil Blackwell, 1971.

Carson, D.A. *The Gospel according to John.* Grand Rapids: Wm. B. Eerdmans Publishing Co., 1991.

Craddock, F.B. *John.* Atlanta: John Knox Press, 1982.

Hoskyns, E. *The Fourth Gospel.* 2 vols. London: Faber & Faber, 1942.

Marsh, J. *The Gospel of St. John.* London: Penguin Books, 1968.

Michaels, J.R. *John.* San Francisco: Harper, 1984.

Schnackenburg, R. *The Gospel according to St. John.* 3 vols. New York: Crossroad, 1990.

Smith, D.M. *John.* Philadelphia: Fortress Press, 1976.

Monographs and Articles

Alter, R. *The Art of Biblical Narrative.* New York: Basic Books, 1981.

Argyle, A.W. "Wedding Customs at the Time of Jesus." *Expository Times* 86 (1974–75): 214–15.

Arias, M., and A. Johnson. *The Great Commission.* Nashville: Abingdon Press, 1982.

Ashton, J. "The Transformation of Wisdom: A Study of the Prologue of John's Gospel." *New Testament Studies* 32.2 (1986): 161–86.

———. *Understanding the Fourth Gospel.* London: Oxford University Press, 1993.

Bammel, E. "The Trial before Pilate." In *Jesus and the Politics of His Day,* ed. E. Bammel and C.F.D. Moule. Cambridge: Cambridge University Press, 1984.

Bammel, E., and C.F.D. Moule, eds. *Jesus and the Politics of His Day.* Cambridge: Cambridge University Press, 1984.

Barrett, C.K. *The New Testament Background: Selected Documents.* New York: Harper & Brothers, 1957.

Beacham, R.C. *The Roman Theater and Its Audience.* Cambridge, Mass.: Harvard University Press, 1992.

Behm, J. *"parakletos."* 5:803 in *Theological Dictionary of the New Testament,* ed. G. Kittel and G. Friedrich. Grand Rapids: Wm. B. Eerdmans Publishing Co., 1964–76.

Belle, G. Van. "Les parenthèses johannique." Pp. 1901–33 in *The Four Gospels 1992,* FS F. Neirynck, ed. F. van Segbroeck et al. Louvain: Leuven University Press, 1992.

Bjerklund, C.J. *Tauta Egeneto: Die Präzisierungssätze im Johannesevangelium.*Tübingen: J.C.B. Mohr (Paul Siebeck), 1987.

Blinzler, J. *The Trial of Jesus.* Westminster, Md.: Newman Press, 1959.

Boismard, M.-E. *Moses or Jesus: An Essay in Johannine Christology.* Minneapolis: Fortress Press, 1993.

Bonhoeffer, D. *The Cost of Discipleship.* New York: Macmillan Co., 1963.

Borgen, P. *Bread from Heaven.* Leiden: E.J. Brill, 1965.

———. "God's Agent in the Fourth Gospel." Pp. 67–78 in *The Interpretation of John,* ed. John Ashton. Philadelphia: Fortress Press, 1986.

Breytenbach, C. *Anfänge der Christologie,* ed. C. Breytenbach and H. Paulsen. Göttingen: Vandenhoeck & Ruprecht, 1991.

Bruns, J.E. "Some Reflections on Coheleth and John." *Catholic Biblical Quarterly* 25 (1963): 414–16.

Buechner, F. *The Life of Jesus.* New York: Weathervane Books, 1974.

Bühner, J.A. *Der Gesandte und sein Weg im 4. Evangelium.* Tübingen: J.C.B. Mohr (Paul Siebeck), 1977.

Bultmann, R. *History of the Synoptic Tradition.* Oxford: Basil Blackwell, 1963.

Burge, G. *The Anointed Community: The Holy Spirit in the Johannine Tradition.* Grand Rapids: Wm. B. Eerdmans Publishing Co., 1987.

Burridge, R. *What Are the Gospels?* Cambridge: Cambridge University Press, 1991.

Culpepper, A. *Anatomy of the Fourth Gospel.* Philadelphia: Fortress Press, 1983.

Dahl, N.A. "Do Not Wonder! John 5:28–29 and Johannine Eschatology Once More." Pp. 322–36 in *Studies in Paul and John.*

Daube, D. *The New Testament and Rabbinic Judaism.* London: Athlone Press, 1956.

Dodd, C.H. "The Framework of the Gospel Narratives." In idem, *New Testament Studies.* Manchester, 1953.

———. *The Interpretation of the Fourth Gospel.* Cambridge: Cambridge University Press, 1953.

———. *Historical Tradition in the Fourth Gospel.* Cambridge: Cambridge University Press, 1963.

Domeris, W.R. "The Confession of Peter according to John 6:69." *Tyndale Bulletin* 44.1 (1993): 155–67.

Dunn, J.D.G. *Christology in the Making.* Philadelphia: Westminster Press, 1980.

Eppstein, V. "The Historicity of the Gospel Account of the Cleansing of the Temple." *Zeitschrift für die Neutestamentliche Wissenschaft* 55 (1964): 42–58.

Fee, G.D. "On the Text and Meaning of John 20:30–31." Pp. 2193–2205 in *The Four Gospels 1992,* FS F. Neirynck, ed. F. van Segbroeck et al. Louvain: Leuven University Press, 1992.

Fortna, R.T. *The Fourth Gospel and Its Predecessors.* Philadelphia: Fortress Press, 1988.

France, R.T., and D. Wenham, eds. *Gospel Perspectives.* Vol. 2. Sheffield: JSOT Press, 1981.

Franck, E. *Revelation Taught: The Paraclete in the Gospel of John.* Uppsala: C.W.K. Gleerup, 1985.

Freed, E.D. "Theological Prelude and the Prologue of John's Gospel." *Scottish Journal of Theology* 32 (1979): 257–69.

———. "John 1, 19–27 in Light of Related Passages in John, the Synoptics, and Acts." Pp. 1943–61 in *The Four Gospels 1992,* FS F. Neirynck, ed. F. van Segbroeck et al. Louvain: Leuven University Press, 1992.

Furnish, V.P. *The Love Commandment in the New Testament.* Nashville: Abingdon Press, 1973.

Gese, H. *Essays on Biblical Theology.* Minneapolis: Augsburg, 1981.

Harris, M. "The Dead Are Restored to Life: Miracles of Revivification in the Gospels." Pp. 310–17 in *Gospel Perspectives,* vol. 6, ed. D. Wenham et al. Sheffield: JSOT Press, 1986.

———. *Jesus as God: New Testament Use of Theos in Reference to Jesus.* Grand Rapids: Baker Book House, 1992.

Harvey, A.E. *Jesus on Trial: A Study in the Fourth Gospel.* London: SPCK, 1976.

———. "Christ as Agent." Pp. 239–50 in *The Glory of Christ in the New Testament,* ed. L.D. Hurst and N.T. Wright. Oxford: Oxford University Press, 1987.

Hengel, M. *Crucifixion.* Philadelphia: Fortress Press, 1977.

———. "Hymns and Christology." Pp. 78–86 in *Between Jesus and Paul.* Philadelphia: Fortress Press 1983.

———. *Studies in the Gospel of Mark.* Philadelphia: Fortress Press, 1985.

———. *The Johannine Question.* Philadelphia: Trinity Press International, 1989.

———. "Psalm 110 und die Erhöhung des Auferstandenen zur Rechten Gottes." Pp. 43–73 in *Anfänge der Christologie,* ed. C. Breytenbach and H. Paulsen. Göttingen: Vandenhoeck & Ruprecht, 1991.

Hooker, M.D. "The Johannine Prologue and the Messianic Secret." *New Testament Studies* 21 (1974): 40–58.

Horbury, W. "The Benediction of the *minim* and Early Jewish Christianity." *Journal of Theological Studies* 33.1 (1982): 19–61.

Horsley, R.A., and J.S. Hanson, *Bandits, Prophets, and Messiahs: Popular Movements at the Time of Jesus.* Minneapolis: Winston Press, 1985.

Jeremias, J. *Jesus' Promise to the Nations.* London: SCM Press, 1958.

———. *The Eucharistic Words of Jesus.* London: SCM Press, 1966.

———. *The Rediscovery of Bethesda.* Louisville, Ky.: Southern Baptist Theological Seminary, 1966.

———. "Zum Logos-Problem." *Zeitschrift für die Neutestamentliche Wissenschaft* 59 (1968): 82–85.

———. *The Parables of Jesus.* 2d ed. New York: Charles Scribner's Sons, 1972.

Käsemann, E. *The Testament of Jesus: A Study of the Gospel of John according to John 17.* Philadelphia: Fortress Press, 1968.

Kinast, R.L. *If Only You Recognized God's Gift: John's Gospel as an Illustration of Theological Reflection.* Grand Rapids: Wm. B. Eerdmans Publishing Co., 1993.

Kümmel, W.G. *Introduction to the New Testament.* Rev. ed. Abingdon Press, 1987.

Kysar, R. *The Fourth Evangelist and His Gospel: An Examination of Contemporary Scholarship.* Minneapolis: Augsburg, 1975.

Lewis, C.S. *Mere Christianity.* New York: Macmillan Co., 1952.

MacMullen, R. *Enemies of the Roman Order.* Cambridge, Mass.: Harvard University Press, 1966.

Martin, R.P. *Carmen Christi: Philippians 2:5–11.* Grand Rapids: Wm. B. Eerdmans Publishing Co., 1983.

———. "Some Reflections on New Testament Hymns." Pp. 37–49 in *Christ the Lord: Studies Presented to Donald Guthrie,* ed. H.H. Rowden. Leicester: InterVarsity Press, 1982.

Martyn, J.L. *History and Theology in the Fourth Gospel.* Nashville: Abingdon Press, 1979.

McRae, G.W. *Faith in the Word—the Fourth Gospel.* Chicago: Franciscan Press, 1973.

Mead, A.H. "The *basilikos* in John 4:46–53." *Journal for the Study of the New Testament* 23 (1985): 69–72.

Meeks, W. *The Prophet-King.* Leiden: E.J. Brill, 1967.

————. "The Man from Heaven in Johannine Sectarianism." *Journal of Biblical Literature* 91.1 (1972): 44–72.

Metzger, B.M. *A Textual Commentary on the New Testament.* London: United Bible Societies, 1971.

Milne, B. *The Message of John: Here is Your King!* Downers Grove, Ill.: InterVarsity Press, 1993.

Minear, P.S. " 'We Don't Know Where . . .' John 20:2." *Interpretation* 30 (1976): 125–39.

Mlakuzhyil, G. *The Christocentric Literary Structure of the Fourth Gospel.* Rome: Pontifical Institute Press, 1987.

Moeller, H.R. "Wisdom Motifs and John's Gospel." *Bul ETS* 6 (1963): 92–100.

Moltmann, J. *The Crucified God.* New York: Harper & Row, 1974.

Moule, C.F.D. *The Origin of Christology.* Cambridge: Cambridge University Press, 1977.

Mussner, F. *The Historical Jesus in the Gospel of St. John.* New York: Herder, 1967.

Neyrey, J. *An Ideology of Revolt.* Philadelphia: Fortress Press, 1988.

Osborne, G.R. "John 21: Test Case for History and Redaction in the Resurrection Narratives." Pp. 293–328 in *Gospel Perspectives,* vol. 2, ed. R.T. France and D. Wenham. Sheffield: JSOT Press, 1981.

Painter, J. "Christology and the History of the Johannine Community in the Prologue of the Fourth Gospel." *New Testament Studies* 30 (1984): 460–74.

————. *The Quest for the Messiah.* Edinburgh: T. & T. Clark, 1991.

Petersen, N.R. *The Gospel of John and the Sociology of Light.* Valley Forge, Pa.: Trinity Press International, 1993.

Potterie, I. de la. "The Truth in St. John." Pp. 53–66 in *The Interpretation of John,* ed. John Ashton. Philadelphia: Fortress Press, 1986.

Pryor, J.W. *John: Evangelist of the Covenant People.* Downers Grove, Ill.: InterVarsity Press, 1992.

Rensberger, D. *Johannine Faith and Liberating Community.* Philadelphia: Westminster Press, 1988.

Riesenfeld, H. *The Gospel Tradition and Its Beginnings: A Study in the Limits of "Formgeschichte."* London: Mowbray, 1957.

Robinson, J.A.T. *The Priority of John.* London: SCM Press, 1985.

Sabbe, M. "The Anointing of Jesus in John 12:1–8 and Its Synoptic Parallels." Pp. 2051–82 in *The Four Gospels 1992,* FS F. Neirynck, ed. F. van Segbroeck et al. Louvain: Leuven University Press, 1992.

Sanders, E.P. *The Tendencies of the Synoptic Tradition.* Cambridge: Cambridge University Press, 1969.

Sanders, J.A. "The Psalms Scroll of Qumran Cave 11," *Discoveries in the Judean Desert Journal* 4 (1965): 91–92.

Sanders, J.T. *The New Testament Christological Hymns.* Cambridge: Cambridge University Press, 1971.

Schürmann, H. "Die Vorosterlichen Anfänge der Logien-Versuch eines Formgeschichtlichen Zugangs zum Leben Jesu." Pp. 39–65 in *Traditions-geschichtliche Untersuchungen zu den Synoptischen Evangelien.* Düsseldorf: Patmos Verlag, 1968.

Schüssler Fiorenza, E. "Wisdom Mythology and the Christological Hymns of the New Testament." Pp. 17–41 in *Aspects of Wisdom in Judaism and Early Christianity,* ed. R.L. Wilken. South Bend, Ind.: University of Notre Dame Press, 1975.

Schweizer, E. "Paul's Christology and Gnosticism." Pp. 115–23 in *Paul and Paulinism*, FS C.K. Barrett, ed. M.D. Hooker and S.G. Wilson. London: SPCK, 1982.

Scott, M. *Sophia and the Johannine Jesus*. Sheffield: JSOT Press, 1992.

Segovia, F. *The Farewell of the Word: The Johannine Call to Abide*. Minneapolis: Fortress Press, 1991.

Sherk, R.K. *The Roman Empire: Augustus to Hadrian*. Cambridge: Cambridge University Press, 1988.

Sherwin-White, A.N. *Roman Society and Roman Law in the New Testament*. Oxford: Oxford University Press, 1963.

Smalley, S.S. *John: Evangelist and Interpreter*. Nashville: Nelson, 1984.

Smith, D.M. "Johannine Christianity." Pp. 1–36 in *Johannine Christianity: Essays on Its Setting, Sources, and Theology*. Columbia, S.C.: University of South Carolina, 1984.

———. "John 12:12ff. and the Question of John's Use of the Synoptics." Pp. 97–105 in *Johannine Christianity: Essays on Its Setting, Sources, and Theology*. Columbia, S.C.: University of South Carolina, 1984.

———. *John among the Gospels*. Minneapolis: Fortress Press, 1992.

Staley, J.L. *The Print's First Kiss: A Rhetorical Investigation of the Implied Reader in the Fourth Gospel*. Atlanta: Scholars Press, 1988.

Stauffer, E. *Jesus and His Story*. London: SCM Press, 1960.

Thielman, F. "The Style of the Fourth Gospel and Ancient Literary Critical Concepts of Religious Discourse." Pp. 169–83 in *Persuasive Artistry*, ed. D.F. Watson. Sheffield: JSOT Press, 1991.

Thomson, P.J. "The Names Israel and Jew in Ancient Judaism and the New Testament." *Bijdragen tijdschrift voor filosofie en theologie* 47 (1986): 120–40, 266–89.

Vermes, G. *The Dead Sea Scrolls in English*. Harmondsworth: Penguin Books, 1962.

Vorster, W.S. "The Growth and Making of John 21." Pp. 2207–21 in *The Four Gospels 1992*, FS F. Neirynck, ed. F. van Segbroeck et al. Louvain: Leuven University Press, 1992.

Watson, D.F., ed. *Persuasive Artistry*. Sheffield: JSOT Press, 1991.

Whitacre, R. *Johannine Polemic*. Chico, Calif.: Scholars Press, 1982.

Williamson, H.G.M. "Samaritans." *The Dictionary of Jesus and the Gospels*, ed. J.B. Green and S. McKnight. Downers Grove, Ill.: InterVarsity Press, 1992.

Witherington, B., III. "Women and Their Roles in the Gospels and Acts." Ph.D. dissertation, University of Durham, 1981.

———. *Women in the Ministry of Jesus: A Study of Jesus' Attitude to Women and Their Roles as Reflected in His Earthly Life*. Cambridge: Cambridge University Press, 1984.

———. *Women in the Earliest Churches*. Cambridge: Cambridge University Press, 1988.

———. "The Waters of Birth: John 3:5 and 1 John 5:6–8." *New Testament Studies* 35 (1989): 155–60.

———. *The Christology of Jesus*. Minneapolis: Augsburg Fortress, 1990.

———. *Jesus, Paul and the End of the World*. Downers Grove, Ill.: InterVarsity Press, 1992.

———. *Conflict and Community in Corinth: A Socio-Rhetorical Commentary on First and Second Corinthians*. Grand Rapids: Wm. B. Eerdmans Publishing Co., 1994.

———. *Jesus the Sage: The Pilgrimage of Wisdom*. Minneapolis: Augsburg Fortress, 1994.

Ziener, G. "Weisheitbuch und Johannesevangelium," *Biblica* 38 (1957): 396–418; 39 (1958): 37–60.

Printed in the United States
25346LVS00003B/175-186

Made in the USA
San Bernardino, CA
10 April 2013